COUPLETS

THOUGHT IN THE ACT
A series edited by Brian Massumi and Erin Manning

BRIAN MASSUMI

Couplets: Travels in Speculative Pragmatism

DUKE UNIVERSITY PRESS   DURHAM AND LONDON   2021

© 2021 Duke University Press
All rights reserved

Designed by Matthew Tauch
Typeset in Quadraat and Meta by Westchester Publishing Services

Library of Congress Cataloging-in-Publication Data
Names: Massumi, Brian, author.
Title: Couplets : travels in speculative pragmatism / Brian Massumi.
Other titles: Thought in the act.
Description: Durham : Duke University Press, 2021. | Series: Thought in the act | Includes bibliographical references and index.
Identifiers: LCCN 2021004649 (print)
LCCN 2021004650 (ebook)
ISBN 9781478013730 (hardcover)
ISBN 9781478014669 (paperback)
ISBN 9781478021964 (ebook)
Subjects: LCSH: Experience. | Pragmatism. | Arts—Philosophy. | Political science—Philosophy. | Perception (Philosophy) | Affect (Psychology) | BISAC: PHILOSOPHY / General | LCGFT: Essays.
Classification: LCC B105.E9 M374 2021 (print) | LCC B105.E9 (ebook) | DDC 144/.3—dc23
LC record available at https://lccn.loc.gov/2021004649
LC ebook record available at https://lccn.loc.gov/2021004650

Cover art: Simryn Gill, detail from *Naught*, 2010–. Objects in the shape of zeros found on walks. Courtesy of the artist. Photo by Jenni Carter.

CONTENTS

Note to the Reader vii

COUPLET 1

2019 Extreme Realism: In Sixteen Series 2
1986 Realer Than Real: The Simulacrum according to Deleuze and Guattari 15

COUPLET 2

2000 On the Right to the Noncommunication of Cultural Difference 26
1998 Event Horizon 63

COUPLET 3

2017 Becoming Animal in the Literary Field 72
2008 The Virtual, Double Capture, and the Urban-Architecture Manifold 94

COUPLET 4

2009 Simondon's "Technical Mentality" Revisited 104
2012 The Supernormal Animal 119

COUPLET 5

1997 Sensing the Virtual, Building the Insensible 134
2004 Not Determinately Nothing: Building Experience 158

COUPLET 6

2014 The Crannies of the Present: On the Subject of Decision 177
2018 Dim, Massive, and Important: Atmosphere in Process 188

COUPLET 7

2005   Going Kinetic: What Is Decision in a Post-deliberative Age? 209
2005   Barely There: The Power of the Image at the Limit of Life 232

COUPLET 8

1995   Requiem for Our Prospective Dead: A Participatory Critique of Capitalist Power 286
2017   The Political Is Not Personal: Affect, Power, Violence 315

COUPLET 9

2001   Tell Me Where Your Pain Is: Pointing to the Body without an Image 324
2015   The Art of the Relational Body: From Mirror-Touch to the Virtual Body 342

COUPLET 10

2000   The Parable of the Cave (Blind Version) 359
2003   Panoscopia 376

COUPLET 11

2003   Urban Appointment: A Possible Rendezvous with the City 385
1999   Purple Phosphene 402

COUPLET 12

2007   On Critique 406
2019   How Do You Make Yourself a Proposition? For a Whiteheadian Laboratory (*with Erin Manning*) 410

Notes 427
References 447
Index 461
Sources 485
Image Credits 489

NOTE TO THE READER

The essays collected in this volume span a period of thirty-three years, from among the very earliest I published to the most recent. They have been selected to cover close to the full the range of topics my work has addressed.[1] Most are previously published, scattered in time and far-flung in publishing context. Their content intersects with that of the published books but also supplements them in important respects.

The essays are not presented in chronological order, nor are they necessarily grouped by subject area. They have been paired in order to suggest cross-connections, on the chance that different transversals might form than in a reading process framed by conventional categories or ordered to suggest a linear development of ideas.

There is, of course, no imperative that the essays be read couplet by couplet. They can be traveled in order from the beginning, the last of one couplet connecting the first of the next. Or they may be dipped into here and there in spot visits following the reader's inclinations, composing informal couplets along the way. However the book is approached, it is hoped that transversal connections will emerge among the essays and, for readers familiar with them, with the books. This book is made for meandering.

Previously published texts have not been significantly edited. The changes are largely restricted to updating bibliographical citations (for example, when a book cited in French subsequently appeared in English translation, or an essay later appeared in a collection that became the standard reference). The previously unpublished essays were in various states of incompletion and have undergone revision to round them out. Newly added notes have been enclosed in brackets. The dates attached to each title indicate the year of composition, which does not always coincide with the year of publication.

Couplet 1

2019

Extreme Realism

In Sixteen Series

Series 1

Everything must be somewhere. (Whitehead 1978, 46)

Real is . . .
Located.
But not restricted to simple location.
> The real includes potential. Potential is real. Its mode of reality is "proximate relevance" (Whitehead 1978, 46). Proximate: to a somewhere everything must be. Relevant: in expressing "a fact of togetherness among forms" (32). The fact of togetherness is the relation of the thing that is somewhere to occasions beyond itself: its inclusion in its own "real constitution" (59) of the elsewhere and elsewhen of its being such.

"Everything is positively somewhere in actuality, and in potency everywhere." (Whitehead 1978, 40)

A process set up anywhere reverberates everywhere. (James 1950, 371)

Real is . . .
Relational.

> "This is the direct denial of the Cartesian doctrine, '. . . an existent thing which requires nothing but itself in order to exist.'" (Whitehead 1978, 59)

Series 2

"The vague always tends to become determinate, simply because its vagueness does not determine it to be vague." (Peirce 1992a, 323)

Real is . . .
"Indetermination, rendered determinate." (Whitehead 1978, 23)
    The concrete fact is the here-and-now of elsewhere and elsewhen in potency, tending to become.

Real is . . .
Determined to be determined.
But never so determined as to be without remainder.
    There is always more.

Real is . . .
Excessive.

"While our [all-too-human] motto is *Exactly what is necessary*, nature's motto is *More than is necessary*,—too much of this, too much of that, too much of everything. Reality is redundant and superabundant." (Bergson 2007, 178)

Series 3

"Say 'now' and it was even while you say it." (James 1996b, 254)

Real is . . .
Transitional.

"We live, as it were, upon the front edge of an advancing wave-crest, and our sense of a determinate direction in falling forward is all we cover of the future of our path." (James 1996a, 69)

Real is . . .
Oriented and open-ended.

Its determination to be determined, on an advancing wave-crest, describes a tendency. What it tends toward are "termini."

"These termini . . . are self-supporting. They are not 'true' of anything else, they simply *are*, are *real*. They 'lean on nothing.' . . . Rather, does the whole fabric of experience lean on them." (James 1996a, 202)

"Nine-tenths of the time these are not actually but only virtually there."
(James 1996a, 72)

Real is . . .
Ninety percent virtual.

Series 4

Real is . . .
Even when it isn't.

"To speak of anything, is to speak of something which, by reason of that very speech, is in some way a component in that act of experience. In some sense or another, it is thereby known to exist. This is what Plato pointed out when he wrote, Not-being is itself a sort of being." (Whitehead 1978, 223)

"He is merely thinking of his forms as including alternative possibilities."
(Whitehead 1978, 117).

Real is . . .
Ninety percent alternative possibilities.

"The actual includes what (in one sense) is 'not-being' as a positive factor in its own achievement." (Whitehead 1978, 189)

"Fact is confronted with alternatives." (Whitehead 1978, 189)

Series 5

Real is . . .
Given.

> "In the real world there is always, over and above 'law,' a factor of the 'simply given' or 'brute fact,' not accounted for and to be accepted simply as given." *(Whitehead 1978, 42)*

Real is . . .
Unrefusable.

> "Matter-of-fact is tinged with the notion of a compulsive determinism." *(Whitehead 1968, 7)*

Real is . . .
Stubborn.

> "Reality is insistency. That is what we mean by 'reality.'" *(Peirce 1935, 340)*

Yet . . .

> There is no avoiding alternative possibilities as a positive factor betokening the relation of the given to occasions beyond itself.

Fact is confronted with alternatives. As a matter of fact, it is relationally more-than-necessary.

> "A phenomenon of force is both a fact and more-than-fact, a given and more-than-given, for force directs itself, beyond its present existence, toward a state it itself will produce." *(Ruyer 1948, 142)*

Real is also . . .
What compulsively surpasses the given.

> "'Givenness' refers to 'potentiality,' and 'potentiality' to 'givenness.'" *(Whitehead 1978, 45)*

Real is . . .
The giving of itself of potential.
Not the *thing-in-itself*, once and for all. Instead, the ever *of-itself* of the world's potential, ongoing.

>This is in direct denial of the doctrine of substance.

>"How an actual entity becomes constitutes what that actual entity is. . . . Its 'being' is constituted by its 'becoming.' This is the 'principle of process.'" *(Whitehead 1978, 23)*

>"The universe is thus a creative advance into novelty." *(Whitehead 1978, 23)*

Real is . . .
Process.
Insistently, creatively advancing, to surpass the given, into novelty.

>This is the principle of unrest.

>"Every ultimate actuality embodies in its own essence . . . 'a principle of unrest,' namely, its becoming." *(Whitehead 1978, 28)*

"The alternative to this doctrine is a static morphological universe." (Whitehead 1978, 23)

Series 6

Real is . . .
Expressive.
Always giving of-itself, it is ongoingly expressive (of potential, determined to be determined).

>"It is not experience that organizes expression, but the other way around—expression organizes experience." *(Vološinov 1986, 85)*

>"Expression becomes independent in its own right, in other words, autonomous." *(Deleuze and Guattari 1987, 59)*

Real is . . .
Not in the interiority of a subject. Expression is not of the subject, it is of the world.

Series 7

Real is . . .
Effective.
To be real is to produce an effect. Anything that produces an effect is real.

> The effect expresses the tension inherent in an antecedent activity compulsively conditioning what comes next, in both its unrefusable givenness and its surpassing the given. Even if the antecedent activity is not itself given, it still is, in effect.

"The objective content of the initial phase of reception is the real antecedent world, as given for that occasion. This is the 'reality' from which that creative advance starts. It is the basic fact of the new occasion, with its concordances and discordances awaiting coordination in the new creature" (Whitehead 1967a, 210). The novelty of the new creature's coordination of the activity it inherits from the antecedent world settles into the world to provide the objective content of the initial phase of a next pulse of process succeeding it, in a snowball world onrolling, continually self-producing, in an additive roll-over of variation.

> "There is only one kind of production, the production of the real." (*Deleuze and Guattari* 1983, 32)

> "Real activities are those that really make things be." (*James* 1996a, 182)

Series 8

Real is . . .
Self-affirming and self-explaining.
The "what" of it is "how" it produces (itself).

"Reality is just itself, and it is nonsense to ask whether it be true or false."
(Whitehead 1967a, 241)

Real is . . .
Fundamentally propositional, as opposed to true or false.

> A proposition is as "a lure for feeling providing immediacy of enjoyment" (Whitehead 1978, 184). An event throws off lures like spores to the future. It has the power to do this because, activating real potential, its occurrence is surrounded by a "penumbra of alternatives" (185). This penumbra is its propositional content, surpassing the "objective content" of its conditions of emergence, in a future-looking movement into the new determination of a next pulse of process. This is the real's advancing edge of *speculative* content, not yet subject to any judgment of true or false. What is "entertained" is the advancing potential; what it is entertained by, is process.

"No verbal statement is the adequate expression of a proposition."
(Whitehead 1978, 13)

"It is merely credulous to accept verbal phrases as adequate statements of propositions. The distinction between verbal phrases and complete propositions is one of the reasons why the logicians' rigid alternative, 'true or false,' is so largely irrelevant for the pursuit of knowledge."
(Whitehead 1978, 11)

Real is . . .
An enactive speculation on its own production, as a complete proposition.

Real is . . .
Self-entertaining.
Self-enjoying.

Series 9

Real is . . .
Additive.

Real is . . .
Without negation. It is a complete, self-renewing proposition. Even not-being is being. To say this is not a contradiction. It is a statement about modes of reality.

> "Again everything is something, which in its own way is real. When you refer to something as unreal, you are merely conceiving a type of reality to which 'something' does not belong. But to be real is not to be self-sustaining. Also modes of reality require each other. It is the task of philosophy to elucidate the relevance to each other of various types of existence. We cannot exhaust such types because there are an unending number of them. But we can start with two types which to us seem as extremes; and can then discern these types as requiring other types to express their mutual relevance to each other" (Whitehead 1968, 69–70). Even being and nonbeing.

> "There is not *less*, but *more* in the idea of nonbeing than that of being."
> (Deleuze 1991a, 17)

> "In the idea of nonbeing there is in fact the idea of being, plus a logical operation of generalized negation, plus the particular psychological motive for that operation (such as when a being does not correspond to our expectation and we grasp it purely as the lack, the absence of what interests us)." (Deleuze 1991a, 17)

> "By affirming one thing, and then another, and so on *ad infinitum*, I form the idea of 'All'; so, by denying one thing and then other things, finally by denying All, I arrive at the idea of Nothing. . . . Negation, therefore . . . is an *affirmation of the second degree*." (Bergson 1998, 287)

Not only is there more in the idea of nonbeing than in that of being, in the affirmation of negation there is more than all there is.

Series 10

Real is . . .
Modal.
> Modes of reality require each other. All types require other types to express their mutual relevance to each other.

> "Existence is all existences; it is every mode of existing. In all and each apart, existence integrally resides and accomplishes itself." (Souriau 2015, 187, translation modified)

Real is . . .
Mutual relevance.
Mutual inclusion in self-accomplishing production.

> "The occasion is one among others, and including the others which it is among." (Whitehead 1967a, 180)

Remembering that . . .

> "There are always 'others,' which might have been and are not." (Whitehead 1967a, 276)

Series 11

Real is . . .
Modal variation, inclusive of otherness.
> "The present occasion while claiming self-identity, while sharing the very nature of the bygone occasion in all its living activities, nevertheless is engaged in modifying it, in adjusting it to *other* influences, in completing it with *other* values, in deflecting it to *other* purposes. The present moment is constituted by the influx of *the other* into that self-identity which is the continued life of the immediate past [the given] within the immediacy of the present [the surpassing of the given]." (Whitehead 1967a, 181)

"For modulation is the operation of the Real." (*Deleuze 1989, 28*)

Series 12

Real is . . .
A plenum.
It is conjunctive.

> This is another way of saying that it is relational, and that it continues across the production of relations succeeding each other. Its complete proposition describes a continuum.

> "The relations that connect experiences must themselves be experienced relations, and any kind of relation experienced must be accounted as 'real' as anything else in the system." (*James 1996a, 42*)

Real is . . .
Radically empirical.

> "Radical empiricism does full justice to conjunctive relations."
> (*James 1996a, 44*)

Series 13

Real is . . .
Disjunctive.
Cut.

> "Everything stops dead for a moment, everything freezes in place—and then the whole process will begin all over again." (*Deleuze and Guattari 1983, 7*)

Cut-flow.

> "That is because the breaks in the process are productive." (*Deleuze and Guattari 1983, 43*)

Real is . . .
As separative as it is connective.
> We can start with two types which to us seem as extremes and can then discern these types as requiring other types to express their mutual relevance to each other.

> "Conjunctions and separations are, at all events, co-ordinate phenomena which, if we take experiences at their face value, must be accounted equally real." (James 1996a, 51)

Real is . . .
Enchainment.
Entrainment.

Series 14

Real is . . .
Transindividual.

> "We are more than the individuals; we are the whole chain as well, with the tasks of all the futures of that chain." (Nietzsche 1967, 366)

Series 15

Real is . . .
Felt.
It is felt to be.

> To be is to be felt.

To be real is to have an effect. The effect cannot but be felt. Without being felt, it would be without effect.

> "Experience and reality come to the same thing." (James 1996a, 59)

Real is . . .
Panexperiential.
> This should not be misunderstood as fundamentally being in a subject, in any sense of the word, much less as being limited to a human subject.

>> "By feeling I mean nothing but sensation *minus* the attribution of it to any particular subject." *(Peirce 1931, 332)*

>> "At the heart of the human, there is nothing human." *(Lapoujade 2018, 47, translation modified)*

> Primordially, feeling is not something that an actual entity has. It is what constitutes its very being, in otherness.

>> "Constituting an actual entity is one complex, fully determinate feeling." *(Whitehead 1978, 25–26)*

> A feeling, of the world. Of the influx of the other, modulating the self-identity of the occasion's immediate past. Of the potential to be otherwise that is otherness.

Real is . . .
Prehension.
> A self-constituting grasping of the potential, in whatever mode, whether sensation, perception, or simply a taking account through the registering of an effect, at the heart of nothing human.

>> "I use the term 'prehension' for the general way in which the occasion of experience can include, as part of its own essence, any other entity, whether another occasion of experience or an entity of another type." *(Whitehead 1967a, 234)*

Real is . . .
Grasped philosophically in a "critique of pure feeling" (Whitehead 1978, 113).

Series 16

Real is . . .
Extremist.
It is non-eliminative. It is as extreme as can be in its non-negation. It is all-embracing in its additivity. It is all-proposing, throwing out at every instant a lure for feeling, for immediacy of enjoyment.

Just as philosophy should be.

> "Nothing can be omitted, experience drunk and experience sober, experience sleeping and experience waking, experience drowsy and experience wide-awake, experience self-conscious and experience self-forgetful, experience intellectual and experience physical, experience religious and experience sceptical, experience anxious and experience care-free, experience anticipatory and experience retrospective, experience happy and experience grieving, experience dominated by emotion and experience under self-restraint, experience in the light and experience in the dark, experience normal and experience abnormal." (Whitehead 1967a, 226)

Experience human and experience nonhuman.

Coda

"Life is the clutch at vivid immediacy." (Whitehead 1978, 105)

1986

Realer Than Real

The Simulacrum according to Deleuze and Guattari

There is a seductive image of contemporary culture circulating today. Our world, Jean Baudrillard tells us, has been launched into hyperspace in a kind of postmodern apocalypse (1983b). The airless atmosphere has asphyxiated the referent, leaving us satellites in aimless orbit around an empty center. We breathe an ether of floating images that no longer bear a relation to any reality whatsoever (11). That, according to Baudrillard, is simulation: the substitution of signs of the real for the real (4). In hyperreality, signs no longer represent or refer to an external model. They stand for nothing but themselves and refer only to other signs. They are to some extent distinguishable, in the way the phonemes of language are, by a combinatory of minute binary distinctions (145–46). But postmodernism slurs. In the absence of any gravitational pull to ground them, images accelerate and tend to run together. They become interchangeable. Any term can be substituted for any other: utter indetermination (Baudrillard 1983a, 56). Faced with this homogeneous surface of syntagmatic slippage, we are left speechless. We can only gape in fascination (35–37). For the secret of the process is beyond our grasp. Meaning has imploded. There is no longer any external model, but there is an internal principle. To the syntagmatic surface of slippage there corresponds an invisible paradigmatic dimension that creates those minimally differentiated signs only in order for them to blur together in a pleasureless orgy of exchange and circulation. Hidden in the images is a kind of genetic code responsible for their generation (Baudrillard 1983b, 55–58, 113–15). Meaning is out of reach and out of sight, but not because it has receded into the distance. It is because the code has been miniaturized. Objects are images, images are signs, signs are information, and information fits on a chip. Everything reduces to a molecular binarism: the generalized digitality of the computerized society (56–57, 134–35).

And so we gape. We cannot be said to be passive exactly, because all polarity, including the active/passive dichotomy, has disappeared. We have no earth to center us, but we ourselves function as a ground—in the electrical sense (Baudrillard 1983a, 1–2). We do not act, but neither do we merely receive. We absorb through our open eyes and mouths. We neutralize the play of energized images in the mass entropy of the silent majority.

It makes for a fun read. But do we really have no other choice than being a naive realist or being a sponge? Deleuze and Guattari open a third way. Although it is never developed at length in any one place, a theory of simulation can be extracted from their work that can give us a start in analyzing our cultural condition under late capitalism without landing us back with the dinosaurs or launching us into hypercynicism.

A common definition of the simulacrum is a copy of a copy whose relation to the model has become so attenuated that it can no longer properly be said to be a copy. It stands on its own as a copy without a model. Fredric Jameson cites the example of photorealism (1991). The painting is a copy not of reality but of a photograph, which is already a copy of the original (30). Deleuze, in his essay "Plato and the Simulacrum," takes a similar definition as his starting point, but emphasizes its inadequacy (1990). For beyond a certain point, the distinction is no longer one of degree. The simulacrum is less a copy twice removed than a phenomenon of a different nature altogether: it undermines the very distinction between copy and model (256–58). The terms "copy" and "model" bind us to the world of representation and objective (re)production. A copy, no matter how many times removed, authentic or fake, is defined by the presence or absence in its makeup of essential relations of resemblance to a model. The simulacrum, on the other hand, bears only an external and deceptive resemblance to a putative model. The process of its production, its inner dynamism, is entirely different from that of its supposed model; its resemblance to it is merely a surface effect (258, 262–63). The production and function of a photograph has no relation to those of the object photographed, and the photorealist painting in turn envelops an essential difference from the photograph. It is that masked difference, not the manifest resemblance, that produces the effect of uncanniness so often associated with the simulacrum. A copy is made in order to stand in for its model. A simulacrum has a different agenda; it enters different circuits. Pop Art is the example Deleuze uses for simulacra that have successfully broken out of the copy mold: the multiplied, stylized images take on a life of their own (265). The thrust of the process is not to become an equivalent of the "model" but to turn against it and its world in order to open a new space for the simulacrum's own mad proliferation. The simulacrum affirms its own difference. It is not an implosion but a differentiation; it is an index not of absolute proximity but of galactic distances.

The resemblance of the simulacrum is a means, not an end. A thing, write Deleuze and Guattari, "in order to become apparent, is forced to simulate structural states and to slip into states of forces that serve it as masks. . . . Underneath the mask and by means of it, it already invests the terminal forms and the specific higher states whose integrity it will subsequently establish" (1983, 91). Resemblance is a beginning masking the advent of a whole new vital dimension. This even applies to mimicry in nature. An insect that mimics a leaf does so not to meld with the vegetable state of its surrounding milieu but to reenter the higher realm of predatory animal warfare on a new footing. Mimicry, according to Lacan, is camouflage (1981, 99; cited in Alliez and Feher 1986, 51n1). It constitutes a war zone. There is a power inherent in the false: the positive power of ruse, the power to gain a strategic advantage by masking one's life force.

Ridley Scott's film *Blade Runner* (1982) shows that the ultimate enemy in this war of ruse is the so-called model itself. Off-world replicants return to earth not to blend in with the indigenous population as an end in itself but to find the secret of their built-in obsolescence so they can escape their bondage and live full lives, and on their own terms. Imitation is an indication of a life force propelling the falsifier toward the unbridled expression of its uniqueness. The dominant replicant makes a statement to the man who made his eyes that can be taken as a general formula for simulation: "If only you could see what I have seen with your eyes." If they find out how to undo their preprogrammed deaths, the replicants will not remain on earth as imitation humans. They will either take over or flee back to their own vital dimension of interplanetary space to see things no human being ever has or will. Their imitation is only a way-station en route to an unmasking and the assumption of difference. As Eric Alliez and Michel Feher (1986, 54) observe, the best weapon against the simulacrum is not to unmask it as a false copy but to force it to be a true copy, thereby resubmitting it to representation and the mastery of the model: the corporation that built the rebellious replicants introduces a new version complete with secondhand human memories.

I said earlier that the simulacrum cannot adequately be discussed in terms of copy and model, and now I find myself not only talking about a model again but claiming that it is in a life-and-death struggle with the simulacrum. The reality of the model is a question that needs to be dealt with. Baudrillard sidesteps the question of whether simulation replaces a real that did indeed exist, or if simulation is all there has ever been (1983a, 70–83). Deleuze and Guattari say yes to both (1983). The alternative is a false one because simulation is a process that *produces* the real or, more precisely more real (a more-than-real) on the basis of the real. Simulation "carries the real beyond its principle to the point where it is effectively produced" (87). Every simulation takes as its point of departure a regularized world comprising apparently stable identities or territories. But these "real" entities are in fact undercover simulacra that have consented to feign being copies. A silent film by Louis Feuillade illustrates the process.

Vendémiaire (1919) takes place in the final days of World War I. The plot is simple: members of a well-to-do family from the north of France who cannot fight in the war flee to unoccupied territory in the south to contribute their efforts to the wine harvest. There they meet one of the daughters' husband-to-be and a sinister pair of German prisoners of war who have obtained identity papers by killing two Belgians and try to pass themselves off as Allies until they can get enough money to flee to Spain. The Germans' plan is to steal from the vineyard owners and pin the theft on a gypsy woman who is also working on the harvest. The plan fails when one of the Germans, about to be found out, jumps into an empty grape storage tank. He is killed by poisonous gases produced by grapes fermenting in the next tank. His corpse is found still clutching the loot, and the gypsy woman is saved. His lonely comrade later betrays himself by getting drunk and speaking in German.

The film is bracketed by grapes. The grape harvest supplies the initial motivation that sets up the situation of the plot, and the grapes themselves rather than any human hero resolve the dilemma. The film is not only bracketed by grapes; it swims in wine as its very element. Every crucial moment is expressed in terms of wine: love is expressed by the scintillating image of the faraway wife dancing in the husband's wine cup; the German menace in its highest expression is one of the escapees stomping on the grape vine; heroism is exemplified by an altruistic trooper who braves death to bring wine back to the trenches to give his comrades a taste of the homeland that will revive their will to victory; when victory does come, it is toasted with wine; and the movie ends with a sentimental tableau of the vines and a final intertitle saying that from these vineyards a new nation will be reborn. "Simulation," Deleuze and Guattari write, "does not replace reality . . . but rather it appropriates reality in the operation of despotic overcoding, it produces reality on the new full body that replaces the earth. It expresses the appropriation and production of the real by a quasi-cause" (1983, 210). The undivided, abstract flow of wine is the glorified body of the nation. It arrogates to itself the power of love, victory, and rebirth. It presents itself as first and final cause. But the war was obviously not won with wine. Its causality is an illusion. But it is an effective illusion because it is reinjected into reality and sets to work: it expresses love, and thereby motivates the man to be a good husband and give sons to the nation rising; it expresses patriotism, and thereby spurs the soldiers to victory. That is why it is called a quasi-cause. It abstracts from bodies and things a transcendent plane of ideal identities: a glorious wife, a glorious family, a glorious nation. ("It carries the real beyond its principle . . .") Then it folds that ideal dimension back down onto bodies and things in order to force them to conform to the distribution of identities it lays out for them. (". . . to the point where it is effectively produced.") It creates the entire network of resemblance and representation. Both copy and model are the products of the same fabulatory process, the final goal of which is the re-creation of the earth, the creation of a new territory.

The power of the quasi-cause is essentially distributive. It separates the good bodies from the bad. In other words, it separates the bodies that agree to resemble the glorious illusion as their model from those that do not, and polices for renegade copies operating with a different agenda. The quasi-cause enables the French patriots to unmask the conniving Germans, and it shows up the gypsy for the true, hardworking Frenchwoman that she is despite her apparent otherness.[1]

This account overcomes the polarity between the model and the copy by treating them both as second-order productions, as working parts in the same machine. But it seems to leave intact the dichotomy between the real and the imaginary—until it is realized that the bodies and things that are taken up by this fabulatory process are themselves the result of prior simulation-based distributions operating on other levels with different quasi-causes. Simulation upon simulation. Reality is nothing but a well-tempered harmony of simulation. The world is a complex circuit of interconnected simulations, in which Feuillade's own film takes its place. It was made in 1919, just after the war. Every war, especially one of those dimensions, has a powerful deterritorializing effect: the mobilization of troops and supplies, refugees from other countries, refugees to other countries, families broken, entire regions leveled . . . The film itself is a simulation meant to insert itself into that disjointed situation to help induce a unifying reterritorialization, to contribute to the rebirth of the nation. Vendémiaire is the first month of the Republican calendar.

So what we are left with is a distinction not primarily between the model and the copy, or the real and the imaginary, but between two modes of simulation. One, exemplified in Feuillade's film, is normative, regularizing, and reproductive. It selects only certain properties of the entities it takes up: hard work, loyalty, good parenting, and so on. It creates a network of surface resemblances. They are surface resemblances because at bottom they are not resemblances at all but standardized actions: what those entities *do* when called upon (the gypsy in this respect is as French as the French). What bodies do depends on where they land in an abstract grid of miraculated identities that are in practice only a bundle of normalized and basically reproductive functions. It is not a question of Platonic copies but of human replicants. Every society creates a quasi-causal system of this kind. In capitalist society the ultimate quasi-cause is capital itself (Deleuze and Guattari 1983, 227), which is described by Marx as a miraculating substance that arrogates all things to itself and presents itself as first and final cause. This mode of simulation goes by the name of "reality."

The other mode of simulation is the one that turns against the entire system of resemblance and replication. It is also distributive, but the distribution it effects is not limitative. Rather than selecting only certain properties, it selects them all, it multiplies potentials—not to be human, but to be human plus. This kind of simulation is called "art." Art also re-creates a territory, but a territory that is not really territorial. It is less like the earth with its gravitational grid than an interplanetary space, a deterritorialized territory providing a possibility of movement in all directions. Artists are replicants who have found the secret of their obsolescence.

In *A Thousand Plateaus*, Deleuze and Guattari invent a vocabulary enabling them to discuss both modes of simulation without lapsing into the terminology of representation (1987). The key concept is double becoming. There are always at least two terms swept up in a fabulous process that transforms them both (293–94 and ch. 10 passim). David Cronenberg's film *The Fly* (1986) presents an instance of this, although a failed one. A scientist named Brundle accidentally splices himself with a fly as he is experimenting with a machine that can dematerialize objects and transport them instantly to any chosen location, in defiance of gravity and Newtonian physics generally. When the accident occurs, Brundle does not so much become fly, nor the fly human. Rather, certain properties or potentials of both combine in a new and monstrous amalgamation: a Brundle-Fly that can walk on walls and think and speak well enough to describe itself as the world's first "insect politician." It tries to purify itself of the fly in it by repeating the process backwards but succeeds only in combining with the machinery itself. In limitative or negative becoming as portrayed in *Vendémiaire*, one of the terms is an abstract identity and the body in question must curtail its potentials in order to fit into the grid, or at least appear to. In nonlimitative or positive becoming, as in *The Fly*, both terms are on the same level: rather than looking perpendicularly up or down, one moves sideways toward another position on the grid for which one was not destined, toward an animal, a machine, a person of a different sex or age or race, an insect, a plant. The fabulatory process, though as abstract as subatomic physics, is immanent to the world of the things it affects, and is as real as a quark.[2] The transporting machine is on the same plane as the terms it combines. Its operating principle dips into that world's quantum level, into its pool of virtuality, to create an as yet unseen amalgamation of potentials. It produces a new body or territory from which there is no turning back. The only choice is to keep on becoming in an endless relay from one term to the next until the process either makes a breakthrough or exhausts its potential, spends its fuel, and the fabulous animal dies. Likening this to interplanetary space can be misleading: there is nothing farther from free-floating weightlessness than this. There is no such thing as total indetermination. Every body has its own propulsion, its own life force, its own set of potentials defining how far it can go. And it moves in a world filled with the obstacles thrown down by sedimentations of preexisting simulations of the "real" persuasion. There is no generalized indetermination, but there are localized points of undecidability where man meets fly. The goal is to reach into one's world's quantum level at such a point and, through the strategic mimicry of double becoming, combine as many potentials as possible. Deleuze and Guattari, of course, are not suggesting that people can or should "objectively" become insects. It is a question of extracting and combining potentials, which they define as abstract relations of movement and rest, abilities to affect and be affected: abstract yet real. The idea is to build our own transporting machine and use it to get a relay going and to keep it going, creating ever greater and more powerful amalgamations and spreading them like a contagion until they infect every identity across the land and the point is reached where a now all-invasive positive simulation can turn back against the grid of resemblance and replication and overturn it for a new earth. Deleuze and Guattari insist on the collective nature of this process of becoming, even when it is seemingly embodied in a solitary artist. Revolutionary or "minor" artists marshal all of the powers of the false their community has to offer (Deleuze and Guattari 1986, 16–27; Deleuze 1989, 126–55). They create a working simulation that may then reinject itself into society like Feuillade's wine assemblage, but to very different, though perhaps equally intoxicating, effect.

Returning to *The Fly*, the former scientist's only hope for a breakthrough is to convince his former girlfriend to have a child by him and the fly. His hope, and her fear, is that he will infect the human race with Brundle-Flies, and a new race with superhuman strength will rise up to replace the old. The overman as superfly.[3] Reproduction, and the forging of a new ethnic identity, are aspects of this process of simulation, but they are not the goal. The goal is life, a world in which the New Brundle can live without hiding and repressing his powers. That possibility is successfully squelched by the powers that be. Brundle-Fly is deprived of an escape route. The original formula, as inscribed in the bodies of Brundle and the fly, was apparently flawed. They did the best they could do, but only reached obsolescence.

How does all of this apply to our present cultural condition? According to Deleuze, the point at which simulacrum began to unmask itself was reached in painting with the advent of Pop Art (1990, 265). In film, it was Italian neo-Realism and the French New Wave (1–13). Perhaps we are now reaching that point in popular culture as a whole. Advanced capitalism, Deleuze and Guattari argue, is reaching a new transnational level that necessitates a dissolution of old identities and territorialities and the unleashing of objects, images, and information having far more mobility and combinatory potential than ever before (1987, 448–73). As always, this deterritorialization is effected only in order to make possible a reterritorialization on an even grander and more glorious land of worldwide capital reborn. But in the meantime, a breach has opened. The challenge is to assume this new world of simulation and take it one step farther, to the point of no return, to raise it to a positive simulation of the highest degree by marshaling all our powers of the false toward shattering the grid of representation once and for all.

This cannot be done by whining. The work of Baudrillard is one long lament. Neither linear nor dialectical causality functions any longer, therefore everything is indetermination. The center of meaning is empty, therefore we are satellites in lost orbit. We can no longer act like legislator-subjects or be passive like slaves, therefore we are sponges. Images are no longer anchored by representation, therefore they float weightless in hyperspace. Words are no longer univocal, therefore signifiers slip chaotically over each other. A circuit has been created between the real and the imaginary, therefore reality has imploded into the undecidable proximity of hyperreality. All of these statements make sense only if it is assumed that the only conceivable alternative to representative order is absolute indetermination, whereas indetermination as Baudrillard speaks of it is in fact only the flipside of order, as necessary to it as the fake copy is to the model, and every bit as much a part of its system. Baudrillard's framework can only be the result of a nostalgia for the old reality so intense that it has deformed his vision of everything outside of it. He cannot clearly see that all the things he says have crumbled were simulacra all along: simulacra produced by analyzable procedures of simulation that were as real as real, or actually realer than real, because they carried the real back to its principle of production and in so doing prepared their own rebirth in a new regime of simulation. He cannot see becoming, of either variety. He cannot see that the simulacrum envelops a proliferating play of differences and galactic distances. What Deleuze and Guattari offer, particularly in *A Thousand Plateaus*, is a logic capable of grasping Baudrillard's failing world of representation as an effective illusion the demise of which opens a glimmer of possibility. Against cynicism, a thin but fabulous hope—of ourselves becoming realer than real in a monstrous contagion of our own making.

Couplet 2

2000

On the Right to the Noncommunication of Cultural Difference

In her opening comments at the "Cultures: War and Peace" colloquium in 2000, Isabelle Stengers invoked the need to define what it would mean to construct a "common world."[1] Paradoxically, she emphasized that one of the principal tasks of that collective project would be the creation of "possibilities of distance." It would be crucial to retain, she continued, "a certain indetermination," as well as to recognize the "impossibility of exchanging places." This notion of a "common" that affirms nonexchangeability and presupposes a share of indetermination, and thus untranslatability, runs counter to traditional communicational theories, for example of the Habermasian variety. But it also parts ways with certain vocabularies of the left where the qualifier "common" is attached to an indefinite series of nouns to mark them with the positive sign of a general desire to be fulfilled, devoid of any particular affective inflection: "common language," "common sense," "common framework" . . . The "common" as oddly neutralizing vocable of wish-fulfillment, pointing in the general direction of the future. Taken at its word, it points with unaccented utopian anticipation to a shared destiny of peace, finally achieved: a new cosmopolitan constitution. But does it not surreptitiously imply the opposite? What "common framework" can avoid projecting upon its own path the shadow of a "common enemy" threatening to stand in its way? There is nothing more automatic than for the commonality of "us" to extrude a "them," the circle of communicational inclusion flipping over into a battle line of exclusion.

Michael Hardt and Antonio Negri state it outright: "clarifying the nature of the common enemy is an essential political task," as part of an ultimately "cosmopolitan" project that also requires "inventing a common language of struggles" (2000, 57). But they pivot immediately, remarking that "perhaps this needs to be a new type of communication that functions not on the basis of resemblances but on the basis of differences: a communication of singularities" (57). Stengers takes a step further, developing a counternotion to the cosmopolitan: a "cosmopolitics" indissociably linking the "common" to the "untranslatable," holding them in productively problematic complicity under the sign, once again, of the singular (2010–11). This is the direction this essay will go in, taking another step further by asking why it is necessary to hitch the singular to the common at all. What happens when the emphasis falls squarely on untranslatability? What of differences that have their reasons for refusing to communicate even their singularity? That refuse complicity—*and* the status of the common enemy? What kind of (cosmo)politics is this?

Of Sociality

Take as a starting point a practice of "intercultural communication." A practitioner specializing in intercultural negotiation with an academic background in Japanese studies was asked to reflect on what her experience might say more generally about intercultural communication (Buckley 1998). She responded that in the experience of being in intense negotiation she found an echo of a more distant experience: her stuttering as a child. From this counterintuitive starting point, working with Gilles Deleuze's famous essay on stuttering (1997a, 107–14), she spins an account of intercultural communication.

With stuttering, as Buckley describes it, a collusion sets in between the interlocutors. There is an unsaid—but unhidden—pact to let what so conspicuously sounds pass in silence. An effort is made not to draw attention to the obvious: nothing is said about the difficulty of saying. Both parties, however, are riveted to the difficulty, asymmetrically. On one side is the speaker in difficulty, and on the other their interlocutor who is hard-pressed not to feel the urge to complete their phrase for them, but must refrain at all costs from doing so to avoid the paternalism of that gesture and to avoid further embarrassment. On both sides attention is intense, bordering on the unbearable, a single phoneme fleeing from language, depriving itself of meaning by overzealous self-insistence.

The interlocutors hang on the phrase in formation, hooked in the suspense of its suspension of the onward flow of language. They are joined at the stutter, like two poles of the same desire: to continue. But to will it is not enough. A stutter is what it is because it resists volition. It is a verbal energy stalled in its nascent state, under the thrall of an automatism. In the face of this autonomous force of interruption, there is nothing for it but to wait. The parties are together in the expectancy for a meaning that no power of decision can compel to come, but must be allowed to come. The will to continue takes on the quality of an invocation. Let it come. Let it continue. A moment before, ideas were being exchanged. The speakers were positioning themselves relative to each other. Opinions were being expressed. Strategies were being deployed. Perhaps advantages were being sought. Or a sincere attempt might have been underway to find a compromise to bring a quarrel to an end and make the peace. Seduction, cajoling, exhorting, charming were in the potential repertory. Reason was doubtless convoked, politeness deployed. In an instant, all of that evaporated, everything now in interruption, everything now on hold. The power upon which all human exchange hangs, that of language, is no longer being garrulously convoked to strategic operation. It is being wordlessly invoked. Momentarily deprived of the flow of meaning, communication retracts into this wordlessness, replaced by the unspoken wish that speech resume. The negotiation of differences melts back to the mutual desire to continue in social congress. The fact that sociality has been interrupted does not mean that it is simply absent. It is very much present *in tendency*, no less intensely lived for being struck by suspense.

The terms of social exchange are in suspense, but there remains a social relation of a kind. It is one that articulates nothing in particular and is accorded no value: a dequalified relation. Both parties are provisionally dispossessed of their power to make a determinate difference through the production of meaning. They are no longer in a position to self-define relative to each other. Yet they remain in relation. They are absorbed together into the simple fact of being there together, at this juncture, in relation, provisionally unable to actively define its content. What is felt in the suspension of meaning is this being-together, being-in-relation, without qualities: sociality as such. *Pure sociality*. Bare sociality. Sociality unclothed by ideas, opinions, strategies, compromises, seductions, reasons, and norms of politeness. Undeveloped into determinate expressions. Unadorned by stylistic variations. Unfinished as moves in a game of position. Sociality *as such* appears. It appears only in suspense.

Sociality stutters.

The suspension of social differentiation is not the same as indifference. It is the *holding in reserve* of articulated difference, under the action of an autonomous power that inhabits language without belonging to it: a force of repetition immanent to language, making it desist in its actual operations while it continues to insist on its own resumption, reduced to its own tendency to emerge. In the vocabulary of José Gil, this force that is immanent to language but not of it, that returns language to its nascent state, belongs to the domain of the infralinguistic (1998, 106–45). The infralinguistic, this time in Gilbert Simondon's vocabulary, belongs to the preindividual field (2005). This is not a domain of indifference. It is differently differentiated. It is not made of discrete parts. Nothing in this field is separately articulated. Nothing in it is defined in isolation. In it, there are only beings *of* relation, without the articulated terms *in* relation: tensions, gradients, degrees, torsions, surges, polarities, tensions, without formed words and finished meanings. Nothing detaches, but neither does anything coincide. Nothing completes, but sociality is not at an end.

The asymmetry in stuttering is the polarity "being in difficulty of expression" and "wishing to help someone in difficulty of expression while refraining from doing exactly that." These poles in no way coincide. They delineate an irreducible differential. The interlocutors, the terms in relation on the dialogic level, are mutually absorbed in pure sociality. They are joined together in suspense, mutually invoking a resumption of expression. Although intensely bound to each other by their participation in the interruptive event, they are not in it together indifferently. The irreducible differential between them means that they *cannot be substituted for each other*. The field of sociality is predicated on the integral impossibility of one taking the place of the other. It is a commonplace that society is founded on exchange. This ignores the obvious fact that in the event (whatever the event), there is polarity and differential.

Social intercourse departs from an unsurpassable limit-condition of nonexchangeability, which is also a condition of nontransmissibility—for what can "being in difficulty of expression" and "wishing to help someone in difficulty of expression while refraining from doing exactly that" have in common? Other than coming together in the same event, differently. Other than undividedly belonging to a situation, asymmetrically. Being bound to the situation together while strictly sharing nothing. This is the condition of exchange. When the conversation resumes, the asymmetry will clothe itself in words, meanings, ideas, opinions, understandings, and all of this will cover over the unsubstitutability. One party might be convinced and come over to the other's position. They might come to share a semantic content. An opinion or conviction might have been transmitted. It's not even out of the question that the speakers switch sides, exchanging positions. But this movement of exchange is just apparent. It occurs only on a certain level of articulation. It doesn't erase the differential. In social commerce, we need only scratch the surface to feel the asymmetries that continue across exchange.

Inequalities are everywhere. They come in the form of differentials of capacities, rights, privileges, and powers that condition the conversation and are disseminated through it. They are both sown and reaped by institutions, apparatuses, and automatisms dedicated to the incitation, canalization, and regulation of speech and action. Discourse spins out the asymmetrical limit-condition of sociality into enduring structures of inequality. It gives elaborated expression to the asymmetry, defining the terms in relation held in suspense at the preindividual level of pure sociality. It clothes the asymmetry, translates it into its terms. Discourse brings the social condition of language to expression at the price of losing it in translation. A stream of determinate statements unfolds in discursive order. Where once was only tendency, there now propagates a manifest and manipulable movement. What was implicate is explicated. The in-it-together spaces itself out, extending itself across a chain of discretized communicational packets in an assignable back-and-forth. What was an indivisible being-together in the dynamic unity of the wait now portions itself out into opposable and combinable parts. What was the immediacy of a belonging, asymmetrically or contrastively shared, now divides into shares, subject to negotiation, which is to say mechanisms of mediation. Society is this becoming of sociality, articulately lost in translation.

There is always a kernel of the uncommunicated and the incommunicable in communication. There is a remainder of the untranslatable in translation. There is no common language. This is a banal remark. We all are aware of it every moment of every day, or we wouldn't have to strive so hard to make ourselves understood—and always end up feeling so sadly misunderstood in spite of our best efforts. If we are being honest, isn't this dynamic endemic to what we call our "relationships," which we feel endlessly compelled to elaborate upon and embellish, dressing up the naked relation of pure sociality that remains the ground upon which they move?

Why not set aside the wish-fulfillment of the incantation of the "common" and turn our attention toward the task of positively describing the incommunicability? In addition to elaborating our relationships (the negotiation of that dynamic will never go away), can we not also reimplicate ourselves in the condition of relation and think about the ways we are always also doing that? Just asking that question implies that there are social techniques that apply to the field of relation as such. Their practice would be unmediated and carry a suspensive force. What would the pragmatics of that be?

Simondon's concept of the preindividual field of relation, which can also be called the field of belonging as long as its conditions of asymmetry and nonexchange are borne in mind, can help give an account of that positivity. The preindividual field harbors not only contrastive asymmetries but complex differentiations bound together in immediate variation, as by contact at a distance. For example, in a magnetic field a perturbation occurring in one location, affecting a subset of the magnetized particles, induces an instantaneous global change in the disposition of all the particles belonging to the field. This is a simple example of what Isabelle Stengers and Ilya Prigogine have called local-global resonance (1986, 224–25, 231).

The field, it must be clarified, is not merely the population of particles. The particles are the terms in relation. The field is the relation itself. The mark of relation is the susceptibility of all of the terms that might populate the field to be instantaneously affected together, regardless of the distances separating them, and to express this effective proximity at a distance in an immediate variation that is at once local and global. The field is "preindividual" in the sense that the being-in-relation of the terms is primary in relation to their individual definition. The specific qualities they manifest flow from their adherence to the field, from their eventful belonging one to the other, and one to all. Another way of saying this is that the relation is the *dynamic unity* of what individuates together. Preexisting terms that enter into the field and participate in this dynamic unity are addressed at the level of their preindividuality: their capacity to reindividuate; to express, in correlation with each other, a qualitative change. The result is a collective individuation.

The wager is that there exists a mode of action capable of addressing this dynamic unity as such. Such a mode of action would not constitute a cause in the conventional sense. A classical cause applies to discrete terms, from the point of view of their already formed capacity to propagate effects in linear fashion by local, part-to-part connections. An action, on the other hand, that applies itself directly to a differential being-together, the dynamic unity of a population, has no discrete object. In fact, it has no object other than the local-global instantaneity of its own effect. The change of state occurs directly at that level, without the stepped intercession of a mediate cause. What is effected is an immediate modulation of a field of belonging. Deleuze and Guattari call this kind of action a *quasi-cause*.

In the case of stuttering, a feral quasi-causality is in operation. It breaks into the conversational chain, producing an interval that fills itself with half-formed words, flashes of thoughts, aborted intentions, suspended desires (for continuation and aid), and no doubt judgments of incompetence or handicap that involuntarily arise even when consciously resisted. It's as if everything that could be said, once the conversation resumes, was bubbling up together in the wait. Diverse tendencies collide and commix, fold into and out of each other, mutually inflecting and invoking each other. The suspense of the conversation is a kind of primordial soup of potential continuations of the exchange. Whatever transpires when fully formed words start to flow again, one thing is certain: the course of the conversation will be different, however slightly, from what it would have been had the interruption not occurred. The negotiating of communicational exchange will have been deflected or inflected in some way by the irruption of the event. What ensues is nuanced by the dis-ease of having fallen together into a sociality without expression.

What characterizes the field of belonging, and what internally differentiates it, is this *mutual inclusion* in the same event of *potential* terms of expression. Simondon's preindividual field is populated by embryonic determinations or tendencies, "germs" of forms to come, enveloped together in their difference, prior to the achievement of fully formed individuality. One of the ways the thinking of preindividual relation in communication is "positive" is that it grasps the field of pure belonging, the field of infralinguistic sociality, as the field of emergence of the expressions that will positively constitute society.

Clearly, there is no way of intervening in a field of pure belonging in a precise fashion, guided by an instrumental logic stringing effects down causal chains in a way that can be reliably predicted. There is no a priori logic to follow, due to the simple fact that determinate discursive and social logics are what *result* from the field. They are its effected expression. The field of expression has its own logic, different from theirs. In its anticipation of defined and discrete terms, this can only be a fuzzy logic. The "terms" proper to this logic are neither formed parts nor separable elements, but rather local-global variations occurring in the mode of mutual inclusion. The logic of the field carries an ineradicable share of indetermination. This is the way in which the field in itself has a positivity: that of a load of potential (to be determined). This makes any intervention in the field an essentially uncertain undertaking.

To intervene upon relation tools are needed that meet it on its own level, actioning its logic: techniques of quasi-causality (defined, once again, as the direct and instantaneous modulation of the dynamic unity of a field of emergent determination).

There exists in European thought a concept that is close to quasi-causality. It is the concept of the *performative*. In the philosophy of language, the performative is the capacity to directly and instantaneously transform a state of affairs through words: to "do things" with words (Austin 1975). The classic example is marriage. A marriage does not work separately on the halves composing the couple. It works directly on their relation. When the words "I now pronounce you . . ." are pronounced, a whole interpersonal world is suddenly transformed. What the members of the couple expect of each other changes. What their relatives and their friends expect of them does as well. It is likely that the quality of their lives together will begin to change, "for better or for worse." The pronouncement of marriage does not operate on the level of meaning. It is about as semantically void as a statement can get: a complete cliché. But it does make a real and integral difference. It recomposes a world. The performance of the marriage is a taking charge of a relational field that is as direct and effective as grasping an object in the hand. The performative use of language carries a power of transformation that inhabits language but is irreducible to its form or content. It effects a power in excess over the properly linguistic capacities of language (signifying and discoursing). Its power is directly exerted in the world and on the world, with all the force of an overpowering gesture. The performative carries an excess of efficacity that is immanent to the use of words. It is less a cliché than a dynamic non-sense—an infralinguistic force that is triggered by language but is not internal to its domain, that does not belong to the linguistic, belonging only to belonging itself. Even in the most conventional, regulated, or rule-bound of contexts, there remains a residue of uncertainty as to the ultimate outcome of the performative, in ways that can contradict what minimal semantic content it carries (basically, just enough to angle in on the relation). In the case of the marriage relationship unfolding from the pronouncement of marriage, this uncertainty translates as the implicit presupposition of unfaithfulness as an ineradicable issue and the eventuality of divorce.[2]

There is another, older word in the European tradition that is also close to quasi-causality in its own way. This word has the advantage of drawing "modern" modes of thought into a certain proximity, by contrast, with what they have consistently belittled as "primitive" thinking. Giordano Bruno gives a definition of the word that is useful for this exposition: "the art of alloying knowledge and the power to act" (2000, 12). That is a fair characterization of a performative statement and its need to "know" how to angle in on relation. The word in question is "magic."

Perhaps we're on the trail of a magical practice of politics, of a kind very different from the political rites that presided over the consolidation of what would become the modern nation-state (notably prepared by the quasi-magic ritual and ceremony of the court of Louis XIV), and that in modern times continued to contribute to its legitimation and empowerment. What follows is a contestatory counterexample to this "magic of the State" (Taussig 1997).

Difference and Malediction

It's 1988; the place is Australia, celebrating the bicentennial of the nation's founding. More precisely, it is the celebration of the first major chapter in the European colonization of the continent, with the landing of the first convict ship at what was to become Sydney. To mark the foundation of the colony, a new parliament building is commissioned for the nation's capital in Canberra. The government of the time is led by the center-left Australian Labor Party (on which Tony Blair would later model his "New Labor" in the UK). It is further developing the policy of "multiculturalism" that followed the end of the institutionalized racism of the "White Australia Policy," which excluded the immigration of people of non-European origin up into the late 1960s. A major intent of the policy is to signal a new opening (decidedly more economic in intent than cultural) to the peoples of Asia. Concurrently, the movement for the rights of Aboriginal peoples was heating up. They had been considered less than fully human by the colonizers, so much so that they were deemed too primitive to have a notion of landownership, and thus to be ineligible to enter into treaties. In the first half of the twentieth century, a policy of cultural genocide was visited upon the survivors of white settlement in the name of "assimilation." Aboriginal languages and culture were suppressed by Christian missionaries charged with "civilizing" them. Children were subject to forced adoptions into white homes far from their places of birth, where they were typically forced to work as domestics. Aboriginal people enjoyed no legal status until 1967, when a national referendum accorded them the right to vote and removed a clause in the national constitution that had prevented the government from officially recognizing their existence or enacting laws specifically dedicated to them. After the success of the referendum, Aboriginal political and cultural movements grew rapidly in strength. In the 1970s their struggles centered on the land rights movement and the recognition by the European judicial system of their traditional "law," a system of oral traditions that lay at the core of the oldest continuous culture on earth and, among many other functions, regulated the territorial regime (which of course did exist) in the precolonial era (those sixty-five thousand years of prior inhabitation that make the colonial period a mere blip in time). In 1976 a national law returned close to 40 percent of the Northern Territory to the traditional Aboriginal owners. But outside this federal territory, the movement faced roadblocks. The state governments most concerned, Queensland and Western Australia, were dominated by powerful economic interests representing the mining sector and the white agriculturalists of the interior. An added complication was that urban and peri-urban Aboriginal people who could not demonstrate a continuous cultural tie to the land as a result of the assimilation policies were left in an ambiguous situation.

To address these issues, the Aboriginal rights movement of the 1980s campaigned for a formal treaty with the federal government, which was the only settler-colonial society in the British Commonwealth never to have signed a treaty with its indigenous peoples. The Labor government accepted the principle of a treaty, but was unable to carry through due to white backlash against the new cultural visibility and political presence of Aboriginal people.

It was against this background that the bicentennial celebrations took place. It is not surprising that Aboriginal activists were not in the mood to celebrate. Their movements boycotted the bicentennial, organizing large-scale counterevents and demonstrations under the banner of the Aboriginal Sovereign Treaty '88 Campaign. The government, for its part, wished to use the bicentennial to symbolically mark the dawning of a new age distanced from the White Australia Policy and promising what would later come to be called, in a subsequent phase of the struggles, "reconciliation" between white society and Aboriginal peoples.[3] With this in mind, it was decided that the design of the new parliament building should integrate a work of art representing Aboriginal culture. A large stone mosaic would decorate the ground in the forecourt of the new parliament. It would be executed in the pointillist style of the Central Desert dot-painting movement, which had transferred body-painting and sand-painting traditions onto canvas and was enjoying a growing success on the international art market. Michael Tjakamarra (also spelled Jagamarra) Nelson, a celebrated Aboriginal artist from a traditional community of the Northern Territory who was a central figure in the dot-painting movement, was awarded the commission.[4] His acceptance of the commission was controversial, with some Aboriginal activists accusing him of being a collaborator and of betraying his people.

The day of the grand opening of Parliament House finally arrived, to great celebration. No less than the Queen of England was present, along with dignitaries from around the world—and fifteen hundred Aboriginal protestors. "The Queen spoke of the irresistible ideals of democracy," reported the national newspaper the *Australian* (1988b) in a page 2 article, "and warmly congratulated those participating in the event." Melbourne's *Age* (1988) noted that "although she passed within a few meters of the Aboriginal gathering, the Queen did not acknowledge their presence." Aboriginal activists participating in the irresistible ideals of democracy were evidently not to be congratulated. The official strategy was simply to ignore the protests. The multicultural image the government wished to project was the reassuring figure of the mosaic artist, flanked by the Queen and the prime minister. Despite the demonstrations, the celebrations appeared to have gone well. Was it not appropriate to set aside such differences, just for an afternoon, to celebrate as one all that was right in the nation its white historians liked to style the "Lucky Country"? A few demonstrations weren't going to blow an ill wind on that. To judge from these articles, the government did appear to have been lucky, making it through the day without major incident.

The front page of the next day's national newspaper prominently displayed the reassuring photo of Michael Tjakamarra Nelson in front of the new parliament, in the company of the Queen and the prime minister, admiring his work. It was the wished-for benevolent image reaffirming national unity. But what's this? The headline screamed, "PARLIAMENT MOSAIC 'PUTS A CURSE ON WHITES'" (*Australian* 1988b). It had been announced that woven into the design, invisible to the uninitiated, was a hidden motif: a malediction against the colonizers. The white people of Australia would be cursed until the day they righted the historical wrongs to which they had subjected the continent's indigenous peoples.

An uproar ensued. People were dumbfounded. The curse dominated the evening TV news about the bicentennial and provided grist for radio talk-back shows. The white reaction boiled with indignation. Even white supporters of Aboriginal rights were taken aback. Closet, and not so closet, racists resistant to the movement raged against the impoliteness of the ingrates to whom the colonial society had attempted, evidently without success, to bring civilization. The royal strategy of simply not acknowledging their existence offered a convenient model for white people unwilling to confront the troubling complexities of the context within which the bicentennial celebrations were taking place. A good number of Aboriginal people themselves were worried that this undiplomatic act, which was being characterized in some sectors of the dominant society as "cultural terrorism," might have negative strategic consequences. Whatever the reaction, virtually everyone was interpellated by the event, in profoundly asymmetrical ways. The polarities organizing the social field were made felt, albeit in a quasi-chaotic, more or less inarticulate manner. Boycott and protest are integral parts of the civil society social negotiation that takes place within the framework of the modern nation-state. The threat to leave the negotiating table is a classic stratagem. That's normal. Even understandable. But malediction? That's beyond the pale of civility. Splutter. The performance of the curse exerted an interruptive force that brought the social negotiation (which was already on the way to being detoured from a sovereign treaty to the weaker and as yet undefined project of "reconciliation") close to the breaking point. It made Australian society stutter.

It is not that white people believed in the literal effectiveness of the curse. The effectiveness of the enunciative act did not depend on belief. In fact, among both white people and nontraditional Aboriginal people, its force had more to do with the impossibility of believing in it. White people in particular were confronted with an expression that seemed radically off, off-message and off-key, rising as it did from a cultural ground that was totally opaque to them. How could anyone in this day and age do that, in the presence of the Sovereign no less. How could anyone believe in such things? The casting of the curse was an act of radical noncommunication. It enacted Aboriginal culture, vis-à-vis settler society, as a pure power of interruption. Its triggering was a pure performative the force of which was not dependent on the transmission of commonly understood signifying or informational content. It was the statement of a transformation, and a real transformation was effected, directly by the statement. A powerful act was committed purely in speaking: a whole population was hit with a collective speech impediment. The dominant reactions were more akin to ejaculations than articulations. There was a generalized derangement of discourse.

What the curse effectively did was to problematize. It opened a breach from whose interruptive interval a pressing problem sprang: How to continue together? How could dialogue resume? How could progressive white people face their neighbors again, after their racism had so copiously confirmed itself, so easily pouring forth? How would the white government find a way of moving past this evidencing of racism in order to get negotiations back on track? What modulations might have occurred in the relations between traditionalist Aboriginal activists and those embracing a more modernist discourse? The conditions for communication had been placed in suspense. The social field shuddered and shifted, re-primed and regathered itself. The transformation touched everyone, each differently. It was global and local, in a single strike. The performative operated an integration and a differentiation in the same stroke.

The problem the curse posed bore directly on the being-together and continuing-together of the population. It did not bear on the exact terms of a settlement. Its action targeted sociality as such. It created a situation where, before being able to continue together, everyone had to affirm, in one way or another, their belonging to the social field. Being-in-relation as such was put into play. The performance of the curse was a technical means of directly addressing the level of relation, toward a rolling redefinition of the terms in relation vis-à-vis each other.

It took a few days to begin to discern the general outline of what had occurred. In the commotion of the immediate aftermath, the curse seemed, from the dominant culture's perspective, to have irrupted from the obscure background of traditional Aboriginal culture. It lacked a precise subject of enunciation. Simply, a curse had been cast. The context and subject of the act remained vague in the eyes of most of the people whose reactions had been so strong. When the dust began to settle, it became apparent that Nelson, the artist who designed the mosaic, had not in fact announced the curse. For him, the mosaic was and remained a blessing offered as a token of friendship to white society, in recognition of the progress it was (he hoped) finally making toward redressing the wrongs of the past (*Australian* 1988a). It had actually been a local urban Aboriginal man of the capital territory where Parliament House is located who pronounced the curse. Kevin Gilbert was an accomplished poet and author and a seasoned political activist and leader of the Aboriginal Sovereign Treaty '88 Campaign. It was he who launched the curse at a press conference just before the Queen joined Nelson for the photo op at the mosaic. So then it was a hoax? Could someone so sophisticated believe in such things? Either the curse was a relic of the past that rose from the immemorial depths of "true" Aboriginal culture from its refuge in the Central Desert or it was just a bad joke. It was either the archaic and authentic content rising from the deep cultural interior, headed toward extinction under the pressures of a modern world to which it was maladapted, or it was a superficial, hypocritical, modern manipulation of the esoteric beliefs of others.

Or: neither/nor. Gilbert was a descendent of the original peoples of the capital region, the Wiradjuri and Ngunnawal. He was recognized by them as a spiritual leader and traditional owner, or custodian of the cultural "laws." Doubtless, the meaning of this role is not the same for peoples living in the shadow of the white power center, who suffered colonization early on and as a result had lost their languages and much of the knowledge carried in them, than it is for the more "intact" cultures of the interior like Nelson's Warlpiri people, who had been among the last to be forced to give up their traditional nomadic ways. Be that as it may, Gilbert had accepted that traditional role, seriously fulfilled it, and saw no contradiction between it and the modernity of his political activism. Asked to explain the curse, Gilbert offered a spiritual reasoning, underlining the continuity between his role as the leader of a media political pressure campaign and traditional culture, with a syncretic twist:

> That design in stone became a vehicle upon which energies were focused. There's a creative energy, a spiritual energy—the spirit wind, if you like, or some people would liken it to the spirit of the Holy Ghost—a creative essence. This spiritual energy had been placed in the stone by the women from Papunya [Nelson's home village] who had danced in front of the new Parliament House on Monday morning, and by the large gathering of Christians there at the weekend. These forces are placed in there, making it a judgment stone, a payback. That means not a sinister, not an evil thing has been done, but a wholesome thing that will always work against assailants, murderers, thieves, until there is a pay-back—or an equalizing—of justice. This is our law, this is our culture, and I believe that if you go there you'll see the mosaic with a different energy. (*Canberra Times* 1988)

Was he telling the truth? Did he literally believe in the energies he was invoking? Even if it were possible to know with full certainty, such questions are largely irrelevant. The stakes are elsewhere. It is fundamentally not a question of the truth or belief.[5] From the performative point of view, it is entirely a question of efficacy: what act was accomplished through the pronouncement of the curse, and with what repercussions? The immediate effect was to make society stutter. One of the conditions of that effect was in fact the difficulty of assigning a subject of the enunciation. There was a contrastive polyvocality in the authorship of the overall event, straddling as it did acts by Nelson, Gilbert, and the Papunya dancers. This made it difficult to pin it down to a single intent or exact cultural backdrop, occurring as it did in a zone of undecidability between modernity and traditionalism. The enunciation unleashed a powerful, but strategically vague, force of interruption. Its power did not hinge on the propositional truth of the statement. It had a vagueness that lifted the event out of the domain of propositional meaning, but that did not attenuate the acuteness of its effect. The event did not furnish either the exact semantic content nor the precise cultural context on which a "correct" interpretation would depend. They are precisely what was suspended. This left the field open for other effects to reverberate on other levels: that of affect (the immediate feeling of a troubled belonging, associated with the wish to continue or not) and percept (the imperative to "see with a different energy"). The problem was not the presence or absence of a hidden motif. The problem was not a secret content from a different culture that was impenetrable to the dominant culture. A hidden content is definable in principle. Everything is clarified by a simple communication of information. The problem posed here was not on that level. It was far more embroiled. It was far more problematizing.

The problem posed by the event was *cultural difference itself*. It was established over the next few days that Nelson had not hidden a secret content in the stones. The secret—that there was none—was out. There was no hidden curse motif in the mosaic. What did not change was the fact that there was the performance of the *form of the secret* as *cultural differentiator* between white and Aboriginal culture *in the event*. Traditionally, Aboriginal culture deploys secrecy as central to a social organization based on ritual and spiritual practice. European culture, by contrast, deploys principles of publicity and an ideal of openness in the secular framework of what it calls civil society. By staging the form of the secret as he did, Gilbert "truly" activated Aboriginal culture *in its difference* from European culture, and did so in *a completely contemporary fashion*. There was nothing "archaic" in the produced effect. It was of searing present-day relevance. To judge by the reactions, this act, more than any other at the time, incisively and powerfully manifested what was at stake in the bicentennial celebration. It expressed most integrally the "meaning" of the bicentennial. Or more precisely, it staged most intensely its dynamic.

The staging of the form of the secret as cultural differentiator had nothing hidden about it. All of the gestures contributing to it were executed in the full light of day, before the cameras, and were fully described by the press. The performative effectiveness of the act positively depended on its being *unhidden but nontransparent* (in much the same way that Foucault, explaining the difference between a proposition and a statement, or discursive event, said that the latter is "neither visible nor hidden" [1989, 122]). The performative statement of the curse manifested *without revealing*. It manifested the affective and perceptive lines of force that were at work in the Australian social field as regards race relations and cultural heterogeneity, not by signifying them, not by describing them, but by problematically *reactivating* them en masse. The object of the curse was not negative and exclusive, as it would seem judging only by its minimal semantic content (a curse aimed exclusively at the white population). It was positive, and addressed itself, differentially, to one and all. Its effective object: the triggering into operation of cultural difference in an inclusive, if asymmetrical, field of belonging, as an *open process* whose terms were still to be negotiated and would likely require periodic, if not perpetual, renegotiation as cultures, history, and laws evolved.

Another way of putting it is that the event posed to the whole of Australian society—to its manner of holding together—a problem whose solution was not to be found in a once-and-for-all, matter-of-fact judgment. It was a problem in the sense of a real complication of a lived situation whose truth was the immediately affective charge of the gestures enacting it: the manner in which people found themselves reacting, before they were able to place themselves at a reflective distance. The performative "truth" is not a verifiable content; it is in the dynamic repercussions of the act. Its validity is purely pragmatic: actively expressive of a real complication; making felt a matter of concern; giving a power boost to a process openly and indefinitely underway. Its truth was not declarative: articulating a solution that would dissipate the problem by uncovering a content or verifying a proposition. A pragmatic truth does not take the form of a final assertion proffered from on high. It takes the form of a triggering force that operates upon the whole of a complex field of forces from a situation of immanence to it. It vectorizes the forces in the field, propelling a problematic *continuation* of their playing out. This pragmatic problematization sums itself up in the question: *How* to continue together? Or, in vectorial terms, where should we all be heading? The manner in which this question is *lived out* is the true (pragmatic) "meaning" of the act.

Once the initial shock waned, a flood of information for the nourishing of reflection ensued. The complexity was now translated onto the mediated level of language content, following from its directly felt manifestation on the level of *doing* things with words. The provocation of the event for the reprise of reflective discourse consisted in its asserting, in how it did things with words, that the oppositions that typically frame the question of the relations between Aboriginal culture and white culture were now null and void. These presuppositions can be figured as a branching network of oppositions, all tributary to tradition versus modernity as master trope: religion/civil society, "chieftainship"/representative democracy, black/white, outback Aboriginal/urbanized Aboriginal, secret/public, esoteric/common, simple/sophisticated, hypocritical/sincere, archaic/contemporary, authentic/fabricated, disappearing/progressing, pagan/Christian. To name a few. This is how Australian society has a habit of structuring itself, at least in its self-representations in dominant media and "commonsense" discourse. The circumstances of the curse did not obey these structuring oppositions. The curse was situated at a point of intersection epitomized by the image Gilbert painted for the press a few days later: that of a sophisticated political activist of the capital, recognized as a traditional leader by his modernized First Nation, allying himself with the "authentic" indigenous ritual performed by traditional women of the Central Desert at the entry of the new parliament dedicated to the foundation of the white state, explaining his action by invoking a syncretic vocabulary of "energies" invested in that place by their ritual, augmenting energies already brought to the same site by an assembly of Christians.

If the performative deployment of the form of the secret operated as a differentiator, staging cultural difference as such, the informational statements that followed at the level of reflective discourse effected, for their part, a reintegration of the differentials that had been activated. The circumstances presented the complexity of an image militating against Australian society being so easily reduced to a branching structure of black-and-white divisions. Things actually happen at the intersections between the terms, at their eventful interstices.[6] Australian society is not composed of two (or several) deep cultural interiorities standing in simple opposition to each other. Society lies at a crossroads. There is a single asymmetrical field of complex relation where cultural difference plays out—neither hidden nor transparent—through encounter.

Encounter: proximity, in the act, of what, in principle, is in opposition. The processual continuity of differing.

The genius of the performance of the curse was that it was able to operate on a double register, differentially and integrally at the same time (on different levels, as different phases of the same event). This ability was based first and foremost on a power of interruption that "communicated" not a signification or a proposition (to be verified) but a charge of processual indetermination (to be played out and renegotiated). Secondarily, on the level of linguistic content it translated into such a high degree of complexity, into such a semantic richness, that it was difficult, if not impossible, to evaluate either its propositional truth (hypocritical or sincere? literal or metaphorical?) or its exact political import (will the process unfolding from it end up contributing to an aggravation or a diminution of discord, and in the short term or long term?). Numerous possible propositions were suggested by the curse that did not mutually exclude each other. (That the act was both hypocritical *and* sincere in a certain way was not out of the question, given that the central opposition that authorized this alternative, that of traditionalism versus modernism, was palpably not in force.) A criterion for final judgment was lacking, and is still lacking. The performative indetermination of the act translated into discourse as a propositional undecidability, by virtue of the surplus of significations it unleashed and the abundance of equally tenable interpretations they authorized. It was this processual passage from indetermination to undecidability, the act's refusal to allow itself to be captured with the finality of the all-is-said-and-done, its lack of cooperation with the triage of facts leading to an empirically verified truth, that enabled the curse to target being-in-relation, to problematize belonging, in so intense and pragmatic a fashion. Its stymying of the selective pinning down of its "true" content is what qualified it as a true technique of sociality.

It is perhaps more precise to say not that society has no oppositional structure—it is self-evident that it does, at a certain level of expression (one need only look at the commonplaces that so regularly spring up to see that)—but that the *structure* of society, as fixed in the content of public propositions about its composition, is opposed to its *process*. It is necessary to make the saying of the structure stutter, in order to enable the doing of its process to resume across the flood of words.

In the long term, Australian society seems to have decided to double down on its signifying structure. The social process that had so intensely, instantaneously been kicked back into movement by the curse subsequently stalled. Five years later, the completion of a treaty was nowhere in sight. Collective reflection had turned entirely toward the question of what a "reconciliation" between the First Nations and the white majority might mean in the absence of a treaty. The resistance of certain segments of the white population had hardened, even toward the less radical option of reconciliation. Michael Tjakamarra Nelson, the artist of the mosaic, concluded that his token of friendship had not been honored. In 1993, the year Kevin Gilbert died, Nelson took up the baton of performative practice. He retraced his own steps. Once again, he made the long journey to the capital. Before the mosaic, he made a solemn announcement. He had no other choice, he said, than to retract his blessing (transforming it once again—or doubly—into a curse?). "The government of Australia is not recognizing my people and our culture. It is abusing my painting and insulting my people. It makes my people sad that government does not respect my painting or my people. I want to take my painting back to my people" (Nelson 2000, 482–83). Nelson then defaced the mosaic by removing a section (in an inversion of the inclusion in it of a curse motif that wasn't there; *Australian* 1993a).

Nelson wanted the process to continue. He attempted a new performative triggering. However, the resegmentation of society along conventional divisions seems already to have been too advanced. He succeeded only in leaving an eloquent testimony to the stalling of the process. Now emptied of its "energies," returned by its author to the desert of his ancestors, the mosaic no longer stirred the social field. It became what the government wanted it to be all along: an anodyne decorative motif adding a bit of color to the white edifice of power.

It is not that there was no evolution on the formal level. In 1992, the High Court of Australia annulled the principle that had been the legal linchpin of the justification for the unequal treatment of Aboriginal people for two centuries: *terra nullius*. This was the doctrine that prior to colonization Aboriginal peoples were so primitive that they knew no form of landownership. The complex systems of territorial rights and custodianship obligations that had been in force before colonization were declared nonexistent. The arrival of "superior" white civilization had automatically "extinguished" whatever it was that might have preceded it that wasn't "really" land tenure. Thus there was no need to sign a treaty with so primitively incompetent a people, or to compensate for the loss of the land and its resources they had never owned, according to this fiction. The continent was declared legally uninhabited—a "no man's land," as the phrase has it in Latin—before white settlement. Talk about a performative act! This official performative fiction of the nonexistence of Aboriginal rights had been the governing principle of the process of colonization in all its aspects. The High Court's *Mabo* decision (named after the plaintiff in the case, Eddie Koiki Mabo) reversed the doctrine of terra nullius. Henceforth, there could be circumstances where the rights of Aboriginal people to the land and resources in any state or territory of the Commonwealth of Australia were not extinguished. In practice, those circumstances were highly limited. The decision only applied to government lands that had not been granted in fee simple to settlers, and to Aboriginal groups that could prove a ritual connection to a specific territory that had continued unbroken since the precolonial era. As limited as it was, the *Mabo* decision was excoriated by a good part of the white population. Middle-class white people in particular fulminated against what they considered to be the "preferential treatment" accorded Aboriginal people. White backlash made extremely difficult the effective implementation of new procedures and the establishment of new institutions for articulating the European legal system with Aboriginal traditional law and the newly recognized land title. It was a fraught, years-long process for Aboriginal people seeking to exercise their right to access to their ancestral lands as established by the *Mabo* decision. The High Court victory on the principle led to a pragmatic impasse on the ground of the social field, where the repercussions of the decision were still subject to laborious negotiation, on an uneven playing field. It was in reaction to this impasse, coming out of the failure of the treaty movement, that Nelson retracted the mosaic.

Culture under the Seal of the Public

The year after the retraction, the situation worsened further. The form of the secret was restaged, but in a context where it was impossible to maneuver around a final judgment based on a finding of fact boxing the processual charge into a verifiable content (which is the same as saying "a falsifiable content"). In this case, undecidability was suspended. Decision was demanded.

The problem was a development issue involving an island off the coast of South Australia. The development of Hindmarsh Island was limited because it was accessible only by ferry. White development interests coveted the relatively unexploited island. Obligingly, the local government proposed the construction of a bridge to enable more intensive development. The First People of the area, the Ngarrindjeri, protested. The island, they said, was a sacred site inhabited by ancestral beings of the Dreaming and was of great ritual importance. The construction of the bridge and subsequent developments would profane the sacred site, destroying the spiritual powers upon which Ngarrindjeri life depended. They would do everything they could to block the development. Thus began a dispute that would escalate into a national controversy, dubbed "the Hindmarsh Affair."

Local white people claimed never to have heard of sacred sites on the island. Of course not, Aboriginal people responded: this is secret knowledge. Why ever would you be privy to it? Okay, the riposte came, it's a sacred site: so *prove* it. We can't prove it, the Aboriginal men said: it's secret "women's business." But certain Ngarrindjeri women (who, incidentally, supported the bridge) came out and said that they had never heard tell of it either. Of course not, said other women, opposed to the bridge: it's secret knowledge only our skin group (kinship subdivision) has the right to possesses. Doreen Kartinyeri, the leader of the bridge opponents, recounted how the knowledge had been passed down from her lineage's grandmothers. *Prove* it, repeated the local white people more loudly, heartened by the dissension within the Aboriginal community. The ensuing controversy amplified to the national level and dominated the news related to Aboriginal affairs in the period 1994–96. It has yet to completely dissipate even now.

From the beginning, white opinion was massively in favor of the cynical interpretation that the bridge opponents had simply fabricated the "secrets" in order to block modern "progress." The federal minister of Aboriginal and Torres Islander affairs opened an inquiry to investigate. The conundrum for those who held custodianship of the sacred knowledge, called the "proponent women" in the press, was obvious: a secret that is revealed is not a secret. Women's secret knowledge divulged to men is no longer women's secret knowledge. How could the form of the secret that served as an organizing principle of Aboriginal society be "reconciled" with the need of dominant white society to publicly verify the content?

In order to protect the secret of the island that protected their culture, the proponent women refused to appear before the inquiry. A female anthropologist was engaged to interview them and consult the relevant historical documents and anthropological studies dating from the time when Ngarrindjeri culture, now mostly urbanized, was "intact." She was tasked with returning a judgment on the cultural well-foundedness of the claims. After extensive study, her verdict came back confirming the existence of the secret women's business. She presented her conclusion as a "significant anthropological discovery" of a hitherto unknown domain of women's knowledge.[7] In order to avoid doing harm to Ngarrindjeri culture, she declined to reveal the secrets in public. Her findings were attached to the inquiry's report in two secret appendices transmitted to the Ministry in sealed envelopes, exclusively for the eyes of women in public office related to the affair. The sealing of the envelopes reproduced the form of the secret of the Ngarrindjeri in somewhat compromised form (disclosure would be limited) while translating its content into the object of a public administrative judgment.

Based on the expert report, the minister of Aboriginal affairs blocked the construction of the bridge. The issue was then brought before the courts. The proponent women still refused to appear. It was the sealed envelopes that stood in their stead in the corridors of white power. The case made its way to the High Court of Australia, which in the end reversed the minister's decision and approved the construction of the bridge. Even this was not the end of the affair. The sealed envelopes had one more addressee: a Royal Commission was constituted to determine the truth of the matter once and for all. It ratified the High Court decision against the proponent women. By government decree, it was declared that the secret knowledge was not discovered, but fabricated. The construction went ahead. When the bridge was inaugurated in March 2001, it was noted that the administrative and legal proceedings had cost the "Australian taxpayers" three times more than the cost of the construction itself. Thus came to the close—or so it seemed—a scandal that had lasted the better part of a decade.

As in the case of the mosaic, the Ngarrindjeri women tried to practice a politics of noncommunication of cultural difference. This time, the effect was totally different. The refusal of communication in the Hindmarsh Affair was deprived of its performative force by its capture in the snare of the administrative and judicial systems. These systems have as their principle the incitation of communication: the imperative to self-express that lies at the heart of disciplinary power. And there should be no mistake: communication as it is practiced in connection with state and quasi-state apparatuses of judgment is essentially disciplinary in nature. In this instance, the Aboriginal women found themselves in the situation of having to follow a politics of noncommunication in a context that was fundamentally inhospitable to its performance, and this had serious consequences. The Hindmarsh Affair was an important defeat for Aboriginal struggles across Australia and precipitated a prolonged crisis in the local community, torn apart by internal divisions. The proponent women suffered from the transmittal of their secrets to the government. They attributed serious illnesses in their community to the revelation of the secret contents to non-Aboriginal women. At the same time, their refusal to appear before government bodies to attest to the authenticity of their knowledge weakened their cause, conceding the power of verifiable/falsifiable public speech to their opponents. After the Royal Commission decision against them, the press repeated ad nauseam the accusation that the spiritual importance of the site had been fabricated. The "fact" of the nonexistence of the secret knowledge entered the public domain in the guise of an established truth. Negotiations closed. The Ngarrindjeri women opposed to the bridge had been put in a position where remaining faithful to their own ideas about what constituted their culture, in its difference from that of white people, inexorably led to a betrayal of that culture. At the end of the Royal Commission, their cause lost, they reclaimed the sealed envelopes and burned them. The "nonexistent" secrets returned to the silence from which they came.

The decisive effect of the governmental capture in a communicational frame was to neutralize the role of cultural difference, even as everything that took place revolved around that difference. Translated into the communicational frame, the only operative distinction in the affair became that of truth and falsehood. It then became a question of performing a triage between the authentic and the lying, according to a principle of veridiction with the apparent power to transcend the circumstantial differentiations of the social field. In this exercise of governmental judgment, cultural difference figures only as a colorful backdrop. There were of course anthropologists who argued in favor of the authenticity of the secret knowledge at the heart of this controversy, and who continue to do so today (see Bell 1998). The Royal Commission decision officially placed these white experts on the same side of the operative distinction as the Aboriginal people who were "proponents" of traditional knowledge: the lying side (fakers, colluders, and/or dupes). The sovereign judgment grouped, on either side of a public split, opposing segments of the population, regardless of the cultural differences within each grouping. Only the truth counted, and nothing but the truth: a truth deemed generally applicable regardless. The divided segments were to be forever separated by the triage line drawn by the finality of the government-declared truth.

The performance of the mosaic curse eventfully differentiated cultures in order to integrate them afterward in the same open and indefinite pragmatic field, where the problem of departure (the nature and consequences of differentiations and asymmetries immanent to the social field) would continue to play out and be negotiated. The Hindmarsh proceedings did the opposite. They integrated different cultures into an a priori common frame that is formally closed and deploys a forcefully common language, in order afterward to divide them, with nonnegotiable finality, and according to criteria foreign to the terms in which the problem posed itself. The problem was posed in terms of on-the-ground cultural difference and was answered in the language of truth as a transcendent principle. The noncommunication of the mosaic differentiated in order to integrate differentials. The communicational imperative as it swept through the Hindmarsh Affair integrated under the sign of the same in order to divide. This sums up the difference between a reprocessualization and a restructuring; between an appeal to problematic becoming and a decisive exercise in normative and distributive power.

Given the circumstances, it was probably inevitable that the attempt of the Ngarrindjeri women to conduct a politics of noncommunication in the face of the communicational imperative of disciplinary power would end by calling into question not only the well-foundedness of certain cultural contents, but the reality of cultural difference itself. It was not only a certain set of cultural contents that was disqualified by the governmental and judicial judgments. The form of the secret itself was put on trial. A decisive factor in the affair was the well-known fact that the classic anthropological study on the Ngarrindjeri, which was based on fieldwork conducted in the 1940s, did not seem to confirm the existence of secret knowledge reserved for women. The study went so far as to propose that the traditional religion of the Ngarrindjeri, alone among the seven hundred or so Aboriginal cultures of Australia, did not practice secret rituals, or at most practiced them "minimally" (Berndt and Berndt 1993). These conclusions have been strongly contested by contemporary anthropologists allied to the Ngarrindjeri, but the general "truth" according to which their culture traditionally lacked the form of the secret was as firmly established in public opinion as the specific "truth" concerning the religious insignificance of the particular island in question.

This disqualification of the form of the secret as cultural differentiator between Aboriginal and European culture echoed throughout the Australian social field. It seemed to confirm what many white people suspected all along: all these stories about sacred sites are just ruses to claim unmerited "privileges." At bottom, we are all alike. We are all modern (or should be, if we want to count). The only difference is that there are among us individuals who have no scruples about exploiting, in the most hypocritical fashion, a supposed cultural difference long since erased by the forward march of progress and the loss of cultural contents dating from the "precontact" era. What is important now is economic development. That is what, ultimately, constitutes the common frame uniting us all in a community. But an odd community it is: a community of atomized individuals. For the reigning principle of that cohesion is the private interest of the individual, abstracted from the vanishing collective backdrop of the ancestral culture of the most time-hallowed segment of the community, now relegated to the decorative, folkloric status of an anodyne mosaic. The gravest consequence of the Hindmarsh Affair was to neutralize the power of the form of the sacred secret to make a cultural difference. The very phrase "sacred site" became a term of derision in white society, as if any claim to the right to the differential benefit of land and resources based on a traditional difference in cultural practices was by definition a pernicious manipulation that did undue injury to the only sacred principle generally recognized by white society: the market. In 1998, the federal government, now dominated by a neoliberal coalition, passed a law severely limiting the admissibility criteria for claims to ancestral land title under the *Mabo* decision. The recognition of the traditional law by the white state was to be more symbolic than real.

But there is a third way, between the modern dismissal of traditional culture and the reflex to counter that with support of its unadulterated "authenticity." In this perspective, a culture is not a grab-bag of information or contents of whatever kind. It is a dynamic formation. A culture is defined less by its contents than by its ability to continuously modulate its forms of expression, due as much to the pressure of internal tensions as to intercultural encounters. Intercultural encounters are always occurring and have been forever. The Aboriginal cultures of Australia were in no way isolated before European colonization. The continent's hundreds of cultures had complex, long-term interrelations, making them among the most multilingual populations on earth. For thousands of years there have been contacts in the north with Papuan cultures and, in more recent historical times, with the Macassans of Indonesia. "The necessity," writes James Weiner (2001, 151), "to retain, replace, or reconfigure knowledge in the face of the experience of its loss is an *internal* mechanism" of all living cultures, which by their very nature—as constituting an open, problematic processual field—always find themselves at an intersection, reaching with every step a turning point where they are called upon to self-modulate, to adapt to change, their own components mutually readapting to each other. In this open field, "new myths are constantly being created and tested" (142). Certain historical events that occurred during colonization, for example the Coniston Massacre of 1928, are now a part of the oral tradition of the Dreamtime. These emergent "myths" (a European category that is utterly misplaced here) are tested not against an invariant structure or a cumulative fund of contents, but by the relational consequences of their pragmatic performance.

"What is lost is a certain technique of relationality itself. . . . A form of social life . . . does not reproduce or transmit or pass on information per se. . . . Rather, it reproduces a certain technique of making information visible" (Weiner 2001, 155). Visible, sometimes, without ceasing to be secret; manifested, perchance without being revealed. The rendering visible of the secret as such may induce the retexturing of the differentiations always already at work in the social field—and always still to be determined.

A cultural form, a form of life, is at bottom an empty form—which is what makes it maximally dynamic. It is an immediate form of relation veritably bristling with potential repercussions, as opposed to a form of content full of already given, ahistorical elements. It is not a common language or framing structure for a determinate store of content. It is a dynamic *form of expression*: a matrix for the renewal of cultural content.

A living culture is one that is continually remaking itself through its relational expressions. A living cultural tradition is a continuing lineage of self-fabrication. From this point of view, if the secrets of the Ngarrindjeri were indeed fabricated and were certifiably "false," that wouldn't necessarily make them "inauthentic"—quite the contrary. It would make them signs of cultural life. Humor for a moment the idea that the form of the secret was not traditionally operative among the Ngarrindjeri, alone among Aboriginal cultures, and that the proponent women had borrowed it from other Aboriginal cultures alive in the contemporary social field, adopting it in order to adapt to present pressures. Wouldn't that in itself constitute a continuation of the traditional multiculturalism, in the name of a collective future? "Fabulation is itself memory, and memory is invention of a people. . . . Not the myth of a past people, but the fabulation of the people to come" (Deleuze 1989, 223, translation modified).

The problem is not that the contents might be false. It is rather that the truth is a false problem. Truth as a form of content boxes in, where the pragmatic question opens out (What next connection might be negotiable?). Where the pragmatic question concerns the future (What new variation on our collectivity is to be invented to meet changing circumstances? How does our collective life continue its lineage?), truth turns back to look at the past. As a procedure of judgment, it bears on propositions about the past considered to be amenable to precise determination, revealing the empirical "truth" of a content whose validity depends on its ability to be preserved without essentially changing.

Pragmatically speaking, the issue is not the truth content of propositions, but rather the effects truly achieved by performance. What is important is the present: the dynamics that are at work in it, from the past and newly emergent; the mode under which they might prolong themselves for the collective future; and with what reconfigurative interruptions. The true stakes are immanent to the field of sociality as it presently plays out, and in the way in which it opens itself to modification at every moment. The true problem for the Ngarrindjeri is this: How to reinsert themselves, as an Aboriginal people in close relation with other Aboriginal peoples, urban and rural, into the larger field of a changing Australian society, with enhanced autonomy? The problem for the larger society is this: How to "reconcile" itself with cultural difference, performative of its continuity, but in a finally unassignable way (in the manner of a dynamic form generative of new contents or new modulations on old contents)? How to share a social field with those who wish to connect and participate without assimilating, and whose "laws" perform their irreducibility to the reigning European legal and conceptual framework? These problems are more ethico-political than empirical.

Coda (2020)

The Australian prime minister of the time, John Howard, he who had signed off on the construction of the bridge, was, for his sorry part, a man of truth. Nicknamed by the press "Honest John," he couldn't conceive of and didn't know how to ask for pardon. He visibly lacked inventiveness. He didn't issue the apology many felt to be the precondition for reconciliation. What this gesture did was implicitly repeat the same insult: "prove it."

Howard may have felt vindicated by the Royal Commission decision that opened the way to his approval of the bridge. Except, as mentioned in passing earlier, that wasn't the end of the story. In 2002 (after the original writing of this essay) a civil suit for damages was brought in federal court by aggrieved local whites with commercial interests affected by the bridge controversy. The court found against them. The Royal Commission, it said, had not established proof of fabrication. Now the government got a taste of its own medicine, as the burden of proof was turned against it. Things began to shift. Negotiations continued. Soon an apology was issued (not by Howard, but by a local governmental body), and the Ngarrindjeri were recognized as the traditional owners of the area. In 2010, the government of the state of South Australia accepted that the secret knowledge was a reality (ABC News 2010).

Still, not everyone is convinced. Even some who accept the existence of the secret knowledge argue that it cannot not have been "embellished." The controversy is not extinguished, nor are the differentials at work in Australian society that played out around it. Although the balance of proof has tilted in the direction of the proponent women, there is still an air of undecidability wafting about the affair. On the pragmatic level, the Ngarrindjeri rights to the land are still severely limited by the competing, and framing, principles of European land tenure, economic development imperatives, and resource use, to which traditional practices have no choice but to adapt. The story is doubtless still not over. It sputters along. New outbreaks of controversy are not out of the question. The process continues, on-again-off-again, in interruption and resumption.

The basic struggle remains the right to the noncommunication of cultural difference against the disciplinary compulsion to "prove it": to sign, seal, and deliver self-justifying proof to colonial power. Rather than to continue, rather than go about the process of living the difference and performing it as befits a living culture. Rather than to perform its vitality, problematically, in an integrally open field of evolving social differentials irreducible to a common framework, and for which there never was, nor should there be, a common language.

On-again, off-again, in interruption and resumption: it seems the Ngarrindjeri women did make Australian society stutter after all. They spun the performance of collective memory in the form of the secret into the ongoing adaptive invention of their contemporary form of life, veritably "fabulating" itself into the future of a self-modulating survival of their people to come, in immemorial resistance to the white man's truth.

VECTORS

- The world is not only made of already articulated structures and fully formed beings.
- There are also beings of relation. These have their own mode of existence, which pertains to a different ontological dimension: the dimension of the in-the-making. This dimension of formation or emergence is populated by a spectrum of differentiations without separation: tensions, gradients, thresholds, tendencies, torsions, all in a state of mutual inclusion (reciprocal immanence) conditioning local-global resonances (as by action at a distance). These are the dynamic germs from which articulated structures and formed beings spring, their becoming effected by a triggering event. The triggering event can be characterized as "performative," "quasi-causal," or "magic." A society's sociality is such a being of relation. It is not an already articulated structure or a fully formed being. It is not a thing.
- The constituent dimensions of a being in relation are bound in becoming. They are in-formation, perpetually in the process of taking-form, bound together in transformational passage. The passage is irreducibly evental. It is an irreversible *process*—that of the actualization of potentials that are invented en route.
- It is possible to situate interventions on the level of forms. We do it every day. The smallest useful gesture, the articulation of the most modest verifiable proposition, or the transmission of the tiniest bit of information suffices. But it is possible as well for interventions to situate themselves on the level of the as-yet-unformed, in the

in-formation. In either case, the appropriate techniques must be deployed. The techniques proper to the *in-formation* are different from those appropriate to the level of *information*. The latter are exercises in normative and distributive power. The former are modulations of ontogenetic powers (powers of becoming inventive of emergent potential).

- Among the modulatory or quasi-causal techniques capable of addressing the relational level of in-formation are techniques of noncommunication: techniques of interruption, suspension. The singular mode of functioning of these techniques should be recognized and respected.
- The passage between the levels goes both ways. The levels relay each other and absorb each other's effects. Every social act, even the most expected, is evental, a performative, if ever so lightly. As an interrupter, it creates the conditions for a modulation, however slight. Once these conditions are created, it is not out of the question that the modulation will amplify. The performativity endemic to all social acts carries an ever-present risk of reprocessualization. Chance and the singularity of circumstance play a decisive role. The force of the performative act is subject to chance inflections, across successive event-thresholds. This is what makes not only its triggering, but also its follow-on, eventful.
- It may well be that it is impossible, from a processual point of view, to separate the content from the context of an act (gesture? statement? . . . both at once). Beneath the structures of formed beings—or more precisely, in their interstices (in the empty interruptive form of a matrixial content-context indistinction)—whirrs, barely perceptible, the immanent motor of in-formation, ready at any moment to resume operation. Nothing endures. Structures self-inventively adapt, and fall into ruin. Beings self-inventively adapt, and perish. Although nothing endures, it is also the case that nothing entirely disappears. All that passes leaves a trace, returning to the germinal state, rebecoming virtual, rebecoming tendency and potential, matter for becoming.
- There persists in the world, everywhere and at all times, a remainder that is a standing reserve of potential modulation (of

processuality). This is the field of belonging of beings of relation: the mutual inclusion of that which cannot yet distinguish itself formally on the level of established structures and beings. This germinal dimension of relation should be attended to and cared for. The processual promiscuity of germinal forms should be cultivated. Remainder, reserve: memory of the future. Pure sociality: being-together, in potential. Those who cultivate the field of belonging are *healers of relation*. Their actions are catalytic (triggering). What healers of relation care for, upstream of significations and propositions (the realm of *negotiators*), are affects and percepts pertaining not to particular accommodations but to belonging as such: the preindividual fact of living-together, or falling in with each other.

- If the passage between the levels goes both ways, then it constitutes a rhythm, a systolic/diastolic alternation— in-formation/information, emergence/extinction. This rhythm unfolds onto the level of articulated structures and formed beings, and folds back in to the incipience of each moment, to fill the intervals.
- There must also be a third kind of technique that does not address either one level or the other, dedicated neither to a purely catalytic operation upon the field of belonging nor to a labor of negotiation between established forms. These techniques address themselves to the rhythm of passage between the ontological dimensions, between the as-yet-unformed and indeterminate on the one hand, and the formally established and determinate or determinable on the other. The catalysis of relation can be called the ethical act par excellence (in that it directly touches upon potential being-together in process), and the pursuit of social negotiation can be called the political act (restructuration; the mounting of new apparatuses for the mutual readaptation of formed beings). Techniques of the third kind—the ethico-political art of caring for the rhythm of reprocessualization-restructuration reciprocity—deserve their own name. Vinciane Despret has proposed one: *ethopoiesis*. Ethopoiesis, as the name implies, concerns the self-inventive becoming of forms of life in relation, or the relational vivacity of the in-formation. Isabelle

Stengers's expression, the *ecology of practices*, is another way of talking about it (Stengers 2010–11). For those who practice it, Deleuze suggests the name *intercessors* (1995, 121–34).[8] Their action is also catalytic (triggering), but in a way that already anticipates takings-form from the field of belonging, and encourages them to pace themselves to an emergent rhythm.

- To speak of ethopoiesis is to speak of *ethnopoiesis*. It is always, in one way or another, a question of the becoming of a people who have a rendezvous with cultural difference. The two concepts, ethopoiesis and ethnopoiesis, are so closely linked that they are as good as synonyms.
- Cultural difference is of the nature of an encounter. It lies at the dynamic crossroads of a multiplicity of forms of expression and communication, some of which are dedicated to defining and carrying content. As such, it does not contain anything or transmit anything. It has to do with the resumption of collective process, through a performance that is known only in and as its relational consequences. It has no in-itself. It is only "in" its continuing expressions, all of which boil down to a single meaning: survival, under conditions of change; in transformation. It is an empty form in the sense that it bursts forth as an eventful indistinction between content and context, which is at the same time a performative undecidability between the context and the subject of the enunciation (this is characteristic of all quasi-causal powers). In this interstitial zone or zone of encounter, articulated structures and formed beings are in immediate contact with one another, the boundaries between them having melted down into a fluid field of differentiation. They are no longer themselves. They are in relation, integrally in on it together. It is only in the enacting of difference that there is unity: the dynamic unity of an unfolding becoming-different-together all over again, in a rhythm.
- The imperative to communicate is much more than a simple demand to share information and transmit contents. It is an exercise in disciplinary power that emits an imperative to *translate and be translated*. Every incitation to communication mobilizes

terrible powers of translation whose object is to fill the empty form of cultural difference, in order to neutralize its generative force. The neutralization technique is simple. It consists in boxing a dynamic form into a determinable content, or an event into the possible object of a verifiable proposition. To effect this transformation, it suffices to say "prove it" (and to have at the ready the institutional powers of judgment and ready means to execute the final decision). Just the suggestion of this kind of translation is already a trial.
- The truth is never what is truly at stake in the ecology of practices. Rather, truth is the limiting condition of the ecology of practices. A radical or minoritarian movement, if it is to (continue to) make a real difference, can never content itself with seeking or transmitting a truth, or defending or advocating a belief. Eth(n)opoiesis is radically *anti-ideological*. To accept the truth as the central issue is to accept the neutralization of differential powers of integral transformation. It is to accept the communicational capture of survival and becoming: their disciplinary arrest. To continue, techniques must be deployed of the kind Deleuze calls "powers of the false, " which is to say powers of fabulation (1989, 126–55). These techniques are nontransparent, thus nonverifiable, even if they are unhidden. Their power comes from the form of the secret—even or especially if it is an open secret, one with no finally determinable content. Collective becoming is by nature *clandestine*, in this nonstandard processual sense.
- If one is attached to using vocabulary derived from the European tradition of political thought, speaking for example of a new "constitution" or a new kind of "parliament" (Latour 1993, 138–45), given all that has been said in this chapter, it would be advisable to attribute a fundamental "right" to the would-be inhabitant of the "common worlds" under construction through that vocabulary: the right to the noncommunication of difference. The right to the practice of incommunicable difference is crucial. The correctives that Latour applies to his European governmental vocabulary—such as the "principle of irreduction"—are too easily

glossed over in the commonplace rush to the "common": toward a common "language," "common sense," and common "frameworks" to which we are all sincerely exhorted to adhere. The normative and distributive (exclusionary) triage of those who do not adhere—those who perform "archaic," clandestine, or fabulatory differencings—lurks just around corner. There is a real and present danger in the language of the "common" of falling back into aspects of Western juridical thought that fuel the disciplinary mode of power associated with the historical operations of its same-old nation-state.

- Better to stutter than to s(t)ay the same.

1998

Event Horizon

1. Gone Critical

System. Routine. At a certain conjuncture, the unfolding of the physical system's line of actions interrupts. The system momentarily suspends itself. It has not become inactive. It is in ferment. It has gone "critical." This "chaotic" interlude is not the simple absence of order. It is in fact a super-ordered state. In chaos theory, it is conceived as the co-presence of all of the possible paths the system may take: their physical inclusion in one another.

Criticality is when what are normally mutually exclusive alternatives pack into the materiality of the system. The system is no longer acting and outwardly reacting according to physical laws unfolding in linear fashion. It is churning, running over its own possible states. It has folded in on itself, becoming materially self-referential, animated not by external relations of cause-effect but by an intensive interrelating of versions of itself. The system is a knot of mutually implicated alternative transformations of itself, in material resonance. Which transformation actually occurs, what the next outward connection will be, cannot be predicted by extrapolating from physical laws. The suspended system is in too heightened a state of transformability. It is hypermutable. Hyperconnectible, by virtue of having disconnected itself. The system hesitates, works through the problem of its critical self-referentiality, and "chooses" an unfolding.

When scientists use words like "choice" they are of course not implying that the system humanly reflects, applying instrumental reason to choose from a set of preestablished possibilities arrayed before it and liable to mutual substitution. But it is no exaggeration to call the system's intensive animation thought, defined as "the reality of an excess over the actual." Its possible futures are present, in the system, in its matter. In effect: incipient effect (resonance and interference, vibration and turbulence, unfoldable into an array, an order).

Possibility has, in effect, materialized. The matter of the system has entered a state where it does not extrapolate into an abstract possibility, and instead effectively absorbs possibilities, en masse, into its animated matter. Materially present possibility is potential. The system's criticality, of course, is as actual as any other state. What is in excess is the self-referentiality of the system's critical condition, its doubling back on itself en masse. What the self-absorbed system infolds is materially co-present in that way: in potential.

Implex: potential in-animates the actual conjunction (it is not separable from it). Excess: potential doubles the actual conjunction (it is not reducible to it). Potential is the implicate double of the actual.

Call a form of thought that is materially self-referential as opposed to reflective; that absorbs possibility rather than extrapolating it; that does not imply a distance between successive states of a system, mediated by an intervening action, but rather their immediate proximity to each other, their inclusion in one another; that therefore embodies a super-order of superposition rather than arraying an order of substitution; that materializes an unpredictable futurity rather than abstracting alternate outcomes from itself and from each other; that infolds before extending; that chooses unsubordinated to the established regularities of linear causality—call that kind of thought *operative reason*. Not the purposive analysis-toward-action of instrumental reason: a hesitant self-definition in suspension. Not an extending out of matter into thought-substitution, nor a doubling of perception by thought: a folding of thought into matter, at a point of indistinguishability with perception. Matter self-perceiving, doubling itself with its variations.

Instrumental reason makes thoughtfully, actfully explicit what is materially implied by the criticality of operative reason. Instrumental reason is operative reason's unfolding, its extension. Instrumental reason doubles perception with possibility: thought-out futurities in extrinsic relation to each other; mutually exclusive paths standing outside and against each other. Untangled by routine. Only thought-out, unimplicated. Arrayed in an extensive system whose alternate paths are separate and set. In a word, well-trodden. Already only thought-out, and now anticipating. Reflecting a rethink, in a next act, an anticipated next step. Retrospective-projective, before-after, looping. Possibility is potential extended, in action reflective of, simply repeating, thought. Simplex.

Potential extended: prosthesis of potential. The possible is the out-folded, out-worn double of the doubling that is potential, the simplex thought-shadow it retrospectively projects, in anticipatory action. Potential's intense, implex-excess (complex) vagueness recognized; thought-reflectively repeated. The possible pales to lucidity next to the felt turbulence of the critical. It is the pallor of potential. As a Bergsonian reading of the critical point, or bifurcation point, might have it.[1]

The critical point may be an interregnum between two different orders, two different systemic organizations with their characteristic paths of actions and reactions. Or it may constitute a threshold between disorder and order, an entropically disordered past and a future of systemic organization. The most celebrated example of the latter case is the Bénard instability, which occurs when turbulent patterns of diffusion in a heated liquid spontaneously order into convection cells. The ordering is not predictable in terms of heat diffusion alone. In fact, according to the theory of heat diffusion it is so improbable that, in principle, it must be considered practically impossible (Prigogine and Stengers 1984, 142–43). Yet it happens. Theorists of such "dissipative structures" explain that the self-organizing of liquid into a convection system is triggered because the instability of the situation suddenly makes the liquid "sensitive" to gravity (163–65; Prigogine and Stengers 1988, 59–60). Gravity suddenly registers, and resonates. It infolds. Gravity is no longer an independent variable framing the system. It is a variation of the system. Its registering is one with the event of the system's self-variation. No longer a law of nature: an in-system event-trigger. It is this in-fold sensing, this in-sensing, of a force that up to that point was not pertinent to the system and had been "ignored" that triggers the self-ordering transformation. Operative reason is a notice of force, a call to attention of matter to force, in a self-referential in-acting of the event of its own practical impossibility. Attention: in-tension.

Operative reason concerns the intensity of sensation more directly than the out-wearing of perception. The difference being: sensation is immanent perception (event in-triggering), and perception is sensation acted out (extended into an already only-thought-out array reflected and pre-reflected in action).

2. Habit and Hiatus

The system is you. Reabsorbing possibility, yielding (to) potential. Your life is one long dissipation. The "certain conjuncture" at which criticality is reached is each and every sensation. At every step you ground and orient yourself, using gravity to propel you along your habit-ridden line of daily actions. Midstep, you are suspended: between falling and walking, ground and air, left, right, and straight. Hiatus. Without duration, measureless, less a pose or repose than a pure passing, from one equilibrium-saving footfall to the next, through an ever-shifting center of gravity that has no more extension, is no more actual, than any other mathematical point. But that is no less real for being virtual (governing as it does your potential bodily movement).

Physical laws, says C. S. Peirce, are habits of matter (1992a, 223–24, 277–79). Gravity is a habit of mass. Always already felt. As already felt, each and every sensation is a law unto itself. Laws: law of association arraying before (and after) it a set of familiar next steps, possible follow-up thought-perceptions, personal or conventional; laws of usage of many kinds (next-step possible actions, more likely conventional than personal). Symbol and function. Not yet only thought. Still in action, bound up with perception. In situation. In mix. So familiar, so automatic, as to be ignored. Every sensation is a gravitational pull, grounding and orienting your nextness in pre-arrays of symbol and function. The ambulant germ of the possible: habit.

At the same time, each and every sensation is a virtual center where lines of action conveying pre-arrayed thought constrict into a point of pure passing: hiatus.

Midstep, in passing, something registers and resonates. It hits you where your equilibrium shifts. The virtual point that is the spatial center of gravity is also the durationless, measureless time of impact. Here and now (always already given) before you know it (not already thought-out in action-perception). Where habit meets event.

Arbitrarily restrict the term "sensation" to the impact at virtual center. Call habituating sensation "situation."

Sensations call habit to eventful attention. They impinge with force. They impact. They arrive, and insist (on the practical impossibility of their own systemic envelopment). Sensation is the transformational call-back to feeling of the so-automatic as to be ignored.

Renewal of feeling, feeling of the new, only felt: shock. Shock is the model of sensation, as it happens. Sensation is the advent of the event of potential, from the virtual center of movement, materially called to in-tension.

If habit is a repetitive-reflective loop (between pre-thought action-perception and the thought-out), then in hiatus of the event the loop falls in. It tightens into a churning circuit. Habit circuits in and out, as it happens. It falls into the center governing potential. And no sooner folds back out toward the realm of possibility. In-step, midstep. Possibility into potential, equilibrated reflection into critical self-referencing, repetition into renewal. And back again. Habit and hiatus.

3. Your Freedom and Your Flatness

Midstep, on the way to work, your tired eye catches a sidelong glimmer of spring sun. The beam enters your brain obliquely and instantly suffuses, imbuing the volume of your flesh with the change of season. Riding the beam, a sweet waft of an early bloom accents the familiar petrochemical bouquet of the city in motion. You are transported. The touch of the light tinges you with a fragrance of escape. Then a sudden screech of brakes returns you. Your fatigue has been shaken. It is not in the spot you returned to. It lies ahead, at work, and behind, at home. The thought of it, not here, thrills. The thought of walking back into it . . . All the life unlived. You can do without. Leave it. Start over. A sudden resolve takes hold. You turn from the path. Midstep over the curb your awakened eyes do not even obliquely see the oncoming laundry truck.

The synesthetic sensation of pungent volume-filling light-motion hits you with escape. The sensation envelops what you feel to be your freedom, a veer. Which in the next step envelops your fate, your flatness. The way in which your flatness is enveloped in your freedom is different from the way in which your freedom is enveloped in the sensation, which is different again from the way the well-trodden paths of habit are embedded in the situation. The path to work and back, as well as tried-and-true relative escapes (such as calling in sick for the day), are already-thought-out possibilities constitutive of the situation. They are worn by the inattentive body as it makes its rounds (already-thought-out-worn). On the other hand, the radical escape of a veer from the tried-and-true is unthinkable in the terms laid down by the situation. It hits in a moment of distraction, directly entering the flesh with unexpected impact, demanding attention. Only afterward is it consciously recognized, as concluded by the now attentive body from its material effects. Once recognized, a logical path from the situation of departure to the escape can be easily reconstituted, and subsequently accessed more easily, less intensely, more or less distractedly. A new possibility. But the reconstitution is exactly that: a retrospective construct. The new possibility of the radical veer follows its accomplishment. It is added to the situation after the situation has been taken leave of. Nothing in the situation as such could have suggested it. Possibility is retroactively situated unsituation.

Before being retrospectively possibilized, the veer out of the situation was embodied, unthinkably, in the situation. Potential: unsituation sensibly and unthinkably impacting on the situation. Potential is the out of the situation materialized in situation as an unpredictable but logically recuperable event, felt before being thought out. Sensation envelops potential as a degree of freedom of the situation: its own outside, critically doubling in on it, in-veering from it. Possibility is retroactively enveloped as the thinkably out-worn double of that double.

The crush of the truck is an event of a different kind: a post-veer arrival rather than a departure. The sequence of events leading to it can also be retrospectively reconstituted. But that path will never enter the logic of the situation or of situations like it. Senseless splattering of flesh. The only response to the bloody truth of it is disbelief. Accident. Pure, senseless contingency. If only you had turned and looked. If only the tenant of the first-floor apartment had waited a week to plant those flowers. If only the truck driver hadn't been speeding . . . It was fated. Fated, but not by those facts, or any possible logic of the situation. It was fated by the sensation. The impact of the sensation was the strike of fate, catalyzing an irrecuperable event. The accident, chance catalysis, pure contingency, unfolded from fateful freedom: this is the virtual. But on arrival, as actualized, the virtual is ex-centric: the center of gravity collapsed. Potential movement arrayed on the pavement. Possibility not only worn out, but wasted, utterly exhausted. The out of all situation. "Impassibility" of the event (Deleuze 1990, 96, 100).

If shock is the model of sensation as it happens, and sensation is the trigger of life potential, it is death that is the model of the virtual (Deleuze 1990, 151–53). Which is not to say that the virtual is always so parabolically deadly. Only that death is the most suggestive figure for the actualization of the virtual (of the reality of the inactual). Every chance, every contingency, every senseless out of every situation, is a little virtuality, a modest death, a rupture, an interval of being. After which life continues, still. Possibility and potential reengage. Situation clamps back down. Next steps array themselves. Habitual paths stretch before and behind. Rounds. Return. Recapture. With something having shifted, something having changed. The new. Circuit of transformation.

Possibility, potential, virtuality: sequencing, veering, rupture; linearity, hiatus of intensity, impossible interval; the predictable, unpredictability, the senseless; the thought-out, the thinkable, the unthinkable; the already felt, the felt, the insensate; the possible, the possibilizable, the impossibly real; the possible, the "practically impossible," the impossible in principle; the instrumental, the operative, and the contingent; same, change, chance.

The possible, the potential, and the virtual can be figured as mutually enveloping, in a complex play of doublings, veerings, arrivals, and returns. Ins-outs. It is the virtual that doubly describes the limits of the fold: a shifting center so central as to be inactual; an ex-centering fog of contingency encompassing life in an impenetrably vague ring of eventfulness. The virtual doubly describes the unity of a life, between limits: measureless depth and insubstantial surface, together. Inside-outside limit: immanent limit. Immanent to bodily change, enveloped in potential, outside possibility and predictability. The event horizon.

The unity, or event horizon, of a life is the immanent unsituation of its matter, its body. In situation, by contrast, a life is incrementally pulled out of itself, into habit. It is put to work: death by attrition. Another limitation, this time of the situation, in and of it. This intrinsic, as opposed to immanent, limit is slowly disintegrative rather than crushingly unifying. Accident versus attrition. Ex-centric collapse of the center of gravity versus entropic run-down (infinite dissipation uncountered by critical conditions). Singularity against the most general habit of matter.

Think of the center of gravity as a contraction of the ring of vagueness that is the event-horizon. And think of the ring as an expansion of the center from which the center has been excised. Think of them together, as a simultaneous contraction and expansion, as a center that is its own excision, a pure passing that is pure arrival. Think of them together as a black hole (in actuality, in possibility, and in potential). The "singularity" of a life is a better word than "unity." In cosmology, a black hole is a "singularity" where a point in the universe falls outside it, into "infinite curvature." By dint of material excess. A situated point ins itself out, rejoining the farthermost edge of the universe, burrowing into depths of the universe at the same time as circumscribing its surface, describing a universal no-time no-place where no laws tread, where excess matter is impassible energy, where everything that passes arrives for never and more. That cosmic feeling. The universe sensing itself, touching its limits. In the most critical of conditions, rehearsing the "big crunch" at the other end of the bang.

Couplet 3

2017

Becoming Animal in the Literary Field

Challenging the "Anthro-" in the "-Cene"

In August 2016, the planet's entry into the Anthropocene era was officially declared by the International Geological Congress, confirming that the impact of human activity had left its mark not only on a changing climate but on the geology of the earth itself. Two months later, a new estimate of the damage to animal life already evidenced in this new era was released (World Wildlife Fund and London Zoological Society 2016). The number of wild animals on earth, it was reported, had declined by 58 percent in the previous forty years. In the next four years alone, the toll was projected to rise to two-thirds, fanning talk of a "sixth mass extinction" event in the history of the earth. It seemed to be another beginning of our species' sporadic reckoning with the end—including, it seemed increasingly plausible, its own.

The dominant discourse on how to respond to this crisis, employed primarily at the level of intergovernmental organizations and NGOs (and among national governments, to the paltry extent to which they have risen to the challenge), is technoscientific. Its orientation is toward fostering science-based policy aimed at reducing carbon emissions, mitigating the effects of climate change, safeguarding the remaining fragments of wildlife habitat, and preserving endangered species on various forms of life support. As necessary as this approach is, there is something about it that gives pause. It prescribes as a cure the same instrument that brought us to this juncture: that is, human instrumental reason itself. In other words, it employs what humans have prided themselves most on—their ability to dominate nature as the self-declared "rational animal"—as the corrective to the effects of the historical exercise of this very ability, as it technocratically infused the modern capitalist spirit. This is an approach that mobilizes the dominant self-defining characteristic of the human as a *pharmakon*: a poison that is also a remedy. What gives pause is that this maintains unchanged the human sense of its own nature, and its position at the apex of the pyramid of nature in the wider sense. The human remains master of itself, and of all other creatures, now reduced to the status of dependents in permanent technoscientific foster care, their existence hanging on the tenuous thread of the goodwill of "man."

There are other approaches that take a very different tack, without questioning the need for technoscientific intervention. These approaches aim at changing the ethical framework within which the response to the ecological crisis operates. They call for an attitude of humbleness and respect for nonhuman creatures, and the environment on which their lives depend. The human is called upon to abdicate its apical position of dominance, to recognize its belonging in a horizontal web of interdependencies, and to reposition itself as the steward of those relations. This relational ethos has a long history, from the Romantics through the rise of the conservation movement in the late nineteenth century, to the first wave of the modern ecology movement in the 1960s. Many of its contemporary inheritors call into question the humanism of the underlying "stewardship" model, which appeals to the better nature of the human—but to the nature of the human nonetheless. Current preoccupations point beyond the human as it has known itself up to now, past a relational engagement to a relational becoming. Truly tending to the web of interdependencies cannot fail to change the human's sense of its own species being, and with it the cast of its practical involvement with nonhuman others. This aim for the human to get over itself, if not overcome itself entirely, is not confined to approaches explicitly embracing the "posthumanist" label, which traditionally focus more on the becoming-other of the human in symbiosis with its own technological excrescences than in interspecies intercourse (Braidotti 2013; Hayles 1999).

Approaches bringing the ethical supplement of a relational ethos to the discourse on the ecological crisis are many and varied. One current, particularly strong at the moment and gaining momentum, emphasizes traditional and emerging forms of inter- or multispecies alliance, locally situated and embodied in practical assemblages. It militates for the embrace of new modes of "kinship" extending beyond the traditional form of the human family, and beyond the humanness of the family itself, toward new adventures in "symbiogenesis" (Haraway 2007; Haraway 2016; see also Despret and Porcher 2007; Kirksey 2014; Tsing 2015). Another major node envisions a new "settlement" between human and nonhuman entities, a "parliament of things" recognizing the constitutive role played by nonhuman "actants" of all kinds in the reticulations through which human being and becoming bestir themselves (Latour 1993, 143–45). The discourse of Gaia highlights interdependencies, seeing the earth as a single, complex superorganism (Lovelock 2016; Margulis and Sagan 1997). In Isabelle Stengers's retelling, Gaia becomes a suprahuman force of "intrusion" calling the human to attention, obligating it to rethink constituent (and destituent) powers beyond the human pale, and to reposition itself in relation to them (2015). Also extending beyond the animal to the nonhuman spectrum to which the human and the animal co-belong is the neovitalist "new materialism." Work in this vein often focuses on the quality of "liveliness" incumbent in all that grows and changes, suffusing life and its nonliving associates alike. An increased attunement to the differing livelinesses as they impinge upon each other, or accord with each other in a way that amplifies each other's relational potential for sensing and acting, can lead to the composition of an altered form of life (see especially Bennett 2010; Coole and Frost 2010; Dolphijn and van der Tuin 2012). Relational potential for sensing and acting: sensibility. Lived quality, differential attunement: affect. Sensibility, affect: this is not just the addition of two terms, but of a whole new dimension for which there is no better word than the aesthetic.

The ethics of relational becoming, having supplemented technoscientific problem-solving, can be supplemented in turn: toward an "ethico-aesthetic paradigm" (Guattari 1995). This shift is marked by a bringing into salience of the qualitative in its own right, as harboring values of an aesthetic kind, lived purely for their own sake, that are not in simple opposition to the functionalities and efficiencies of the technoscientific paradigm any more than they are reducible to the "oughts" inherent to traditional ethical frameworks (Massumi 2017b). What follows takes a particular path not often taken in these debates, but in no way foreign to their concerns, toward an ethico-aesthetic paradigm for becoming-animal.

Enter the GoatMan

In the intervening month between the official declaration of the Anthropocene era and the landmark study on the sixth extinction event, a less momentous milestone was marked. In September 2016 two books shared the Ig Nobel prize for biology (Improbable Research 2016). Both had been widely reviewed, both overwhelmingly positively, and had sold remarkably well. Why, then, their ignominy? Ostensibly because each, in its own way, explore the human-animal relations in the qualitative key. The ethico-aesthetic paradigm is not so easily affirmed. The automatic response is: Are you serious?

Any time lived quality is seriously mentioned in relation to differing forms of life, Thomas Nagel's famous, and endlessly alluded to (if much less often read) essay will be brought up (1974). It is in this essay that the qualitative question was most famously posed—and declared basically unanswerable: "What is it like to be a bat?" We will never really know, because the bat is an "alien" (438) form of life whose central mode of experience—sonar—we humans don't even have (not to mention the ability to fly). The battiness of bat existence, the "immediate quality" (445n11) defining what it's "like" to be a bat, is accessible only to bats. Both winners of the Ig Nobel duly cite Nagel—and then proceed to convert his warning into a challenge: to embark on a project of *becoming-animal*, in as literal a way as possible, to put it to the test whether it is indeed impossible to bridge the alien gap. Exploring a serious question does not exclude the pursuit of folly. The books relate the widely different means by which the authors pursue their respective follies. Their compounding of serious questioning with a serious dose of whimsy is undoubtedly what nominated them for the Ig Nobel. That they both vacilate between the serious and the frivolous is a strong indication that the qualitative question is struck by the same ambivalence, making every entertainer of it a candidate for ignominy. At the same time, the strange synchronicity of two books about actually attempting to become animal coming out the same year indicates that, between the Anthropocene and the sixth extinction, there is something in this moment that makes confronting the qualitative question, and the ethico-aesthetic paradigm it implies, newly compelling. Becoming-animal is in the air.

In GoatMan: How I Took a Holiday from Being Human, Thomas Thwaites takes a design approach to the question of what it is like to be a goat (2016). In Being a Beast: Adventures across the Species Divide, Charles Foster tries what is essentially a field biology approach, informed by data culled from third-person observation translated into first-person experimentation (2016). He attempts to embody a series of animals, from badger to fox to swift, lingering on otter, his favorite. He is not shy about professing a hatred for cats (149).

It is hard not to take this element of personal favoritism as a warning sign. It signals the holding in reserve of a proprietary quantum of subjective fiat safeguarding an all-too-human self that will not surrender itself to what it wishes to become, maintaining through it all its peak-mammal prerogative of categorical judgment of other species. Foster's approach to the animals he doesn't hate is to steep himself in the scientific literature about their behavior in the wild and their perceptual and sensory abilities. He then attempts to use this objective information to put his safeguarded self in the other animal's boots. (Had the becoming been more successful, I would have said paws—no apologies for being catty.) The tool for this projection is empathy, "no different from what you need to be a decent lover or father or colleague" (2016, 101). Human empathy is transferable to other animals because there is a certain likeness between the animal and the human owing to similarities in neurological makeup (16). This not only limits the options for becoming-animal to the "higher" vertebrates; it also puts limits on how far the becoming can go. There is, of course, a limit to the similarities, so in the end the animal will essentially remain as "elusive" and "inaccessible" as ever (11). Upon returning to the comforts of his own home after six months of living in a simulacrum of a badger den, his badger colleagues "seemed farther away than ever" (77). But that doesn't mean that the experiment wasn't a success. There's a consolation prize: "Our capacity for vicariousness is infinite. Empathize enough with a swift and you'll either become one or (which may be the same thing) you'll be able to rejoice so much with the screeching race around the church tower that you won't mind not being one yourself" (216). The outcome of the author's essays in the imitation of otherness was that "Charles Foster [became] *more* like himself" (216, emphasis in original). The experience of being "like" animals had ended by making him become more like he always was: "There is some essential I that inhabits my body" (22). It turned out essentially to have been a human self-enhancement exercise all along. This celebratory reconciliation with the distance separating the human and the animal should have come as no surprise to the reader, given that the book's epigram from Jonathan Safran Foer exalts a humanist (synonym for anthropocentrist) position from the very start: "To ask 'What is Animal?' . . . is inevitably to touch upon how we understand what it means to be us and not them. It is to ask 'What is Human?'" Us and not them: home again. Otherness be denned.

Nagel would not be surprised that Foster's approach failed as an approach to otherness. If you try to translate objective knowledge about an animal into an empathetic imitation of the animal, he says, it is bound to fail. "Insofar as I can imagine [what it's like to be a bat] (which is not very far), it tells me only what it would be like for *me* to behave as a bat behaves. But that is not the question" (Nagel 1974, 439). Nagel recommends "another direction": "an objective phenomenology not dependent on empathy or the imagination. . . . Its goal would be to describe . . . the subjective character of experiences in a form comprehensible to beings incapable of having those experiences" (449). In other words, close the subjective gap between the homebound human and the alien animal as much as possible by objective means: exhaustively research the animal's behavioral and perceptual capabilities in order to build as complete as possible an objective understanding of how it inhabits its world. Then *describe*. You'll never close the gap entirely, but the reader's rational understanding will asymptotically approach what it is like to be the nonhuman animal in question.

Nagel seems unaware that, although he has skirted the self-defeating mediation of all-too-human empathy, he has introduced another intervention: language. He seems to assume that description is objective, which amounts to assuming that language is a transparent medium of communication for the literal transmission of referential meaning, against the many advisories sent out by generations of scholars in any number of humanities disciplines that description is a language *genre*. No language use is literal. All language use carries an irreducible *literary* element (understood in a broad sense not restricted to "literature").[1]

This literary element is no stranger to becoming-animal projects. It is evident that both Thwaites's experiments and Foster's were undertaken *in order to* come to fruition in books. Foster, unlike Nagel, acknowledges the literary element in his own undertaking. His use of an empathy-filled descriptive genre ("nature writing") is "a sort of literary shamanism" (Foster 2016, 1). Except that it's not. A few pages later (12–13), he makes this clear by disparaging J. A. Baker's ([1967] 2005) "canonical" book of becoming-animal, *The Peregrine*, for being all but too "shamanistic." By that he means that Baker seeks "self-dissolution" precisely through literary inventivity: the development of a "new language." This troubles Foster (2016, 13). "Who's speaking here?" he asks accusingly. The question doesn't arise in his book. He proudly announces that he will always "maintain a boundary between me and my animals" (13).

If it *is* clear who is speaking, if a point is made of maintaining the boundary between me and "my" animals, how could a becoming-animal possibly eventuate? Perhaps Baker is on to something. If neither human empathy taking itself on a field trip nor "objective phenomenology" spun out as description can go all the way, maybe, just maybe, literary inventiveness can. How paradoxical would that be? Could language, the ability most often cited (however questionably) as what draws the dividing line between the human and the animal, actually be a privileged portal to the becoming-animal of the human? The argument has been made (Deleuze and Guattari 1986, 12–15, 34–38; Deleuze and Guattari 1987, 237–48, 256–60; Deleuze and Parnet 1987, ix, 5–7, 44–49, 75–76; Massumi 2014, 8, 55–64). Understood: it would have to be a "new" language (How would that work?). Baker will have to be added to the mix.

Thwaites provides a bridge. In *GoatMan*, he tries to experience what it is like to be a goat by modifying his own body. He approaches it as a design question. His research into goatliness reveals some basic physical differences: four legs, not two; four stomachs, not one. He is interested in goat perception and sociality (a significant addition), but he fears his access to both is hindered by his bipedalism and inability to graze. How could he begin to understand what it's like to be a goat if he cannot approach the world from their quadrupedal angle and indulge in the feeding activity that occupies virtually all of their waking hours? How could he experience goat sociality when no natural-born goat would ever accept an unabashed biped into its fold? So he goes about developing prostheses that allow him to walk on four legs and eat grass (an artificial rumen). The road is hard, and the returns are meager: he barely manages a day with the herd on the slopes of the Alps. Significantly, he has approached his goal through the artifice of design rather than by an attempt at naturalism. His rumen extends beyond his own body. He chews grass during the day, spits it into a sack worn on his body, then at night processes the grass in a pressure cooker designed to transform the cellulose into a form digestible by humans. The need to share goat activities distances him from imitation. He can approach goatliness only by strategically departing from it and inhabiting the *differential*. No goat wears its stomach on the outside. But that is the only condition under which he can join them in grazing. Similarly, he joins in with the movement of the goats through another inventive differential. He finds it terribly difficult, even with his quadruped prosthesis, to maneuver the steep slopes and to keep pace with his herd-mates. Even with the prosthesis, there is no way for him to move "like" a goat. He keeps falling disastrously behind, which means falling out of any possibility of participating in goat society. "And so I invent a new semibipedal— more tripedal—kind of gait. Using a mixture of sideways on four legs/ frontways tottering on two while using a third leg against the slope for stability, sometimes going backwards, sometimes going forwards, I manage to scramble" to follow the herd (Thwaites 2016, 159). He moves into the gap between bipedalism and quadrupedalism in a way that is if anything more like a crab than a goat. He does not become *the* other: he becomes-other, to man *and* goat. He scuttles into the gap between them, inventing a third term: goatman-crab. No such animal has been seen in nature. Thwaites's methods are not naturalistic. They go against nature.

He ends up pursuing a becoming-different: he becomes neither like a goat, if by that is meant feeling what a goat feels when it roams and grazes; nor more like himself. In fact, becoming more like himself was the last thing he had in mind. The whole adventure begins because he feels a lassitude with being human and yearns to escape his petty "worries of [human] personhood" (15). As the book's subtitle announces, he wants nothing more than "to take a holiday from being human."

Meager as the results are, a breakthrough moment does occur. It happens because he commits a "goat faux pas" (Thwaites 2016, 176). In goat society, being higher on the slope is a sign of dominance. With his prosthetic locomotion, he can move up more easily than down, and his taking the high road is interpreted by the dominant goat as a challenge. Before the situation comes to a head-butting, a third goat steps in and interposes itself between the two. The situation is defused, and Thwaites is careful after that to stay in his place. Goats are not stupid. The dominant goat did not mistake Thwaites for a goat. He was not fooled by some likeness between himself and a hornless helmet-wearing assisted crab-walker. He looked upon Thwaites *as* a goat, at a moment when Thwaites committed a faux pas *as* a goat would, and reacted *as* a goat would in that circumstance: with anxiety. The "as" here connotes not a resemblance of form, but the singularity of a *mode*. Goat and modified man entered a goatly mode of relation together, across their differences, without equalizing what, in general, it feels "like" to be one or the other. They fell into an attunement with each other's actions and affect, at a very precise *crossing point* between their species. This did not make them alike, as to the forms of their bodies or their inner life. It inducted them together into the same event. This is becoming-animal, against the grain of the settled categories of nature: a mutual enactment of difference in motion; a differential attunement co-triggering an event. This is an asymmetrical process. It is enabled by one of the two terms that are moving into relation having already moved toward an unimaginable unknown third term, neither the one nor the other. Becoming-animal as "heterogenesis": a difference-becoming (Guattari 1995, 50, 108, 127). Here, otherness is not a problem. It is the necessary condition for the event. It is what goes into making the event, and comes out no less other than it went in. Under its conditioning, a thirdness emerges. Another otherness. Anothering of others occurs.

This can happen because there has been a transmission of *character*. This is where likeness does play a role. It does not figure under the equal sign but in chiasmus. As part of his research, Thwaites had visited a neopagan shaman in Amsterdam (2016). He is intrigued but cannot relinquish his rational knowledge that no matter what mushroom he eats, under whoever's ritual supervision, he would not "actually" become an elk. But is it not possible, he asks, to change one's "relationship with the world . . . so that, for a moment, the elk and the person were also the person and the elk"? (143–44). The human regards the elk as a person, at the same moment the elk regards the person as an elk. In this cross-eyed exchange, their natures cross. This is what ended up happening in the top-goat incident. Thwaites regards the dominant goat as a person in the sense that Thwaites's participation in the event is predicated on his having immediately, unreflexively attributed to the goat intention, desire, meaningful gesture, and a spirited adherence to a system of values. The goat is regarded as more than a mere goat. He directly figures, in the encounter, as a nonhuman person: the subject of his own life. The goat does the same thing for Thwaites when he regards him as a rival for top-goat status. This chiastic transfer of character—or more accurately, this simultaneous cross-positing of personhood—does not in any way vitiate the otherness in play. The exchange occurs across an inexpungeable species difference that remains intact, even as it becomes oddly irrelevant to what is happening. The two do not leave the encounter more similar than they went in. They similarly cross-subjectify each other without becoming alike. The attribution of likeness that both cross-perform *preserves* the mutual otherness, anothering.

The attribution of personhood should not be interpreted as an act of anthropomorphism. That would be to forget the goat's co-responsibility for the event. What it actually does is distribute personhood across the animal and human divide, so that neither side has a monopoly on it or can claim sovereign rights to it. It actually *dehumanizes* personhood, by placing it in a chiastic zone of indistinction between the animal and the human.[2] The chiasmus involved is life-altering. The goat's life has become otherly goatly by virtue of having entered into society with a man against the natural slope of the order of things; in the same stroke, the human has become a bit more than a man, by virtue of having lived a remarkable intensity of experience in goat-mode. *Double becoming* (Deleuze and Guattari 1987, 304–7). Both terms in the reciprocal relation are altered. Trans-becoming. But neither term "actually" becomes the other. *Something else* has happened. An anotherness on top of the two involved—a thirdness—has slipped in *between* the two, taking effect at the insubstantial intersection that is the chiastic crossing point: a reciprocal self-differing irreducible to one or the other, as goat gets otherly goated and man more-than-humaned in one and the same event.

This *something else taking effect in the thirdness of the in-between* is the becoming-animal. It is in a sense abstract: it isn't concretized in a separate form. It is consubstantial only with its own event of reciprocal self-differing. It is the occurrent reality of the cross-eyed differential at play in the event. As Deleuze and Guattari would say, a becoming-animal has occurred—without there *actually* being an animal become (1987, 238).

Thwaites brushes up against becoming-animal, in this in-between sense, through design practice. Baker gives it perfect pitch in his writing. What greater artifice, what greater anothering abstraction, can be achieved than in the literarity of writing? The fact that nonhuman animals don't write books is no obstacle to a differential becoming-animal whose necessary conditions are fundamentally asymmetrical, even though they take effect at the reciprocal crossing point of a chiastic exchange of character similarly performed.

The Accidental Falcon

Thwaites consciously sets out to become goat, choosing it as a goal. This voluntarism represents a residual humanism in his project. His usual un-cross-subjectified human personhood leads the way. In *The Peregrine*, Baker does not choose his becoming-falcon.[3] He slips into it, as if softly possessed. He notices the seasonal presence of peregrines in his little patch of England. It is in the early 1960s, when peregrines are on the verge of extinction due to DDT. He is drawn to them, fascinated at first, it seems, more by the ephemerality of their existence as they fly in the face of their looming extinction event than by any describable solidity of their species being. The prospect of their disappearance (fortunately staved off by the budding ecology movement's first great success with the banning of DDT) makes them already a future abstraction, like living ghosts of themselves. Baker is drawn in by that eerily present abstractness in the future tense. Little by little, he is overtaken by it. He does not subjectively choose, the better to become cross-subjectified.

This is what Foster, from his self-centered perspective, misunderstands as "self-dissolution" (the simple opposite of his supposedly "essential I"). Echoing Nagel: that is not the question. The question concerns eventful intensities of relational experience in becoming. Following Baker into the field of the hawk will give a new perspective on what was just said about personhood. In *The Peregrine*, there is something in the air that calls into question the centrality of intention, even if desire, meaningful gesture, and immersion in a system of values remain. When personhood enters the zone of indistinction between the animal and the human, affect replaces intention as the arbiter of character.

As Robert Macfarlane remarks in his introduction, Baker "had to forge a new language of description" to produce this book "in which very little happens, over and over again" ([1967] 2005, xii). There is no narrative arc: no intrigue or dénouement. The narrator goes into the fields to find and observe peregrines. Dawns rise, dusks fall. Days pass, seasons change. Birds appear and disappear, flock and scatter, circle, rise, and roost. Peregrines hunt. That's about it. And it's gripping. There is uncommon intensity in the very little happening of this book.

The language has a poetic terseness. What is described, over and over again, are first and foremost movements. Contrasting and coordinate movements draw lines and curves across the pages. "A peregrine rising and falling. Godwits ricocheting across the water, tumbling, towering" (Baker [1967] 2005, 51). "As a tern rose, the peregrine stooped" (46). The birds draw movement across the sky. They figure as movement. They *are* movement figures: activation contours cutting shapes on the surface of the sky. "He created beautiful patterns and doodles in the sky, as swiftly evanescent as the swirling shapes of waves upon the shore" (103).

Second to movement come light and color. The play of light and color brings the qualities of the individual into relief. "The hawk shone in the amber light and color, every feather sleek and burnished" (Baker [1967] 2005, 168). Light and color highlight the individual figure but also refract it into its background. "He fused into the white mist of the sun" (82). These passages, mergings and emergings, are effected by movement. "Moving down through sunlight, he changed color like an autumn leaf, passing from shining gold to pallid yellow, turning from tawny to brown, suddenly flicking out against the skyline" (97). In the color passages, birds not only emerge from and merge into the background, they refract each other, taking on and shedding each other's aspects. One of the "distant pigeon-like birds, that had until then always proved to be pigeons, was suddenly the peregrine" as it flew "crisp and golden in the sunlight" (96).

Movement and color themselves merge with and emerge into and out of each other. "Movement is like color to the hawk" (Baker [1967] 2005, 102). This does not mean that the hawk equates or confuses movement with color on the basis of "what" they look "like." It sees in one what the other can *do*: effect passages. They are alike not in *what* they are but in *how* they operate transformations. Similarly operative, they can combine forces to co-effect transformation. This occurs across their difference. Movement still does what only movement can do, as does color. Different as they are from each other, they remain always *for* each other. Each holds a standing invitation from the other to join forces for combined effect. They are less like two separate things than two qualitatively different dimensions, each defining its own axis of variation, stretched between poles describing optimal and pessimal limits beyond which it fades out and loses its defining quality (light and darkness for color, rest and infinite speed for movement). Each axis is amenable to the other in the midrange of its polarized stretch. Always in the middle, the invitation stands. Together in their middlings and alone in their respective movements to the limit, they form a matrix of transformation.

Everything in *The Peregrine* is "like" this. An individual bird is defined less by its species than by the "style" (Baker [1967] 2005, 126) with which its movements carry it through the matrix of transformation, taking on color and aspect, alternating light and dark, rest and acceleration. An individual *is* its pattern of matrixial transformation. It is the figure it cuts across and among dimensions. Passages in the book are legion where the peregrine takes on the figure of another species of bird by varying its style of movement (for example, 71). Just as numerous are passages where the hawk emerges into its own figure from a flock of birds of a different feather, or shears away from its own into their fold (for example, 86). The "the" of *The Peregrine* functions as an indefinite article. "The" peregrine is sometimes two. Then it pairs its movements with its own kind, arabesquing together. When it is one, it is often hard to tell if it is the same one. The "individual" is actually "dividual": a multiplicity of qualitative fissions and fusions continually varying its figure. Not a particular, but a singular self-populating.

The description does not follow a particular bird in a narrative line moving horizontally through the book. It follows a plethora of passages to the limit, mergings and emergences, appearings and disappearances, across many a middling qualitative transformation, through a constantly shifting panorama of manyings and singlings out. The world of *The Peregrine* pulsates with these passages. It sets its own pulse, following the continual variation of the movements its figures cut in their dance with each other and with the elements. Intensities rise and fall, each pulse pumping new life, in rhythmic variation, at the slightest flicker of a movement.

What is gripping is being lulled into the rhythm of the book's not-much-going-on-over-and-over-again, to be carried away by the pulse. It does not take long to sense that not much in particular is going on not because there is nothing eventful, but because *everything* is happening all over again, on something like a vertical axis perpendicular to the spinning out of narrative progression. On that intensive axis, the entire world is composing and recomposing itself, accordioning into and out of itself, pulsing with life. This is the pulse of the world reemerging anew at each beat, from its own matrix of relation. It is not a creation out of nothingness. Rather, it is a co-creation out of repeated relation. The cut of each figure is inflected on the fly by the movements of those around it, and by the mood swings of the elements. The world rearises, in time with the beat of the wings of the figures in movement, varying in concert. It is not about this or that specific event. This is *the* event: of worlding. Particular events do stand out, but in the manner of motifs integrally woven into the matrixial fabric. The dominant motif, this being the world in which the hawk flies supreme, is predation.

The "the" of the event carries the same multiply singular tenor as "the" peregrine: the paragon. The ambit of the peregrine's movements are the largest. It can rise to the zenith (Baker [1967] 2005, 95, 139) on an upswell, fade to a speck (86, 11, 141, 139, 163), then disappear, merging no longer with other avian figures—other birds have been left behind, far below, just minion specks in the commanding surview of the peregrine's eye—but with the very element of the sky. The peregrine can swoop from the zenith to the nadir of its world at inconceivable speed—as good as infinite for this world, from any prey species' perspective—disappearing now into the dampness of the field, to chance a coating of mud that might hold it sodden to the earth, bird now merging with the terrestrial element (65, 85).[4] The peregrine has many becomings with other birds, and other birds themselves have their own figural transmogrifications, if in a more limited, less exemplary ambit. But the peregrine, and the peregrine alone, cuts its figure into becomings elemental.

It is this status as elemental animal that makes it the focal point of the becoming-hawk of the human.[5] The peregrine is the linchpin of this world's co-creating.[6] "The most exciting thing about a hawk is the way," when it swoops to kill, "it can create life from the still earth by conjuring flocks of birds into the air" (Baker [1967] 2005, 106). Life arising at the point of death. With each swoop of the falcon, a life in this world in the balance—just as all of life in our empirical world today is in the balance, on the brink of the sixth extinction. Will a new world of life be conjured from the jolted earth of climate change? If so, who or what will cut the peregrinal figure for a retaking flight of the flocks of life?

The point isn't the overused, and overly general, one of the poignancy of the dialectic of life and death. As always, it is about what happens in the middle, *between* life and death. It is when a life is in the balance, already figuring its own death, at once itself and the specter of itself—and pulsing all the more for that with intensity—that the world's matrixial plenitude is most hauntingly felt.[7] This is life, at a ghostly distance from itself, living its own abstraction, at the utmost edge of intensity.

Writing the World Anew

The world of *The Peregrine* is not a description of the empirical world. The peregrine of the book is not the empirical referent of traditional descriptive language. This is not "nature writing." It is creative writing in the most forceful sense of the term.

The world of *The Peregrine* is abstractly composed of elements, dimensions, and figures, conjured up in language. They are no less real for that: abstract yet real, as Deleuze liked to say (Deleuze and Guattari 1987, 255). The components of *The Peregrine*'s world are real, if abstract, *forces*. The movement figures the novel stages are integrals of affect. They are defined by *how* they do and, in their doing, by how they affect and are affected by what else is figurally (not figuratively) a-wing in this world. They are swirls of relation. The author has gone to field every day for a year to observe empirical interactions, embodied beings affecting each other, in the co-composing orchestral movements of nature naturing. He has then abstracted from the observed interactions the affective *manners*—the modes of *affectability*—exemplified in them. These he re-embodies in words. The birds' movements continue in the novel, their manner intact, their style preserved, transduced into words. They cut the same figures abstractly in language as they did in the field. The empirical creatures have been translated, by the offices of literary artifice, into abstract *characters*. Each exemplifies an integral of affect in matrixial imbrication with others.

Reembodied through words: the reader's body is intensely involved and activated by the abstract figure's movements on the page. The book is gripping because it really, abstractly awakens the kinesthetic sense. "Lilting, surging, rushing, boring, dipping, swaying, carving-up" (Baker [1967] 2005, 143). The words vibrate with movement. Experience pulses with the movements of the characters. With each merging and emerging, hover and dart, not-quite visions and smells and touches and flickerings of movement populate experience. These incipient actions no sooner appear than disappear, like a hawk soaring and swooping, merging and emerging, now from the element of language.[8] These flockings of feeling flit on the uttermost edge of perception, in the balance between the empirical and the abstract, just as life balances on the brink of death.

They quasi-occur, liminally: they are felt, but not fully actualized. This makes them all the more real. This is experience, at a ghostly distance from itself, living its own abstraction, at the utmost edge of perceptual intensity. The affects of the birds are at one and the same time the percepts of the reader. There occurs a transfer of character between them.

The reader's experience pulsates with the rhythm of the words. She is affected by the spectral movements across the page *as* she would be had she been in the field in the presence of flesh and blood. As: not "like." The co-composing of affective forces has been recomposed in another element, with all the artifice native to that realm. It is their *mode* of affectability that transfers, straddling the differential gap between field and book. The force of the book hinges on artful differencing rather than on any naturalistically rendered likeness. It hinges not on likeness in representation, but on anothering. Field and book, across the gap of their reciprocal alienness to each other, effect a spectral third of liminal experience. Their mutual otherness is not an obstacle but a necessary condition. The *Peregrine* performs a double becoming-literary of the world of the hawk and of the human reader.

It is a choice to pick up the book, but it is not a choice to be carried away by it. Lulled by the words, the reader falls in with the rhythm, riding the figural movement as a hawk rides the wind. A nonvoluntary—but not simply involuntary—merging into the movement of becoming occurs. This is *sympathy*. Not empathy. Empathy is what my "essential I" does when it maintains the boundary between myself and "my" others, and feels *for* them, producing a disingenuous feeling, a demonstrably false feeling, of being "like" them. Sympathy is when the boundary of the I is dissolved—but not the difference on either side of it. Sympathy is a bodily falling in with a feeling-with, at the edge of perception. It does not dissolve the self. It produces another, of self and other, across their difference, in the liminal thirdness of affective co-composing. "Sympathy is what things feel when they shape each other" (Spuybroek 2016, 3).

The becoming-literary of the world of *The Peregrine* is ethico-aesthetic. It is aesthetic in its literary artifice. And it is ethical in its reliving of relation. It is all the more intensely ethical in that it refuses I-centered motivation. Sympathy is not intended: it *takes*, both in the sense of setting in of its own force, and of being a force of possession. It is larger than the self it sidelines, and more powerful. In sympathy, The Peregrine powers beyond humanism, and the inveterate anthropocentrism inscribed in the very word. It does this in a way only humans can: literarily. It is in literary language, with its artificings of abstraction, that the human can breach its own nature, most liminally, the experience of the world in the balance. It is in literary language that the human can enter with utmost real-yet-abstract intensity into other-becomings, exemplarily including becoming-animal. This is by no means to say that literary becoming-animal is the only kind, or the "best."[9] Only that it marshals for this undertaking the highest powers of abstraction. When there is a becoming-animal without there being an actual animal become, it is that the becoming-animal is all in *expression*. Literary becoming-animal brings becoming-animal into pure expression. This element of expressionism puts a certain distance between the approach analyzed in this essay and the new materialist current: here, becomings-animal brink on the incorporeal (suggesting an incorporeal materialism).

The becoming-animal in The Peregrine takes in a way not unlike the chiastic double becoming of goat and man in Thwaites. Goat looks at man and man at goat, and their eyes cross. At that moment, they regard each other as persons. In this event, they directly, nonreflexively posit each other as having character. This is where the meaning of "person" changes, under the spell of sympathy. Sympathy subtracts intention from character. You still have desire, meaningful gesture, and valuation. You still have qualities of experience, both joy (Baker [1967] 2005, 10) and fear (66). But you have them not as persons in the usual sense, but as figures, abstract integrals of affect. Literary writing is figure-full of character, and characters.

The narrator is one of them. He begins as a representative of his species. He is a man and, like all men, the enemy of all animals, none more so than the endangered peregrine. Animals flee from him. They fear him, in so intense a way that it cannot be far from hatred (121). But as he eases his way into the world that is becoming, and as the relational pulsings of that world wash through him, he begins to figure, for his animal others, as just another creature of the field. The animals gradually begin to lose their fear of him. The peregrine, which had avoided all acknowledgment of his presence other than the withholding of his own, now engages with him. He enters into the peregrine's ambit. He is now in the scope of that lofty eye.

On several occasions, the peregrine acts toward him *as* he would another creature of this world. He does not, however, see him as another peregrine. The peregrine, after all, is the paragon figure; the exemplary animal; the most fully, affectively forceful of animals in this world. This world is not big enough for two peregrine figures. There can only be the indefinitely multiply singular one of his figure. No other can be "like" him. As did the goat, the peregrine sees the man in his own terms, with an attribution of character. But to see in peregrine terms is to see the other not as a cohort, but as prey. At times the peregrine harries the man as he would a pigeon or a mouse (Baker [1967] 2005, 154–55, 172). With this gesture, the narrator is posited by the hawk as a character in the same world, but not of his ilk. The narrator is sucked into the raptor's relational world of predator and prey, as Thwaites was inducted into the society of goats. He takes joy in the peregrine's movements (143). He feels peregrine joy in the soaring to the zenith, and thrill in the speed of the descent. He can almost taste the peregrine's kills (111). As the eyes of the peregrine settle more often on him, he begins, chiastically, to see with them. From on high, the keenness of a hawk eye can take in the full compass of this world, in lofty surview. The narrator's view flickers between the on-high of the paragon predator and the low-to-the-earth that is the station of his prey. He does not resolve the flicker into a single image, as if he were coming to coincide with the peregrine, in a becoming like him. Instead, he inhabits the differential. The distance is not overcome in the comfort of a unifying synthesis. Man and hawk remain as different as the zenith of the sky and the nadir of the earth. They stand across from each other, respective specks between which lies the whole stretch of the world. Affective distance, the asymmetry of otherness, the unease of difference, is honored.

In the literature of becoming-animal there is an episode that might seem to work similarly. In David Abram's *Becoming Animal*, there is an epiphanic moment in which the author describes seeing through the eyes of a hawk. He looks down and sees nothing other than . . . *himself* (2010, 258). He doesn't flicker unresolvedly between on-high and low-down. He occupies both stations at once. The self enlarges into an "encompassing awareness" (216). For Abram, to become animal is to "come home to myself" from afar (222). Otherness mystically melts into a synthetic sentience, experienced in the first-person: a bigger, better world-me. Everywhere is the center of experience, and at every center of experience is I spying me. This reflexivity smooths over the asymmetries of otherness and short-circuits the refractivity of animal figures into their collective other of the elements. Here, the ethico-aesthetic undertaking of becoming-animal operates as a subjective phenomenology, steadfastly cleaving to the "concreteness" of first-person experience. The result is a hypostatization of empathy. This is very different from Nagel's hypothetical "objective phenomenology," no less so than Baker's steadfastly abstract sympathetic approach. When Baker sees through the eyes of the peregrine, he does not see his homebody self. He sees himself as different: as the raptor prey he never was (except really abstractly). Baker does not come home, he goes to field.

In *The Peregrine*, the relation to the other is no longer empirical, but does not go so far as to turn mystical. It is superempirical: in surview.[10] In surview, the encompassing point of view is that of the *writing*. It is liminal. The center does not hold. It cleaves as a differential. The *distance* between affective perspectives is enveloped in the movements of language. This is what makes it truly relational, annexing the self to a liminal world of becoming, rather than annexing the world to the self. It is only under these conditions, of encompassing asymmetry, that the intensest heights of double becoming can be attained. The affective force of *both* sides of the becoming is intensely felt *because* the separating distance is not finessed. They are mutually included in the same relational weave, as the differences that they are. Nature denatures, transforming from natural landscape to artificed affectscape. It is only on that condition that it renatures—pulses with self-creative tension, rearising.

Nature in its concreteness provides no encompassing perspective. The human, in its humanism, fools itself, as does Nagel with his objectivism, into thinking that its rational, descriptive mind can indeed embrace the whole, asymmetries dissolved, differentials resolved. This is the last conceit of the human. The intrusion of Gaia disabuses us of that. It makes it palpable that the human has no possibility of synthetic encompassment. As a species, we are fatally immersed in the goings-on of nature. However, with consummate artifice, language can mobilize more-than-human affective force—in a way that returns the human not to its familiar home, but to its difference-engined animal becoming. It is by exercising one of the very capabilities that has been used historically to alienate the human from other animals that the human can rejoin the relational matrix of trans-becoming. This is not meant to imply in any way that nonhuman animals are excluded from language.[11] Languaging is on a continuum, stretching all across the range of animality, from pole to pole. It is an axis of animal life, constituting one of its differential dimensions. The human takes wing at one pole of the continuum. By carrying its special abilities in this dimension to their highest power—literary language—the human can contrive to overcome its own conceit. It can remit itself to the creative movement of its own animality. For creative movement, creativity in movement, is something all animals embody, relationally co-composing. It is called evolution: continuing qualitative transformation, in which individual figures of different species stand out against the matrixial background of all-embracing asymmetrical relation. Nothing characterizes animality more than its capacity for creative evolution (Bergson 1998), displayed in the boundless proliferation of variations on the theme of animate life that has continued through all of the earth's eras, across every extinction event. The more more-than-human the human becomes, drawing to its utmost on its ownmost capabilities, the more intensely animal it also becomes. Language, taken to the literary limit of what it can do, gives the human all the more animal character. By bringing becoming to pure expression, literary language *dramatizes* the creative forces of self-transforming nature, distilled into word-borne movements of characteristic affective force.[12] The *how* the forces of nature do—their *mannerisms*—come into superempirical relief.[13] This makes the expression abstract in an exemplary way: in a way that gives it the potential, were it to jump the gap between field and book in the reverse direction, of playing, sympathetically, a piloting role in the composition of new, actual manners of relating.

Yes, life will rearise. After the sixth extinction, new flocks will stir forth from the scorched fields and flooded plains. New characters will cut their figures in patterns of movement no hawk or human has ever seen. New manners of being will emerge. It's not a choice between life and death. It is question of which ones will die—and what role the human will choose to play in those deaths, and in setting the conditions for new life. Although "choose" is not the right word. It is no better an idea now than it was at the beginning of the Industrial Revolution to place the fate of the world in the hands of human choice. And yes, rational choices well grounded in functionalist technoscientific understanding have a crucial role to play, as will the relational ethics of empathy with other creatures. Yet there is a need for something more than these. The ethico-aesthetics of sympathetic becoming can provide that more-than.

Baker does not choose to become animal as an intentional act. He falls into it, in sympathy, and rides the winds of becoming. He rejoices when these bring him to a place where he ceases to feel like a man among men ([1967] 2005, 95). He rejoices in the becoming different of his humanity. There is nothing heroic in this journey, although there is much that is gripping. It can involve—must involve at times—feeling as small as a mouse in the eye of the hawk. A generous dose of this modesty would become the human.

So take to the field, however that presents itself to you, with mud and stubble or in concrete and steel. Hone your affectscapes. Re-how your manners. And not just in writing. What would it mean to learn, literally, to *live* literarily, as an ethico-aesthetic adventure toward parts more-than-human? Is such a thing actually possible? By what artifice of nature? Would it involve large-scale peregrinization, wafting at the zenith of predatory surview?[14] Not on your life, Gaia admonishes. Then what other options are there?[15] How can we, as a species, not-choose them?

2008

The Virtual, Double Capture, and the Urban-Architecture Manifold

JASON NGUYEN/MARK DAVIS: *Historically, a Western understanding of the material world has relied on a desire to understand things for what they "are." But the work of Deleuze and Guattari proposes an ontology rooted in "becoming." Paradoxically, this way of thinking debases the singular moment of instantiation, elevating instead the abstract collection of circumstances that intersect to produce it. What is the role of the "Virtual" in this ontology, and how does it differ from the Platonic "Ideal"?*

BRIAN MASSUMI: An effort of thought is required to prevent the Deleuzian "virtual" from slipping into the Platonic ideal. The concept automatically shifts in this direction the instant it is separated from "the singular moment of instantiation," or in Deleuzian terms the "actual." It is the virtual which is debased by being separated in thought from actuality—not the actual which is debased by its association with the virtual. The two are inseparable. They must be thought strictly together. From a Deleuzian point of view they have no philosophical meaning apart from their dynamic embrace of each other. The movement of becoming is not on one side or the other: it is the result of their coming together. "Dynamic" and "movement" are the key words. There would be neither dynamism nor movement were the virtual and actual in separate realms. There is one world, and it is they.

The virtual separated from the actual would be utterly "sterile" because it would have nothing through which to express itself. Unexpressed, it would not give itself to thought. The actual apart from the virtual would be absolute stasis, because a thing in change is like a Doppler effect through the present of a just-past moving into the future. The past and future are precisely what are inactual, so they fall to the virtual.

The moment you think change, you have actually appealed to the virtual. Think the actual without the virtual, and you have fixity.

Deleuze needs a concept of the virtual *because of* his project of thinking the actual. The starting point of that project is the Heraclitean observation that the only constant is change. Deleuze needs the actual to hold the reality of the virtual to this world. Deleuze considers his thought, including the thought of the virtual, to be a variety of empiricism. He accepts the dictum that everything that can be considered real must in some way be experienced, with "experienced" minimally defined as having effects or taking effect. The actual is nothing other than the taking-effect of the virtual. A supernal virtual—a virtual that is "out of this world" as Peter Hallward (2006) misunderstands Deleuze's to be—could never get past the post of this effective philosophy.

This is just a first approximation. The virtual is a slippery concept. It is by nature elusive. I call it "recessive." It does not expend itself in its effect. It withdraws back into itself, constituting in the same stroke the just-past of that effect, and the to-come of the next. It is always in the gaps between chronological moments, in a nonlinear, recursive time of its own: just past–yet to come; future-past. When the virtual withdraws back into itself in the gaps in the actual, it has no "place" to go. It goes only into its own return. You can only think it across its iterations, and the mark of each iteration is an actual change. Each such change can be expressed as a modification of an order of juxtaposition of actual elements. In other words, the virtual, by nature elusive in a time-like way, takes effect as a spacing. It does not take effect without its effects taking *place*.

This is where the paradox of Deleuze's thinking lies: not in an alternative between the actual and the virtual, but in how they come together. The way in which they come together creates a space-time tension that is difficult to model conceptually because our habits of thought tend both to dichotomize space and time (treating them as independent variables) and to erase their difference (for example, by construing time as a "line"). It is difficult to talk about the virtual without falling into one of these traps, or most often both at the same time. For example, the suspicion that the virtual is a Platonic ideal has already spatialized it as a realm apart, a higher plane or other world.

Deleuze has two base strategies to deal with this slipperiness of the virtual in its relation with the actual. First, he multiplies models for it. A given model may tend toward spatializing the virtual. He will immediately undermine it with a temporalizing countermodel. If you put the two together, you get a space-time tension, or even a paradox. You are making progress. None of the models is meant to be an adequate description of the virtual. They are conceptual tools meant to assist in following the movement of the virtual into and out of the actual. This movement will be different in each case. And in each case, a particular set of models will have to be mobilized. The virtual is most adequately expressed in the interference patterns between them. The thought of the virtual is all about process, and must itself *be* a process. It can never come in one go.

For example, Deleuze often speaks of the virtual as being composed of sets of "pure singularities." These are point-like, and taken together form "constellations." Taken that way, the virtual begins to resemble a fixed space-like structure. So Deleuze will go on to say that the singularities "extend" toward one another. This undoes the fixity by adding a vector aspect carrying a time connotation. The constellation is starting to feel like a projective geometry (in which points and lines are interchanged, and the plotting of space requires a time of transformation). Then just as you're getting used to that he'll say that each singularity "includes" all the others, in the dynamic form of its extensions toward them. The singularity is now sounding like a curve: an integration of singularities. We're now in a calculus model, each singularity an integrable differential. If you try to put the models together, you get points stretching out into lines, lines curving, curves folding back into mutual inclusion—a the whole bending into a topological model. Point, set, structure, vector, curve, differential, integral, topological transformation. All these are the virtual. And that is only a few of the mathematical models you might appeal to (there are others: Riemann space, Markov chains, fractals, and on and on). There are also physical models (the singularity as quantum of event). Biological models (rhizome, phylum). Geological models (strata, plateaus). Military models (war-machine, "fleet in being"). The models never end. Their multitude is only limited in the working out of a particular conceptual problem. Each problem approached will take its own selection of them. The materials and formations in question will simply not be able to bear the embarrassment of conceptual riches. The models will shake down, under pressure, into a restricted set. The movements into and out of the reduced plurality of models that are left will mimic the actual pattern under study. The problem will have been processed in thought. Thought will have mimicked its actual object in and as its own process—making that process analogical.

The thinking of the virtual is always analogical, in an irreducibly complex way. This is what I meant in *Parables for the Virtual* by the "superiority of the analogue": that the only approach to the virtual is analogical, and it is only by virtue of the virtual that we have change and intensity (Massumi 2002, 133–43). Simondon has an ugly name for this kind of analogical thinking of and with complexity (2005, 529–36). He calls it "allagmatics" (from the Greek word for "change"). Here it means you can never model the virtual once and for all. And that you can never simply apply the models of it that you produce. You have to put them to work. You have to work through them, and work them through, differently in each case, under problematic pressure. You have to enact them. It's a real process.

Mistrust anyone who privileges any one model of the virtual. They are standing back from the process. It is a common tactic of critics of Deleuze to take one of his proliferation of models for *the* model, and then on that basis critique the concept of the virtual as inadequate. This is like amputating someone's thumb and then criticizing them for not living up to the definition of the human by failing to display opposable digits. You can't grasp the virtual without a full conceptual hand. You can't actually grasp it at all. It's more like prestidigitation. You make the moves that conjure it up performatively as a thought-effect.

JN/MD: *As Deleuzian-Guattarian preoccupations seep in to architecture, practices are emerging which adopt the process of formation as a philosophical datum. But while Deleuze and Guattari have shifted emphasis from the static being of "form" to the infinite process of "formation," the architectural expression of this philosophy must still confront the mostly static nature of the built environment. Is it possible to reconceive of the discipline of architecture entirely as an art of temporal, rather than spatial, organization? What are the implications of such an agenda?*

BM: Approached processually, there is no contradiction between form and formation, stasis and transformation, or even time and space. The most useful way of approaching these "oppositions" is to treat them as phase transitions. We do not say that ice "contradicts" water. Water becomes ice, and ice water. They are processual extensions of each other. Each contains the other as its own potential. They are in a state of "mutual inclusion" in the same line of variation. They belong to the same "phylum." Their starkly different formal qualities, it is true, commit them to different destinies. Water enters prioritarily into regimes of flow, ice into regimes of rigid accumulation. However, the formal differences do not belie their belonging to the same phylum. Quite the contrary, they *express* it—differentially. The transitions from one phase state to another give the process to which both forms belong the opportunity to express itself more fully. The potentials each phase state contains appear differentially, in a distribution bringing to expression at the same time what the process immanently includes, and its engagement with external conditions belonging to other processes. The ice-form expresses at the same time a potential of the material phylum to which it belongs, and an environing set of weather conditions. The expression of the potential of the water process is *conditioned* by another, more encompassing process. The second process takes the first up into itself. It sets the conditions under which a specific form belonging to the first process will present itself in it. This is what Deleuze and Guattari call "capture."

Capture is always "double capture," because, as I noted, the process taken up has something to say about what happens, and co-determines the more encompassing process that determines what form it takes. Today's weather conditions wouldn't be what they are were water not part of the phylum it is. Weather conditions may determine which of water's potentials will appear, but the weather is dependent on water's offering up those potentials for it to be what it will have been on any given day. It's the difference between rain and snow. The point is: even "static" or frozen forms belong to processual continuums populated by phase transitions between related forms which express the same process in starkly different formal qualities. Which form presents itself with what precise qualities, when, where, and how, is determined in dynamic encounter with another process that is more encompassing than the first but with which the first is nevertheless in a relation of co-determination.

The design process, what the question calls "formation," is architecture's liquid phase. The "static" form that emerges from that phase is the built structure. The weather is the urban environment (including all its constituent dimensions or strata: zoning, circulatory patterns, commercial pressures, cultural preferences, trends in taste) providing the conditions for that building. Urbanism and architecture are in a relation of double capture. To be thought fully, neither can be thought apart. They are co-determining. The determination doesn't end at the erection of the building. The urban process that takes it up may continue to bring new architectural potentials contained in the building to expression. How a building takes effect, what architectural-urban effects it has, varies according to what passes through it, how it is inhabited, and what goes on around. A building may be repurposed, qualitatively changing what difference its formal qualities make in the life of the city—the architectural equivalent of snow or rain, a city chill or urban warming trend. An entire architectural genre might modulate which potentials actually appear, even without explicit formal reconfiguration, in response to economic or cultural changes redefining the prevailing "weather" conditions of the urban environment. The building next door might be demolished and replaced, changing the local urban fabric in a way that modulates the remaining building's lived qualities and perhaps, as a consequence of that, its program. The street in front might evolve into a pedestrian mall, changing patterns of circulation, those changes in their turn entraining others. The building may deteriorate, contributing through its very breakdown to the conditions for urban renewal. The possibilities are infinite. If you look at the larger picture of the double capture of the built form and the urban environment, over the long term the fixity of the "static" form reliquefies. All that is concrete melts into city.

The "static" form is only a provisional stop in the architectural process. It is better conceived of as a threshold in a process that continues past it, and sweeps it up in a co-determined movement of continuing transformation. The architectural process is ongoing for two reasons: (1) following the principle of mutual inclusion, each form (or phase) virtually "contains," in processual potential, all others belonging to the architectural continuum; (2) through the encounter with the encompassing, conditioning process of the city, different sets of these architectural potentials are serially expressed, with or without actual formal modification (sometimes relationally, much the way one color modulates another by its proximity).

The question, then, is: How can the design process pre-adapt itself to the continuation of process, which is in any case inevitable? How can it build into its built result as yet unexpressed architectural potentials, enriching or intensifying the way it lends itself to re-uptake and recursive reforming by other processes (double capture). How can it multiply its own co-determining contributions to the double captures it engages? As Lars Spuybroek argues, answering these questions requires shifting the vocabulary from, for example, "ambiguities" of code or meaning, to ontogenetic "vagueness" (2004). Ontogenetic vagueness is not a lack of definition. It is a surplus of it: a mutual inclusion in the same actual form of potentially divergent takings-effect belonging to different phases of the same process. Greg Lynn also speaks of this surplus-determination when he calls the produced architectural form the dynamic "shape of a multiplicity" (1999, 20). This question of the surplus-determining continuation of the architectural process is the problem my own work on architecture has focused on.

Surplus-determination has to do only marginally with what is most commonly taken to be the "content" of architecture: the typologies of constituted form defining styles which can be infused with new meaning through a recoding or cross-coding of their component formal units. It is less concerned with architecture's formal disciplinary understanding of itself than with its *living through* the encounter with its outside. There is a particularly important "outside" of architecture that the built environment actually contains: the body. It cannot be forgotten that the living-through of the architectural process is always, and always variably, embodied.

There is a third "double capture" in close embrace with the two already discussed. The material phylum of the human body, with its immanent process of experience-formation and all the potential that process holds, enters into complex relations of co-determining continuation and recursive reforming with the built structure. The built form is to the body as the built environment is to the building. The qualities of the built environment are the weather conditions for embodied experience.

A logic of perceptual emergence, of experiential ontogenesis, must be added to the larger picture. What experiential phase transitions does a passing or inhabiting body engage in in double capture with the built form? How do these continuous transformations feed back into urbanism? Or back into architecture, at its interface with urbanism? What unexpressed potentials are capacitated, at what thresholds, and to what effect? How can architectural form surplus-determine perception and qualities of experience? Arakawa and Gins (2002) answer that question by adapting the concept of "affordances" from James J. Gibson's (2015) "ecological" approach to perception theory. The unit of architecture, from Arakawa and Gins's processual perspective, is not a formal unit of style. It is the "landing site": the way in which an architectural element beckons the body to actualize one of its experiential potentials. Or many at once. When there are several, without one necessarily being privileged over another, the architectural element has become surplus-determining: the unitary form of an experiential multiplicity whose conditions of emergence are an architectural encounter with the phylum of the body, that encounter itself enfolded in the urban encounter with architecture: triple articulation.

It cannot be emphasized enough that this foregrounding of perception and experience is not a call for a phenomenology of architecture. Phenomenology returns experience to a form of interiority (the transcendental ego) or a closed loop (the "flesh" of the world as prereflective of subjective expression). Here, experience is but an echo. In the ecological approach I am advocating, experience is an emergence. It returns the body to a processual field of exteriority (encounter). The same goes for architecture itself. The model at all levels is what I have called "relational autonomy": the emergent expression of a process's singular potentials in a dynamic of encounter with its processual outside. Applied to architecture, this undermines the explanatory power of any approach that begins by separating the inside of the discipline from its outside, as if architecture itself were effectively a form of interiority defined by historical periods, a repertory of styles, or a set of characteristic procedures. All of these change. All are under continual variation. Architecture as a "discipline" is what passes through these ongoing phase-shifts. It is in the gaps between chronological moments. It is in the surplus-determination of elements of style in virtue of which they carry an in-built, or immanent, potential for modulation. It is in the invention of new procedures which retool its interface with other processes. Architecture is the indiscipline flowing through its own complexly co-determined iterations. It is not an edifice itself. It is not a structure. It has no definitive content. It is a living process. As Deleuze and Guattari were fond of saying, escape is the lifeblood of process. A creative discipline is defined by how it *escapes* its past content and internal constraints. It renews itself through the rigorous indiscipline of its effective couplings with processes other than its own.

Couplet 4

2009

Simondon's "Technical Mentality" Revisited

PARRHESIA (ARNE DE BOEVER, ALEX MURRAY, AND JON ROFFE): *In our preliminary discussion, you said that Simondon's thought on technical objects cannot be understood outside of the context of his theory of individuation. Could you explain this a little bit further, perhaps by drawing from the essay "Technical Mentality" that is published in this issue of* Parrhesia, *no. 7 (2009): 17–27?*

BRIAN MASSUMI: The essay "Technical Mentality" is a fascinating case in point and might very well occupy us for the rest of the conversation. On the one hand, it is startlingly contemporary in its concerns, linking as it does the question of the nature of the technical object to the evolution of the network, long before the developments we have all experienced since Simondon's time—most notably, the rise of the internet—had created a general awareness of the necessity of that move. His evocation of the technical object evolving through the network into a postindustrial "open object" frames the discussion in a way that is of the utmost relevance to today's situation. On the other hand, the essay employs a good deal of vocabulary which, read in isolation from the rest of his work, can come across as terribly anachronistic, if not downright off-putting. He speaks of a technical mentality "harnessing nature" through increasingly norm-based functioning structurally embodying the proper "cognitive schema" so as to eliminate the "proliferation of the inessential" that comes when consumer choice interferes with design. This comes after a discussion of the difference between the Cartesian mechanism, with its structured hierarchy ordered by an ideal of stability, and the cybernetic model of the continuously self-adapting system regulating itself through feedback mechanisms horizontally linking recurrent operations as a condition of possibility for any functional hierarchy. Simondon falls, of course, more to the cybernetic side, which he praises for its kinship with a "true realist idealism." A rapid reading might well be forgiven for mistaking Simondon's "technical mentality" for a scarily normative vision of ultra-rationalized technocratic cyber-control. It would be just that, though—a mistake. While Simondon is unarguably closer to cybernetics than to Descartes, his theories diverge from cybernetics in fundamental ways, and his ethics also turn out to be anything but normative and technocratic.

It's complicated to untangle what he's getting at from a single essay addressing a specific question concerning the technical object, particularly one as thorny as its "mentality," in isolation from the larger theoretical context he develops in his books. For example, in this essay Simondon mentions a water turbine invented by Jean Guimbal, which managed to miniaturize key components while ingeniously solving the associated problem of overheating. He refers in this connection to the "schema of concretization which brings the invention into existence." It would be natural to identify the schema of concretization with the cognitive schema he mentions far more frequently in the essay, and to understand the cognitive schema as an abstract model in the mind of the engineer that comes before the object and guides its construction. By that understanding, the origin of the technical object is purely cognitive and entirely internal to the human thinking subject. Human thought pre-cognizes a solution, then externalizes it by finding a way to mold matter to the form of its pre-thought solution. The practical finding of that way would be the technical process: the set of mediating actions shepherding the abstractly thought object into concrete embodiment. Invention would move from the past of a thought, cognitively fully formed, toward the future of an embodiment materially repeating the original thought's abstract form. The relation of the technical object to its cognitive origin would be one of resemblance: conformity to a formal model.

This is clearly *not* what Simondon means by concretization. If this were all there were to the story, Simondon would be trafficking in "hylomorphism." Hylomorphism, or the idea that the generation of form is reducible to the imposition upon inert matter of a pregiven abstract form, is the philosophical enemy which Simondon endeavors to undo throughout his work—not least in the opening section from *L'individuation psychique et collective* (Psychic and Collective Individuation; 1992) published in this issue (*Parrhesia* 2009, 4–16).[1] There may indeed be an abstract model in the mind of a human engineer that, as Simondon says, "presupposes that the problem is resolved." But that is not what interests Simondon. He sees something else that takes him in very different direction.

PARRHESIA: *Could you explain this a bit more, perhaps again by means of an example?*

BM: Just how far away his own thinking moves from any conventional cognitive model that might be applied to invention is signaled by the fact that he scrambles the causal order it assumes. In the section of *On the Mode of Existence of Technical Objects* following his discussion in that book of the Guimbal turbine, he links invention to an *action of the future on the present* (2017, 60). What can this mean? The veritable moment of invention, he says, is when a circular causality kicks in. In the case of the Guimbal turbine, it has to do with the potential for the oil in the turbine and the water around it to each play multiple roles. The water brings energy to the turbine, but it can also carry heat away from it. The oil carries the heat of the generator to the housing, where it can be dissipated by the water, but it also insulates and lubricates the generator and, thanks to the pressure differential between it and the water, prevents infiltration. There are two sets of multifunctional potentials, one in the water and the other in the oil. The moment of invention is when the two sets of potentials click together, coupling into a single continuous system. A synergy clicks in. A new regime of functioning has suddenly leapt into existence. A threshold has been crossed, like a quantum leap to a qualitatively new plane of operation. The operation of the turbine is now "self-conditioning" (53–59). It has achieved a certain operational autonomy, because the potentials in the water and in the oil have interlinked in such a way as to automatically regulate the transfer of energy into the turbine and of heat out of it, allowing the turbine to continue functioning independently without the intervention of an outside operator.

Before the passing of the threshold, there were two discontinuous energetic fields. The oil and the water were separated by differentials of temperature, pressure, viscosity, and pattern of movement. The respective energetic fields of the oil and the water were in a state of what Simondon calls "disparity." When the synergy kicked in, the disparity rolled over into an emergent continuity. The differentials between the two fields are still there. But there is also something else, which has leapt into existence. There is a circularity between them, a recurrent feedback that has crossed a threshold to bring another plane of operation into existence. That plane of operation—of self-maintenance—is continuous. But its continuity moves *across* the difference. It comes into itself across the difference, from which it simultaneously separates itself to claim an operative autonomy as a qualitatively new regime of functioning. The new quality of operation arises as an "effect" of the disparity. This is not the same as saying that the disparity is the cause. What brings the new quality of operation into existence is the circling into each other of the multifunctionalities of the energetic fields of the oil and the water: their entering into a dynamic relation.

What matters for Simondon is the paradox that before the oil and the water entered into relation, the respective multifunctionalities were not in effect. They were nowhere. They are not to be found in the past. It is when the relation kicked in that they were determined, by that very event, to *have been* the potential for what has come. If the potential was not effectively there in the past, there is only one place it could have come from: the future. The respective multifunctional potentials of the oil and the water came into existence at the very instant their disparate fields clicked together into automatic relation. The potentials in the oil and the water for the turbine have been *invented* by the relation's energetic kicking in. Invention is the bringing into present operation of *future* functions that potentialize the present for an energetic leap into the new. The effect is a product of a recursive causality: an action of the future on the present. This is why Simondon insists that the technical object is not the product of a hylomorphic causality moving from past to future. A technical invention, he says, does not have a historical cause. It has an "absolute origin": an autonomous taking-effect of a futurity; an effective coming into existence that conditions its own potential to be as it comes. Invention is less about cause than it is about self-conditioning emergence.

This completely changes how we must think about the "mentality" of the technical object. The fact that there was an abstract model of the turbine in the mind of the designer is in a way secondary. The idea for the technical object is finally dependent for its effectiveness on the autonomous taking-effect of the relation. Either it clicks in or it doesn't. The designer can bring the two disparate fields of the water and the oil to the brink of relation, but the passing of the threshold belongs absolutely to *their* potential. The designer is a helpmate to emergence. He can put the pieces in place, moving through a linear series of steps progressing from the past of abstract conception to a present on the brink. But the passing of that threshold to invention depends on the potentialization of the elements presently in place as a function of their future. The newfound potential expresses itself as "operative solidarity" between the elements, across the disparity of their fields. That solidarity is not the result of a simple step-by-step accumulation, or of piecemeal adding together of elements. It is nondecomposable. It is holistic. It's not a structure, he says. It does not add elements together to form a structural unity. Rather, it is a holism-effect that adds a whole new dimension of existence to the elements' diversity.

PARRHESIA: *You seem to be going directly against Simondon's first postulate of the technical mentality here. It appears that for him, "Technical Mentality" is precisely about leaving the holistic mentality behind; it's about the decomposability of the technical object.*

BM: Yes, I should pause here for a moment to say something about why I am using the words "holistic" and "nondecomposable" in spite of Simondon's bitter criticism of holism in the essay, and his listing of the decomposability of the elements as the first postulate for a thinking of technical mentality. Simondon insists at the same time that the elements remain decomposable *and* that they give rise to an "effect" that consists in a "mode of functioning" (2017, 50) characterized by an operational "solidarity" (30, 69)—and thus an effective continuity. These two propositions must not be seen to be in contradiction. As Deleuze liked to say, the whole is not of the parts, but *alongside* them and in addition to them. Whitehead also has a formula for this: the many become one, and are increased by one. What I am calling a holism-effect is just that: an effect. The word "effect" is taken in a sense akin to the optical "effect." Deleuze, under Simondon's influence, also speaks of scientific effects attached to the proper names of the scientists who invented them. He takes the optical effect as a model. An optical effect is an excess effect of a visual whole that detaches itself from the diversity of the elements conditioning its appearance, without in any way annulling that diversity. An example is an optical illusion that suddenly "snaps-to," carrying the perceiver in one nondecomposable go across a threshold to a new unitary appearance. Simondon's bitter critique of "holism" in the "Technical Mentality" essay applies to philosophies that replace the diversity of conditions from which an effect arises with the nondecomposability of the arising whole, annulling their diversity and attributing a foundational ontological priority to the whole rather than rightly placing it on the level of emergent effect. This is one example of one of the most original aspects of Simondon's thought: his endeavoring to always think discontinuity and continuity *together* (an orientation he shares with William James's radical empiricism). This endeavor is encapsulated in his emphasis on the *quantum*, borrowing from physics. A quantum leap in physics is nondecomposable as a movement across a threshold. But its nondecomposability takes off from one set of diverse and decomposable conditions (a collection of particles in a particular configuration) and leads to another (a collection of particles in a changed configuration). The dynamic wholeness of the quantum event (the all-or-nothingness of its occurrence) interposes itself between two diversities, whose discontinuity it marks by a change in level accompanied by a qualitative change in the defining properties of the system (a passage, for example, from one element of the periodic table to another). For Simondon, all transition, all change, all becoming, is quantum.[2]

Now to return to the role of the cognitive schema as preexisting abstract form, in relation to the absolute origin as quantum event of emergence. Following intermediary steps suggested by the cognitive schema, the designer organizes diverse elements, moving through a process of past conditioning, to the brink of the present. At that "critical point," the future effect takes over. It takes care of itself, making the automatic leap to being a self-conditioning system. That moment at which the system makes the leap into operative self-solidarity is the true moment of invention. The past-conditioning by the designer is boosted into a new dimension of existence by the sudden taking-effect of a future-conditioning. Potentialities snap into place, enabling a new regime of functioning, anticipatorily useful for the future, from whose own back-action they effectively came into being.

It is crucial to understand that the "schema of concretization" is the snapping-to of the emergent operative solidarity. That is why Simondon says in "Technical Mentality" that the schema of concretization is the multifunctionality of the oil. He means it literally. The oil, in its potential coupling with the water, in operative solidarity with it toward future uses, is the schema of concretization. The schema of concretization is the effective entering-into-relation of the oil with the water. It does not conform to the cognitive schema that was in the mind of the designer according to a principle of resemblance, as copy to model. It effectively takes off from it into a new dimension of existence—which is that of the technical object's relation to its own autonomy. The snapping into operative solidarity of the coupled multifunctionalities of the formerly disparate energetic fields of the oil and the water is the schema of concretization. The instant of the schema of concretization's entering holistically into effect is the absolute origin of the technical object. It is not a cognitive form imposed from outside. It is flush with matter. It's the taking-effect of a new order of relation *of* matter. The taking-effect reenergizes matter, across the diversity of present elements and the disparity of their fields, propelling it onto a new emergent plane of operational solidarity, a new level of material existence. The schema of concretization is *immanent to matter's becoming*.

PARRHESIA: *So how does Simondon's thought on technology depend on his theory of individuation? It seems that we still haven't quite addressed this point.*

BM: Although Simondon never defines the term "technical mentality" in On the Mode of Existence of Technical Objects, and in fact doesn't use it in any of his published books, it is not hard to give it a meaning in keeping with his overall philosophical system—which is to say a definition that is fundamentally *noncognitive*, flush with matter, for which human cognition would be a special case. Given the lack of explicit development of the concept in Simondon's own work, it is perhaps not out of order to turn to another thinker to lend a hand. For Whitehead, each taking-form involves "the swing over from reenaction to anticipation" due to an "intervening touch of mentality" (1967a). He speaks of the reenaction in terms very similar to Simondon, as an "energizing" of a given set of conditions inherited from the past. The swing-over to anticipation introduces novelty into the world. A taking-form "arises as an effect facing its past," no sooner to turn away from its past to become "a cause facing its future": a future cause (192–94). The snapping-to exemplified in the taking-effect of the self-conditioning operational solidarity of this new existence *is* the "touch of mentality" (it constitutes a "subjective form," in Whitehead's vocabulary). Whitehead also talks about this in terms of the passing of a quantum threshold consisting in the becoming of a qualitatively new existence. Saying that the becoming ends as a future cause does not mean that the invention, once it arises, takes its place in a linear chain of causality, as the historical origin of a reproductive series. The causation is always indirect, passing through an interval of immanence: that snap-to of concretization whose schema is immanent to active matter. Each subsequent exemplification of the mode of existence must return to the "absolute origin," to come back to Simondon's vocabulary.

Technically speaking, it is this return event of formation—and not the form—that repeats itself. It is less that a form is reproduced than that an invention repeats itself. If the repeat inventions fall into a strict pattern of conformity with each other, then it is necessary to explain the serial production of this repetitive resemblance-effect. The collective conformity of a population of serially produced technical objects to the cognitive schema in the mind of the designer does not explain anything. It skips over all the "intermediaries"—the chain of past actions bringing the elements to the threshold where they holistically take effect facing their future. It skips over the diversity of the elements. It skips over the disparity of their resident fields. It skips over the quantum leap of becoming that crosses the disparity, in the coming to effective existence of a new level. It skips over the touch of mentality. It forgets the action of the future. It forgets just about everything that is effectively an ingredient of the event of invention. Far from explaining anything, the reproduction of resembling forms exemplifying an invention is precisely what is in need of explanation. What it indicates is that the inheritance of past conditions have built-in constraints that limit the degree of novelty of each retaking effect of the invention. Simondon accounts for these limiting conditions that serially restrict exemplifications of an invention to formally resembling each other in terms of *standardization*. The technical object is an individuation—an event of taking-form—whose past conditioning pre-contains the coming potential of its functional autonomy within certain parameters. The parameters are homeostatic, or equilibrium-tending. The technical object has only the margin of functional autonomy allowing it to maintain itself homeostatically. The key point is that the moment of technical mentality—the *technicity* of the technical object—is always immanent to a material event of taking-form. This event occurs at a critical point where the past effectively swings over into a futurity of functioning. The event of self-futurizing serially repeats itself. The potentialization in which it consists repeats, with a past-conditioned latitude of becoming. The difference between the technical object and the living thing is a question of how great a latitude of becoming their past conditioning will permit. There is life when taking-form maintains itself at the brink. Life lives on a moving threshold of metastability, of fragile, provisional equilibrium that is subject to constant perturbation, from whose jaws it must repeatedly snatch its homeostasis. The living thing is an individuation that has no choice but to *continue* its invention, or face dissolution. Its homeostatic equilibrium is not a simple self-maintenance, but an ever-renewed achievement.

PARRHESIA: *Do you see a connection here with Simondon's theory of physical, vital, and psychic (and collective) individuation?*

BM: Psychic individuation is a further continuation of the achievement of vital individuation that widens its latitude of becoming. Psychic individuation is when vital individuation continues across a quantum leap that brings into existence a new level of operation on which homeostasis does not necessarily have to be maintained, or even renewed. Of course, a homeostatic equilibrium must continue to be renewed on the vital level, to which psychic individuation remains coupled as a necessary condition of its taking effect. Its quantum leaping to its own level moves with life's moving equilibrium. But it takes effect with a qualitative difference. It has the latitude to continue its invention across changes in operational parameters. It can continue inventing itself in such a way as to continue becoming *different*. Maturation is the lowest degree of the psychic individuation of life. The invention of cognitive schema exemplifies a higher degree. The invention of axiomatics—schema for the translation of cognitive schema into each and out of each other—is a still higher degree. Allagmatics, the metaschematizing of axiomatics, is the highest degree, corresponding to what Deleuze and Guattari call conceptual invention, and Guattari in his solo work "metamodelization."

The crucial point is that all of these are *individuations* in their own right. There is an individuation of modes of thought, by the same token by which there is an individuation of modes of physical, technical, and vital individuation. There is no linear causality between any of them. Each is an effective invention bringing into existence an autonomous level of operational solidarity. None can be adequately explainable without reference to an absolute origin. Each must return in its own way, at every iteration, to the absolute origin: an interval of immanence where taking-effect is flush with a self-formative activity of matter as immanent cause. Their coming to existence cannot be explained without eventfully factoring in this immanent cause.

All of the key terms of Simondon's philosophy revolve around the moment of inventive, eventive, taking new effect. In *L'individu et sa genèse physico-biologique* (The Individual and Its Physico-biological Genesis; 1964) Simondon calls the holism-effect that clicks in at this point a *resonance*.[3] Then he defines *matter* as this very resonance. Matter is thus defined in terms of a *form-taking activity* immanent to the event of taking-form. Nothing could be further from the form-receiving passivity of matter according to the hylomorphic model. *Nature* is then the universality of this immanent form-taking activity that is matter: that is, its immanence to each event of form-taking, as the principle of individuation animating every coming into existence. The disparity between energetic fields, from the point of view of the potential that their synergistic taking-effect brings into the present from the future, Simondon names the *preindividual*. The disparity itself is *information*. Then there is a specific term for the clinching into synergistic relation of a diversity of elements, across the disparity of information and toward the emergence of a new level of functioning realizing the potential of the preindividual. This he calls *mediation*.

The definitions could go on indefinitely to cover the entire Simondonian repertory, all revolving around the same critical point of absolute origination. All of the familiar words that come back around that point take on startlingly new meanings which it is crucial to hang onto if one is to follow Simondon's thinking. Simondon's "mediation," for example, has nothing to do with the meaning of that term in communication studies, media studies, or cultural studies. In Simondon, the term carries ontogenetic force, referring to a snapping into relation effecting a self-inventive passing to a new level of existence. It would in fact be much more precise to call it *immediation* (Massumi 2019). Information, for its part, pertains to the "preindividual" preparatory to that passage. Information—Simondon is unambiguous about this—has no content, no structure, and no meaning. In itself, it is but disparity. Its *meaning* is the coming into existence of the new level that effectively takes off from the disparity and resolves the discontinuity it exhibits into a continuity of operation. Information is redefined in terms of this *event*. As for Gregory Bateson, information is a "difference that makes a difference": a disparity that actively yields a new quantum of effect, and whose meaning is the novelty-value of that effect. What differentiates Simondon in general from the cybernetic and information theory traditions out of which Bateson was working (in particular, what differentiates him from Wiener and Shannon/Weaver) is that for Simondon this differencing process can in no way be understood in quantitative terms and is not susceptible to any kind of stable formalization. The differencing process is not describable in quantitative terms because although a quantum leap does coincide with the discharge of a measurable amount of energy, it also coincides with a passing of a threshold to a qualitatively new level of existence. That qualitative crossing is the crucial point for Simondon. It requires for its understanding the mobilization of a whole stable of concepts beyond the pale of quantitative method. The process is not susceptible to any stable formalization because it is continually giving rise to new operational solidarities that did not exist before, and therefore exceed all prior formalization. The "mentality" of the process always avails itself of a *potential energy* of invention, in relation to which quantification and formalization are constantly playing a perpetual game of catch-up. Neither ever catches up. Quantification is always laboring under a deficit of potential, and formalization under an energy deficit. Even working together, they can only get as far as the possible—according to Bergson, nothing more than an anemic, back-cast shadow of potential.

PARRHESIA: *Could you talk a bit more about the significance of "potential energy" in Simondon's thought?*

BM: It is Simondon's insistence on the centrality of the concept of potential energy that makes his philosophy a "realist idealism." It is what he himself points to as differentiating his thought from information theory and cybernetics. The potential of the energetic taking-form that is Simondon's individuation is *real* in the sense that it always comes to pass in the material clinching of an effective event. It is *ideal* in the sense that it comes into the effective present of that energetic event as the action of its future. The real and ideal are two facets of the same event. Together they make the event of individuation more resonantly material than any mere formalization, and give it more of a mental "touch" than any set of quantities could ever have. What differentiates Simondon from Bateson himself is that Simondon never lets the touch of mentality hypostasize into a "Mind" that is one with Nature. There is no "Mind" immanent to Simondon's Nature—only form-taking informational *activity* (with as yet—that is to say until its own future occurs to it—no content, no structure, no meaning). There is no "one" but always a one-*moreness*: a "more-than-one," everywhere energetically in potential.

Returning to the question of technical mentality in Simondon's article, the relation between the cognitive schema and the schema of concretization can now be better understood. The cognitive schema resembles the schema of concretization that is the effective invention of the technical object not because it effectively molds it, but in the sense that it underwent an individuation that is *operatively analogous* to it. It also took emergent effect, from a preindividual field of thought (consisting in an unresolved disparity between perceptions, some present, some appearing only possible). It also passed a quantum threshold across which its operational solidarity came newly into existence (inventing the emergent meaning—the cognitive schema itself—capable of resolving the preindividual perceptual disparity into a well-formed anticipation energetically facing its own effective future). Thus effectively formed, the cognitive schema was able to follow the recursive traces of its anticipatory emergence back to the future from which it came, strategically guiding the setting in place of elements piece by piece, progressing step by step to the very brink of invention. But not beyond. At that point, it can do no more. It has prepared the preindividual field. But it cannot take the ultimate step. Because that step involves the arising from the preindividual of a new autonomy: the coming into self-maintaining existence of a brand new mode of functioning. Only the technical object can clinch that for itself. The cognitive schema must pass on the baton of invention to the schema of concretization, and step back. For the next step is the point of absolute origination at which the technical object, formatively touched by its own mentality, emerges onto its own level of reality. It is the point at which the technicity of the object takes effect. Its taking-effect takes a whole new form, through which it effectively declares its ontogenetic independence from the cognitive schema. It snaps-to its own effect, immanent cause of its technical future.

The cognitive schema and the schema of concretization are in operative analogy with one another in the sense that it is this form-taking *process* that is repeated between them. It is not, strictly speaking, a form, or even a structure, that is reproduced by one for the other. A thought does not resemble a turbine. A disparity between perceptions present and possible is not structured like a disparity between water and oil. But the taking-effect of the operational solidarity of the cognitive schema in thought, and the taking-effect of the operational solidarity of a schema of concretization in turbine-technicity, do "resemble" each other in the sense that they exemplify the same ontogenetic process. Their comings-to-be follow the same process of individuation. In addition, one coming-to-be ends up passing the processual baton to the next, ending as future-facing as it began, at the point of its own absolute origin. The two individuations are not only in operative analogy. They form between themselves a *transductive* series (a forwarding of futurity down the processual line of absolute originations relaying each other, in operatively analogous takings-form).

When this transductive process is taken into account, what Simondon means by the cognitive schema "harnessing nature" takes on a completely new meaning. It carries an inventive connotation that distances "technical mentality" from any technocratic vision of rationality. The "recognized, measured, normalized" thresholds of functioning he invokes at the end refer specifically to the standardization that past-conditions the serial emergence of the technical object. His point is that when the technical object under consideration takes the form of the postindustrial *network*, the standardization is actually the past-condition for an *opening* of the technical process to an unheard-of future latitude of becoming. Through network standardization the technical object in fact accedes to some of the same natural potentials "harnessed" by psychic individuation. It "maintains itself" not in a homeostatic equilibrium but in a "perpetual actuality," wherein its inventive individuation is "eminently apt to be continued." More and more, it comes to "carry its own line of prolongation on its own plane" of operational solidarity, in operative analogy with psychic individuation. The "touch of mentality" that constitutes its technicity intensifies and expands. Technical mentality ideally-realizes itself more fully. It is "augmented, continued, amplified."

As this happens, technical individuation and psychic individuation come to the very brink of each other. They enter into a relation of transduction. In concert, they rejoin Nature, without "disfiguring" it the way that Simondon considers that the opposition between the "affective modalities" of the artisanal and the industrial has done. These technicities were in affective disparity. They were antipathic. Which made their disparity ineffective. Instead of clinching forward over a threshold to a qualitatively new level of existence, they stubbornly clung to their antipathy for one another, prolonging their disparity. They remained in "inessential," that is to say ontogenetically ineffectual, naturally uninventive, preindividual tension. This locked out any resolution of their disparity through a quantum leap of future-facing potential snapping-to, to newly individuating effect. The lock-in was to a relative level of collective ontogenetic stupidity.

If the stubborn disparity between artisanal and industrial technicity can be said to have defined post-Enlightenment humanity, it was as its own perpetual crisis. The period was locked in an ineffectual dialectic between nostalgia for the simpler, more bucolic "humanness" of artisanal production and the "progress" of the human bought at the price of its own fragmentation at the mercy of the manic Taylorist drive for industrial efficiency. Does the "amplified" technical mentality of the "postindustrial" network presage a more intelligent taking-form *beyond* the human? Do technical individuation and psychic individuation not only brink upon each other, but transductively merge into a single lineage? In postindustrial technicity, will the cognitive schema and the schema of concretization finally converge? Simondon doesn't explicitly pose this question, much less answer it. But it is a measure of the effective potential of his own conceptual inventiveness that he came to *its* brink, so far ahead in anticipation, and in a way that furnishes us today with future-facing resources apt to assist us in coming to our own response, as an expression of an ethics of becoming.

Personally, I shy away from posthumanist discourse. For me, a Simondonian ethics of becoming is best to be found not in a next "posthuman" phase but in the *nonhuman* at the "dephased" heart of every individuation, human and otherwise. What I mean by the nonhuman is the ontogenetic clinching of the preindividual that catapults it over the threshold of becoming. I mean the individual—that nondecomposable solidarity of occurrent existence—at the brink. Just coming eventually to be what it will always have been, at a level where it has, as yet, no content, no meaning, no structure, only past-conditioning future-facing. The really-ideal "absolute origin," as a function of which every quantum of individuation effectively ends where it causally begins, so as to emergently interlink all individuations in that vast network of transductive more-than-oneness that is the process of Nature.

2012

The Supernormal Animal

Instinct is sympathy. If this sympathy could extend its object and also reflect upon itself, it would give us the key to vital operations.
—Henri Bergson (1998, 176)

The athletic grace of the pounce of the lynx. The architectural feats of the savanna termite. The complex weave of the orb spider's web. We admire these accomplishments as marvels of the natural world. The wonder resides as much in the automatic nature of these animal accomplishments as in their summum of technical perfection. Instinct: an innate condensation of ancestral wisdom passed from generation to generation, acquired through random mutation, retained through adaptive selection, unfolding with such regularity and efficiency as to rival the most skilled of human artisans (and in the case of certain social animals, apt to put the most well-oiled human bureaucracy to shame). Standard stimulus, normative output. Signal, triggering, performance, following one another in lockstep, with no second thoughts and without fail. Pure mechanism, all the more trustworthy for being unreflective. Instinct: the instrumentality of intelligence wrapped into reflex. So masterful it is in its functionality that it gives luster to utility. The productive beauty of the hive. The automatic aesthetics of adaptive stereotype.

Such is instinct . . . by repute. But instinct has always been hard-pressed to live up to its reputation. From the very first systematic investigations dedicated to it by the nascent science of ethology, it has betrayed a most disconcerting tendency. The same drive that so naturally leads it through to its normative accomplishments seems to push it, just as naturally, to overshoot its target. Instinct seems called upon, from within its very own movement, following its own momentum, to outdo itself. Its instrumentality envelops an impulse to excess. This suggests a very different natural aesthetic—or a different nature of the aesthetic—than the beauty of utility.

It is not for nothing that for thinkers such as Gilles Deleuze, Félix Guattari, Raymond Ruyer, and Étienne Souriau the theory of the animal is bound to the theory of art. The link between animality and artfulness necessitates a reevaluation of the neo-Darwinian notion that selective adaptation, consolidated by instinct, is the sole motor of evolution. Deleuze and Guattari supplement adaptive evolution under pressure of selection with the concept of becoming as the pilot concept for the theory of the animal. Becoming is taken in the strongest sense, of emergence. "Can this becoming, this emergence, be called Art?" (Deleuze and Guattari 1987, 316).

Called "art," the formative movement of animal life is no longer analyzable exclusively in terms of adaptation and selection. Another name is called for: expression. In what way do the animal and the human, each in its own right, as well as one in relation to the other, participate in this expressive becoming? Together in what natural animal "sympathy"? If this natural sympathy is moved by an instinctive tendency to outdo itself in expressive excess over its own norms, what does this say about the nature of the animal? The nature of nature? And if this sympathy could extend its object and also reflect upon itself, providing the key to vital operations, what would prevent us from finding, at the self-extending core, something that could only be described as a primary consciousness? A germinal consciousness flush with life's continuance? Might it be instinct which, against all expectations, obliges us to say, with Ruyer that "consciousness and life are one" (2019, 174)? That "consciousness and morphogenesis are one and the same" (160)? A consciousness flush with the unfolding genesis of forms of life: a creatively lived dynamic abstraction. Abstraction? How is that animal? How animal is that?

It is only possible here to stage a first move in the direction of these questions, through a replaying of instinct.[1]

It was Niko Tinbergen, one of the pioneers of ethology, who first noticed that all was not right in the automatism of instinct. Tinbergen was researching the instinctive behavior of the herring gull (Tinbergen and Perdeck 1950). A red spot on the female beak serves as a signal or "trigger" for feeding behavior. It attracts the peck of the chick. The execution of the peck intensifies the chick's begging behavior and triggers the corresponding behavior in the adult, namely the regurgitation of the menu. Tinbergen was interested in knowing what precise perceptual quality constituted the trigger. He built decoy gull beaks presenting variable characteristics in an attempt to isolate which characteristics were essential to triggering the instinctive behaviors.

His method was guided by four assumptions: (1) the signal as such is a discrete stimulus (the colored spot); (2) the stimulus stands out in its discreteness against a supporting background, with that form imprinted in the young gull as an innate schema (the geometry of the adult's beak and head); (3) the hungry chick's response follows mechanically from the appearance of the spot against the background of an actual shape formally resembling the schema; and (4) the response is a sequence of purely automatic actions operating as a reflex. The assumed mechanism was the triggering of an automatism by an instinctive recognition following a principle of formal resemblance.

What Tinbergen found was quite different. Against expectations, the decoys most resembling actual seagull beaks and heads exerted the *least* force of attraction. The most "natural," or naturalistic, forms left something to be desired. Tinbergen decided to push the experiments further by extending the range of variation of the presented forms "beyond the limits of the normal object." This included decoys that "did not look like a good imitation of a herring gull's bill at all" (1965, 67). Certain decoys exhibiting a noticeable deficit of resemblance were among the most effective of all. Tinbergen himself was forced to recognize something: that instinct displays an inherent tendency to snub good form and overshoot the limits of the normal in the direction of what he dubbed "supernormal stimuli." The question then became: Precisely what perceptual qualities press beyond the normal?

There was a strong correlation between the color red and the triggering of feeding behavior. The absence of red, however, did not necessarily block the instinctive activity. A spot of another color—even black or gray—could do the job, provided that there was high enough contrast between the spot and its background. High-contrast red proved the surest signal. But the fact that black or gray could also do the job meant that the effect didn't hinge on a discrete color quality, not even red. What the effectiveness of the presentation hinged on, Tinbergen concluded, was an *intensification* effect, in this case produced by the relation of contrast. The color red exerted a supernormal force of attraction to the extent that it lent itself to this intensification *relation*. Gull chicks may have a predilection for red, but even where red was present, there was supernormal pressure toward forcing red into an intensifying relation of immediate proximity with another color, the more contrastive the better. It was this proximity of differences in quality, this qualitative *neighborhood*, that dynamized the force of attraction, pushing the instinct to surpass what had been assumed to be its natural target.

The term "supernormal" thus does not connote a simple opposition between what is normal and what is not, or between the natural and the artificial. What it connotes is a plasticity of natural limits and a natural disrespect of good form. It indicates a tendency toward deformation stretching behavior out of shape, from within its own instinctive operation—a transformational movement naturally pushing animal experience to artificially exceed its normal bounds. Supernormal stimuli express a natural tendency toward an affirmation of excessiveness. "Supernormal dynamism" is a better term than "supernormal stimulus" because it better reflects this tendential movement and the relational tenor of its triggering.

The term "trigger" needs revisiting as well. If the signal functioned purely to trigger an automatic sequence of actions, it would be naturally resistant to the intervention of the supernormal dynamism. It would be firmly under the jurisdiction of the laws of resemblance governing good form and its well-behaved representation. The supernormal dynamism would come in contravention of the laws, relegating it to the status of a simple negative—an infraction—rather than recognizing it as an affirmation of what exceeds the bounds of behavioral norms. It also consigns it to the status of an externality, like an accident whose occurrence doesn't rightfully belong to the nature of the situation, and simply intrudes. But the supernormal tendency clearly pushes from within, as a dimension of the situation. It does not accidentally come up against. It pushes across, with a distinct air of exaggeration. It doesn't just throw the behavioral functioning off its form. It makes the form of the functioning behaviorally vary. It twists the situation into a new relational variation, *experientially* intensifying it. What is in play is an immanent experiential excess by virtue of which the normal situation presents a pronounced tendency to surpass itself.

The fact that Tinbergen was unable to predict which characteristics were determining testifies to the fact that what is at stake is not resemblance to a specific schema serving as a model. The triggering "stimulus" was not in fact isolatable and was not subject to the necessity of corresponding to a model.

The most that can be said is that red as "stimulus" is *bound* to contrast. The same applies to other qualities ingredient to the situation. If they are likewise treated as linked or indissociably bound variables—in other words, as relata—the bounds of potential variation are stretched. The plasticity of the situation is complicated with additional dimensions. The unpredictability grows with the complexity. For example, the geometric variables of length and thickness of beak, and beak size in comparison to head size, enter into relation with contrast, yielding a color-linked geometry in motion. The rhythm and pattern of the movement express a collective co-variation, shaken into further variation by changes in aspect accompanying the quasi-chaotic movements of the hungry chick. The sum total of the qualities ingredient to the variation do not add up to a gestalt. There is no reliable background, any more than there is a fixed figure to stand out against it. When one quality changes, its proximity to others in the directness of their linkage entails a simultaneous variation affecting them all, in something like a relativist curvature of the space-time of behavior. Any variation reverberates across them all with a contagious force of deformation. "Such 'relational' or 'configurational' stimuli," Tinbergen observes, "seem to be the rule rather the exception" (1965, 68). There is no privileged element capable of extracting itself from its immediate neighborhood with the totality of linked qualities. The color red may well be a favorite of the gulls. But its preeminence can even be endangered by mousy gray. An element that is normally foregrounded is perpetually at risk of sinking back into the gregariousness of the moving ground from which it distinguished itself. Any discrete quality may be swallowed back up at any time in the tide of collective variation. Given this general condition of co-variant linkage between qualities in immediate experiential neighborhood, it is no wonder that the ethologist was rarely able to predict the response to models including a supernormal element. Even after the fact, it is impossible to identify with certainty which linkage the relational intensification was due to. "So far," Tinbergen writes, "no one has been quite able to analyze such matters; yet somehow, they are accomplished" (68).[2]

At most, it is possible to discern passages toward plastic limits, with periods of relative stasis along the way: vectors of supernormality punctuated by stases in the unfolding of instinct's internal dynamic. In Deleuze and Guattari's terms, it is more a question of "consistency"—that is to say, processual "self-consistency"—than it is a question of a gestalt or perceptual form in any normal sense. The philosopher of science Ruyer uses the word "auto-conduction," which again has the advantage of connoting the dynamism.[3]

The upshot is that there is an inexpungeable element of unpredictability in instinct that pertains not to the outside intervention of accidents but to the self-consistency of its experiential dynamic. Self-consistency, as distinguished from the accidental, is not a synonym for predictable, regularized, or law-abiding. Ruyer makes much of the fact that instinct may trigger in the absence of any stimulus because it demonstrates a capacity for *spontaneity*. The difference is that spontaneity is not a slave to external circumstance. If it is as unpredictable as the accident, it is because it is auto-conducting, to excess. Ruyer holds that the capacity for spontaneity, which he qualifies as "hallucinatory," must be considered a necessary dimension of all instinct (2019, 98). Although the spontaneity of instinct cannot be reduced to the accidental, accidents nevertheless play a role: "We must consider that an animal in a complex, accident-rich environment would have little chance of survival if it could only avail itself of stereotyped movements, even if they were corrected by orienting stimuli. Of far greater importance are responses that are improvised directly upon the stimulus . . . acting as a kind of irritant rather than as a signal" (98, translation modified).[4]

The lesson of the accident: if instinct really lived up to its reputation as a reflex mechanism, it would be downright maladaptive. For this reason, Ruyer replaces the notion of the trigger-signal. The "stimulus" irritates, provokes, stirs. It is a processual "inductor" (2019, 91). It jump-starts an active process, inducing the performance of an "improvisation." If we put the two terms together, we get a replacement for both "trigger" and "accident" in one terminological stroke: *induced improvisation*. The improvisation is an integral modification in the tendential self-consistency of animal experience, correlated to the externality of an accident-rich environment but governed by its own stirring logic of qualitative variation. An improvisation is a modification rising from within an activity's stirring, bringing a qualitative difference to its manner of unfolding. It is immanent to the activity's taking its own course.

The animal's observable behavior change in the environment is the external face of this immanent modification. In the immanence of its stirring, the modification is hallucinatory: it is "improvised *directly*" on the percept. It operates in all immediacy in the experiential domain of qualitative neighborhood. The physical environment and the qualitative neighborhood are in close processual embrace, but their dynamics remain distinct. Their difference in nature is never erased. The environment, or external milieu, does in the end impose selective constraints. Its selective principle is and remains that of adaptation. And yet instinct opposes to the law of adaptation an auto-conducting power of improvisation that answers to external necessity with a supernormal twist. The improvised modification of the instinctive tendency, although externally induced, takes its own spontaneous form. As an improvisation, it is formally self-causing. Evolution is and remains subject to selective pressure. But that is not the question this episode from Tinbergen's research raises for ethology and by extension for the philosophy of science.

Conceptually, the question pertains to relation. Adaptation concerns external relations between an animal and its environment. Selective pressure exerts an external judgment on the fitness of a modification. By contrast, what an improvisation concerns directly, in the tendential neighborhood of its ownmost activity, are *"internal" relations*: co-varying experiential qualities that come of a block, indissociably linked.[5] For Deleuze and Guattari, as for Ruyer and Bergson, there is another dynamic generative of variation besides the accident. There is a positive principle of form-generating selection operating in its own neighborhood, autonomously of selective adaptation to external conditions. The peck of the herring gull expresses an inventive power of artifice immanent to the nature of instinct, no less than instinct is immanent to nature.

To the adaptive imperative of conformity to the demands of selective pressure, instinct opposes an immanent power of supernormal invention. Faced with a change in the environment, like the sudden appearance of a red-spot-sporting beak on a head, it turns tail, folding back on itself to return to its own neighborhood, there to renew the ties of its native tendency. The accident-rich environment preys upon the instinctive animal. In answer, animal instinct plays upon the environment—in much the sense a musician plays improvisational variations on a theme. Bergson made the point: instinct, he said, is *played* (*joué*, translated as "acted") more than it is represented (1998, 180). The ludic element of instinct pries open a margin of play in the interaction between individuals and between the organism and the environment. The blind necessity of mechanistic adaptation selecting schema of automatism is just half the story. Instinctual behavior is ringed, in Ruyer's words, by a "fortuitous fringe" of induced improvisation (2019, 94). Deleuze and Guattari refer to a "creative involution" occurring on that fringe, a phrase itself playing on Bergson's "creative evolution."

Involution: "to involve is to form a block that runs its line 'between' the terms in play and beneath assignable relations" (which is to say, external relations; Deleuze and Guattari 1987, 239). Between individuals, and between the organism and the milieu, runs a tendential line in the direction of the supernormal. It plays directly in the unassignable register of internal relations: immediate qualitative linkages in a solidarity of variation, mutually deforming as a plastic block. The tracing of this "line" of plasticity is unpredictable, but is not strictly speaking accidental or aleatory, being oriented: toward a spontaneous excess of creative self-consistency.

The tendency toward the supernormal is a vector. It is not only oriented, it carries a force. For example, a cuckoo chick possesses supernormal traits encouraging the female of another species whose nest the cuckoo parasitizes to take it under its wing and nourish it. The host female, Tinbergen says, isn't "willing" to feed the invader. No, she positively "loves" to do it (1965, 67). She does not just do it grudgingly. She does it positively with passion. The force of the supernormal is a positive force. It is not a force in the mechanistic sense. A mechanical force pushes up against a resistance to deliver an impulse determining a commensurate movement in reactive conformity with the quantity of applied force. What we have with the supernormal is a force that pulls forward from ahead, and does so qualitatively: an attractive force. Supernormality is an attractor that draws behavior in its direction, following its own tendency, not in conformity but deformedly and, surpassing normality, without common measure. Supernormality is a force not of impulsion or compulsion, but of *affective propulsion*. This is why it is so necessary to say that instinct involves the inducement of an effect rather than the triggering of an automatism. It is more stirringly about effecting from within than being caused from without. To do justice to the activity of instinct, it is necessary to respect an autonomy of improvised effect with respect to external causation.[6] Instinctive is spontaneously *effective*, in its affective propulsion. It answers external constraint with creative self-variation, pushing beyond the bounds of common measure.

Deleuze and Guattari have a favorite word for affective force that pulls deformationally, creatively ahead, outside common measure: *desire*. Desire is the other, immanent, principle of selection. Deleuze and Guattari define desire as a force of liaison, a force of linkage conveying a transformational tendency. Desire has no particular object. It is a vector. Its object is before it, always to come. Desire vectorizes being toward the emergence of the new. Desire is one with the auto-conducting movement of becoming. Becoming bears on linked experiential qualities in a solidarity of mutual modification, or what Deleuze and Guattari call "blocks" of sensation.[7] It plays upon unpredictable relational effects. It is the improvisation of these deformational, relational effects that constitutes the new. As Deleuze writes, "form is no longer separable from a transformation or transfiguration that . . . establishes 'a kind of linkage animated by a life of its own'" (2005, 104).[8]

Creative life of instinct: vital art. Ruyer remarks that it is the nature of instinctive activity to produce an "aesthetic yield" (2019, 94).[9] After all, what is a force of mutual linkage if not a force of composition

(Deleuze 2005, 104)? Deleuze and Guattari ask, "Can this becoming, this emergence," this composition animating the genesis of new forms with a life of their own and producing an aesthetic yield, be called "Art" (1987, 316)?

We've entered another immediate neighborhood, that of art, the animal, and becoming (evolution played upon by creative "involution"). In this immediate proximity, Deleuze and Guattari write, "what is animal . . . or human in us is indistinct" (1994, 174). For if we can call this Art, it is because the human has the same self-animating tendency to supernormality. Only when we experience it in our own desiring lives do we arrogantly tend to call it culture as opposed to nature, as if the animal body of human beings was somehow exempt from instinctive activity. As any biologist will tell you, the human body is on the animal continuum.

Instinctively, as Deleuze and Guattari might say, we humans are in a "zone of indiscernibility" with the animal (1987, 273, 279, 293–94, 305). Paradoxically, when we return most intently and intensely to that neighborhood "we gain singularly in distinction" (Deleuze and Guattari 1994, 174, translation modified). It is when the human assumes its immanent excess of animality that it becomes all the more itself. Brilliantly so. "The maximum determination issues from this block of neighborhood like a flash" (174, translation modified).

Addendum: Project Notes

A preliminary indication of the direction in which this replaying of the theory of instinct might move, along lines suggested by the opening quote from Bergson, can be provided by glossing the concept of desire in relation to Gabriel Tarde's notions of "belief" and "appetition."

Belief for Tarde has no content in the sense of fundamentally referring to an external object. It is a force of liaison binding a multiplicity of lived qualities into a primary perception that is self-effecting (Ruyer's "hallucinatory" activity). It does not belong to a subject. It is a belonging conditioning the subject's emergence (Tarde 1880, 152–56). The subject does not have or possess belief. Rather, belief is a "possession" (Tarde 2012, 52–53; Debaise 2008). It is the possession of a multiplicity of life qualities *by each other*. It is this immediate qualitative linkage that constitutes the real conditions of emergence of a subject of experience.

In Bergsonian terms, this immediate possession of life qualities by each other can be considered a primary sympathy. Once again, sympathy is not something that is had by a subject. It is not a subjective content of animal life. It is a self-effecting qualitative movement constitutive of the life of the animal. *The animal does not have sympathy, it is sympathy.*

"Appetition" for Tarde is the movement from one such sympathetic perception to another, following a tendency toward expansion (Debaise 2008, 6, 11–12). The tendency toward expansion is an "avidity," corresponding in the present account to the "passion" of the supernormal tendency to excess. The passion of animal life is its creatively outdoing itself. It is the vital movement of animality's self-improvising, energized by the sympathy that it is. Since this moves animality to surpass what it normally is, it would be more precise to say not that the animal "is" sympathy, but that its becoming is sympathetic.

Together, belief and appetition constitute a pulse of "pure feeling" (Tarde 1880, 153). This feeling is pure in the sense of not yet belonging to a subject, but rather entering actively into its constitution. This is the "block of sensation" for Deleuze and Guattari (1994, 164, 167), or William James's "pure experience" (1996a, 4, 15, 25–26, 39–91).

The concepts of belief, desire, and pure feeling ground Tarde's thinking in always already ongoing "minimal activity" (Debaise 2008, 10) rather than any a priori foundation, objective anchoring in external relation, or substance. The possession of belief and the movement of desire that orient sympathetic becoming are immanent to this minimal germinal activity. This is what I call elsewhere "bare activity" (Massumi 2011, 1–3, 10–11, 22, 23, 27). The subject *issues* from this immanence: it is, in Whitehead's terms, a "superject."

Tarde uses "desire" as a synonym for "appetition." In this essay, desire refers to the co-operation of belief and appetition in Tarde. As employed here, the concept of desire also includes an essential reference to Ruyer's definition of consciousness as an experiential solidarity between perceptual qualities indissociably bound in "primary liaison" (2019, 123, translation modified). Primary liaisons are nonmechanistic and, as Deleuze and Guattari emphasize, "nonlocalizable" (1987, 413).

They are not therefore "connections" in any usual sense of the term. At the level of life's minimal (germinal) activity, consciousness is one with the desiring movement of pure feeling.

It is only when this primary consciousness comes to fold back onto itself—"reflect" on itself, as Bergson had it in the opening quote—that it secondarily "extends its object." More precisely, life's folding back on itself recursively *constitutes* an object. The object emerges as an effect of this recursivity. The object, Whitehead says, is *that which returns* (1920, 143).[10] This should not be taken to imply that there is a preconstituted object that returns for a subject. It is not so much that the object returns, but rather that life recurs. It cycles back to an already improvised block of sensation, periodically reiterated with a negligible degree of variation—a variation within the bounds of what, for practical purposes, can be treated as the "same."

Thus the object, as it happens, is not one. It is a recursively emergent, reiterative *event*. What distinguishes an object-event from other species of event is that its reiterability enables it to stand as what James calls a "terminus": an attractor for life-composing movements of appetition (1996a, 13–15, 55–82). When the object is not actually present, it has not "withdrawn," as object-oriented ontology would have it. It is attractively present as a virtual terminus. It is quietly exerting a force of potential.

The objective movement of return of events to negligible variation settles in as a countertendency to the supernormal tendency. The already improvised gels into a nodal point. In tendential orbit around points of return, life's movement can take on regularity. The "sameness" of the object is the harbinger of this regularization. Through it, the object-event becomes a pivot for life reexpressing itself, with a higher quotient of repetition than variation. Thus it is less that "consciousness extends its object." It is more that life extends its own activity into objective-event mode. A plane of regularization bifurcates from life's self-expressive coursing. Life activity settles into a reiterative ordering of itself, a level of organization holding variation to an orbit of negligible variation. Regularization, normalization: it is on this object-oriented level that life's activity comes to *function*.

This object-oriented normalization of life constitutes what Deleuze and Guattari call the "plane of organization" (1987). The plane of organization of function is in reciprocal presupposition with the "plane of consistency" of desire (9, 21, 70–73, 251–52, 265–72). This gives life a *double-ordering*. Pure feeling is doubled by object-oriented perception, in a play of supernormal tendency and normalizing countertendency: of qualitative excess in vectored becoming, and objective leveling in recursive return; of passion-oriented "minimal" activity, and regularized object-oriented action; of creative spontaneity, and organized function. Always both, in a complexity of mutual imbrication.

Evolution cannot be thought apart from this mutual imbrication of contrasting planes of life and the dynamic tension of their always coming together, never dissolving into each other, never resolving their difference. Evolution is differential. Functional adaptation is only half the story. The other half is spontaneous and creative. On this side lies the primary origination of forms of life (which are nothing if not intensely qualitative, tending to excess in an immediacy of germinal activity).

This double-ordering implies that what we normally call "consciousness" is a derivative of a primary, nonreflexive, non-object-oriented consciousness corresponding to a radically different mode of life activity, as yet in no subject's possession. This primary consciousness is not *of* something. It is something: sympathy. It "is" the immediacy of sympathetic becoming—also called intuition.[11] From primary consciousness's recurrent becoming comes, paradoxically, its countertendency. The mode of this derivative or secondary consciousness is *recognition*. Recognition takes recursive return for identity. It constrains recurrence to the same. Organization and normalization are predicated on object-oriented countertendency running circles around desire.

PROJECT:

Index the animal to its unrecognizability.

Find in the human the passion of the animal.

Induce human being to recur to its animal becoming.

Take it to heart that "at the heart of the human there is nothing human" (Lapoujade 2018, 47, translation modified). For it is in the eminently objectless, immediately relational, spontaneously variation-creating activity flush with instinctive animality—this tendency the human shares with the gull—that the human "gains singularly in distinction," attaining its own "maximum determination" in a passionate flash of supernormal becoming.

Take it to heart: animal becoming is *most* human. It is in becoming-animal that the human recurs to what is nonhuman at the heart of what moves it. This makes its surpassingly human. Creative-relationally *more-than* human (Manning 2013).

Put that in writing.

Remember that supernormal becoming is a "minimal activity" of life's exceeding itself. It is modest, to the point of imperceptibility. In the nest or in writing, it is a modest gesture, vanishing even, no more than a flash. Yet vital. Potentially of vital importance. Because it may resonate and amplify and shake life's regularities to their object-oriented foundations.

Consider that in the primary consciousness of the immediate intuition of animal sympathy "the act of knowing coincides with the act that generates reality."[12] Not: correlates to. *Coincides* with. Thought-matter (Deleuze and Guattari 1987, 43). The reality of animality *as* abstraction. Abstraction *as* the movement of the real.

Improvise on that.

Couplet 5

1997

Sensing the Virtual, Building the Insensible

The "virtual," it is hard not to notice, has been making a splash in architecture. Its full-blown entry into the discourse was somewhat belated by comparison to other fields. This has been to architecture's great advantage. For the poverty of prevailing conceptions of the virtual, in its popular compound with "reality," have become all too apparent: beginning with their inability to earn the name. "Virtual reality" has a short conceptual half-life, tending rapidly to degrade into a synonym for "artificial" or "simulation," used with tiresome predictability as antonyms for "reality." The phrase has shown a pronounced tendency to decompose into an oxymoron. It was in that decomposed state that it became a creature of the press, a death warrant on its usefulness as a conceptual tool.

There is a countervailing tendency to use "virtual" without the "reality" tag—not because the virtual is thought to have no reality but because its reality is assumed, the only question being what mode it takes. It is in the work of Gilles Deleuze and Félix Guattari that this current gains its most elaborated contemporary expression. The advantage of architecture is that the virtual has been introduced into its discourse by theorists and practitioners cognizant of the impasse of earlier appropriations of the concept in other domains, and conversant with the alternative Deleuze and Guattari's work represents.

Deleuze and Guattari, following Bergson, suggest that the virtual is the mode of reality implicated in the emergence of new potentials. In other words, its reality is change: the reality of the *event*. This immediately raises a number of problems for any domain of practice interested in seriously entertaining the concept. If the virtual has to do with change as such, then in any actually given circumstance it can only figure as a mode of abstraction. For what is concretely given is what is—which is not what it will be when it changes. The potential of a situation exceeds its actuality. Circumstances self-abstract to the precise extent to which they evolve. This means that the virtual is not contained in any actual form assumed by things or states of things. It runs in the transitions from one form to another.

The abstractness of the virtual has been a challenge to certain discourses, particularly in the interdisciplinary realm of cultural theory, that make a moral or political value of the concrete. This is not the case with architecture, even though its intimacy with the concrete is quite literal. Architecture has always involved, as an integral part of its creative process, the production of abstract spaces from which concretizable forms are drawn. The challenge that the virtual poses for architecture lies more in its transitional nature than its abstractness. How can the run of the in-formation be integrated into a process whose end is still-standing form?

The answer for many has been: topology. Topology deals with continuity of transformation. It engulfs forms in their own variation. The variation is bounded by static forms that stand as its beginning and its end, and it can be stopped at any point to yield other still-standing forms. But it is what happens in-between that is the special province of topology. The variation seamlessly interlinking forms takes precedence over their separation. Forms figure less as self-enclosures than as open co-dependencies of a shared deformational field. The continuity of that field of variation is inseparable from the forms populating it. Yet it exceeds any one of them, running across them all. When the focus shifts to continuity of variation, still-standing form appears as residue of a process of change, from which it stands out (in its stoppage). A still-standing form is then a *sign*: of the passing of a process. The sign does not in the first instance signify anything. But it does imply something. Or better, it implicates. It envelops in its stillness a deformational field of which it stands as the trace: at once a monument of its passing and a signpost of its potential to be repeated. The variation, as enveloped past and future in ceasing form, is the virtuality of that form's appearance (and of others with which it is deformationally interlinked).

Topology has exerted a fascination on certain contemporary architects because it renders form dynamic. This has important consequences for both the design process and the built form to which it leads.

The topological turn entails a shift in the very object of the architectural design process.[1] Traditionally, form was thought of as both the raw material and the end product of architecture, its origin and telos. Form bracketed design. Approached topologically, the architect's raw material is no longer form but *deformation*. The brackets swing open. Form falls to one side, still standing only at the end. Form *follows* the design process, far from enclosing it. Far from directing it, form *emerges* from the process, derivative of a movement that exceeds it. The formal origin is swept into transition. Followed by the architect.

One thing swept away is the popular image of the architect as autonomous creative agent drawing forms from an abstract space of Platonic preexistence to which he or she has inspired access and artfully dropping them into the concrete of everyday existence, which is thereby elevated. The architect's activity becomes altogether less heroic—and the abstract more palpable. For the architect must follow the same process that the form follows. The architect becomes a prospector of formative continuity, a tracker in an elusive field of generative deformation. The abstract field of variation takes on a certain post-Platonic thickness, in and by its very elusiveness, by becoming a field of hands-on exploration and experimentation. New form is not conceived. It is coaxed out, flushed from its virtuality. The architect's job is in a sense catalytic, no longer orchestrating. He or she is more a chemist (or perhaps alchemist) staging catalytic reactions in an abstract matter of variation than a maestro pulling fully formed rabbits of genius from thin air with a masterful wave of the drafting pencil.

Le Corbusier outlines the antithetical position in an early manifesto:

> The goal of art is to put the spectator . . . in a state of an elevated order. To conceive, it is first necessary to know what one wishes to do and specify the proposed goal. . . . Conception is, in effect, an operation of the mind which foreshadows the general look of the art work. . . . Possessed of a method whose elements are like the words of a language, the creator chooses among these words those that he

will group together to create a symphony. . . . One comes logically to the necessity . . . of a logical choice of themes, and the necessity of their association not by deformation, but by formation. (Le Corbusier and Ozenfant 1920, 65–67, 62)

Here, creation consists in the masterful composition of aggregate forms, drawing on a preexisting vocabulary of combinable elementary forms. Creation is an individual expression of the artist at the same time as it accedes to universality. The "pure" artist possesses a superior combinatorial logic allowing "him" to articulate the "universality" of "man": a "capital point, a fixed point." Forms, in this account, are elementary, and elementary forms are "words" signifying "universal" principles of fixity. The completed forms are as far as could be from the asignifying signs, materially enveloping singular conditions of change and emergence, toward which hands-on topological experimentation moves.

Those hands, of course, are now on the computer keyboard. In a most unCADlike way. The computer is not used to prefigure built form, in the sense of presenting an anticipatory image exactly resembling it. The whole point of the topological turn is to catalyze newness and emergence rather than articulating universalized fixation. Of course, topological transformations are just as formalizable, in their own way, as are classical geometric forms. Chance must be added to truly yield change. The computer becomes a tool of indeterminacy. Abstract spaces are no longer neutral screens for imaging what has already been seen in the mind's eye. They must be actively designed to integrate a measure of indeterminacy. As a consequence, the space of abstraction itself becomes active, no longer merely prefiguring. The abstract space of design is now populated by virtual *forces* of deformation, with which the architect must join forces, to which he or she must yield in order to yield newness. The design process takes on a certain autonomy, a life of its own.

From the "artful genius" perspective, this may seem like a cowardly abdication of creativity to autonomized machinic procedure. In fact, the arbitrary returns. Its first point of reentry is the way in which the activity of the abstract space is programmed. There is no such thing as pure indeterminacy, certainly not in a programmed environment. Indeterminacy must be designed to emerge from an interplay of constraints. What constraints are set to interact will be an arbitrary decision of the architect, working from a more or less explicitly developed aesthetic orientation, and taking into consideration the functional parameters of the desired end product as well as client preferences on a number of other levels (including cost). The manner in which such "analogue" traits are translated into topological terms informs the programming but is not itself preprogrammed. It is the point of entry, into what is nevertheless still an autonomic process, for the architect's decision.

The process does not of itself generate a completed form. It generates a proliferation of forms. The continuity of the deformational variation can be cut at any point, any number of times. The constraints can be tweaked and set in motion again to experimentally generate whole new series of formal separations. The outcome of any given run cannot be predicted. But a choice must be made: a set of forms must be selected to provide the foundation of the actual design. The second area of arbitrariness is in the selection. The overall process is an *analogue* one. Such constraints as taste, function, preference, and cost are analogically translated into virtual forces, which are then set into variation, and analogically translated back into taste, function, preference, and cost *as embodied* in the final, composite sign-form. The movement is not from the simplicity of the elementary to the sophistication of the complex. Rather, it is from one arena of complexity to another. Complexes of complexity are analogically launched into interaction. Each complex is separated not by a self-enclosure but by an analogical gap that the process must leap. The art of the architect is the art of the leap.

Integrating topological procedures involving indeterminacy does not replace creative freedom of expression with machinic necessity. To begin with, the absolutes of "freedom" and "necessity" are endemic to the "creative genius" approach of the Le Corbusier quote. They do not apply to the topological approach, which works instead with arbitrariness and constraint, dosed rather than absolute, and locally co-functioning rather than in Promethean struggle with one another as universal principles. The opposition between the absolutes of freedom and necessity was never, of course, itself absolute. The creative freedom enjoyed by the "purified" artist was predicated on allying himself with a higher necessity (unchanging, universal, "primary" order). His "elevated" activity consisted in giving that necessity formal expression in the "secondary" world of the dirty, ever-changing, individually varying, everyday. The artist separated himself from the everyday in order to return to it, reorder and re-form it. The world itself was his raw material, as if he himself could freely stand outside and against it as pure, formative activity. This elevating mission might be seen as typical of "high" modernist approaches to cultural production.

To the topologically inclined, things are very different. Arbitrariness and constraint are internal to the process. They are variables among others, in a process that is all variation and that separates itself into phases, across analogical gaps, instead of separating the "artist" from the world, the better to impose order upon it. The "impurities" of the everyday—personal taste, dirty function, preference enforced in part by social convention, and, most vulgar of all, cost—enter the process, across the analogic gaps. The translation into and out of virtual force lays everything out on a single, complex, deformational surface from which form emerges as a certain kind of stoppage. The architect's activity is swept up in that complexity, its triggering and stoppage. It works at a level with it. The architect yields dosed measures of his or her activity to the process. The "arbitrarity" of the decisions that enter and exit the process are more like donations to its autonomy than impositions upon it. Rather than being used to claim freedom for the architect, decision is set free for the process. The architect lets decisions go, and the process runs with them.

"Arbitrarity" might not be the best term for the decisive activity of the architect as process tweaker and form-flusher, since that role requires "following" the process, and following the process requires having a certain "feel" for its elusiveness, for its running, for its changeability: a feeling for its virtuality. The old and abused term "intuition" perhaps fits better than terms such as "arbitrarity," "freedom," "inspiration," or "genius." "Intuition" is the feeling for potential that comes of drawing close enough to the autonomous dynamic of a variational process to effectively donate a measure of one's activity to it. Intuition is a real interplay of activities. It is neither a touchy-feely dreamlike state nor an imposition from on high of form on matter, order on disorder. It is a pragmatic interplay of activities on a level. The "donation" involved should not be construed as an "alienation" of the architect's activity, because what is donated is returned in varied form, ready for insertion into a different process, or a different phase of the same process (building).

None of this has anything to do with purity. Everything is mixed together at the beginning and comes out just as mixed. Impure all the way. Constraint enters as conventional strictures and professional expectations, client preference, cost projections, and so on. Each of these involves more or less static forms, as well as their own dedicated matters of variation. Arbitrariness or "freedom" enters in the way those constraints are set into interaction, and how an end-form is extracted from the interaction. That end-form must in some way accommodate itself to the constraints of conventional strictures and professional expectations, client preference, cost projections, or it will be "pure" in a very down-to-earth sense: not built. Everything that is present at the beginning comes out in the end of the actually built. Only different. The success of the exercise is not measured by any godlike ability to create something from nothing. It is the more modest ability to extract a difference from a variation (a standing difference from a running variation). It all depends on what happens in the middle. Cultural production becomes the art of the prevailing middle.

This is not really a "low" modernism against Le Corbusier's "high" modernism, since it interactivates those categories as well. Neither is it exactly a postmodernism, since the sign-form is primarily a sign of a material differentiation rather than a citation, and it implicates a process rather than referring intertextually. The architectural activity associated with the topological turn is not unrelated to such modernist adventures as Cage's experiments with chance or Burroughs's cut-up and fold-in. It might well be considered a neomodernism, although it has become more accepted to refer to it, along with its modern antecedents, as neo-Baroque, defined by Deleuze (1993) in terms of the "fold to infinity" (the mutual processual envelopment, on a single abstract variational surface, of complexes of complexity). It mixes procedures evocative of the modern avant-garde with an admitted complicity with vulgar worldly constraints. It might be recalled that Baroque art was an art of patronage. Today's commercial constraints on architecture are different, but just as strong. Maintaining a stance of "purity" toward them is not a test of political mettle. It is a test of intellectual honesty. It goes without saying that no architect can build without being in complicity with commerce and industry. The choice is not between complicity and purity but between a politics that maintains the relevance of the distinction and one that recognizes that creation in absolute freedom from constraint was only ever a self-aggrandizing myth. An architectural politics that admits "complicity"—the co-functioning of arbitrariness and constraint in the extraction of a standing difference from a running continuity of mixture—is what Deleuze would call an ethics, in distinction to the heroic moralism of the teleologically fixated.

Labels are of limited value. They tend to stereotype, as "high" modernism inevitably has been in this account for purposes of exposition. The stereotyping can easily extend to both "sides." It is just as important not to lump too hastily all architects using techniques akin to the ones described here as belonging to the topological turn into one rubric, as if they constituted a school, as it is to recognize the simplifications abbreviated accounts like the present one visit upon the topologically challenged. The ways in which the analogical gaps described earlier are negotiated by architects who are topologically engaged with the virtual will vary widely. There are no constants. The signature engagement with computers is not even necessarily a constant, since allied processual effects may be produced by other means (as indicated by the Cage and Burroughs examples, as well as the architectural precedents of Frederick Kiesler and Frei Otto). A fluid typology of post-heroic architecture could be delineated along multiple gap-leaping lines of variation, in what may be an expanding field of futurity already prospecting the architectural present (or what may, alternatively, be just a blip). Whatever the fate of contemporary currents, it is more important to multiply productive distinctions than lump camps.

Although the inherited antinomy of freedom and necessity ceases to be the central problem it once was, the topological turn produces ample problems of its own. The originality of a cultural process is measured by the complexity and productiveness of the new problems it creates, not the neatness of its creative solutions. For in complexity there is life. A good problem is a gift of life, the provision of an opening for others' activities, for uptake by other processual dynamisms, a contribution to the collective surface of continuing variation. By that standard, the topological turn in architecture is already a success.

Foremost among the problems it produces is the nature of the actual relation between the built forms that emerge from its process and the process as it happened. In other words, if the idea is to yield to virtuality and bring it out, where is the virtuality in the final product? Precisely what trace of it is left in the concrete form it deposits as its residue? What of emergence is left in the emerged? If the end form is a sign that does not signify, then what does it do and how does it do it? What is the relation of the asignifying sign to its event?

The problem raised is a semiotic one that neither architecture nor current discourses in cultural theory are well equipped to handle. To be appropriate to its field of application, this semiotic problem must be posed in terms of singular potential, material emergence, and event, rather than the tried-and-true terms of universal (or at least general) signifying structure and individual decodings or interpretations variously conforming to it.

The difficulty of the problem is that it points to the continuation of the architectural design process outside of itself, in another process. The outside of architectural design is in a very real sense its own product—the building itself: the life of the building. The building is the processual end of the architectural process, but since it is an end that animates the process all along, it is an immanent end. Its finality is that of a threshold that belongs integrally to the process, but whose crossing is also where the process ceases, to be taken up by other processes endowing the design with an afterlife. The most obvious after-processes are two: looking and dwelling. The exterior of the building takes its place as an object in the cultural landscape, becoming an unavoidable monument in the visual experience of all or most of the inhabitants of its locale. And the building becomes an experienced form of interiority for the minority of those people who live in it, work in it, or otherwise pass through it.

There is resistance from many quarters in architectural discourse to highlighting the experience of the built form. There are very good reasons for this reluctance. Talking about it in signifying semiotic terms of decoding and interpretation clamps the brackets closed again. It reimprisons the architectural process in preexisting formal structure, consigning it to intertextual referral, for those who are familiar enough with and care enough about the collective conventions, or to the banality of metaphorical "free" association on the part of those operating "below" the structural level of citation, on the local level of "individualized" variation. The latter is in fact entirely prepackaged, since all of the "individual" variations preexist as possible permutations of the general structure of signification. The variation is punctual. It does not emerge. It is "realized" (conceived) at structurally spaced intervals, at predictable "positions." In the end, there really isn't so great a difference between the in-the-know structural irony of the citationalists and the heartfelt "personal" metaphors of "naive" associationists. How many times do we have to "read"/"discover" a face in a façade? The uptake has been into a process that assumes an opposition between the constant and the variable, and can therefore hope, at best, to achieve a sterile dialectical synthesis between imposed form and "freely" chosen preauthorized variations ("discovery" deconstructively unmasked as "really" being a "reading"). Quite different is continual variation, in which everything enters the mix and in which there are no constants (even though things may occasionally stand still) and no structural preexistence (even if there is ample systemic feedback), and thus neither dialectic nor deconstruction (only deformation and emergence). This is the true alienation: when the immanent outside is not only taken up but is taken away by a process so legibly alien to it.

Another receiving-end option is phenomenological. The way of phenomenology posits a "raw," unprepackaged substrate still perceptible, if only one knows how to "return" to it, beneath the structure of referral and association. The substrate is construed as "intentional," or as prefiguring subject-object relations. The experiential substrate, it turns out, is not so much unprepackaged as it is packaged by a structural prefit between the body and the world. This has the merits of avoiding imprisonment in signification and of reconnecting with material processuality. But it consigns everything to function, hypostasized as the ontological ground of lived experience. "Intentionality" is another word for function, glorified as the ground of all experience.

This transcendentalization of function encloses process in organic form. Another not-so-great-as-it-is-made-out-to-be difference: between "high" modernism and existential phenomenology. For both, experience is formally prefigured. The difference is that in the first case the form is purely, otherworldly geometric, and in the second, rawly organic, "lived," and one with the world (the world made flesh). The great rallying cry of Deleuze's view of creativity, as drawing on the virtuality of process by yielding to it, is the Spinozan slogan "We do not know what a body can do." Phenomenology cannot yield (to) the virtual, whose "body" is emphatically "machinic": an autonomized processuality (if not necessarily a high-tech one). It cannot take the machinic indeterminacy of the virtual, even when it takes its own topological turn (as in Merleau-Ponty's last work on folding and gapping, or "chiasmus" [1968]). It cannot step over that threshold. It can only stand a "return" to the well-trod ground of possibilities for organic functioning. The divergence between Deleuze and phenomenology is summed up in another slogan: to the phenomenologists' "Consciousness is always *of* something" (cognitive prefit), Deleuze responds "Consciousness always *is* something" (ontological emergence).[2]

The topological turn in architecture must avoid these directions, and does. But does it live up to the project of drawing on the virtual to draw out the new? The question remains: How could it if its end product is recognizably still standing-form? By virtual definition, the built form does not resemble its conditions of emergence. It does not resemble the virtual forces generating it, or the analogical gaps its generation leaps. Unlike a structure of constants and variable realizations of it, the asignifying sign-form does not conform to its own event: there can be no conformity between the product and its process, no one-to-one correspondence between the end result's formal features and the steps of its deformational emergence. Virtuality cannot be seen in the form that emerges from it. The virtual gives form, but itself has none that is fixed (being the in-formation of transition). The virtual is imperceptible. It is insensible. A building is anything but that. A building is most concrete.

This impasse has led to the frequent complaint that the architecture operating in the topological field is formally indistinguishable from modernism: that there is nothing so "original" about it, nothing to it but a lot of techno-tricks in the design process that leave no visible trace in the built form, at least none that anyone not directly involved in the design could be expected to notice or care about. Isn't it still a building, to which a style can be attributed, that is recognizable as belonging to a particular category of building, that fulfills the typical functions of its kind? Where is the newness? In the computer gadgetry? In slight variations on existing architectural themes?

There is no way of effectively responding to this criticism as long as the afterlife of the design process in the life of the building is not seriously attended to. Taking the looked-at, lived-in life of the building into account does not fatally entail a surrender to the structural reduction of the signifying sign or to the phenomenological apotheosis of organic form and function. There is, perhaps, a way out of the impasse. But only if there is a willingness to reentertain questions about perception, experience, and even consciousness that have been anathema for some time now to many in architecture, as well as in other domains of cultural theory and production.

Although the virtual, Deleuze explains, cannot itself be seen or felt, it cannot *not* be seen or felt, as other than itself. What he means is that in addition to residue in static form, the formative process leaves traces still bearing the sign of its transitional nature. These are not virtualities but populations of actual effects that more fully implicate changeability and the potential for further emergence than self-enclosed forms or ordered agglomerations of forms realizing a rigid combinatory logic to produce citations, associations, or, most ubiquitously, stock functional cues—formal compositions following laws of perspective and resemblance designed to awaken habitual patterns of recognition and response. In even the most ordered formal composition there are accident zones where unplanned effects arise. Nonperspectival, unresembling, they are just glimpsed, in passing, as anomalies in the planned interrelation between actual forms. They are surprising, perhaps mildly disorienting, sometimes, just sometimes, shocking. They are less perceived than side-perceived; half-felt, like a barely palpable breeze; half-seen, on the periphery of habitual vision. They are *fogs* or *Dopplerings*. Patches of vagueness or blurrings presenting to the senses an insensible plasticity of form. Flushes of freshness, a-run in concretized convention and habit. Recalls of emergence, reminiscences of newness.

Fogs: actual traces of the virtual are often light effects. Although we tend to think of the perceptual dimensions of light as clearly distinguishable and almost boringly familiar, they are not so docile on closer inspection. Experimental psychology, even after decades of trying, is still at great pains to set even the most "obvious" boundaries between different light-related phenomena. What is the relation of white and black to lightness and darkness? Are the shades lying in a continuum between those extremes shadows or achromatic colors, intensities of light or gradations of gray? How can the distinction between chromatic and achromatic colors be maintained in the face of such everyday effects as the colored shadows so lovingly catalogued by Goethe? Is there a simple relation between color, light intensity, and illumination? Where, for that matter, is the boundary between one color of the familiar spectrum and another? What sets the boundary between glimmer, white, and clear? How do reflectance and translucence enter into the equation?[3] The boundaries we set and distinctions we function by are habitual. According to many theorists of vision, they do not replace the infinitely complex perceptual fog that is our originary and abiding experience of light. They occur with them, alongside, in a parallel current or on a superposed abstract perceptual surface, in a perpetual state of emergence from the continuum of light-dimensions that one frustrated would-be tamer of visual anomaly termed "the brightness confound" (Bornstein 1978, 132).[4]

The "brightness confound" can become a conscious percept through a concerted effort of unlearning habits of seeing or through a simple accident of attention. When it does, the confound is contagious. It strikes depth: three-dimensionality, argues the "ecological" school of perceptual theory (Gibson 2015), is an effect of complex differentials of surface lighting played out in ever-shifting proximities of shadow and color, reflectance and luminosity, illumination and translucence (it is not, as traditional theories of perception would have it, the product of mysterious calculations of relative size and distance—as if the eyes could count).

Depth is a surface effect susceptible to the brightness confound. When it goes, so goes separable form. Not only do the relative size and distance of objects flutter, their boundaries blur. They cease to be separate figures, becoming not entirely localizable zones in a fuzzy continuum. In other words, they cease to be objects, becoming what they always were, in the beginning and in parallel: fluctuations. Visual runs. Experiential transition zones. The distinctions of habit fold back into the always accompanying level of the more-than-three-dimensioned light concurrence from which they emerged. The fixed boundaries and "constants" of our habitual perceptions are emergences from an experiential confound to which they can return, and must return. For they are not in the final analysis structural constants at all, but continually regenerated effects, predicated on the variation they follow and emerge from, as its perceptual arrest. They rest entirely on variation.

Architecture, Deleuze will say for this reason, is a distribution of light before it is a concretion of forms (1986a, 57). Its basic medium is light. It uses concrete and stone, metal and glass, to sculpt light in ways that either direct the fixations of attention steadfastly away from their confounded conditions of emergence or, on the contrary, enable it sporadically to fold-back into them. The separation between "primary" sensations (i.e., depth and forms) and "secondary" sensations (in particular, color and lighting) is untenable. Since perception is a matter of complexes of complexities played out in surface relations, the more useful distinctions are, again, topological (cuts and continua; boundaries and transitions; fold-outs and fold-backs) and processual (aflutter or stabilized; a-run or still-standing; refreshed or habitual; functional or eventful). One of the direct implications for architectural practice is that color need not be dismissed as essentially decorative. As a dimension of the brightness confound, it is as primary an architectural element as the cube—if not more so.

Dopplerings: actual traces of the virtual are always effects of movement. When it was said that the separations between the perceptual dimensions of light were habitual, what that really meant is that they arise from movement. Depth perception is a habit of movement. When we see one object at a distance behind another, what we are seeing is in a very real sense our own body's potential to move between the objects or to touch them in succession. We are not using our eyes as organs of sight, if by sight is meant the cognitive operation of detecting and calculating forms at a distance. We are using our eyes as proprioceptors and feelers. Seeing at a distance is a virtual proximity: a direct, unmediated experience of potential orientings and touches on an abstract surface combining pastness and futurity. Vision envelops proprioception and tactility, by virtue of past multi-sense conjunctions whose potential for future repetition our body immediately, habitually "knows," without having to calculate. Seeing is never separate from other sense modalities. It is by nature synesthetic, and synesthesia is by nature kinesthetic. Every look reactivates a many-dimensioned, shifting surface of experience from which cognitive functions habitually emerge but which is not reducible to them. It is on that abstract surface of movement that we "live" and locate. We cannot properly be said to see, or experience, three-dimensional space and the bounded forms filling it. Rather, it is they that emerge from the abstract surface of experience, as reductive concretions and relative stoppages of it. Our seeing *stops* with perspective and form. We do not see or experience perspectival forms from the outside: they occur to our experience and in it, as arrest events that befall it. We ourselves, as spatially located forms in regular interaction with other forms, as embodied subjects in reciprocity with objects—we ourselves must be co-occurrences with depth and boundary, co-emergences of concretion and stoppage, companion arrests, fallout of the befallen. "We" ourselves are stoppage events in the flow of experience.

The relation between space and movement must be inverted, along with the relation between form and lighting. When the relation between space and movement inverts, so does the relation between ourselves and our experience. Experience is no longer in us. We emerge from experience. We do not move through experience. The movement of experience stops with us. And no sooner folds back on itself. And continues, alongside us, in parallel: doubling, as a superposed abstract surface in repeated interaction or intersection with the stoppage we have been. Our existence is an ongoing topological transformation of a complexifying abstract ontological surface: separation, fold-back, doubling, intersection, reseparation, fold back over again, redoubling, resection. . . . Confound it.

The confound of light envelops form, and with form it envelops space, at which point everything becomes movement. Didn't Bergson argue in *Matter and Memory* that we are beings of light, effects of its differential movements (2004, ch. 1)? That our bodies, or for that matter all of matter, are interactions of light with surface dimensions of itself? That the "abstract surface" is light in itself, interacting infinitely and absolutely with itself, registering or "feeling" its own variations as form-effects? Contemporary physics would not disagree.[5]

All of which carries us rather far afield. To return: this essay began with the maxim that the virtuality or changeability of a form exceeds its actuality. The point of the detour through the existential brightness confound is that if we apply that maxim to our own life forms, our "experience" onto-topologically exceeds our being. In a word, experience is our virtual reality. It is not something we have. It is a transformability that has us, and keeps on running with us no matter how hard we try to stand still and no matter how concretely we build. It is our continual variation. Our becoming. Our event: the lightning whose thunder we are.

The suggestion here is that the philosophical correlate of the topological turn in architecture is the idea that the ongoing of experience exceeds being. Or put another way, that feeling conveys potential and change (the corollary being that the feeling is absolute in the sense that it is immanent only to its own process: the feeling in and of itself of a matter of variation, emergent stabilities of form effectively aside). This philosophical orientation was dubbed a "radical" empiricism by William James and a "superior" empiricism by Deleuze. What it means for architecture and other plastic arts is that they can rejoin the virtual and take experience into account in the same move.

For architecture to rejoin the virtual and take experience into account in the same move would mean its aspiring to *build the insensible*. If in any composition of forms, however rigid, an accident of attention can return experience to its confound, then it must be possible to make a project of building-in just such accidents of attention. In other words, built form could be designed to make the "accidental" a necessary part of the experience of looking at it or dwelling in it. The building would not be considered an end-form so much as a beginning of a new process. Stable forms can be designed to interact dynamically, as bodies move past or through them singly or in crowds, or as sounds mute or reverberate, or as relations of surface and volume change with the time of day or season, or as materials change state with levels of moisture or temperature, or as the connection between inside and outside varies as an overall effect of these variations in concert with the rhythms of activity pulsing the city or countryside as a whole. Forms can be composed to operate as catalysts for perceptual events returning experience to its confound. A building can harbor foci of implicative vagueness, lucid blurs, dark shimmerings, not-quite things half-glimpsed like the passing of a shadow on the periphery of vision. Architecture can locally and sporadically return experience to that part of itself that can never be perceived as being (since it has only becoming) but cannot but be felt (in passing). Architecture can accept as part of its aim the form-bound catalysis of the in-formation (the deform).

The vagaries in question here have to do neither with trompe l'oeil, optical illusion, nor ambiguity. Trompe l'oeil is fully subordinated to formal resemblance. More distorted (anamorphic) or unanchored practices of simulation play on resemblance, but in needing it to play on, hold fast to it.[6] Optical illusion also never leaves the formal level, being an oscillation between two forms rather than a rhythm of recursion between form and the in-formation. Ambiguity, for its part, belongs to signifying structure. It is nothing new for architects to build-in ambiguity in order to make an event of standing form. But ambiguity still addresses the conventional function of the sign-form. It activates citation and association in order to push them toward a critical reappraisal. It operates on the level of conventional sign-form in order to deliver it to critique. Building-in ambiguity may succeed in catalyzing an event—but the event is still a meaning event.

The asignifying or processual sign-form of the onto-topological turn catalyzes experiential potential rather than meaning. It is a sign of material dynamics of variation, pointing in two directions at once. On the one hand, it recalls the elements of indeterminacy and chance of the design process itself. It is an echo of the experimentations of the architect. But it does not resemble or in any way conform to them. Rather than referring explicitly to them, it refers them to another process. The architect's processual engagement with the virtual is taken up in an alien process: the life of the building, the looking and dwelling of those who pass by it or through it. This process continues from the design process's point of cessation. The virtual is fed forward into the final form. But in final form, the way the potential is yielded (to) bears no resemblance to what befell during the design process, from which, it must be remembered, it is separated by analogical gaps. The feed-forward of virtuality delineates a continuity, but it is a leaping continuity of differentiation. The architect, who donated his or her activity to the autonomization of a process, now lets the product go, into another process. Architecture as a gift of product for process. The sign-form fundamentally means nothing. It is meant to stand at the threshold between processes. The middle prevails.

The aim of onto-topological architecture has no end. The aim may nevertheless involve many ends: critical, citational, associational, functional, profit-making. In fact, it necessarily involves all of these: it involves them with each other. It adds them to the catalytic mix. Like stability of form, pre-operative conventional sign systems feature as constraints added to the complex mix out of whose interaction the new rearises in the design product. The aim of processual architecture doesn't stop at any end. It takes everything from the middle again. The intuitive aim is to middle the end-mix. The product is re-process.

Although there is no formal resemblance between the re-process in which the product is taken up and the process that produced it, there is a certain correspondence between them. Were there not, the leap across the processual gaps would not earn the name "analogical." The correspondence in question doesn't concern the nature of the forms in play, or even the qualities of the event they mix to make. The correspondence is a processual retake. It is the process of generating the new from an intuitive interplay of constraints and arbitrarity that keeps the continuity across the leaps. The correspondence pertains to the conditions of emergence rather than the actuality of the emerged. In other words, it is virtual. The identity analogically stretched across the gaps of differentiation is "machinic": what is repeated is autonomization; same process, different at every take.

Philosophy and architecture have always been on intimate terms, in a mutual embrace passed on from Plato's city of the republic to Augustine's city of god to Leibniz's monad-house to Heidegger's house of being to Virilio's bunkers (to name just a diverse few). Formalist modernism's high-moral attachment to purity and geometric harmony can only be understood as a concerted philosophical sortie waged through architectural means. Conversely, architectural achievements have often stood as exemplars for philosophy. Architecture flourishes with philosophical infusions; philosophy exemplifies in monuments. Architecture and philosophy are drawn toward abstract-concrete symbiosis with each other (which contributes more of the abstract, and which more of the concrete, is not as straightforward as it may seem—so long has the reciprocal exchange gone on).

The basic question of this essay has been: What philosophy can or might enter into a symbiosis with architectures engaging with the virtual, in particular by topological means? The answer seemed to lie in a "radical" or "superior" empiricism. What such a symbiosis would mean for architecture is a willingness to bring into even more pronounced expression its processual dimensions. That in turn means theoretically and experimentally reevaluating the separation between the "primaries" of form and depth and "secondaries" such as color and illumination. That further entails an inversion in what is traditionally assumed to be the relation of form and movement, subject-object structurings and experience, constancy, and variation. Where it all leads is to a semiotic of singular potential, material emergence, and event: a semiotic for which the abstract is really material, and the sign-form's material appearance is not only seen. Vision, following this path, must be grasped as directly inhabited by the other senses, and the other senses by vision. In such an asignifying semiotic, all perception figures as synesthetic, and synesthesia is seen as a creature of movement. Perhaps most controversially, a distinction is maintained between movements in the actual world between fixed forms, and the absolute movement of process self-feeling, from which the world itself emerges. A tall order. A tall, autopoietic order. But the theory is not without precedents, and the experimentations have palpably begun.

NOTE ON TUNNELING TO THE FUTURE. Most palpably, they have begun in the integration of digital technology into architecture. Although computerization is not a necessary condition for topological experimentation in design, its forecast integration into built form may bring us to a new threshold in the sensing of the virtual in built form or the building of the insensible. Proponents of "ubiquitous computing" look to the day when digital media become architectural: no longer furnishings or infrastructure, but an absolutely integral part of the building. When the digital display becomes as structural architecturally as a window, looking and dwelling will be transformed. But not as completely as when digital media learn to forgo the display and the analogy of the window and the interface is able to go anywhere, responding no longer only to mouse- or keystrokes anchored to the screen but to gestures, movements, and sounds, dedicated, roving, or ambient, compounded or uncompounded with visions and information.

Electronic media offer, in principle if not yet in practice, an infinite connectibility of spaces. It is crucial to be clear about this: it is not the abstract informational content of what the media might connectively deliver, or even the abstract space of the "infosphere" from which it is drawn, that is virtual. Although the virtual is a mode of abstraction, the converse is not true. Abstraction is not necessarily virtual. It was argued earlier that the possible (or the permutational: encompassing information no less than signification) and the simulated (of which trompe l'oeil and anamorphosis are the simplest examples) are abstract without being virtual: the first because it pertains to a generative matrix whose actual permutations preexist in it; the second because it retains in one way or another a fundamental link to formal resemblance. What is virtual is the connectibility: potential (the reality of change). It cannot be overemphasized that the virtual is less the connection itself than its -ibility.

The assumption is often made that increasing the sheer number and variety of media connections between locations constitutes a virtualization. This is to confuse the virtual with the technological thing. If the virtual is not the informational content or its infosphere, neither is it the physical implantation of technology. The distinction between the virtual and technological actualization is paramount. Comparing two qualitatively different ways of digitally connecting spaces brings out the distinction. *Windowing* is one. Windowing provides a framed and tamed static perspective from one local space onto another that remains structurally distinct from it. The connection established is predominantly visual, or at most audio-visual. Features from or of one locale are "delivered" into another as information, prepackaged for local understanding and use. Windowing is communicational. What characterizes communication is that it is designed to be "transparent": no conversion is supposed to take place by virtue of the connection in and of itself. For the information to make a difference, the receiver must be primed to make it make a difference, to interpret or exploit it. Information is a feed. Neutral packets ("data") are consumed on one side of the window (or screen) to feed a process already understood and underway, with known effect and intent. Nothing new. What is on the other side of the window stays on the other side, and is not affected by the consumptive conversion operated delivery-side. The "conversion" is not really a qualitative change because it just augments something already primed and in place there. The connection is segregated from the conversion.

It is for this reason that communication is termed a mediation or "transaction" (rather than an action). Whether communication ever really lives up to its transparent aspirations is doubtful. But that is not so much the issue here. The issue at hand is rather to think of another way of connecting spaces that doesn't even make the pretense. Call it *tunneling*. Tunneling cuts directly into the fabric of local space, presenting perceptions originating at a distance. Not data prepackagings: perceptions. The perceptual cut-ins irrupt locally, producing a fusional tension between the close at hand and the far removed. As the distant cuts in, the local folds out. This two-way dynamic produces interference, which tends to express itself synesthetically, as the body returns vision and hearing to tactility and proprioception in an attempt to register and respond to a structural indeterminacy. "Returns vision and hearing to tactility and proprioception": vision and hearing are *transduced* into other bodily modes of activation. Tunneling is not communicational, but transductive. The connection is unmediatedly a conversion. As a consequence, it takes on a thickness of its own. It isn't just a transparent delivery. It *is* something, and its something is a doing: a direct conversion. A qualitative change. Something is happening here: action. But is it here? It is not only bodily modes that transduce. Space itself is converted, from the local-or-distant into a *nonlocal*. Distant cut-in, local fold-out: the irruptive perceptions retain as much "thereness" as they take on "hereness." Distance as such is directly presented, embodied in local interference. Two-way movement, between near and far. Between: unplaceably in the midst.

Architecturally speaking, tunneling builds-in the prevailing middle of the experiential confound. It makes structural the transductive irruption of the structurally indeterminate. The opposition between the structural or formal and the accidental is disabled. The "fogs" and "Dopplerings" are no longer peripheral and adventitious. The periphery becomes central, the adventitious of the essence. Structure opens onto the potential of the not-yet-known or -intended. Melding connection with conversion, tunneling builds-in -*ibility*. The opening is not onto "the" new: like a new thing. It is onto new*ness*: the reality of transition, the being of the new, quite apart from any*thing* new. Tunneling may still yield information and function, interpretation and opportunity to exploit in the service of the augmentation of the already-here, or perhaps even its purposeful growth into some*thing* new. But it does so in a second phase. It ends up that way, after a second conversion: when its interfering stills and the newness settles into things. Settle it will. But first it stirs. Deforms. Any information-function or even invention that emerges, emerges from the deforming in-formation, singed or tinged by it, as by the lightning its thunder was.

Since tunneling catalyzes deform conditions of actual emergence, it must be considered ontogenetic. The connection is an onto-topological cut-in/fold-out that builds-in a phase-space of indeterminate potential. The potentializing cut of the distant into the out-folding local can actually combine with communicational deliveries or in-foldings from the "infosphere," paradoxically expanding the confound itself to include information as such (if not function, which always follows the deform). The only proviso is that the materiality of the signs encoding the information stands out. In other words, that the signs be as insistently blips of light as they are letters, as insistently sound wave as voice: forces of perception. When the communicational medium ceases to be transparent and perforce stands out in its materiality, information blends into perception. Information then precedes its understanding: it is *experienced* as a dimension of the confound before being understood and used and perhaps lending itself to invention. The understanding, use, and invention are then already a repetition. Of something they were, but emerged from, diverged from, and do not resemble: transductive perceptual forces, forced *-ibility*, necessarily sensed virtuality. Information takes on a genetic relation to its confounded and *in situ* self. This is a far cry from communication. But it may still be considered citational. Tunneling information builds-in what might be called a vertical mode of citationality, in which the citation has a different ontological status from that which is cited, as emergent actuality to repotentializing confound. The relation of the citation to the cited is asignifying and direct, if divergent. The connection between them is processual, more fundamentally experiential than it is cognitive or functional (which are what the experience becomes when it self-diverges).

This kind of self-differing citationality could do with a name to distinguish it from the "horizontal" postmodern version, in which everything has already been said (delivered) out there somewhere, and delivering it again over here only leads to the conclusion that nothing new has happened, only repetition (no matter how many new inventions have hit the market in the meantime). The name "self-referentiality" will do as well as any for the emergent or becoming version, in which something does occur. Or "recur." "Recursion" might be a better word than "repetition" for what happens to information in the process (reemergence, renewal, tinging with potential). Information transductively "recurs," across a "vertical" or *in situ* distance from itself (a concretely abstract self-distance, or self-emergent nonlocality). A new arena of self-referential artistic activity calling itself "relational architecture," developing under the influence of figures like Stelarc who set up transductive linkages between the body and the internet, experiments with this kind of recursive confounding of informed experience in the built environment.[7]

Much of what may come of these experimentations is still the province of science fiction, or at best futurism. But as digital technology develops and slowly integrates with architecture, it may be helpful to keep three points in mind: (1) No technology in itself is virtual or virtualizing. It is always possible to window new media, and there will be strong cultural and economic pressures to do so. Windowed, digital technology limits itself to the insufficiently-abstract of communication, falling short of its transductive capacity to concretize the abstract as such, to confoundedly actualize the virtual. Virtuality is a mode (-ibility). It is not in the "what" of the technology (its specifications and implantations) but in the "how" of its composition with other formations such as architecture (its modal conditioning). (2) The postmodernists were in a way right when they said that nothing ever happens here (or there). Because it all happens in the middle. Another way of making the point about the "how" is to say that newness and new things are not the same. No matter how many inventions there have been, it doesn't mean that an event or real transition has occurred. If invention grows from a communicational feed, and then gives itself over to communication, qualitative change is neither here nor there. The reality of change is transductive—which may occur with or without invention. And with or without, may be built. (3) What points 1 and 2 add up to is that technology, while not constituting change in itself, can be a powerful conditioner of change, depending on its composition or how it integrates into the built environment.

Technically, the "tunnelings" somewhat futuristically evoked here as actualizations of the reality of change require fiber optics. It is no surprise to the Bergsonian that the actualization of the virtual in built form rides on waves of light. So what? The metaphysical assertion that our body and matter itself are constituted by light interacting infinitely with itself as its own hyperabstract surface, feeling absolutely its own variations, has little or no importance in itself. It can, however, act as a reminder: to bring it all back to perception. To perception, understood positively, as actually productive of existence, or as virtually preceding existing separations of form. To perception, in continuity with the world (deform). The reminder is: don't content yourself with all-too-easy negative formulations such as "distance has been abolished," or with structural descriptions of how already constituted forms in already separated spaces technically, even inventively, communicate. Bring it all back. To the abstract concretely. Confound it: transduce it.

2004

Not Determinately Nothing

Building Experience

Postponing the Image

> For me the main question was: can I make the content of the paintings, the perception of them, be the architecture itself?
> —Lars Spuybroek (2000a, 127)

In the *WetGRID* design for the Musée des Beaux-Arts in Nantes (1999–2000) Lars Spuybroek sought to extend the architectural program of the exhibit into a meta-architectural exploration of the interconnection between perception and construction. The goal was to build the exhibit's theme by making a literal "Vision Machine" that effectively fed the content of the photographs and paintings on display into the experience of the installation space. This was no metaphor. The aim was for the experience of the art and the experience of the building to be brought into active proximity with each other. For this to happen, a shared ground, on which there was already an implicit entwining, would have to be extracted from both sides and brought into view. It was immediately clear that this would be a "ground" which is not one, and a more-than-optical "view."

There is no doubt in Spuybroek's mind as to how this shared ground is to be accessed: through movement. This may seem paradoxical at first, since movement is the last thing we normally think of as the content of still images. Naively, we think of the visual content of the image as representations of the form of objects. Many of us have been schooled to think beyond this commonsense approach to see the content as the acquired cultural codes enabling us to recognize arrays of paint or chemical pigments as referencing objective forms. Neither of these approaches to image-content works in this connection. Both impose an alien becoming on architecture. To meet painting and photography in representation, architecture would have to become pictorial (suggesting a centrality of decoration). To meet them in cultural coding, it would have to become language-like (suggesting a centrality of message decoding). Although this latter route was widely followed in late twentieth-century architecture, it backgrounds the undeniable role of construction as a spacing and timing (channeling, filtering) of embodied movement. Movement, not message, is the actual content of architecture. Acknowledging this, however, would seem to oblige the still image to become diametrically other than it is: moving. To work a way out of the predicament a zone of proximity needs to be found where image meets architecture without either ceasing to be itself.

Spuybroek suggests that common ground is *potential* movement. Potential movement is "abstracted into" the architecture, he says, "and that abstract movement loops back and relates again to people's movement" (2001a, 111). Potentials for movement are extracted from actual movement, then fed back into it via architecture. We normally think of abstraction as a distancing *from* the actual, but here potentials are being "abstracted *into* it." This means that elements are built into the design that trigger the movement actually underway into a state of overlap with changes in its register, with possible continuations, or with alternatives to itself. If potential movement could similarly be extracted from the still image content and hooked on the same architectural triggers, then not only would actual movement in the building overlap with potential movements, but the potentials of architecture would overlap with those of painting and photography. The clarity of the actual movements underway would be shadowed by a vagueness of what they could be, at the abstract intersection of building content and image content.

To achieve this, it is necessary to "postpone the image" (Spuybroek, 2001b): to suspend the recognition or decoding of a finally and fully determinate content by building potentializing hesitations into the predictable channeling of movement through the building.

> The room one enters maps directly onto one's tentativeness. . . . One's sporadic linkings with features of the architectural surround thread . . . into the pulsed arraying of possibilities.
> —Arakawa and Gins (2002, 42)

Tending Perception

> Our agenda should be to short-circuit action, perception and construction.
> —Lars Spuybroek (2004, 358)

Take a seat, lean back, stop fidgeting. Short-circuit action. Purge your thoughts of the daily course, things done and to do. Attend to the peripheries of your vision as much as to its center of focus. After a moment, from the heart of the visual stillness, you will start to feel a faint commotion, a hint of a pull. It is as if you were being drawn out of your recliner into the center of your visual field. The center is no longer a simple optical focus. It has become an attractive force. That is because the periphery is not a distinct boundary. It is a cloudy ring-around: a 360-degree horizon where your vision fades into indistinctness in all

5.1 *Field of View*, from Gibson (2014).

directions. The peripheral fade-out gives a strange tunnel-like feel to the whole of the visual field which funnels you toward the center with a feeling of slight vertigo. If you try to shake the feeling by moving your head, say to the right, the effect is only heightened by the ski-jump of your nose suddenly leaping into view, no longer in its anatomically middle position, but as a promontory protruding from the peripheral vagueness and unshakably suggesting a slalom down your legs, the only clearly visible part of your mostly occluded body. The funnel effect is also heightened by the beams of the ceiling and the pattern of the floor tiling, both of which converge toward the window to which the feet at the far end of your legs are also pointing arest their ottoman. Out the window, a path leads from your up-ended toes toward a vanishing point at the earth's horizon. The center of visual attraction is where your feet, the windowsill, and the path meet, connecting the periphery of your field to the vanishing point at its center. The toe-point connects two horizons of different orders, the lateral horizon of the earth and circumference of your visual field, in a continuous sweep running across your incompletely appearing body through the geometry of the room. The toe-window-path convergence is an invitation to stroll. It visibly suggests a potential transition from the slalom of stillness into which your reclining thoughts stirred you, to a calming walk through the garden.

The garden path is what Arakawa and Gins call a landing site. A landing site is a possibility of convergence that unconsciously exerts a pull, drawing the body forward into a movement the body already feels itself performing before it actually stirs. When it does stir, it relays between sense modes in a habitual fashion, recognizing itself in the renewal of the familiar relay, which in turn locates it along a path marked by an ordered sequence of further landing sites. Each landing site governs a tendency drawing the body forward, away from where it is, further down a familiar path presenting an ordered unfolding of the variety of its experiential modalities.

The entire sequence is pre-felt, more or less vaguely, in the stirring of the tendency. A view of the garden is the already-feeling of the soles of the feet relaying from the sight of the path into tactile contact with it. It is the intervening proprioceptive pre-feeling of the flexing of the muscles and joints. It is the kinesthetic presentiment of the flow of your body

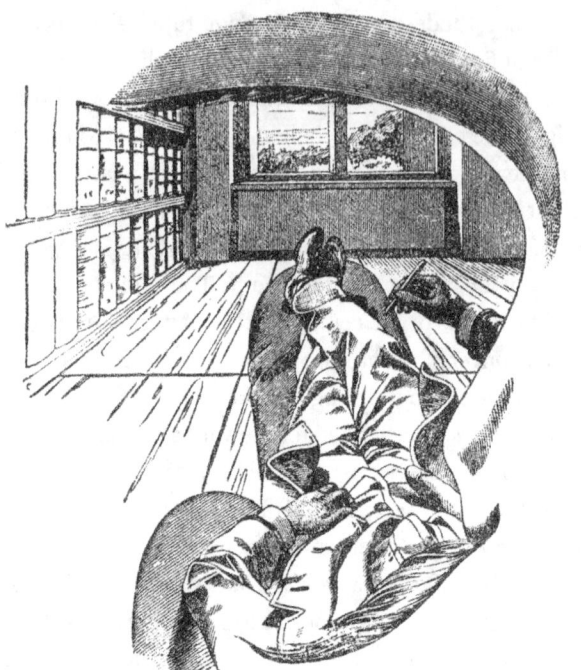

5.2 *Self-Portrait*, Ernst Mach (1886).

past the flowers. It is the succession of anticipated relays into pleasant new sights which for now, from the recliner, remain occluded by the window frames and in the path. There is a familiar function to be fulfilled by the stroll down the path. That function, stress relief, can be fulfilled in advance simply by the presentiment of it. The variety of sensings that would relay in the actual movement of the walk is already included, in germinal form, in the seated suggestion of the movement triggered by an errant glance out the window. It was the pull of their pre-inclusion, their already stirring without yet actually coming about, that made an event of that simple sitting. Sitting still is the performance of a tendency toward movement. The tendency is already a movement, without the actual movement. And it is already a sign of the fulfillment of the conventional function, without the actual fulfillment. It is the pre-performance, in potential, of the movement and its function. In potential, the movement is already in the world without yet having extended itself along its actual path. It is in intensity.

> The important thing to keep in mind is that the tendency to respond determines the perception.
> —Lloyd Kaufman (1979, 378)

If the tendency to respond determines the perception, then holding back the response while holding onto the tendency postpones perception. The image fails to advance into its own determinateness. Its perception and the action it governs are short-circuited, held, incipiently, in their own potential. The pre-feeling of the landing sites and their sequencing continues indeterminately, in intensity.

One of the ways this postponement can be achieved is by gesturing to perspective with intimations of depth while at the same time undermining its full deployment. The undermining can be achieved by bringing two of the fundamental structuring elements of the field of vision into resonance. The periphery of vision and the vanishing point can be abstractly connected, across the actual content of the image. In the recliner, this contact between the circumference of the field of vision and its central vanishing point was already established by the draw exerted by the toe-window-path convergence. Its attractive force animated the visual field with an inward activity: a funnel-effect dizzying down the nose and sweeping along the legs. This immanent activity is itself an experience of potential movement, connected to but distinct from the sequencing of anticipated garden-path-variety landing sites and supplementary to the object recognition, decoding, and function fulfillment associated with them. It is abstract in the sense that it corresponds to no actual features of the image. It is contained in the image, but is not its content. The periphery of vision and the vanishing point are poles determining an abstract, vortical, potential movement affecting the field of vision in its entirety. The ease with which they tend to join belies the stability that the field of vision exhibits when it is functioning on the familiar ground of content recognition and decoding.

The potential movement enveloped in the vanishing point toward which the toe-window-path convergence gestured has already been described. This potential movement is comforting to the extent it brings a presentiment of the fulfillment of the soothing function of the stroll, and is attached to more or less predictable content. But it is destabilizing inasmuch as it betokens infinite continuation beyond fulfillment of that function and any particularizable content. At the limit, it extends into a smudged array of potential intersense relays receding indistinctly to an infinitesimal scale beyond any actual perception's powers of resolution.

The periphery of vision can also be destabilizing when it ceases to function as a framing of the field of vision and instead betokens a completion never reached. For it promises, at the mere turn of the head or a swivel of the body, a filling-in of the field of vision, whose partiality can be disturbing. But with each movement seeking its completion, the periphery and the partiality return. They persist as a draw from vision into kinesthesia and proprioception, turn and swivel. Vision is not in fact framed. At its edge lies a 360-degree horizon of potential movement, into which it is constantly advancing. But as it advances, it succeeds only in displacing this moving limit. Vision never reaches the limit—or is always already at it, in its tendency to reach beyond itself.

Vertigo is experienced when the circumferential fringe of vision swirls in on the perspectival vanishing point in a vortex of potential experience, like turbulent water around a drain. The lateral horizon toward which the vanishing point recedes, and which grounds experience on the gravitational plane of the earth, rotates chaotically with the vortex, destabilizing not only the body's station but its relation to any vertical elevation rising perpendicular to the ground.

Dizziness is always intensely disorienting because it is never just an experience of vertigo but always also a vertigo of experience: a vortex sweeping away the stability of experience's very structuring and the repeatability of its recognizable functions. Even the most genteel vertigo affecting the most domestic visual field radically ungrounds the ground of experience. The variety of other-sense potential that it sweeps in from the fringe, and toward which it centrally drains, forbids reducing vision to its manifestly optical content (especially when vision is trained on the multisensory body itself).

> The body-image is never a complete structure; it is never static; there are always disrupting tendencies.
> —Paul Schilder (1950, 287)

Even the most smoothly strolling of experiences contains a minimal degree of vertigo. Each relay from vision to an other-sense experience such as touch or proprioception carries vision across its functional limit. This necessarily occurs at every step along any line of actual movement. When vision makes the transition, vision must be marked, however slightly, by the turbulence of passing its limit, or of its limit passing into it. There is a micro-vertigo immanent to the interconnection of the senses that accompanies all movement. Vertigo, then, is not qualitatively different from the potential for actual movement. The actualization of potential movement is a vertigo of experience, by the same token as vertigo is the experience of potential movement.

> Given a number of dimensions of feeling, all possible varieties are obtainable by varying the intensities of the different elements. Accordingly, time logically supposes a continuous range of intensity in feeling. It follows, then . . . that when any particular kind of feeling is present, an infinitesimal continuation of all feelings differing infinitesimally from that is present.
> —C. S. Peirce (1992, 323–24)

Experience always gives a number of dimensions of feeling. And it always presupposes time, in the indefinite continuation at its center and the deferred completion at its periphery. All possible varieties of experience inhabit every vision, enveloped in movements whose actualization would take time but whose variety is already intensely present in potential. All possibilities of feeling are obtainable by varying the intensities of the different elements. This means, for example, that the degree to which the vertigo of potential movement is experienced in a built environment can be varied by varying the nature, strength, or frequency of the visual cues for such things as distance, station, direction, framing, and perspective that are made available for recognition and decoding, and through the nature and allure of available landing sites for familiar function. Construction can short-circuit action and perception, in the sense of feeding them into each other on the level of their potential (un)grounding. They can be extracted or abstracted from their content in such a way that their immanent activity, the movement of their potential, is vertiginously abstracted into architecture.

Surface Depth

In *WetGRID*, Spuybroek went straight to the nub of the issue: vertigo. His strategy was to build degrees of vertigo into the experience of the exhibit in a way that connected the content of the architecture—the visitors' actual moving through—with the content of the paintings by making them meet in a common element of abstracted potential movement.

In order to build in vertigo as potential movement it was necessary to build out shadow, perspective, and horizon, and to retool framing. Framing as normally used in art and architecture neutralizes the danger of the periphery by replacing its indefinite fringing with an unambiguous boundary that divides inside (content) from outside (context), forbidding the destabilization of a turbulent flow that would intermix their potentials. The horizon founds tectonics by grounding action on a perceptual plane parallel to that of the earth, in rectilinear contrast to station and vertical elevation, often considered the essential dimension of architecture, whose nature is then to uplift through resistance to the force of gravity. Rather than privileging rigidifying forces of material resistance, Spuybroek seeks a "liquid" architecture (un)grounded on potentializing forces of lived variation, abstractingly immanent to both perception and action in their constructed interconnection. He wants to build buildings in a way that is a rebuilding of experience rather than the simple erection of a tectonic structure. Although perspective, for its part, harbors at its center the potential perceptual danger of the vanishing point's infinitesimal recession, it neutralizes this danger by focusing on the predictable middle distance, where one step distinctly follows the next, from one recognizable object to another, the intersense relays between pacifyingly yoked to familiar functions. Shadow goes hand in hand with perspective. The occlusions that shadow presupposes imply an ordering of objects in a distinct succession along a navigable perspective line receding controllably into a middle distance. Shadow presents perspectival depth, whether or not a vanishing point is manifestly operative.

To sidestep these conventional architectural limitations, in the design for the Vision Machine exhibit Spuybroek avoided any hint of shadow and any right angles between the horizontal and the vertical planes. This divested perception of the possibility of orienting itself according to perspective and rendered unfamiliar the culturally encoded function of the gallery space. Visitors to art galleries are accustomed to strolling on the horizontal plane of the floor and seeing on the vertical plane of the wall, on which the pictures are hung and against which they are framed. The sequential hanging on the same plane of distinctly separated, framed images governs an ordered movement of the feet in the service of the studied eye's progression through the content of the show.

In the absence of right angles between the horizontal and vertical planes of construction, it becomes uncertain where the floor ends and where the wall begins. Their sharp distinction is replaced by a continuous curve, setting the construction on the oblique. The lean of the

5.3 *WetGRID*, overview, exhibition design for Vision Machine, Musée des Beaux-Arts Nantes, 2000. Courtesy of NOX/Lars Spuybroek.

construction makes for a lack of shadow, which in turn prevents perspectival depth. The curvilinear, semi-translucent tunnels composing the installation still clearly occupy volume. But the geometry of the volume is not graspable at a glance. It is all continuous surface, folding in and away, invaginating and exfoliating. The foldings offer a kind of surface depth, without perspective. Upon entering the gallery, it is not at first apparent whether a given portion of the surface volume is offering a landing site for feet or for eyes, or what kind of progression along the surface, into the depth of the exhibit, is being afforded. Visual perception and the action of walking enter into a disorienting zone of indistinction. They dizzyingly loop into each other, only sorting themselves out over the duration as the visitor hesitantly moves around the installation. Even after exploration, at every bend they threaten to fall back into intermixing. In order to gain purchase, the eyes must follow the feet, themselves assisted by the occasional touch against the structure and an unaccustomed attention to the proprioception assisting balance and posture in the unfamiliar surrounds. Different-sense perceptions fold into and out of each other, as perception folds into and out of exploratory action. The threat of vertigo taking hold gives pause to each advance in the installation's experience. In that hesitation, the sense-modes are suspended in potential relay. There is an indecision as to which relay will actualize next, and whether its actualization will land with enough purchase to determine a next action. In the same hesitation, perception and action come together in constructed postponement.

> What emanates from the body and what emanates from architectural surrounds intermix.
> —Arakawa and Gins (2002, 66)

The construction has succeeded in building-in a mutual abstraction of the modes of perception, and of perception and action, in such a way that they loop into each other, meeting in their potential relays. The experience of the exhibition has been effectively placed on a vertiginous common ground of potential movement that is as much in abstraction of any particular mode of perception as it is in abstraction of any actually determinate action. The building has in fact managed to extract a common element from its lived content, in a way that enables it to loop into the still-image content of the paintings and photographs on display.

The content of many of the images is itself abstract or willfully vertiginous, sometimes to a hallucinatory extreme. This match between the content and the context is not a mirroring or coded reflection of what lies outside the frame.

> There is no clear distinction between inner and outer orientation. . . . They are integrated into one system.
> —Lars Spuybroek (2000b, 157)

The frames of the images in the exhibit do not separate them from their built surround. They connect them to it. Bernard Cache reminds us that a kite is a frame (1995, 109). A kite is not separate from its turbulent milieu. It is responsive to it. It is dynamically connected to it in a way

5.4 *WetGRID*, interior, exhibition design for Vision Machine, Musée des Beaux-Arts Nantes, 2000. Courtesy of NOX/Lars Spuybroek.

that it receives and visibly expresses the forces moving through it. The images toss in the turbulence of the installation's experience like kites in stormy skies, hanging, seemingly precariously, at odd and oblique angles from the curved architectural surface of uncertain definition, wall-floor. They respond to, receive, and visibly express the force of the architecturally abstracted potential movement on which they toss. They offer a floating landing site, not for repeat function fueled by habitual object-recognition but for the architecturally induced vertigo of movement's potentializing abstraction from these. Rather than reflections or representations of their surrounds, they are operative analogues of the process unfolding in the built environment, into which it cumulatively feeds forward, adding itself to the properly artistic process of abstraction already at work in the frame. Transmitted into the art, other-sense movements are even more thoroughly held in potential. Only optical experience can actualize itself on the ungrounded landing site offered by the image. The nonvisual senses remain potentialized, but their readiness to land, to actualize in a next relay, is radically short-circuited. The harder they press, the more deeply they are held in potential. They cannot not continue to be felt, but only in the vision, wholly invested in sight, divested of any shred of their own actuality. Other-sense potential movement is packed into opticality. Vision becomes intensely imbued with the "infinitesimal continuation" of the nonvisual senses.

The Vision Machine is the coupling of a certain architectural ungrounding with a turbulence-sensitive artistic framing that transmits the force of nonvisual senses into purely optical experience, making it visible in a vertigo of potential movement at amplified intensity.

Building Experience

The exhibition architecture is literally a machine and, like all machines, has been engineered and constructed. The perceptual processes described earlier have been "abstracted in" to construction during the design process, long before bodies were in actual movement through the installation-to-come and there were wall-floors on which paintings could hang. The design would have to have the ability to address bodies on the level of their potential movement, that is, below the level of object recognition, familiar function, and cultural decoding (even if all of these must necessarily continue to operate at least sporadically or "postponed," suspended in their incipiency). This means connecting to them on the level of force. The force would have to be at once deforming (able to separate bodies from the habitual form of their experience), transformative (converting actual movement into potential movement), and transitive (capable of being abstracted into the architecture and from there of moving into the picture frame to merge with the deforming and transformative forces native to painting and photography). In a word (Simondon's), the force would have to be transductive.

In this project, Spuybroek's approach was to make the design process itself a series of transductive steps which can then transfer directly, machinically, to the final construction. He began by programming abstract forces of deformation on the computer. Control vertices were connected to flat strips of simulated rubber, at their edges. The vertices were then connected to each other by strings, with virtual springs attached to the intersections of the threads. A force of rotation applied to the springs would transmit a vortical force to the attached strips, which would continuously deform into an undulation in which concave curves would appear. At places, the strips would come together to suggest a fusion into a more extended concavity, or they would split apart. The concavities, having elevation, were taken as proto-interiorities, and the splits as proto-openings. This proto-architectural effect of the application of vortical force was then materialized in a model made of paper strips mapping the computer simulation. A small number of rules were applied to further the transformation in the same direction it was already taking. These manual "algorithms" involved placing paper clips at certain strategic points to connect the paper strips in such a way as to augment the concavities and openings, taking a step further on their way to becoming (somewhat peculiar) architectural elements (nonstandard rooms and entrances). The vortical effect was thus amplified and transmitted to a new material, in which it prepared the way for an analogous transformation taking further the process begun in the material of departure. The vortex was transduced. The paper model was then returned to the computer in order to be rematerialized in a third transductive step that would take the vortical emergence of architectural form into the actual building. The model was digitized and its surface was cross-sectioned top to bottom. Segments of the cross-sections were selected to form a skeleton, then milled in wood by computer-controlled machinery. The pieces of the wood were then joined by semi-translucent cotton fabric to reestablish the continuous undulations of the curvilinear surface.

In the transduction to wood, the proto-architectural form gained the ability to be self-supporting. It could now stand as architecture. But its resistance to the force of gravity was not the motor of its design. It was an emergent property of a transmitted transformative force-effect, as were the nonstandard architectural elements that finally took form. Because of this, the final structure was defined more by the imprint it bore of the nature of the abstract originating force than by any conventional architectural coding. The vortical nature of that originating force meant that the form that finally emerged across the series of transductive steps was undulatory. It had no corners between walls or between wall and floor, no edges to occlude and cast shadow, no linear vanishing points to anchor perspective. An architecturally habituated body entering it could not but feel a certain vertigo. The abstract force of the programmed vortex had been effectively transduced into embodied vertigo. It had jumped from the computer, through paper, wood, and fabric, to the architecturally contained, art-enjoying human body. A common ground had indeed been found where architectural and artistic perception, action, and construction dynamically meet. Potential movement had advanced all along the transductive line to find visible expression in an experience of anomalously framed viewing.

Not Determinately Nothing

Spuybroek does not design form. He guides a form-taking process that moves abstract forces through a series of transformations toward architectural embodiment. The resulting structure is a built expression of the nature of the force, whose transduced imprint it continues to bear. It also bears the abstractness of the force of departure and the flexibility of the intermediary materials the force passes through. The abstractness and flexibility persist as a vagueness in the structure forbidding too determinate an object identity being pinned to it. For example, the walls of the Nantes exhibit are not formally distinguished from the floor. The columns produced by the skeletal wood sections are not processually separate from the wall. The curvaceousness of the overall form is enfolding rather than enclosing, leaving an indecision between interior and exterior. The structure is not codifiable as a traditional architectural form. But it retains an unmistakable quality of buildingness by virtue of the fact that it has been constructed, is freestanding, and is at a scale that a human body can be moved through it and be contained by it. The installation is a proto-architectural form nonstandardly occupying a generic architectural place.

> I materialize many undefined things.
> —Lars Spuybroek (2000a, 126)

The relatively undefined nature of the final form is a derivative of the openness of its process of emergence, which was an experimental playing out of the effects of a force through successive transformations and material transfers. The playing-out of force-effects that drives the design is also a transitive thinking-through of the potential movements they carry in seed and can disseminate. The algorithms applied to the paper model make it a literal analog computer, akin to Gaudí's Sagrada Familia suspended chain studies. The thought elaborated by the process is how to continue the experimental openness of the transductive design into the experience of the building.

> Tentativeness: feeling and thinking combined.
> —Arakawa and Gins (2002, 82)

The vagueness Spuybroek's process materially thinks through in order to build-in is not a simple lack. It is the dynamic presence of Peirce's "continuous range of intensity" in transductive thought/feeling. Although it hinges on suspending habitual action and inculcated decoding in order to "postpone" the image in potential movement, it is not for all of that determinately nothing. It is the incipience of a something transductively to come.

174 COUPLET 5

> Potential means indeterminate yet capable of determination. . . . The vague always tends to become determinate, simply because its vagueness does not determine it to be vague. . . . It is not determinately nothing.
> —C. S. Peirce (1998, 323–24)

Determined to Be Determined

In every vagueness there is a tendency to become something determinate. In other words, vagueness is the sign of a potential movement toward definite form-taking. The vague is a positive state of intensive activity enveloping all possible varieties of experience. The tendency to take form may be suspended and held in intensity. This was the aim of the *WetGRID* project, which occupied a generic architectural function, that of housing art, with a built experience that overspilled the expectations of the genre. Traditionally, one consolidated set of possible experiences can be selected and abstracted into the design of a determinate form so that its form recognizably exhibits the conventional characteristics of its type, for example, the office building, and definitely fulfills its associated function.

In his *SoftOffice* project, Spuybroek seeks to invent an in-between state where a generic function is fulfilled, but flexibly. The aim is to design an office building with internal differentiations associated with different activities. But instead of mapping generic functions to rooms with forms to match, Spuybroek recategorizes the activities that will be housed according to the patterns of behavior that are involved, and extracts from this a different topography. Certain patterns of behavior recur in relation to different functions. For example, certain functions not usually grouped together might demand one office worker to be alone, and others to group together for collaborative work. Some require sitting still before a desk, others moving about. Collaborative work may be creative or rote, movements choreographed or somewhat stochastic. There are often expected rhythms of movement between different patterns of behavior implied in the stages required to fulfill a function. Now if, instead of mapping dedicated functions to separate rooms, you map similar patterns of movement to shared spaces, the architectural problem suddenly shifts.

The problem that the *SoftOffice* project set for itself was to design a limited set of flexible spaces lending themselves to different functions sharing certain patterns of office behavior, and then build in transitions between the flexible spaces that encourage spontaneous movements from one to another. The idea is to try to build in the creative synergy that comes from cross-connections between usually compartmentalized activities and from chance variations in function-filling progressions. In order to achieve this, as in Vision Machine, the design for *SoftOffice* had to take the embeddedness of potential movement in perception as its architectural object, and similarly seek a zone of proximity between perception, action, and construction. However, more determinate landing sites would have to be built in for a more limited set of possible experiences than was the case in Nantes. The landing sites would in addition have to be more stably attainable in order to limit the scope for the vertigo inherent in intersense relay making the architectural experience fly off its axis or lose too much perspective (not usually desired for office workers). A certain vagueness would be retained. But, in the words of Arakawa and Gins (2002, 97), it would have to present a "plausible indeterminacy": in other words, one determined to be determined as leading profitably to the development of a saleable product (in the area of media and entertainment).

For *SoftOffice*, Spuybroek employed a similar technique as in *WetGRID* but involving in the analog computing stage a lacquer and wool-string apparatus adapted from Frei Otto. The resulting proto-architectural curvilinear forms embodied the same form-taking process as in Nantes. But the determination of the form had to be taken one step further. More definite program elements had to be mapped to the resulting spaces, given the commercial development research function of the building.

SoftOffice prolongs *WetGRID* in a way that adapts Spuybroek's experimental design process to the requirements of commercial architecture, without changing the basic nature of the process. It is in fact a transduction of *WetGRID* as a whole that transforms its motive force of vertigo into a force of functional flexibility and transmits that flexibility to an existing genre of building conventionally lacking in creative form and creatively lived content. *SoftOffice* is part of a transductive dissemination of the creative form-taking process Spuybroek developed in such projects as Vision Machine. It expands the range of the building types it can plausibly occupy and of the architectural functions it can fulfill.

Couplet 6

2014

The Crannies of the Present

On the Subject of Decision

In the past twenty years there has been a burgeoning of research in experimental psychology on nonconscious perception. Much of the impetus for this activity has come from Benjamin Libet's troubling experiments on the formative interval of perception.

Libet experimentally verified a half-second lag between the brain activity initiating a movement and the conscious registering of the "decision" to act.[1] What was troubling about this—what generated prolific and ongoing debate—is that the very act assumed to be most definitive of reflective consciousness, and to fall most incontrovertibly within its compass, fell instead into a gaping hole in the weave of experience. Not only is what occurs in the gap unavailable to consciousness, but the very fact that there is a lag is itself nonconscious. The "decision" was found to be retrospectively "backdated" to coincide with the onset of brain activity, so that no gap is consciously experienced. Which only makes sense: how could an interval of nonconsciousness be consciously experienced? The very idea, however, introduced what many found to be an intolerable asynchrony into the heart of experience. The present of reflection, many a critic moaned, cannot be a "fiction." If the present is already a was-there, then consciousness is always a beat behind itself. Who knows what mischief might be doing in the off-beat of conscious suspense? If we can never catch ourselves in the act, we'll never know—until it's too late. How can we ever trust ourselves again? If we don't know what we're doing while it's doing, how can we choose to act conscientiously? Is there no free will? Freedom and morality seemed to go down the gaping drain of fractured consciousness, whose effective presence to its own event can no longer be sustained.

Things only got worse. Soon after, a similar delay was found to affect all action-perception, not just volition. Attention was shown to "blink out" for up to a half-second after the registering of a perceptual event, which in the laboratory context typically meant the flashing of a cue card. Conscious registering of the cue came at a lag, as did any bodily response to it. What is more, it was found that a second cue arriving in the interval cannot enter consciousness. There is a blackout period in which conscious thought and bodily response are held in suspense, absorbed in "readiness potential" for what comes next and is already welling: shock (Broadbent and Broadbent 1987). Perception is perforated by an unending stream of nonconscious microshocks. Although the second cue striking during the interval of shock is excluded from consciousness, it is not excluded from having an effect. It can still modulate the coming experience. It can operate as a "prime."[2] This strikes another empirical blow to the notion of a self-present, self-deciding consciousness. The lag is not a simple lapse of attention. Shock is positively built into the physiology of the eye in the form of "microsaccades." These mini-jerks of the eye occur without cease, and after each there is an even mini-er blackout of perception than that of attentional blink. Gaps within gaps. Saccadic holes within attentional holes. It gets positively fractal.

How, then, to explain the felt continuity of our actions and perceptions? The usual way of explaining it is to say that I smooth over the rapidly proliferating gaps with backdated "in-fill" that I "add" to the stimuli that actually manage to get through in order to "complete" them. The continuity is "really" an "illusion." Far from the lucidly self-present decider I pride myself on being, I'm just an illusionist, running after my shockingly perforated perception as it gurgles down sinkholes, desperately painting the canvas of experience to connect the black dots and keep it afloat. Artistic, perhaps, but a tad less exalted than the Enlightened subject of yore. To add insult to enlightened injury, an incipience of attention can be found in the saccadic holes within the holes in attention. It turns out that microsaccades are not purely random and chaotic, as had long been thought. They are quasi-chaotic. When the eye is focused, the distribution of the microsaccades gapping the field of perception point in the direction of the next focus with significant probability. Microsaccades are acts of "covert attention" (Hafed and Clark

2002). Who is covertly paying attention in the gaps in my attention? Am I possessed by a speedy mini-me lurking in the fractal gaps like a foreign agent on a covert mission to mislead me into thinking that I pay my own attention? For that matter, to whom does the stimuli needing completion get through? Who is there to receive them? Who paints in the filler? With what ungapped eyes does this elusive illusionist see the holes? Who I is this? And where does he store my canvases? It just gets worse and worse.

It was not always so bad. James's "specious present" predates by a hundred years the backdating Libet lag that rediscovered it for modern neuropsychology: "Say 'now' and it *was* even while you say it" (1996b, 254). James, however, took it in his philosophical stride. As did Whitehead. Midstream between James and Libet, Whitehead advised that "in considering our direct observation of past, or of future, we should confine ourselves to time-spans of the order of magnitude of a second, or even fractions of a second" (1967a, 192). So much comes of this "confinement" that it soon starts looking like a wondrous opening. The here-and-now of immediate experience, Whitehead continues, directly overlaps with the was-there of the immediate past. The immediate past is a "group of fused occasions, which enters into experience devoid of any medium intervening between it and the present immediate fact" (181). The past that is immediately co-present is "roughly speaking . . . that portion . . . lying between a tenth of a second and half a second ago. It is gone, and yet it is here." The "present occasion while claiming self-identity, while sharing the bygone occasion in all its living activities, nevertheless is engaged in modifying it, in adjusting it to *other* influences, in completing it with *other* values, in deflecting it to *other* purposes. The present moment is constituted by the influx of *the other* into that self-identity which is the continued life of the immediate past within the immediacy of the present" (181). This is a busy present, also entertaining futurity. "Immediate experience requires the insertion of the future in the crannies of the present" (191) in order to fulfill its engagement to modify, adjust, revalue, and deflect—in a word, modulate—the world from which it emerged. "Cut away the future, and the present collapses, emptied of its proper content" (192). It is the extension of the past-present toward a future modulation that makes the lived moment.

The felt present, this specious present, is a vector-feeling produced by the fusion of the fused past-present with an "aim" at futurity (Whitehead 1967a, 181, 191, 192). It is the felt momentum of that tending-toward. The specious present is triggered into action by the futurities "inserted" into the interval by the nonconscious priming of the cue. The notion of the "cue" must be extended to include everything that has the power to hit in the off-beat of experience, in the flicker of forming consciousness, to potential effect. Not only an actual image fleeting by: wafts of half-formed memories, inklings of alternative aims, self-reactivating habits, the postures that come with all of these, virtually—not to mention the resonances and interferences between them, as they come together in a crowd, clamoring to prime their way into the modulating of action. Incipient actions, all, one with perception's dawning. In fusion-upon-fusion, in-forming experience. A particular cue, such as a flash image, or a chance detail in the field of vision, or a singular coming-together of details in a configuration, serves as the leading edge of experience's in-forming. What effectively comes to prime enters on the cue's comet's tail of passing experience.

This fusion-upon-fusion is not yet a chronological order. The leading edge of the primary cue (when there is one that is isolatable) always brings a grouping of long-past iterations forward, in the form of already operating tendencies and already contracted skills and habits. The cue's galvanizing cutting-in fuses the multiplicity of these unfoldings into an absolute identity of the just-was-there of the immediate past and the here-and-now of the fractal present. The "two" fusions, of the contracted past with the here-and-now of the present, and of this immediate past-present with the future, come together in the infra-instant. They add up not to quantitatively more but to dynamically one: potentiation. They are differential aspects of the same integral enactment.

The terminal attractions contributed by the future's insertion tip the dynamic balance of the self-identity between past and present. The blacked-out gap in perception is not a lack. It is sparkingly intense, to excess. Something has to give. What gives is a "present" feeling of transition: an extension-effect. The felt-extension synchretically straddles the gap. It has leapt into the world of effect, held aloft by its own integral momentum. It does not collapse immediately back into intensity, as the past and present fractally collapse together in the gap, no sooner to rise out in phoenix-like in-fusion. It does, however, drop—into the modulating field of experience, where it extends its emergent effect. It joins the quasi-chaotic cascade of welling effect, a ripple on the surface of occurrent world-space. It has now registrably transpired. The emergent perception is not a noun (an in-filled image). It is an event: an effective action-perception. As a content taken up into a subsequent moment of retrospective reflection, its self-creative leap out of the interval into emergence will figure not as an "illusion" but as a drop of real life.

Is this cued emergence of the moment and co-creation of life-content, in and out of the infra-instant, so terribly injurious to our human pride? It may well temper our confidence in our self-reflective capacity to decide our actions in subjective isolation from the outside "influence" of nonconscious priming. But look what we get in return. If we take it all in Jamesian and Whiteheadian stride, we feel the interval to have been teeming with "living activity." We get activation. We get potentiation. We get welling intensity. We get emergent occurrence. From the shock of the cue-cut comes the surprise of an extended experiential creation. Something happens when something's doing in the gaps in our perception. Every life moment becomes eventful. We may not be able to live reflectively in the interval as it's doing, but we can't not live it out as it happens. That could be interesting: to ride out the ontogenetic waves. "The barest start and sally forwards, the barest tendency to leave the instant, involves the chasm and the leap," writes James (1996a, 70). That could be exciting. Self-reflection, less so. It is difficult to surprise oneself with one's own reflection.[3] The occurrent world, on the other hand, is bubbling with surprises. It is endlessly self-creative of its own variation. Whatever we may feel that we have lost in the laggardly shock to our self-reflective pride, we get back in the wonder of the creativity of the everyday. Whitehead held that all of metaphysics crowds into the infra-instant of "present" experience.[4] All of history and all of psychology course through its restless fractal crannies. As does everything else that is awash in the world, including the murky currents of contemporary politics and war (Massumi 2015a; see also Couplet 7 in this volume).

If in their own work James and Whitehead take the infra-plunge in stride, it is because they take the problem in the terms in which it poses itself and work constructively from there. The problem imposes itself in terms of time and "readiness potential": time and the formation of experience. Posing the question instead in terms of free will assumes the necessity of a "rational," reflective, deliberative subject, and the unthinkability of life as anything other. This begs the whole question. The deliberative subject figures in the debate as already formed. It is pre-thought. If it is concluded to exist in spite of the humiliations, it is found to be still there, well-formed and standing steady on terra firma just as suspected, somehow in spite of the leap and chasm. If it is concluded that it does not exist, then all that has been achieved is to negate an already formed idea. Which leaves you with the same idea, under erasure. Ideas under erasure, as Derrida shows, have a way of surreptitiously returning. So it's either still there, or it's there again. The negated subject surreptitiously returns in this debate whenever the brain is said to "pick up" or "access" information or "receive" an image. The implicit subject of the perception may no longer be standing so high and mightily self-directing, but there it is again, peering at the canvas of life in a much reduced form. The hated "homunculus."[5] No matter how many times it gets killed off in the literature, it implicitly returns, again and again. The homunculus is the cognitive undead of neuropsychology. It sometimes takes demonic form, as in the covert operations of the attention-paying mini-me of the crannies.

In short, making free will the problem makes it a false problem. A false problem begs the question by deflecting the terms of the problem into a preformational dead end. Pragmatically what this does is to activate tendencies running counter to those the problem proposes, in the terms in which it poses itself. In this instance, the countertendencies start with the subject. The preformed subject of decision reciprocally presupposes preconstituted objects. This in turn presupposes that conformity is more fundamental than differential and variation, all the more so when the subject is assumed to act "rationally," that is, in accordance with conventional criteria of what is reasonably needed or morally obliged. It is only in the course of its acting in accordance with these normative criteria that the subject is acknowledged to effectively enter into the company of others. This further presupposes a logical priority of the simplicity of the individual alone in its decisive skull over the multiplicity of others together in a surprisingly complex world. At best, what all of this accomplishes is to save subjective normality from the jaws of the abyss. Creativity is left to fend for itself.

None of this is meant to belittle the importance or validity of the experimental findings in neuropsychology. On the contrary, it is an appeal to take them with the seriousness they are due. This does not involve proceeding without presuppositions. It requires proceeding in accordance with presuppositions confluent with where the terms in which the problem poses itself propose to take it. These are the terms: One, time. Two, time lag. Three, "covert" or nonmanifest activity in the lag, in the synapses of the brain, in the nerves, in the muscles, in the eye—and in their respective and collective milieus of life. Four, a potentiation in the lag embodied in this activity; "readiness potential." Five, a capacity on the part of the nonconscious lag-activity to trigger an unfolding from the potentiation into a registrable action and perception. Six, the susceptibility of that unfolding expression of potential to be varied or modulated by cue-strikes falling into the gaps between registrable action-perceptions. Seven, a "backdating" of the modulated action-perception such that it is felt to have straddled the lag. Eight, the inescapable fact that what is consciously felt to have transpired bears no resemblance to and does not represent or reflect the complex conditions under which it was produced. These are lost in the cracks of experience.

Present felt awareness is then a variational creation expressing its conditions of emergence only in effect, and its effective emergence is the making of a difference. Time figures here as a lag: a differential interval. In the interval is activity. The activity embodies potential. The potential is for variation. The variation appears as a felt present. The felt present emerges from the differential interval to register an integral difference. The integrated differing is a creative event. Suppose that the creation is not "just" an illusion but a surplus-value production of reality. Suppose that consciousness is not *of* a prior something reflected, but rather *is* this productive event really contributing a registrable more to the world of experience, in spite of the abyssal self-withdrawal from awareness of the conditions enactive of the production (Deleuze 1986a,

56). Suppose that the felt present is not so much *in* the world as it is a pulse of the world's worlding. Suppose that the present feeling *is* the enactive solidarity of its multiple aspects, past, present, and future, in the same creative event. Suppose a time-variable world of complexity and emergence. Suppose that the perceptual event's registering itself as a modulation in the world's worlding is sufficient reason for it, that it is self-standing in its own relief, aloft the lag, effectively real, needing nothing, already subjective, lurking in the cracks or holding it in its self, to rationally validate its reality. Take it as it comes. Don't get ahead of the problem by jumping forward to things made. Suppose, with James, that the world itself is but "things in the making." "Put yourself *in the making*."[6] Suppose that what subjects, objects, and norms of activity there are afoot in the world are makings: derivatives of a primary perceptual process of self-standing ontogenesis that does not wait for or require your rationally evaluated support for its becoming, being perfectly capable of valuing itself ontogenetically, thank you anyway, in *how* it makes experiential time for itself and *how* it takes its worlding place, and to what cascade of effects. Follow the how.

Then, and only then, ask *what* attributes, such as free will or demonism or passivity or rationality, these makings may be said to have. By then, the very definition of freedom and will have undergone a complex variation. The terms will have returned, this time with a difference, in coevolution with others actively involved in the playing out of the problem. Don't negate anything. Co-involve everything in the process. At most, if necessary, hold certain terms in suspense until circumstances propitious for their reinvolvement impose themselves as forcefully as did the initial terms of the problem. This is the radically empirical approach. Take everything to be real. Take everything real to be just as it appears.[7] Catch everything that really appears in its just-appearing; that is, in its own complex, co-involved in-the-making. Your terms themselves will then appear with the problematic force to move thought forward. This is one way to affirm the problem in thought with the constructive seriousness due it.

A tool for purifying the terms of the problem of parachuted-in countertendencies is the concept of what James calls the "terminus" of an experience.[8] The terminus is the effectively real, ideal limit of the processual momentum enveloped in the terms of the problem. It is an extrapolation of the oriented potential incumbent in the operative solidarity between the terms. This potential is enacted to varying degrees of achievement, or to varying processual intensities, in each action-perception belonging to the tendency governed by the terminus. Every situation is transhabited by a multiplicity of terminal tendencies in complex, coevolutionary, mutual embroilment. The infra-instant figures then as the reserve of potential always "left-under" the passing-through into an emergent action-perception of the terminus's force of attraction. It is in the infra-instant that the orienting force of the terminus takes effect. It is active, really if abstractly, as a creative co-factor in the emerging of the experience toward the horizon of its processual limit. The off-beat in experience is the dynamic gap-point at which the terminus recurs to the here-and-now. It then turned back around in no-time, returning forward in the direction in which its coming had the tendency to go.

The infra-instant of off-beat experience that the terminal momentum leaves-under its continuing onward is also a really abstract, processual limit. It figures a different limit, in contrast and creative tension with that of the terminus. Rather than extrapolate experience ahead, it interpolates itself. It is intervallic, falling recessive rather than arcing on. It is where experience falls out of itself into the groundless ground of its own abstract making. Experience in the syncopated making is abstract because, not yet having emerged into itself, it is not yet registrable in time or space. Its emergence makes a drop of world-time in which to take place. To construe it any other way would be to fall victim to what Whitehead called the "fallacy of misplaced concreteness." This is the presumption that a something doing can be construed as having "simple location." If ontogenetic activity had simple location, its product in-the-making would already have defined attributes. It would be pre-standing steady, a formed substance or subject already in the world brandishing its essential attributes, even if its "accidental" properties might undergo change. This is begging the question again.

The infra-instant is nonlocal. Not because it is a simple void or negation. It is nonlocal by dint of overfullness of potential. It is the kind of no-time/no-where that is everywhere/always in the enactive cracks of coming action-perception. "In a certain sense, everything is everywhere at all times. Every location involves an aspect of itself in every other location," Whitehead writes (1967b, 90, 71). "Each volume of space, or each lapse of time, includes in its essence aspects of all volumes of space, or all lapses of time." The infra-instant is the essential co-involvement of all places taken and moments made, under certain of their aspects. The aspects are those of potential. The termini and tendencies in-forming the world cue into the infra-instant and course through its fractal gaps. They all crowd in, overfilling the interval with readying potential, until one crowds out, into the clearing of its own extrusion.

The infra-instant is the point at which everything turns into process as process turns toward emergence. Interpolated, in-turning, in infinite potentiating recession from the action-perceptions that will nevertheless phoenix forth, everywhere and all the time: the infra-instant is the *immanence* in each of its crannies of the unbounded-whole world of experience. It is that world's all in the-making, in-forming the ubiquitous off-beat. This prompted Félix Guattari to call it the "navel" of the world (1995). The immanence of the infra-instant is the processual umbilicus of the world's quasi-chaotic renewal or "chaosmosis" (112–13). The terminus is the outside limit of experience. The infra-instant is its immanent limit. Dynamically, the immanent limit extending-out into a specious present strictly coincides with the outside limit's turning-in. Quite some twist. The answer Whitehead gives to the question of where continuity is to be found: in the twist. In the crowded immanence of experience.[9] "In continuity" is quite some worldly commotion. It is this commotion that is of the "essence": experience's ontogenetic essence as *abstract activity*. Lost in the in-most recesses of the everyday and every place, where we might be sorely tempted to seek a misplaced concreteness of experience, we find instead the most dynamic and unbounded of abstractions: the world's expression in perception, catching its commotional breath.

Like the terminus, the infra-instant is a limit-concept. It is barely thinkable, yet advances itself with troubling force as a problem for thought. If the value of a philosophic concept is what it does, if its effective meaning is the difference it makes, what does plumbing the navel of the world do for thought? One of the differences it makes immediately is to suspend the false problem of the subject, and whether it can be attributed free will, over a chasm of abstract activity. This deflects the issue initially not only away from reflection but also away from cognition generally.

2018

Dim, Massive, and Important

Atmosphere in Process

> It is not true that there is a definite area of human consciousness, within which there is clear discrimination and beyond which mere darkness. . . . The basic fact is the rise of an affective tone originating from things whose relevance is given.
> —Alfred North Whitehead (1967a, 164, 176)

"Dim, massive, and important" (Whitehead 1967a, 270). These are the adjectives Whitehead combines to describe the background of experience that enters the "definite area of our consciousness"—to the degree that it does—as what we call atmosphere. Of the three, the first will seem most apt at first approach. We are dimly aware, on a continuing basis, of an environing of our thoughts and activity. This we rarely attend to, content to let it murmur softly through the moment like a halffelt breeze caressing our bodies (but without the actual movement that would signal a corporeal nature of its own). When we do attend to it—which is when it draws our attention to itself—it expresses as a global affective tonality, unimputable to any given element of the surround. Even if the atmospheric effect seems to emanate from or pool in the vicinity of one or several elements more than others, it skirts their exclusive ownership. It is they that express at its bidding, serving as indicators or amplifiers, like weathervanes for invisible breezes registering signs of change in the air. If the affective tone "originates from things whose relevance is given," the things are not determinately given. Their relevance is nothing so sharp as to invite a judgment of *particular* importance. It is rather the atmosphere that has importance, after its own manner: that is to say globally, as a general space of surround from which *something* of relevance that may prove pointedly important might next appear. Calling it a "space" is to say too much. An atmosphere envelops like a space but lacks the definite boundaries and coordinate locations of spatial structure. It is certainly space-like, but it doesn't surround us without also infusing us. Its ability to pervade our feeling gives it an air of subjectivity, at the same time as it is experienced as being in the world, giving it a vaguely object-like presence. Space-like, occupying a gray zone between subject and object, the ontological status of atmosphere eludes the usual categories. However "heavy" the atmosphere, when we focus on its status, it melts into air, more sprite-like than "massive" in any usual sense of the word. It bears down without weight.

In order to understand what motivates Whitehead's characterization of the background of existence that we experience as atmosphere as not just dim but also massively important, it is necessary to look more closely at the nature of its peculiar mode of existence. Atmosphere eludes the usual categories of space, subject, and object because of the way it presents as *quality*. Atmosphere is the global quality of the moment, cutting across the registers of all that populates it, as generally enveloping as it is singularly infusing. The word "quality" is called for, but with it comes a danger: that of collapsing atmosphere back into one of the categories it eludes. That category, of course, is the subjective.

No current of thought has inquired into atmosphere in as much detail and as astutely as the "new phenomenology" advanced by Hermann Schmitz (2016; Schmitz, Müllen, and Slaby 2011; Böhme 1993). New phenomenological discussions of atmosphere display an acute awareness of the uniqueness of its mode. Their rich phenomenological descriptions converge with the brief sketch just offered. Except in one important respect: their phenomenology. Common to phenomenological approaches, new and old, is the positing of what Whitehead called "the basic fact" as an "originary mine-ness." For the new phenomenology, this "primitive present" is an "undifferentiated pure presence of mine-ness" in which the five elements of "*here, now, being, this* and I are fused" (Schmitz, Müllen, and Slaby 2011, 249). In other words, all of the dimensions of first-person subjectivity are present, but without self-identity as yet. All of the prerequisites of self-identity are in place, even anticipated, by a primitive self-awareness. This undifferentiated subjective ground of first-person experience is described as a "mine-ness" that is self-aware, but without "self-ascription" as yet (248).

For Whitehead, to the contrary, the "basic fact" is not in subjectivity, even one so pure and "primitive." It is, rather, *in the world*, in all its messiness: "Our primitive perception is that of 'conformation' vaguely, and of the yet vaguer relata 'oneself' and 'another' in the undiscriminated background" (1985, 43). This positing of *relation* as the primitive of existence asserts the "basic fact" not as an undifferentiated, a priori subjective slate but as an eventful *participation* rough with an irreducible element of *otherness*.

The present, for Whitehead, does have a self-identity, but it is not of the subject of consciousness with itself. It is of the present with the past: "The present occasion while claiming self-identity, while sharing the very nature of the bygone occasion in all its living activities, nevertheless is engaged in modifying it, in adjusting it to *other* influences, in completing it with *other* values, in deflecting it to *other* purposes. The present moment is constituted by the influx of *the other* into that self-identity which is the continued life of the immediate past within the immediacy of the present" (1967a, 281, emphasis in original). The "continued life of the immediate past within the immediacy of the present." This swivel from the subject to time places atmosphere, as expression of the undiscriminated background of experience, in the world of *process*: self-modifying, self-adjusting, self-deflecting, and, for the pulse of the moment, self-completing. The basic fact is the processual inheritance, by the present, of the activity of the immediate past. The genesis of the here-now-being-this-I that will come to recognize itself in the moment's self-completing and ascribe it to itself arises from an *elsewhere-elsewhen-becoming-thus-and-other* primitively *departing* from self-identity that is not in the first person. The self-identity is the world's taking a breath to catch up with itself, past superposed with present for an immeasurable beat, before continuing its course to the future.

Whitehead speaks of the "vector nature" of this departure from self-identity in the direction of an added difference, calling it the "emotional" basis of experience (1967a, 271). It is the feeling-itself into form of a new drop of experience detaching from the background continuity of the world's ongoing, to cut its own figure. Carried in the "emotion" is a feeling of "derivation" from the given antecedent world, as genetic background of this and all other occasions. This is the vague "relata of 'oneself' and 'another' in the undiscriminated background" to which Whitehead refers. The background continuity is no sooner felt in its continuity than it is cut into by an influx of "other" influences. These form a wider background: that of the potentials, infinitely more capacious than any direct inheritance, proposing themselves to the new occasion as lures for its taking form. The moment of self-ascription comes at the end, in the occasion's self-completion, separated from self-identity by a genesis. The self-completion of the occasion precisely coincides with its "perishing." "So, that's what it was!" says a pulse of the world, in an expiration of climactic "self-enjoyment." "So that was me!" (Deleuze and Guattari 1983, 20).

In this schema, self-identity is not an already-mine. It is a force of the world, collecting itself for the beat of time. It is an unmeasured offbeat in the force of time's forwarding, conditioning continuing. It is the world's in-breath, bracing for a change of direction. The self-ascription is the expiration of what emerges from that veer. The departure point of self-identity is *retroactively* owned by the experience completing. Mine-ness is divergently emergent. In the "basic fact," the relation is prospective, "oneself" to come, felt in an immediacy of hindsight. The ascription of "oneself" in derivative relation crowns a departure from self-identity.

Finally owned, the sense of mine-ness perishes at the instant of its feeling, to make way for its own transcendence in a successor self-identity. Self-identity is punted farther down the road of process to form the point of departure for a new vector-pulse of experience selfdiffering that will retroactively own it in its turn. Subject to the force of time, I has no time to enjoy myself. To paraphrase William James, say mine, and I is already past: "We live, as it were, on the front edge of an advancing wave-crest, and our sense of a determinate direction in falling forward is all we cover of the future of our path" (1996a, 69).

What is at stake here is an *ontogenetic* movement, vectoring the creative force of time in "other" directions. There is no unmoving *ontological* foundation, certainly not in the first person. There is no clean slate of mine-ness upon which I reflexively inscribes me, in a circle of self-recognition.

It is the "emotional" feeling of the vector force of in-the-world derivation accompanying every experience that gives atmosphere its Whiteheadian massiveness and importance. The importance is, first, the inheritance of the weight of the world's past, in presently passing self-identity with it. Next, it is the final bequeathing to the world of a difference effectively made, weighting what comes next. The massiveness is the weight of the world's continuing. But even more, it is the excess weight of potential that comes with the influx of otherness. This supplement of background is what empowers the continuation to depart from self-identity and differ.

Atmosphere is the background of massiveness and importance. The importance hits vaguely, in the off-beat between pulses of determination. The massiveness wafts airy, undiscriminated, as good as sprite-like.

In today's vocabulary, we might tend to say "affective" rather than "emotional," in recognition of the distinction between affect and emotion that is the hallmark of one of the constitutive tendencies of what has come to be known as affect theory. Significantly, the new phenomenology also qualifies its "primitive present" as an "affective involvement" (Schmitz, Müllen, and Slaby 2011, 245–46). But after "affective involvement" comes the qualifying phrase "of the subject of consciousness." When process-oriented currents of affect theory bracket the foundation of mine-ness, the affective involvement figures as the unmediated participation of pulses of the world's process *in each other*, subject only to the force of time. "The whole of nature," writes Whitehead, is "involved in the tonality of the particular instance" of emergent experience coming to pass (1967b, 83).

The task for a process-oriented account is to understand atmosphere as the expression of an affective involvement in the whole of nature, as ontogenetic background of experience. The involvement is expressed as a "tonality." Tonality is "character," for example of a piece of music or a color. It is a qualitative concept. The process-oriented account of atmosphere must confront the experience of atmosphere in the directly qualitative terms in which it presents itself, as an expression of the ontogenetic background.

The mainstream philosophical approach to the concept of quality cleaves it in two. "Primary qualities" (solidity, extension, figure, number, and motion) are considered real and objective. As such, they are the province of classical empirical science. "Secondary qualities" (color, sound, tastes, etc.) are impressions in the mind of a perceiver, endogenously produced upon impact of a bodily stimulus. Secondary qualities are purely subjective, taking off from the body into the interiority of a subject, and irrevocably consigned to that private zone. By this account, secondary qualities are epiphenomenal. They have no ontological status of their own that can be counted as real after its own manner. They are simply "mental additions," fancies of the mind. As such, they are untrustworthy. There is no guarantee that they correspond to what is actually "out there." It goes without saying that by this reckoning, atmosphere, which has no definite extension, figure, or number, and thus no measurable motion, and no solidity at all, falls to the side of fancy. It is "merely" subjective, not the stuff of serious thought.

This account is profoundly unsatisfying to both phenomenology and process philosophy, due to its fundamental Cartesian dualism and its institution of a correspondence theory of truth. Whitehead blasts the division between primary and secondary qualities as the cardinal gesture behind what he calls the "bifurcation of nature" (1920, 26–48). This is the sundering of nature into two fundamentally uncommunicating domains. It precludes a process-oriented nature philosophy, the orientation of which must be radical-empirical. By that is meant taking everything as real after its own manner, and inquiring into what that manner is (what qualitatively different mode of its existence is involved). What is "radical" about this is that the "real" is extended to include relation, and the affective registering of relation comes immediately of the basic fact, or primitive, of existence. A nonbifurcated philosophy, Whitehead insists, must be a "critique of pure feeling" (1978, 113). The thinking of atmosphere has a natural place in it.

In this account, the mark of the real is indubitability (Whitehead 1967a, 181). This is an indubitability that comes first, not after an interregnum of cogitation. It is not a product of reflection and reason. It is an event of direct perception. It is the indubitability of what comes to consciousness as already there, and as already having made a difference, so that we find ourselves in the midst of the differencing. It is the inability to second-guess. We never second-guess atmosphere. As a directly perceived expression of the temporal self-identity upon which the world's continuing hinges, it corresponds to nothing other than itself, and needs only itself as its own interpretation. When we find ourselves finally here-now-being-this-I, we are already swaddled in it. It is a given, for the moment, always such as it is. It has already always arrived true to itself, regardless of what we may think of it afterward.

An atmosphere may be ambiguous. In fact, it is of its nature to be vague. But this makes it *the truth of an ambiguity, not an ambiguity about the truth*. We might walk into a room and feel a slight, unascribable tension. No doubt about it, that is just what the atmosphere of the room is—because it has been felt to be so. Atmosphere is all in the feeling, and the feeling is a given of unfolding experience.

Whitehead considers this immediacy of a qualitative experience that surrounds and pervades, and is directly given, as the "primary phase" of all experience, coinciding with the self-identity at the origination of each and every pulse of experience. Neither a primary nor a secondary quality in the classical-empirical sense, it has the status Peirce called Firstness: Quality "in no way refuted or refutable," "embryo of being" (1998, 177, 269). For Peirce as for Whitehead, the basic fact of affective tone, of which atmosphere is a species, is more primitive than sense perception understood as the cognition of isolatable objects possessing clear attributes and occupying a determinable location in space. Sense perception, according to Whitehead, is a higher-order development, present only in the more complexly evolved organisms.

Although vague, affective tonality is not formless. It skirts the form/formless dichotomy, as it does the dichotomy between subject and object. It carries what Whitehead, a bit confusingly, calls a "subjective form."

What Whitehead means by "subjective" in this phrase is not what is meant in bifurcated nature: that is, belonging to a subject or being in a mind. By subjective he means being "nothing else than what the universe is for it" (1978, 154). This mirrors Peirce's definition of Firstness as "that which is such as it is positively and regardless of anything else," as zero degree, or germinal threshold, of consciousness (1998, 267). From a Whiteheadian perspective, the "regardless of anything else" means "fully absorbed" in its manner of infolding the "antecedent universe" into a feeling that is positively such as it is, and only thus. The zero-degree thusness gives the enveloped universe to a new occasion, for its unfolding in a next pulse of process. This is in keeping with Whitehead's idea, mentioned earlier, that in its purely qualitative being the primitive affective tonality is already a "relatum." It is a double relatum, once in the way it enfolds its antecedent world, and again in the way this enfolding prospectively anticipates a constitutive influx of otherness, toward the renewal of the world in the emergence of a new self-difference.

We are dealing with a paradox. Relation, for Peirce, is precisely not Firstness but Thirdness. The paradox, taking the Peircean terms with a Whiteheadian twist, is that there is a Firstness *of* Thirdness, a primitiveness of relation. Peirce's simple Firstness, like its Whiteheadian correlate, the simple "eternal object," is a limit-case, never actually encountered. It is a virtuality, or pure potentiality, real without being actual.[1] In actual fact, the unicity of Firstness, its being absolutely and positively such as it is, thus and only, regardless, is that of a temporal integration. It is the self-identity of the present and its immediate past, ripe for an already brewing influx of other influences, other values, and other purposes that will culminate in a new self-ascription. This self-identical openness for what will come (to itself) is the outcome of the last such influx, hinging to next. It is this unique, unrepeatable *integral openness* that is nothing else than what the universe is, for—and as—this one occasion forming. An eternal object is always in point of fact a "complex eternal object" singularly enveloping contrast and difference (Whitehead 1978, 24, 34, 114, 186). Otherness in the process of integration, in departure from self-identity, is the very stuff of subjectivity, as integral world-quality. This, in Peirce's words, is the absolute subjectivity of a "mere feeling that has the dark instinct of being the germ of thought," one with the pulse of the vector-force of time.[2]

Whitehead's primary phase of self-identical integral openness corresponds to James's "pure experience." This term was James's translation into his own vocabulary of Peirce's Firstness. James defines pure experience as "a primitive stage of perception in which discriminations afterwards needful have not yet been made." Speaking of a focus of experience, James continues: "a piece of experience of a determinate sort is there, but there at first as a 'pure' fact." In a clear indication that the concept of pure experience is not restricted to limit-case simplicity, James gives the example of reading. In language strangely prefigurative of Blanchot's "il y a" (1949, 320n1), he writes, "'Reading' simply is, is there; and whether there for some one's consciousness, or there for physical nature, is a question not yet put" (James 1996a, 145).

"'Reading' simply is, is there": this changes the meaning of the word "form" in Whitehead's phrase "subjective form." The occasion, coming into its own qualitatively, is fully absorbed in its own *activity*: "reading simply is, is there." The form is a dynamic form, a pattern of activity. It is not a substantial form or abstract figure. This saves quality from the substantialism and idealism that are the twin enemies responsible for the bifurcation of nature, glaring at each other from opposite sides of the breach they have imagined. It allies quality to notions of dynamism, even to energetics. Whitehead speaks of the "primary phase" as an "energizing" of a new pulse of world-process (1967a, 182–83). "Energy is sheer activity" (Whitehead 1968, 137). More than that, "the energetic activity considered in physics is the emotional intensity entertained in life" (168). The rise of an affective tone whose relevance is given in the background is the basic fact of all occasions of nature, even those containing a "germ of thought" not of the persuasion to rise into a reflective consciousness and explicitly self-ascribe.

Atmosphere is the vague but integral qualitative feeling of the background of all existence. *Worlding simply is, is there*. In the case of atmosphere, the question of whether it is for someone's consciousness is already, vaguely, put: the worlding simply is, is there . . . to *have been for me* (in some as yet unascribed way). Atmosphere is the vague but integral qualitative feeling of the background of all existence as it will necessarily, retroactively relate to me, in an outcome of emergent mineness from the "pure fact" of a self-identity that is nothing else than what the world is for it.

Each occasion infolds the background of its integral activity into the pattern of its unfolding, in a manner so singular to it as to be just so, regardless of all else. Each dynamically accounts for the background, in modulations of its subjective form. These include traces of the unfolding dynamic form's turning-away from paths not taken. For the background is always redolent with more potential than can be effectively infolded and finally determined in the precision of a self-patterning. But only certain occasions, among them those of the human kind, feel the background as atmosphere. For them, the unmistakable vagueness of atmosphere vibrates with the remainder of unactualized potential. Atmosphere shivers with potential, felt in excess of what the occasion can fully determine and precisely pattern, foretokening a remainder that will be left after the occasion's activity runs its course. Enveloped in the quality of an atmosphere is the otherness of nonhuman experience, along the full spectrum of nature, experienced as a vast reservoir of vague but indubitable potential coursing with the force of time.

There is no place for passive reception upon a subjective slate in process philosophy. There is always activity, energizing more activity—action upon action. The feeling of an affective tone, or processual quality of experience, coincides with the transmission of a dynamic form, including its manner of integrating into its own subjective form the background of potential from which it stands out. The word "transduction" would be better than "transmission," because the self-completion of a pulse of experience is the springboard for a next that will differ from it. The coming pulse is under processual obligation to commence in the primary-phase self-identity of its immediate past with its dawning present. But it will no sooner introduce some degree of novelty and immediately deviate from its point of departure—earning it the status of an event. It will come into its own subjective form, as a singular occasion of experience, fully absorbed in the immediacy of its own coming about.

The way the event carries its background of potential with its own dynamic form calls other, co-occurring events into a felt participation in the spectrum of potential it is busily absorbed in transducing. The germ of this felt participation is the "rise of the affective tone" coming out of the primary phase of an experience to which Whitehead referred. The affective tone accompanies the occasion's self-forming as its atmosphere, integrally surrounding and all-infusing it. It is as immediate as any focal element it wraps around and runs through, only vaguer.

The focal occasion of a speaker delivering a lecture, for example, fills the room with a directly felt sense of the potentials parsed by the situation, equally distributed around and infusing its occupants' correlated occasions of listening. In a case such as this, where a conventional genre of activity is in practice, the parsing of potential is analyzable in terms of "habitus." But the potential in the air also includes the potential for novelty: always a possibility is an unheard-of idea, a comical slip of the tongue, an outbreak of pathos, or a scandalous pronouncement—any number of departures from the habits and conventions of comportment coded into the situation. These outlier potentials are included in the complexion of the atmosphere. Their potential inflections of the course of things are what give the occasion its sense of eventness, however generic the occasion may be. Atmosphere is never reducible to habitus or social coding.

The atmospheric feeling of parsed or parseable potential, though liminally conscious, is as immediate, in its own mode, as the stand-out sensation of a lecturer giving a speech or the strained attention of the auditors. Process philosophy's insistence that all experience is direct perception rehabilitates the category of immediacy, even for something so apparently tangential as atmosphere. Its attention to the force of time and the transductive nature of every occasion signposts that *immediacy* cannot be confused with the *instantaneity* of a sense-impression. The present of process is not a widthless point in time. It is a transductive smudge, diffusing atmospherically through space as part of its vectoring across the dimensions of time, as each succeeding present dawns in self-identity with its immediate past and heralds its own difference-making passing-on the baton of potential to a next pulse.

Whitehead uses the example of anger to explain how a focal event or element is embedded in a more encompassing process (1967a, 183). How, he asks, does a man in anger know he's angry? He doesn't have to reflect upon the situation to know. He doesn't have to summon a memory of the previous moment. He just finds himself in his anger. The affective tonality of the anger of the moment before has lingered into the dawning of the present moment—and there he finds himself. The anger's continuing served as a hinge of transitional identity, or what Whitehead calls "conformation," between the immediate past and the dawning present. Processual identity is not a separating off. It is a falling into continuity. It is what ensures the quality of relation between moments of time. For Whitehead, this is not a passive slippage. It is a "reenaction," as if process had passed over a measureless break to actively take up again from where it left off, in no time flat. The reenaction is not an act of the angry man. It is not in his subjectivity, understood in the traditional sense. It is an act of process, in its world-continuing activity. The man knows he is angry because he finds himself already acting, on the other side of the break, in the qualitative continuity of the relation ensured by the reenaction. His knowledge that he is angry requires no separate act of cognition, and it is not in response to any particular sense-impression. The reenactive self-identity of his present of anger with its immediate past is *nonsensuous*. There is no specifiable sense-impression or set of sense-perceptions corresponding to it, because the continuity came not from a localizable source in the world but rather from the break in time reenergizing its worlding. The knowledge of the anger is an immediate thinking-feeling of the quality of that worlding: its processual *character*. The man's knowledge is precognitive and prepersonal, a direct infusing of his actions and feelings with that character. Incoming from an immediate past that is already no longer, the anger has rearisen, into its own dynamic character, ready for an influx of otherness. In this pulse of its continuing, it will self-modulate. It will take on something new, perhaps a diminution of intensity, or an alloying with "other" affects, or a crescendoing in an unreflected action that just comes of the anger, as if of itself. However the anger plays out in the new occasion, the man will just know he is angry, with a sense of derivation—not one of personal ownership. Anger simply is, is there, as having been, surrounding and infusing. It will only be afterward that the man owns up to his anger-laden feelings and actions. At which time he will be apt to argue that he was "beside himself." So . . . *that* was me? (Cringe.)

The thinking-feeling involved in the transduction enacted by affective tonality is a mode of abstraction, in two ways. First, because the continuing is nonsensuous, and what is nonsensuous can only be abstract by definition. Second, because the past moment influencing the present is no longer. It is already gone the moment it is reenacted for now. A basic definition of abstraction is the effective presence of what is absent. The man's knowing himself to be angry is a concrete grasping, in direct perception, of an abstract dimension of the real, of the world, of process, rebeginning for a concretely felt abstract influx of otherness.

The reenaction of the anger passes to the present the subjective form of the moment just-past. Enveloped in the man's finding himself in anger is a pattern of activity that reseeds itself and continues to unfold across new variations, like a musical piece refraining its motifs across the breaks between movements. The anger is this subjective form, this dynamic form, self-expressing as affective tonality.

The movement is a co-motion, from the point of view of potential. For enveloped in the influx of otherness is a crowd of "vague presences," filling out the relational tenor of the experience (Whitehead 1985, 43). Mixed in with the anger are almost-feelings of many things, half-sketched, but still contributing to the feeling. With the anger come ghosts of confrontations with past lovers, brushing up against outbursts against long-dead parents, echoing words of hurt heard in other situations, not to mention insecurities and fears for the future. All manner of things in a throng, resonating together, in quasi-chaotic half-voicing, in a background hyperactivity of affective glossolalia, barely but insistently there. Their commotion adds overtones and undertones to the overall affective tonality. This conflux of qualitatively variant other-angers forms the wider background of the anger in which the man finds himself.

The anger that clearly expresses itself is the leading edge of this capacious background, making itself felt. It is the breaching of the background, rising to the foreground of the present moment in the singular form of this anger, just thus, thence to recede into the background again, from which the following words and actions will stand out differently, in their turn. The vague presences are indistinctly felt, as potentials for reenaction. It is precisely as potentials that they agitate the anger: actions sketching themselves, incipiently, without being carried out, contributing something of their feeling tone nonetheless; contributing something of their subjective form. Only one will actually irrupt in speech or gesture. When it does, it will resolve their echoing multiplicity into the arc of a single, irreversible stream of action. The other-angers are still almost-felt, in their multitude, to graded degrees of vagueness. Their conflux corresponds to a gradation of the potential proposing itself for the occasion.

It is the gradation of potential that is "massive": the contrasts between the other-angers, and the contrast between them collectively and the singularity of the actually expressed anger, constitute the intensity of the occasion (Whitehead 1978, 234). Other-angers massively contribute to composing the intensity of the experience, and participate in delineating its importance. Importance is not just the practical impact of what eventuates. It is also the feeling tone of the impact taking practical effect: the quality of impactfulness. That quality is nothing without the feeling, in addition to the impact itself, of the contrast between what this occasion effectively became and its dimly present could-have-beens (extending not just to other-angers but even to other-than-anger affective tones, on a graded qualitative continuum of varietal differences).

It is this contrastive tenor that makes the anger, however singular and self-absorbed, however absolutely just itself, a relatum. The contrasts virtually expand the field of relation, present in germ in the primary phase of time-making self-identity, to a full-spectrum gradation of potential that is far more encompassing than the connections between things actually present and the actions practically impacting them in the making of their moment. The actions make the moment, such as it will have been, positively and regardless of anything else. If the actions make the moment, their contrasting dim presences contribute to making the moment momentous. In concert, the clearly felt foreground actions and their vaguely felt background of graded potential are nothing else than what the universe is for this occasion.

The vague presences contribute to importance because they are suggestive of potential alternatives. They have the weightless weight of lures, propensities, tendencies, betokening other influences, values, and purposes. They act as an incorporeal flutter of forces, which the unfolding experience vaguely takes account of in its dynamic taking form. They are co-energizers of the occasion, their undertones and overtones exerting a modulatory influence on its self-completing. They contribute to the affective tone that peaks in the clear and unmistakable subjective form of anger, as cutting edge of the occasion.

The sharpness of this cutting edge can be called, following Daniel Stern, a "vitality affect" (1985, 53–61). This is the quality of feeling accompanying the irreversible arc of the action, pregnant with the background of potential from which it issued, and carrying the complexion of its minor tones. The vitality affect is the lived dynamic form of the occasion of experience, its actually occurring subjective form. It is not a linear playing-out, however clear the action and however strongly the dominant tonality insists on its own centrality. Much can change on the fly. Intervening side-perceptions or micro-gestures, or a previously unattended-to detail that suddenly pops out, can aggravate, deviate, or flatten the feeling. These interventions are able to modulate the feeling because their sensuous presence overlaps with and is supplemented by the nonsensuous influx of lures, propensities, and tendencies dimly present. The complexity of this overlap creates a margin of indetermination that makes the playing out of the primary phase of reenaction an improvisation. This is what gives the coming experience the character of a creative act, however generic it may be. The impetus of the reenaction, together with the flutter of potential felt on the fly, are formative forces. They are creative factors, conditioning the occasion without linearly determining it.

The distinction between vitality affect and atmosphere—between a dynamic cutting edge occupying the foreground of the event and its ontogenetic background—is not a hard boundary. *Atmosphere is diffuse vitality affect, and vitality affect is contracted atmosphere.* They are in mutual, inter-involved embrace, gradients of each other. Their ratios differ, on a continuum. Atmosphere can take over, experience remaining in its incipient co-motion as germ of thought and embryo of being, with no stand-out form or dramatic contour. This is what Deleuze calls "haecceity," from the Latin *haec*, "this" (Deleuze and Guattari 1987, 260–65). Haecceity: thisness. A sunset: this sunsetness. A storm: this storminess. This five-o'clock-of-a-summer-afternoon-ness. Haecceities are full of dim, potentialized and potentializing presences, softer, vague, more multitudinous still, than in the case of cutthroat anger. What makes itself felt is a certain quality of openness, a vague opening to formative forces, a susceptibility to influences, propensities, tendencies only hinted at, not sharp enough to pierce through and irrupt, not urgent enough to demand or command irreversible action.

Swaddled in haecceity, we are suspended in a world of potential. Or more precisely, in this region of the world of potential. This weather, this season, this age. Everything is background, and the background has risen to the foreground, activated, but diffusely, in a co-motional lull, reenacting nothing in particular. Here there is nothing but the quality of feeling this, just thus, in and for the moment. There is nothing but how, qualitatively, this is.

Atmosphere, as haecceity, is a pure expression of background potential. It does not compel action, but actions may bubble up. When they do, they are *free actions*: conditioned, influenced, even induced, but not caused per se. We may find ourselves taking a photo of the sunset; or sitting back, hardly noticing the five o'clock apéritif we poured; or musing about the passing of youth and the autumn of life. Actions of this kind, that we are lulled into, resonate with the atmosphere. They are felt less as separate expressions than as aspects of its expression. Their relation to the atmosphere, like the relation of atmosphere to the world, is expressive rather than causal.

Atmosphere, as haecceity, is not itself active exactly. Aflutter with vague presences, it cannot be dismissed as passive either. It has the tenor of an event, without actually being one. It is eventlike in its ephemerality. Like an event, it passes. It is an eventness without the actual event.

This is not a subjective impression. Atmospheres, like moods, according to Gilbert Ryle, "are not occurrences and do not therefore take place either publicly or privately." Moods, he says, are propensities of persons, "not acts or states" (1949, 83). They are the correlate of atmosphere on the level of the individual body. *Atmospheres are propensities of the world. Moods are atmospheres of the body.* Both are direct perceptions of a multitude of liminal motions and brewing potentials, stirring in indiscriminate co-motion.

It is more accurate to say, as Ryle says of moods, that an atmosphere is not so much an event as a *collection* of events. "Unlike motivations, but like maladies or states of the weather," they are "temporary conditions that in a certain way *collect* occurrences, but they are not themselves extra occurrences" (1949, 83, emphasis in the original).

The weather: a multitude of micro-events restlessly astir. Movements of particles, bodies, and rays, billows of winds and shifts and shafts of light, reflections and sounds, echoes and contrasts, overshadowings, all coming-together in a singular feeling. This is not a question of a mere collection, or a simple aggregate. It is an interweaving, to resonant effect. It is a coming-together in reciprocal activity, enveloped en masse in a background, surrounding and suffusing. The atmospheric feeling is the reality of the envelopment, resonantly expressing all of the contributory elements, but indiscriminately, wrapped in a global quality. The quality, neither act nor state nor extra occurrence, directly expresses the elements' *manner* of coming together, just now, just thus: the feel of the "how" of this collecting-together to expressive effect.

Atmospheres are *elemental* in this sense: locally composed in co-motion, indivisible in effect. The effect is of the nature of the *aesthetic*: a question of expression; of quality, of manner, style. Atmosphere is the elemental art of the world's surrounding and suffusing with potential, collecting in propensity, without extra occurrence.

The direct perception of atmosphere, neither public nor private, is not, as phenomenology would tend to style it, a "disclosure" of the world. It does include what has been, in that self-identity that is the immediate past as it now conditions what is coming next. But it also includes what could have been—and what will never be. The crispness of autumn is populated by sprites of lost loves and specters of futures dashed, vague presences, haunting and hinting, enticing and taunting.

Whitehead makes this point in relation to history. Every standout event of history is surrounded by an atmosphere. The atmosphere expresses the manner of that event's punctual occurrence. But it also converts the event from a point in history into a smudge: a historical field. It makes it vaguely epochal. Whitehead speaks of a historical event as being surrounded by a "penumbra" of potential that persists like a halo around its every recollection, giving it new life—in a sense making it immortal. Consider the Battle of Waterloo, he writes:

> This battle resulted in the defeat of Napoleon, and in a constitution of our actual world grounded upon that defeat. But the abstract notions, expressing the possibilities of another course of history which

would have followed upon his victory, are relevant to the facts which actually happened. We may not think it of practical importance that imaginative historians should dwell upon such hypothetical alternatives. But we confess their relevance in thinking about them at all, even to the extent of dismissing them. But some imaginative writers do not dismiss such ideas. Thus, in our actual world of today, there is a penumbra of eternal objects [qualitative potentials], constituted by relevance to the Battle of Waterloo. Some people do admit elements from this penumbral complex into effective feeling, and others wholly exclude them. Some are conscious of this internal decision of admission or rejection; for others the ideas float into their minds as day-dreams without consciousness of deliberate decision; for others, their emotional tone, of gratification or regret, of friendliness or hatred, is obscurely influenced by this penumbra of alternatives, without any conscious analysis of its content. (Whitehead 1978, 185)

Waterloo lives on in every present, in a penumbral complex of reciprocally intricated potentials whose vaguest, and most encompassing, expression is an obscurely influencing emotional tone lacking any conscious analysis or well-defined content. The sharpness of the emotional tone continually varies, as it journeys through history. At every stop, it holds a shifting kaleidoscope of futurity, in self-identity with the past—in this case an increasingly distant past, making serial ingress back into history, through an endless series of immediate pasts coinciding with new dawnings of the present. In some occasions, Waterloo resharpens into a fully determinate variation on its theme, honed into conscious focus, pointedly cutting its figure again, quivering with history-reshaping vitality affect. In others, it remains atmospheric. Waterloo accordions into and out of its penumbral complex.

In its punctual expressions in particular presents, as selectively reexpressed, the complex is transhistoric. But considered in itself, across its serial expression, it can only be considered unhistoric: because it is not all in any one of them. It is never fully actualized as a whole. As a vague, open, ongoing whole, it overspills the punctuality of any and all historical events. Its penumbral fringe tapers off in all directions into the virtual. Pure potential. Its transhistoric passage is the actual movement of the virtual through history. Through it, but never fully in it. It is the path of things, fellow-traveling, things that are of the world but not effectively in its history, because they bide their own time in potential: "eternal objects." Which are neither: neither eternal (rather: untimely) nor objects in any normal sense (because potential). This adds another to the list of oppositional categories with which this account began, that atmosphere falls between. One more to add:

The penumbral complex that expresses most globally, and vaguely qualitatively, as the affective tone of an epochal atmosphere is, ontologically speaking, "a hybrid between pure potential and actuality" (Whitehead 1978, 185–86). This is the mode of existence that Whitehead calls "propositional." He makes it abundantly clear that the proposition is not reducible to a logical statement. It is a proposition of potential, by the world, for this time and times to come, in serial turnover and penumbral variation. It is a traveling propensity of the world to make a qualitative difference, over and over again, grounded in the serially continuing identity of a self-varying event that in actuality was once and for all, but in potentiality is for all times.

Atmosphere is the *untimely*. It is the expression of the untimely character of the world. Nietzsche: "The unhistorical is like an atmosphere within which alone life can germinate and with the destruction of which it must vanish" (1997, 63–64).

Epochal atmospheres are the unhistorical of history, just as moods are the impersonal of subjective life, and weather the conditioning background of the events of nature. Neither subject nor object. Neither act nor state. Not an extra occurrence but the collecting of occurrences in qualitative expression. It is from the atmospheres of (through) history that a new event self-germinates, recharacterizing history by qualitatively changing its course, slightly or grandiosely as the case may be. Likewise, on the level of the individual body. The rise of an affective tone, and its global accompanying of the occasion's playing-out in the subjective form of mood is the *impersonal* elemental ground (surround) from which personality germinates. And serially regerminates to vary across the series of punctual events composing a life. Nature (weather; or, most globally, climate); history (untimely penumbra); individual life of the body (moody rise of an affective tone) . . . object (*aura*).

An object is obviously not subjective. But if atmosphere is the elemental reality of the envelopment of potential surrounding and suffusing a locus of occurrent becoming, then objects have atmosphere. If objects have atmosphere, and atmosphere is neither subjective nor objective, then we are paradoxically compelled to say that, propositionally speaking, an object is not objective. This is not a pipe. This is a pipeness. This is a pipelike nexus of qualitative variation. This object, in addition to its sharpened functions, obscurely influences through the manner in which it carries a penumbra of alternatives whose edges will never be exhaustively charted. The feeling of the inexhaustibility of the object, in process and as propensity, is its aura: that by which it outdoes its utility and, more generally, exceeds intentionality.

None of this occurs, exactly. But it all effectively appears. *It is not a question of reality versus appearance. It is a question of the reality of appearance.*

This account of atmosphere, and its vicissitudes, adds up to a serious challenge to ideological theories of historical transmission, as well as to any linear causal framework. Factoring the penumbral potential carried by atmosphere into the equation broadens the focus from the simple determinateness of the discrete to the complexity of the field conditions of its appearing, thus, such as it is, and always will have been. Again: conditioning, not causality. The difference, philosophical and practical, is enormous.

A process take on atmosphere makes its appearing an element of the real. More than that, it makes it elemental to the real. It obliges us to reconcile ourselves, practically and philosophically, with the untimely power of the vague.

Couplet 7

2005

Going Kinetic

What Is Decision in a Post-deliberative Age?

Freight Train of the Real

0.1 *The freight train comes down the track and it's filled way over there, and until it runs to the end, you can't see what's inside of it. And every time you try to reach in, it's like putting your hand in a gear box, because this depends on that, and this depended on that, and each piece depended on something else. And you think you're making a wise decision if you grab in the middle of it, but in fact, if all the layers that led to those things are not readdressed back up, you end up with a situation that is kind of ad hoc; it is—it's a perfectly responsible, isolated decision, but if you make a series of them, they end up random; they don't end up with coherence. And so all this appetite to kill this, or do that, or start this, my attitude is, look, we'll do it the best we can. And as I look back, I say to myself, "Not bad."*—Donald Rumsfeld, U.S. Secretary of Defense, 2001–6 (2002b)

1. "It's an iterative process," the strategist says. Making decisions, that is. The problem is that what you're making decisions about is on full throttle at high gear, in continuous forward hurtle. To get a handle, you try to back up. You try to uncover all the variables. But the backtrack isn't linear. The lines cross and divide into too many bifurcating paths. The paths buckle and fold into mutually obscuring layers. This depends on that, and this that depended on that other that, and everything depended on something else. The variables are all dependent. It's a tangle of interrelation. And although you're right in it, it's not in a stable way. It's more like you're thrown to the periphery by the centrifugal force of the advance. Your hands are not on the steering wheel. With one hand you're holding on to the roof, trying not to fly off and fall under the wheels. With the other you're reaching into the gear box to try to steer in some way by fiddling directly with the mechanism, hoping your fingers don't get crushed. All the while, you're wondering what the cargo is and if it's dangerous. If you're really good, you can make a perfectly responsible decision based on the best available information analyzed according to the most impeccable logic and causal reasoning. A perfectly responsible decision. The next time you're ready to make a decision the momentum has already carried you further down the track. In the meantime, the variables have reentangled. You're back where you were: smack in the middle of it. Only further down the line, moving that much faster. You begin to suspect that all you're doing with your high-powered analysis is grabbing at straws. It's all looking a tad less responsible and impeccable. In fact, after a series of the most well-considered decisions your steering is as good as random. The problem is that you have been acting serially along a linear-logical track, whereas the track itself has continued on full throttle at high gear putting everything all over again into an interdependence so closely knit that it's foolish to think you can extract one thread without pulling several others into a knot. After a certain point, it's clear that it's irresponsible to make responsible decisions. It's you that has to change gears. You have to draw on other resources. You don't just have information, logic, and analysis to go on. You have *appetite*. "Kill this," the strategist said. . . . "Not bad."

0.2. *[Secretary of State Colin] Powell, for one, saw that Bush was tired of rhetoric. The president wanted to kill somebody.*—Woodward (2002, 53)[1]

The Political Uncertainty Principle

2. *You can't know. You get all these leads and somebody says I think this or maybe he's there. And so you work it out, and eventually if everything works out, you catch him. And in this case [Osama bin Laden], we have not caught him. Therefore, we obviously are not close, or we are close, but we don't know, because we haven't caught him. We'll only know when he's caught how close we were.*—Rumsfeld (2003b)

3. You never know in the present. You can't know. You can only know retrospectively, when all is said and done. So why wait until the facts are in? After a year's study and planning and deliberation, you will be exactly as ready to make the decision as you were when you began.

0.3. Reporter: *We were ready to make those decisions last year.* Rumsfeld: *Sure. You're ready to make them before they're decidable.*—Rumsfeld (2002b)

4. It is not only that you are ready, it is right to decide before the decision is decidable. In a complex world, the freight train of the real doesn't stop for dawdlers. Every decision is in any case pre-ready: already as ready as it will ever be. There's no time to establish the facts beyond a reasonable doubt. Politics must operate according to an uncertainty principle proper to its level. Its cipher for Rumsfeld was the missing Osama bin Laden, Schrödinger's cat of political physics.

0.4. *Either he's alive and well, or alive and not well, or not alive.*—Rumsfeld (2002c)

5. The political uncertainty principle is thorough and inescapable. The epistemological status of the knowledge available to inform a decision at any particular moment is undecidable. Today's facts will always turn out to have been tomorrow's dead cat. To put it bluntly (in Ronald Reagan's [1988] words), *"facts are stupid things."* We might be close but not know it and get nowhere, or we might not be close and happen to pull on the right levers and end up right where we wanted to be. Only the future will tell. Rumsfeld explains that people who think they have sufficient knowledge in the present to make a certainty of their decision are assuming that they're "omniscient" when they are really only "free associating" (Rumsfeld 2002a). President Bush concurs. It amounts to the same thing if you base your decision on logical analysis of the facts or if you don't. As he said of his 2000 presidential campaign rival:

0.5. *The fact that he relies on facts—says things that are not factual—are going to undermine his campaign.*—Bush[2]

6. It did, and he lost.

0.6. True decision simply must operate in a different dimension to that of factuality. In the present, the status of one's available knowledge is always essentially undecidable. For all present intents and purposes, the factual and the nonfactual are in a state of overlap. Given this factual indistinction, what has *not* happened is always as pertinent to a decision as what *has* happened. A decision must be based on *both*.

7. Rumsfeld: *Reports that say that something hasn't happened are always interesting to me, because as we know, there are known knowns; there are things we know we know. We also know there are known unknowns; that is to say we know there are some things we do not know. But there are also unknown unknowns—the ones we don't know we don't know.* Reporter: *Excuse me, but is this [the fact that Saddam Hussein has weapons of mass destruction] an unknown unknown?* Rumsfeld: *I'm not going to say which it is.*—Rumsfeld (2002a)

Readiness to Anticipate

8. Sure. You can elaborate the epistemological categories of political reason. But it doesn't make a difference because you never know in advance which category will have applied to a given case. The best you can do is be *ready to anticipate*, in the words of philosopher Gilbert Ryle (1949, 230). Or in Bush's words, to "stay ahead of the moment" (quoted in Woodward 2002, 118). The object of political decision is not this fact or that fact but, again in Bush's phraseology, "any unforeseen event that may or not occur."³

0.7. *He is ready to anticipate, though he need not actually anticipate, how it will look, if he approaches it, or moves away from it; and when, without actually having executed any such anticipations, he does approach it, or move away from it, it looks as he was prepared for it to look. . . . No extra thinking or pondering, no puzzlings or reminiscences need be performed. . . . He need not wonder, make conjectures, or take precautions; he need not recall past episodes; he need do nothing that would be described as the thinking of thoughts.*—Ryle (1949, 230)

9. Ryle is describing the recognition of an object perceived in the present. He is concerned with what will have occurred prior to the event of recognition, at a level that belongs necessarily to the perception but is not yet it, not yet a recognized this or that. His example is a thimble. The point he is making is that there is an *infra-perceptual* preparation necessary to the emergence of a full-fledged perception. He calls it a *predisposition* or *propensity*. The propensity to perceive is not the thinking of thoughts. Yet when the perception does eventuate, "there is a sense in which he is thinking and not merely having a visual sensation" because the perception "is having a visual sensation in a thimble-seeing frame of mind" (1949, 230). Although the perceiver need do nothing that would be described as the actual thinking of thoughts, she is poised to have a thought "if there arises any call to do so." She is now ready to anticipate thinking, just as in the approach she had been ready to anticipate the perception.

10. Ryle is arguing, first, that when a perception actually occurs it is because it anticipated itself, only without the actual anticipation: purely in propensity. Deleuze would call this a virtual occurrence. The virtual event is the *propension* of the perception. It is the way in which perception always "stays ahead of the moment" of its occurrence. But the staying ahead is inseparable from the actual occurrence. It only *will have been* the propension of *this* perception once the perception has formed. The virtual occurring of perceptions is the perpetual "will have been" of *this* or *that* actual perception. It is the way that every perception has of always having been "ahead of its own moment." But the "ahead" of the moment is *of* the moment. It is of the nature of a present perception to arrive in the mode of already having been, purely in propensity. In other words, the way in which a perception precedes itself is not on a linear time line. The "pre-" is not a prior actual moment. It is the "pre-" of *this* moment *in* it. The "pre-"ing is the perception's immanence to its own occurrence: its always alreadiness for itself. This is less a *pre-*occurrence in the usual sense than an *infra-*occurrence: an infra-momentous perception; an infra-perception.

11. Ryle goes on to assert that the infra-perception envelops a thought that will potentially take conscious form. The propension of the event is as much an infra-thought as an infra-perception. When the perception actually occurs, the consequent thought will have already occurred as a virtual thought: there is a definite sense in which *the perceiver is thinking without the thought actually having to have occurred.* The infra-moment of the virtual event envelops a perception in propension, and the perception in turn envelops a thought. The thought doesn't need to actually occur, but it is *ready* to occur if *called upon.* The thought can be actualized as a conscious recognition, *if it is summoned.* A summoning comes from outside. It is extra to or in excess of what it addresses. The actual thought will occur if it is determined to do so by an extraperceptual summoning.

Ryle indicates the nature of the extraperception that draws the event of perception into actual thought. He specifies that the actual thought will occur if the perceiver is "linguistically equipped." It is language calling. Language calling culminates the perception in the form of an actual thought. Thought will have occurred virtually in any case. But when language calls, its occurrence culminates in an actual thought which carries the perception's event over into discourse. At that point, it will have occurred virtually *infra-linguistically*. The perception has left its immanence to itself to carry over into an immanence in language. It has become a recognizable content of discourse. It is important to note that this implies that *thought is actually collective*. Perception culminates in a fully articulated thought only when called upon to do so in interaction with language: in language interaction.[4]

12. The infra-moment of the event is as much the will-have-been of perception as the may-be of the thinking of thoughts. It is where thought and perception are held together in mutual propension. But it is also where they are held potentially apart. The perception may actualize without the thought being called upon to actualize as well. Where perception will have been, actual thought may be. Thought and perception always occur virtually together, but their virtual co-occurrence is also their potential divergence. The infra-moment is their mutual inclusion in a potential differentiation.

13. The infra-moment of co-occurrence is infra-perceptual, infra-conceptual, and infra-linguistic. It is infra-perceptual and infra-conceptual *spontaneously*, which is to say *necessarily*. Every perception that has been ready to anticipate itself will have also readily anticipated a thought. Every perception that actually comes to pass will have already passed through the virtuality of thought-in-perception. On the other hand, the co-occurrence is infra-linguistic *imperatively*: having been called upon; under the order of language. The thought-in-perception is an order-word.

0.8. *The order-word is the variable of enunciation that effectuates the condition of possibility of language. . . . We may begin from the following pragmatic situation: the order-word is a death sentence; it always implies a death sentence,* *even if it has been considerably softened, becoming symbolic, initiatory, temporary, etc. Order-words bring immediate death to those who receive the order, or potential death if they do not obey, or a death they must themselves inflict, take elsewhere. . . . Death, death; it is the only judgment, and it is what makes judgment a system. The verdict. But the order-word is also something else, inseparably connected: it is like a warning cry or a message to flee.*—Deleuze and Guattari (1987, 106–7)

0.9. "... the President wanted to kill somebody ..."

Preacceleration

14. All that is readily anticipated infra-temporally comes to pass through movement. What is anticipated without actually being anticipated, Ryle specifies, comes actually to pass through an "approach toward" or "a moving away from" the actuality it will have been. It is movement that induces the actualization. The readiness to anticipate then must have mutually included virtual movement in the same propension. When the movement actualizes, the infra-perception does as well, carrying with it its virtual charge of conception and the conception's potential answer to its calling into linguistic expression (a thought). The passage of virtual movement toward actuality is the active differentiator of what will have become separable dimensions of experience: perception, conception, and linguistic expression.

15. What Ryle called a "frame of mind" is a readiness to anticipate *movement*. It is more a *frame of body* than a frame of mind. Except that it isn't a frame either, it's an immanence. "Mind" as such only enters in, if it does, at the movement's last stop. The final answer to language calling is a thought. An actual thought comes last. When it comes, it will retrospectively determine the movement that led to it as having been a *movement of thought*. The movement of thought arises in a bodily premovement, infra- to any determinable category of experience. It is what Erin Manning (2009, 13–28) has called a bodily "preacceleration."

In an Enemy Frame of Mind

16. Ryle is talking about what immanently prepares perception in the unproblematic case where a perception that one was ready to anticipate will have actually come to pass. But what happens if you are not looking for so docile a thing as a thimble? What if what you are looking for is more like a needle in a haystack—except that you don't know that it's a needle? This is the situation of political decision, post-9/11, after it has taken security as its object and declared its mission to be "war on terror." The "terrorist" could be anyone, anywhere, coming from within or without, attacking by any means, at any time.

0.10. *When I was coming up, it was a dangerous world, and you knew exactly who they were. It was us versus them, and it was clear who them was. Today, we are not so sure who the they are, but we know they're there.*—Bush[5]

17. The terrorist is the unspecified threat.[6] *"It is increasingly difficult to determine exactly where a threat's going to come from"* (Rumsfeld 2002b). We are not sure who the they are or where they're coming from, but we know they're there and on their way: the terrorist is the *certainty of indetermination*. Military strategy and political decision must face that certainty.

18. *"The American people need to know that we're facing a different enemy than we have ever faced"* (Bush 2001)—a *"faceless enemy."*[7] Life-or-death decisions must be made in the face of the faceless enemy, or what Rumsfeld calls the *"virtual enemy"* (Shanker 2002).

0.11. *Reporter: What you do in this building [the Pentagon], what the military does, is completely real and solid. What are some of the new things you think this building and this military have to learn to fight an enemy that's virtual?*—Shanker (2002)

19. What do you do when what you're doing is real and solid but what you're doing it for, or toward, is virtual? The terrorist is loath to show his face. If one terrorist happens to show, there is certain to be another further down the tracks, no one knows when, where, or in what guise. The actual visual sensation Ryle speaks of is continually deferred, even when it occurs. When all is said and done—nothing ever is. You're never at the end of it. You're always in the middle. You're always ahurtle, trying not to be thrown off. All that decision has to go on is the preacceleration of an occurrence that will never fully eventuate, whatever may come. All that decision has to base itself on are incipient approachings-toward and movings-away-from in a perpetual infra-moment. *The propension of the event holds sway. The propension is indefinitely in suspension.* Whatever actual perception appears in the present, and whatever that perception allows actually to be anticipated, the essential is not there. The enemy has always already moved on. The essential is in the always elsewhere of an infra-momentous anywhen. Decision must act not on actual perceptions or even on actual anticipations. It must act in the element of the readiness to anticipate the actual. Its element is now infra-.

20. All decision is left with is the event's preacceleration. All it has to go on is the pre-movement of thought at a point where it is as yet virtually indistinguishable from a perception, and where it is already a movement, but only in propension.

0.12. *The enemy is not only a particular group, Bush said, but a frame of mind.*[8]

21. Except that it isn't a frame of mind, it's a frame of body. Except that the frame isn't that, but an immanence. And the unframed immanence of the body is a preacceleration of collective events, poised for the marching call of language, ready to anticipate the story.

0.13. *Everyone's so eager to get the story, before in fact the story's there, that the world is constantly being fed things that haven't happened. All I can tell you is, it hasn't happened. It's going to happen.*—Rumsfeld (2003a)

Predecision

0.14. *America will act against emerging threats before they are fully formed.*—Bush (2002a)

22. What you do is hold onto the propension. You pre-act on the threat's *emerging* in such a way as to prevent its fully forming. You *preempt* the threat. You reach into its propension and suspend it. That way, it never passes into an actuality. Although something else, following from your precipitate action, will eventuate. Preemption is productive, just not on a linear path, following a predictable line.

23. Preemption is what Rumsfeld was talking about when he said that the true decision is made before it is decidable. It is right to prejudge. If you wait for the evidence you will need to make a judgment based on what is actually decidable, you'll be too late. You will have handed the virtual enemy an ontological advantage. If you act in the actual, if you act on the factual, you will be in ontological complicity with the virtual enemy. It is imperative that you stay ahead of the moment. It is not only right to predecide, it is *only* right to predecide.

24. Lodging decision in the "pre"-ness of the infra-moment gives rise to a time paradox, as judged by the actual linear course of things. The *ahead* of the moment is in and of the moment, immanent to it. But in the case of threat what is ahead *of* the moment is also an indeterminate futurity. To preempt the threat you have to act on that futurity in the present. To the extent that you are successful, you have kept that futurity from ever actually being present. In other words, you have consigned it forever to the past. A suspended propension is a pure futurity arrested in its "pre"-ness so as to become a purely past futurity. To preempt threat, you must *act on time*—to deviate the time line. You must act in the infra-moment to arrest the unfolding of the present, and by so doing suspend the moment's future-tending in the past. Acting on time becomes a life-and-death political issue.

0.15. *If you are a terrorist, beware, because your last day was yesterday. . . . We are coming to arrest you.*—Leaflet dropped by U.S. Marines before the siege of Falluja (CBS 2004)

25. If you are terrorist, I can tell you today, you're dead yesterday, because we're coming to arrest you tomorrow.

0.16. *I have made good decisions in the past. I have made good decisions in the future.*—attributed to Bush[9]

26. "Good" decisions are future-past.

0.17. *I think what you'll find is, whatever it is we do substantively, there will be near-perfect clarity as to what it is. And it will be known, and it will be known to the Congress and it will be known to you, probably before we decide it, but it will be known.*—Rumsfeld (2003a)

The Tautology of Political Reason
(or the Politics of Tautological Reason)

0.18. *We will defend the peace by fighting a war.*—Bush[10]

27. The time paradox of right decision translates into a nonlinear logic, one that does not observe the rule of excluded middle. Like the ontological level it intends, its element is mutual inclusion. The logic of right decision favors three propositional forms. Each expresses as a particular form of ambiguity the undecidability of the time-loop into which decision must slip in order to operate in the infra-. Each form of ambiguity holds together in solidarity the difference between the futurity to be preempted and the predecision that will have preempted it.

28. The first propositional form is *oxymoronic*. This is the form favored by Bush, whose strategy as commander-in-chief is summed up in the proposition that ensuring peace means making war. The oxymoronic short-circuiting of logical progression can telescope into a reduplicative or a sheer redundancy, or exacerbate into a stark contradiction.[11]

29. Secretary of Defense Donald Rumsfeld specialized in the two other nonlinear logical forms, which are more technically demanding. One is a form of *equivocation* that consists in an intensive variation of the same proposition presented simultaneously in the negative, the positive, and the interrogative moods. We're close, we're not close ... can you tell which it is? The moods that are intensively varied correspond to the different moments of preemptive action that virtually coincide in the inframoment. The success of the preemption (he's dead) is held together with its failure (he's alive) in a way that presupposes preemption as the logical context. Thus this way of equivocating is in fact a practical device for *asserting* the principle of preemptive decision: what is presupposed goes without saying.

30. The third propositional form is the *tautology*: a suspension of linear reasoning in a logic-loop where the conclusion is already contained in the premise or the cause in its effect. This was practiced brusquely and to all appearances knowingly by Rumsfeld, who, to judge from his frequent musings on the status of knowledge, fancied himself the administration's resident epistemologist. It was also practiced with great regularity by Bush, in a more untrained but often also more poignant way.[12]

31. All of these are expressions of the temporal uncertainty principle that now governs political decision. As it appears on the logical level, the uncertainty principle generates a proliferation of nonlinear propositional forms which in their aggregate may be broadly termed tautological.

Blowback and Bow Waves

32. It is only right to predecide. Failing to do so exposes the nation to two mortal dangers. The dangers are courted when decision lodges itself in the present of its making rather than in the infra-momentous dimension of its future-past. If decision actually coincides with its own moment, it locates itself on a linear time line. At first sight this may seem safer than being swept up in the whirl and hurtle of the infra-moment. This is a misconception, because decision's lodging itself in the present moment does not segregate it from the past or future. It simply denies their immanent influence. Although it is indeed highly risky, predecision gives a fighting chance of success. Actually making a decision in time, rather than in such a way as to act on time, ensures failure. The problem is that the infra-moment of the future-past is immanent to any and every moment on any time line. The infra-moment is temporal compression or time-intensity: the immediate presence to each other of time's different dimensions. It is by virtue of this mutual inclusion that acting in the infra-moment is to act on time as such. If decision-making practice neglects or denies this complication, it is obliged to express itself extensively *along* the time line. It is simply displaced onto that axis. This manifests in one of two ways, both of which are triggered by making the mistake of actually anticipating rather than maintaining a perpetual state of readiness to anticipate.

33. *Reflexive pull-back* is a complication of the present caused by over-anticipation of future problems that a given decision might provoke. "Reflexive pull-back" is a Rumsfeldian term of derision used to describe

Bill Clinton's decision-making style, and by extension that of all liberals and Democrats (Woodward 2004, 19). Pull-back is a form of blowback. The undecidability of the present is segmented into a set of discrete possibilities which are then projected anticipatorily into the future. The future, of course, is still undecidable. The only difference is that now there are a host of very specific possibilities to be afraid of. The unspecified enemy is now a shadow army of thought-out consequences issuing from one's own decision-making process. We have met the enemy, and it is us. The more the decision is belabored, the more the past is studied in order to understand how it led to the present juncture, the more effort is made to extrapolate that line of development into the future, the more specific and scary the possible consequences become. The future possibilities swarm back on the present. You pull back reflexively. You are paralyzed by the future backwash. You hem and haw and end up not really deciding anything in particular, only hedging your bets.

34. The motto of reflexive pull-back is the Clintonian refrain: "*I feel your pain, I feel your pain*" (*New York Times* 1992). Pull-back is an affective malady of decision. Pull-back is affective blowback from anticipated future consequences. Its vector of infection is empathy. The underlying condition is an insufficiently developed appetite to kill, otherwise known as the "wimp factor." The wimp factor had been a major issue—if not the major issue—in the 2000 presidential campaign. Clinton, before passing the baton to Gore, had been dogged during his entire tenure as president by the perception, fanned by the neoconservatives who would achieve dominance in the Bush administration after 9/11, that he was un-warworthy and thus a danger to the security of the country. A president was a president only if he had the "right stuff" to be commander-in-chief. Try as he might to shake the perception that his decision-stuff wasn't right by intermittently dropping bombs (Somalia, the Iraq no-fly zone), Clinton never overcame the wimp factor. It spread by political party association through the 2000 presidential campaign to John Kerry in 2004. By then, the "war on terror" had made the role of president synonymous with that of commander-in-chief. Suffering from reflexive pull-back was henceforth interpreted as a sign of weakness. It opens an empathetic door to enemy attack. In a particularly effective Bush campaign television ad, the danger of reflexive pull-back was depicted as a swarming pack of wolves. It was obvious at a glance that they did not lack the appetite to kill. There is little doubt as to the fate of the frolicking American children whose only sin, we surmise, had been to be too young to vote for Bush.

35. With reflexive pull-back, the political uncertainty principle appears as a movement back from the future on the linear axis of time: the reverse movement of affective blowback from possible futures. The other linear decision disorder moves uncertainty forward from the present into the future in a *bow wave*. It is what happens when you make the procedural mistake Rumsfeld warned against of making studied decisions in serial fashion, as if you could steer a clear course in the troubled waters of the world when you know you will inevitably drift and founder.

36. To understand this danger, you have to transfer to a boat. You're no longer on a freight train rushing headlong down the tracks. You are navigating in a ship, hands firmly on the helm. You look around, assess the situation, studiously anticipate all the variables you can, and logically factor them in. You make perfectly responsible decisions. For the present, it's clear sailing. The problems come later, in the "*years uncovered now in the future.*"[13] What you haven't factored in is the unpredictable follow-on effect of today's decisions on tomorrow's complexity. Your decisions will come back to haunt you because when you cover present contingencies you inevitably *uncover* future ones. This is because you have addressed a specific set of actual contingencies by building upon certain capacities for response that you already have, when what you are trying to respond to is the unspecified threat of a virtual enemy whose capacities for attack are indeterminate.

37. *Uncovering the future* means that you make certain maneuvers in preparation for the future. You specifically prepare to meet expected challenges, perhaps by commissioning particular weapons systems. This gives your navigational decisions a forward momentum. As you plow through the murky waters of the present toward the future, the thrust of your bow throws a forward wake whose amplitude is proportional to the weight of your onboard decisions. For example, if you are carrying a given number of stealth bombers that you responsibly opted for over developing bunker-busting nuclear missiles, the weight of that decision uncovers contingencies that might otherwise have been covered. Farther ahead, it will be too late. You won't have them when you need them. The weight of the decision to take stealth bombers on board has sent forth a bow wave that has pushed aside the possibility of responding to bunker-bustable threats when you need to.

38. The bow wave disorder is a follow-on effect rather than a blowback effect. It moves forward from the present to the future, rather than backward from the future to the present. It limits possibilities rather than massing them into a swarm. Its vector of infection is not empathy but measured decision. It is a rational malady rather than an affective one. It is not paralyzing, but can be just as lethal. What it shares with reflexive pull-back is that it projects political uncertainty onto a linear time-axis by neglecting the necessity for predecision.

39. The right decision is to have done with linearity. In a way, this brings you back into the moment. But the moment is not the discrete present. It is an indeterminate *something doing*.—James (1996a, 161)

0.19. *All of a sudden, here we are. Once in awhile I'm standing here, doing something. And I think, "what in the world am I doing here?" It's a big surprise.*—Rumsfeld[14]

40. Right decision is not deliberative. It does not develop incrementally in step-by-step consideration. It strikes like surprise. It cuts into, or lurches out of, the flow of the present. But the present is not an ordered flow from past remembered landmarks in the direction of an intended future destination: all of a sudden, here you are. Your being here is no more a presence of mind than it is a conscious navigation through a landscape. What in the world am I doing here? You're standing there, in what can only be—given that you find yourself again secretary of defense of the most powerful nation on earth—a most decisive frame of body. It is not that the present is readying itself to call up a decision. Rather, your reawakening to yourself in a posture of decision has called the present to attention. The present is less formative of the decision than it is predisposed to it by a flash of alertness. Left to its own devices, the present is an indeterminate something doing, more an eddy of being than a laminar flow of reflection, more a vague agitation than an orientation, or perhaps an unfocused background without a foreground figure, or a medium of nothing doing in particular. The present only takes shape in, and as, the imminence of a decision that will have surpassed it. *Surprise* is how the future feels when it strikes against the present. Sudden alertness. A tensed readiness to anticipate anything, against a vaguely apprehended background of an ongoing of activity. Surprise makes the present pass before its time. Barely there yet, and already interrupted by the knock of the future. Just awakening to itself, and instantly thrown into the past of the flash decision obliged by surprise. The something doing drops back before a something suddenly done.

41. "*I think we agree, the past is over*" (Bush).[15] The actual recollected past, the one you are tempted to readdress as you sail through the landscape of a deliberative present, that past is over. Suddenly, here we are, in the future-past.

0.20. *The first step to take, then, is to ask where in the stream of experience we seem to find what we speak of as activity. . . . Now it is obvious that we are tempted to affirm activity wherever we find anything going on. Taken in the broadest sense, any apprehension of something doing, is an experience of activity. . . . Bare activity then, as we may call it, means the bare fact of event or change. . . . The sense of activity is thus in the broadest and vaguest way synonymous with the sense of "life."*—James (1996a, 160–61)

42. The art of governing is to *have decided* the "bare fact of event or change." Governance must then make itself, in the broadest and vaguest way, synonymous with life as *bare activity*. Or more surprisingly, with its decisive *interruption*—the bare fact of event or change preemptively cut into.

0.21. *The word "decision" is used in its root sense of "cutting off." . . . "Decision" cannot be construed as a causal adjunct of an actual entity. It constitutes the very meaning of actuality.*—Whitehead (1978, 43)[16]

43. Right decision is not pulled-back, blown-back, or bow-waved. It is in actuality "future-leaning" (Rumsfeld, quoted in Woodward 2002, 19) in the sense of *proactive* (in the strong sense of active before the fact).

0.22. *I will not wait on events.*—Bush[17]

Going Kinetic

0.23. *You know, which I find amusing. But I'm also—I've been to meetings where there's a kind of "we must not act until we're all in agreement." . . . Well, we're never going to get people all in agreement about force and the use of force. . . . But action—confident action that will yield positive results provides a kind of slipstream into which reluctant nations and leaders can get behind.*—Bush[18]

44. Action is confident action. Confident action is the use of force. The use of force is decision. Agreement, on the other hand, is decision-*making*. Although they share syllables, decision and decision-making are opposites. As the participle indicates, decision-making is open-ended. It eddies in the present, interminably, bogged down in indefinite activity. It's not only not confident action; it's no kind of action. It doesn't know how to interrupt bare activity with a decisive cut. It spins its wheels in the quicksand of deliberation. This sinks decision. Agreement must be predecided, or it won't float. A decisive cut through decision-making has to be made.

45. "Action" is not really the right word. Action carries connotations of well-aimed intent and follow-through. "A man of action" never asks "What in the world am I doing here?" The traditional figure of the man of action knows where he is, where he wants to go, and how to go about getting there. He is confident in this sense. He doesn't dally, but neither does he charge heedlessly ahead. Although he doesn't charge heedlessly ahead, he never second-guesses himself. He does not stop to understand your pain. He is capable of being deliberative and consultative, but when time is of the essence and force of circumstance bears down, he can skip the mediation and take the helm directly. He is decision-making retracted into a single body, standard bearer of the wisdom of nations. Churchill in World War II was a man of action. George W. Bush in Iraq and Afghanistan is no Churchill. "Action" and "confidence" as applied to him must have a different meaning.

0.24. *Slipstream, n.: area of reduced air pressure and forward suction immediately behind a rapidly moving racing car.*—Webster's

46. "Going kinetic" is the right term, rather than "action." "Rumsfeld and other White House insiders used the term for the active response" (Woodward 2002, 150). Decision as active response in the preemptive context cuts through decision-making. It is a launching straight into movement. It cuts in upstream of action, flush with its preacceleration. It does this in such a way as to catapult readiness to anticipate that is bare activity straight into kinetic, even frenetic, movement. Decision in a flash. The cut and run.

47. Forget the boat. The flash of decision is the streak of a race car in instantaneous acceleration. To be "forward-leaning" in decision is to be forward-sucking in movement. Rather than plodding a bow wave, you jump the gun. You take leave so abruptly of present company that you leave a vacuum in your wake. This area of low communicational pressure creates a slipstream into which the other parties fall, swept up in the momentum of your preaccelerated departure.

48. The other cars at the starting line either fall in behind you or fall behind events. If they fall in, they keep pace. They remain as immediately behind you as your departure was suddenly ahead of the moment. The vacuum in which they find themselves is that of the present, voided of its participling content: deliberat*ing*, negotiat*ing*, persuad*ing*, implement*ing*. This is a vacuum-unpacked present, reduced to a speedy immediate-past twinning a flash-forward acceleration.

0.25 *Induce, vt. (fr. L in + ducere to lead—more at "tow").*—Webster's

49. To lead, to tow. Going kinetic is to lead others to fall in by producing a powerful movement with its own tow. The slipstream "into which reluctant nations and leaders get behind" is the present evacuated of its articulable content in such a way as to convert it into pure impulsion, high-pressured compulsion.

0.26. *We'll let our friends be the peacekeepers and the great country called America will be the pacemakers.*—Bush[19]

50. The vacuum, being nothing, does not move. Being empty, it has no motive or locomotive force. Its impulsion is not mechanistic, in the manner of a linear cause pushing at a point of application from behind. What falls into the slipstream is moved by the pressure *differential* between its sudden emptiness, the racing ahead out of nowhere, and the turbulence left to either side in the wake of that precipitate movement. In other words, the follow-on movement sucking in those behind is a *field effect*. Its triggering is *relational*, not part-to-part mechanistic in the old plodding, classical empirical way. A field effect is a *quasi-cause* acting on the actual at the level of the virtual (by cutting into the readiness to anticipate).

51. Race car or no, we are still riding the freight train of the real. But we have made a vacuum of its movement. We have levitated it from the rails. Enough of that linearity. We are now fielding the real as we hurtle along. Others have no choice but to relate to that. Their future-past must fall in with our cut and run.

0.27. *The [president's] aide said that guys like me [a journalist] were "in what we call the reality-based community" which he defined as people who "believe that solutions emerge from your judicious study of discernible reality." I nodded and murmured something about enlightenment principles and empiricism. He cut me off. "That's not the way the world really works anymore," he continued. "We're an empire now, and when we act, we create our own reality. And while you're studying that reality—judiciously, as you will—we'll act again, creating other new realities, which you can study too, and that's how things will sort out. We're history's actors . . . and you, all of you, will be left to just study what we do."*—Suskind (2004)

Gut Going

0.28. *I'm not a textbook player. I'm a gut player.*—Bush[20]

0.29. *I'm also not very analytical. You know I don't spend a lot of time thinking about myself, about why I do things.*—Bush[21]

52. That's the kind of confident he is. He has the confidence of the gut: a feeling, not exactly a perception, let alone a well-deliberated thought. Because if you can't wait on events, you can't wait and see. There is no "discernible reality" to study. Just the reality to be created by the slipstream of the decision. Decision can only make the cut by entrusting itself to intuition.

0.30. *I'll tell you this, we don't sit around messaging the words. I got up there and just spoke. What you saw was my gut reaction coming out.*—Bush[22]

53. Leading by gut feeling pertains to Ryle's readiness to anticipate: "No extra thinking or pondering, no puzzlings or reminiscences need be performed. . . . He need not wonder, make conjectures, or take precautions; he need not recall past episodes; he need do nothing that would be described as the thinking of thoughts." However, the cut of the gut performs a preemptive twist on this. The general formula for readiness to anticipate was given earlier as "*the will-have-been of perception as the may-be of thought*": thought enveloped in the preacceleration of an anticipated perception. Reformulated by the gut for "confident action," it goes: "*the may-be of thought as the will-have-been of feeling.*" Perception is short-circuited, and with it anything that would normally be described as the thinking of thoughts, including the clear memory of past perceptions. To feel, perchance to think? (Or something like it, in its place?)

The Thought Bovine

0.31. *Then I went for a run with the other dog and just walked. I was able to—I can't remember what it was. Oh, the inaugural speech, started thinking that through.*—Bush[23]

54. I don't spend a lot of time thinking about things. It's a bit fuzzy. I was running. But I was walking. Other dog. Can't remember. Oh, thinking.

55. When the decider goes kinetic under leisure conditions and there is no immediate decision to be made, there is something like reflection that kicks in and rides the slipstream, merging with the vacuum it produces. Movement launches something like thinking, as gut feeling launches movement. Movement is to reflection (or something like it) what gut feeling is to the movement of decision.

0.32. *Bush does not like chitchat when he jogs. . . . Spotting a herd of cattle, he says simply "bovine." Minutes pass before he says another word.*—Dowd (2002)[24]

Ruminations

0.33. *I'm the commander in chief—see, I don't need to explain—I do not need to explain why I say things. That's the thing about being the president. Maybe somebody needs to explain to me why they say something, but I don't feel like I owe anybody an explanation.*—Bush (quoted in Woodward 2002, 126)

0.34. *I think if you know what you believe, it makes it a lot easier to answer questions. I can't answer your question.*—Bush[25]

0.35. *If you don't stand for anything, you don't stand for anything. If you don't stand for something, you don't stand for anything.*—Bush[26]

Conclusion

0.36. *I think the precedent is bad of having to go out and make your case publicly because we may not have enough information to make our case next time, and it may impair our ability to preempt against the threat that may be coming at us. . . . Are we going to have to make a case every time?*—Rumsfeld[27]

0.37. *We don't believe in planners and deciders making the decisions on behalf of Americans.*—Bush (quoted in Mitchell 2000)

0.38. *I'm the decider.*—Bush (CNN 2006)

Coda (2020)

In thinking about post-deliberative politics, or what is now commonly called the post-truth political world, it is important to remember that it did not begin with Donald Trump. Nor did it begin with George W. Bush. It passed a threshold with Ronald Reagan, and had more than a little to do with the administration of George H. W. Bush and the Gulf War.[28] The prefix "post-" is misleading. It is less that we have passed a turning point where all that came before has become obsolete and a whole new period has dawned. Instead, a mode of political operativity—an operative logic—has reached a threshold of consistency that has consolidated it in the sense of *potentializing it to recur*. The operative logic described in this essay haunts the social field, ready to rise to relative dominance on the political level, while propagating into new varieties in other domains (military theory, the economy, to name just two).[29] The "post-" is not an ever-after. It is decidedly more like a "Not again?!"

What has been enunciated here through the words of the Bush administration is an iterative force. It recurs, in a punctuated series. A mode of consistency has gained an ever-ready potential to return. Its operation short-circuits deliberative decision-making by a cut of decision returning to the infra-level of bare activity, where feeling, perception, thought, and discourse are stirring together, not yet fully formed, in readiness to anticipate. It is itself a readiness to anticipate. It is a looming. It lies in potential, ready and waiting to strike and set the dominant rhythm for a time. It lies in wait as a processual affordance that can be "called upon" by force of circumstance playing out in a complex ecology of other modes of power. This is what makes it definitive of this period: its ever lurking. Its always potentially affording itself. Its haunting of the social field, as a dominant rhythm in waiting. A shorthand for this mode was chosen in this essay to emphasize that when this rhythm actuates its mode involves a future-past action on time itself. The shorthand term is "preemption": politics preaccelerated.

For each case in the iterative series the conditions allowing this operative logic to "take," to rise to relative dominance, will vary. The exact texture it presents will be unique. It is not one thing. An operative logic is a matrix. Each return the matrix generates has to be thought through in its own right. It does not suffice to content oneself with defining it in the negative, simply as lacking the deliberative decision-making and "reality-based" approach that is purported (rather far-fetchedly) as having effectively been in force in the pre-"post." The singularity and positivity of each iteration needs to be looked at. The Trumpian iteration of post-deliberative politics is no exception. There is still a long way to go before the terms are found in which to express its singularity and mutant positivity. Currently, few accounts go further than characterizing it in negative terms, moralistically mourning what is "no longer."

The distraught tone palpable in this essay—a kind of time capsule of the affect of a certain horrified observer of the Iraq War period—should not be interpreted as proposing a return to the deliberative politics of yore. The representative democracy it was synonymous with, and the public sphere upon which that notion of democracy was built, have fallen apart at the seams. To say that they are "in crisis" is an understatement. They are ready for the undertaker. They lack the vitality to compete with "deciders" of the Bush or Trump kind. They lack the wherewithal to brake the neofascisms following in their slipstream. The tone of distress in this essay should be understood as a call for a specifically antifascist political counterpractice of the infra-.[30]

2005

Barely There

The Power of the Image at the Limit of Life

Barely There

A near absence, or borderline presence, dominated US politics for the first three months of 2005. Terri Schiavo was "barely there" (Ulick 2005) and looming large, at the vanishing point of life's expressive powers, on the borderline between life and death, consciousness and oblivion, where thought and language flicker, barely, or just fade away. The political and social forces at play in the United States, from the local to the federal level, rallied around and rearrayed. It was not the first time, nor would it be the last, that this vanishing point would be the organizing point of politics and power in the United States. In fact these descents into the vanishing point occur so frequently, in so many forms, to similarly far-reaching effect, that it appears that the "barely-there" marks the threshold of a mode of operation of power. No longer sovereign, disciplinary, or even biopolitical (to borrow Michel Foucault's typology),[1] this regime draws on all three in a field defined by no one in particular among them. Paradoxically, the serial descent into the vanishing point of life positively constitutes, on the rebound, a mode of thought correlated to the new regime of power—one that is no less rigorously pragmatic for being directly collective.[2]

Terri Schiavo had starved herself into a coma. In 1990 she suffered a cardiac arrest as a consequence of anorexia. Her brain was severely damaged by lack of oxygen, leaving her in a "persistent vegetative state" from which doctors said she would never recover. Rehabilitation efforts having failed, she was kept alive on a feeding tube. Her fate became the focus of an intense and extraordinarily complicated debate that drew out into a fifteen-year struggle involving an array of concerned parties approaching the issue from different angles. The core issue was whether to remove the feeding tube. Michael Schiavo, Terri Schiavo's husband, said yes. He argued that it had been his wife's explicit wish that she not be kept alive in the event she fell into such a state. He became her legal guardian in order to obtain legal power to make this life-and-death decision. Terri Schiavo's parents, Mary and Bob Schindler, said no. They pointed out that she was a devout Catholic and would never act against the Church's teaching on suicide. For them, it was an issue of the sanctity of her soul. The medical profession, more attuned to the life of the body, came down on Michael Schiavo's side. From the medical perspective, a person whose vitality had ebbed to a vegetative state and who had no prospect of improvement had no "meaningful quality of life" and was (although they would never say it in so bald a way) as good as dead. It would be a mercy to let her die all the way. The conservative Christian right-to-life movement mobilized its considerable resources in support of the Schindlers. On the other side, the right-to-die movement, which shares the medical profession's criterion of quality of life and militates for the right to "die with dignity," pushed for Terri Schiavo's apparent wishes on the matter to be honored. The disability rights movement countered the medical profession's "as good as dead" perspective with the pointed rejoinder "not dead yet." They raised a host of questions, including who is in a position to judge quality of life, what the nature of a minimally conscious state is, how dependable a diagnosis excluding recovery in coma cases is, and the danger of a slippery slope where the same logic used in this case to justify proxy life-or-death powers might be extended to disabled people of many kinds (Johnson 2005). Practically, the movement was in political alliance with the Christian right but coming from a completely different set of concerns. They were not calling for an intercession of sovereign power but for a biopolitics limited to the first clause in its formula (to make live) severed from the second clause accepted by the medical establishment (to let die).

What happened in early 2005 was that the controversy amplified to the highest levels of government, peaked, and came to a resolution. A state appeals court denied a petition from the Schindlers to reopen the case after Michael Schiavo won a long series of court battles over his right to remove the feeding tube. Prodded by the Christian right, the state legislature of Florida, where the Schiavos and Schindlers lived, passed an emergency bill authorizing Jeb Bush, the state governor and brother of President George W. Bush, to intervene and order the feeding tube be reinserted, which he did. The law was subsequently ruled unconstitutional, and the tube was withdrawn. Now the US Congress stepped in. A law was passed, cosponsored in the Senate by a supporter of the disability rights movement (Tom Harkin) and a supporter of the Christian right (Rick Santorum). It gave the Schindlers, and only the Schindlers, a special right to a federal court appeal after they had lost at the state level and the US Supreme Court had refused to take the case. This unprecedented act was dubbed "the Palm Sunday Compromise" to underline the religiosity of the act. It was eagerly signed into law by President Bush, but was quickly declared unconstitutional. Elsewhere, the waters had been muddied, and the integrity of the pro-life forces called into question, by the release of a confidential memo written by a Florida Republican operative arguing that the case offered a golden opportunity for the party to exploit in order to shore up right-wing support in an important battleground state. Governor Bush, however, did not intervene further, in spite of intense lobbying from the right. The tube was removed again, and Terri Schiavo died.

This is a very brief sketch, omitting many episodes and details, of an epic political story. The reason it is brought up here is not to take sides or assess the merit of the arguments, but rather to point out the number, diversity, and complexity of the arguments, underlining the fact that this thicket of political forces was activated around a point of indiscernibility between life and death, thought and vegetation. Terri Schiavo's silence, at this point of undecidability, became a cacophonous *node of collective expression*. Many lines of expression, discursive and affective, were energized by it, taking off from it into their own circuits and circling back on each other to engage in struggle. A whole field of power swirled around one woman's borderline animate body and the near absence, or minimal presence, of her own powers of expression. The multiple lines of expression that burgeoned around her implicated different modes of power, co-activated in their agonistic difference from each other, but also in potential co-composition, all in orbit around a "barely-there" at their collective heart.

Michael Schiavo was claiming what can only be called a *sovereign power*, defined by Foucault as the command power to put to death or to let live.[3] Significantly, he was claiming that sovereign power as a private individual. This privatization of sovereignty is a defining characteristic of the current landscape of power. Sovereignty has been interiorized. It can be exercised with the approval of a justice system and as an internal variable of it, devolved to a private sphere that is no longer on a scale with the territory of the state, but cuts to the contours of the individual body. In this incarnation, the sovereign power to command death can only be exercised over the life of a body at the limit, close to a point of indistinction with death. This is the point at which the medical profession's life-sustaining powers reach their limit, and are recognized to be at that limit by the juridical system. The sovereign power takes over when the medical-juridical system's power for life, or biopower, passes it the baton of the feeding tube. The figure of sovereign power in play here is thus circumscribed by biopower. Biopower relinquishes its hold and passes on the baton at what it medically deems a *natural* limit of the life, after which it would be "artificial" to sustain it. Sovereignty is defined not as politically salient but as naturally redundant. Its redundancy with nature is the condition laid down for its legitimacy by the larger biopolitical system as a province of which it is exercised.

The executor of the sovereign command power, on the other hand, acts as a responsible subject of law. He or she is presumed to have internalized such norms of behavior as are judged necessary for managing one of the private decisional spheres that is assumed by, and subsumed under, the umbrella of a well-ordered public sphere. In other words, the individual's accession to sovereign power is predicated on his or her interiorization of *disciplinary power* in the guise of the normalized citizen subject. The relay point between biopower and sovereign power coincides with an instantiation of disciplinary power, the history of which is chronicled by Foucault (1977) in *Discipline and Punish* as its progressive becoming-immanent to the social field.[4] One terminus of that history is arrived at here. It becomes nested into the fabric of a heterogeneous field of power, at the level of the normativized individual.

At this point where modes of power complexly overlay one another in a such a way as to enable a gear-shifting between them, Terri Schiavo's parents argued that the gears should be disengaged. The Schindlers located the case at an equally complex overlay, but in relation to a different limit. They argued that the medical-juridical system should be strictly held to its biopolitical calling of exercising power *for* life. Foucault's celebrated formula for *biopower* is "the power to make live or let die" (2003, 241). The Schindlers, like the disability rights movement, wanted to hold it exclusively to the first clause. All measures, however extraordinary, should be taken to keep their daughter alive. This stance, however, was not legitimated by recourse to a logic internal to the law of the land, nor one pertaining to biopower as such. It appealed to a different figure of sovereign power, one which, far from being a dependency of government or interiorizable in the individual, is transcendent to human affairs. The concern was not life at a natural limit, but life beyond nature, everlasting. Human government should shelve its own principles and bend to the supernatural command of the will of God. The Schindlers were returning to an absolutist model of sovereignty, of the highest order. Historically, it was this highest-order sovereignty that had descended to earth to become-immanent to the social field, taking mundane shelter in the interiorized judgment of the well-disciplined individual subject wielding Cartesian control over a normalized body. Schiavo's parents were ascending the path disciplinary power had descended, returning it to its transcendent source. In the contemporary context, that amounted to demanding that government cease gear-shifting and suspend its own operations, so that extraordinary measures could be taken to sustain a life. In other words, it was demanding that government act, exceptionally, as the executor of God the Sovereign's will by ceasing to execute its own and letting those acting according to God's wishes to step in unimpeded. The appeal was explicitly addressed to political leaders claiming a personal relationship with God: Governor Jeb Bush, President George W. Bush, the religious right contingent in Congress, and the Christian right generally. These politicians were being called upon to act as God's servants rather than as public servants.

What was being suggested corresponds to Foucault's definition of the coup d'état (2007). In the history of state sovereignty, the coup d'état is not the forcible transfer of state power. It is precisely a *"suspension of* . . . laws and legality," an "extraordinary action" whereby the state acts "on itself, swiftly, immediately, without rule, with urgency and necessity, dramatically," responding to "a pressing and urgent event" due to which it must "of necessity free itself" from the law (261–62). Foucault's absolutist coup d'état is the "state of exception" that Giorgio Agamben (1998), following Schmitt, sees as the constitutive act of sovereignty: "decision in absolute purity," in this case moral purity, where "the law is outside of itself." "The exception that defines the structure of sovereignty . . . does not subtract itself from the rule; rather, the rule, suspending itself, gives rise to the exception. . . . The exception is a kind of exclusion. What is excluded from the general rule is the singular case" (15–17).[5] The Schindlers and their fundamentalist Christian allies wished the state to act, as if from outside of itself, on the *singularity* of Schiavo's case (with respect to her unique immortal soul). The law passed by the US Congress was a special act that suspended normal governmental principle and procedure and applied *only* to her. This suspension of the law was foiled in the end by the highest level of the judiciary, but not before producing a dramatic breach rife with political reverberations. The law that actually passed was a "compromise." Rather than commanding that the feeding tube be reinserted, it mandated an extralegal supplementary go at the courts, as an exception applicable only in this case.

The Schindlers and their allies were operating at the point where biopolitics meets sovereign power flowing directly from its transcendent source, in contravention of the normal course of government. This was sovereign power reasserting itself from that absolute limit where it comes to itself from outside the state's rule of law, swooping down from above via congressional fiat to shunt aside the interiorized figure of sovereignty as immanent to the social field, whose secular margin of maneuver is cramped by disciplinary normativity and biopolitical regulation.

"The situation created in the exception has the peculiar characteristic that it cannot be defined as a situation of fact or a situation of right" (Agamben 1998, 18). Sovereign command is not a situation of empirical fact because the measures taken do not follow necessarily from their immediate antecedents as a logical next step. They are not the orderly effect of a causal chain. They effect themselves, quickly, immediately, and rulelessly, in suspension of the ordered progressions organizing the social field. Because they suspend legal principle as well as the orderly progressions flowing from it, they do not constitute a situation of right. Neither empirical fact nor deduction from juridical principle, the singular situation breaks into logical and discursive unfoldings, to interrupt them. The state of exception irrupts. Its irruption is not empirical, juridical, or logico-discursive.

Gut and God

President George W. Bush, who played a prominent role in the Schiavo affair through his moral support for and emergency signing of the law, was a frequent point of irruption of exceptional measures. The most far-reaching example was the command or "pure decision" to commit his country to war in Iraq. Like all of his major decisions, it did not come as a logical end-conclusion. It was a foregone conclusion. As early as November 2001, just weeks after 9/11, Bush was asking Secretary of Defense Donald Rumsfeld what the invasion plan was for Iraq (Woodward 2004, 1–8). This was before there had been any discussion in the cabinet or National Security Council on the issue. In fact, "at no time did the president sit down with his war cabinet and discuss" the merits of an invasion (Thomas 2004). Secretary of State Colin Powell was advised of the decision months later, in January 2003. "The whole conversation took twelve minutes. That was what passed for debate in the Bush war cabinet" (Thomas 2004, 22; Woodward 2004, 269–74). As the leak of the infamous "Downing Street Memo" recounting British and American intelligence discussions would later verify, the decision to go to war was a pre-decision, made months prior to its announcement, with the intervening time used to "fix" the facts about the presence of weapons of mass destruction in Iraq.[6]

This approach was not peculiar to the 9/11 context. After resigning as head of the Environmental Protection Agency in May 2003, Christine Todd Whitman complained, "In meetings, I'd ask if there were any facts to support our case. And for that, I was accused of disloyalty!" (Suskind 2004). "Did he ever explain what he was doing? 'Of course not,' he said, 'I'm the commander—see, I don't need to explain—I do not need to explain why I say things. That's the interesting thing about being the president. Maybe somebody needs to explain to me why they say something, but I don't feel like I owe anybody an explanation'" (Woodward 2002, 126). When issues did come up in policy meetings, rather than explaining or debating or weighing evidence or establishing principle, Bush saw his role as "commander." What this meant to him was asking "questions that aren't worth asking" in order "to be provocative." He watched how his advisors reacted to the provocations, and then made a gut decision based on their reactions. "With Bush," explained Secretary of Defense Dick Cheney, "it's all gut; it's visceral" (Gibbs 2002–3). Bush had absolute intestinal faith.

Bush had undoubting confidence in his visceral decisions because he was convinced they came to him through divine guidance. But "I'm surely not going to justify war based on God" (Thomas 2004, 23). Although he experienced his decisions as faith-based, he did not justify them doctrinally. The divine inspiration behind their irruption was no secret, but their mode of public appearance was more the manner in which they struck: bodily, affectively, as a gut feeling that came less as a conclusion than directly in the form of confidence.

For members of what Bush and his aides disparagingly called the "reality-based community"—defined by a senior advisor as people who "believe that solutions emerge from judicious study of discernible reality" (Suskind 2004)—it came as little comfort that the dispensation from situations of fact and situations of right came with a blessing on mental blankness. One Republican congressional ally, Newt Gingrich, remarked that when Bush encountered new situations, "he cue[d] off things he probably [didn't] even remember" (Brookhiser 2003, 63). With little need to build or orient according to logical and discursive progressions, memory becomes expendable. Gut decision-making works reflexively, rather than reflectively: automatically on cue, like a bodily reflex.

George W. Bush operated as a presidential barely-there practicing intestinal sovereignty.

They Said She Said

The implications of this concatenation of contrasting barely-theres, Schiavoist and Bushist, for the nature of the contemporary field of power are complex. One indication is that the sovereign power of absolute decision has learned how to embed itself at the very heart of the field of power, but does not define its overall mode of power. It gets miniaturized and privatized, enveloped in the biopolitical functionings of the public sphere and the administrative state. It can be gear-shifted back into exercises of disciplinary power, or in the exceptional event trump both biopower and discipline with a suprapersonal transcendence. But even the transcendent exercise of sovereign decision has to make its peace with the immanent fabric of the social field by filtering back down for its implementation, through the innermost folds of the body in Bush's gut case, or through the executive or legislative branches of government to the ground-level policing of individual actions in the case of the Schindlers' strategy. In both cases, but in different ways, its deployment revolves around the barely-there—where life is at the limit of its ability to affect and be affected. To get at what the overall mode of power might be today, it is the political operationalization of this affective limit that must be understood. We might begin by listening to Terri Schiavo, speaking (barely) from there.

It is indeed reported that she spoke.

This is what she said: "Ah . . . waaaa. . . . Ahh waaaa."

This is what that said to her parents: "I [with a Southern accent] waaaaant . . . water." In other words, I want to drink the liquid of life. I want to live.

Where did the "water" come from, one might ask? "Ah waaaa": *agua*. It had to have been suggested to the parents by the Spanish for "water," perhaps influenced by the prevalence of Spanish in South Florida, where they resided. Terri Schiavo's parents parsed the twice-repeated syllables to produce a contrast between them, and from the contrast meaning arose: "ah . . . waaaa" (I [Southern accent] want) "ah waaaa" (agua). They did a creative intercultural reading of the utterance in order to extract from the sounds a surplus-value of meaning, emerging out of what other parties in the controversy would characterize as nonsense. Meaning rose renascent, from the affective barely-there. This extracted surplus-value energized a political movement whose voice not only reached into every corner of the country but resonated with the highest levels of government and was heard across the world.

To the medical ear, and to Michael Schiavo, the sounds were not words. They were reflex vocalizations resulting from spontaneous nervous system firings. They were autonomic agitations, mere tics expressing nothing more than nervous irritability. Not life, but the machinery of life, still kicking, still running, but residually, at its lowest level of intensity, where it no longer has any meaning. At the point of indistinction between the organic and the inorganic, animate and inanimate. Life at the vanishing point, where human choice slips into a vegetable slumber where it is indistinguishable from essentially inert but irritable matter. The stuff of twinges. "It would be absurd," Gilbert Ryle writes, "to ask someone what he had a twinge for. . . . Neither my twinges or my winces, neither my squirming feelings or my bodily squirmings, neither my feelings of relief, are things I do for a reason. . . . It would be nonsense to say that someone tried to have a twinge" (Ryle 1949, 105–6). But then, do people try to have a surplus-value of meaning? Do not their twinges, squirmings, and spasms of relief regularly supplement themselves with semantic expression, in a way that is not so clearly the opposite of reflex? Is this not always to some extent a creative act producing a surplus-value of meaning? Reduplicative syllables and vaguely articulated word-like sounds are well known to automatically fuse into a perception of meaningful words.

Maybe Schiavo's parents' supplementation of her sounds was on solid grounds, and Schiavo was having a twinge for a reason, Ryle notwithstanding. Research on residual consciousness in people in a vegetative state has confirmed an ability to understand language and even respond, given the means, in a surprisingly large minority of cases. This calls into question the clear-cut nature of the distinction between meaningful life and irritable matter, blurring the boundary between consciousness and unconsciousness, twinge and reason. But maybe the doctors were right and this was not her case. Perhaps her parents were unilaterally extracting a surplus-value of meaning from the sounds, in just as autonomic a way as the doctors said Schiavo herself reflexively "spoke." The courts sided with the doctors.

Whatever way you go, what gets staged is the paradoxically expressive power of the barely-there at the shared affective threshold of life and language, the enveloped (immanent) limit of the field of power where consciousness flirts with oblivion. What occurs at that threshold is not the sort of thing that feeds consensus. It is too ambiguous. Too supercharged with potential meaning. It is by virtue of its supercharging that it becomes a collective node of differential expression that energizes affective and political circuits while mobilizing multiple regimes of power.

Surplus-Value of Organization

What we are confronted with is a *singular point*: a problematic nexus around which tendencies animating and animated by different modalities of power form relays that work themselves out agonistically to produce stark bifurcations in the course of events: to die or not to die. A singular site of struggle, whose outcome is not precast. A point of productive paradox, in more ways than one. First, this singular point is multiple. If it comes once (Schiavo), it no sooner comes twice (Bush). It has a singular power of repetition, or more precisely self-iteration: of variation and displacement. It is also a paradox in the sense that it cannot fully be described by any one logic. It falls between them, belonging partially to many. It is productive precisely because its paradoxical nature is not the lack of a logic. It is a surfeit of logics. It lies at the intersection of multiple logics that clash and resolve themselves to each other in ways that generate potential. Their coming together as a knot generates a tangle of possible forking paths, belonging to different possible worlds. There is the possible world in which the cooptation of the issues by the Christian right aids in the reelection of a Republican governor, positioning him for an eventual shot at replacing his brother in the White House. There are possibilities for the Christian right to turn that around and consolidate its hold on the Republican

Party, rather than the Republican Party's using the Christian right as an electoral tool. There are possibilities of a reenergized disability rights movement succeeding in renegotiating the terms of the biopower formula and reconfiguring the relays to sovereign and disciplinary power in which it participates. There are possibilities of the right-to-die movement making a gain. This is just to mention a few. At the problematic point, these forking paths are activated en masse. Not all of the possibilities are equally foregrounded or equally probable. They are graded: present in variable intensities. And of course they may not only fork. More than one—but not all—may be realized. They may co-actualize, tolerating or even boosting each other, mutually adjusting to reach a new settlement that modulates the parameters of their playing out. The new settlement, and emergent mutual adjustments, partially resolves the paradox, but never erases it.

The paradox of the singular point is that, however things squirm and shake down, it will have enveloped forking paths that proved incompatible, leading to possible worlds that are *incompossible*. The germinal dis-ease of the forking paths with each other, their co-agitating at the singular point, sets a process in motion. Different tendencies enter into tension. The tensions stir various formations active in the social field into action. There is a commotion. When the dust settles, one tendency has won out. Or more than one have found a way to co-function where before they couldn't. They have produced possibility, invented a *compossibility*, which will be added to the mix as a new tendency, one that will then be ingredient to the next stirring. When the singular point irrupts, its ingredience will be ready and waiting to enter the fray.

The production of a possibility is how Deleuze characterizes the movement of the virtual. Different tendencies, none of which has the strength to immediately assert itself, enter into interference with each other by packing in to the same point, making a dynamic paradox of it. From the differential working-out of the tendencies' striving to express themselves, a new possibility emerges, which, through a pattern of iteration, can settle into the world as a new formation. The new formation, in its nascent state, is fusional: it adds its tendency to the world, and superadds, by feedback, to the coming-together of differential tendencies at a singular point. It is iterative: striving to reexpress itself. Like the expression of Terri Schiavo's intercultural thirst (or her nonexpression of bodily reflex), it is reduplicative. It no sooner activates at a nexus than it comes again at another. It is irritable. It is agitational. It pushes toward a bifurcation point, but may fall into formation. Its drive toward expression lends itself to the production of a *surplus-value of organization*—an emergent co-functioning—analogous to the surplus-value of meaning to which Schiavo's voice gave rise in her parents' ears.

Such is the matrix of events: a singular vanishing point, where actual formations and the differentiated levels of functioning to which they belong accordion into each other, before accordioning back out. A point of collapse where what is in actuality mutually exclusive comes together in immediate proximity, perchance to unfold again, to inventive effect. Language struggling to generate meaning. Language falling silent into meaninglessness, bringing the humanity of the speaking subject into reflexive neighborhood with the plant, the animality of the human at a point of indiscernibility with the vegetable, the organism with mechanism. The organic bordering on the inorganic. Life flickering with death. All of the above, and more, in infinite, uneasy proximity, with a dis-ease as irritating as a nervous twitch. Too much going on where not enough is happening for any common perception or consensual interpretation to settle.

The singular point is a vanishing point of intensive suspension that draws attention to itself by virtue of its charge of indeterminacy: its not being decidably one thing or another, yet. No kind of power, yet. Just a black hole into which attention falls. A power to capture attention without offering it an object, there being as yet only affectability. On the horizon of the black hole, tendencies actually belonging to different formations agitatedly circle each other. The media register the stir and amplify the agitation. Shock waves travel to every corner of the social field. An event bursts. Some tendencies escape, like black body radiation, rippling the field. The media field. The wires and air waves plug into the irritation, becoming an extended nervous tic of distributed attention. What is most powerfully transmitted is not "the" meaning of any particular act or state of affairs, but the forcing of attention: an indeterminacy squirming to be determined.

The media plug the body into the singular point, and hook-line the singular point into the body. All of society is on the media feeding tube. The individual body and the field of power resonate together, operational analogues of each other, to the degree to which they hang on the same event. The social field ripples end to end with the same irritability. A hyperactively inert collective body—irritable matter of politics—stands at agitated attention. Political business as usual stops, suspended, exceptionally, for a beat.

On the next beat, things rejig. Positions are taken, lobbying is pursued, suits filed, memos written, judgments passed, legislatures called into action, politicians and government officials called to task. It may take years to process the impact of the event, whose practical meaning will only emerge over time. One thing that is certain is that the composition of powers, in this case among the Republican and Democratic parties, the Christian right, the right-to-die movement, the pro-life movement, and the disability rights movement, will come through the event changed, qualitatively. The event is a shock-to-the-system of qualitative change, working itself out.

The media do not transmit a meaning or content. They transduce the singularity of an event into emergent meaning. They detonate a charge of indeterminacy in an overcrowded field, compelling it across a threshold of change. The transduction induces a power modulation of the social field. It produces a global reintegration event amplifying from a micro-singularity, radiating a state of exception that gradually, agonistically, settles into formation.

In this cultural epoch, to say "event" is to say "media event." But the media event by nature overspills the media. The media event transduces into a surplus-value of organization. By whatever channels, the event always potentially leads to the modulation of already operating actual formations. The media event that is not just a media event, but also a surplus-value of organization, is also not just a human event. It may also call supernatural forces into active duty, as in Schiavo's case. And it is not just a life event, because it starts at a point where life and death are in immediate proximity with each other, in a zone of indistinction.

In the Schiavo affair, the micro-social singularity of the family drama swirling around a hospitalized body triggered a macro-event amplifying the singularity. Dead center was an ambiguous sign of potential life, a may-be expression, an affectively charged vocal indeterminacy that was as real as can be, but not assignable in its actuality, packed as it was with incompossible potential pathways and meanings yet to work themselves out: as good as virtual. Terri Schiavo's "ah . . . waaaa" was the *virtual center* of the amplifying event. At a virtual center—germ of process—the actual collapses for an immeasurable interval into a point of indeterminacy. Here, the off-beat of the actual strictly coincides with its next surplus-value producing up-beat. Rising-falling of potential. The breath of a life on the brink, so close to the limit that it is hard to tell if it is taking leave or rallying a return. In the end, it takes leave. But as the individual body dies, the event transduces into the reanimation of a social body. The field of power tenses, modes of power flex their muscles, in operative analogy with the individual body. Then the field of power settles back into itself, under qualitative change—which is to say, in becoming. The virtual center of the change dissipates into its transmitted force of organization settling the becoming of the social field into formation.

What is new about the regime of power now reaching a threshold of consistency is that the field of power has reorganized itself around the serial repetition of the process just described. If this is indeed the case, the field of power does not center on a structure, but rather on a reappearing vanishing point that transmits a charge of indeterminacy transducible into an organizing force. The transduction pulses through the media, operating as an extended nervous system riveting attention. In the process, individual bodies resonate with the field of power, in the becoming of a body politic.

The overall mode of power, once again, is not sovereign: the power of deciding the exception, to make die or let live. Nor is it disciplinary: the power to apply a gridded overlay onto life, to inculcate morally acceptable norms and police them. Nor is it biopower: to make-live according to norms molded to the biological, or to let die; to make survive or abandon to wither. Sovereign and disciplinary power are, each in its own way, powers *over* life. Biopower, for its part, is the power *of* life. In contrast, the new mode of power at issue here is a power to make life reemerge: to make become. It is an ontogenetic power operating at the very limit of life: an *ontopower*. It kicks in where the breathing is labored and the body politic is almost out of oxygen. It takes as its object not the subject (sovereign power) nor the citizen (disciplinary power) nor even the surviving human organism in the "natural" environment of its sustaining population (biopower). It dips beneath the object of biopower, to access the expressive powers of the vegetative body, where the animal body is in a rhythmic zone of indistinction with the twitching of inert matter. At the same time, it rises out of that zone, to reanimate sovereign, disciplinary, and biopower, in their sometimes agonistic, sometimes symbiotic mutual embrace, always to be renegotiated: it appeals to supernatural and gubernatorial powers of sovereign decision, kick-starts judicial proceedings, draws discursive and interpretive battle lines, relays toward legislation, commands attention, distributes attention, fires incommensurable passions, so that out of the commotion surplus-values of meaning and organization are produced (along with many other kinds besides). It touches just as directly on the human as the vegetable, and the vegetable as the animal; on the organic, mechanical, and material; on the technological and the divine. All together in the self-amplifying event. If a one-word qualifier for this mode of power were required, it wouldn't be autarchic, moral/normative, or vital. It might be called cosmological, in that it dips into life's conditions of emergence, for another cycle.

This mode of power is intimately linked to the human body and its transduction by the media apparatus. But it doesn't take the human body per se as its object, so much as its irritability, its agitability, its activatability: its *affectability*. The object of this power is not one: it is the indeterminate activity that stirs the body and its field, in micro-macro resonance. A pure, unspecified, not-distinguishably-anything-as-yet activation. The *whatever-activity* of affect at the vanishing point from which everything rearises and in rearising, renews.

The human body as such may not be its object, but it is its host. Ontopower enters the cosmological stage by striking the body with affect, at a singular point of intensity where appearance is seen disappearing. The September 11 attacks were another such activation point. *Ground Zero*: human life collapsing into inorganic rubble, pulverized to a point of indistinction with dust. Gaping, wordless, gasping. Implosion. The collapse no sooner amplified by the media into a far-reaching global reconfiguration of just about every formation active in the social field, under the aegis of a new organizing principle going by the name of "preemption." From Ground Zero, appearing from the disappearance, indistinctly at first as the dust begins to clear, is seen a body extricating itself from the rubble (fig. 7.1), then a face (fig. 7.2), and finally a tattered American flag (fig. 7.3).

With the flapping of the flag, life palpably stirs again. The horror is now transduced, by media means piggy-backing on the power of the stirring image, into a restoration of national "confidence"—the kind that is predicated on fear and ineradicable insecurity and asserts itself as a reaction-formation to them.[7] That kind of confidence can actually build a remarkable degree of consensus (or its functional equivalent, the muzzling of dissent). The path the consensus enables involves the military operationalization of ontopower, down the forking path of preemptive war. Not just one war: one war blurring into another, indefinitely. The "Long War." Endless war. Iraq blurring into Afghanistan blurring into an ill-defined "war on terror" that converts the globe into a special operations "threat environment" studded with American bases

7.1 Ground Zero, September 11, 2001.

7.2 Facing tragedy, September 11, 2001.

in dozens of countries, with the backwash pooling on the "domestic front," home of the afraid (which only makes it ripe for serial restorations of confidence).[8]

The Exemplary Body

Once (the story goes), political leaders were masters of persuasion, stirring the citizenry with feats of artful speech. Their well-honed discourse presented a coherent worldview that swept people up in its promise. The rhetoric swept them away in a collective course of action, implemented through a machinery of government as well-oiled as the words were silver-tongued. The aura of the rhetoric transferred to the person of the orator. The charismatic leader was the exemplary embodiment of the nation on the forward march. The people saw themselves reflected in his image. When he gazed back, he saw in them the unity of the nation. They identified. They glimpsed, in the mirror of his eyes, their own individuality, completed in the reflected image of the body politic, superimposed upon their multitude by his all-embracing gaze.

7.3 Confidence rises from the rubble, September 2001.

They saw as if through his eyes. This identification hinged on the body and image (body image) of the leader as peak individual: as exemplary individual embodying the unifying perspective of the state. The identification set in the glue of ideological adherence.

How far away this seems. And yet the same vocabulary is still used: identification, unifying completion, charismatic leadership, the "masses" carried away with ideological fervor powered by affect. In the regime of ontopower, all of that has changed. Except that affect is still the key. The completion-effect it brings, however, is singularly troubled. It no longer hangs on the inspirational coherence of words. If anything, it is more the opposite. Discursive incoherence focuses the affect on the exemplary body. The completion is a supplementation of that body's disappearing to a limit more than an effective unification around a center that holds firm. What occurs is a completion-effect, in the way we speak of optical effects: a surplus-value of appearing emanating out of a disappearing into the barely-there. George W. Bush was no charismatic leader. He was a presidential barely-there. By the time he entered the scene, the body of the leader was already moving to a different rhythm.

In a strange way, the exemplary body of the leader becomes exemplary of Terri Schiavo. And both resonate with the collapse of the Twin Towers. The confidence snatched from the void of the Towers is an emotional surplus-value. It emerges from the whatever-activity of the agitation of the event, transducing the abyss of affectability it opens into the production of surplus-values of meaning and organization analogous to those expressed by Schiavo. In the insecurity of the new threat environment, any number of other analogously operative singularities are apt to pop up without warning, at any point in the social field, now synonymous with an unpredictable bubbling of life-troubling events. Life, constitutively insecure, haunted by fear, catches its breath at the brink.

The body of the leader still plays a hinge role, as it did in charismatic leadership. But rather than anchoring a solid identification with an exemplary image of wholeness set in the glue of a mesmerizing flow of self-coherent rhetoric, it embodies an exemplary instance of the barely-there. Rather than individuals in the social field imitating the exemplary life of the leader, the leader mimics life at the limit. His image extracts politically operative effects from the approach to that limit, as exemplary social-field-shaking event. The analogous singularities distributed across the field resonate in time with this, mimicking the event in their own distributed manner. They embody the event at their own site and scale, in their own different but correlated ways, animated by its respiratory rhythm. The insecure lives of erstwhile citizens—now denizens of the threat environment—form a distribution wave of the rhythm of the barely-there.

The body of the leader is now in the role of resonator-in-chief. It is still central in a sense. It is a central node in a distribution wave rippling off in all directions: the hub of an operative analogy bubbling across the social field. Events figuring the barely-there, from Schiavo to the Twin Towers to any number of others, resonate with the body of the leader, and through it with each other. They disappear into the shared limit of that exemplary black-hole body, before radiating out again, amplified, rippling into a field-wide event. Rather than a centralized structure of unification peaking in the head of state, there is a differentiating rhythm of proliferation across a field of events.

When everything gets riveted to a macro-event, like 9/11, the body of the leader must step into the pall of that event in such a way as to extract from it a surplus-value of legitimation for the exceptional acts that will be required under the exceptional circumstances. The identification with the leader, if that is still the right word, is now not with the content of the image, as registered in visual form. It is not with the discursive content of a well-stated ideology. It is in the distribution of surplus-value effects through media amplification and contagion. It runs with the event, via the exemplary embodiment of it by the leader. The leader is now less the helmsman navigating through events than a parasitization of their potential to take life to the limit where it enters a zone of indistinction with the end of expression that is also its bestirring. The leader is the peak parasite of event-potential. Wrapped up in that potential are amplifiable releases of energies of surplus-value production that propagate and vary, more contagional than identificatory. The body of the leader has an aphasia for the language of Weber. It now speaks fluent Tarde (1903).

To understand the hinge role of the political image in this new regime, it is necessary to reassess what an image is. The question of the regime of power raises the question of regimes of vision. This is particularly true at this juncture, in the aftermath of 9/11, where the power of the image was immeasurably boosted by cable TV, riveting the world to the event (just as TV was beginning to relay into a media ecology with a fast-developing internet).

All Our Distortions

There is a concept in perception studies called "amodal completion" (Michotte, Thinès, and Crabbé 1991). It is sometimes called "filling in." One of the things it refers to is the fact that the eye is beset by blind spots. The inputs it collects are so hopelessly riddled with holes that it is empirically impossible to hold to the old idea that the eyes transmit to the brain an actual image for higher processing that faithfully reflects the form of objects in the visual field. Vision is not pictorial. There is no reflective conformity or illustrative correspondence between what the light bounces off of surfaces out there onto the surface of the retina, and a matching image in the "mind's eye." What the eye transmits are scraps. Eyelids blink. There is a blind spot on each retina. There is a blind spot between the retinas, occupied by the sense of smell. There are blind spots between the rods and the cones all over each retina. The inputs reaching the optic nerve for transmission to the brain puncture and fragment the light array reaching the eye more than they use it to mirror the surfaces off of which the rays reflect.

Yet when we look, we don't see punch-outs; we see a whole, seamless object. It is as if the image has been filled in by the brain. That completion is "amodal" in the sense that it does not correspond to input in any particular sensory mode. Vision can effectively function if it is completed by a process that is not only not visual in the narrow sense, but is not in any sense mode at all. That process can only be of the order of thought or imagination. Two vision researchers, J. Kevin O'Regan and Alva Noë (2001), have recently revisited the concept. They point out that it can easily lend itself to the oldest fallacy of perception studies: the so-called homunculus theory. If the eyes did transmit an image to the brain, who would be behind the brain to see the image? If thought or the imagination fills in the holes between what shreds are actually transmitted, who is looking at the fragments to think the punctured picture complete? The homunculus fallacy returns if the completion is conceived of as a supplying of lost visual detail, a summoning into being of missing visual stimuli by a faculty of the thought or imagination "behind" the perception.

O'Regan and Noë (2001) suggest that there is no actual filling-in mechanism. They suggest instead that we see *with* the holes in vision (§5.5, 950–51). To understand how that might be, you have to add movement. Movement, in fact, is pre-added: the eye is in constant motion. Its voluntary movements of focusing take place over the top of what are called "saccadic" movements: continually occurring, involuntary little flicks and micro-jerks. This continual motion smears the reception and transmission of the light stimuli. It also moves the blind spots over the field of vision, turning the holes into trails of unseeing. It all seems hopelessly scrambled. Except that there are repetitions and variations. A stimulus that was in front of a hole comes back after it as the eye moves on. A smear comes again backward as the eye reverses course. The field of vision snaps back after a blink, its reappearance accompanied by a saccadic movement. There are *patterns of scrambled appearance and disappearance*. Seeing is not in any supposed pictorial content supplied by the stimuli. It is in the *rhythm* of incomplete or *proto-appearance* and disappearance, which allows the brain to *anticipate* returns and repetitions of variation.[9]

What is "seen" is not the image as such, understood in the pictorial or representative sense. It is the anticipation of variation. Seeing is the anticipation of eye movements. In anticipation, we see the eye's potential movements. We see potential: visual experience is made of virtual images.

Say you're looking into a room through a doorway at a chair and a desk. In addition to all the holes just mentioned, there are occlusions or blockages. The chair occludes part of the desk, for example. Both objects have hidden sides. The doorway frames them both. Experiments have been done where subjects are asked to draw a framed scene including occlusions after a certain observation time. Their pictures show things that could not have actually been seen. The reported vision typically not only fills in the holes, but edges around the occlusions to show what was blocked out. Occluded parts of the desk are shown: more of the desk and chair are shown than the angle of sight would allow to appear. Areas outside the frame are shown that give a more complete picture of the ensemble. The subjects have seen more than met the eye. Subjects *remember* seeing more. They have effectively experienced seeing more. They have seen more, but virtually.

What they are seeing are potential movements that were not executed: advances to and through the door; peeks around corners; approaches and circlings; turns of the head to take in more of the scene. These movements are not just of the eye, but of the whole body. Their anticipation registers potential kinesthesia. The completion of the image is not only a virtual seeing. It is a virtual seeing whose content is more directly nonvisual than visual. In other words, virtual seeing is the translation into visual terms of what is virtually experienced in other sense modes: not just a potential sight, but a potential sense of whole-body movement toward and around, as well as potential touches of what might become unoccluded through the movement. The real, virtual image that is effectively experienced is *amodal*: occurring *between* senses, in their interrelation. Vision does not just support, but positively requires tactile and especially kinesthetic completion. It cannot function otherwise.

The analytic philosopher Gilbert Ryle observed that the viewer is perpetually "ready to anticipate, though he need not actually anticipate, how [the scene] will look, if he approaches it or moves away from it" (1949, 230). The viewer need not actually anticipate because, as the experimental psychologist Lloyd Kaufman asserted, what is actually perceived is not the content of actual sense-data, but rather the *tendency* to movement (1979, 378).[10] What is a tendency if not a "readiness to anticipate"?

Vision is always looking ahead, amodally preempting itself. Of course, there is a contribution of the past as well. Tendencies are acquired as habits and are consolidated by memories. So when vision looks ahead, it sees its past before itself. What we see are not so much present stimuli as an amodal future-past.

Visual form appears virtually against the background of its own nonpresent variations. Included among those variations are continual translations from other sense modes. Each sight is the actual presentation of a virtual continuum of variation: a full-spectrum perception.

The ongoing stream of perception tends to go on nonconsciously as long as its anticipated continuations link seamlessly to one another according to habit, corroborated step by step by the proprioceptive, tactile, and visual senses successfully completing each other in a smooth progression from scene to scene. What is seen tends to enter consciousness when habit is frustrated and the progression is cut into by something unanticipated. Consciousness, Whitehead says, dawns in surprise. "The general case of conscious perception is the negative perception" (1978, 119). Hey, this is *not* . . . what was expected. Consciousness, where it occurs, occurs at a point of discontinuity in the ongoing amodal completion. Something that doesn't fit demands attention. A sensory perception then kicks in, in a specific mode: "Hey, this rock is gray." The sensory input throws a check. "I thought I was picking up a white rock. . . . Now where is it?" The virtual continuum is shaken and reels, unsure of where its amodal completion should be tending. Movement soon resumes, along an altered path, relaying differently among the senses than it would have otherwise, gradating them differently in relation to each other, in this case perhaps foregrounding touch as we ponder in our hands the stone of a different color. Consciousness occurs only "fitfully, partially" (53), at pivot points reorganizing the relation of the senses to each other, modulating the amodal completion that occurs between them.

Considered from this point of view, the holes, saccades, and occlusions of perception are less interruptions of consciousness than *micro-openings* for it: *micro-checks* occurring in the nonconscious background of experience. The stop/check of conscious perception is an *amplification* of the base state of discontinuity that gets smoothed over by amodal completion. There are the *immanent conditions* of vision coming up and out. The image is not the sensory grayness we recognize as representative of the stone once the surprise subsides. The image is the *process* of the immanent conditions of perception interrupting and recuing its amodal completion. The image is a complex pulse. It does not represent a stable display; it presents a *syncopated rhythm* of movement.

The rhythm is a tripartite composition.

1. There is the *down-beat* of habit, or amodal completion continuing unchallenged. Its course is modulated by the impact of micro-checks passing below the threshold of conscious attention. These are smoothed over by amodal completion into the continuity of an unfolding progression.
2. Each micro-check is an immanent *off-beat* of experience, amplifiable at certain junctures into a macro-awareness of an interruption as registered in sensory perception and inducing a recue.
3. The recue is the *up-beat*, coinciding with a resumption of amodal completion following an altered path.

The off-beat is *underperception* (unperceived, nonconscious, but productive of perception; its immanent condition). The down-beat is *overperception* (perception supplemented into a virtual ongoing whole that sees-over the discontinuities, over-seeing a continuing-across them). The up-beat is the *fitful irruption of the condition of underperception*, a micro-cut jogging a macro-awareness in the shock of the "not" (not smoothly continuing), jigging a recue of overperception. Which is to say, the production of a *surplus-value of perception*.

Perception as reception, as the sensory registering of determinate forms, far from being the base state of perception and the foundation of experience, is an artifact of overperception. O'Regan and Noë say that a perceptual shape is not a stable form, but rather "the set of all the distortions" a form potentially undergoes (2001, 975). This inverts the relation between static form and movement. "What is meant by stationary," write O'Regan and Noë, "is one kind of sensory change" (949). Stability is an effect of movement. Completion rests on discontinuity. An image resides primarily in the invisible regions of the spectrum of experience. It is more virtual than sensory: amodal infra-thought.

This does not make vision an illusion. It makes it an activity: a creature of movement. The overperceived amodal completion of the visual image in continuous movement, overseeing discontinuities, is the way perception transduces its generative force—its restless readiness to anticipate—into an actual path whose completion is prospective: always taking the shape of a next step. Vision preempts itself in the production of a surplus-value of perception. Its sensory character is glossed over in the amodal completion of the present of experience by its forming future. We are on the edge of an advancing wave-crest, as William James says, and our determinate direction in falling forward is all we ever recover of our continuously forming future path (1996a, 69). We fall forward, it might be added, because we trip over a micro-cut, already past by the time it is amplified into a macro-awareness (if it is). The present of perception as perpetual future-past.

Government of the Barely-There

The political operationalization of the barely-there in the context of state power passes through the image understood in this way, as it attaches to the body of the leader. The barely-there is experience's immanent limit of underperception, where all our distortions are together in readiness to anticipate, in cut toward recue for the production of a surplus-value of perception and, in its wake, surplus-values of meaning and organization. Ontopower is the mode of power that moves to this syncopated rhythm, using the recue potential of its amplificatory upbeat to modulate a collective field.[11] It operates by cuing into the off-beat of affectability. When ontopower flows through the exemplary body of the state, its transforms the social field into an affective body politic, in the sense of a correlated, collective individuation.

The amodal completion of the image is central to this dynamic. The completion effect is not an artifact of projection, as it is in the case of the identificatory dynamic of charismatic leadership, where the light cast by the eminence of the leader overlays an image of unity and feeling of wholeness upon the social field, in which the individuals populating the field delusionally recognize their own image. Instead, it functions as a diffuser, gathering in agitatibility to its central node, and then spinning surplus-value production back out across the field. The centrality of its node produces a concertation among its distributed effects, but not a homogenization. What it distributes are spurs to forking paths, and germs of potential relays and overlays among them. The effect is *differential*. The individuals of the field are correlated, hanging together on the image-event, but in tendentially different ways. This process of differentiation was described in the forking paths and emergent com-possibilities of the Schiavo affair. In Schiavo's case the operationalization of the barely-there hung on an ordinary body, one not exemplary in the way the body of the head of state is. The political operationalizations were of a different order, and the differential nature of the effects was unmissable.

In the case of the exemplary body of the state, with its centralized imagery, there are circumstances under which the effects of the process are so tightly correlated that the differentials may be muffled and over-looked, so that something approaching a hegemony is achieved. This was the case with 9/11 and the body of Bush. Still, it is crucial to bear in mind, in order differentiate this hegemony-effect from charismatic leadership, that what is diffused is not a stable image of unity, but a syncopation. The amodal completion of the leader's body image offers a vision of wholeness, but it is stroboscopic: it oscillates with the off-beat. The agitatibility and affectability always to be found at the immanent limit of the image are diffused with it. This means that the vision of wholeness, and the hegemony-effect it may produce, are constitutively unstable. The vison of wholeness producing a concertation in the body politic is self-undermining. It is, at bottom, an affective attunement, not an ideological adherence. Seeds of affect are sown, and with them tendencies whose unfolding can never be entirely predetermined. The off-beat hits as a shock to the system, a cut into continuity interrupting habitual unfoldings. From the surprise of the off-beat, new up-beats may rise, settling perhaps into new, habitual, down-beat over-seeings, marching to a different rhythm.[12]

Ontopower is always fundamentally a *heterogenesis*: the concerted production of a field of correlated differentiations. Any hegemony-effect is provisional and precarious. For it to endure, it must be regenerated. Which is to say, it does not in fact endure. To appear as enduring, it must be repeatedly re-produced across a *series* of images.

The media do not function primarily as diffusers of pre-formed sensory images. Their apparatus is *productive* of the image in an extended sense. The image is not just the punctual visual display. It is distributed by its very nature, straddling the barely-there of the body (in a commotional zone of indistinction with dead matter), the exemplary body of the state (as central node fielding amodal completion), and the body politic (the becoming affectively-correlated of the field). A rock dropped into a pond forms a ripple pattern propagating across its entire surface. The image is not just the rock. It is rock and the ripple. As part of a series of drops. The ripple pattern of the next drop in the series will form interference and coherence patterns with the last, in not entirely predictable ways. The media ecology is a never-resting rock-throwing machine rippling the surface of the social pond. The continually varying patterning of that surface at any particular moment is the body politic. The body politic is more a wave phenomenon than an identificatory structure.

An image is a *pulse* of this complex, serial, distributed *process*. An image is not punctual. An image is a potentially social-space-filling propagation. The body politic is not one. It is the interference and coherence effects affecting the many, collectively correlated, each in its individual way, to the drop and ripple of the image-event. Events, always occurring, may prove no more than a micro-shock. They may be no more intense than a flitting shift of attention, as thin as a computer click. They may even pass under the radar. Or they may immediately amplify to cross the threshold of focused perception into the surprise of the "not" dawning differentially into a new moment of consciousness at innumerable correlated points in the social field.

The image process, as attached to the body of the leader, takes over the *legitimation* functions formerly the province of ideology and the reason of state. Legitimation, suspended on the barely-there, becomes a matter of affectability and its eventful propagation, before it unfolds into a question of ideational or organizational content.

The content of an image has no meaning or organization in abstraction from its ripple-effects, which are a constitutive part of the image. There is no image in isolation. An image *acquires* its content, which takes the form of the surplus-value effects ensuing from its hit and spread. The iconic content of the image taken in isolation is nothing more than the minimal set of conditions for its taking effect as a pulse in process. It is more a *prospective index* of the propagation of its coming surplus-value production—smoke of future fires—than a transmitted content whose contours are pregiven. The image, in its iconicity, precedes itself. The image as a pulse of process is productively preemptive—a precessive force productive of future effects.

Every image says "ah . . . waaaa" in its own way.

See Bush Run

What did Bush do when the image hit: when the buildings crumbled and the earth moved? He ran for a hole. He put down his book. Yes, he was reading at the time. It is already difficult to remember that he had tried, up to that point, to style himself the "education president." When word of the attacks on the Twin Towers came, he was visiting a kindergarten reading *The Pet Goat* with the future patriots. News photos would show him stunned by the news that had just been whispered into his ear, the look of a deer in the headlights on his face. Fate would have it that he would not become the "education president." The idea was already quite a stretch to begin with given Bush's much-discussed struggle with the English language and the coherent construction of ideas. A news media trend and cottage publication industry had already formed around his incoherencies, popularly dubbed "Bushisms." He made a quick segue from foregrounding language, into movement. He hightailed it to the presidential plane, Air Force One, and ran for the safest hole. He was quickly whisked away to a bunker in the Midwest that had been prepared for this kind of contingency. Along the way, for example at a stop in Louisiana, he made brief, stiff—to call them jerky (in all senses of the word) would not be exaggerating—television appearances. The statements he made when he popped up for these surprise appearances were exceedingly vague, even by his usual content-thin standards of discourse. They were certainly not of the rousing sort to inspire confidence at a moment of sudden crisis. It was as if he had gone AWOL. The nation nervously waited, left with nothing to fill the hole of despair that opened where the foundations of the Twin Towers once stood because Bush had disappeared into one of his own.

The next day, September 12, he headed back east to the White House. The saccadic, jerky rhythm of his television appearances continued. The saccades continued for the next few days, but September 13 marked a turning point. On that day, he stood before the press and spoke of "war" (Barron 2001). The nation was, from that moment, engaged in the "war on terror" that would lastingly define his presidency, much more than any education initiative could ever have. The president ducked away again, popping up two hours later at the Washington Cathedral to deliver his first major speech since the attack. It hammered in the declaration of war. Two days later he popped over to Ground Zero, where he reviewed the troops, met with "mud-streaked rescue workers and inspected the smoking mountain of rubble that had been the proud World Trade Center. . . . 'U.S.A.! U.S.A.! U.S.A.!' they chanted. The president spoke only briefly" (McFadden 2001).[13]

The declaration of war stood out as a *performative* against the saccadic background of a general discursive terseness. Before the speech, there had been almost complete bafflement as to how to categorize the event. The first people interviewed reacting to the attacks could only compare them to a Hollywood disaster movie. There was no nonfiction category immediately available to express its enormity. The category it came to fill was one pertaining to the mode of being of the image, rather than a category of image content: the spectacle. "It looked just like the scene from a movie" echoed countless times in person-in-the-street interviews. The word "war" was bandied about, but so were alternative categories, such as "crime." The image was still undecided. It was still vibrating in its spectacularity and had not yet settled down into a content category.

Bush's declaring it war made it so. The image now fell in line with its future content. Its event, from that point, will have been nothing other than an act of war. The image, at the ground zero of its impact, had preceded its assignable content. Now, suddenly, it will have been nothing other than what it was henceforth from the very beginning. The performative exercised a recursive force for the future. The unassignability of the image of the Twin Towers falling was back-gridded into the category of war, for all time.

7.4 Agape, September 11, 2001. Photo: Patrick Witty.

Agape

Before the performative, people were agape. They were bereft of words before the enormity of the spectacle and its sudden interruption of the progression of their everyday lives. One image in particular, widely reprinted, captured the reaction (fig. 7.4). The image of the buildings' collapse was itself repeated ad nauseam on cable TV. Its repetition restlessly propagated the bereftness. The image was an agitation, opening and reopening a wound of affectability. Image commotion, radiating out of the barely-there. Bodies appeared, exiting from windows to plunge to the ground from the dizzying heights, over and over again. Bodies disappeared, engulfed in the flames that simultaneously revealed and occulted their agony, unseen but no less felt for that. Bodies disappeared, in shreds and fragments, beneath the rubble, underseen. Over and over again, survivors appeared from the cloud of dust billowing out from the site of the collapse like gray-cloaked ghosts returning to life.

Life at the limit, on continuous loop. Life vibrating in absolute proximity to death. Spectacle of the barely-there. Ground Zero.

You've Got to Look

The effect was a lot like what happens when you repeat a word over and over again trying to grasp its meaning in some essential way, but the very opposite happens. The words disintegrate into strangely hollow soundings, bearing only an uncanny afterimage of their former capacity to carry meaning. By dint of compulsive repetition, language implodes. It is reduced to inexpressive sound matter—which is less the opposite of language than its material potential, and the possibility of its resuscitation.

Watching the Towers collapse time and again as the images replayed in endless looping produced a similarly uncanny feeling. Human life reduced to its material ingredients—but not as its material potential. Irreversibly instead, without a hope for resuscitation. Onlookers were compulsively drawn to the site. One, interviewed on CNN a few days later, still could hardly speak. She just sobbed, repeating, "You've got to look, you've got to look."

You've got to look, but you don't see. The image of the falling bodies (fig. 7.5) was quickly pulled from viewing, but the memory lingered like a specter, resurfacing from time to time, particularly around the anniversaries of the event (Flynn and Dwyer 2004). Even the disappearance of the bodies tended to disappear. Reduplicative black hole of death.

Attention turned to the recovery of the corpses. There was a grisly deathwatch for glimpses of body fragments being pulled from the rubble. The entire neighborhood was scoured for months afterward, every tiny fragment of human matter collected and catalogued. Fewer than expected were found. Most of the bodies had simply "vaporized," "rendered into dust."[14]

In a sense, this withdrawal of actual seeing was truer to the event than explicit showing would have been. Because what was being compulsively sought for sight was death. People were trying to register the incomprehensibility of it. They were craning to see an essential invisibility—something which, for sensory seeing, could only be and remain virtual. They were straining their eyes to see a ground zero of vision itself.

7.5 Falling.

This ground zero of vision was the point of emergence of a new level of Bush-centered imagery that overlaid the invisibility of death and the disappearance of human life with an amodally completed image of vitality—paradoxically via a declaration of war, with its far more palpable promise of more death.

Afterimage

It was the performative of "war" that stopped the endless looping. It straightened the vibration into an action path, heavy with consequence. The details of that path were not yet certain. But there was no question that the freight train had departed the station.

The effect of Bush's performative statement, reduplicated at his saccadic appearances around Washington and at Ground Zero, was immediate. There was an upswing in the mood. The shattered nerves of the nation were already on the up-beat. The effect rippled across the social field. Agitation self-converted into resolve and confidence: *surplus-value of emotion*. Much flag-waving, yellow-ribboning, and patriotic trumpeting ensued. There was a rallying around national "heroes": first responders, police, the military, not to mention, of course, the commander-in-chief, whose popularity saw a meteoric rise. Even the dead were "ordinary heroes" by virtue of having been at the wrong place at the wrong time, and so were their family members, by virtue of having been at the wrong place at the wrong time at one remove. Weather-worn national narratives kicked back in with new vigor: *surplus-value of meaning*. The passage of the Patriot Act and the foundation of the Department of Homeland Security, among other consolidations of the security state, were already on the horizon: *surplus-value of organization*.

The effect was remarkable, not least because Bush had not given the public a reasoned argument as to why the attack meant war, what manner of war this was, whether it was containable in space or time, and whether it was winnable. He had no historical rationale for his declaration. All he had given was a pattern of official movement, a pattern of bodily appearance and disappearance mimicking the appearance and disappearance of the bodies at Ground Zero—with one difference that made all the difference. The bodies of Ground Zero, like all highly affective images, short-circuited amodal completion. This induced the impossible imagining of annihilation, total negation; vaporization and reduction of life to combustion gases and bone fragments. The amodal completion of an image with death is a contradiction in terms. The image of death is self-extinguishing. It is impossible to think absence. Pure negation is unimaginable, because you have to think of what was present to think its absence. So the image flickers. It vibrates between a ghost presence and absence, at the joint limit of life and the thinkable.[15] The image is a black hole, oscillating between absolute implosion and ghost-body radiation. The effect is a traumatic oscillation between life and death, turning away and staring in horror, the alternation itself exerting a fatal allure. This is an agitation that cannot be mastered. It can only be repeated, drawing in all that is around, over and over again. This was expressed in the obsessive-compulsive repetition of the image and the semi-articulate exclamations of those riveted to it. A pained collective "ah . . ." without the "waaaa." Because not even the sweetest water can slake a traumatic image thirst.

Enter Bush, popping back up to utter his performative. Suddenly another image rose from Ground Zero: that oversized flag hoisted up a flagpole rising dramatically from the rubble, unmistakably evoking the celebrated photo from Iwo Jima that serves as a single-image shorthand for American patriotism and the nation rising again from the dust of tragedy. Bush's performative operated as an *affective gear-shift mechanism*. It flipped the amodal completion from death to life renascent. Bush had given no content for this. He had given little more than dynamic holes. It was up to the people to complete the picture—which they did by invoking the wholeness of the nation and the vitality of its "ordinary heroes" in a panoply of conventional images and discourse. The newly formed newly militarized figure of President Bush was now defined by his role as commander-in-chief. His accession to that role would in no way hinge on his personal qualities, or any proven ability actually to fulfill that role. He *appeared* to fit the image, in the literal sense: as an artifact of his saccadic movement of appearances. His syncopated rhythm of appearing and disappearing mimicked the barely-there of Ground Zero, but at the same time displaced it, from the smoldering site of the attack to the exemplary body of the state. He went physically to Ground Zero to stand by that hole, superposing his own image over it, as if taking a gravestone rubbing of it. Then he went on his way in his newly assumed role as commander-in-chief, carrying the trace with him. His movements moved the dynamic trace into new contexts and bumped it to a different level. They created the perceptual conditions for a collective counter-amodal completion.

The conditions were those of the production of a virtual image of wholeness, completing the incompleteness of his presence, and filling in the saccades of his actual appearances like the spokes of a revolving wheel merge into a continuous afterimage. Since his image was now superimposed upon the image of Ground Zero, the fill-in of continuity overlaid that originary black hole. The trauma was still felt, but it was now seen-over as the wellness of the nation becoming whole again, overseen by a commander-in-chief. The incompleteness and rarity of Bush's body image were the conditions for this transduction. They created an allure not unlike that of the appearance and disappearance from Ground Zero, still flickering in the background, imperceptibly leaking out in the intervals between images of wholeness. Bush's appropriation and transduction of the 9/11 amodal completion process was still powered by the implosive energies of the event. There had been a heightened anticipation as the world waited for him to step up. The country was in dramatic suspense as he did his rabbit-in-a-hole routine. The amodally completed image was a fusion of the public's anticipation and their past habituation to figures of public leadership in times of war. The rush of patriotic fervor hit an up-beat with the surprise awareness of a changed affective direction—already primed to settle into the down-beat of familiar expressions of nationalism as the country habituated to the long slog of war and the home-front security that would bring the war back home. The lesson of Vietnam had been learned. This time, images of returning coffins from the foreign front would be banned. Disappearance of the disappearance of death again, the emptiness filled with surplus-value productions of patriotism.

A hegemony effect was soon produced. A taboo was immediately set in place on commentary and analysis. Any attempt to bring out the historical background to US foreign policy that may have created the context for the attack was shouted down in outrage. Prominent cultural figures such as Susan Sontag and Karlheinz Stockhausen who dared raise dissident voices were viciously attacked and ostracized.[16] Any attempt to suggest that "war" was not the only conceivable response, or that a "war on terror" was a suspect concept, were silenced. In the following months, artworks were routinely censored, in particular if they showed bodies falling or other images giving a sensory presence to death (see, for example, Edwards 2002). Nerves continued to be so raw that a man was arrested a full year and a half later for wearing a "Give Peace a Chance" T-shirt to a shopping mall (Morrow 2003). The immediate response of many public figures to the attack, including Bush, had been to exhort the American people to keep shopping as a patriotic act and sign of continued life. If shopping was an expression of patriotism, antiwar sentiment displayed in the act of shopping could only be tantamount to treason. "Families of 9/11," an association of relatives of the fallen, gained prominence and used their high profile to function as a shrill moral police against any insufficiently hushed and pious discussion (see Senior 2002). Looking back, it is difficult to comprehend the violence of the silencing—and the complicity of the mainstream media and the majority of American academics and political figures, Democratic as well as Republican.

This is not to say that there were no voices of opposition. It's just that where they were they not silenced, they could not be heard above the din. The move toward war with Iraq was met with some of the largest demonstrations in US history. But the images disappeared behind the beat of patriotic 9/11 imagery. They were outshone. They were incapable of inducing a counter-counter-amodal completion producing a different kind of body politic signposting alternatives to the path of war.

The hegemony effect was not a consensus. It was a struggle. It was held in place by speech and image policing, not shy to censor where self-censorship was not sufficiently effective. The refound "unity" of the nation was only as deep as its virtual image. The hegemony effect was a repressive effect of anything that might trouble that image and uncover the black hole it oversaw. It was not a "natural" falling into harmony. It was an achievement of disciplinary power piggy-backing on the ontopower of the syncopated image process.

Vitality Redux

To understand how this reinvention of Bush, post–*The Pet Goat*, was possible it is necessary to return to his pre-9/11 imaging. His formal presidential appearances are only half the picture. The most eye-catching appearances were the informal ones. These took place against a backdrop not of terse words or even verbal performative, but of ceaseless, often senseless, activity. He golfed, he chopped trees on his Texas ranch in memory of Ronald Reagan's bush-clearing prowess, and above all he ran, six miles a day. These activities involve saccadic movements in their own right: jerky, repetitive, serially executed moves, with gaps of action between. Analogous to his movement in the days following

9/11. Bush would appear, provide a vigorous photo op, then run like a rabbit. His practice was to give very few interviews or press conferences. Words, his nemesis, were kept to a minimum. He would often just offer a repeat soundbite, then direct attention to his activity. The exemplary display of Bush's discursive minimalism was the jogging cow incident (discussed in the previous essay). "Bush does not like chitchat when he jogs," wrote the reporter who accompanied him on the run. "Spotting a herd of cattle, he says simply 'bovine.' Minutes pass before he says another word" (Dowd 2002).

Discourse subsides. It is still indexical, but more verbal cud-chewing than oratory. Language steps aside to make room for what his image is indexing. And, appropriately for the process, Bush's visible appearance is indexing something that isn't visible: exercise. Activity for its own sake, pure of function and meaning. Unspecified vigor. The kind of vigor it would take for a wordsmith to try to keep up with him on a run (which the cow incident reporter, by his own admission, was sadly lacking). It is no accident that one of Bush's favorite repetitive cud-chews is the sound-bite he inherited from his father: "This will not stand." This must go kinetic. The reporter was barely standing by the end of it.

What the reporter's unusual access to the president in movement had allowed him to gather was less a scoop than a stoop. He had experienced a differential in vigor highlighting the president's vitality. Vitality as such, as discursively contentless as possible, as semantically pure as cows in a pasture. Bare(ly there) vitality.

It is this vitality that Bush offered to his fellow Americans for their amodal completion. "Bush's Obsession with Exercise Borders on Creepy," went a not-untypical newspaper headline of one of many articles concerned about his jogging. "He Loves to Work Out, and Wants Other Americans to Do the Same," continued the subheading (Chait 2005). Bush's coursing of activity straightened the oscillatory implosion of the Ground Zero of vision and the nation with an action line, a vector-line of movement. It transduced the energy of the void into a kinetic energy that keeps things moving along the performatively signposted path. Retrospectively, after the 9/11 affective conversion, what the public had always seen in Bush's visible form was the ceaseless activity that is the potential for active human life taking its course. From agitatibility to activatability.

Bush's movement pattern was an invitation to amodally complete his syncopated image to fill the void of words created by the collapse of the Twin Towers with vitality, overspilling directly into action. Expressing in speech is bovine. Expressing in action, leaving the pasture behind in the dust, is a herald of a heroism to come. The journalists and historians who bide their time in the wordy pasture of the "reality-based community" will be left behind without being given more of a second thought than Bush likely gave the cows as he ran toward his presidential destiny as a maker of history (and a breaker of the world). Appropriately, the Los Angeles Times article that the Montreal Gazette reprinted with the added qualifier "creepy" was originally entitled "The (Over) Exercise of Power" (Chait 2005).

The surplus-values of meaning and organization produced were entrainments from the surplus-value of vitality produced by the Bushified image process, bumped up to other levels. All the levels run on the energy of that font of vitality gushing from the barely-there. It is also what gives the wholeness of the amodal completions the affective tonality of wellness and potential. Surplus-value productions now gear into each other like nested dolls: the virtual image-wholeness of the individual reappearing from the abyss of death that had been threatening to engulf life and above which newfound confidence now proudly waves in red, white, and blue; the virtual image-wholeness of the commander-in-chief as exemplary of each individual's vitality across the social field; the virtual image-wholeness of the nation symbolized by the flag, around which disciplinary mechanisms rally to translate the newfound confidence into the hegemony effect of an apparent unity. All of these levels telescope into and out of each other, forming imagistic, discursive, and organizational relays. Each relay echoes the gush of vitality from the barely-there, repeating it more or less agitatedly. That repeated capture of the energies of the barely-there accompanies every iteration belonging to the process, across levels and the series of actions and expressions composing, like a portable origin.

Governmentally, the surplus-value production of vitality translated as the right and capacity to exercise unilateral, arbitrary force: a redux of Schmittian sovereign decision. This was rationalized by a revitalization of the "unitary executive" doctrine of US constitutional law.[17] But in practice, it amounted to the exercise of powers of exception, which by nature need no justification, being the force of law, before the law (and in its cracks and syncopated holes; Agamben 1998; Schmitt 2007).

7.6 Facialized kiosk.

Put a Face on It

There is another gear-shift mechanism specifically dedicated to making the relay from activity as such to unfoldings of speech and meaning and depth of human emotion overseeing the commotion of affectability. That mechanism is the face.

Among the most affecting images to come out of the collapse were of faces emerging from the cloud of smoke that rose from the rubble as the buildings imploded. These had a prolonged afterlife with many reuptakes. In one of the most iconic (fig. 7.2), a figure is caught just emerging from the cloud, one hand raised as if in a feeble attempt to wave away the encompassing cloud of dust in which it had just been enveloped and against the background of which it is becoming visible: terrified, but alive, squinting forward, away from the devastation, to a future of life continuing. Face shots of missing family members were plastered across every surface of the city, from fences to storefronts to kiosks (fig. 7.6). An abundance of votive candles was arrayed around, converting the sites into improvised shrines.

In a particularly odd bit of disaster serendipity, an ad on a bus shelter seemed to show a man falling, arms akimbo, screaming in terror, above it the word "infinity" (fig. 7.7). The surface of the ad was also plastered with faces of the fallen. It turns out that it was an ad for the Gap clothing store distributed by the Infinity outdoor advertising company. It showed Will Ferrell on the floor on his back, legs and arms in the air, vocalizing not in terror but presumably in an excess of joy at his

7.7 Infinity. Photo: Robert Spencer.

outfit. We can not only shop to support the nation, we can shop to be (Massumi 1993, 3–38).

The overlay of faces was fitting. The faces affixed to the ad's fallen-body-that-was-not-one graphically expressed the hope that the dead might be found alive after all. They buoyed the image of the body, raising it back toward the well-grounded life of consumer society, preserving the person of loved ones from the void. Here, as elsewhere, the image was being used as an antigravity device floating life above the void.

The face personalized the unbearable. The photos plastered over the compulsion to see death, and the impossible need to comprehend absence, with a visible present reminder of a past life—an individual life, with a face and a name. Putting an identifiable face on the void allowed the unspeakable excess of affect released by the event to be detoured away from the black hole to be absorbed elsewhere: in grief, mourning ritual, reminiscence, spiritual comfort, hope renascent—if not sustainable on the individual level then displaced onto the collective level of the nation rising again. The excess of affect was absorbed in emotion, becoming a content of individual lives, in reminiscence and retelling. Speech was reinitialized, in the first person. Its dominant mode was not persuasive or argumentative discourse but the first-person narrative. The makeshift altars where face shots of the lost covered fences and street corners by the hundreds enacted a *piety of the personal*: a collective individuation of a spectrum of human emotions, overspilling into innumerable personal stories told with a sanctimoniousness usually reserved for religious observance (as indicated by the near universal use of the word "altar" for the sites of remembrance). Commentary and analysis were widely squelched on the grounds that they were disrespectful to the departed. After all, it's impolite, if not downright violent, to tell someone they're not feeling what they're feeling. Changing the subject, or moving to a different affective tonality or level of discourse, was equated with negating what people were feeling. It was not infrequently compared to killing the dead all over again. Affect, translated into this manner of emotion, was given the power of always having the last word, effectively silencing other expressions. This channeled into the affective politics of confidence in force at the national level, creating a privileged relay in the political operationalization of the event. The piety of the personal that drew strength from 9/11 had been a factor in American culture for a long time, and no doubt has a long life ahead of it, on the identitarian left as well as the right.[18]

Bush played the piety well. When he appeared at Ground Zero to bolster the morale of the rescue workers, he was met with an intensely personal response. He later remembered being particularly affected by a rescue worker who pointed straight at him as he walked by and yelled out, "Don't let *me* down." In the background, the workers' chant of "USA-USA-USA" performed a generic Americanness as the backdrop for an affective individuation resonating between the individual subject of the state and its exemplary body. Bush waded into the crowd of family members seeking news of missing relatives, asking one person after another, "Tell me about yourself." Each of them, he later said, "believed that their loved one was still alive" (Woodward 2002, 69).

The compulsive looking into the void of death was converting into a voluble belief in life. The despair of not knowing how to respond to the event, not even knowing how to categorize it enough to talk about it before it was performed into a category, the shocked paralysis and standing agape, was converted into a background of generic confidence in generic American national strength and vitality, against which the "heroism" of the ordinary American would stand out in its individuality: exemplary body, body politic, and individual life-body, staged together on different but interconnecting levels, collapsing amodally into each other's completion, and accordioning back out to plug into level-specific action lines and narrative conventions, all vibrating imperceptibly with the underseen agitation of the barely-there. One particularly popular trope was the American flag painted on someone's face as it cheered (the commander-in-chief, no doubt), expressing the interconnection between the levels.

The someone on whose face the flag was painted was, inevitably, white.[19] "Generic" means whiteness: the supposedly neutral background of humanness against which an individual's particularity stands out, the degree of that individuality's participation in the quality of humanness measured by its similarity with the generic standard. Deleuze and Guattari maintain that the personalizing device of "faciality" is the very mechanism of whiteness (1987, 167–92). Generic whiteness marks the unmarked, codes what passes for uncoded. The way it presents itself as the collective visage of the human goes without saying. It functions as the ground from which it is legitimate to speak. Any body departing from the generic, facialized standard is coded as other and a danger.

In a word, the renascent body politic that emerged from Ground Zero as from a displaced national origin was virulently racializing. The terrorist was the "faceless enemy," a danger so ubiquitous and unpredictable as to lack all determinate human characteristics. This enemy was less than human. Black and brown bodies are indeed endowed with faces. But in generic eyes, the face might prove to be a mask that might be torn off at any moment to reveal the generic anti-visage of the faceless enemy beneath. Anti-Arab racism went viral and tended to overspill into racism against all racialized bodies. On the evening of September 11, during one of his pop-up appearances before the performative of war had set, Bush blurted that on that morning "freedom itself was attacked by the faceless crowd." Subsequent to the declaration of war, the "crowd" had settled into the "enemy," and an oscillation between the faceless and the brown-faced, the masked and unmasked, the unspecifiable and identifiable, agitated and affected the social field, mimicking the vibratory alternation of appearance and disappearance characterizing the syncopated political rhythm operationalizing the event.

Through facialization, conventional macro-level codings returned with a vengeance: implicit or explicit racial hierarchies, discourses of the "clash of civilizations" and European superiority, a revamped version of the "white man's burden" ("America, policeman of the world"). The "unity" of the body politic was predicated on a fragmentation of it—as is always the case.[20] This is the analogue, at the level of the image of the nation, of the fragmentary conditions of perception itself. It is part of the working process: the more the danger of the fragmentation is felt, the more vigorously the amodal completion of the nation as "unified" (read "homogenized") has to be renewed by image production and propagation, cut and recue. The lack of coherence in the image has to be systematically overseen by the serial refrain of its process.

The "faceless enemy" was capable of hiding behind a seemingly ordinary face of a different color. It was also capable of being worn on an exemplary body. Saddam Hussein was the anti-Bush. The two exemplary leaders were twinned in antithesis, facing each other down. The face-to-face of the leaders provided another structuring element productive of surplus-values of emotion, meaning, and organization. It is at this level that the identificatory dynamics associated with the old charismatic form of leadership kicked back in. The interpersonal conflict between Hussein and Bush was a passion play of "good against evil." Guess which is which.

Affective Conversion Circuit

The woodenness of Bush's facial and verbal expressions only helped. It made him all the better as a vessel for the process of facialization, which, paradoxically, is an impersonal process, though productive of personalizing effects. At Ground Zero he became a lightning rod for affect, propagating affectability and its channeling into action paths and lines of expression, fueled by the vitality his image also channeled. The syncopated rhythm of the image process now coincided with an *affective circuit*. The circuit linked Bush's inarticulate, ceaseless exercise and the saccadic beat of his appearances with the people's virtual completion as a body politic, their facialization, and the associated productions of surplus-value. Along the way, people's inexpressible excess of feeling was translated into channelable, if not entirely controllable, emotion. Each individual body captured by the circuit, hooked in through their fascination with the underperceived barely-there, completed Bush with the charge of personality he constitutionally lacked. His exemplary body image, in turn, gave them the collective vitality they feared they had lost.

The affective circuit effected a change of valence. The negativity of the black hole of affectability flipped into the positivity of the nation's coming alive again with renewed purpose, out for revenge, operationally united, by dint of hegemony effects, in the fight against a "common enemy." The gaping emptiness of Ground Zero was converted into collective resolve and a newfound confidence in the face-to-face with the enemy.

Once again, all of this was accomplished in the immediate aftermath of the attacks without concerted discursive construction or persuasive argument embodying systematic governmental reasoning. It was directly catalyzed on a predominantly visual register by the transmission of televised images, in a final heyday before television's merging into a wider media ecology. Television, informational and communicational technology in general, was no longer mediating (if it ever really was). It was directly accessing. It was plugged directly into the real conditions of emergence of the image, down to its physiological ground(lessness), in ways that channeled its virtual powers of amodal completion toward emerging political ends.

This represented a watershed. Political legitimation would henceforth be predominantly affective. The collective confidence and thirst for revenge that the affectively fueled image process enabled was self-justifying. It needed no other logic than its own operation of magically reaching into the rabbit hole of despair and pulling out an eagle of confidence. It worked for Bush.[21]

From now on, a political physiology of perception must be a part of any theory of state legitimation.

Power Regime of Vision

It was by this time already a commonplace, at least since the Reagan presidency, to say that "image" has taken precedence over "substance." This affirmation is almost without exception framed in mass-psychology terms of identification, presupposing the model of charismatic leadership. The usual implication is that image should be a visual assist to full speech (ideologically replete). By this account, there should be a coherence between image and ideational content: strong image, effective leader; image of corporate responsibility, practice of corporate responsibility. Image and ideation should coincide. They should be consistent. They should be true to each other. The image is in a clearly subordinate role, second to the message, which it merely strengthens by making it more vivid. It is considered illegitimate—a distortion or manipulation verging on political malpractice—for the image to slip out from under its well-reasoned linguistic subordination. In this line of thinking, the word "image" is not being used in any strong visual sense. Political visibility is reduced to the status of a logical reflection or illustrative enhancement. Under no circumstances should the image visually assert itself—that is to say, assert the (onto)power of its visuality, independent of or against coherencies of speech, and thereby enter a different regime of its own.

The point of view suggested here is very different. With Reagan's political ascendancy a new *power regime of vision* started to bootstrap itself into operation, reaching a new threshold of consistency around 9/11. I have argued elsewhere that Reagan's exemplary body-of-the-leader image beat a syncopated rhythm of disappearance and appearance, fragmentation and unification, verbal incoherence and surplus-value producing expressive power that set in motion a similar affective conversion circuit, to similar hegemony effect (Dean and Massumi 1992; "The Bleed: Where Body Meets Image," in Massumi 2002, 46–67). The role of vitality and vigor, in oscillation with mental and physical fragility, seen-over in a dynamic afterimage of apparent continuity, was also a feature of Reagan's tenure. It is a little known fact that Reagan (1983) was the first president to market an exercise video while in office, between hospital visits for polyps.[22]

Over this period, political visibility took power. More precisely, the *more-than-vision-of-the-visual* took power. The image in the extended sense, including its virtual other-sense completion, took power. As it did, it backgrounded traditional political discourse, altering the very ground upon which political legitimacy is built. It was only with the second Bush presidency that the regime of vision/more-than-visual reached full deployment. The principles of its operation cannot be found in any conformity or correspondence between image and discourse. Nor can it simply be reduced to the negative, a breakdown of that solidarity. Political visibility has a positivity. It has its own mode of operation, against speech and beyond belief. Its operative principles are to be found literally in vision: immanent to its syncopated operation in its conditions of emergence, as propagated by the media, in particular television. It is no accident that Reagan made the transition from television personality to president. Or that rumors circulated that Bill Clinton was testing the waters to make the transition from president to television personality. Or that the defining event of George W. Bush's presidency was televised live and endlessly rerun. The revolution in political legitimacy *was* televised.

The Art of Eye-Catching Speech

The lesson of Reagan was consciously embraced by political operatives. "Nothing counts more than what your eye can see," said Rich Galen, a Republican Party consultant, summing up the early Bush presidency's approach to public relations. It's "a lesson we all learned from the Reagan years." The newspaper article quoting this statement is headlined "Bush Message Edited to Few Words" (Bazinet 2002).

It was a conscious strategy of the White House communications office to structure President Bush's formal speaking appearances around brief, two- to five-word slogans. The slogans were displayed on giant canvases hung directly behind the podium, carefully sized and positioned in such a way as to make it impossible to delete them from camera shots. The "message serves as an eye-catching backdrop" to the appearance of the president. That message, of course, is strenuously low-calorie, displaying a proud conceptual thinness and studiously maintained policy vagueness. "A Home of Your Own," goes one. "Corporate Responsibility" is another. "The camera-friendly speech backdrops, which roll up into tubes for easy transport, are the brainchild of Emmy Award–winning producer Scott Sforza." "Scott is an artist, plain and simple," Galen gushes.

Sforza's Hollywood art of politics consisted in reducing political discourse to a *visual* backdrop to the presidential *appearance*. The words are more indexical than meaningful. This is now the business-as-usual default. The communicational logic lies less in the slight ideational content of the words than in their indexical *repetition*. There were only a limited number of slogans circulating at any one time, each endlessly repeated, their redundant deployments marking the president's PR pilgrim's progress across the land.

Serving as backdrops to his presence, visibly marking his successive appearances, the verbal phrases were less transmitters of message content than traveling *image* assists: eye-catchers, indexing the person of the president; presidential highlighters. Their ideational content, impoverished by redundancy and displacement, ceded primacy to vision. The backdrops were designed more to *show* than to mean. They were less words shown to be read than signs seen to show. It's just that what they show is more complicated than meets the eye.

It is no exaggeration to say that the words literally form part of the president's visible image. It was a truism of Gestalt psychology that a unified form is visible only against a background from which it stands out. That figure-background coupling is the minimal unit of visual form. This essay tackled the question of what it means politically, from a broader view of regimes of power, that Bush's presidential appearance, his politically visible figure, backgrounds linguistic meaning, that it backgrounds the ideational—and therefore *ideological*—content of discourse. That the Bush presidency visibly stood out *against* speech. An attempt was made to forge a political account of vision that returns it, ontopowerfully, to its imperceptible conditions of emergence, at the limit of life.

This morphed en route into a question of the legitimation of power. The eye-catching function of speech overshadows political doctrine and *belief*. If belief is no longer proposed as the principle of identificatory allegiance to the political figure, then what is? What replaces it as a basis for the electorate's support and fidelity? If political doctrine is structurally backgrounded, what publicly justifies governmental decisions? The art of presidential appearance fundamentally reformulates the question of political legitimacy. How legitimation functions is always a key question, but all the more pressing in times of war. On what basis were the American people drawn into an ill-defined "war" against terrorism, including subwars in two countries, Afghanistan and Iraq, and special operations in many more? How were they captured and netted into this ill-fated adventure? With what by-catch? With what lasting ripples on the home front?

The answer was barely there all the time. It was vibrating in affectability, at the limit of the livable, on the trembling threshold of the sayable. To take a nation there, television had to show much more than the eye can *actually* see. Bush's secretary of defense Donald Rumsfeld sums up with characteristic aplomb:

> Things will not be necessarily continuous. The fact that they are something other than perfectly continuous ought not to be characterized as a pause. There will be some things that people will see. There will be some things that people won't see. And life goes on. (2001)

Coda (2020)

Rumsfeld was right. Life did go on, and there was much that wasn't seen. And there was also sometimes too much that came to view: the Abu Ghraib photos; the cages at Guantanamo; the 2007 Wikileaks "Collateral Murder" aerial video of civilians being gunned down from a US military helicopter in Iraq. Much water has passed under the afterimage bridge, and many joggers have run by many a bovine, since this account was written.

The power regime of vision described here proceeds in saccades. It blinked out under Clinton, then again with Obama. The Democratic side of US politics tends no less toward affective means of legitimation involving facialization (Clinton's personalizing "I feel your pain"; Obama's individually inspiring "audacity of hope"). But they do so in a different mode (Clinton jogged *and* spoke volumes), with a different balance between the discursive and the imagistic, reason of state and affective-conversion circuiting. That is precisely what the question of regimes of power is all about: modes. There are tenuous indications that the mode described here might infect Democrats. The 2020 Democratic Party candidate Joe Biden has differentiated himself from Trump in his response to the COVID pandemic. His choice to follow public health advice by "sheltering in place" and addressing the nation from his basement, coming out intermittently and haltingly with his face half-obscured and words muffled by a mask, have created great hilarity among Trump supporters. Trump has tried to capitalize on this as he himself was making a "comeback" from his own saccadic COVID-19 pattern of appearances by dubbing him "Barely There Biden" (Wolffe 2020): "Joe doesn't know he's alive" (Rucker and Sonmez 2020). Are we now entering a period of dueling barely-theres? The power regime of the image does not rest. It is always moving on to more variations of itself.

If the issue is the vicissitudes and intermixings of mode, it is not one of periodization, or the transition from one dominant structuring to another. Society is not a structure. It is a differential field: a polarized field harboring competing attractors governing tendencies toward different modes of experiential synthesis toward the production of surplus-values of emotion, meaning, and organization. In each instance, a diagnostic evaluation must be made of the relative strength of the attractors and their corresponding tendencies, and of the interference and resonance effects produced by their dropping image rocks to ripple the surface of the social field.

The Trump anomaly seems less the anomaly when seen from this angle. The attractor of a preemptive politics of fear experienced a visible surge when counterinsurgency-trained federal law enforcement repatriated the Iraq-honed tactics of the "war on terror" to the home front on the streets of Portland in the summer of 2020. Ostensibly intended to contain Black Lives Matter protests, the deployment quite predictably only stoked them to higher intensity, in a further illustration of the principle that preemption paradoxically produces what it purports to fight (Massumi 2015a). Trump has pushed rule by exception to an even greater extent. He has detoured around the legislative branch through the systematic use of executive orders; systematically sheltered behind presidential immunity to violate laws regarding conflict of interest, self-dealing, and the use of the office of the president for partisan purposes; hollowed out the government bureaucracy and regulatory bodies and subordinated them to his personal diktat (excluding not even the weather service, whose hurricane charts he famously bent to what his advisor Kellyanne Conway approvingly dubbed his "alternative facts" with the decisive stroke of a magic marker; Cappucci and Freedman 2019); and systematically stacked the judiciary. John Yoo, the architect of the George W. Bush administration doctrine of torture and leading advocate of the "unitary executive theory" justifying its exceptional practice, attempted to rehabilitate himself from the ignominy into which he had deservedly fallen in order to provide the semblance of a legal rationale for Trump's overreach (Marcus 2020). These refluxes notwithstanding, the Trumpian exemplary image also exhibits highly original characteristics. The radicality of its deconstruction of reasoned discourse and demolition of evidence-based policy, the radically reactive tenor of its affective tone, the compensatory brashness of its exemplification of individual deficiency requiring virtual completion, the explicitness of its undermining of the very notion of legitimacy, and the constancy of its agitations of the social field through syncopated image-and-text bombing on Twitter in symbiosis with Fox TV News, the right-wing internet echo chamber, and the alt-right web—all of this requires a new set of newly sharpened theoretical tools to do its processual composition justice. To be (amodally) completed.[23]

Couplet 8

1995

Requiem for Our Prospective Dead

A Participatory Critique of Capitalist Power

Shoot to Feed

In the beginning was a screen. Dead center, a figure. It is black. And shriveled, as if shrinking from its surroundings, the menacing emptiness of which is attenuated only by a sprinkling of crumbs. Is it an ant, at the extremities of exhaustion, foraging far from the safety of the nest? Concentric circles ring the end of an outstretched limb. A target. No, an insect wouldn't be worth the ammunition. Now we see. It's not an ant—it's a Somali. "Aim for the bowl," says a corpulent figure standing beside the screen, pinpointing the spot with his confident baton. It is none other than General Norman Schwarzkopf. The "hero of Desert Storm" himself. He has returned from retirement to make a fantasy appearance in another desert "theater," whose unforgiving sun will now have to compete with the caring afterimage of his shining glory. Your life is in my sights, the fantasy knight-errant of the New World Disorder seems to be saying. What is "life," in a world in crisis, but an armed stay of execution? Your human potential is beggary gone ballistic. My philanthropic bullet delivers the coup de grâce.

This political cartoon appeared in North American newspapers on New Year's Day 1993, two weeks after US marines arrived on Mogadishu beach to begin what would be the most heavily publicized humanitarian mission in US military history, and two weeks before President George H. W. Bush went out with a bang, resuming his bombing of Iraq on the eve of Bill Clinton's inauguration in a fond farewell to his relished role as commander-in-chief. The legitimation of state violence in those early days of post-Soviet America hovered in the air midway between Mogadishu and Baghdad, and in the airwaves between "terrorist" "thug" and starving nonwhite child, as it straddled the transition between Reagan Republican and "New Democrat."

These images belong to a particular moment in recent American self-fashioning in the world theater (the rest of the world figuring, in the accustomed American way, as a dark backdrop for the drama of the country's reassertion of its official self-image, primarily for domestic consumption, toward home-front political ends).

According to a self-congratulatory formula widely circulated at the time in the US press, under American leadership the world was on the verge of making the old call to arms obsolete: henceforth, "thugs" aside, the armed forces would no longer "shoot to kill" but "shoot to feed." It is nothing new for the military to justify itself with the claim that it slaughters in the service of life. What is more remarkable is the tendency to blur the very boundary between life and death, even between the organic and the inorganic—and with it the distinctions between war and peace, civilian and combatant. The Gulf War, Baudrillard tells us with characteristic overkill, did not take place (1995). He is obviously not speaking from the obliterated point of view of the estimated 350,000 Iraqis—two-thirds of whom were civilians—who died in the live-feed spectacle.[1] He is speaking as a Westerner watching on TV from a safe distance. From that vantage point, it was in fact easy to come away with the impression that the Allied forces, self-proclaimed upholders of international law, had taught the "criminally insane" "butcher of Baghdad" a lesson he would remember, without shedding real blood. It played in the media as a clean war. Military censorship tightly controlled reporters' access to the front and for the most part successfully discouraged transmitting images of dead or wounded Americans. Coverage was limited as much as possible to Department of Defense footage of fireworks and hardware and polished PR performances by baton-wielding top brass supported by the latest in business presentation equipment. It looked from a distance as though the only combatants were remote-controlled ballistic automatons who were not, however, without social graces. At least on "our" side. American missiles "serviced" their counterparts. The enemy was a scofflaw client who needed a bit of "punishment" in order to recognize the benefits of rejoining the international "community," on its terms. For "community," read "marketplace." Everyone knew on some level that the "crime" for which Saddam Hussein was being punished was not against "humanity." His gassing of Kurdish civilians before the war was passed over in silence by Western governments, as would be his postwar cruelty to the Shi'ites in the south.[2] The crime that fit the punishment was against the economic status quo. No one pretended the war was not over the oil that fueled the proudly displayed military machinery. The human suffering on the Iraqi side disappeared into the geopolitical relay circuits automatically connecting, among others, the oil market and the weapons market, and in the automatic feedback circuit of Western opinion polling, which installed the launch button for the missiles abroad into television remote-controls at home. The most haunting images of destruction entered America's living rooms at the end of the war. The miles of burned-out Iraqi vehicles, serviced into immobility along the "highway of death" as they attempted a panicked return from Kuwait, contained charred human remains. These were graphically displayed. But the uniform color of soot clothed the organic and inorganic in a surface sameness. The aerial pans showed a still: one automatic feedback that had dead-ended, dry as the desert, no more flow, any blood that may have warmed the veins of the vehicle operators boiled away in the blasts. In that stillness, the blackened ex-human became visibly a part of the circuitry.

American suffering, for its part, was not lost from view. But neither did it splash in liquid abandon on the antiseptic battlefield (American casualties were counted in the low hundreds). It skipped over the actual conflict. This was not just because the high-tech hardware of war was made to stand in, as much as possible, for flesh-and-blood fighters. Human presence on the Allied war front had not simply been replaced with machinic body-doubles. The warring present, the time of human suffering, had been translated from a haunting past directly into a function of futurity.

The dead have always played an active role in American politics. During the 1980s they came to be one of the most powerful political constituencies in the country. This is not because they voted, as they had done in an earlier era of American democracy, and are still rumored to do from time to time in Chicago. It was because they had felt. The constant reminder of their death agonies made them a potent lobby. By the 1988 presidential election, it had become difficult, if not impossible, for a politician on the national scene to admit to having had doubts about the US role in Vietnam. Draft-dodging or antiwar activism or, in the case of the older generation, failure to serve in Korea or World War II meant political suicide if combined with anything approaching a peaceful outlook on US international relations or with "softness" toward designated internal enemies (in particular, terrorists, thugs, drug users, and welfare recipients, fused into the figure of the "criminal" or social "cheat," which in turn overlapped with any number of figures of "deviance," most of which were dark of skin but could range anywhere from women exercising their constitutional right to reproductive freedom to anyone implicating their organs in unauthorized couplings). The taint of pacifism was a disqualifier for national service because it indicated an unworthiness or unwillingness to authorize the casual use of force to protect American "interests" (read "markets") in crisis-prone overseas locations, and domestically to extend police powers in response to the growing chaos of what was perceived to be a disintegrating social order in North America. Being "soft" on "crime" or insufficiently aggressive toward Third World "thugs" (read "otherly complexioned heads of state") was itself portrayed to be a violent crime. It was violence against the dead. It retrospectively sullied the purity of fallen heroes. "Our boys" in Vietnam did not die in vain, even though that war was lost. Their angelic "sacrifice" would only be in vain if the "lessons of Vietnam" went unheeded, and the next wars—including the "wars" on crime and drugs—were lost as well. As Sylvester Stallone had established in *Rambo*, the "boys in uniform" didn't lose the war in Vietnam. It was lost by pusillanimous bureaucrats in Washington who didn't have the "right stuff" to cheerfully blow the Vietnamese away, as Bush would do with the Iraqis to near universal acclaim from the US electorate. The American soldiers in Vietnam were killed by their own leaders, as surely as if they had pulled the trigger. Their bureaucratic successors kill them all over again every time they go "soft," heaping a cross-generational accumulation of "shame" on their warmly remembered stone-cold memorials. US soldiers in Vietnam died less from their wounds than from a lack of "resolve" and "pride" that was passed like a plague from grassroots pacifists to politicians. Antiwar activists were serial killers-at-a-distance whose attacks were relayed through the mass media to the battlefield, in the form of protest-motivated bureaucratic inaction. They killed fifty thousand in Nam, and would doubtless kill again, barring preemptive measures. "Can we win next time?" "Ronbo" Reagan had asked plaintively, echoing that other bad actor.

Throughout the 1980s, this necromantic legitimation of state violence functioned primarily in retrospect. By the time of the Gulf War, the constant appeals to remember the "lessons of Vietnam" for the future well-being of the country had given it prospective force. The preemptive measure was to accuse any potential critic of the eventual use of armed force by the US government of signing and sealing a death sentence against the "boys" at the theoretical front. Commemoration of sacrifice had buckled into anticipation of risk. Now premeditated slaughter by high command was justifiable as the prevention of death.

This weapon was used so effectively in the buildup to the hostilities in Iraq that expressions of dissent when the war did come were muffled. It is not that there were no protests; rather, the surprisingly widespread protest that did occur (including spontaneous walkouts by high school students across North America, and in San Francisco an organized blockade of the Bay Bridge and rioting downtown) was downplayed or passed over in silence by the press. Media coverage of protest had been reclassified as accessory to murder. After the war, doubts would emerge about the wisdom of the violence or the truth-value of government claims and statistics. But before and during, mum was the word. The popular wisdom that was picked up by the press, in interminable person on-the-street interviews, was a chorus of "we have to support our boys," regardless—'cause their lives depend on it. They're ready to make the supreme sacrifice, and we're duty-bound to support them. Bring out the yellow ribbons.

The Vietnam War–era slogan "America Right or Wrong" had been personalized as "Our Boys Right or Wrong." The moral imperative of the state no longer needed to be grounded in an assertion of the innate superiority of the "American Way of Life"—a claim that had long since deconstructed itself in economic stagnation and endless social strife. Now there was an easier way to access moral rectitude for reasons of state.

You needn't think, or assert a claim that you might be called upon to support with an argument. All you need do is feel—a oneness with the prospective dead hero and, based on that, hostility for the hypothetical enemy. The legitimation of state violence would now operate preferentially on an affective register, through the mass media. Both moral reasoning and critical thinking would fall out, in favor of the mutual amplification of empathy-based aggressiveness and government policy in a direct feedback loop between formal and informal opinion polling and military strikes. The legitimation of state violence would no longer ground itself in the originary rectitude of "founding fathers," nor even a clear and present danger faced by their sons. Legitimation was now up and moving. It hinged on an affective circulation centering on a vague eventuality blurring the difference between politics and crime, past and future, protest and social degeneracy, accessory and first degree, action and inaction, even life and death as being in this world was reduced to a stay of execution selectively granted by nonparticipants by dint of not judging. What of those with no reprieve? At this distance, it all seems so hypothetical. We don't have to dwell on the mess, let alone dwell in it. We'll just enjoy the light shows over Baghdad. End of story. Moral and political reasoning are short-circuited, along with collective memory, by a kind of magical thought by default. The punctual, hierarchical, command-based exercise of power is enabled by horizontal mass-media flows of necromantic not-doing. The Zen of state slaughter. Legitimate violence is now more ritualistic than reasoned.

The indistinction between life and death brings us back to the starving Somali. The death of the enemy has been visually absented in the theater of war by the link-up of high-tech imaging and weapons circuitry, and displaced from thought through the mass-media-exorcized suffering of the hero. The emptiness of that death twice-removed goes to Somalia and dons civvies. Rags. In peacetime, the unseen of war— the legitimated boiling of blood and morally color-corrected body rot— assumes the figure of a rapidly disappearing life-force that is nevertheless plainly visible as a blot on the evening news. The marine's bullet aims for this well-publicized vanishing point of humanity. Now it is the bullet that is hypothetical and it gives life back its substance, and at the same time its dignity, instead of taking them away. Biopower scoops up the commander's baton, as grain showers the bottom of the bowl. Shoot to feed. Bull's eye.

In spite of the (at best) implicit racism of this postcolonial revival of the theme of the white man's burden, a certain complicity is produced between the white Americans who made up the television target audience and the black Africans in the soldier's humanitarian sights. The wartime television viewer had accorded the soldier a stay of execution, which is now peacefully transmitted to the Somali. The deficit of those who do not not-do, the a priori guilt of government critics, comes out the other side of the media relay as a surplus of virtue positively expressed by soldiers as life-affirming action in the civil sphere. The threat of death becomes fully visible as armed force affirms life, and the imminence of death reenters thought, after a fashion. Both the misery of the famine victim and the risk run by their brave saviors are lavishly screened for contemplation. Not analysis: contemplation. It won't be asked too loudly what role Cold War–era US foreign policy played in creating the crisis in Somalia by propping up a brutal dictator until all-out civil war forced him into exile. It won't be asked what consequences the UN's decision to arrive in Somalia under the auspices of a longtime adversary of the exiled Siad Barre, one General Mohamed Farah Aideed, whose power base at the time of the UN operation was clan-based in a country breaking at the seams with ethnic rivalries.

Rather, it will be marveled: How tenuous is life! Mortal danger is the great leveler. It makes an empathetic "us" of the soldier (white or black), the famished black African, and the riot-stunned white American viewer more or less explicitly targeted by TV programmers and advertisers (and who may well have difficulty mustering the same measure of sympathy for black heroism and black suffering closer to home). The obvious political and economic differential signaled by the fact that it is the philanthropy of the fantasy white-knight, represented in the opening cartoon by a now-mythic General Schwarzkopf, that seems to give the black American soldier the potential for heroism and purports to put the black African's very humanity back on the menu is overshadowed by an implied community of victimization. Whether in the famine-stricken Horn of Africa or opulent LA, "we" are scurrying about as helplessly as ants under the glare of a panoply of life-threatening forces. These may be natural or social or, increasingly, a combination of both, and run in both directions in infinite regress from the human scale: the ever-present specter of the "terrorist" and the "thug" stands at the scalar intersection between AIDS and global warming, threats microscopic and cosmic (Ewald 1993).[3] The variety and unpredictability of the threats seem to place them outside the control of ordinary mortals.

For a moment, however, the omnipresent threat of death appeared to have been localized in Somalia and neutralized. If it could be neutralized once there, the operation could be repeated elsewhere. A promise of life begins to circulate through the media. Why can't civilians on the home front be given the same promise? Done. When there's a riot in LA, who you gonna call? The army. A hurricane hit? Who you gonna call? The army. The drug war getting you down? Why not call the army? There are cultists prowling around your schools conspiring to steal your children? Incite a gun battle, then call any one of a number of rapid-response paramilitary shock troops available on the state and federal level for high-profile special assignment.

War and nonwar are getting harder and harder to tell apart, as the provocative title of Baudrillard's Gulf War book points out and as Paul Virilio, writing two decades earlier, predicted would happen (1976). The mass-media circulation of violence-legitimating affect conditions a seriality that makes questions of origin and sequence moot points. Whichever came first, war or nonwar, hot war or cold, shooting peace or peacetime war, whatever it is, it is here and it is now, in our anticipatory present, transported from the trauma of a reconstructed collective past directly into the insistent here-now futurity of "our" implied community at risk. "We" seem to be in a New World Reorder that has shuffled not only "our" feelings and contemplations but "our" very temporality, henceforth nonlinear. With the fall of the Soviet Union, Virilio's "total peace" is already upon us. "Total peace," also known as "pure war," is history deprived of the teleological frameworks once assured by now exhausted mythologies of democratic progress and ideological macro-battles between power blocs in dialectical embrace. The blurring of the distinction between war and peace to the extreme squeezes out any possibility of mediation.

Command and Control

The mass "media" do anything but mediate. They directly instill and effectively circulate politically and morally operative affect. Electoral politics no longer represents the will of an actual community, if it ever did. It functions to attach legitimating affect to caricatural personalities carefully shaped with the help of marketing expertise, in a way that enables the entrenched machinery of government to continue its autonomic functioning. The end of the Cold War has coincided with a rapid decline in the ability of Western legislatures to govern. In the United States, a wave of popular referenda is attempting to limit many legislators' terms in office. The president is valued most as commander-in-chief, and there is a popular expectation (not always satisfied) that at least in the early months of his tenure the Congress is duty-bound to pass his legislative initiatives largely unmodified, in what amounts to electorally sanctioned rule by decree. The growing clamor for a line-item veto is another expression of the trend to push the presidency's civil rule in an autocratic direction reminiscent of military leadership. In spite of the long-term trend toward strengthening of the executive branch, neither the commander-in-chief nor the legislature can accurately be said to govern. It is more that their periodic replacement through the electoral process gives an entire landscape of collective autonomic apparatuses participating in political legitimation and decision-making a chance to readjust themselves to one another. These include all governmental branches at every level (the military services, the intelligence agencies, the many layers of administrative bureaucracy, the regulatory agencies, the foreign service and diplomatic corps, the state legislatures vis-à-vis the federal government, the courts); paragovernmental bodies (not-for-profit organizations, think tanks, lobbies); supposedly nongovernmental technological apparatuses such as communications systems (including but in no way limited to the mass media) and weapons systems; and even apparently nongovernmental nontechnological apparatuses, such as commercial markets. Each of these can be seen as a self-reproducing system hermetically sealed from the would-be expression of "popular will" by decades of accumulated procedure, giving it a vested center of gravity. Each self-reproducing collective apparatus is an orbit caught in an inconceivably complicated web of multilateral alliances and antagonisms implicating every other apparatus. Each apparatus implants command centers that radiate spheres of influence and patrol jurisdictions, sinking control basins into the collective landscape. The command centers multiply and disseminate nodes of autocratic decision, in other words of "negative" power, the power over life modeled on the right to kill. Every command is a little death because its interdictions subtract a potential from life. The control basins are eddies of "positive" power, the power to target life and reinforce or even produce certain of its potentials.

The ever-complexifying web of orbit-obeying powers over life and powers to enliven automatically readjusts itself at election time. The election is a forced interruption of the continuous functioning of this interlinking of self-reproducing systems. It is a rigged event injecting a measure of contingency into the web. That contingency becomes the focus of a mutual readjustment of a system that is so complicated that it cannot be described as a structure, but only as a metastable, self-organizing system of systems in a continual struggle to integrate interruptions, planned and unplanned, ranging from the relatively minor to the catastrophic, into periodicities, or regularized rhythms of functionings. All of the periodicities generated by the system of systems revolve around the periodicity of the electoral process in various ways. Elections are the periodicity of general reference.

If all this adds up to a structure, it is a dissipative structure combining a multiplicity of periodicities in a fluctuating set of highly complex differentiations that are locally implanted following divergent patterns, but resonate globally. This is chaos. Each self-reproducing system in this generalized production of order out of chaos combines modulations of what could be called, broadly, the "political" dimension (command, in its relation with control) with the "economic" dimension (all submit in one way or another to monetary criteria of productivity and efficiency), and contributes in a way that could be called "cultural" to the binding of selected affect sequences to more or less predictable pathways of thought assigned a territorial base (what is commonly referred to as an "identity"). For lack of a better word, the chaotic co-functioning of the political, economic, and cultural dimensions could be dubbed the "social"—although all of these designations are fairly arbitrary at this point.

What happens to "civil society" in this chaotic social landscape? It falls into the cracks between command and control. Between command and control, as between the systems implanting and perpetuating them, there can be no mediation, only resonation and autonomic readjustment. That is "communication": interference between autonomic systems and the modes of power they accrete, not exchange between autonomous individuals. The possibility of unweighted negotiation between equal civil entities is lost in the web of vested procedural power. When control procedure hits a snag, a specialized autocratic function rises up from the horizontal web and swoops down on the problem in a sometimes spectacular command-center assault. If well orchestrated with the mass media, this does produce a consensus of sorts, but not of the Habermasian variety: it is an affective consensus that legitimates the premeditated but unmediated application of state violence in a way that can only be qualified as innocently but thoroughly sadistic. Civil society disappears in the rhythmic rumble of self-reproducing autonomic systems going about their daily business, punctuated by impatient outbursts of excessive violence. Life and death on Ranch Apocalypse. In Waco, negotiation went up in smoke, for once and for next.[4]

It would be a mistake to make too much of the fondness in the mass media, and in some theoretical circles, for apocalyptic imagery. The conflagrations accompanying disproportionate deployments of state violence are spectacularized versions of the modest command decisions percolating the social on a daily basis. The power of death, the power over life, is utterly mundane. It is tripped into operation a thousand times a day on any number of levels, to varying degrees of intensity, any time the autonomic functioning of a self-reproducing system is jolted by a temporarily unassimilable event requiring it to readjust itself. Excessive displays of the power over life occur when interruptions affect more than one autonomic system, the mass media among them. Interruptions that cut across several of the semi-autonomous levels, or strata, composing the social threaten to send amplifying shock waves through the resonating network. This is especially so when the interruption of the day-to-day calls into question the generalized affective legitimation of state violence operated by the mass media. For example, when large numbers of "ordinary" Americans find themselves sympathizing, in spite of themselves, with gun-toting, child-molesting cultists under siege. The disproportion of the response, the excessiveness of the sudden state violence, its overflow of all reasonable bounds, changes the status of the situation. It lifts it entirely out of the sphere of the mundane, elevating it to the level of ritual. This trips the mechanisms of exorcistic affective legitimation into operation. The force of the conflagration is funneled toward normative ends.

What stands out is less the rupture of apocalypse than its periodicity, its seriality. State violence has the ability to leap from one outburst to the next, as if its excess was transported directly from the past into the future without bothering to detour through the present, understood as a continuous flow of time providing the duration necessary for processes of mediation to run their course. Negotiation short-circuits in a burst of sparks, or it is never even undertaken with any expectation of a successful outcome. The delay between exercises of state violence is less a present than a suspense, a dramatic tension running a tightrope over the void between the past and the future, on which nothing can be sustainably grounded.

The suspension of linear time characteristic of state violence short-circuits not only negotiation but apparatuses of ideological mediation as well. Bill Clinton's first election aroused hopes in some quarters that US foreign policy might follow a less interventionist course. Those hopes were destined to be disappointed. What are one man's personal convictions against his public conviction—for mass murder. Clinton was among those guilty of nonviolent homicide. The stigma of his student activities against the Vietnam War nearly derailed his presidential campaign and haunted him during his crucial first four months in office. He was unworthy, it was argued, of the all-important role of commander-in-chief. The heckling that greeted him at a visit to the Vietnam War Memorial in Washington seriously undermined him, contributing to his record low showing in the polls at the four-month mark and prompting a *Time* cover story, "The Incredible Shrinking President" (1993). Only a military adventure would save him. The Gulf War had worked wonders for Bush, taking him from some of the lowest poll ratings ever recorded for an American president to some of the highest in a matter of weeks. Clinton made a go at Bosnia but was rebuffed by fears in Europe and in his own administration of a prolonged Vietnam-style engagement. Somalia afforded some short-term relief when victim status rebounded on the UN forces, and "shoot to feed" reverted to "shoot to kill," "peace-keeping" to war-making, in another demonstration of the convertibility of these functions.[5] But what really did the trick was that trusty standby, Saddam Hussein all over again. Bush's nonassassination (the alleged Iraqi plot to kill him during a visit to Kuwait) provided the perfect exorcistic pretext. A majority of the American public declared through the polls that they would have supported the punitive strike ordered by Clinton in retaliation for a crime not committed even if it had been known in advance that there would be civilian casualties, thus confirming—if more confirmation were needed—that blurring the line between civilians and combatants, action and inaction, life and death, participant and onlooker, guilt and innocence, was a perfectly legitimate state function.[6] The light show resumed in the sky over Baghdad. (Or was that replay footage?) Clinton's ratings recovered enough to put his domestic agenda back on track. According to a *New York Times*/CNN poll (June 30, 1993), Clinton's ratings jumped eleven points to 50 percent in the week following the attack. This placed him in the strongest position of any of the G-7 leaders for the 1993 Tokyo trade summit held two weeks after the attack. Clinton's Tokyo performance in turn strengthened his hand with Congress in the debate over his domestic economic package and saved an ambitious education reform, unveiled three weeks after, from the oblivion to which it might otherwise have been consigned. Clinton had paid for domestic reform in the currency of displaced death. In spite of his ideological differences with his predecessors, when it came to neocolonial violence he had taken up exactly where Bush left off.[71] Bush had continued the Reagan series, adding Panama and Iraq to Granada and Libya. The series will doubtless be prolonged long into the future, regardless of whether it is the Democrats or Republicans who hold the White House. This in spite of the short-lived success of Clinton's Bushification. By the second half of his term, Clinton's ability to direct domestic policy had been almost completely undermined by a Republican sweep of the 1994 legislative elections, won on a campaign highlighting his "waffling," or the lack of affective constancy in his media image. His ability to generate legitimating foreign adventures had withered under the combined weight of television images of dead American soldiers dragged through the streets of Mogadishu, an uncelebrated withdrawal from Somalia that left the country in worse shape than the American troops found it in, frustration over the failure of the UN forces in Bosnia to prevent continued hostilities, a mysterious illness affecting Gulf War veterans which in its concrete incomprehensibility resembled nothing more than the virtuality of risk made flesh, and the new visibility in Congress of conservative politicians with more convincing militarist credentials than Clinton could ever muster. Bosnia gave Clinton a fleeting, gun-related feel-good incident when a downed American pilot was rescued by American forces in the spring of 1995. However, the sheen of the occasion was soon entomologically tarnished. The relish with which Captain Scott O'Grady related how he had survived by eating insects didn't go down easily. Bugs are not what come first to Americans' minds when they hear the TV slogan "the breakfast of champions." Subsequent revelations that the culinary "hero" had made every mistake in the book, and that his own incompetence as a flyer was what landed him in his predicament in the first place, did not help (*Australian* 1995). Clinton and heroism just didn't mix. The president was left to pursue nonwar by other, more mundane means (trade war with Japan). What had started in Kuwait with a well-oiled bang ended with a whine heard round the world, emanating from the general direction of Detroit: from crude to cars.

Perhaps most significant, the Waco incident had incubated in American grassroots populism. The existence of a widespread local militia movement allied with the gun lobby, and nurtured on racial hatred and resentment against welfare, burst into public view in the media follow-up of the bombing of the Oklahoma Federal Building on the anniversary of the Waco conflagration in April 1995. The disproportion of the government response to the Branch Davidians had become a potent symbol for a significant minority of mostly white, mostly rural, and mostly male Americans. Far from affectively legitimating the head of state, for this segment of the population any muscled government action only stoked an already growing disaffection from centralized government in any form. Waco began to be ritually invoked at cross-purposes to its mainstream function, in a spontaneous combustion of affective attachment to the government. The excess that was Waco changed signs. The command-and-control legitimation loop that had been in continuous, virtually unopposed operation from at least the beginning of the Reagan years through the first half of Clinton's term, was now under contestation from a radical movement for whom, fantastically, the highest legitimatable level of collective organization was the county. The militias' combination of traditional right-wing elements (isolationism, vigilantism, international conspiracy theories targeting Jews, a general scapegoating of racial and ethnic minorities, a focus on moral issues and defense of the patriarchal family) with orientations that in recent American experience have been associated with the far left (an anarchistic rhetoric of direct democracy; volatile, decentralized forms of sometimes clandestine organization) was a shock to the system. In the lead-up to the 1996 presidential campaign, the most active political tension was no longer between Clinton and the Republicans but between two wings of the Republican Party: statesmanlike political veterans invoking, yet again, the hallowed name of Ronald Reagan (who for many was now on the liberal end of the political spectrum!) and upstarts trying to ride the wave of radical populism. The center of political imbalance had shifted markedly to the right and beyond, threatening to leave Clinton out of the loop. Only a Dole candidacy was able to save him.

Although the affective legitimation of command, in its articulation with control, has fallen into relative quiescence, it is not a political "moment" in the sense of a simple phase in a linear development that is now past. Social time is nonlinear time. It is the nonfunctioning of the Baghdad-Mogadishu legitimation mechanisms described earlier that is the political moment in the sense of a present that will pass. Command-and-control is woven in the social fabric as a pervasive mode of power. Its fortunes do not hinge on any one political figure or election. Its macro-level ability to legitimate itself may have been interrupted for a time, but it will take more than a bomb to dislodge it from its pervasive micro-implantation in the social field. Baghdad-Mogadishu legitimation is quiescent, not obsolescent. It takes no soothsayer to predict its return. The difference is that the next time it happens, its renascent statism will most likely be warding off a threat from the grassroots right rather than from the liberal left. The main point is that the seriality of the command attacks is the product of an autonomic repetition-compulsion embedded in the political machinery of government as a dimension of the social—not the continuity of a personally invested ideological framework, on the part of the leader or the voters. Although nothing prevents the commander-in-chief or a mere civilian from investing in the violence ideologically, command and its legitimation are currently produced by means that are fundamentally nonideological, in the sense that belief does not necessarily enter into the equation at any stage, either on the part of the perpetrators of the violence or their domestic audience. Affective concurrence suffices. Subsequent to the fall of the Soviet Union, the eternal recurrence of state violence has all but lost its pretense of serving ideological ends. It no longer presents itself as a principled defense of a well-grounded totality with an a priori right to survive. It presents itself as a life-giving "service" to a community that is not a people, and is not actually unified. The operative "community" is a fractious and fissile global market, upon which the well-being of the national home audience is seen to hang. The attacks do not always have a well-defined geopolitical objective over and above their legitimating aim (even if they always have a geopolitical effect in their area of application). When they do have a geopolitical objective, it is now more decidedly than ever economic. The army doesn't fight; it does market maintenance work using cruise missiles as a grocery store janitor would a broom. It is all part of the balancing act among and within trade blocs that is now the primary concern of foreign policy.[8] To say that the mediations of civil society have disappeared is to say that every aspect of life and death, at home and abroad, is now directly capitalized. The "radical right-wing" militias earn the "radical" of their media label by dimly opposing the world capitalist order embraced by every other media-visible political tendency, taking as their weapons delirious international conspiracy theories and an isolationist survivalism whose utopianism is as economically unformed as its resurgent ideology is politically anomalous. Reagan Republican and "New Democrat" vie to steer the same, prevailing social dynamic (as if a self-organizing system were really steerable). The militias opt out. The countervailing movement of which they are a part is too embryonic to say what precise mode of power it will grow into, given the chance to develop the social dynamic it envelops. One thing that is certain is that the resulting sociality will hardly qualify as "civil."

The Singular-Generic

This account has come full circle, several times, just as Clinton, Bush, and Reagan did. There is a limit as to how far the kind of analysis set in motion here can go. The emphasis in the analysis of affective legitimation was on blurrings, reversals, repetitions, disappearances, displacements, fusions: mutual convertibilities. This strategy was not followed in order to reach a sublime evocation of postmodern implosion or deconstructive aporia. Quite the contrary, it is meant to preface an appeal for the construction of theoretical tools tuned to levels of complexity to which cultural theory as a whole has not yet adapted. The mutual convertibilities are not negativities, and while they operate on the representational level in mass-media imaging they are not confined to that level. They are rhetorical figures, and more: they are positive operators of the self-reproducing system-of-systems that is contemporary capitalist sociality. The figures we see on TV are distilled enactments on the level of representation of processes occurring at all levels, throughout the social field. The autonomic supersystem of global capitalism works by making ever-finer differentiations as part of a continuing, generalized process of adaptational recomposition which reshuffles the cards and changes the rules of the game at every turn, in response to frictions arising from its own functioning (trade-related nonwars) as well as to perturbations from without (antigovernment isolationism). The "implosions" and "aporias" are real, supersystemic elasticities enabling the recomposition and mutual readjustment of constituent subsystems. Contemporary capitalist power is metaconstructivist, as must be its critique. And all critique of power must participate, directly or indirectly, lucidly or deliriously, in the critique of capitalism, or risk falling into instant obsolescence in the ever-changing landscape it governs.

A few tentative principles for a capitalist critique of a kind, it is hoped, that no populist militia would ever think to embrace:

1. Capitalism, following Marx's metaphor, is vampiric. It sucks value from preexisting formations, but in killing them endows them with an eternal afterlife. Capitalism, to paraphrase Deleuze and Guattari, is the "motley collection of everything that has ever existed." Tribal societies, for example, are relegated to reserves, which then become bases for the expansion of the burgeoning worldwide tourism market. Elements of their art, music, and dress are extracted from their ghettoized societies to circulate indefinitely through the periodicities of the entertainment and fashion industries. The strategy is one of circulatory stratification: shreds of a precapitalist formation are conserved by the institutionalization of a vested territory, which may or may not correspond to a tract of land but is always legally or procedurally formalized as a distinct social stratum. That stratum is then completely subsumed by processes of capitalist valorization involving deterritorialized circulations ("representation"). The level of deterritorialized circulations itself constitutes a stratum, that of communication, defined as extractive interference. All of this might be called the principle of capitalist additivity.

2. You can't shuffle without cutting. This is the principle of separation. Every convertibility that is produced through communication, on the level of deterritorialized circulation, is predicated on a transformative separation (an extraction). For example, the figure of the "thug" is extracted from the civil sphere and imported into diplomacy, producing a fusion of "enemy" and "Third World head of state" under the sign of the generic "criminal." This feeds into codifications of punitive international law on the one hand, and on the other into a mass-media-borne backwash of the new composite figure into the domestic civil sphere from which it was extracted. Domestic political "enemies" will now tend to be filed under "criminal," feeding into a preexisting tendency to reinforce police powers. This produces further fusions between the "criminal" and "drug addict" or "welfare recipient" or "terrorist"—a word that gained currency at the beginning of the twentieth century in connection with ideologically motivated anarchist "propagandists by the deed," but is now an all-purpose term for those practicing non-legitimated, stateless violence. A new stratum is produced: that of generic criminality, which migrates between strata. On each stratum it fuses a different mix of already functioning figures. These figures do not disappear. They continue to function parallel to the generic, but more suggestively are also stockpiled in the generic figure, from which they can always be re-extracted as needed. The "enemy" is still lurking, and can always be called upon or reassigned. Each of the constituent figures of the generic overfigure are available for reactivation at new sites at any time, thus can be swiftly adapted to changing circumstances. The fusion of figures in the generic is less a "confusion" than the production of a generative matrix composed of fissionable atoms of figurability. The generic is not an absence of determination, but the continuity and coexistence of determinabilities defining a virtual range of sociality. Each determined figure that is re-extracted from the generic mix serves as a point of subjectification (in other words, a gravitational pull around which competing orbits of affect and thought are organized) and at the same time as a nucleus of power (a gravitational pull for competing bureaucratic bodies of control procedure and political command centers). Once again, communication—in this case the circulatory production of generic figures of sociality in the mass media—is more concerned with the creation of interference patterns than with either transparencies or black holes. Baudrillardian "implosions" are in fact productive interweavings that can be analyzed functionally in terms of convergences, bifurcations, and resonations (interference patterns) that are auto-generated within an expanding and complexifying chaotic supersystem. Any of the "confusions" evoked earlier can be approached in this way. It would be absurd, for instance, to argue that linear time has become extinct, replaced by a nonlinear temporality based on recursive causality between past and future. Linear time is very much with us. But now so is nonlinear time. The question is: in what mix, to what effect, at what levels.

3. The principle of separation brought us, through the generic, to the next principle, that of determination. The object of capitalist power does not preexist the exercise of that power. Productive power is exercised on points of indeterminacy: on molecules of genericness fusing singular atoms of sociality in an unstable primal soup of power. The figures are determined enough to be perceived and to attract the attention of autonomic apparatuses of power. But they are not determined enough to fall unambiguously into an already codified procedural or political category. They are unqualified, nonspecified. They are not yet determinations, but determinabilities (Deleuze 1994, 168–76). The exercise of control-and-command power qualifies, specifies, determines: in other words, it extracts a codifiable figure from the generic soup and attaches it to a territory. The territory is less a tract of land or an individual body than a class defining possible sites and embodied objects of power. The virtual singularity of the generic is classified as a particularized possibility for the exercise of power. Newly emergent social sites and embodiments, or mutations of already existing ones, will not be immediately classifiable and will fall under unclear jurisdiction. They will be competed over. In the end, they will be determined as belonging to a given class, or as requiring the creation of a new class. Once classified, they fall under the auspices of one or more apparatuses of power. Productive capitalist power operates on the supersystemic level as an apparatus of capture feeding social escapes back into the web of interacting power systems. The determined sites and embodiments also form the basis for claims of freedom or privilege on the part of the bodies to which the class or category is applied. Negotiation has not become entirely extinct, any more than linear time has. It has been reshuffled. It has been internalized into the supersystem's mechanisms of expansion and adaptational self-reproduction. Forces of existence that coalesce enough to begin to define new social sites or embodiments are perceived by the supersystem as indeterminacies that are then competitively determined by the supersystem's constituent systems in a way that assimilates them into the existing social landscape with minimal disruption. Ontological emergence is hijacked.[9] Emergences creating the conditions for serious conflict are funneled into normative channels setting carefully controlled parameters of negotiation. Not only do these emergences not disrupt the supersystem, they feed it. Every socially recognized class is a potential market. Productive capitalist power is directly a market-expansion tool, and conversely, every market-expansion tool is directly a form of capitalist power. The creation of a niche market through advertising is the creation of a niche power-object that is also a potential political constituency. Social emergence, the irruption of new forces of existence, are precapitalized. In other words, the power to exist has been transformed into an internal variable of the capitalist supersystem. This subsumption of life itself under capital is expressed in different ways on many levels. Biotechnology and the Human Genome Project are the most literal examples. On the level of capitalist diplomacy, it involves the singular-generic "humanity" that enters into mass-media circulation, disappearing and reappearing following a complicated rhythm. We saw earlier how the "humanity" of the Iraqi war dead disappeared into the machinic circuitry. We also saw how "humanity" reappeared in Somalia thanks to the philanthropic gesture of the military white-knight who shot to feed. Life and death are fused in the generic figure of "humanity" in crisis, then are reparticularized, reimplanted, proceduralized, and valorized in a variety of ways. This vastly increases the reach of power, but also expands the potential for negotiation and advocacy under the banner of "human rights" and "humanitarian aid." The stakes are real. The importance of human rights advocacy cannot be underestimated and should not be seen to be belittled by critiques of "humanism." But by the same token, it is not in itself a site of "resistance." It is a site of adaptational capture—a far better option for the starving Somali than obliteration. Adaptational capture is the only other option open in the absence of conditions for resistance. Resistance, if it is still at all possible (and I think it is), will take a different, most likely posthuman route.[10] Critiques of "humanism" could very well prove useful in opening that path. This is an argument for an additivity of political strategies on the part of those who desire to change the capitalist supersystem, to match the additivity of capitalism itself. It is crucial to begin thinking in terms of non-mutually exclusive strata of political action (including identitarian politics) and how they may be coalesced into supersystemic contestation.

4. It is as artificial to separate command from control as it is to separate death from life. Command (power over life, power of death) and control (power to enliven), though really distinct, co-function. They are interwoven into the fabric of everyday life, and their uneasy ground-level mixes

can be seen to lie along the same continuum of power. On that continuum, the quality of their respective effects converge. On the one hand, the command subtraction of a potential provokes a reflexive evasion or adaptive alteration: command is also productive of life; control is its by-product. On the other hand, the field of operation of the noncoercive, incitative power of control channelings is punctuated and porously delimited by command attacks, to which it regularly appeals in self-defense. Command and control are reciprocal by-products, as are life and death. "Death becomes multiplied and differentiated, endowing life with the singularities, and thus the truths, from which life believes its resistance arises . . . death as coextensive with life, and as composed of a multiplicity of partial and singular deaths" (Deleuze 1986b, 95, translation modified). The interpenetration of life and death, of course, is a characteristic of all modes of power, even the "negative" power of absolutist command the evocation of which opens Foucault's *Discipline and Punish* (1977), and whose object is sovereignty. Foucault's disciplinary institutions can be seen as normative command centers radiating control, productive less of sovereignty than of eddies of social order. Biopower takes the interpenetration of life and death, control and command, to a new level. It integrates disciplinary power into a new social landscape marshalling the partiality of death, subdivided and multiplied, toward the goal of enlivenment, the multiplication of life's productive powers. Unleashed production replaces order as the object of power (in Marxist terms, this coincides with the "formal subsumption of labor" under capital). Deleuze suggests that contemporary capitalism must be seen to function under yet another regime. A "crisis of enclosure" has occurred (the "crises" long heralded in the media, among which the "breakdowns" of the family, the judicial and prison subsystems, and the school subsystem figure prominently). When the walls come down, disciplinary command functions are not dismantled, but rather released. They disseminate and vary, coming to be even more finely distributed throughout the social field, bringing death, subdivided and multiplied, and life channelings into even more intimate embrace. Deleuze applies the name "control" to the regime of power growing out of the ultimate fine-meshing of command-and-control, because the overall tenor of the system is one of positive channeling and incitement. In spite of its "productive" nature, he contrasts this mode of power to "biopower." This is because it actually bears more directly on circulation than on production—to the extent that this distinction still holds. The society of control corresponds, in Marxist terms, to the "real subsumption of society" under capital. Real subsumption is characterized by a blurring of the boundary between circulation and production (every deterritorialized circulation expressing and creating a surplus-value). "Control" is best taken in a sense close to its cybernetic sense: systems control of input, output, and the transformative operations effected in the autonomic machine—applied to bodies (defined as broadly as possible, to include images) rather than to information. In this view, "input" and "output" combine into one function, as a channeling across a threshold (a residual wall that came down). The threshold is not between an inside and an outside but between two juxtaposed outsides in an open field. The transformative operation does not follow the crossing of the threshold; it is the threshold. Emergence is serialized in successive passages. It is processed. The object of this mode of power is not sovereignty, order, production, or even circulation per se; rather, it is the circulatory modulation of all of these (and more).[11] Control involves the assimilation of powers of existence, at the moment of their emergence (their phased passing), into a classificatory schema determining normative orbits around which procedural parameters for negotiation and advocacy are set. It has to do with the production of socially valorized normative entities. The normative undergoes rapid inflation, as classificatory and regulative mechanisms are elaborated for every socially recognizable state of being, including illness (support and advocacy groups for people living with particular health conditions: the socialization of disease) and death (euthanasia: the properly social, as opposed to political, production of death). "Normal" is now freestanding, no longer the opposite and necessary complement of "abnormal," "deviant," or "dysfunctional," as it was under disciplinary power, except in limit-cases. The meaning of "normative" has changed. Normativity becomes synonymous with collective visibility and social operativity— with living itself (and with illness and death "with dignity," in other words actively transformed into an affirmation of life). Command, for its part, is a militarized police function that is activated in the limit-case by a transgression of an existing norm (that is, by a failure or refusal to be assimilated to a new norm). Command takes over at the point at which the normal rebinarizes with the "abnormal," "deviant," and "dysfunctional." That point is fluid, under constant renegotiation. The mass circulation of figures of criminality, and their police-figure complements, applied to heads of state as well as their subjects, is not as gratuitous as it might have seemed.[12] Crime is itself the figure of the limit-case (particularly crimes "against the community" and "against humanity," which by their generic nature tend to subsume all other varieties). It is in the domain of crime that the continually displaced parameters of command are constantly reset. The vagueness of the generic figures of crime, criminal, and cop clearly expresses a general function of the capitalist supersystem. Command and control are the fissionable and fusionable atoms of capitalist power (the singular-generics proper to it). They reciprocally generate each other, and disappear and reappear into each other following a complicated and fundamentally unpredictable rhythm covering the totality of social space. The principle of modulation states that the capitalist supersystem must be characterized, globally, as a modulatory social control system conditioned by and conditioning command (the "political" defined narrowly as autocratic decision backed by effective force).[13]

5. Normative control systems and command centers are collective autonomic apparatuses, as are their interlinkages. So although humanized intentionality, as expressed through negotiation and advocacy, also appears and reappears and disseminates throughout the social fabric, it does not characterize the system as a whole. Like life itself, human intentionality has become an internal variable of capitalist power. What mediations continue to function are incapable of founding anything approaching a civil society that could ground a consensus-based decision-making power. The dream of a civil society that could serve as an equilibrium-seeking, democratic counterpull to the profoundly undemocratic, crisis-ridden, creative chaos of the capitalist supersystem is just that: a dream. This is the principle of complicity, or untranscendable control. Mediation-based strategies, whether of reform or of dialectical struggle, are now bit players on the global scene of power (which does not preclude their retaining important roles locally). If the human disappears and reappears locally and primarily affectively, globally it is relegated to the status of a reflexive machinic relay. For example, instant opinion polling elicits human reflex responses that are relayed via the autonomic apparatus of the mass media to other apparatuses, where they legitimate or enable certain autonomic operations.[14] In the case of the Gulf War, human response was relayed through the executive branch to military command centers, where it was translated into decisions to shoot, this time to kill. In such autonomic surroundings, it is vain to mourn the passing of moral reasoning and philosophies of right. Our social existence is affective and reflexive, and it serves little purpose to deny it. Any movement aiming to breathe new life into ideological power mechanisms in the name of humanity, or even a county-size portion of it, is working against an enormous posthuman tide.

6. Although capitalist control endlessly produces norms and normativity, although capitalist command polices them, although controlled assimilations of sociality give rise to codifications and recodifications, although the generic figures it circulates may give grist for symbolic orderings, the contemporary capitalist supersystem as such is neither normative, codifying, nor structural-symbolic. This is what distinguishes it from earlier regimes of power. On the formal level, contemporary capitalism's constituent elements are indeterminacies that are determinabilities that are singular-generics—the very convertibilities that were argued to constitute positivities. They are the positivity of the supersystem in its formal dimension. This amounts to saying that the system is formally undetermined but gives rise to determinations; that it is ungrounded, yet grounds. Capitalist power is determining (of norms, codes, and symbolic structures) in effect. But its every ground-effect is no sooner implanted than uprooted. Deviance, decoding, and structural escape are also, in effect, determined (as channeled transformative passage, captive social fluidity productive of new norms, codes, symbolic structures). The emphasis on multiplication and fluidity should not be taken to imply that formal analysis of contemporary capitalism is impossible, that its formal dimension is unthinkable. All that it means is that contemporary capitalism is not definable in the framework of traditional logic. Fortunately, there exist new logics, as well as metalogics. The latter are formal supersystems not averse to productive paradox whose constituent elements are, precisely, the excluded middles of indeterminacy, determinability, and singular-generic. Although the formal expression of such axiomatics is of little value to cultural theory, their conceptual scaffolding may well have contributions to make to a metalogical description of capitalism.[15] Mainstream social sciences are already employing axiomatic method. The open-systems theory of Niklas Luhmann can be seen as an axiomatic conceptualization of the self-reproduction of social systems. Luhmann's analyses of "autopoietic" self-referential systems describe the formal dimension of what are being called here "autonomous apparatuses of power."[16] In the deregulatory environment of contemporary capitalism, every apparatus of government power is under intense pressure to reinvent itself as a self-reflective, self-reproducing system subordinated less to the will of a "people" than to measurable output criteria defined in directly capitalist terms ("productivity" and "profitability"). "Metatheoretical" approaches to cultural studies often attempt to map possibilities for global contestation. Their problem is not that they are too "meta," but that they are not "meta" enough. Cultural theory has to be raised to an entirely new level of abstraction in order to be able to grasp the utter and increasing concreteness of capitalist power. Because the reality of that power is in flux. The supersystem has no constants. It is a field of continual variation, each modulation of which combines a superabstractness with an infra-empirical concreteness, at the border between life and death: once again, the fickle figure of "humanity" and the marketable mapping of the human gene provide suggestive examples. Enlightenment "Man" has deterritorialized and bifurcated. Torn from its metaphysical mooring in any putative human essence, uprooted from any stable existential territory, it enters circulation. Ex-"Man" circulates on the one hand as a singular-generic "humanity" that can be shot to be fed or shot to be killed, can become a military staging ground, as ant or enemy, or a machinic disappearance. This is a "humanity" that, as a collective, affective, generative matrix, is too essentially changeable, too multiply determinable, to be attributed the pallid integrity of "moral personhood" that is the presumption of any enlightened ideology of emancipation. On the other hand, ex-"Man" circulates as a generative (genetic) matrix embedded in the materiality of the human. The singular-generic human genome lies at the point of capital indistinction between the biological and the chemical, where the "human" is more closely akin to a saleable virus, neither dead nor alive, than a reasonable animal standing at the pinnacle of earthly life-forms, one step below the divine on a ladder of perfection. Moral-rational integrity is lost in a human self-concept struck with the metalogical mutability of affect; species integrity is lost in a biochemical code expressing the mutability of human matter. Capitalist power operates on that double-edged mutability. Its preferential domain can be said to be where the far side of abstraction meets the underneath of the concrete—where concept becomes affect (and thus returns to the body as seat of affective actualization); where body becomes code (and thus conceptual); where the conceptual becomes corporeal (where reflection becomes reflex), and vice versa, in a double becoming no sooner splintering "Man" into singular-generics than fusing these in a shared capitalization on a global scale; and no sooner fusing them than launching them into differential circulation on distinct empirical levels (the mass media and biotechnology). Only an axiomatic can grasp this super-infra mutability, this systemic capacity for differential fluctuation, as a positivity rather than an aporia. The axiomatic principle holds that the thinking of late capitalist power as autopoiesis—or better, "heteropoiesis" (Guattari 1995)—should not be left to state apologists such as Luhmann but redirected with a view to resistance.

7. Resistance, if it is possible (and again, I think it is), needs to be reinscribed in the generic. As it is usually conceived, resistance starts from a particularity and either defends or deepens that particularity. But particularity is an effect of the very system of determination that resistance is meant to resist. It is a reductive embodiment of the singular-generic in a serially determinate, normatively specifiable entity. Resistance must be reconceptualized as an operation on the generic: its direct embodiment as multiply singular.[17] The tactical embodiment of the groundless ground of capitalist power would short-circuit its channelings. It would dephase controlled emergence: in other words, envelop locally the globality of its phasings (this is the technical definition of "singularity" in chaos theory). Resistance would be the condensation of vital powers of emergence—and multiple deaths. In other words, it would define itself less as an oppositional practice than a pragmatics of intensified ontogenesis: at life's edge. This is the countercapitalist principle of vitalist metaconstructivism. This principle can only be fully theorized through its own pragmatic application. In other words, through experimentation.

8. A final principle might be dubbed the autonomy of affect (Massumi 2002, ch. 1). Affect constitutes a social stratum. It is no less a social automaton than any other apparatus of capitalist power. And apparatus of power it is: the circulation of affect through the mass media is in and of itself a normative control mechanism (a channeling of attention). It feeds into other control systems operating on other levels, and which is directly convertible into fuel for command systems. It must be borne in mind that affect, in the continually varying capitalist landscape, is an impersonal flow before it is a subjective content. That is why the sadism of affective legitimation was earlier characterized as "innocent." It is everyone's, but no one's in particular. If there is criminal guilt here, it is fluid and generic. Affect is an internal variable of the system. Like every such variable, its variability is predicated on a deterritorialization, but its determination involves a reterritorialization. It is a crucial task of capitalist critique to redefine affect, to reconceptualize the processes by which affect is deterritorialized from its historical territory—the supposedly autonomous subject—and reterritorialized in a variety of autonomic apparatuses—including but not limited to innocently complicitous bodies. Such a redefinition of affect would have to find a way of describing deterritorialized circulation in terms of forces and movement (forces of existence, intensive movement), retaining a derivative role for signification (coding and symbolization). This done, there is no reason why complicitous collectivities could not or should not intervene pragmatically on what then appears as an eminently pragmatic register. Affective intervention could take place on the level of capitalist communication, perhaps even through the mass media. This insider, or immanent, resistance might play on the nature of communication as productive interference. Productive interference patterns that fail to resonate with capitalist legitimation, either by excess or by deficiency or with humor, are at least momentarily unassimilable by the supersystem and seem, from its point of view, to be simple negativities, "vacuoles of noncommunication," to quote Deleuze (1995, 176). Tactical noncommunication might take a ritualistic form, mimicking the ritual legitimation of capitalist power, to very different effect—and affect. For it would not be sadistic, but joyful; not exorcistic, but invocational, calling forth what are, again from the point of view of the supersystem, vague and alien powers of collective existence whose determinations escape.

This essay itself is meant to be such an invocation, however hesitant and unformed. It began with what was essentially an expression of my complicity, my involvement in the Gulf War and Somalia, as an American television viewer reflecting back on the intensely ambivalent reactions I had at the time to what I saw those many years ago (so close, so far). For there was no option simply to step outside the Reagan-Bush/Clinton legitimation of state violence. The only "outside" my Gulf War television experience admitted of was a criminalized Saddam Hussein–General Aideed: so evidently an outwardly projected, distorted image of the "inside" in which I found myself. This "outside" is a relative outside that is the inside's own creation (through the mass media, through foreign aid). No, I am in, and the only way out is through to an absolute outside, an as yet barely thinkable, still inexistent outside that would amount to an immanent conversion of capitalism. Critique is not an abstract distancing of the self from its concrete "object"; it is a superabstract, infraconcrete distance to—to an outside, of the self and its system of objects (capitalism). That outside is the potential, contained by capitalism, for its own collapse. It is a pure virtuality. I do not affirm the opposite of Reagan-Bush/Clinton (Hussein-Aideed). I affirm the extinction of that opposition as a mode of capitalist power. The "principles" outlined here were affectively inflected concepts taking faltering steps toward the threshold, in a manner meant to match the mode of operation of capitalist power, without buying into it. They are less "principles" in any strict sense than pragmatic "pointers" in which I invest not my "self" but my affect, my body (my thought as affect-body). This an investment in a future money can't buy. It is complicity—but not toward retirement.

2017

The Political Is Not Personal

Affect, Power, Violence

BRAD EVANS: *Amongst the many contributions you have made in your work, you are particularly known for innovatively developing the concept of affect. How do you understand this concept and why is it relevant for understanding power?*

BRIAN MASSUMI: I appreciate the question, because there tends to be a misunderstanding that affect is only about personal experience. Because of that supposed emphasis on the interiority of the individual, it is often thought that affect is by nature apolitical. For me, it has always been the exact opposite. I was attracted to the concept because of how directly political it is. It is a power concept through and through.

The basic definition that I keep coming back to comes from Spinoza, who spoke of "powers to affect and be affected" as what defines a body and a life. A power to affect and be affected is a potential to move, act, perceive, and think—in a word, powers of existence. The "to be affected" part of the definition says that a body's powers of existence are irreducibly relational. They can only be expressed in dynamic relation with other bodies and elements of the environment. The power to affect and the power to be affected are inseparable; they are two sides of the same coin. They are reciprocals, growing and shrinking as a function of each other. So from the start, affect overspills the individual, tying its capacities to its relational entanglement with others and the outside. Affect is fundamentally transindividual.

The word "power" here is in the first instance not power-over. It is power-to. Affect grasps life from the angle of its activity, its exuberance, its drive to express always more of a body's powers of existence or potential to be, in an always irreducibly relational way, in attunement with the affordances of the outside. It is an expansive concept, and a concept of expression. Each act expresses powers of existence, and varies them, affecting and being affected in a way unique to that circumstance, so that every act of being is also a modification that takes its place in an ongoing becoming. Power-to is the power to change. That is the starting point: a nonlimitative concept of power as life-enhancing, and life-changing, through an openness onto the outside.

The problem then is to account for power-over, which limits power-to and curtails becoming through repression or the normative channeling of activity. By this account, power-over is emergent. It is not foundational. It is not a general, abstract force, or Law with a capital L. It is a particular result, a kind of achievement. Like every achievement, it can come undone, or be undone. It has to continually work to maintain itself. This means it is always manifesting its weaknesses, even as it exerts its sway. This is empowering politically, because it makes change and the affirmation of powers of life primary, and attributes to them their own power—as a kind of directly affirmative, primary resistance.

BE: *Through this conceptualization of power, what you also seem to be proposing is a different concept of politics and the political.*

BM: This concept of power expands the realm of the political beyond its usual connotation of formations of domination, containment by institutions, and channeling by norms. It extends it to a level of emergence where positive powers of existence are stirring and vying to express themselves, laying claim to an autonomy of becoming. Power-to is a strange amalgam: it refers to a relational autonomy. This extension of the concept of power is often spoken of in terms of a distinction between "the political" (the autonomous expression of relational powers of existence as primary resistance) and "politics." Politics is the capture of powers of existence, turned against their own expansion and enhancement.

This might sound very abstract, but it's actually all about intensities of experience. There is a third part of the definition which says that a power to affect and be affected always manifests itself eventfully, in a transition, a passing of a threshold across which a body's powers of existence are either augmented or diminished. They are raised to a higher power or curtailed. This transition to a higher or lower power-to is felt as a shift in a body's intensity of existence, its capacity to be all that it can express, and express more of what it can do.

With affect, *the political becomes directly felt*. This has all kinds of implications for political practice. For one thing, it opens the way for a fundamentally *aesthetic* approach to politics, taking aesthetic in something close to its etymological meaning as pertaining to qualities of experience. But it also closes the door on the limiting idea that if you are talking about qualities and intensities of experience, you are talking about subjective interiority. Here, you're talking about intensities of relation that register individually, while directly making a difference in the world. These pertain to the individual's autonomy of expression of its powers to be, but only to the extent that that expression is participatory, directly and dynamically entangled with the outside.

BE: *I'd like to bring this conceptual insight directly to the question of violence. What does the word "violence" mean to you from a political and philosophical perspective?*

BM: It is clear that the concept of violence cannot be reduced to direct, bodily violence. Violence is not only in the act. It also acts in potential. It operates even when it doesn't pass fully into action. This is widely acknowledged in political discourse concerned with "structural violence" and "micro-aggression." But from an affect philosophy perspective, the concept of structural violence is questionable. It is too broad. It makes violence into that kind of general, abstract force that underlies every situation and every act like an inescapable foundation.

This is a profoundly disempowering notion. It puts the individual at the mercy of forces that are not just circumstantially more powerful than it is by several orders of magnitude, but are essentially so. It is hard to see how what is founded—the individual life—can escape or counteract its foundation: it's formatting by power in that overpoweringly abstract understanding of it.

The concept of affect offers two strategies here. The first is to define violence as power-over: the curtailment of the power-to. This acknowledges that violence is not reducible to the punctual acts that bring it to full expression in bodily aggression. It can act in and as its own potential. Violence can be as oppressive in the way it looms over us as an unspoken threat that is applied unequally, depending on the color of a body's skin, its gender, and other conventional markers that the exercise of power-over uses selectively to trigger itself into operation.

The second is to say that even though violence looms everywhere all the time, it never does so in a general way. Even as a threat, it is a particular *operation*. Or more accurately, a particular way of being in pre-operation. To have any effect, the threat, as potential for violence, has to *make itself felt* in some way. To make itself felt, it has to introduce itself into each situation into which it moves. It has to make ingress, and it does this affectively. "Structural" violence is no less an event than the swing of a club. But it is a directly affective event, which diminishes a body's expressive powers of existence even without actually lifting a finger. "Priming" is a way of talking about what kind of event this entering into pre-operation is.

Priming is the way in which the *conditions* set up for a situation implant certain tendencies in it. That is what I meant by pre-operation: being present in tendency. This conditioning-in of tendencies is contingent on signs, including but not limited to the bodily markers I just mentioned. Violence in the broader sense affectively "in-signs" itself into situations. The priming of the situation is the way it signposts that a *conversion of the power-to into an exercise of power-over* is imminent, looming over every action, on the brink of coming fully into act.

As I said, this in-signing is itself a kind of act, or event. This means that it is possible to respond to the violence making potential ingress on the same plane on which it operates: that of live events. There may be an inkling of a potential to alter-prime the event toward a different set of conditions, activating different tendencies. This amounts to taking back potential. To act politically is to occupy potential.

BE: *Might we not also apply this logic of violence as potential to the concept of resistance?*

BM: Yes, violence is everywhere all the time, effectively in potential—but so is resistance. There is a primary resistance that is always churning, always vying, always pushing toward the augmentation of powers of life. And this can be *performed*. It can be *enacted* in a way that it is attuned to the ingression of violence in that particular situation, countering it head-on or clandestinely evading it. This brings things to a down-to-earth tactical level, which can save us from the paralysis that the overarching general concept of structural violence can easily create. How can a mere part resist such a foundational whole? How can you fight a generality when your existence is always local?

The idea here is that the "general" violence has to make itself enter into each particular situation in which it wants to hold sway, but that ingression is always already met with primary resistance—and where there is resistance there is some degree of freedom in how a body is affected and can affect. The need to make ingression, rather than just being in place a priori, introduces a degree of play, in the sense in which we say a mechanism has play, which can potentially be exploited in situ to confound the operation of power-over. It opens the way for an affirmative "micropolitics" in response to the ever-renewed background conditions of micro-aggression and the punctual macro-explosions of outright violence that they hold in ready reserve.

The trick is to avoid responding on the same general level on which the violence seems to operate. Don't take it at face value. That only gives it more power. Always remember that power has to adapt itself to each situation, and that means that there is always a chance that resistance can counteradapt itself on the fly—if it is affectively attuned to the *singularity* of each exercise of power. To do this, you have to live out the situational intensity of *this* experience, here and now, in all its complexities and sinuosities.

Principles are not enough. Critical judgment is not enough. Being "woke" is not enough. These are necessary, but they are raised to a higher power if they are used not as ends in themselves, and not as general strategies, but as avenues toward an affective attunement to the event in its singularity. That sets the conditions for more than a frontal response, in reaction to the threat of violence—which just weds you to the form of the aggression. When you think about it, reacting is just a contrary a way of being constrained by what you are reacting against.

Affective attunement sets the conditions for a *tactical* power to *improvise* a response that is not dictated by the aggression as a reaction to it, in mirror-image form, but rather claims its own positivity, in eventful autonomy and relation, artfully playing to what is concretely being insigned and enacted, refusing conversion by power-over while avoiding embodying its negative image. The emphasis then is on affirming counterpowers of moving, acting, perceiving, thinking that decide their own form as they enact themselves.

This gives resistance a plastic power-to in the face of power-over's ability to insinuate itself into every situation. It requires honing different modes of action, creating new sets of affective skills and tactics that are as aesthetic—because they are improvisational and affirm intensities of experience—as they are directly political—because they are by nature relational and are all the more plastic and power(-to)ful the more relationally attuned they are and the more collectively they are mobilized.

BE: *So how does this notion of relationality relate back to your concerns with the personal?*

BM: Personalizing narratives actually occlude this affirmative power of resistance, because they are focused first on defining the present event in terms of the individual's past, and only then look to opening the collective future in a break from narratives from the past. Yes, the personal is political. The personal is never untouched by the accumulated effects of power. It is never free of power effects and the traces of their violence. These are part and parcel of its very constitution. But precisely for that reason, the converse is not the case: *the political is not personal*.

The political is a collective break from the accumulating effects of power inherited from the past, claiming the right of ingress in the present. The political is what breaks through the personal, shattering the hold of the accumulated power effects that are part and parcel of its constitution, liberating self-affirming powers of primary resistance that co-occur with identity but do not belong to it, that are not contained in it but pass through and around it, that open instead onto the outside, onto new affective vistas of collective becoming. We live toward the future transindividually, in excess over our personhood. The political is not coming home to a familiar face. The political is estrangingly intensive. It is rewilding. In its movement, we are strangers to ourselves. We meet ourselves anew as the animal we are just now becoming. The political acts in the name of a life we have *not* lived. It acts for the life we have *yet* to live.

BE: *Connecting this to the rise of Donald Trump in the United States, how can we make sense of this phenomenon, especially in terms of the liberation of prejudice?*

BM: Trump is an extreme example of the power of the personal, and the personal *as* power. When I say that I mean something very different than it might sound like. I don't mean that he embodies the "rugged individual" of American mythology, or the old civic model of upright personhood, like the nineteenth-century ideal of the sovereign, self-governing individual as paragon of capitalist virtue providing a moral compass for entrepreneurial activity with which others identify and strive to emulate. This is the traditional theory of political leadership based on "identification" with a charismatic figure.

Nothing could be farther from the Trump post-truth. There is nothing either particularly rugged nor morally upright about him. His personality is not a bulwark against the excesses of capitalism. It's an opening of the floodgates. He does not stand in his person against capitalism's excesses—he flows with them. It is he who is identified with those excesses, rather than others who are identified with him. He won election precisely because of his supposed capitalist prowess, in one of the most corrupt sectors of the economy. He is the *personification of capital*.

This is precisely how neoliberalism strives to redefine the person: as "human capital," or what Foucault calls the "entrepreneur of himself." But what is this "himself"? It has no consistency. Trump says one thing one day, something else the next. The center does not hold. There is no center. There is just an eddy of bluster on the roiling seas of social media. Trump personifies the deregulating tendencies of neoliberal capitalism. Through him, the "creative destruction" at the heart of capitalism's movements extend to the emotional composition of the person, now borderline, post-normative, trading in cartoonish exaggerations of the erstwhile norm, refracted through the distorting prism of a white hypermasculinity bloated to absurd dimensions. It is hard to take Trump seriously as a person. This is reflected in the colloquial use of his name as a common noun: the Donald.

The Donald embodies a certain hypercapitalist overcoming of the person. His followers do not identify with him in the sense of recognizing themselves in him. Through his bluster, they identify themselves with capitalism's deregulated overspilling of the norms. They embrace the ideal of being "entrepreneurs of themselves," in "politically incorrect" excess over regulated norms of behavior. By what criterion is there an identity or sameness between a billionaire born into wealth and privilege and a middle American in the Rust Belt with the fear of God in them about falling into poverty (if they are not already in it)? Weirdly, it is less that Trumpians are recognizing themselves in his sameness than that they are *recognizing their own difference* in his distorted mirror. They are seeing what they experience as their own *exceptionalism*: what makes them special as Americans, vis-à-vis the hated "un-American Americans" ("liberal progressives," the "mainstream media," the "deep state" establishment, immigrant "job-stealers," "entitled" African Americans—the list is long).

This occurs not through Trump's person in any traditional sense, but through his *persona*. His obsession with Twitter and cable TV makes him a single-body media node. He lives for it. His life-form is inseparable from it. His person is an ongoing media irritation: an affective resonater, nodally positioned. He receives with a shudder waves of social and political static, and no sooner sends them back out with a Twitter spasm, in a self-perpetuating cycle. This operates in a way that primes the social field for just the kind of ever-present threat and violence I was talking about earlier. The Trump-figure is an *affective converter* of power-to into a contagion of power-over disseminating through the social field—a one-man epidemic of reaction-formation. But this is the strange phenomenon of a proactive reaction.

Here, reactivity is affirmed as such. It is practiced as an offensive sport, or better, a war-machine ever on the attack rather than in self-defense. This is beyond "prejudice." It is a veritable mode of existence, affectively primed. There is no time left to go into more detail about this. The main point is that an affective approach to politics might offer some new conceptual tools for understanding the originality of the Trump phenomenon. We do ourselves no favors if we try to respond to it with obsolete conceptions about politics and persons. We are in uncharted, post-truth, deregulated territory, and we need new modes of understanding and resistance to be equal to the challenge of collectively reopening the potential of our quickly foreclosing future.

Couplet 9

2001

Tell Me Where Your Pain Is

Pointing to the Body without an Image

Where Does It Hurt?

My child, as a toddler, shook my sense of space. The purpose of this essay is to convey that disruption into adulthood. The question is: What will it be when it grows up?

Here is what happened. Toddling along, as toddlers do, he fell, slapping a knee against the pavement in a painful reminder of crawling. Nothing more banal. The expected tears began to flow. The time-honored ritual of parental soothing was called for. "Kiss it better," he pleaded as I pulled him to his feet. "Where does it hurt?" I asked, following protocol. "There!" he said, pointing. His voice betrayed the mildly exasperated but indulgent tone we use when those less astute than we require us to state the obvious.

He was pointing to the pavement in front of him.

I often wonder what effect it would have had on his development if I had kissed the ground at his feet. Not feeling quite that devoted, I kissed the scraped knee and pronounced it better. As we toddled on, I wondered: Where *does* it hurt? I would lose all credibility if I told my tottering child that it doesn't hurt where he hits the ground. On the other hand, hadn't he accepted the healing kiss to the knee? His resignation to where my lips found the pain indicated that he was taking an open-minded approach to the problem. The idea that there was a "there" to the pain seemed to be a point we could agree on. What we agreed on was in the assumption that the feeling had some kind of voluminousness or extension that made it meaningful to ask where. What we disagreed on was where "there" was.

The child's "there" could be two places. He was prepared to locate the pain both on the ground in front of him and in his leg. He took it in his stride that his feeling should be multiply located. I didn't. I knew where his nerve endings were. I knew the pain to be there: in the organic object. My son was not locating the feeling in a single, objectively defined location. He was locating it in *its event*. The ground he fell upon marked the culmination of the event. It was only natural that he should locate the fall's effect where the event that brought it terminated. The event began in a misstep: an accident that happened because its triggering went unperceived. If he had had the wherewithal to specify at what point the accident tripped in, he could have seen it coming and it wouldn't have happened. Now that it happened, what emphatically stood out was where it brought him to.

In the logic of the event, there is no contradiction in humoring the adult and saying that the pain is also in the knee. A characteristic of events is that they have extension. They have a span (they straddle a splay of factors) and they are extendable. The end point of an event is always the starting point for a new phase in its unfolding. The pain extends across its culminating ground and the walking away from that encounter of the uprighted organ. It stretches between those two locations, organic and inorganic, and their two times: the already-past of the event and its ongoing present. My son was understanding the voluminousness or extension of his feeling to include the places we had collaboratively pointed out, the theres of the pavement and of the knee, as well as including the immediate past of the event and its on-flow in the present. For him, the "extension" of the event of pain could not be reduced to what we think of as spatial emplacement. It included duration. Including duration makes for vague extension. You can say with confidence that the ongoing pain-event *passed through* the falling-ground and the knee's walking away. But it began in an accident, whose onset was by nature unperceived. So you can't say with confidence just how or where it started. Neither can you say how far it will go. Will it end when it reaches the merry-go-round in the park? Or will it linger and resurge at bedtime, at the anxious edge of sleep, to be relived in dream? The event emphatically marks a before-after, but its limits are vague.

If you think of it, the confidence of my initial response was a false one, even on its own terms. True, the feeling can be objectively verified to have been in the knee. But from there it went up the nerves to the spinal column, and from the spinal column it reached the brain and fanned out across trillions of synapses. Where was it by then? In their fractal interval? In memory? Point to that. Now where did it begin, objectively speaking? Every pain recalls and recapitulates past pains, as well as echoing feelings of other kinds. Like soothing. No feeling is an island. A feeling reverberates across an indefinite string of iterations that its event plays like a harp. Against the score of that rhythmic inclusion, that echoing connection, a feeling strikes its note. Its specific quality is both effect and expression of its moving inclusion.[1]

So: Where *does* it hurt?

A feeling begins in an unplaceable unperceived, and never really ends. Hurts don't die, they just linger and resurge. Despite this indefinite extension, we can still point and say: the pain passed here. That much is clear. There are regions of clarity in the feeling-event's ongoing. The problem is, there are two of them, and they splay. If you ask where the feeling "really" was, you have to choose one or the other. That means discounting aspects of the event as it was felt. The child really did feel the pain to be on the pavement. You can only give a definitive answer to the where of a feeling-event if you are willing to subtract feelings from it. Yes, there are regions of clarity, but if you try objectively to locate the feeling in a region of clarity you run into trouble. You have to dismiss as unreal elements of the event that effectively figured in it. You have to practice a cognitive cleansing of the felt event.

If you can't locate the feeling in a region of clarity, why not locate the region of clarity in the feeling? This is what the child's open-mindedness was suggesting. William James agrees with the infant. "When a [newborn] baby's toe aches," he writes, "he does not place the pain in the toe. He makes no definite movements of defence, and may be vaccinated without being held" (1950, 187–88n). This is because the baby doesn't yet know he has a toe. The pain is a world unto itself. As the needle penetrates the flesh, nothing else exists.[2] Not knowing where it came from or when it will end, the child's entire being is absorbed in the excruciating intricacies of the feeling. But say that the nurse strokes the limb,

> awakening the pain every time her finger passes towards the toe; let him look on and see her finger on the toe every time the pain shoots up; let him handle his foot himself and get the pain whenever the toe comes into his fingers or his mouth; let the moving leg exacerbate the pain,—and all is changed. The space of the pain becomes identified with the part of each of the other spaces which gets felt when it awakens; and by their identity with it these parts are identified with each other, and grow systematically connected as members of a larger extensive whole. (187–88n)[3]

The pain is indefinitely extended across an open multiplicity of movements. But it figures in each movement as a moment of clarity or recognized intensity of feeling. The repetition of the feeling in different ways by different movements weaves a web of feeling paths. The pain stands out as a spot of intensity, an "emphatic point" (James 1950, 185), where the paths intersect in a refrain: note struck; rhythmic inclusion in a pattern of transition.[4] The identity of the organ is a differential of feeling tracks, traced in duration by a multiplicity of movements. The pain's location arises as the global effect of a web of connections movingly brought to the same feeling. Behold, the toe. It gradually emerges against the backdrop of that vague, complex extent of movement, rising emphatically from the intersections, where one movement cuts across another. It emerges *as a feeling locus* standing out in a pattern of repeated emphasis. The regularity of the potential for that standing out begins to take on a stature of its own. The emphatic point settles into a body part, poised for pains (and pleasures) to come. It has become separately identifiable—and speakable. The parental voice chimes in: "Get your toe out of your mouth." Point of protocol. The infant will eventually agree that some intersections are better than others.

James is vigorously shaking our sense of space. He is saying that *in order to place the pain in your toe, you first have to place the toe in your pain*. The toe as a locatable object emerges as a differentiation of the pain.[5] Once it emerges, it is easy to point to or suck on, revisit and discourse upon, as a place of feeling. Apply that principle to every body part. *In order to locate an experience in the body, you must first locate the body in experience.* The body as a locatable object emerges as a differentiation of a vague, complex extent of movements cross-cutting, including some that will later separate out as belonging to other people. There is an open-ended, processual whole of collective experience, a *"simple total vastness"* (James 1950, 145, emphasis added) that precedes the body's locatability and speakability.[6] There is a field of experience that precedes bodies' physical and cultural positioning. It is unbounded, of vague extent, but highly differentiated in its own, eminently eventful, intersectional way, full of before-afters.

This is nothing less than a Copernican revolution in our understanding of the body and its space. You cannot understand the body's placement and partition if you assume a preexisting space within which it feels. The body doesn't feel its way through a space it navigates. It doesn't move through a pregiven spatial frame of experience. Rather, experience moves through, not at first a body, but its own vague voluminousness, the unbounded extent of its self-echoing event. The body, its parts and places, space itself in its difference from time, are emphatically spotty derivatives of that passing-through. They are encompassed by the global volume of the interplay giving rise to them. The Copernican revolution consists in the realization that *the world does not contain feeling, but that feeling instead contains worlds*. Worlds emerge from and are delimited by feeling. We are all perpetual infants subject to ongoing vaccination. At every step we feel the needle passing through, and our entire body, the whole world, contracts into the sharpness of that point. "Place is not different from what passes through it" (Deleuze 1991b, 3).[7]

A Critique of Pure Feeling

A corrective is necessary here. It is accurate enough to say that the world does not contain feeling but that feeling contains worlds, but this can be taken in the wrong way. It can easily be taken to imply a subjectivism: that the world is in our heads. James, however, is saying something very different, something very close to the opposite. The nurse passing her finger over the leg of the child can do so because her finger has long since arisen from the background of her life's movement to stand out as a body part. Its standing out can be traced phylogenetically back to regions of the future nurse's developing embryo feeling each other out. The feeling is not only on the side of the child. It is on both sides, and all the way back. The intersection between movements is a point of encounter between two worlds of feeling meeting at their extremities. But then, could not the same be said of the sidewalk? My son fell and scraped his knee because the particles of the cement were adhering to each other, feeling each other into a common form. That form was lying in wait for the knee because the aggregate of the particles was feeling gravity, and the subsurface of the earth beneath. Again, the intersection of the event is a point of encounter between two worlds, or two fields, of feeling, understood in the widest sense. The world "does not contain feeling" because it is *made of feeling*. This is the point of Whitehead's refashioning of philosophy as a "critique of pure feeling" (1978, 113) and James's radicalizing of empiricism in terms of "pure experience" (1996a). The world is made of feeling, which we appropriate into the feeling of our body parts and their movements. We do not interiorize the world in our minds. We contract its vastness into local emphases that we appropriate to build the pattern of our lives and its registers of expression around us. These emergences we effectively own—at the same time as they remain fundamentally *in and of the world*. They are eventful expressions of the world that we take (up) to compose our life's expressions. They are not "contained" by the world, because they retain a trace of the vastness from which they emerged. They hang by the memorial thread of their own emergence to the aboriginal vastness, umbilical cord to the beyond. "Ouch" is a cosmic expression.[8]

Reorienting the "Space" of Experience

It may seem counterintuitive that location and the discreteness of things are contractions of a simple total vastness of moving experience, as opposed to the extensiveness of experience being built up from discrete, simply located building blocks that we mosaic together into a static spatial schema, as classical empiricism would have it. But this is supported by recent research into how people orient.

The commonsense assumption is that people orient by putting the positions of objects together to form a mental map and memorizing key "landmarks." The assumption underlying that assumption is that the map is a cognitive copy of a pregiven spatial frame through which experience passes. The researchers started with this assumption, but were startled by their own results. After extensive experimentation they concluded that people *do not orient by the location of objects* (Epstein and Kanwisher 1998).[9] How do they orient, then? Where are they when they orient? If you take objects out of space, what are you left with? Empty positions? What is a space composed of empty points? A simple total void. Where are you when you are in a void? You're in a vague voluminousness, vast enough not just for you but for the world to be lost in. Then how do people orient?

The answer is simple if you close your eyes. Wait as the visual memory of the configuration of the objects in the room starts to fade. Now imagine getting up from your seat and making your way to the door. Now what are you orienting with? Twists and turns. You're orienting in a space composed entirely of *movements, minus the positions they connect*. The positions are the problem: they have faded from view. You solve the problem of position by trying to sequence the movements from within a vague sensation of voluminousness. For example, you "instinctively" go through a number of twists and turns, not exactly sure where you're going. Just as you're starting to feel totally lost, you bump your nose against a wall. Emphatic point: you know immediately which way to turn to reach the door. Locatable objects and the paths between them have reemerged from their loss. You have located yourself in your pain. The map unfolds from the accidental emphasis of feeling. The touch of the doorknob kisses the world better.

Of course, this assumes a *previousness*: an experience of the room that can be reawakened. Although appealing to memory doesn't get us very far. The fact is, you forgot. When you closed your eyes and the visual image of the objects in the room faded away, you forgot. You could summon no precise memory of their configuration. When you fell into a spaciousness preceding any determination of position, you also fell into a memoryness preceding the reemergence of any particular memory. It was into that memoryness that you emerged from the womb. It is the neonate universe. When you close your eyes, you are neonate all over again.

A memoryness preceding any particular memory: where you go to orient is a memory-like spaciousness that exists only as "the *potentiality* of being distinctly localized" (James 1950, 155, emphasis in the original). What you have reaccessed is less a pregiven space mapped by a definite memory than a *spaceability* together with a *memorability*. Both are contracted into an accidental *quality* of feeling (the pain) from which determinate space and actual memory unfold. Space is made of being lost, as memory is of forgetting.

What is this spatio-memorability before you have found yourself in your pain and succeeded in sequencing the movements to the door? Each twist and turn still exists, or subsists, in vague memorial form, as a dormant, practiced action. They can all in principle be reawakened. But they are out of sequence. You don't really know which way to go. The twists and turns are all "there," but they are adrift not only from objective configurations but from each other. They exist as dynamic atoms of sequenceability, without the sequence yet: as yet unconnected connectabilities. The movements composing the space of experience are *pure transitions*, with as yet "no order of parts or of subdivisions" (James 1950, 146). They must be considered to coexist in the same potentiality, but without mixing, as though superimposed upon each other on a single, vaguely ontological plane: a "simple total vastness." Composed as it is of transition, the vagueness of the plane is as timelike as it is spaceable. The atoms of sequenceabilty comprising it are timelike precursors of position. At the emphatic point of pain, they unfold from the plane, well-placed memories rearising. They return from spatiotemporal dormancy to a definition they have lost. They become visualizable. You hit your nose against the wall and get a visual image of the door relative to where you are. As the atoms of transition unfold from their plane, they separate from each other. As they separate, they gel into the form of objects connected by known paths. They reappear as a set object configuration. They float, frozen in place, before your unseeing eyes, like paralyzed performers. You make the movements, guided by them, as by a map. You are orienting in an abstract space of object mapping that your orienting effort has called forth. The map unfolds from the effort of orientation. Only then can the orienting follow the map. *In order to orient in space, you must first spatialize orientation.* This is what Bergson meant when he said that objective frames of experience are extractions, or abstractions, from a preobjective dimension of duration.

In this example, the sequences and positions were already arrived at, but were then lost. They were then refound by returning to the dimension of spatio-memorability from which they derived, and rederiving them. James's infant toe example recounts the process of derivation. It indicates the "preobjective" dimension of duration as equally *presubjective*: the sense of self grows with the sense of the body's contours, its feelings coming to be owned by an emergent me.[10] "Only virtually or potentially either object or subject as yet" is James's formula for pure experience (1996a, 23). That dimension accompanies the orienting of all subsequent experience, underpinning its ability to find itself again. But it also preceded it as its *pure* potential for being localized: pure previousness, memorability in itself, as ultimate ground of differentiation, upon which we all fall to our emergent knees. This is Bergson's "pure past" (Deleuze 1991a, 59). We can't just speak in terms of duration because it overlooks this dimension of the pure past. But isn't this also the ultimate "space" of experience?

It is hard to know what to call it. It doesn't obey our categories. It is a level of emergent experience where time and space, like subject and object, are not yet differentiated from each other: a timelike spaceability. This plane of emergence is not exactly an emptiness. It is brimming with atoms of past-felt and future-felt intensity just waiting for the before-after of an accident to emphatically unfold. If this "space" of experience is a void, it is a quantum void, from which all the dynamic particles of experience emerge and no sooner return, and where they abide in transitional potential. It is not empty. It is the map that is empty. The map is abstract. It is composed of ethereal object forms frozen into abstract configuration. It is empty of movement. Your orienting with reference to its paralysis adds movement back in. But the added-in movement as such never features on the map. The movement flows invisibly through practiced actions of unfolding transition. These are no sooner executed than reforgotten. With their forgetting, your experience has returned to its dynamism. When the next accident befalls, a revised map will unfold from the renewed emphasis of feeling. New lines are traced. One step, you are in the dark of pained potential. The next step, you are triumphantly navigating paths with the aid of the empty clarity of visual abstraction. This rhythm is your world. It is the world as you contract it, almost in the sense in which you contract a condition, and exactly in the sense you contract a habit.[11] Your experience does not take place in the objective frame of space and time and visible objects. Space and time and objects rhythmically rise into your experience, just as surely as your experience periodically falls out of their frame.

Movement-Vision

Open your eyes. Walk out the door. Do you see your movement? Not really. You see changing object configurations. Movement as such is invisible.[12] It is what happens between objects and between body parts, and between those betweens. Movement is nonlocal dynamic relation. It is purely transitional. Everything that was just said in the dark applies in the light of day. Think of it this way: The rhythm quickens. The unfolding of a map and its emphatic renewal occur quicker than you can open and close your eyes. You might think you see your movement. But what you are experiencing is a visual Doppler effect. The serial unfolding of maps occurs so quickly that the frozen configurations blur together into an image of continuity. That image overlays the invisibility of movement. As we walk through the world, we are effectively in both "spaces" simultaneously, the objective and the preobjective, subjective and presubjective. The abstracted forms of visualization are superimposed on their potential. The rise and fall of the rhythm of experience proceeds apace.

The continuity of transition is effectively experienced, but fundamentally nonvisually. It is experienced by senses dedicated directly to movement: proprioception and the sense of balance of the inner ear. The sensation of movement, or kinesthesis, is generated by these senses working in concert. It is a form of synesthesia. This kin-synesthesia bleeds into vision. It fills in the gaps between frozen configurations. Our visions are smoothed over by invisible kinesthetic filler. In the psychological literature, this is called "amodal" perception: nonvisual visual in-fill (Michotte, Thinès, and Crabbé 1991; O'Regan and Noë

2001).¹³ It can even be argued that there are no properly visual presentations, frozen or otherwise: that all of vision is syn-kinesthetic in-fill. Think of the space between your eyes: what do you see there? Think of the blind spot on your retinas. Think of the spaces between your retina's rods and cones. What do you see in the gaps in your vision? The same thing you see when you close your eyes and try to find your way to the door: other-sense experience struggling to translate itself in visual form. When we see ungapped objects with smooth paths between them we are seeing with other senses than our eyes. Vision *is* other-sense abstraction to the extent that it presents locatable forms. Space and the objects we see "in" space *are* other-sense abstractions: syn-kinesthetic contractions.

A consequence of the vision of objective forms arising in experience at a contractive remove, as emphatic points against a background of pure transition, is that there is an inexpungeable shiver of indistinction between vision and imagination, and between vision and hallucination, not to mention memory.¹⁴ The memoryness of the skills and habits, through which "practice becomes perception," is typically considered by experimental psychologists to be the major in-fill operation. It can be experimentally demonstrated that you actually see what you might habitually expect. The fact that in amodal perception you see what experience has taught you to expect means that memory can exhibit futurity. The triggering into action of a habit is a memory of the future. The necessary role that the memory of the future plays in visual perception makes it as difficult to hold it in sequential time as it is to contain it in bounded space. It also explains why the success of memory is predicated on forgetting. Habits work by going dormant and then getting triggered. Our entire ability to anticipate is an elaboration of habit. Without the forgetting that is formative of habit, memory would have no future, and no present of transition to it. There would only be an eternity of pastness. Which is to say, nothing, a void even of atoms of experience. This is a very different void from the "pure past" as experiential ground of previousness just discussed. Previousness implicates nextness: future-past. Vision falls out of its objective frame, into its own future-looking previousness. In order to sequence itself, it must access an open-endedness: its own potential continuation. It must fall back imperceptibly from sequencing into sequenceability. In doing so, it falls from space and time into transition. It falls out of its objective spatiotemporal frame, but doesn't see that it has, or that all that it has, ultimately, is transition: the passing present, redolent of previousness, already expectant with nextness; the passing-through the present of the self-opening field of experience.

Vision can afford to overlook its fall to the ground, into its own openly invisible process. That is because it can bend back on itself. Once in-filled objects appear with smooth paths between them, you can visually revisit them. Now that you know how to get to them, you can return to them. You can extract at leisure the outlines of the objects. You can plot paths between them. You can re-present the plot-lines or outlines on a page or screen for all to see. You can extract forms and construct actual maps or even more abstract schema re-presenting their locatability. In short, you can generate a geometry of experience from your kinesthetic in-fill. Geometric forms and mappings are visual abstraction raised to a higher power: the power to express its self-derived lineaments in its own visual terms. It is the power of vision to reference itself. Vision can close itself off in a loop of self-reference. This gives vision a Euclidean independence from the other-sense in-fill from which its objective consistency actually emerges. Referenced to itself, it can afford to ignore its connection to its kin-synesthetic ground. It can pretend to be its own ground, standing alone on its supposed receptivity to pre-completed form, purified of the heterogeneity of other-sense dependencies. The forms and mappings it generates in this way are abstractions twice removed—which is to say, raised to a higher power. What they are twice removed from are the invisible dimensions of experience from which vision arises. They are twice removed from their own emergence. What they are higher powers of is the process of abstraction that starts in the standing out of points of emphasis amid the simple, total vastness.

Lived Relation

It is as if we lived in two dimensions or orders of reality at once. One, the visual order, is built upon emphatic points of intersection that stand out from the flow of experience. These are extracted from the flow as freeze-forms, composed of other-sense in-fill. They can then be mapped to one another by the second-order abstraction of Euclidean spatialization. The visual order stands at a remove of abstraction, twice over. It is the product of positive powers of abstraction, based on the contraction of the complex background of transition into an emphatic point that stands out as a "local sign" lending itself to the second-order operation of mapping and other forms of formalization (James 1950, 155–61). The other dimension, inhabited by transitions, is invisible. It is immersive, containing everything that appears on the visible level, but in a continuity of transition, flush with the self-opening of experience in and of the world. The plane of the visual self-reflectively detaches itself from its kin-synesthetic encompassment. The kinesthetic immersion above which it abstractly rises is in continuity with the dynamic plane of potential that was described earlier as the durational space of experience. That plane of potential is composed of sequenceabilities and connectabilities. It *is* continuity. Continuity is defined precisely by its cuttability. Separations cut away from continuity, into separations from it.[15] These occur at points of emphasis that eventfully emerge from intersections of continuous movements of transition to provide the material for habitual sequences and oriented connections. Lifted from the flow as local signs, they further provide the material for mapping and framing. The plane of visual organization of objective forms with specifiable positions is an abstract image of continuity, twice removed. We live in those two dimensions of reality at once. On the one hand, the well-lit theater of visual organization with its higher-order abstraction: *derived image of continuity*. And on the other, a blind immersive immediacy of pure transition, pure potentiality without an image, directly felt, in the falling of experience back into its reorienting emergence: *immediate continuity of imaging*. More precisely, we live *between* those dimensions, in the rhythm of their separation, presupposing their participation. We live in their relation.

However complex this is already, it is not the whole story. Many senses, including hearing, smell, and touch, have been left out. Touch is especially important because it functions as a hinge between vision and the other major mode of experiential abstraction: language. When my son scraped his knee, we shared our objective mappings by pointing and uttering demonstratives. "There it is. . . . No, it's over there. . . ." The pointing indicated location as the promise of a touch. The demonstratives doubled the gesture in language. Pointing your finger and saying "There" is a way of indicating the possible transition to touching what you see.[16] This cross-referencing of sensings gives both greater anchor-weight and shareability. Words are cross-referential pointers. Speaking conjures up possible sights and touches at increasing remove. Words can indicate transitions between sight and touching even in the absence of both. They can also jump ahead or backward, skipping intermediaries in the habitual or conventional sequencings. Language is a mode of abstraction taken to a highest power, at an abstractive remove at which it can cross-reference experience with close to random-access versatility.

Language, of course, is not only cross-referential. It is also self-referential. The self-referentiality is already nascent in its cross-referential operation. The demonstrative "There" of the knee-scrape incident was implicitly repeated in "Kiss it better." A command always implicates a demonstrative. The reverse is undoubtedly also the case: a demonstrative always implies some sort of command. The most apparently innocent demonstration carries an implicit obligation. This is the "protocol" of the situation referred to earlier. The protocol consists of a shared recognition of a precedent for what comes next and an expectation that the precedent will be repeated. Every demonstrative utterance brings to bear on its situation a repetitive force of obligation borne in words. In conveying that obligation, language translates itself directly into event: the utterance of the words immediately triggers a sequencing of actions, orienting what happens. All language is performative: things are done with words.

The priming of a situation with an implicit protocol is what Deleuze and Guattari (1987, 75–110) call an "order-word." An order-word is cross-referential in that it is borne by language but is not linguistic per se, since it directly plays into and across a number of nonlinguistic registers of feeling, activity, orientation, and eventfulness. But it is self-referential in that it relates registers of language to each other: the demonstrative to the imperative, for example. The order-word is a kernel of a linguistic system. It is as much a node of connection among linguistic registers as it is of language's crossing into nonlinguistic dimensions of experience.

Language, of course, also conveys protocols bearing on itself. Like vision, it bends back on itself. You can speak and write about language, and in a way that uses it to extract from itself obligatory forms and mappings all its own: grammar. The order-word hangs on a kernel of grammar (a minimum of semantic content and grammatical construction serving as a trigger). Formal logic and linguistics are endeavors of extracting that self-referential dimension of language from the cross-referential kernelling of experience, to give its structure abstract expression on a plane independent of its eventfulness.

The emphasis in the account of language just given concentrates on the entrainment of a nextness from a previousness in a way that orients the coming event according to expectations. Language also carries prodigious powers of invention. It can abstract a nextness from its dependence on its immediate antecedents, deviating toward a different arc of unfolding, tending toward unaccustomed—even virtual—end points. It can invent new destinations, whose attractive force brings new tendencies into the world.

A philosophy of language, as opposed to logic or linguistics, would have to take into account all of its dimensions: its kernelling in integral experience, its sense-mode cross-referencing touchingly hinged to a potential kinesthesia, and its self-referential mapping as formal system. Further, it would also have to concern itself with how these relate, and how powers of invention can carry them away.[17]

How they relate is simultaneously through pointed removal (conjuring up possible punctual sights and touches at increasing remove) and extractive uptake (conveying transitions between sight and touching even in the absence of both, that absence enabled by and enabling the skipping of intermediaries and the remixing of orientations). The uptake of sense-mode cross-referencing is a taking-up of synesthesia. Language extractively takes up synesthesia, still wet with the kinesthetic ground of potential immersing all experience, into the self-closure of a formal system. Formal logic and linguistics are designed to abstract-out the kin-synesthetic side of language, along with the demonstrative-imperative operation it kernels with, as well as the potentials of invention that build from there. They miss the syn-kinesthetic side of language, and with it language's experiential share of transitional reality. They list to the form side of self-referential closure. A philosophy of language that rights the bias must be as concertedly a philosophy of experience.

The issues raised by language at the cross-roads of sight, touch, and socio-linguistic order are numerous and important, and lead in many a direction. For now, back to the main arc: objects, configurations, paths; extracted forms, mappings, geometries; space and time themselves. The point is that these are derivatives of a dynamic field of experience, of a simple total vastness of transitional reality that they can never hope to encompass, only contract—for the simple reason that it encompasses them. The inescapable conclusion is that *any explanatory or creative procedure that relies on notions of form derived from visual order, or on operations of mapping expressed in a (Euclidean) geometry from the forms in turn derived from visual form, or on any other formalizing structure, is missing the larger part of reality*. It's missing the encompassment of the world of locatable form by the spatio-memorability of pure transition. It's missing potential. It's missing immersion. It's missing emergence. It's missing the accident. It's missing the event. It's missing experience in the making.

Lived Abstraction

We started with the body: scraped knees, sucked toes. Everything that has been said about space and time applies to the body to the extent that it is understood as a visible form, appearing as an object among others. We tend to think of the body as being mappable in the same way as the spatial frame through which it is seen to navigate over time. The body is thought of as our little self-enclosed patch of space. This conception of the body is expressed in the idea of body image. The notion of body image has been exported from psychology to other domains, including cultural studies. It treats the body as a configuration of objective parts that are looked upon by a contemplative subject ensconced "inside" it. This subject presumably experiences its body-object as if from a distance. How the animating principle or dynamism of the body could be at a visual distance from it is never explained. If the subject were at a distance from its body, it would be at a distance from all its objective parts, including the eyes. The subject would somehow see with abstract eyes behind the eyes: a mind's eye. This is not imagination or even hallucination. This is pure fiction, cognitive fiction. In this fiction, experience is what mediates between the peering subject and its body-object. That is what we are implying when we say we "have" experiences as we seem to watch as our body goes about its business "in" space and time. But if what has been said here has any validity, we don't "have" experience. *Experience has us.* It is all-encompassing, and through and through.[18] Experience is not in the mediated between of the subject and its body-object.

Say instead that the body is between visual form and invisibility. Say that the body is their hinging on each other, in all its dimensions. Say that the body is their rhythmic participation in each other. Say that it is the making-present of their transitional relation. Say that it is the making-visible of the presence of transition. Then there is nothing between the body and anything else. The body is the between, in all immediacy. The making-visible is not itself visible. The relation between the visible and the invisible cannot be seen. *The body is fundamentally without an image. That imagelessness is the real subject of experience.* Everything else is objective filler or formalized abstraction. The body is its own subject, and both are one with all-encompassing experience passing through: sight unseen. *Abstractions can be built upon the body because the body is abstract.* All the way down—and then some. The ground of experience is groundless: essentially in movement; always a transitional reality.

These inversions in the concept of the body are versions of what was called earlier a Copernican revolution in our understanding of body-space. If it still seems counterintuitive, try it this way. If there was a cognitive subject inside the body navigating its way around by looking out on forms and mapping them relative to each other, then a simple geometric conversion of its already acquired visual space would not fool it. For example, you might put lenses over the eyes behind which the wily subject was lurking that inverted the view, so that was up was now down and what was left was now right. A cognitive subject would surely be too smart to fall for such a simple trick. After all, it has a ready map. All it has to do is use its mind's eye to turn the map upside down, and then laterally transpose it. The second operation would be the more difficult, like reading letters in a mirror. Is that really so difficult? Surely all will be right again in the world of vision from a distance. Wrong. What happens is total disorientation: "I was unable to recognize my surroundings" (Schilder 1950, 109). Total disruption of motor skills and habits: the body is completely "torn up" (113). Nausea. Total disorientation and total disruption enveloped in utter nausea. It takes eight days for the world to right itself. Little by little, a functional space of orientation unfolds again from the nausea. As obvious a conversion as this simple reversal returns the world to its neonate state of envelopment in preobjective feeling. The space of orientation has to be rebuilt from the swirling ground(lessness) up. The world has to grow up again out of an encompassing quality of moving experience (in this case, of a distinctly Sartrean variety).[19]

Repeat: in order to orient in space, you must first spatialize orientation. Until you've accomplished that, don't be surprised at the "looseness with which the parts of the body are connected with each other" (Schilder 1950, 114): that there is "primitively at least no order of parts or of subdivisions" (James 1950, 146). Don't be surprised if gaps appear in or between your body parts. For example, if your limbs detach from your trunk, or your chest and shoulders appear empty (108). Don't expect to be able to get anywhere in that body image. A body wracked by irruptions of invisibility isn't going far. It is too close to the event of experience. It will have to linger a while in the proximity of transitional experience before it gets its land-legs back. Do expect some scrapes before it fills itself back in.

Question: If the map changes, where is the change on the map?[20]

Change is not on the map. Change is in the making of the map. The map-making is not itself on the map.

Place by itself does not make a change (Leibniz 1995, 133).[21]

2015

The Art of the Relational Body

From Mirror-Touch to the Virtual Body

Primitively our space-experiences form a chaos, out of which we have no immediate faculty for extricating them. Objects of different sense-organs, experienced together, do not in the first instance appear either inside or alongside or far outside each other, neither spatially continuous nor discontinuous, in any definite sense of these words. . . . This primitive chaos subsists to a great degree throughout life so far as our immediate sensibility goes. . . . The general rule of our mind is to locate in each other all sensations which are associated in a simultaneous experience, and do not interfere with each other's perception.
—William James (1950, 181–84)

Corresponding to every feeling within us, some motion takes place in our bodies.
—C. S. Peirce (1992a, 44)

A process set-up anywhere reverberates everywhere. . . . Every possible feeling produces a movement, and that movement is a movement of the entire organism, and of each of its parts.
—William James (1950, 371, 380–81)

There must be a continuity of changeable qualities. Of the continuity of intrinsic qualities of feeling we can now form but a feeble conception. The development of the human mind has practically extinguished all feelings, except a few sporadic kinds, sounds, colors, smells, warmths, etc., which now appear to be disconnected and disparate. . . . Originally, all feelings may have been connected in the same way, and the presumption is that the number of dimensions was endless. For development essentially involves a limitation of possibilities. But given a number of dimensions of feeling, all possible varieties are obtainable by varying the intensities

of the different elements. Accordingly, time logically supposes a continuous range of intensity in feeling. It follows, then, from the definition of continuity, that when any particular kind of feeling is present, an infinitesimal continuation of all feelings differing infinitesimally from that is present.
—C. S. Peirce (1992a, 323–24)

In mirror-touch synesthesia the sight of a touch to another's body elicits the feeling of the touch in the corresponding location of the observer's body. This effect is frequently discussed in the literature as a spatial "confusion" or an "error" in the ability to discriminate self and other.[1] Construing it in this way carries an implication, whether intended or not, of a "normal" cognitive base-state of a private subject peering out on the world and representing it to itself, anchored in the safe house of a discrete, clearly positioned body container. The labeling of the phenomenon as "mirror"-touch synesthesia, rather than "sight-touch" synesthesia on the model of other synesthesia nomenclature (sound-color, color-grapheme, shape-taste), encourages that implication. A cognitive mistake must be occurring, the name says, of the kind mirrors produce. As when we catch a glimpse of ourselves as we pass a mirror that we didn't know was there and experience the sudden jolt of seeing another person who looks just like us. Or when we use a mirror to tweeze an errant hair and find ourselves spatially confused as to which direction is left and right. The first description of mirror-touch synesthesia in the scientific literature, in 2005, took place around the same time another discovery with the same first name was beginning to register in a major way in popular knowledge and imagination. It is rare to find a discussion of mirror-touch synesthesia that does not also mention mirror neurons: specialized neurons that respond when the movement of another body is perceived by firing in a pattern that is identical to that which occurs when performing the action. Same name, same "confusion," same "error." Same implied bias: that our perception is fundamentally a passive reception of an image constituting a private representation of the world, which under normal conditions is then cognitively corrected to purify it of illusions of perspective and other unthinking errors.[2] But the passive-reception model upon which the cognitive model of representation is grounded is precisely what the discovery of mirror neurons irrevocably calls into question, in a way that has important implications for mirror-touch synesthesia. Before drawing conclusions about the implications for art and culture of either mirror neurons or mirror-touch synesthesia, it is important to purify the perception of these perceptual phenomena of the nominative mirror bias. It is self-evident that our perception *participates* in the world before it can be said in any way to *mirror* it. To understand the way in which mirror-touch synesthesia participates in the world, it is necessary to reconsider it in the larger context of synesthetic experience in general, its role in the formation of perception, and what that says about the nature of the body.

Many tools for this reconsideration are found in the literature on mirror-touch synesthesia itself. But since the scientific literature is less focused on reformulating fundamental questions about the nature of perception than it is on identifying neural correlates to the experiences under investigation, an assist from philosophy is needed. As the collage of opening quotes indicates, philosophy (or, in James's case, psychology before it had completed its separation from philosophy) knew of phenomena like those associated with mirror neurons more than a hundred years before their scientific discovery, and was already thinking about them in relation to multisensory experience. Concepts similar to those articulated by James and Peirce in the opening quotes were central to the thought of Bergson ("nascent action") and Whitehead ("reenaction" as the primary phase of perception). This early philosophical inquiry, whose orientation can broadly be described as process philosophy, situates the question in a different conceptual trajectory than is usual for the contemporary scientific literature. The direction it indicates is consonant in many ways with the contemporary theoretical currents of embodied cognition and enactive perception studies. But it significantly diverges from them in two important ways. First, in calling into question the very category of cognition, bumped from its position of primacy by what can only be described as aesthetic categories. Second, in insisting that the genesis of perception can only be understood using a radically different conceptual tool set than that used to describe its fully formed structures and functions—and this applies even to such basic notions as the concepts of space and position. The following discussion will follow the trail of some of the conceptual links made in the opening quotes in order to open the discussion beyond representation—even beyond cognition—toward an artfulness of the body, in the genesis of perception, occurring in an emergent domain with a texture all its own.

1. "Development essentially involves *a limitation of possibilities*" (Peirce). A body's capacity to produce determinate experience is acquired through a process of limitation. Neurophysiologically, this translates as a developmental passage from a neonatal "exuberance" of "functional hyperconnectivity" to a "pruning away of unused connections," completed by age nine, and a strengthening of the remaining connections through learning (Maurer, Gibson, and Spector 2014, 46–47). It has been experimentally demonstrated that the quantitative neuronal hyperconnectivity of early life corresponds qualitatively to a field of perception that is characterized by an exuberance: of multimodal sensations. "Children's perception should resemble that of adults with synesthesia" (50). The "inhibition" of synesthesia in adult perception is not complete. This is particularly true of clinical synesthetes, who retain conscious awareness of certain cross-sensory associations. But "remnants of these associations appear to exert unconscious influences in non-synesthetic adults" as well (51).

This suggests that the difference between neurotypical perception and synesthetic perception cannot be construed in terms of a deviation from the norm. Synesthetes do not *add* a deviation from the normal path of development. They just *prune* the same developmental path less fully. They consciously retain remnants of the developmental exuberance of experience (and often put them to use, for example as mnemonic devices). Neurotypicals prune to the trunk.[3] They inhibit multimodal experience from rising to the level of consciousness, retaining only single-channel perception: vision that is only sight, separated from what is felt by touch; an audition that is only a sound and not a color. The separation of experience into perceptual modes corresponding to the separate physiological channels of sensation is not fundamental to experience, and is not a developmental destiny. What is primary is in fact a lack of separation between the senses. This is not a simple confusion. Rather than a lack of distinction or indifference, it is an exuberant hyperdifferentiation, in continual variation: a "continuity of changeable qualities" (Peirce). Primitively, experience comes as a "continuity of intrinsic qualities of feeling [of which] we [neurotypicals] can now form but a feeble conception. The development of the human mind has practically extinguished all feelings, except a few sporadic kinds, sound, colors, smells, warmths, etc., which now appear to be disconnected and disparate. . . . Originally, all feelings may have been connected in the same way, and the presumption is that the number of dimensions was endless" (Peirce 1992a, 323–24). The original continuum is composed of an infinity of varieties of multisensory fusions, in continual qualitative variation. The difference between the synesthete and the neurotypical is that the synesthete consciously retains a wider swath of the fusional continuum (albeit not much more of its changeability, since among clinical synesthetes the retained associations tend to become coded so as to appear invariant; Maurer, Gibson, and Spector 2014, 54–55). The fact that the full continuum persists unconsciously despite its "practical extinguishment" in "normal" perception means that "when any particular kind of feeling is present, an infinitesimal continuation of all feelings differing infinitesimally from that is present" (Peirce). Neurotypicals remain neurodiverse in potentia.

The cross-connection between senses is not fully "extinguished." Peirce says that it is "practically" extinguished. The separation of the senses is a tendential limit never actually reached. What normally pass for monosense experiences are in fact cross-modal fusions presented in a dominant sense. For example, to see the shape and texture of the object is to perceive, in vision, its potential feel in the hand. To feel that potential touch is to see the potential kinesthetic experience of walking toward the object (Berkeley [1709] 1957, 13–86). Sight envelops potential other-sense experiences and would not achieve its own definition as a determinate vision without them. It is well known, for example, that object vision cannot develop without movement. Every "single" sense experience is the envelopment in a dominant mode of appearance of an "infinitesimal" (virtual) continuation of other-sense experiences. Every perception is a *composition* of the full spectrum of experience, "practically" appearing as if it were disparate and disconnected from the continuum.

Each perception normally comes in a dominant experiential key. That dominant mode of appearing, however, is imperceptibly held aloft by a multisensory composition without which it would have no purchase and take no determinate shape. In the final analysis, the "limitation" necessary for the development of determinate experience is more a question of relief—strata rising by gradations to a pinnacle—than of either/or. A sight held aloft in vision by a virtual touch. The touch enveloping a kinesthesia. Perceptual strata in composition: a geology of experience. What distinguishes clinical synesthetes from neurotypicals is that in the experiential mode in which their synesthesia presents, their conscious perception peaks not in a monosense experience but in the broader stratum of a particular cross-modal connection. Clinical synesthetes and neurotypicals have it in common to background the infinite changeability of the continuum of qualities of experience. This is done through codings that become second nature, forming a repertory of perceptual habits and skills (Maurer, Gibson, and Spector 2014, 54–56). They attend preferentially to their respective peaks of experience.

If a perception is a composition, there is an artfulness to it. Neurotypicality and synesthesia are each in their own right arts of experience. Their respective pinnacles of experience rise from the shifting ground of changeable qualities whose continual variation is habitually and skillfully overlooked at that experiential height. However, "given a number of dimensions of feeling, *all possible varieties are obtainable by varying the intensities of the different elements*" (Peirce). A number of dimensions of feeling are always given. Thus experience can always be *recomposed* by varying the intensity of its elements. The artfulness of experience can be built upon further, leading to the formation of new perceptual habits and skills.[4] In the process, new varieties can be obtained. This amounts to a continuation of the development of perception, evolving toward new peaks, presenting itself in new determinations that are in principle infinite in their variety. While this artfulness of experience is in no way limited to the institutional domain of art, its expansion is one of the things art can do, when it earns its name. It earns its name by bringing intensive variations into relief—when it takes as its mission to vary the "geological" intensities formative of experience (rather than combining already determined forms).

Since the defining limitation of the normal composition of experience is achieved through inhibition, it stands to reason that the reintensification of perception is enabled by disinhibition. This means that the composition involved cannot be achieved entirely voluntarily. The full-spectrum complexity of experience must be *released* before it can be rebuilt upon. The operation of artfulness of experience cannot be fully voluntary. In fact, it escapes the opposition between the voluntary and the involuntary, the self-effecting and the intentional. If one brings one's perception to the edge of release and inhabits the resurgent complexity, has one acted upon experience—or released oneself to be acted upon by it? Has one composed a perception—or been composed by the process of perception's taking form? In that process, is one's will and conscious thought but one element on the continuum, entering into the fusional mix?

2. Mirror-touch synesthesia is a composition of experience that entertains the same relation to the shifting geology of experience as other varieties of synesthesia. Like all peak determinations, its effect appears from the compositional background of other-sense textures that do not themselves appear.[5] The specificity of mirror-touch synesthesia is that its vision-touch fusion immediately raises questions concerning the space of experience. It seems to collapse the distance between two bodies. To put it that way, however, assumes that the space of perception at the formative level is structured according to the same spatial schema as peak neurotypical perception, and that mirror-touch synesthesia "errs" by deviating from that schema, ending up spatially "confused." But is not the perception of space also a composition (see Couplet 9, "Tell Me Where Your Pain Is," in this volume)? Is not the ability to project an invariant spatial grid on the world of perception the abstract product of a certain multisense fusion consolidated into a skill and a habit? Our everyday navigation of the world occurs through the interoperation of the visual signposting of punctual landmarks and kinesthetic dead reckoning on a roiling proprioceptive sea. Our sense of living in a coordinate grid is a formalized, geometrical abstraction from this multisense complexity which, once it has been acquired as a skill, is consciously overlaid upon experience. There is no reason to say that a phenomenon like mirror-touch synesthesia arises from a defect in spatial experience.

Given what was said earlier about the continuum of experience and its relation to synesthesia, it would be more precise to say that it returns to the conditions from which neurotypical spatial perception arises, and peaks from them otherwise. This raises the question of how the potential for spatial perception according to an abstract geometric gridding is enveloped in the continuum of intrinsic qualities of feeling of which we normally have but a feeble conception, but from which all definitive experiences nevertheless rise. What are the precursors of spatial perception on the continuum?

"Primitively our space-experiences form a chaos, out of which we have no immediate faculty for extricating them. Objects of different sense-organs experienced together, *do not in the first instance appear either inside or alongside or far outside each other, neither spatially continuous nor discontinuous*, in any definite sense of these words" (James). The potential for the experience of space is not fully extended (it is a "simple total vastness"; see Couplet 9, "Tell Me Where Your Pain Is"). In other words, there is no preoperative schema of juxtaposition arraying points in external relation to each other, as on a coordinate grid. The potential for spatial perception is enveloped on the multisense continuum. The sensations of the senses which will compose themselves into space-experience do not appear in the first instance outside or alongside each other. With no outside or alongside, "inside" has no meaning. Neither does continuous or discontinuous in the usual senses (as applied to already determined forms). An infinite continuum, it must be remembered, is not an actual formation of smooth transition. If it were, it would be extensive. That would make it a space. The continuum of potential experience is not a space. It is not composed of points, but rather of qualities. It is a qualitative domain.

A qualitative domain is intensive. It is defined less by continuity in the extensive sense than by potential cut and recomposition. A qualitative continuum is one whose nature is to be cut into, in order for a limited expression of the potential it holds to definitively appear. Uncut, it is too intensely full of itself for anything in particular to come of it. At each cut into the continuum, it is as if the qualitative domain folded over on itself, like origami. With each refolding, it presents a new facet. A standout form held aloft by an imperceptible organization of subfolds stands out in experiential relief. A tectonics of folding must be added to the idea of a geology of experience. A qualitative continuum is defined as one that cannot be cut without changing in nature.[6] It cannot origami itself into an experiential prominence without re-expressing itself with a difference. To conceive of the continuum in itself, outside any unfolding from a cut, it is necessary to think in terms of *mutual inclusion*: a simultaneity of infinite qualitative varieties that are "located in each other" and "do not interfere with each other" (James). In Bergson's vocabulary, they are in a state of mutual "interpenetration." In Deleuze's vocabulary, they are in a state of "reciprocal presupposition."

This mutual inclusion of an infinite variety of qualitative varieties is a limit-concept. The reality of the continuum in itself is unactualizable. It is virtual. This virtual "chaos" (James) might more accurately be renamed, using one of James's own signature terms, a *confound*. The continuum is not chaotic in the sense of an unformed mess. It is a virtual form of hyperdifferentiation of potential qualities of experience, found together, each in the other, confounded, fused together, in simultaneity, without one excluding the other. This is not a mess. It is a hyperorder of qualitative varieties in mutual interpenetration, ready to express—always in a standout facet, limitatively expressing the infinite variety of the continuum, in a particular composition of the geology of perception, with its own relief.

How, if "we have no immediate faculty for extricating" an expression, is the cut ever made? How do we not implode into the intensity, lost in the infinite virtual folds of potential experience?

In a word: through *movement*. Every movement makes a cut: it brings certain elements of experience into relief, origami-ing the continuum on the fly. Originally, it is not we who move our body volitionally. It is our body that is moved, by the variation of experience in the making. The infant body is a chaos of involuntary fits and starts. The baby is possessed by movement; it is a creature of undirected activity. Our body's potential for development is this primitive chaos. We begin bodily lost in the intensity of the qualitative confound of experience. Far from being a chaos in the sense of pure randomness, the confound of experience in-the-making is hyperfull of differentiations pre-tracing potential orders too numerous and changing to be able to register yet. Little by little, by dint of repetition, certain multisense connections start to stand in relief: a touch on the lips and a taste of milk; the sound of footsteps announcing the imminent arrival of a touch on the lips and a taste of milk; a texture against the skin; a shape suddenly registering in a blindly groping hand; a sight settling on the shape. From this limited, chaotic self-organizing, nexuses of intersense experience gradually appear and come to stand out against what has become, by this very standing out, the experiential background of the confound of experience. The nexuses register. They crystallize into objects. The objects return in a pattern of juxtapositions, disjunctions, and conjunctions, forming a web of extensive relations. From that web a sense of an abstract extensive order finally emerges: an order of alongsides, outsides, and insides. Space has come. It has come out of movement, patterned by its repeated variation.

There is a primacy of movement. Primitively, the movement is undirected. But as objects appear, so does directness. It is not at first so clear as a willing-toward. The body is still being moved, but gradually the moves become less random and more patterned. The body is first moved, outside its own control, by a chaos of appetition. The appetition settles into preferential directions, as perception settles into objects designating termini for appetition's striving. Appetition starts out uncontrolled, but becomes directed. It starts unconscious, but rises to consciousness with the emergence of the system of objects and its extensive spatial order. This extensive ordering enables directionality by enabling discrimination: limited focus on a delimited locus. The primitive chaos of the body is now more composed. It has been captured, by and for appetition's directional channeling. The body can now orient itself and navigate the confound. Our sense of self is the product of this capture.

Once again, the achieved directedness is not so clearly a question of voluntary control, taking over from involuntary activation. It is not so much that we now control our impulses, matured into desires and intentions. What has happened is that our appetitions have become self-possessed of their own emergent patterning. It is less we who possess self-control than that our appetitions *emergently self-possess us*. Before we can be said to be in any way subjectively in possession of ourselves, we are bodily possessed of movement coming into possession of its own orientability, mapping its emergent patternings into an extensive order. We are self-composed by this process of emergence, predicated on movement's patterned relation to itself, bootstrapping itself from the infinitely open qualitative domain that is the confound of experience, in a developmental order-out-of-chaos effect. Our possession by this emergent order-out-of-chaos effect "subsists to a great degree throughout life" (James). We continue to be self-possessed of our appetition's patternability and, as a function of its self-patterning, its orientability. The primitive chaos of the body follows us throughout life, providing a ready field for reemergence. If this were not the case, our world of experience would lose its intensity and plasticity. It would mineralize into the gridding that emerged from it. It would plateau in it, and content itself with the directional predictability of its own flatness.

The importance of this for mirror-touch synesthesia is that although the phenomenon seems to pertain to space, it must be understood more fundamentally to concern *movement*.[7] In view of the role of movement in the genesis of experience and of the self, the supposed spatial "confusion" involved in mirror-touch synesthesia must be conceived of very differently.

3. "Corresponding to every feeling within us, some motion takes place in our bodies" (Peirce). Physiologically, the motion in our body accompanying every feeling is the firing of mirror-neurons recruiting an extended network of activations throughout the brain. But this is just the somatic tip of the experiential iceberg. As Raymond Ruyer says, the movements in the brain are but the form in which experience most directly appears to the outside observer. In other words, they are the registering of experience as an extensive system of movement, apprehended as such by a learned observer schooled in spatial gridding. The imperceptible regions of the iceberg are the intensity of experience from which the extensity of spatial experience peaks. In itself, experience is an unlimited confound of infinite, self-folding complexity (physiologically registered in the extensive folds of the brain). In intensity, movement is not activation at a point in a grid, or displacement between two points on a grid, or even the co-activation of a network of points. Qualitatively, experience is "a process set-up anywhere" that "reverberates everywhere" (James), rippling through the confound of experience.

"Every possible feeling produces a movement, and that movement is a movement of the entire organism, and of each of its parts" (James). But "organism" must not be understood as limited to the physiological tip of the iceberg. It must be understood to include the virtual "tectonics" of the confounded domain of potential variation from which all determinate experience rises.

The mutual inclusion of potential takings-determinate-form of experience has an order that does not map one-to-one to the system of extensive orientation to which it gives rise. All of the variations are in absolute proximity to one another, registering all the others in its own changeability. A change in one variety ripples into a change in all the others, in mutual deformation, like the rubber band Bergson uses as an example of the "qualitative multiplicity" that experience is aboriginally (1998, 265).

The complexity of the hyperorder, of which we can give ourselves only a feeble conception, can be intuited if we imagine every variety of potential experience moving simultaneously, with infinite speed, into all others, passing thresholds between sense modalities and forming multisense fusions in profusion as it goes. This is movement in place, without displacement. An imperceptible vibration of potential variations on experience, rehearsing themselves, in intensity.[8] The displacements of the physiological body in extensive displacement in space is doubled in intensity by a vibratory virtual body of pure variability. A determinate experiential form origamies into relief when an actual movement cuts its patterning and orientation into the vibratory intensity of the virtual body, drawing out a determinate standout expression of the potential it enfolds. This moving act of composition is action upon action, actual movement cutting into the continuity of intensive movement, to extensively unfold its own discrete form from it.

The closest geometrical approximation to the hyperorder of the virtual body is not the extensive grid defined by the Cartesian coordinates. It is topological. Topology is the geometry of continuous deformation. It is the mathematics of folding. A topological form is not limited by boundaries in Cartesian space. It is limited by events: by cuts. A topological figure comprises all of the foldings and stretchings and refoldings that fall within the limits of two cuts, as when a rubber band breaks.⁹ The rubber band of experience "breaks" when extensive movement cuts into the vibratory intensity of the virtual body, throwing out a shard of experience, which then stands out for itself against the integral background of the variability of experience from which it came. From the point of view of this discretely appearing, limited form of experience, the continuum of experience against which it stands out is not a background in any spatial sense. It is the field of emergence of experience: its genesis, its imperceptible interval of formation. The topology of experience can only be thought by resituating spatial experience with respect to the interval of its genesis in the topology of experience. Topological transformation implies a virtual time of transformation: pure process.

Extensive geometry is exoreferential: it enables points, and the objects occupying them, to be located in relation to each other according to a system of external relations. Topology is *endoreferential*: it concerns the processual mutual inclusion of variations. These are defined by what are called "internal relations," although the term is misleading because the concept does not connote insideness, but rather mutual interpenetration: a mutual inclusion that is "in" nothing but the infinite, incessant passing into and out of each other of the ungriddable qualitative variations whose simultaneous in-each-otherness composes the timelike process-space of the virtual body. Not the inside of experience, but experience's *immanence* to its own changeability.¹⁰

From this point of view, the mirror-touch synesthesia effect of a touch that is at two places at once is completely understandable. Mirror-touch synesthesia retains the passing into and out of each other of two modes of experience, vision and touch, bracketing exoreferential positioning on the spatial grid as well as movement as extensive displacement on that grid. *The mirror-touch effect occurs on the virtual body*, where the nonlocality of such spooky action at a distance is the norm, by processual dint of the mutual inclusion. To say that mirror-touch has to do with a spatial confusion is to be confused about the fact that the physiological body is at the tip of the iceberg of the virtual body. Instead of registering a determinate stand-alone experience on the spatial grid, mirror-touch synesthesia contrives to double-register the same experience simultaneously at two different points in extensive space-perception.¹¹ This is the result of a folding of vision and touch into each together on the virtual body, their in-each-otherness immediately refracted onto two points on the coordinate grid of developed experience. The mirror-touch effect is a limited expression of the integral, everywhere in-each-otherness of the infinitely, qualitatively multiple transformations of the virtual body. The expression is limited, to two. But that is still more multiple than one.

Understood in this way, mirror-touch synesthesia is not an error in spatial perception. It is a less limited than normal expression of the truth of the body (the truth of the body's virtual doubling by its own potential for variation).[12] Neither is mirror-touch synesthesia an error in self-other distinction. A synesthete does not come out of the experience of mirror-touch confused as to where the touch can be located spatially. It is just that before the touch is located spatially, it refracts at infinite speed into two locations, so that the *qualitative nature* of the event immediately registers. The spatial gridding of experience is bracketed for an imperceptible interval so that the truth of its genesis in ceaseless qualitative transformation may express itself in the defined form of a touch that as directly concerns me as you. As directly concerning me as you is a definition of *sympathy*. Sympathy is the qualitative nature of the event.[13]

What mirror-touch synesthesia makes palpable is the fact that the genesis of experience is fundamentally sympathetic. The virtual body is the very process of sympathy, by virtue of which any transformation anywhere on its continuum by nature reverberates everywhere. In the genesis of experience, a transformation cannot solely concern you and not me, or vice versa. Such distinctions belong to the plateauing of fully developed experience in the diminished intensity of extensive perception. But this does not mean there is a confusion between you and me. It means that in the genesis of perception there is a mutual inclusion in the virtual body, whose topological complexity is afold with experiences' forming, flush with what in developed experience will selectively concern only one as opposed to other. You and I, self versus other, are cut from the same immanence of experience unfolding into spatially distributed, determinate expressions. Distinctions like self and other are but the tip of the iceberg whose imperceptible topological vastness is, processually, as much in one's development as another's, in that both are in each other's potential to mutually transform by virtue of their co-implication in the same event. The formative *relation* of co-implication in the same events is the changing ground of experience. If the virtual body can be said to represent anything, it is this relationality of the life of the body.

The scientific literature speaks of the simultaneous in-each-otherness of two experiences in mirror-touch, and more generally of the operations of mirror neurons with which it is associated, in terms of "empathy." The concept of empathy implies an interiority of experience. Etymologically, "empathy" means "in-feeling," as opposed to sympathy's "feeling-with." The connotation of an interiority of experience suggests a base state of separation from the world and from other bodies that must then be overcome. That overcoming is usually conceived in terms of identification. Anywhere notions of identification are employed, the notion of a private world of interior experience is reactivated, whether this is intended or not. Identification assumes the coordinate grid of spatial separations as an a priori given. It further assumes that the selves "inside" of which experiences occur are separated subjectively from each other in much the same way as points in space are. These separations are overcome—actually illusionarily disavowed in this account—by projection. One self projects its experience across the spatial divide and "mistakes" what belongs to the opposing self as being "inside" of itself. There is no doubt that identification happens. But it is a secondary process, occurring on the derived stratum of extensive relation.[14]

The primary process is the nonlocality of sympathy: the immediate relationality, such that what is set up anywhere reverberates everywhere. This is the generative level of all experience, and the seat of all development, which continues to exert an at least unconscious influence. The same must be said of this aboriginal sympathy as was first said of synesthesia, and then of the "chaos" of spatial perception: it subsists throughout life. Its process doubles all bodily experience with a virtual body representing the capacity of experience to vary through events of relation. Although the virtual body cannot be said to "exist" in space or in metric time as the measure of displacement across space, it is as real as relation. It "subsists" immanent to all spatial location and moments of time, in the topological recess of experience's in-the-making.

Mirror-touch synesthesia stands as a reminder of the primary process of the origami of experience. Its here-and-there, simultaneously in-me-and-you effect points to the imperceptible activity of the virtual body folding out into determinate experience. It signposts the body's continual endoreferencing to its own relational variations and to its inexhaustible, eventful capacity to change. The mirror-touch duality, instead of being denigrated as a defect, can be seen as an index of the more encompassing—in fact, indefinitely mutually inclusive— qualitative multiplicity that is the floating geology of the living, moving body, its processual iceberg. It can be appreciated as a gateway opening back onto the formative complexity of experience: to the artfulness of the body's self-possession of experience.

Mirror-touch synesthesia's artfulness of the body can be an example to art, in the sense of a specialized arena of activity. It is a reminder to art that, given a number of dimensions of feeling, all possible varieties are obtainable by varying the intensities of the different elements: that experience can always be recomposed, if what is attended to is its formative intensities rather than its already acquired forms. Art, attentive to the relational complexity of experience's in-the-making, can make itself the experimental practice of composing new peaks of perception expressing the living, moving body's qualitative multiplicity, unfolding in new variations its capacity to change.

Couplet 10

2000

The Parable of the Cave (Blind Version)

Begin if you please by imagining a closed cave bounded on all sides. . . . I will suppose that this cave is pitch dark. I will also suppose that you can swim about in the air regardless of gravity. I will suppose that you have learned this cave thoroughly; that you know it is pretty cool, but warmer in some places, you know just where, than others, and that the different parts have different odors by which they are known. I will suppose that these odors are those of neroli, portugal, limette, lemon, bergamot, and lemongrass,—all of them generically alike. I will further suppose that you feel floating in this cave two great balloons entirely separated from the walls and from each other, yet perfectly stationary. With the feeling of each of them and with its precise locality I suppose you to be familiarly acquainted. I will further suppose that you formerly inhabited a cave exactly like this one, except it was rather warm, that the distribution of temperature was entirely different, and that the odors, in different localities in it with which you are equally familiar, were those of frankincense, benzoin, camphor, sandalwood, cinnamon, and coffee, thus contrasting strongly with those of the other cave. I will further suppose the texture-feeling of the walls and of the two balloons to be widely different in the two caves. Now, let us suppose that you, being as familiar with both caves as with your pocket, learn that works are in progress to open them to one another. At length, you are informed that the wall of one of the balloons has been reduced to a mere film which you can feel with your hand but through which you can pass. You being all this time in the cool cave swim up to that balloon and try it. You pass through it readily; only in doing so you feel a strange twist, such as you never have felt, and you find by feeling with your hand that you are just passing through one of the corresponding balloons of the warm cave. You recognize the warmth of that cave, its perfume, and the texture of the walls. After you have passed backward and forward often enough to become familiar with the fact that the passage may be made through every part of the surface of the balloon, you are told that the other balloon is now in the same state. You try it and find it to be so, passing round and round in every way. Finally, you are told that the outer walls have been removed. You swim to where they were. You feel the queer twist and you find yourself in the other cave. You ascertain by trial that it is so with every part of the walls, the floor, and the roof. They do not exist anymore. There is no outer boundary at all. . . . The shape may be further complicated by supposing the two balloons to have the shape of anchor-rings and to be interlinked with one another. . . . In passing through one of the balloons you have a choice of twisting yourself in either of two opposite ways, one way carrying you into the second cave and the other way into a third cave. That balloon surface is then a *singular surface*. You can readily understand that nothing but a rigidly exact logic of relations can be your guide in such a field. I will only mention that the real complications of the subject only begin to appear when continua of higher dimensionality than three are considered. For then we first begin to have systems of relations between the different dimensions. (Peirce 1992b, 252–53)

"All this," concludes Peirce, "is quite contrary to the geometry of our actual space" (253).

Or is it? A classic phenomenological description by Albert Michotte concludes that the lived space of the body is "a somewhat shapeless mass or volume."

There is very little by way of internal organization or connection between the parts. There is no clear marking off of the head, trunk, and limbs by precise lines of demarcation. The link between them is rather like that between the "head" and "tail" of a [creeping] caterpillar. Instead of any precise line of demarcation we find a number of regions with extensive connections between them gradually merging into one another. We can with some justification look on the body as a sort of *kinesthetic amoeba*, a perpetually changing mass with loose connections between the parts, and with the limbs constituting the pseudopodia. There are, however, very marked differences between this kinesthetic amoeba and the amoeba seen under the microscope. The latter has a contour separating it from its background, while this feature is clearly lacking in the case of a body in isolation. The "volume" of which it consists is not limited by a clearly defined surface, and there is no "contour." This is a point of considerable interest, and it necessarily follows as a result that the *whole* of the kinesthetic field of bodily sensations is filled by the body. In these conditions, there can be no question of any distinction between figure and ground such as occurs in the visual field, where the ground provides impressions of the same modality as that of the figure. The limit of the body is like the limit of the visual field—an imprecise frontier which has no line of demarcation, and which indeed cannot without absurdity be imagined to have one. . . . The body takes on a very wide range of different forms. Not only does its shape change, but its whole structure varies appreciably according to the circumstances. . . . [It] seems to float in a more extensive space, without its boundaries being at all clearly marked. (Michotte, Thinès, and Crabbé 1991, 204–6)

A kinesthetic amoeba . . . Try designing a house for that. Try designing a computer interface for the human pseudopod. Start by mapping its "positionality." Just try.

While you're working on it, temporary quarters for the amoeba might be found in Peirce's cave. The cave could be taken as a topological description of the "more extensive space" in which Michotte's amoeba "floats." Peirce's "logic of relations" might provide a description of Michotte's "shapeless" body "mass" in positive terms: as a "system," a complex system composing a boundless continuum of "appreciable" variation.

What does this cave look like again? That's just it. It doesn't look like anything. It's pitch dark. Plato would be utterly lost in it because it has no visible form, nothing to be seen as true or debunked as illusory, no copies to be matched to originals. It is the darkness that begins at the "limit of the visual field." Although dark, it conceals no secrets. It is no more, no less than what you *feel* it to be. Its truth is in the groping. You are groping something you are already familiar with. It's just like a place you have been and know as intimately as the inside of your pocket. It is the already inhabited. There's a *previousness* to it (see Couplet 9, "Tell Me Where Your Pain Is," in this volume). Although it is formless, it is not undifferentiated. It has the fog-bank differentiation of odor, coupled with the gradient differentiation of temperature. It is divided into regions defined by a smell synesthetically coupled with a degree of heat. But "divided" and "defined" aren't the right words. If the logic of the cave requires an "exact" logic, it is neither an analytic logic of division nor one of definition, if by "definition" is meant a fixed and stabilizing demarcation. Its principles are to be found elsewhere. This cave is a work in progress, and the progress is toward integral openness, complexly differentiated.

A gradient is continuous, presenting ordered variations as you move through it. Odor wafts, and heat concentrates and diffuses. They both come in gradients. At any one moment, you are at the intersection of a variation in each. At each moment you are already almost-feeling the next degree of temperature crossed with a varying nuance of odor. The next that you know to be coming is felt enveloped in the one before, the last in the penultimate. Fog banks and temperature gradients don't have sharp boundaries. They fade in and out and continuously transition. Although they don't entirely envelop each other, and never entirely coincide, they can and do overlap, forming thresholds between different nuances or degrees. Even without prior knowledge of the cave, you would feel a certain nextness in the variation composing the threshold.

This continuity of variations is what gives the cave-space its *unity*. The gradient differentiation runs through the fogs and temperature variations, equally across their overlap and disjunction. In the absence of visible contour, it is only by virtue of double-gradient continuity of variation that the disjunct fogs and successive nuances of warmth are experienced as belonging to the same space. If the gradients give the space its unity, the disjunctiveness of imperfect overlap between the fog banks, coupled with differences in temperature, is what gives the cave-space its *heterogeneity.* As you transit the regions, you feel *both* the unifying continuity of the gradients *and* the disjunctive overlapping of their regions. Your moving-through fuses the gradient differentiation with the fogbank differentiation, yielding a doubly *heterogeneous unity.* A "place" in the double gradient field is not defined by an abstract system of coordinates externally applied to it. It occurs in it, as an odor-temperature coupling. It is in it and of it: of the same stuff, of the same order of things.

The smells in each cave are of a family: they are *generically* alike. If the gradients' co-continuity of variation determines them as belonging to the same "space" (using the term advisedly), the smells' affinity with each other determine them as belonging to the same *kind* (lemony). Their "of a kind" is *qualitative.* "Lemony," as a quality, is inextensive. But it takes on extension across the successive and overlapping gradients of the different fragrances it generically envelops. These couple again with gradients of temperature, with its varied continuum of degrees of coolness ("warmer in some places"). The heterogeneous unity produced by the fusion of these qualitative gradients composes not a space in the usual sense but a *field.* This is a term used by both Peirce and Michotte. In light of the foregoing description, we can specify it as a field of *qualitative intensity.*

The field of qualitative intensity is too varied to be particular. But its move-through patterning of coupling, continuity, overlap, and disjunction makes it too singularly complex to be universalizable. The field is too generic (lemony) to be particular, and too singular (heterogeneous in its unity) to be universal. The cave-field is a *singular-generic*: member of no class other than itself; a being that is as it is felt to be; multiply differentiated; movingly unified.

The lemony cave is linked to another field of a different generic. Its aromatic gradient envelopes a variation from frankincense to coffee, passing through cinnamon. Call it cinnamony. Its range of temperature is different too, this time on the warm side. The nature of the link between these two singular-generics is significant. The singular-generic span of the lemony cave and the cinnamony cave are unmistakably different from each other. They comport a "strongly contrasting" smell family, a different temperature range, and thus different fusions felt in the moving-through. Yet they are still "familiar," in that they are both organized in the same mode, precisely as heterogeneous unities of fusion. You already inhabited the cinnamony cave before finding yourself in the lemony cave, which presented itself as analogue of the first, in a different key of odor-temperature cross-gradation. However, the link between them which allows each to become present again, their previousnesses becoming reciprocal through a back-and-forth, is far from familiar. It is a "strange twist." The link is an *event* of anomalous *movement*: as good as accidental. This movement-event is utterly unique, something you have "never felt before." It is a *pure singularity* as opposed to a heterogeneous singular-generic.

The strange twist opens onto a discovery. The texture between the central balloons of the two singularly generic caves was different to the touch. You're in the lemony cave and feel that the boundary of the balloon has become as thin as film. You pass through it—at which point you realize that on the other side the texture of the film of the balloon corresponds to that of the cinnamony cave. The centers of the two caves coincide! The fact that they are qualitatively differentiated allows them to be *superposed*. If you interpreted their extensiveness in the usual spatial terms, you'd have to say that they occupy the same space. And yet they remain as qualitatively different as before. Qualitative fields can interpenetrate. They constitute a pre- or proto-spatial *fielding* of the world: an infra-space of experience's extensiveness.

Of course, Peirce is not one to leave well enough alone. There are in fact two central balloons in each cave, and their centers are empty: they are anchor-rings, which is to say torus-shaped. The two balloons in each cave are fused to form a double torus. Why this seemingly gratuitous detail? It can only be because it undermines the uniqueness of the "center." Each center is already a variation on itself, and the surrounding field conditions flow through the empty center of the centers. If there were a single center, the heterogeneity of the cave-field would be arrayed around it. This would anchor it to a structuring element belonging to the familiar geometry we attribute to space. The double-torus conceit complicates this irredeemably, introducing variation and heterogeneity into the center. The back-and-forth movement between caves achieved by moving through the wall of the central balloon would have to negotiate the complexity. There are just too many variables of entry and transition to make the twist that performs the moving-through more than a particular movement-form. It has to negotiate its variations on itself. A move that takes account of its own variations in its every performance is a singularity, not a particularity: it is operating with a superposition of alternatives, negotiating its own potential. This is what makes it a "strange" twist.

The link between the cave-fields is not itself extensive. It is as thin as a film with no appreciable thickness. For its part, it has no previous familiarity. There is no previousness to it. It is a novel feature, and has the novelty of surprise. Its mode of reality is different from that of the gradient fields. It has the twisted nature of deformational movement referencing its own variations in its every performance. It is singular without being generic. It has no quality other than the strangeness of its movement. It has only *movement quality*, and movement quality is sui generis, singular: "There are a thousand smiles, a thousand getting-out-of-chairs, a thousand variations of performance of any and all behaviors, and each one presents a different vitality affect" (Stern 1985, 56).

Michotte warned us that "there can be no question of any distinction between figure and ground such as occurs in the visual field, where the ground provides impressions of the same modality as that of the figure." What we have instead in Peirce's caves is a difference in modality. Two fields that are analogous to each other (similar in mode but different in kind) are linked by a twist of a different nature. They enter into twisted relation, without grounding or backgrounding each other. If standing out from a background is the definition of a figure in Michotte's sense, borrowed from Gestalt, these fields are *nonfigural*. They are complexly ordered, each in its own right and in connection to each other, but remain informal in the sense that they cannot be mapped one outside of the other. The fact that they are superposed makes them spatially indistinct. They defy the spatial distinction marking the separation of forms or figures. It is part of the definition of space that it is composed of transitions of the same nature: smaller segments of space adding up to a larger expanse. Space is homogeneous. The mode of linkage of these qualitative fields, on the contrary, is ontologically different. The fields are heterogeneous, and so is the singularity of their linkage, including at it does in its performance a multiplicity of variations on itself (it is a *multiple-singular* in contradistinction to the singular-generic).

The link is a limit. It is a *limit-event* more than a spatial boundary. When you enter the singularity of the balloon movement, neither field can be placed in relation to the other, except in terms of the transition between them. Their relation is that of *pure transition*. They can't be juxtaposed like separate forms. They can only be come-into. The fields are *in-comes* from across each other's limit. When you are in one cave, the other does not exist in an adjacent space. It exists only as a potential in-come, across a threshold of event. Having no figure, there being no form or ground, there is no way of taking an actual distance on one when you're in the other. Neither has a proper place to be apart from its eventful implication in the other. They are in an *absolute proximity of qualitative differing*, separated only by an event. The double-torus center of one is the complex other side of the double-torus center of the other. When you move from one to the other, the event is more like a movement in place—a *vibration*—than it is an extensive movement of displacement. In other words, it's an *intensive movement*. The *extensiveness* of the fields (their gradient spans) are *intensities of each other*.

There is no outside perspective on intensive difference. You can't get a view on one field of intensity from another. You cannot plot the relation between them spatially. You cannot measure their difference, since what defines the fields' respective singular-generic character is a moving fusion between the qualitative dimensions of smell and temperature.

Your *movement is their differentiator*. Their distinctness hinges on the strange twist. That movement is what operationally differentiates them. Its event is all that effectively separates them. *Their effective separation is an artifact of their connection*. They are separately presented through their connection. The differentiator of movement *actualizes* them.

Peirce is full of surprises. As soon as you discover the connection between his caves, you learn that the outer perimeters of the caves have dissolved. If you "swim" to that "outside" limit, things get downright "queer." You discover that this event-limit also leads to the other cave. *The center of each cave coincides with the perimeter of the other*. It's not just that you twist between them. They twist into each other. The center is not defined spatially but *topologically*. They are continuous transformations of each other. Their centers turn in on each other at their outer limits. Their outer limits fold back in to each other's centers. The strange twist at the center is itself superposed upon the queer twist at the perimeter. They lead to the *same event*. They are not centers in the usual spatial sense. They are *virtual centers*: distributions of the differentiating event. They are *processual* centers: hinges for the process of orienting to a change between the qualitatively different fields.

Now with no actual perimeter, but only a limit-event, the caves are fields of *immanence* with no outside. They are *pure interiorities*. Monads. There are no windows between them, but they are linked by the event. The event occurs at the limit of the interiorities, not as a spatial boundary but as the threshold of their folding in and out upon themselves and each other. It doesn't belong to either of them. It belongs to their transition. It is their *transitional reality*.

If the fields are pure interiorities, the transitional reality of the event is the *pure exteriority* of the dynamic connecting them. The event is exterior not in the sense that it is outside relative to a cave's interiority. On the contrary, it is no less at the heart of each cave than it is at their periphery.[1] That is why what transpires is always an "in-come" and never an "outcome." As James says of the world of pure experience, "transitions and arrivals (or terminations) are the only events that happen" (1996a, 63). The event is a processual center immanently "exterior" to the spaces it is in. It is an immanent difference of modality across which a difference between fields unfolds. When you begin a twist, you *tunnel* into the difference between the fields (also on tunneling, see Couplet 5, "Sensing the Virtual," in this volume). Upon exiting the twist you untunnel, coming out-into one space or the other. Having differentiated the spaces by your strange twist, you earn a "swim" of familiar sniffs. Once you have experienced the novelty of the strange twist leading from one to the other, you can make your way back to the boundary-film and repeat the feat. The boundary is marked by a third, tactile quality added to the mix: the texture of the diaphanous film that is barely there. The touch of something barely there is a near-touch. This almost-touch indexes what cannot be touched: difference.

If at the center it is strange enough, at the periphery it gets downright "queer," Peirce says. Now the walls of the cave completely disappear. Presumably, the boundaries of the central balloons have also, given that these transitions fold around to superpose. Depending on how you do the twist, you either end up at the center of the other cave—or you arrive in a third cave, again analogous to the other two. The queer twist is an intenser strange twist, enveloping in-comes into three fields in its eventfulness rather than two. Since you can't feel the walls any more, and everything is darker than dark, how do you know what move you're making in this complexifying labyrinth? How do you differentiate and select? Your body is in a dynamic in-between, coinciding with a pure (multiple) singularity composed of an overlay of deformational movements leading to different in-comes. How do you move in a superabundance of potential movement? How do you orient in pure transition?

Through *proprioception*: the muscular- and joint-sense registering the movement of parts of the body in relation to each other. Proprioception registers the immanent relationality of the body. It does not directly concern the body parts themselves or their positions, so much as their changing configuration, and the changes from one configuration to another: the differential order of their co-relative movements. Proprioception fields the body as a milieu of pure transition made up of twists and turns interrelating. In itself, it has no sense of space or place, only a complexity of contortions folding into and out of each other to compose their own field of indefinitely multiple transformation. This field has no external reference. It has no nose or skin surface or ear for exteroception. Each of its component contortions are sui generis, pure (multiple) singularities.

It is only by cross-referencing its component differentials to incidents of touch, hearing, and vision that it can participate in the experience of position and contribute to orientation in a field other than its own. When Peirce threw us into his cave, he abandoned us to proprioception. It was only by indexing the gradients of odor and temperature to proprioception that it could be possible to begin orienting in the total darkness of the unknown cave. Imagine being in the very first cave. Certain landmark intersections, or fusions, between the gradient fields would begin to stand out from the sequence of swimming motions.

These could be found again, and paths intuited among them. The possibility of following a learned order of contortions to move back and forth between already experienced feeling intersections became the basis of an enactive map of the cave. But this origin story is a fiction. When is there not previousness? To have a body is to have always already fielded previousness. There is no specifiable origin, any more than there is a simply located center.

Be that previousness as it may, at whatever cave in the analogue series you find yourself, what is enactively mapped is not an external space but rather the complex order of contortions. Through exploratory movement, the body's field of immanent relationality *exfoliates* into a field of active orientation (Gil 1998, 114–36). The cross-sensory intersections are indexed to the body's field of immanent relation and, through it, to each other. The first two sense modes other than proprioception to enter into the act in the Peircean fable of the cave, smell and the skin-sensing of temperature, came in the form of an immersive gradient field. Although exteroceptive, they could not anchor to a spatial framework, if by space we understand a metric system of juxtaposition composed of discrete positions, fixed in their particularity, with fixed distances separating them. They came as fields whose composition was closer to that of the proprioceptive field itself than that of an external space: subject to a continuous variation. The gradient fields were composed of regions lacking the exactitude of fixed frontiers. Instead of simply being separated by boundaries, their regions were separated *and* connected by thresholds, where differences fade into and out of each other in a fusional dissolve. The cave experience was characterized by the singular contortions composing the proprioceptive field coming swimmingly together with the singular-generics of odor and temperature. This kinship in mode of composition—consisting in continuous variation—created an operative alliance between the proprioceptive and odor-temperature fields: a three-way fusion. Proprioception was essential even before the linkage between caves—the glue that holds everything together—revealed itself to be purely proprioception, at the limit of pure transition, in multiple-singular variation.

The only fixed anchoring to a set position by an exteroceptive sense that Peirce allowed us was through touch. The walls of the central balloons and the perimeter had different textures. But then the center and the periphery overlay upon each other, before dissolving. There is no longer even anything that could be mistaken for a unique center (already double-torused). There is only a virtual center—without simple location, and as much at the perimeter as at the center. This is more an event-locus than a particular place. It is an event-locus constituting a hinge dimension between fields of experience.

At the strange twist leading between the two caves, and even more intensely so at the queer twist adding a third, we return to where we began when we were thrown into the cave: we are remitted to proprioception operating purely on its own. How do we orient in that intensely singular relational in-between? *By indexing proprioception to itself*. By folding its contortions strategically into and out of each other. We are orienting directly in and with the field of immanence of the moving body. Since this field is composed of nothing but transitions, it can operate only *as* a transition: a reality of pure transition. This most singular of singular points is what acts as the hinge dimension. At the end of Peirce's parable, it is the only thing holding the expanding field of caves together. Their separation-connection hangs on a contortion: "You can readily understand that nothing but a rigidly exact logic of relations can be your guide in such a field" (1992b, 253).

"All this," Peirce warns, "is quite contrary to the geometry of our actual space" (1992b, 253). Our "actual space"—as habitually experienced and conventionally understood—is a Euclidean space. It is anchored prioritarily to the exteroceptive sense of vision. Positions in it are occupied by objective forms and figures apprehended at a distance. These stand out as landmarks, upon which we take a distant perspective through our eyes. The landmarks and the possible perspectives on them at different distances and angles of approach can be distilled into an abstract schema holding their variety in a uniform frame defined by a Euclidean coordinate grid. The logic of this classically perspectival grid is at bottom more a positional logic of juxtaposition and ordered succession than a contortional logic of relation. Of course, all manner of geometric relations are implicit in the positional grid, but these are derived by *adding movement back in* (trajectories, rotations, etc.).

It is this geometric frame, with its positional logic into which movement has to be poured as an extrinsic addition, that we take to be the "actual" space of our experience. This is to forget that it is an abstraction from the proprioceptive field in its fusional coming-together with the gradient fields of other senses. What Peirce has given us with the cave is a thought experiment taking us back to the primitive *field of experience*, of which the *experience of space is a derivative*. The thought experiment gives us a taste of what it would mean to experience experience-in-the-making as tributary to a logic of relations that *begins* with movement rather than adding it artificially back in, and that is made of transition more fundamentally than position. This return to the field of experience inverts the relation between movement and position. Movement takes priority.

When we feel we live in the box-frame of a (Euclidean) space of experience, our relation to the outside is fundamentally *quantitative*. If positions are set, then the space they share is defined by the measure of the distance separating them. This is an essentially metric space. In Peirce's cave, on the other hand, there is no distance in the Euclidean sense (as tied to a system of external relation between positions). The caves are superposed. The distance from one spot to another within each cave is "measured" by sequencing contortions. Which is to say, it isn't measured. It's enacted. Everything takes place in a field of pure interiority lacking the kind of extensive relations that reign in Euclidean space. There is extension, of a sort. The different odors and variations of temperature overlap, but are also offset from each other by thresholds of transition, giving them a *span*. There is a continuous differentiation obliging orientation to operate with an *intensive* understanding of the field: one that works with singularities of fusion and transition which co-envelop what it being transitioned to and from. The span in question is defined in a fundamentally *qualitative* manner: as the transitioning across qualitative variations. The span is one with a qualitative *spectrum*. The gradients composing the fields have their generic feeling quality, spanning a range of nuances. The intersections between the gradient fields that co-texture the field also have their own, fusional, felt quality. The strange and queer twists, for their part, are unique in their kind: genera of one (multiply singular).

The field that Peirce has given us is *experience as a qualitative field of differentiation*. The composition of that field is entirely different from that of a Euclidean space. It is still subject to a rigorous logic of relations, but one we can only do justice to if its principles of composition are taken at their word (or more precisely, at their contortion). What the contortions say is that the field of experience is *topological*, not geometric in the Euclidean sense. To understand its principles, we have to forget Plato's cave.

Plato's cave is only apparently immersive. There is no immediacy of feeling. There is no fielding, in the immediacy of movement, of experience-in-the-making. There is no movement. No one is swimming free of gravity. Everyone is chained in place. Projected on the surface of the wall, at a perspectival visual distance, are pregiven forms. This is an anaesthetic space, the farthest thing from a space of qualities of feeling. It is empty, filled with no richness of fragrances flirting with each across thresholds. Is it cold? Is it warm? If it has any temperature gradients, they are irrelevant, not considered worthy of mention. Fixed in position in their seats, no one can touch the wall. It has no texture that matters. There is no cross-sensory-mode referencing. All there is is vision, purely receptive of form at a distance. Everything is pregiven, not just the forms but the entire setup. The cave dwellers are not in active complicity with the space. They suffer its structure. They compose nothing.

One thing that we Peircean cave creatures can agree on with the prisoners of Plato's cave: yes, Plato's cave is an illusion. But when we exit it, we are not blinded by the light. We are not immersed in the conditions of vision, having to learn from the very beginning again to see truly. When we exit Plato's cave, there we are again in our experience's previousness, happily paddling in the aromatic Peircean darkness—freed at last (again) to experience experience as a qualitative field in the making. We are proprioceptively immersed in the cross-sensory conditions of qualitative experience.

Once again, there is no outside to the Peircean cave. You don't exit, you're always in-coming. There are event-limits between its caves, which are monadic, or more precisely transmonadic continuations of each other. There is no limit to them. It's not an inside-outside scenario. It's a *labyrinth*. The continuing keeps on going as we keep in-coming to experience. Cave upon cave. Two caves, three caves—no limit to the calving of caves. There is no reason to stop at three. There could be any number, Peirce says. There could, potentially, be an infinity. Each cave transmonad is a region of continuous variation. The caves' superposition defines a larger, unlimited continuum. Continua on a continuum, stretching out of and contracting into each other, playing the accordion of life: the life of movement.

"A continuum," Peirce notes, "may have any discrete multitude of dimensions whatsoever" (1992b, 253–54). Each cave, being limited, is a "discrete multitude" of gradations, thresholdings, and singular-twist opportunities. Now, "if the multitude of dimensions surpasses all discrete multitudes"—as is precisely the case for the continuum of continua taken to the infinite limit—"there cease to be any distinct dimensions." What there is is "the *uralt* vague generality of the most abstract potentiality" (254).

The qualitative field of experience is a *continuum of infinite differentiation* adding up, not to a bigger space, but to greater and greater superpositions of potentiality, greater and greater intensity, approaching the abstract limit. Occupying the limit is the "simple total vastness" that James remarked was our proto-experience of space: space as pure experience (1950, 136; see Couplet 9, "Tell Me Where Your Pain Is"). When the qualitative field of experience accordions to its greatest extent, approaching the pure experience of itself, it is *extending into intensity*. At the apogee of that movement, it surpasses all discreteness by carrying itself to the limit of its potential. It abstractly approaches the ur-continuity of its own potential.

That is where experience comes from, and where it swims toward: *intensive potential of qualitative differentiation*.

This is the home of Michotte's kinesthetic amoeba.

We tend to speak nonchalantly of the "shape" of the body, as if it were an objective form in Euclidean space, with definite contours and a determinate position at every moment. The shape of the body, however, is isomorphic to the shape of the field of experience. They are, in fact, subsets of each other (mutually enveloping in the way the perimeter of Peirce's cave folds into and out of its centers). The *shape of the body is qualitative* (transmonadic). The uralt nature of unbound potential amoebically infuses all of experience and can easily come back out for itself from under the presumed objective form of the body with its presumed Euclidean life-space.

For it to come back out, all you need to do is sit still. In stillness, the body relaxes into its intensive potential. It subsides into a kind of absolute rest, one that is in no way the opposite of movement. It is, rather, the zero degree of movement. There is no other side to a degree zero. It only has an upside. Everything rises from it. The zero degree of movement is the ultimate in-come point. From it, variations on the qualitative continuum rise back up into the labyrinth of experience's moving, to take contortionist topological shape.

James echoes Michotte on the objective vagueness of the body. For both, the body's fundamental lack of spatial order forbids any structurally complete image or mapping of it, making the notions of "body image" and "body schema" so often, and so often so lazily, relied upon in cognitive studies and phenomenology little better than conceptual straightjackets.

James also echoes Peirce on the idea that the principle of the body's composition lies in the fielding of qualities of feeling. These are no more subjective, exactly, than they are distinctly objective. Because if we are not careful to hold onto them with all our attention, with almost superhuman self-structuring effort, they will sink away from us. They have a will of their own to redescend into the background of the vague generality of most abstract potentiality from which they rose, toward the zero-degree of the kinesthetic amoeba. To rejoin the upside is easy: just move. You needn't overdo it and self-structure. Just swim. You will exfoliate heterogeneous cross-sensory worlds, blooming monadic one and all, all the more interconnected for having no windows.

> *Different feelings may coexist in us without assuming any particular spatial order.* The sound of the brook near which I write, the odor of the cedars, the comfort with which my breakfast has filled me, and my interest in this paragraph, all lie distinct in my consciousness, but *in no sense outside or alongside of each other.* Their spaces are *interfused* and at most find the same vaguely objective world. . . . There are moments when, as we lie or sit motionless, we find it very difficult to

feel distinctly the length of our back or the direction of our feet from our shoulders. By a strong effort we can succeed in dispersing our attention impartially over our whole person, and then we feel the real [as objectively defined] shape of our body in a sort of unitary way. But in general a few parts are strongly emphasized to consciousness and the rest sink out of notice; and it is then remarkable *how vague and ambiguous our perception of their relative order of location is*. Obviously, for the orderly arrangement of *a multitude of sense-spaces* in consciousness, *something more than their mere separate existence is required*. What is this further condition? they must appear as parts in *a vaster sensible extent* [a continuing; a continuum] which can enter the mind simply and at once [in abstract potentiality]. I think it will be seen that the difficulty of estimating correctly the form of one's body by pure feeling arises from the fact that *it is very hard to feel its totality as a unit at all*. (James 1950, 146–47, emphasis added)

2003

Panoscopia

The popular success of the painted panorama in the nineteenth century hinged, according to the social historian Stephan Oettermann, on its popularization of the controlling gaze (1997). By climbing to a vantage point such as a hill, tower, or rooftop, an artist could command a sweeping 360-degree view of a city or landscape. The aim was to deliver that commanding view to the paying public. Great pains were taken to reproduce the scene as accurately as possible on an immense, circular canvas. A specialized architecture developed to house the bird's-eye images, brought to ground. The open-air vantage point was replaced by an indoor observation deck, separated from the wrap-around wall upon which the canvas was stretched by an intervening space. The gap recreated a sense of distance vision in the closed exhibition space to which the open sweep of society and nature was now profitably confined.

Formally, the scene was a composite of a number of segments, each ordered according to the conventions of perspective, with its own vanishing point. The vanishing point was the anchor of traditional representational order. In framed painting, it created a privileged axis in the dimension of depth running from the eyes of the viewer to a point where the representational space receded into an infinite distance. The infinite regress extended the principles of linearity and symmetry governing the foreground composition indefinitely to all of space, making the scene shown a selected segment of a universal order. On the opposite end of the same axis, in the viewing space before the canvas, lay a corresponding vanishing point where the same order was back-projected into the mind's eye of the observer, receding into the infinite proximity of subjectivity. The reciprocity of the two poles assured the participation of the subject and the object of sight in the same representative order. The painted panorama extended that order horizontally beyond the traditional frame by linking perspectival segments to encircle the viewer. Mathematical formulae were used to correct the distortion created by bending the flat perspectival surfaces into a curve. The vanishing points of the joined segments stood out as privileged viewpoints through which the viewer could pivot to take a representational tour. The panoramic image did not in fact break with traditional perspective, but multiplied it. Order now radiated laterally in all directions for the untraveling visual tourist, treated to an awe-inspiring view of a particular place at the same time as a representational performance of universalized knowledge.

Contrast with that the present-day panoramic photography of Luc Courchesne. The images are captured automatically rather than constructed using rule-bound procedures that would give them an air of representational authority. They are lifted out of the flow of the artist's everyday life using a 360-degree camera lens attachment, more like chance samplings than logical segments. Each bears a date, tethering them to a singular moment. The moments link together as an itinerary through lands foreign and familiar. Since the images do not on the whole present recognizable landmarks or follow a conventional rule of progression, such as a tourist trip, their spatial order comes across to the viewer as ephemeral as their dating. The viewer is not positioned, as in the painted panorama, to enjoy the spectacle of the particular, awe-inspiringly integrated into universal order. The images compass a seemingly chance itinerary, a life-drift. The viewer, rather than being masterfully positioned, is invited to enter the drift.

November 2, 2000: Two blue railings bracket the center-point like metallic lids. The center-point is composed of two differently shaded concentric circles, a gray iris and a black pupil. The pupil is not part of the image per se. It is its formative blind spot. It is the spot occupied by the camera mounted with a panoramic lens. It is the black hole of representation, standing in the image for its mechanical origin as well as for the artist's body, eclipsed by the lens to which he owes the image. The double origin of the image, mechanical and human, is twice removed. Taking the place of the traditional vanishing point, this black hole attracts the eye, drawing the observer into the image at a paradoxical point

378   COUPLET 10

10.1   Luc Courchesne, *Journal Panoscopique, Ogaki City,* November 2, 2000.

where its emergence coincides with its eclipse, and where the body of the artist, the imaging apparatus, and the eye of the observer collapse together. Rather than projecting a universal order, the image implodes.

The eye, however, is no sooner drawn in than a countervailing centrifugal force pulls it back out. The horizon pulls back from the centerpoint to the periphery. This third concentric circle is less a line than a fringe. It has a blurred thickness, across which the image fades infinitely into the distance in all directions, fringing the image with its own fading out. Unlike the painted panorama, the distortions produced by projecting a curved surface onto a flat surface are not corrected for. The persistent distortion forbids the fade into the distance from coming across simply as an objective representation of an external view. It marks it as belonging to the image and its process of production. The image has unfolded from the inward collapse at its core only to envelop its own distance.

By folding its outer limit back into itself, the image asserts itself as a form of interiority. It is not so much a represented segment of an outside objective sight as it is a *monadic sampling* of vision. The monad, says Leibniz, has no windows. It is a pure interiority. Yet it connects with the outside: by enveloping it in itself. The point at which the outside enters appears as an interior emptiness. The black hole of representation at the heart of the image is the trace within it of the process of its production and of the principle of its form. The enfolded tension between the center and the fringe sets a visual rhythm in motion. The eye of the observer tends to swing back and forth between them across the photographic scene. When the eye pauses on that scenic content, the eye's oscillation continues in place, as if the seen enfolded that movement as well as presenting itself. The bipolar attraction to the fringe and to the center transforms into an immobile movement or pulsing: a kind of formal giddiness animating every point in the image with a pull in two directions at once, without any actual displacement. The effect of this *immobile pan* is slightly dizzying. A *virtual* visual movement has been induced by the paradoxical form of the image as a monadic whole.

The hint of dizziness in the image activates the viewer's sense of balance by gently throwing it off. Recent studies have shown that the sense of balance always works by gently throwing itself off. The body generates continual kinesthetic noise, quasi-chaotic micromovements. Its sense of balance is its constant nonconscious correction of this sway. What we experience as the stasis of standing is a minimal degree of nonconscious kinesthetic activity in place, ready to unfold into actual movement at any moment: activity on the verge of emerging. The quasi-chaotic nature of this nonconscious experience of emergent activity only enters awareness when a troubling of the body's active capacities short-circuits the actual emerging into action. This short-circuiting of action in its incipience enters awareness as vertigo.

The dizziness in the panoramic image triggers a conscious experience of the body's base state of emergent activity. In so doing it gives a kinesthetic content to the virtual visual movement. The pulsing of vision in the image is doubled by this intersense switch to the kinesthetic sway of active incipience. The sight seen is inhabited by a virtual movement of vision, seconded by proto-activity in a nonvisual sense register that is felt short of actually emerging: a twofold virtual dynamic. The image is thus internally dynamized, in and out of vision, without actual activity or interaction. This intersense pulse-switch-sway is a kind of itinerancy *of* the image. This itinerancy in place recalls intensively, interior to each image, the life-drift sampled extensively across the photographic series.

This has an important consequence for the nature of the photographic series. If the images in the series had the naturalistic representational order of perspective painting that had been multiplied in the traditional panorama, then they would potentially connect at their peripheries. A spatial order would radiate from each image, suggesting a logically mappable connection between them. There would be no obstacle in principle to filling in any gaps in the representation. In Courchesne's photographic series, on the other hand, the gapping is constitutive. The periphery does not extend outward in orderly geometric fashion, but folds distortedly back in. This gives the image a virtual dynamic that is *felt* in vision but is not itself visual. Its content is thus not reducible to the visual scene and cannot be fully rendered as a spatial form. There is something time-based in it (pulse-switch-sway) that is irreducibly experiential. They are *images of experience*.

The form of the images is a monadic dynamic that draws the viewer in for an experience: a truly, effectively *immersive perspective*. This is not a perspective in the traditional sense of an outside view onto a naturalistic scene. It is an interior perspective on life, as technologically image-assisted. Although Courchesne's panoramic photographs are actually still, the virtual dynamic they contain qualify them as interactive. Not just snapshots: *still interactions*.

And then there is the hand. It cups the black hole-iris in its palm, as if to steady the image and deliver it from its own giddiness. Another nonvisual sensing is added to the process. The seer is invited to become a toucher. His or her hand can extend toward the artist's hand in the image, and give the glass plate on which the photograph is mounted a spin, countering his apparent steadying. The image is put back in motion, but it is a derivative movement that is applied to the image from the outside rather than arising in the interiority of the image. The vision-kinesthesia switch relays again into tactility. At this juncture, the image folds out of itself without folding back in. The viewer is seeing actively in front of the image, at a safe distance from which it can be manipulated. This issuing into action stills the virtual dynamic interior to the image. The tactile interaction has transformed the live interactive still into an objectively spinning still life. The invitation to touch and spin the glass plate unfolds the image in an actual interaction. This constitutes a *translation* of it into another dynamic, in which the image features as an object, approachable from the outside. It is regiven to an outside perspective where sight at an objective distance can relay into a touch.

The interaction inside the 360-degree screen apparatus Courchesne calls the Panoscope is another actualizing translation of the immersive perspective. The projection of the image in 360-degree surround places the viewer in a situation more similar to that of the traditional panorama observer. The body is free to actively swivel to take in the view. The whole-body swivel repeats the spin of the plate, translated from a movement of the seen object into an objective movement of vision. The transformation into a traditional panorama does not, however, go all the way. The small scale of the surround screen sets up a tension between close and distance vision. The fact that the represented distance is seen close at hand, without the traditional panoramic device of the gap between the observation platform and the canvas, gives an odd feeling of being swaddled in visual distance, as if the touch of the hand to the photographic plate had changed direction and returned optically to the body. This sets up a pulsing between near and far and between the visual and the tactile not unlike the virtual movement of the fringe folding into the immanent center of the photographs or the pulse switch to sway. The effect is heightened by the fact that the viewer enters the apparatus through what in the photographic disk was the black hole tracing all at once in an overfull void its human authoring, mechanical process, and monadic principle. The Panoscope, as a result, remains more intensely immersive than the traditional panorama, even as it plays on its conventions.

As images of experience, Courchesne's installations cannot be reduced to their visual content. They must be approached as on-site performances,

10.2 Luc Courchesne, *Panoscope V.1*. Photo: Richard-Max Tremblay.

even in the absence of actual interaction. The photographic stills are fully a part of Courchesne's interactive art practice. There is a reciprocity between aspects of the work that requires each of its elements to be understood in translational terms in relation to the others. They repeat the same immersive dynamic, but differently in each case, depending on the apparatus and the installation. This means that the installations for which Courchesne is best known, in which the Panoscope is fitted with a voice-command video interface that is interactive in the usual digital sense of the term, are best understood if they are not seen in isolation but in relation to the interactive-still pieces. The concept of interaction needs to be expanded to account for virtual dynamics capable of inwardly animating an immobile surface.

Couplet 11

2003

Urban Appointment

A Possible Rendezvous with the City

To catch the city in a different light, the situationists recommended making virtual appointments (Debord 1996, 26). A group member was asked to show up at a certain corner at a predesignated time. Neither party knew who the other was. Steeped in uncertainty, the encounter was destined to remain merely a possibility. Merely a possibility? Fully a possibility. Think of what it feels like going to meet someone you have never seen before in a public place. Every person walking by might be about to step into your life. The slightest of gestures amplifies into an emergent sign of recognition. The space around is no longer a neutral frame. It is charged with anticipated gazes leading potential approaches.

> Arrival supplants departure; everything arrives without necessarily having to depart.
> —Paul Virilio (1987, 19)

Your peripheral vision sharpens to catch the subtlest flutter of arrival at every angle all around, giving a much more palpable sense of immersion than you normally feel. Space thickens, liquefies, and stirs. Wavelets of possibility fill it like a fourth dynamic dimension.

> Transitions and arrivals are the only events that happen, though they happen by so many sorts of path.
> —William James (1996a, 63)

The device of the virtual appointment is designed to make possibility movingly palpable, in a city space now defined as much as an overcharge of potential paths of human encounter as by its geometrical and geographical properties.

> *The experience says "more," and postulates reality existing elsewhere.*
> —William James (1996a, 67)

The HUMO workshop made a virtual appointment, not between individuals in the city but between a collectivity and the city.[1] Twelve artists were invited to Linz, Austria, for the week of February 3–7, 2003.[2] Waiting for them was the world's most powerful projector mounted with a power generator on a 12-ton truck. The projector is capable of throwing an image over sixty by sixty meters, large enough to cover the façade of a large building.[3] HUMO = HUge and MObile. "The project," Rafael Lozano-Hemmer's call for participation announced, "will consist of rapid deployment of strategic images to transform urban landscapes. Logos, emblematic buildings, quotidian spaces, suburban malls, advertising billboards, etc., will be the targets of unannounced, unregulated ephemeral interventions . . . below the radar of potential regulators." The Ars Electronica FutureLab was placed at their disposal for the preparation of digital images and their transfer to acetate slides for rapid-fire open-air projection.

Like the situationist *dérive*, or experimental urban "drift," for which the possible rendezvous was one tactic, HUMO was a plan to exceed the expected. A truck-borne band of artists would roam the city making stealth image attacks on buildings, factories, fields, and highway underpasses, onto anything and everything. The locations would be scouted ahead of time or chosen on the spur of the moment in passing. They would be as central as a main plaza or as marginal as an industrial slag heap. In either case, art would leave the walls of the gallery behind to flit for a moment on the periphery of official urban vision, out of place, out of scale, out of nowhere. The image's arrival would momentarily alter the perceptual conditions of the local space, crystallizing at least a vague sense of the unaccustomed possibilities it enfolds. Even if no legible message was sent, the anomaly of the image's very presence would signal a "more" postulating the existence of an elsewhere, beyond the conventional logic of that place.

11.1 HUMO image projection. Image: Anya Lewis.

In the everyday course of things, the sites of the city can be trusted to keep their appointments. A skyscraper can be counted on to be in the right place at the right time in order to serve as a landmark. A train station or government building will faithfully fulfill its promised function, on schedule. There are regions of known possibility surrounding each of the building types or infrastructural elements composing the city—ways of featuring in the lives of those who enter them or pass them by that are as conventionalized as the types are generic. For each generic, there are regulated rhythms of passage into and out, more or less predictable patterns of circulation around, and strict zoning and ownership limitations on what can affix to the external envelope that stabilizes its public mode of appearing. The regularity of a building's regime of transition creates a backdrop against which any unexpected arrival will stand out. The background, however, does not simply disappear under the weight of the anomaly. In fact, it rises to the surface and reasserts itself in and through, in addition to, the unaccustomed gesture. For example, projecting an inside scene on an outside wall actually strengthens the feeling of exteriority. Nobody is fooled into thinking that it is no longer a façade. But few seeing it will be untouched by the strangeness of seeing the inside out. The uncanniness of the feeling brings a sharpened awareness of the façade's exteriority, but with a twist: not as it normally presents itself. Exteriority reasserts, with new and added effect: in a special effect.

When an artist makes an appointment with the urbanly unexpected, this must be taken into account. There is no simple displacement or re-placement. There is no straightforward inversion, contradiction, or even combination. The accustomed persists in background conditions contributing to a special effect which is not reducible to a logical operation on the generic type, a message about it, or even a visual recontextualization of it. This is because the sensorimotor specifications of the human body are built into the city on several registers at every site. The city's amenities offer what James J. Gibson calls "affordances" and Arakawa and Madeline Gins "landing sites" (Gibson 2015, 119–35; Arakawa and Gins 2002, 5–22).

Landing sites are offers of useful connection and platforms for possible action pre-fit to the needs and capacities of the human body. Each landing site offers the body one of its own functions, stored in objective form. A park bench, for example, is a storage of repose. It has been sculpted to that function. Its objective form is that function in urban reserve: an available mold for its civil reliving. Each landing site beckons the body from a particular angle of its unfolding experience, to which it affords a response. The park bench beckons the body from the angle of its city-caused exhaustion, affording rest in response. For the footweary the sight of a bench is not just a visual image of a recognizable object. Compressed into the visual image is a palpable anticipation of the additional steps it will take to reach the state of rest, a pre-sensation of knees flexing and body plopping at destination, an advance on the pleasure of tired muscles relaxing throughout the body—already tempered by the coming hardness of slats against vulnerable bones.

The landing site already includes an anticipatory feeling, stretching across perceptual registers other than vision, of the experience of affording oneself of the offered function. The sight of the bench invokes movement-feeling (or kinesthesia) as well as postural feeling (or

11.2 HUMO image projection. Image: Harald Schmutzhard.

proprioception) and tactile sensation (texture, pressure, hardness). These other-than-visual sensings are included in the image, in nascent form, as inklings or pre-feelings of a promise kept. They inhabit the sight and are as present in the recognition of the object as its properly visual form. The recognition is not a merely cognitive act triggered by visual form. It is a veritable pre-living of the process leading to the enjoyment of the promised function. Fused into the visual presentation of the object are nascent experiences in other sense registers, whose pre-feeling compresses into the presence of the image their own unfolding over time. The bench sighting is *fusional* (an integral experience whose overall quality is attributable as much to touch and other senses as to vision) and *durational* (presenting not just an object but an unfolding).

The façade of a building is also an affordance. Enfolded into the sight of an apartment complex is the feeling in the legs of winding down corridors and the drop in the stomach of ascending in elevators and the touch of a doorknob and the slip of a key and a swaddling in warmth and artificial light: a nascent, multiregistered experience of arriving home, already presented, in fusional duration, in the façade's visual attributes of flatness and verticality. We cannot not experience home arrival, from one angle actually and integrally in potential, at the sight of the apartment façade. It is built into our learned relationship to that generic building type. Every city sight, at any moment, is an arrival of this kind without, as James would say, any necessity of departure.

Because there is perceptually built into every city feature an acquired relationship that has taken time to develop and takes time to unfold, Lozano-Hemmer emphasizes that urban art is not site-specific but *relationship-specific*. The relation always arrives, coming to us through a leading perceptual edge—usually visual—in advance of its next sequential unfolding. In other words, its arrival is a promised *event* that has yet to occur: an appointment with a known but not yet actually afforded outcome. To afford oneself of the outcome is to eventuate the relationship, to *perform* it: to follow through with its actual step-by-step unfolding.

Urban art, as a relationship-specific practice, approaches the external surfaces of urban elements such as buildings as *performance envelopes* already presenting potential events. It *suspends* the unfolding of those events for its own duration. For example, as long as a citizen has stopped to experience a strange art image on a familiar façade, he is not affording himself of home. The promised home-appointment is still perceptually enfolded in the façade, but its step-by-step fulfillment is temporarily suspended. For that duration, the event is held in its potential: the appointed outcome remains virtual. In place of the beckoning event, what unfolds is an unsought art experience. The art *parasitizes* the expected event with its own happening. The situationists also had a name for this practice of inserting unexpected encounters-with-potential into existing landing sites: *détournement* (hijacking or detouring).

Urban art intervention involves holding virtual appointments in a parasitic event. It affords a temporary detour from accustomed paths leading to known landing sites. The detour, like the unfolding it suspends on arrival without erasing, is not a merely cognitive act. Even though it always involves a combination, displacement, or replacement of forms, and these procedures often suggest inversions or contradictions of message and meaning, the art event cannot be reduced to its formal procedures or semantic content. The accustomed event it detours is a fusional duration which is irreducibly experiential, in that it compresses into itself perceptual continuations that are really, if nascently, lived. In order to effectively substitute its own event for the expected event, the art intervention must be of the same nature as it. It is also a fusional duration, compressing in itself multiregister experiential potential. But since there is no expected outcome in particular, what that potential might unfold as remains unspecified. The already known, normally expected event is thus wrapped in a parasitic *indeterminacy*. The art intervention's *special effect* is an added parasitic twist to the pre-fit experience habitually associated with the site type and the promised outcomes its form generically enfolds. This special indeterminacy effect is *felt* without being recognized.

In the example of an interior scene projected onto a façade, the nascent other-sense experiences of being inside are already elicited on the outside that normally promises them only after an unfolding. Their arrival comes too soon. The spatial displacement of the interior and its combination with the exterior presents a temporal distortion whereby two unfoldings find themselves occupying the same surface. The presence of the disjoint durations produces interference between the multisense patterns each enfolds. It is this excess of interference that is felt as the event's added special effect: a surplus of undefined potential. This extra indeterminacy effect has its own experiential quality arising from the coming-together of its component durations: the feel of unaccustomed potential taking up residency in the joints of the familiar. More other-sense nascencies pack in, less distinguishably affording: the promise of more promise, without landing. A performance envelope has been differently activated, without, however, anything in particular eventuating.

The felt suspense of this eventuating of a public nothing in particular could be the whole art event. Or it could just be a first phase. The event can be framed in such a way as to invite its viewer to become a participant. Platforms using motion detection, tactile interface, or sound activation may offer actual other-sense opportunities to interact with a hijacked visual surface as well as with other participants. This actuates unaccustomed intersense linkages, which may crystallize into suggestions of as-yet unrecognized affordances inhabiting landing sites to come. Rather than reexperiencing a generic type, the participants will have performed a *prototype* of experience. And they will have done it together. From the leading edge of a perception, the event has drawn the participants into a collective unfolding, however vague to begin with, of their own *sociality* as such.

Urban art intervention is not best fit to reflect the reality of the city—for the simple reason that it is better suited to revise it. It has its sights more immediately on the augmentation of urban reality than its representation. It is a *social laboratory*: a performative platform for provisional group definitions of potential, in a public innovation of affordance.

The setting in place of a provisional performance envelope is complicated by the fact that the relations which the art event parasitizes always in fact include a *nonlocal* dimension: all the more reason why the intervention cannot be site-specific. Every generic type composing the city is iterative and distributive. Home buildings, for example, repeat themselves at any number of sites, with variation, in an ever-developing distribution, as houses sprout and apartment complexes are razed and rebuilt. The same applies to storage tanks, highway underpasses, industrial slag heaps, and museums; to every urban element. The art intervention pertains as much to this process of elemental distribution and variation inherent to the city, on which its ability to regenerate itself is based, as it does to any particular si(gh)ting. The art event is addressing not just the specific site, but through that site a general urban dynamic, a way the city has of being and rebecoming itself—a city *mannerism*.

Urban art intervention addresses *citiness*, the city itself, from the mannerist angle of one of its constitutive self-iterations. That is why whatever kind of interaction eventuates from the art event's special activation of a performance envelope is prototypical. If distributive conditions are right, the parasitism may inherit the host site's potential to repeat elsewhere with variations. The design of the event platform can take measures to accommodate this mannerist possibility. This is the role of *documentation*. Documentation is the art event's park bench: the form in which it rests. Except that documentary rest is for transport, since it is in documentary form that the event may move from one "park" to another. Documentation as vehicular event benching. To vehiculate the event, the documentation cannot be conceived merely as reflecting or representing it. It must be thought of as, and designed to be, the event in seed form.[4] If the documentary germ falls on fertile urban ground, the performative prototyping may well resprout. *Documentary design* is an integral component of urban art as ongoing *process* dynamically addressing the city from a local angle on its generality (its translocal iterability). It is the event's way of angling itself, or generally affording its own rehappening.

There is another way in which nonlocality features in an urban art event, in particular one employing the strategy of image projection. The urban surface is itself a generic type. Every surface in the city onto which an image might be affixed or projected already affords a recognizable, nonlocal function: advertising. An urban art event cannot avoid being, simply by virtue of deploying *public* imagery, an engagement with *publicity*. Advertising makes every urban surface a potential billboard. And every urban volume can now be transected in a way that resolves it into a configuration of newly available surfaces. Any and every city space can in principle be sliced into so as to multiply indefinitely the number of publicity surfaces it can host. This is the leading edge not just of a perceptual mode—visuality—but in the same stroke of a global system: capitalism. Through the ubiquity of advertising, capitalism is continually breaking and entering the lived volumes of urban experience, parasitizing them in its own profitable way. This public breaking and entering of the city by visible expressions of capital is what Paul Virilio calls *effraction* (1987, 25). It "overexposes" the city to capital-intensified sight. New digital technologies have provided advertising with effraction tools of inestimable power. They offer previously unseen possibilities: variations of scale, from the smallest of miniaturizations to a new gigantism, in addition to new dimensions of mobility and angles of attention-getting. The logo is as much a component part of the urban landscape as the apartment block.

An advertising image brings *transnational* arrivals to the city. The logos more and more attach to multinational companies of global reach. Their presence betokens connections between each city locale and local sites across the globe. As Saskia Sassen argues, the contemporary city is a global city in the sense that it connects outwardly and horizontally, through or beneath its vertical integration in a nation-state, to form an economic and social network filigreeing with other far-flung urban centers and their associated rural reaches. Cities are part of a "new geography" that "links subnational spaces across borders.... This is a space that is both place-centered, in that it is embedded in particular and strategic locations, and transterritorial, because it connects sites that are not geographically proximate yet are intensely connected to each other" (2000, 137).

Not all the finely webbed connections are made visible in the advertising image. There are many its sponsors have an interest in *not* envisioning. The arrivals to the global city are not only consumer goods bringing purchase choice but also people bringing labor power. Immigrants of all kinds, including political and economic refugees, flow into and out of the cities as part of a mass human migration of unparalleled magnitude. Their life histories, memories, and maintained economic and cultural links connect back to areas of the world where the structural effects of nineteenth-century European colonization are still playing themselves out, as new forms of imperialism daisy-chain with them. The sweatshops and child-labor practices targeted in recent years by boycott campaigns are emblematic of the kind of operative imperialist connections that go unsighted by advertising. A giant Nike ad that recently occupied the entire multistory façade of a large building in the center of Rotterdam is a case in point. Featuring Edgar Davids, a Dutch soccer star of African ancestry born in Suriname, it makes visible a structural effect of colonial history that can be publicly and profitably affirmed (the cosmopolitanism and increasing ethnic and cultural diversity of global cities that make them a social factory for the creative emergence of new skills, styles, and modes of expression that are then subject to appropriation and logoing) while backgrounding others that are troubling (the increasingly unequal distribution of wealth in the global economy and the dependence of companies like Nike on exploitative labor practices in other corners of the world in order to maintain their profitability in an intensely competitive transnational economic environment). Like all urban perceptual events, an advertising display presents in the now of the moment an other duration, and in the here of that now a potential unfolding elsewhere. The desired unfolding from the Nike ad is toward the elsewhere of a shoe store and the time of a

11.3 Nike ad featuring Edgar Davids, Rotterdam.

purchase. It is not a step-by-step retracing of the connections leading to sweatshops, possible labor action in Asia, and domestic boycott.

An urban art event employing image projection engages with this dimension of advertised nonlocality in the global economic environment, whether it wants to or not. Consciously or not, it will embed decisions about how it can or will deal with that engagement in the very form of the platform it designs for itself, the performance envelope it actuates, and the documentary follow-up tactics it adopts. Will it ignore all that, at the peril of further blurring the boundaries between art and advertising, already called into question by the cannibalizing of what were once avant-garde artistic strategies by an increasingly style-savvy public relations industry? Will it consciously try to suspend the consumer unfolding for a moment by producing perceptual interference patterns that detour participants' actions and deflect attention toward other unfoldings? Or will it exploit its parasitizing of potential advertising sites to ironize or explicitly comment upon the kinds of connections that the advertising normally occupying and multiplying urban surfaces makes a concerted practice of not envisioning? Or will it combine strategies, either in different phases of its eventuating or integrated into each phase as different levels of itself (giving it a multilayering effect, like an event-depth or spacing proper to the time of its performance)?

The strategy of explicitly displaying unvisualized connections suggests a second pole or orientation of urban art intervention. The first orientation was the perceptual/experiential pole tending toward a prototyping of sociality as a self-disseminating process that is itself essentially urban in nature. The second orientation is ideological, asserting missing logical connections and transmitting a message that is not urban itself but is rather *about* the city and its elsewheres, "speaking" from a principled distance on them. Every urban art project operates at both poles, to different degrees or intensities. Every such intervention must prepare the perceptual conditions for its own occurrence and at least momentarily suspend site-specific affordance, and to the degree that it does it operates at the experiential pole. Every intervention is also a comment on generic urban practices like advertising, if only by virtue of unexpectedly occupying a city surface, and thus carries a certain weight of ideological analysis and comment. It is a question of emphasis, or what is preponderantly conveyed. If what is vehiculated is primarily an idea or message content about the city and the connections between the local and the global, the conveyance is *communicational* or informational and parks itself toward the ideological end of the urban art spectrum, toward the iteration of a principle. If what is vehiculated is primarily a self-seeding performance of sociality, it is preponderantly *contagious* or mimetic, and parks itself at the perceptual end of the spectrum, toward the iterative dissemination of a new experience-type.

The work of a given artist is likely to tend more toward one pole or the other. Lozano-Hemmer's work tends toward the social contagion of experience pole, while that of Krzysztof Wodiczko tends to the ideological communication of a message pole. In most instances, to the extent that an urban art practice operates at one pole, it backgrounds or disengages from the other. If it emphasizes one pole, it is because it has set specific mechanisms in place to uphold that orientation. Every practitioner or project will display a selective emphasis or signature mixture of these tendencies. Either tendency may be staged in a way that empowers participants to appropriate the event's outcome for themselves, toward their own ends.

The perceptual/experiential pole was presented as the base state or default setting of urban art intervention not because the genre in any way excludes communicational strategies, but because the communicational function it can play is not unique to it but is shared with other arts (it can be practiced in print, online, and in the gallery). It is through its communicational aspect that urban art intervention itself communicates with other arts, and through its necessary treatment of perceptual/experiential urban landing sites that it drifts off on its own as an autonomous art practice.

The members of the HUMO workshop came from a variety of art practices and represented a healthy mix of these strategies. The broad range of participant approaches and disciplines was essential to the workshop conception. The exceeding of the expected was meant to be part of the workshop experience itself, and to feed forward into the on-site projections. Group heterogeneity can produce positive feedback fostering the emergence of unplanned synergies. This notably occurred in the HUMO workshop, at least in part in response to other contingencies. As with the situationists, chance and constraint were not considered contraries. The attitude was that they could work hand in hand, as in the tactic of the possible rendezvous where the arbitrary imperative of being at a particular time and place for an imposed purpose gives rise to an intensified living of potential. Working under unchosen imperatives, friction in the procedural machinery, and obstacles encountered en route can gel perceptions that might otherwise remain peripheral and crystallize creative tactics that might have been overlooked. Unsuspected avenues open, constraint transforms into a new chance to advance, blockage into a new opportunity. This thinking informed the workshop concept: what was being offered was not a class, but an adventure. And an adventure it was.

Sure enough, obstacles began to be encountered almost immediately. It soon became clear that in order to hijack a city site with an image, you have to deal with the possibility that the image might be hijacked by the site. There is no such thing, the group soon learned, as a simple 2D projection on a found city surface. A building is not just a bigger screen. Its surface has a shallow depth of its own due to the texture of its construction materials, which can give the image a strange, almost tactile thickness. The building also imposes in places its own form and configuration. Windows, for example, can swallow pictorial elements like black holes, significantly altering the overall visual effect, to the point sometimes of undermining the comprehensibility of the image. Just the fact of being blown up in scale can turn some images monstrous while neutralizing others. Which way a given image will go is not as easy a call to make as one might expect. Scale comes into its own as a problem. Unpredictable plays of ambient light and weather conditions can also significantly affect image quality. Further, a building in its urban context, unlike a screen or canvas, is essentially unframed. It is impinged upon, even visually altered, by its surroundings. The presence of neighboring buildings, for example, may impinge upon an image by casting shadows, and even alter its perceived form by peripherally entering into a gestalt with it. Street and security lights dapple the scene. Trees grow, sometimes in the vicinity of fences, in league with which they can make finding an optimum line of sight—or even any line of sight—difficult. Visibility can be hard to format. This was brought home to the group when it realized that the first projections, which were barely discernible on site, had been so striking a kilometer away that people driving on the highway had started to pull over in large numbers to watch. One participant, Johannes Gees, summed up the general group feeling following the first projections: "It's amazing how a building can get in the way of an image."

There are two responses to the indiscipline of buildings. One is to learn how to gain a measure of control over site-interferences by developing a sensitivity to them and a feel for assessing their parameters, and then adopting or inventing technical procedures to eliminate contingencies where possible or, for those that cannot be eliminated, to minimize their impact. The second response is to embrace the unpredictability of the context as a collaborator, treating the contingencies as nonhuman image coauthors. The accidental swallowing of the pictorial element of an eye by a window, for example, can produce a strikingly unplanned effect of face and façade morphing into each other (according to another participant, Harald Schmutzhard). Projecting onto a highway underpass fractures an image onto disjunct surfaces at different depths from the projection point, creating an eerie amalgam of surface and volume that gives a sense of motion in stillness that cannot be achieved in a nonurban medium. When on top of this the image is of a building interior or a human body, the scene is weirdly, almost ineffably affecting. The strongest image-enfoldings of multisense feelings, and the most

11.4 HUMO image projection. Image: Maja Kalogera.

intensely suspending special indeterminacy effects, seemed often to arise at fortuitous conjunctures.

The HUMO group developed both the control and embrace responses. On the control side, composition and printing techniques were found to sharpen image resolution to withstand certain ambient interferences. Devices were employed to enable the artist to fit the image precisely to a site configuration. One device was a preparatory trip during which a coordinate grid composed of white lines on a black background was projected onto the site. The resulting site map was then digitally photographed. This created a digital template. Back at the lab, an image could be superimposed upon the template, allowing it to be scaled to the site with its constituent elements exactly positioned. This control device actually yielded chance results of its own, as the group started spontaneously responding to certain grid projections as works of art in themselves. Templates were also produced manually using a camera obscura to outline the scene in perspective. In the lab, the perspective outline was scanned into the computer to be used as a template in a fashion similar to the gridded photograph.

Once these control procedures had been perfected, the workshop members could go back out into the field with a mix of controlled and uncontrolled images to test at different sites under variable conditions. A spirit of image experimentation effectively took hold. Group members no longer felt that the buildings necessarily got in the way. But they also did not necessarily feel a compulsion to prevent them from doing so. There was a creative margin of play between the image hijacking the site and the site hijacking the image, in which the group quickly learned to operate artistically.

The overall response of the workshop members to the barrage of obstacles they encountered in the beginning was to rally around each other, and each other's images, facilitated in large measure by the expert motivational orchestration of Lozano-Hemmer. Participants worked together around the clock to respond to the challenges. A mutual aid ethic took hold. One form it took was an informal assembly-line set up to shepherd each artist's images from screen to acetate to projector to landing site. The collaborative nature of the work loosened somewhat proprietary feelings of individual authorship. By the last night, the mood

11.5 HUMO image projection. Image: Anya Lewis.

had upturned to euphoria, despite the accumulated exhaustion of a week of sleeplessness and endless hours huddled around the truck late into the night in subzero temperatures. Some participants were already talking about bringing urban art intervention techniques back to their home terrain, in the hopes of seeding a translocal community of inquiry and experimentation into the practice. If the seeds grow, the virtual appointment with the city will have been kept, by many and multiplying paths.

The experience says "more" . . .

1999

Purple Phosphene

When I close my eyes, I see lights. Spirals of different brightness curling like phosphorescent puffs of smoke. If I "focus" on the smoke it swirls into color. Sometimes the entire background will take on a glow, often orange or green, of unimaginable richness. Bubbles of other colors form, always in movement and just as glimmeringly rich, like none I have ever seen with open eyes. I never painted, out of despair of ever capturing those colors.

"Phosphenes" is the inelegant name they have been given. My favorite phosphenes are deep blues, but most of all purple. Purple. Purple is the rarest and most resplendent: my unicorn of vision. It appears only when I have been so engrossed in color play, and so calmed by it, that all voluntary thought has ceased. With purple comes a change. The silent monologue that accompanies my every waking moment, and that I please myself to call my thought, ceases. A thinking that is not my thought begins. Apparently random snippets of conversation float by, Dopplering across the phosphene field. The voices are almost recognizable, as if I have heard them before. The words also: they could have been things I heard that day. So mundane. Yet they carry an aura of unspeakable profundity (in spite of which I have persisted in writing). The words are almost visible. I have the sensation that if I "focused" just a little bit harder, I would see them floating by, curlicues of verbal light slowly streaking across the field of color, leaving an illuminated comet's trail visually repeating their Dopplering.

Rarely, rarer than a unicorn, in the midst of the phosphenic conversation, a perfectly round color bubble will float into the field from the right. Inside it will be a miniature scene of astounding clarity. It is as if all the colors in the swirl had settled themselves, with a sampling of verbal streaks, inside a single bubble where they have taken on shapes, their phosphorescence slightly dimmed but nothing near extinguished. The still glowing scene is always social, featuring a group of people. I feel that if I were only able to leap into the bubble it would present a lucidity of inexhaustible detail I could spend a lifetime exploring: a whole new world. Except I have the sense of already having inhabited it. For the scene, like the words and voices, is very close to recognizable. I feel if I could join in the conviviality my belonging to that singular congress would be like living the aura of color. The bubble world, however, remains closed. It slowly floats left out of field. (I wonder: is phosphening handed?)

When I first experienced this strangely familiar worlding on my retina as a young child, I was convinced by its almost-recognizability that the scenes were actual memories that I had forgotten and that were attempting to return in order to tell me something unspeakably profound about my past. I would exert all my mental faculties toward retrieving the memory. When I realized that I would always fail at this memory quest, my proto-Freudian preoccupation turned to prophecy. I became convinced that the scenes were actually from my future and would reveal something terribly important about my destiny. This proto-theological preoccupation also soon faded, as the scenes themselves inevitably did. I found it impossible to hold on to them for long, as if they were not of this world, past or future, only of and for their own: the field of color itself. I knew now: they were not mine, not anybody's. They were not in the possessive. They expressed themselves in the genitive absolute: from and "of" themselves, wholly and only. I felt privileged to have been a witness to their wholly only "of"-ness. I subsequently noticed strikingly similar experiences when dropping off to sleep. That led me to the conviction that all of this had something beautiful to say about the borderland between waking and dreaming: about a region that neighbors both, in which both participate, but doesn't belong to either.

That region is populated by emergences passing from variable brightness to color to shape. They are triggered by or index the arrival of speech. They represent nothing, but still evoke a memory, of the future if not of the past. Given this indeterminacy of tense, they are perhaps best termed "memory-like": memorial in a way that collapses futurity into pastness. The waking world trails into them, almost recognizably. Like a foretaste of dreams to come. Their emergence cannot be willed. It is spontaneous, or nothing, levels of auratic nothingness fading from experience. This borderland between waking and dreaming is "memory-like" in that it cannot be recalled. It only recalls *itself*. You cannot hold onto it, or call it back. You can only return it to its own event. Close your eyes. Maybe go to sleep.

Perhaps that's the way to enter the phosphene after all. Perhaps that's what dreaming is: returning the bubble of perception to its own event. Unheld, unbeckoned, total and alone. Sleeping phosphene, living color. Color and brightness, wholly and only. Borderland all round. Like the circle of the horizon compressed into its own dimensionless center point: self-earthed horizon. Self-encompassing groundlessness. How can a body be in that?

It can't. You can't hold it or be in it or be it. You can just let go and be "of" it. You can be the earth "of" it, the absent ground "of" it. Gravityless: let go and float. Eminently bearable lightness of being, in the genitive absolute.

The dream: the beauty.

The truth? How wrong was the poet.

Beauty lies.

In sleep it lies, afloat.

Couplet 12

2007

On Critique

I wanted to follow up on the discussion thread about the organization of the event.[1] As a co-instigator of the series of events and a member of the organizing committee, I bear a large share of the responsibility for the "noncritical" approach. In view of this, I thought I might explain some of the background to the adoption of that approach, as I have understood it. For me, there were three principal starting points. The first was the distinction that Deleuze makes between criticism and critique. The second, entirely related to the first, was a statement by Isabelle Stengers that she rarely accepts invitations to academic meetings because they are normally structured in a way that ensures that nothing "important" (in Whitehead's sense) can happen. She went on to say that she only accepts when she has a sense that the interaction is prepared so that something actually happens that is truly an "event." Since she made this statement in response to an invitation Erin [Manning] and I had just tendered, we figured we'd better start thinking fast and seriously about what it might mean for an academic or artistic meeting to be an event, and pragmatically how you go about setting in place the conditions for its occurrence. Isabelle did come, and these questions became the core of intense discussions with her that grew to include a number of people who would later become participants and co-organizers of last year's *Dancing the Virtual* and the upcoming *Housing the Body*.

The third jumping-off point was the sense that part of the response to the problem Isabelle posed might be found in the "radical" empirical call for our thought-practice to "be true to the conjunctions as well as the disjunctions." I think that Isabelle's aversion to the usual academic practices is rooted in her acceptance of Deleuze's assertion that critique, if it is to be eventful, must be an "immanent" critique. One of the things this means is that everything that enters the interaction must do so actively, not by proxy, as represented, simply spoken for, or even transmitted (in short, not as an already constituted content). It must become equal to the coming event by performing itself in and for that particular assembly, so it enters actively into the constitution of what happens as a co-creative factor. Its "critique" is then not the opinions or judgments we have of it. It takes place on an entirely different plane. The critique is not an opinion or a judgment but a dynamic "evaluation" that is lived out in situation. It concerns the tendencies that the introduction of that factor actively brings into the situation. It is the actual, eventful consequences of how that factor plays out, relationally with any number of other factors that also activate tendentially, and in a way that is utterly singular, specific to those situated co-expressions.

That is why Deleuze speaks of critique as a "clinical" practice: it is the diagnostic art of following the dynamic signs of these unfoldings, which can then be actively modulated from within the situation, immanent to it. The modulation can be augmenting (taking a certain tendency to the limit), diverting (deflecting it into a different tendency), transmutational (interacting with other tendencies in a way that invents a whole new direction as a kind of surplus-value of interaction)—or it can lead to a clash that stops the process. Any furtherance, convergence, becoming, or blockage that happens actually happens: it's an event. This kind of eventful, affirmative critique is very different from criticism, or what I would call negative critique.

In a negative "critical" situation, rather than asking the factors entering the situation to be "true" to the coming event (asking that they actually take the risk of putting themselves into play, accepting that they may exit the event having fundamentally changed), it is the people entering the situation who are asked to be true to what they represent—their pre-existing positionings, as encapsulated in already arrived-at opinion and judgment. These necessarily enter the situation as generalities, because their pre-encapsulation prepares them for representation in any similar situation and not just the one at hand. The only singularity is the way in which the legitimacy of the general representation in question is performed. In other words, the only difference affirmed is rhetorical, and what it fundamentally asserts is the personal prowess, in that situation, of the defender. It's all about legitimation and ascendancy.

This leads, in the best of scenarios, to blockage. Blockage is the best that can be expected because the interaction is formulated a priori (if only "humorously") in terms of a war of position assuming an enemy-friend distinction the playing out of which takes the form of a victory or defeat. If there is no blockage, it means that one set of positions has "won" and another has been disarmed or annihilated. It's a war of "disqualification," in Isabelle's terms. And whichever way it goes, it is a nonevent, because the most that might change is a reversal of fortunes within a pregiven positional structure. Deleuze's belief that debate and conversation are anathema to thought, to the extent that thought allies itself with emergence and becoming, I think relates to this. Debate is the war of annihilation practiced as a form of politeness (where the annihilation remains symbolic).

I entirely agree that there are many academic meetings that are far more "critical" than *Housing the Body* is proposed to be. That is why I, endorsing Isabelle's attitude, tend to avoid them as much as possible. Responding to Isabelle's challenge in no way means adopting a fake attitude of harmony. It doesn't mean wishfully seeing only conjunction and denying disjunction. But it does, I think, mean launching into the event from a certain kind of conjunction: a set of shared initial conditions that is experienced by all participants, putting them on the same event "plane," as one participant put it, so that whatever disjunctions occur do just that—actually occur—rather than being represented and legitimated in a proxy war.

The conditions that the organizing committee has set—no transmission of content (no presentation of pre-completed work), a common set of challenging readings, a certain pre-collectivization of tendencies entering the situation in the form of open "platforms for relation" ready for activation, and so forth—are meant to be techniques for creating a shared frame for the activation of differences, as creative co-factors for what will become the multiple singularity of this event. The idea is close to that of structured improvisation in music, where enabling constraints are put in place not in order to impose sameness but, quite the contrary, to foster unforeseeable differentiations. The idea is not at all that everyone will arrive at the same conclusions, or even to "agree to differ." If successful, the enabling constraints have placed the coming event on an entirely different plane than that of debate or discussion. Rather, the hope is that the ways in which we differ will pass together through the generative filter of the enabling frame: that we will continue to differ—all the more so—but together, for the moment at least, in creatively "impolite" but not disqualificatory ways. The hope is that together we can invent new modes of academic and artistic encounter that don't endlessly reproduce the same critical debate model, and that those new ways might contribute, in some small way, to a change in the culture of intellectual and artistic "exchange."

I was truly touched by the generosity and openness of last year's participants, and by their willingness to set aside the rhetorical war posture. That I consider "important." I deeply appreciated people's willingness to take the risk of entering a situation where it was clear that whatever was going to transpire could transpire only if they actively brought it to fruition—that there was no product being offered to them, the only product being the process they would make together. I learned a great deal from *Dancing the Virtual*, and what I took away energized me in a way conventional conferences never do. I am looking forward to this year's event with great expectation, knowing that last year's momentum is poised, due to many people's efforts and talents, to make a new event of itself, with all sorts of emergent differences due to the passage of time, the playing out in the meantime of off-site interactions flowing from the last event, and the addition of new participants who will bring their own tendencies and talents creatively and affirmatively into the mix.

2019

How Do You Make Yourself a Proposition?

For a Whiteheadian Laboratory

(WITH ERIN MANNING)

Propositions, Whitehead proposes, "are not primarily for belief, but for feeling at the physical level of unconsciousness. They constitute a source of the origination of feeling which is not tied down to mere datum" (1978, 186). The Whiteheadian proposition, of course, may rise selectively to consciousness and filter through judgment to form a derivative "intellectual belief" answering more recognizably to what in everyday life, and in other philosophies, responds to the same name. Few domains are as dedicated to this filtering as academe. Few genres are more in the thrall of intellectual judgment and belief than the academic conference. To raise the question of what it might mean to practice academic discourse propositionally in the Whiteheadian sense, specifically in the context of a conference, is apt in most quarters to elicit primarily disbelief. Originating feeling at the physical level—seated stiffly on a panel? Unconsciousness—in the atmosphere of intense self-consciousness so often setting the dominant tone of the room? Not tying oneself down to the datum—in other words, surpassing the given—in a context tailored to the transmission of the judgmentally already-arrived-at? Not a proposition likely to fly.

If it would fly anywhere, it would be at a conference of the Whitehead Research Project (WRP). It was with this belief that SenseLab accepted the invitation to contribute to the planning of the WRP's December 2016 conference. At the previous year's Center for Process Studies international conference, Roland Faber had responded to a presentation of SenseLab's (decidedly un-conference-like) activities by saying that it was as if SenseLab styled itself a "Whiteheadian laboratory." Flattered, and feeling an immediate kinship in the mere evocation that such a thing was, first, possible and, second, desirable, we were ripe for the lure. So it was natural for the group to accept the invitation when it came. SenseLab received the invitation as a challenge to transport some of SenseLab's techniques into the conference context to see if the compass of the genre could be gently inflected a degree or two toward a propositional practice in the Whiteheadian sense. How, SenseLab asked the conference-to-be, do we make ourselves a proposition?

This question—how do we make *ourselves* a proposition—arose from one of the most striking characteristics of the Whiteheadian proposition. Unlike the conventional, or merely logical, proposition, it does not enshrine a separation between the subject of the statement and the subject of the enunciation. In the conventional proposition, the subject of the statement is the logical subject, or what the proposition is about (essentially, the grammatical subject). The subject of the enunciation is the producer of the statement. The action of the subject of the enunciation, say, a philosopher, is to designate the logical subject and make a statement about it by attaching a fitting predicate to it ("mortal," "three-cornered," "on the mat," to take the classic examples). The action itself of the subject of the enunciation does not figure. It is bracketed, sequestered from the logical proposition, as if it went just as well without saying. The statement is treated as if it resided in a realm of pure thought, outside the world of workaday philosophers whose mundane lives inspire them to think of no better examples. In a word, the conventional proposition is generally specifying (qualifying a class of being in the abstract). This schema is transposed into the academy in the treatment of the subject of study as a neutral content of general validity separate from the subject of the teacher or researcher enunciating it. This sequestering of logical content—nowadays degraded to the status of information—enables the transmission model of teaching and scholarly communication. The transmitter figures only in the role of master of propositional ceremony: expert designator and predicator, to the general edification of the information's recipients.

Ostensibly, that is. There can be a prestige that attaches to that role (hence the self-consciousness of the conference milieu). The prestige relies on the separation between subject of the statement and subject of the enunciation that makes of the proposition a neutral content to be mastered in the abstract, and at the same time belies it. It implicates the subject of the enunciation concretely in the proceedings. It makes it palpable that the fitness of the statement is not the only thing at stake. The status of the speaker himself is as well. The speaker (or writer) performs herself. The performance can be felicitous, or it can go bad. It plays out. This makes it something of an event. The communication of a logical proposition is never a pure transmission. It plays out, event-like, in a way that fatally binds the subject of the enunciation to the proposition. The moment of separation was only ever abstract. The artifice of its abstraction only succeeded in deferring the nonseparability between the subject of the statement and the subject of the enunciation, displacing it from the production of the proposition to its reproduction in transmission. Concretely, the bare neutrality of the logical content of the proposition is always clothed in the finery of a performance. In the event of the performance, all manner of elements enter in. Feelings of many a kind may originate: pride, shame, shyness, bluster. These feelings physically implicate the speaker, with sweat and tics, or, on the contrary, bodily signs of self-possession. Much of what is at stake in what is at stake remains unsaid, even unconscious. What is at stake is the prestige of mastery. What is at stake in what is at stake might lend itself to psychological analysis, in terms, for example, of mimetic rivalry, whose feeling of competition is famously just the tip of an unconscious iceberg. In short, in practice, the *generality* of the conventional proposition surreptitiously *personalizes* the proposition, down to its unconscious concomitants. The non-Whiteheadian proposition lives uncomfortably in the element of the generally personal. The discomfiture resides in the latter's disavowed dramatization of what it contrives to neutralize.

Where the conventional proposition personalizes, the Whiteheadian proposition historicizes. It does this most importantly not in the usual sense of making statements about the past, even less by concerning itself with a purportedly linear descent through time, but more radically by removing the emphasis in the first instance from the statement and placing it squarely on the event. When Whitehead launches his discussion of the proposition in *Process and Reality*, he moves quickly to a historical example, the Battle of Waterloo (1978, 185; in what follows, all page numbers not otherwise credited are from this work). What most immediately interests him is not the truth-value of a statement about Napoleon's defeat. He does not subscribe to the logician's (and commonsense) creed that the "one function" of propositions "is to be judged as to their truth or falsehood" (184). Their primary function, rather, is as "a lure for feeling providing immediacy of enjoyment" (184). Propositions are to be *entertained*, more fundamentally than they are to be judged.[1] What interests Whitehead is the event's fecundity in spinning off lures for feeling, its affording occasions for entertainment beyond its own occurrence. An event throws off lures like spores to the future. It can do this because its occurrence is surrounded by a "penumbra of alternatives" (185) to its truth—or truths. As he explains, the statement of every proposition, even the classic examples, carries a degree of ambiguity. "'Socrates is mortal' . . . may mean 'The *man* Socrates is mortal,' or 'The *philosopher* Socrates is mortal.'" The basic statement "Socrates is mortal" presupposes a "relational system" that "can be carried further than the mere requirements of indication" (195). The statement's truth is surrounded by a penumbra of alternative nuances. These are an integral part of what the statement proposes and cannot fail to be activated each time it is stated. Not only are they integral to what is proposed; they constitute propositions in their own right.[2] Every proposition is complex, carrying a multiplicity of implicit variations on itself. So much so that this multiplicity is essential to our understanding of what a proposition is. Not even the simplest proposition can be reduced to what its statement says in so many words. The "form of words symbolizes an indefinite number of diverse propositions" (195). "No verbal statement is the adequate expression of a proposition" (13). "It is merely credulous to accept verbal phrases as adequate statements of propositions. The distinction between verbal phrases and complete propositions is one of the reasons why the logicians' rigid alternative, 'true or false,' is so largely irrelevant for the pursuit of knowledge" (11).

Now, credulity toward verbal phrases as adequate statements of propositions is precisely what defines academic communication. The Whiteheadian understanding of the proposition lays down a challenge to its relevance, to the extent that it insistently fails to make the distinction between verbal phrases and the complete proposition (the proposition in Whitehead's broader conception). The challenge is all the harder because the penumbra of alternatives composing the proposition can extend much farther than nuances on what is being indicated, or what the predicate ("mortal") is being applied to. It can extend as far as alternative courses of the world. What is relevant to, and therefore presupposed by, the statement, includes what "might have been, but is not" (226). The "impress" of these alternatives is felt differently—with different emphasis, different gradations of felt germaneness, at the limit fading off into what amounts to an exclusion—depending on the mode of entertainment characterizing the occasion in which the proposition is repeated.

One person, Whitehead says, may daydream a Waterloo, in which case the alternatives of its penumbra "float . . . without consciousness of deliberate decision." In this case, the alternatives are "admitted" into entertainment by an "internal decision" (185). This can only mean a decision internal to the proposition itself—to its own pressing to make an impress. The complex of relevant alternatives carries a propositional *force*, such that it is essentially self-proposing. This force is what makes the proposition a lure to feeling. The pressing to make an impress beckons some manner of attention, awakens a degree of interest. The gradation of the penumbral complex of alternatives it introduces into the dawning occasion now coming to entertain it "obscurely influences" how it will play out. For some, more attentive than the daydreamer, the influence may be felt in an "emotional tone . . . without any conscious analysis of [the] content." The tone may vary widely, from one "of gratification, or regret, of friendliness or hatred," depending on the conditions (185). The tone is not determined solely by the force of proposition as given, but also by how it is taken up. It marks how the lure for feeling that the proposition has impressed upon the circumstances is transduced by the arising occasion into the first stirrings of an *aim* providing its impetus toward self-completion.

Peculiar things happen when the aim is a professedly dispassionate judgment. The floating of alternatives is arrested as much as possible. The emotional tone is bracketed. The proposition is nailed to what it indicates, gradating away the relevance of alternative courses of history, nuances held to the background as much as possible. But this is a rearguard action. The penumbral complex will have already exercised its strike force. It will have already made the internal decision to set the lure of daydreaming. Although this provocation is declined, it cannot but have made itself felt after a manner (if only through the effort of turning them away, in negative prehension).[3] And it will already have exerted an obscure influence clothing itself in emotional tones, which the dispassion of judgment will have to strip from it as it admits the proposition into consciousness for logical analysis. By the time the proposition has reached the level of conscious judgment, its field of relevance will have been whittled down, to the point of making the proposition, however true it is judged, largely irrelevant to the pursuit of knowledge. That is, if knowledge is understood to concern itself with the composition of the actual world as it happens—in other words, as it is eventfully influenced by a propositional *force of thought* that is internally decided to make felt alternative courses of its own realization, in aim-inviting excess over any particular verbal phrasing of it, and in emotional surplus over any supposedly neutral analysis. "The conception of propositions as merely material for judgments is fatal to any understanding of their role in the universe" (187).

The notion of the proposition as a lure for feeling relaying into an aim providing an impetus for the self-completion of an arising occasion dramatically changes our sense of what a proposition is. It makes the circumstances, normally conceived as externalities that can be safely disregarded for all logical intents and purposes, into an *internal variable* of the proposition itself, part of its very warp and weft. Propositions don't hover in an ether of general thought. They have a "locus." By Whitehead's "ontological principle," every thing that is must be somewhere. The locus of the proposition is the somewhere of the event of its entertainment. The locus "consists of those actual occasions whose actual worlds include the logical subjects of the proposition" (186). This is a proliferating series. Propositional force is fertile.

Take Whitehead's second historical example, Caesar's crossing of the Rubicon (195–96). The locus is the "society" of occasions forming a nexus around that event. The defining characteristic of the society is the manner of the two logical subjects, Caesar and the Rubicon, coming-together for the crossing. That defining characteristic subsists as a complex eternal object—a composite relational potential. This can be "conjecturally supposed to be prolonged up to the contemporary world with the judging subject, or, even more conjecturally, into the future world beyond the subject." In other words, the relational potential is re-realized in the contemporary world for a later subject re-feeling the propositional force of the event. When this happens, a variation on the proposition occurs. Whitehead evokes an old soldier from Caesar's army sitting on the banks of the Rubicon many years after the crossing he witnessed as a youth. His world now also contains Caesar's having been assassinated, inextricably linked, in an extended nexus, with his having crossed the river. The emotional tone of this later-life, peacetime entertainment is markedly different from the same soldier's experience of the crossing as it happened in his youth. Among other things, a dramatic new logical subject figures: enter Brutus. Another predicate, "having been assassinated," links itself to "having crossed." The composite of relational potential carried by the proposition has expanded and complexified into a *propositional field* folding in a multiplicatory set of interwoven logical subjects and predicates, partially disjunct but overlapping. Each predicate is a thread that can be extricated from the weave to stand out in and as a separate proposition, as different as crossing and being assassinated. The penumbral complex has expanded to include all this, and more—stretching on as far as daydreaming can rove. At each entertainment, the complex of relational potentials is re-graded to include more or less in its focal length. The propositional field telescopes in or out, encompassing more or fewer logical subjects and predications, in differing patterns of emphasis. Think of a traveler sitting on the banks of the Rubicon today, and all this contemporary world includes. Think of the differing emotional tones those inclusions invite. Think of the diversity of aims that the once again varying proposition might now incite with its lure for feeling. The proposition is so much more than a statement. It is nothing less than a worlding. It is a serial iteration of the world's complexing, and re-complexing, of its own relational potential. The proposition is the force of thought gone worlding.

Not only are the circumstances of the entertainment an internal variable of the proposition; so too is the entertaining subject itself.

"Everything" in this worlding "depends upon the differences in direct perceptive knowledge" which the iterations presuppose for their entertaining subject (196). "The particular subject of experience can, in the nature of the case, never be eliminated from the experienced fact" (195). This is "the doctrine of *the inherence of the subject in the process of its production*" (224).[4] The separation between the subject of the enunciation and the subject of the statement safeguarding the neutrality and generality of the proposition in its conventional modeling is brushed aside. Each variation on the proposition in its series of avatars becomes irreducibly *singular*—unisolatable from the circumstances in which its lure is felt—and irrevocably *interested*—formatively inflected by a renaissance of aim, born in direct perceptive knowledge.

What constitutes transmission is also complicated, in a way that removes it from the passive/active dichotomy. On the one hand, the proposition is self-proposing, in its alluring beckoning of attention. In its role as lure for feeling, it is playing the role of provoker. But it is nothing outside of its taking up into an aiming of the coming occasion toward its own self-completion, for whose coming it is patient. It "awaits its logical subjects" (188)—which now include among their number the entertaining subject itself, recognized as an internal variable of the proposition. The proposition as datum—in its givenness to an occasion—is simultaneously active and passive, provoker and patient (Whitehead 1967a, 176). The entertaining subject also displays this combination of activity and passivity. It receives the lure at the same time as it actively transduces the lure into an aim. The two active-passive syntheses overlap on the threshold to the new event in which the proposition will play out. The dividing line between the entertaining subject, or subject of the enunciation, and the logical subject, or subject of the statement, falls away in a dual act of origination, singularly occurring. The proposition awaits its subject, and the force of its strike kickstarts the subject's actively coming into itself. Just thus, with just this emotional tone, for just this lure-begotten aim, constituting just this event in the series that will continue past it.

The entertaining subject *does not preexist* the entertainment. It emerges in it and as it, one with its event, in a singular manner. "It is new, *a new type of individual*, and not merely a new intensity of individual feeling. That member of the locus [that is the entertaining subject] has introduced a new form into the actual world" (187). The proposition is a real *individuation*, serving as the focal point of an actual reworlding. The individuation is a *speciation*: the veritable invention of a new *type* of individual. Rather than transmission, *creation*. Rather than linear progression, self-complicating seriation. Or, if this is transmission, it is the transmission not of statements about the truth, but truly of creative events.

Creation is *affirmed* before it is judged true or false. The proposition "enters, as *a value*, into the satisfaction [self-completion] of that subject; and it can only be criticized by the judgments of actual entities in the future" (191). In the event, it is a pure affirmation, in the sense of the direct, perceptive, "intuitive judgment" of "what is," prior to any "intellectual judgment" of what is "true or false" that may be brought to bear later.

The term "individuation" should not mislead. The proposition is "not restricted to that individual experience" (191), referring to the singular experience coming into itself in response to the lure. To the extent that the new individual that emerges is the recipient of the proposition's self-proposing, it integrates into its coming-to-be a "nexus whose relatedness is derived from the various experiences of its own members and not from that of the judging experient" (191). The patience of the entertaining subject is the immanence in its emerging character of the relational character of an indefinite multiplicity of others. "There are always others" (including, it must not be forgotten, those "which might have been and are not"; Whitehead 1967a, 276). The individuation at issue in a proposition is fundamentally a *collective individuation*. A proposition is societal, both at origination and in destination. For the subject now emerging will add itself to the extended nexus, as it conjectures itself beyond this occasion toward the future. The many will have become one, for more to come, as the occasion "objectively conditions the creativity transcendent beyond itself" (Whitehead 1978, 221).

Can academic practice cross the Rubicon of the Whiteheadian proposition into the empire of collective individuation? Is it capable of making the crossing, or is it here that it meets its Waterloo? What would it mean for academic "communication" to integrate the propositional force of reworlding "intuitive judgment, couched in direct perceptive experience," into its mode of operation? How do we make ourselves a proposition, taking the question literally. Not: How do we make a proposition *for* ourselves? But: How do we really make *ourselves* a proposition—how do we creatively, collectively individuate, into a new academic type? How do we originate new forms in the academic world?

SenseLab's practice has grappled with this question throughout its fifteen-year history, even before it learned to articulate it in terms of the Whiteheadian proposition. Earlier, the articulation was in the convergent terms of the Bergsonian "problem," as propositionally relayed by Deleuze (1991a, ch. 1). From the beginning, SenseLab activities have revolved around the making of events. The question the always-evolving group took as its point of departure was what it would take to make an academic or artistic meeting, conference, artist's talk, exhibition, live up to the name of the event. The answer, as Whiteheadian as Deleuzian, was the emergence of the new, the origination of novelty. A movement of thought would be set in motion that could lead to the formulation of thoughts previously unthinkable. This could not be a neutral or general "newness": generality activates the conventional proposition and settles into the element of mere intellectual judgment. The process would have to be oriented, interested, a matter of appetition as much as of intellectual curiosity. In short, to be worthy of the event of thought, the gathering would have to begin by setting a lure to feeling apt to transduce into a collective aim.

Preparatory meetings and interactions, live and online, around readings, artworks, movement, and materials are necessary for the setting of the lure. This is because the lure is propositional in the Whiteheadian sense only if it self-proposes, in that region of indistinction between activity and passivity, provocation and patience. It cannot simply be a verbal statement of a theme or topic. It has to emerge of its own from the complexity of a preparatory process open enough to embrace the full range of attentional modes, from daydreaming to the intensest study of the precisest of metaphysical concepts, and to activate their interstices. It would emerge from this entangled complexity not as a thematic topic but as a problematic: a propositional field carrying a penumbral complex of relational potentials ripe for the re-complexing, ready to telescope in and out to find the patterns of emphasis crystallizing it into a new, self-completing variation on itself.

Then procedures must be set in place to pass from the preparatory phase to the gathering event that will perform the variation. The crossing of that threshold will have to bring the lure into the gathering place, respecting the fragility of its dual nature, with its superposition of activity and passivity, provocation and patience. It must be palpable, at the literal threshold to the gathering, that the transmission model, with its own dual nature of generalizing and personalizing, will not be in force. The threshold must be a making-collectively-felt of the lure, inviting its transduction into a collective aim in the course of the activities. By "collective" is meant indivisibly relational: emerging as an excess of effect, an effect that is more than the sum total of the actions of the individual contributors, emergently more than the sum of the parts, and directly felt as such. The society of this "emergent collectivity" is what will constitute the entertaining subject, not restricted to individual experience. The sensation on the part of the participants will be one of having been swept up in a movement of thought washing through them, and sweeping them along, their own individual experience and cogitations forming a cellular eddy in the societal stir.

The way in which the emergent collective conjectures itself beyond this occasion toward the future will need to be attended to. The event will have been singular, but not single: events seriate. The process must proliferate, in order to be faithful to its own event. For it will have selectively re-graded the penumbral complex, foregrounding some of its logical subjects and predications, backgrounding some of the relational potentials while bringing others into salience. As is the case with all events, in their character as worldings, the "full sweep" (189) of this relatedness will be bequeathed to the next event in the series, for its own singular re-worlding. Attending to the way in which the event has conjectured itself into the beyond of the next event involves finding ways of making felt the full sweep of the relational complex under variation, including the elements of it that were backgrounded, or negatively prehended, in this iteration, and extending to alternatives that might have been but were not (yet still might come to be). This is a question of curating the event, in a completely new sense. The curating of the full sweep of the event, as it passes into self-completion to potentiate what lies beyond it, is a practice SenseLab has intensely explored under the name of the "anarchive" (2016). The way of the anarchive is the caring for the penumbral complex.

Over its lifetime, SenseLab has experimented with a panoply of "techniques of relation" for propositional event-making (Manning and Massumi 2014, 83–151). The term "research-creation" was adopted as the most flexible academic category for them. The term was just beginning to be institutionalized in Canada as SenseLab launched. As practiced by SenseLab, research-creation is a performative practice, staging a propositional movement of thought couched in direct perceptive experience and uncontained by conventional disciplinary boundaries. The work locates itself at the crossroads of philosophy, art, and activism, in a multivectorial movement between collective reading practices and movement- and materials-based explorations.[5] A concept of "immediation" (Manning, Munster, and Thomsen 2019) has been collectively developed to conceptualize the move from the traditional transmission model to this event-based model, for which the operative concept is *transduction*: not the transmission of already formulated stated content, but the passage of a self-reformulating relational complex from one set of event-producing conditions to the next, across an evolving series of occasions in an expanding nexus.

It was against this background that the invitation to contribute to the organization of the WRP conference came. At that moment, SenseLab itself was at a crossroads, exploring the possibility of spinning off from the university into a community-based Three Ecologies Institute (named after the eponymous book by Félix Guattari [2014]). The three ecologies refer to the conceptual/mental, social/political, and environmental/technological. The WRP's long-standing engagement with ecological thought in a similarly extended paradigm was an added lure. It was clear, however, that SenseLab techniques could not be imported wholesale into a different milieu, especially in the absence of the sustained collective preparatory work toward the passing of the threshold into the event and the setting in place of techniques of relation serving as a springboard for the ensuing interactions (this phase of the collaborative setting of conditions is even more crucial when different organizational cultures are coming together). It was also clear that making a dramatic departure from the conference format was not appropriate for the proposed convergence between SenseLab and WRP. What the circumstances seemed to call for was a modulation of the existing conference format nudging it in a propositional direction.

The strategy adopted was to prepare a call containing choice quotes from *Process and Reality* where Whitehead most provocatively sets forth the differences between his notion of the proposition and the conventional view, and inviting prospective participants to join in an exploration of what a conference taking the difference seriously might look like. Presenters were encouraged to avoid the usual conference paper format. Three alternative formats were suggested:

> *Knot*: a paradox or temporary impasse in your work, life, thinking, or creative practice that might become newly productive if staged in a way that opens it to a collaborative exploration, in language or between language and other modes of expression.
>
> *Juncture*: a known conjunction reopened for further exploration through new techniques reconfiguring its potential. Such a juncture might be a given theoretical perspective, a set of established techniques informing a particular practice, an already-operating collaboration or project, or an existing disciplinary, interdisciplinary, or intermedia platform, restaged with a new inflection.
>
> *Vector*: a move out from known junctures into a wander-line that is oriented by a proposition, and in that sense directionally constrained, but is at the same time open-ended in way that invites new takings-form on the fly.

It was assumed that not all of the presenters would take up the invitation of an alternative format (which indeed proved to be the case), but it was hoped that enough of a critical mass would for the event to have a palpably different tone. The idea was for the presentations to offer themselves from the angle of their incompletion: incomplete, but already in the middle, the arc of an aim toward self-completion interestedly en route. This would make the presentation's point of entry into the event problematic: unresolved, but striving appetitively toward a resolution.

Others would be invited into this movement of thought and to share the appetite, in the hope that this multiplication of entertaining subjects might jog the movement of thought contributed by the presenter toward a fitting outcome, but one the presenter alone would not have otherwise arrived at. Such a resolution is unlikely to occur in situ, especially in an environment such as the conference setting, already choreographed with the expectations of mastery and self-presentation.

SenseLab's proposition *to make ourselves a proposition* by orienting thought toward knots, vectors, and junctures would facilitate a different way of coming-into-relation. We would meet in the constellation of thought's incompletion, in the very movement of thought. There would be no pressure to conclude, still less to reach a consensus. The technique is anarchival, bearing on the force of thought's ongoing. Its aim is to plant seeds of potential that may sprout into alternative courses, perhaps after having lain fallow, perhaps even without their effect being specifically felt. It may come of a re-grading of the penumbral complex, altering its quotient of negative and positive prehension. It may come in interference or resonance patterns in regions of the propositional field that are liminal to the presenter's consciously attended-to central focus. Or it might percolate up as from nowhere as a sudden realization at a later date, as when a key piece of a preoccupying puzzle comes of its own in a dream. The exercise will have been a success if, for example, the article later prepared for the conference publication carries something derived from the direct perceptive experience of the presentation and discussion into its final form, like an imperceptible birthmark. Or if a new way of formulating an aspect of the problem surfaces unexpectedly in the teaching context. In short, the openness of the problematic mode suggested for the presentations was not meant to be closed by the presentation. It was meant as a technique for the openness to keep working conjecturally beyond it.

To model this kind of collective enunciation in an ongoing openness of relation, it was suggested that among the invited participants there be a certain number with a history of working together collaboratively who would make joint presentations. The hope was that a knot, juncture, or vector from an ongoing collaboration collectively presented would act as a lure for the audience's feeling the potential of their own implication in the movement of thought crossing through the room. Budget constraints did not allow as many collaborations as originally desired, but it was possible for a certain number to contribute.

Another technique for setting in place the conditions for a more propositional event was to ensure the presence of a large contingent of people from SenseLab, all of whom had experience in alternative-format academic/artistic events and who had been involved in the internal discussions around how the convergence with WRP might best be staged. SenseLab funded twenty-five of its participants from its Canadian, European, Brazilian, and Australian hubs to come to Claremont.[6] This was done in recognition of the fact that the modes of response to presentations on the part of audience members are important determining factors for whether the propositional force of the thinking is empowered or disenabled. Responses oriented toward individual judgment of the verbal phrasing of statements neutralize the collectively individuating force of thought that Whitehead's theory of the proposition brings to the fore. The conventional mode of response in academic contexts comes down on the side of individual judgment, taking debate for its fundamental paradigm: a battle for supremacy between individual verbal phrasings, their propositional stakes replaced by the personal stakes of owning the room by getting one's own formulation across the most forcefully. Of course, this is rarely practiced in so bald a manner. It is mostly practiced with politesse, in the attenuated forms of the "exchange of ideas," "friendly commentary," and "conversation." But the essentials—mistaking a verbal statement for a proposition—remain the same in these more genteel variations. SenseLab participants have a years-long practice of moving in concert to the complete proposition, and share an allergic reaction to debate, echoing Deleuze's oft-quoted (and almost as often misunderstood) saying that nothing is more inimical to thought than conversation.

Most of the SenseLab participants did not give presentations but were considered full participants in the event through their responses to the presentations, not only during the sessions but also around them. It is a widely commented truism that in the traditional conference setting, nothing ever happens in the sessions but only in the corridors, during breaks, or afterward over food. The hope in this case was that something would indeed happen in the sessions, but that in addition, the interstitial and ambient spaces would also be activated and resonate propositionally. SenseLab participants were primed to function in those spaces, as well as in the sessions, as guardians of the penumbral complex. Their way of fulfilling this role could be "atmospheric": barely perceptible, operating through "minor gestures" (Manning 2016) inflecting the potential of the event by modulating its emotional tone. This participatory activity in a minor key was meant to be an essential contribution to the event. For it is in an event's minor gestures that its anarchival force is couched: aspects of its relational complex that might not have been (fully, directly, or globally expressed) but still may be (in some manner determining, perhaps surfacing after having long lain fallow). So involved were SenseLab participants in this role that in sessions where presenters did not take up the challenge to make themselves a proposition by trying out one of the alternative formats, the disappointment was palpable, at one point breaking out into a dramatic eruption. The way of the proposition is sometimes rocky.

The third conditioning technique SenseLab brought to the gathering was a particular practice of collective reading that it has employed since close to its beginnings. Instead of a presentation session, the first regular time slot was dedicated to a "conceptual speed-dating" séance.[7] This is a practice where a text, no more than twenty pages in length, is circulated in advance and everyone is urged to read it carefully before arriving. The attendees are divided into pairs to discuss the text, and at five-minute intervals one person from each pair moves to a next person and the discussion is continued across the interval. A particular concept, of a particular kind, is chosen as a focus for the discussion. The concept must be a "minor" concept—the textual equivalent of a minor gesture. This is a concept that might not even be noticed as a formal contributor to the conceptual weave of the thinking moving through the text, but once attended to appears integral to the weave, and even essential for making the other concepts hold together. The concept must be minor in order to avoid activating already-arrived-at conclusions and ingrained presuppositions about the text that participants may have brought to the gathering, luring them into a renewed engagement. The strict time limit that cuts off each mini-discussion in midstream and the pressing need to find a quick way back into the discussion with each new interlocutor pressurizes the experience. It creates a slightly altered mental state where one's overactive tendency to dominate one's own thoughts and one's discussion with the other is quietened. There is not time to self-present or to contextualize one's individual approach to the problems raised. It is necessary to go straight into the rethinking. This instills a receptivity to what the *concept* is saying: how, in this occasion, it is revealing and recomposing its propositional field. Conceptual speed-dating is a technique for fostering patience for the movement of thought. After a few moves, it can be difficult to remember if a particular thought came from oneself or another. This is the sign of a collective enunciation: a collective individuation of thought in the making. If the exercise has been successful, the whole-group discussion after the session has a very different feel from the usual plenary discussion. The just-emergent collectivity of thought can be felt in the air, and its aftertaste can potentially move into and obscurely influence subsequent interactions. In the case of this particular exercise—a gathering of Whitehead experts—it was deemed crucial *not* to use a text by Whitehead. This was because everyone present would have entered with a finely honed set of established understandings that it would be difficult to reopen for renewal. The approach had to be sideways (like the SenseLab members' guardianship of the penumbral complex in the subsequent sessions' question-and-answer periods and in the conference's interstices). A set of carefully curated extracts from Nietzsche's *Late Notebooks* (2003) was chosen that had strong and, doubtless for many, unexpected resonances with Whitehead's thought, and in particular with his concept of the proposition and its evental nature. The extracts dealt with the limits of consciousness and the affective basis of thought, will and the zones of indistinction between activity and passivity, the implications for our notions of causality of what in Whiteheadian terms is formulated as the inherence of the subject in the process of its production, the fiction of individual expression, and the self-proposing force of thought.

The conference has now passed. One of the futures it conjectured has now occasioned this book (Faber, Halewood, and Davis 2019). Have anarchival traces of the gathering made their way between the lines? If so, we can say together that we have made ourselves a proposition.

NOTES

Note to the Reader

1. The exception being the recent work on value (Massumi 2017b, 2018).

Couplet 1. Realer Than Real

1. Parenthetically, it is no accident that there are two German escapees: the simulacrum is a multiplicity that poses a threat to identity and is traveling a line of flight that must be blocked at all costs. Here, the multiplicity is reduced to a doubling because under the Oedipal procedures of capitalism the nonidentity within identity takes the form of a splitting of the subject into a subject of enunciation and a subject of the statement: one of the Germans is obliged to remain mute. On the subject of enunciation and the subject of the statement, see Deleuze and Guattari (1983, 265; 1987, 129).

2. On the "Real-Abstract," see Deleuze and Guattari (1987, 142, 145–46). "Real" in this context has a different meaning from the definition given earlier: here, it refers to the "intensive" realm of the virtual that "subsists" in reality understood as an extensive system of actualized simulations. On the concept of virtuality, see in particular Deleuze (1991a, 29, 55–61).

3. The allusion to Nietzsche is not gratuitous. For Deleuze (1989, 131), the "power of the false" is another name for the will to power, and what I have been calling positive simulation is described by Deleuze and Guattari (1983, 330–31) as the eternal return.

Couplet 2. On the Right to Noncommunication

1. Colloque de Cerisy, "Cultures: Guerre et Paix," organized by Tobie Nathan, Olivier Ralet, and Isabelle Stengers, Centre Culturel International de Cerisy, France, August 23–30, 2000. Proceedings, including the French original of this essay, published as "Propositions de paix," ed. Isabelle Stengers and Tobie Nathan, special issue, *Ethnopsy: Les mondes contemporains de la guérison*, no. 4 (April 2002).

2. The account of the performative here is inflected toward Deleuze and Guattari's concept of "incorporeal transformation" in the "Postulates of Linguistics" chapter of *A Thousand Plateaus* (1987, 75–110). The main difference is that the

incorporeal transformation does not require the same "felicity" of convention as Austin's performative. It is broadened to cover "illocutionary forces" of all kinds, assuming only the immanence of a differential field of tendencies or implicit presuppositions.

3. For details on the history of the Aboriginal rights movement, see Attwood and Markus (1999). On the politics of reconciliation in the 1990s in particular, see Grattan (2000).

4. On Nelson's life and art, see Vivien Johnson (1997).

5. Tobie Nathan, the originator of a form of ethnopsychiatry that concertedly avoids projecting Western categories of judgment onto non-Western cultures, emphasizes the inadequacy of belief as it is usually understood as an explanatory category for arenas that by Western reckoning fall under the rubric of religion, spirituality, or superstition: "Beliefs are not strictly approachable through questions: *they are not contents!* They manage bonds, and as such are only available to investigation through their enactment." Belief is "an active process of delimitation" distinguishing the "self" from "non-self," always "in an active manner" (1996, 98, emphasis added).

6. "A domain of *culture* should not be thought of as some kind of spatial whole, possessing not only boundaries but an inner territory. It is located everywhere upon boundaries, boundaries intersect it everywhere. . . . Every cultural act lives essentially on the boundaries. . . . We can speak about [it in] its autonomous participation or participative autonomy . . . that is, in its unmediated . . . orientation" (Bakhtin 1990, 274).

7. *Transcript of the Royal Commission*, 5330, cited in Weiner (1999, 197).

8. *Intercesseurs* is unfortunately translated as "mediators," losing the eventful immediacy of the transformation.

Couplet 2. Event Horizon

1. For Bergson's critique of the possible, see "The Possible and the Real" (Bergson 2007, 96–112).

Couplet 3. Becoming Animal

1. On the "literary quality" of even the most apparently bare-bones demonstrative use of language, see Whitehead (1920, 7).

2. The chiastic exchange underpinning becoming-animal, predicated on a cross-subjectification in the mode of personhood, taken in a more-than-human sense, is a key point brought out by recent Amazonian anthropology in relation to shamanic practice. See Viveiros de Castro (2004); Kohn (2013, ch. 4, "Transspecies Pidgins").

3. Birdwatchers and readers of the book will know that a falcon, properly speaking, is a female peregrine, and a tiercel a male. I'm using the word here in a generic sense.

4. "Mud stagnant, mud evil; mud in the clothes, in the hair, in the eyes; mud to the bone. . . . Mud is another element" (Baker [1967] 2005, 98).

5. It also extends becoming-animal toward nonhuman becomings involving inorganic animacies, the outermost horizon of becoming.

6. In Deleuze and Guattari's terms, the peregrine is the "Anomal" (1987, 243–47).

7. On "a" life, see Deleuze (2007, 384–90).

8. On incipient action, see Massumi (2002, 30, 106–8, 114, 124, 208–10).

9. Abstract yet real becomings-animal may take flight from any number of human-animal assemblages, including, under the right conditions, those involving companion animals, service animals, and even work or food animals, not to mention animal images, photographic, filmic, or oneiric. Of all becomings-animal, it is those produced by traditional shamanistic practices that are most powerfully worlding, and world altering. In a different register, play is a privileged leavener of becoming-animal in everyday contexts. In "Another Regard," Erin Manning analyzes the double becoming of a chimpanzee and a human in play at a zoo in a way that accords closely with the account of becoming-animal developed here (2013, 232–55).

10. This is a reference to Raymond Ruyer's concept of *survol*, often translated as "self-survey" (2016, 90–103).

11. That there is a continuum of language stretching across the spectrum of animality is a central argument of Massumi (2014).

12. Deleuze, "The Method of Dramatization" (2004, 94–116).

13. On nature's essential mannerism (which opens it to unnatural participations—artifices of becoming that run superempirically against its established grain)—see Debaise (2017).

14. Nietzsche's animal becomings in *Thus Spoke Zarathustra* occur between the optimal and pessimal limits of the eagle and the snake, Zarathustra's special animals. But in the becoming more-than-human of Zarathustra, the predator-prey relation is overcome: "An eagle cut broad circles through the air, and upon it hung a snake, not as prey but as a friend" (2006, 15). The passage to the "overman" is marked by the lion becoming a child, predation turned to *play* (15, 17, 48–49).

15. In a move similar to Nietzsche's turn to play, Deleuze suggests the way of fabulation (1989, 150–54, 222–24, 279; 1995, 125–26, 174). ("Fabulation" is unfortunately translated as "story-telling" in this book.)

Couplet 4. "Technical Mentality" Revisited

1. [The entirety of this book is now available in English translation as part of Simondon's masterwork, *Individuation in Light of Notions of Form and Information*, vol. 1 (2020, 257–380).]

2. [The emergence of self-conditioning quantum holism "effects" is further developed under the concept of the "semblance" in Massumi (2011).]

3. [This book is now available in English translation, also as part of Simondon, *Individuation in Light of Notions of Form and Information*, vol. 1 (2020, 21–256).]

Couplet 4. The Supernormal Animal

1. For a more lengthy account, see Massumi (2014).

2. "There is no absolute distinction between effective sign-stimuli and the non-effective properties of the object. . . . The full significance of supernormal stimuli is not yet clear" (Tinbergen 1951, 42, 46). Tinbergen, however, does not integrate these observations into his theory of instinct overall. They remain isolated musings. Deleuze and Guattari critique the predominance of the stimulus-trigger-automatism model in Tinbergen's thinking (1987, 327–28).

3. "This is a question of consistency: the 'holding-together' of heterogeneous elements. At first, they constitute no more than a fuzzy set" (Deleuze and Guattari 1987, 323). They characterize life itself in terms of a "gain in consistency," for which they use "self-consistency" (*auto-consistance*) as a synonym (335). They go on to define consistency as a "surplus-value of *destratification*" (336). On auto-conduction, see Ruyer (2019, 7, 39, 143).

4. Ruyer says the same of internal "signals" such as hormones, which according to his account induce a relational effect of co-variation that is in every respect analogous to what occurs in the case of fields of external perception.

5. On expressive qualities and internal relations, see Deleuze and Guattari (1987, 317–18, 329).

6. On cause and effect as belonging to different orders, see Deleuze (1990, 6–7). Deleuze ties the independence of effects to language. The present account does not follow him in this regard.

7. On blocks of becoming, see Deleuze and Guattari, "Becoming-Intense, Becoming-Animal, Becoming-Imperceptible . . . ," in *A Thousand Plateaus* (1987, ch. 10) and "Blocks, Series, Intensities," in *Kafka* (1986, ch. 8). On the associated concept of blocks of sensation, see Deleuze and Guattari, "Percept, Affect, Concept," in *What Is Philosophy?* (1994, ch. 7).

8. In the English translation, the French phrase "une liaison animée par une vie propre" is rendered as "a love affair kindled by a decent life." I take the phrase much more literally. The word *liaison* is used throughout Deleuze's and Deleuze/Guattari's work in reference to and in resonance with Ruyer's thought to mean an unassignable (nonlocal) "linkage" (or "bond"), and the idea of an immanent life of form ("animated by a life of its own") fits the context of this passage, which is working from the thought of Wilhelm Worringer.

9. The English translation refers to an "aesthetic result" where the French has "aesthetic yield."

10. "Objects are the elements in nature that can 'be again'" (Whitehead 1920, 144).

11. For an excellent analysis of intuition and sympathy in Bergson (which in Bergson's texts are not actually as synonymous as they are presented to be here), see Lapoujade, *Powers of Time* (2018).

12. Bergson (1972), quoted in Lapoujade (2018, 24).

Couplet 5. Sensing the Virtual

1. [Issues of topological design in architecture are returned to at length in Massumi (2019, ch. 1).]

2. "Things have an internal equivalent in me; they arouse in me a carnal formula of their presence" (Merleau-Ponty 1964, 164).

3. The classic treatise on the perceptual vagaries of light is Johann Wolfgang von Goethe's *Theory of Colours* (1970). For an appropriately confounding catalogue of relevant philosophical conundrums, see Wittgenstein (1978). See also Jonathan Westphal's gloss on Wittgenstein (1987).

4. [The "brightness confound" is discussed at length, with an emphasis on its envelopment of nonvisual dimensions of experience, in the chapter of the same name in Massumi (2002, 162–76).]

5. In relativity theory, "it is the light figure that imposes its conditions on the rigid figure" (Bergson 1965, 126). See the discussion in Deleuze 1986 (58–61). Both Deleuze and Bergson seem to be using "light" in an extended sense comprising the continuous or waveform aspects of all physical phenomena. "Einstein proposed that the particulate nature of matter may be explicable as concentrations and knots in a fundamental, continuous field" (Bohm and Peat 1987, 73). "Blocs of space-time [whose topological torsions constitute rigid bodies] are figures of light" (Deleuze 1986a, 60).

6. The reliance of the simulacrum on resemblance, if only in order to falsify it, is why Deleuze later dropped the concept, after earlier work had championed it in such well-known essays as "Plato and the Simulacrum" (1990, 253–65) [see Couplet 1, "Realer Than Real," in this volume]. "I have totally abandoned the concept of simulation, which has very little to recommend it" (Deleuze, "Lettre-Préface," in Martin 1990, 8).

7. [For an extended analysis of the work of Stelarc, see Massumi (2002, ch. 4, 89–132).]

Couplet 6. The Crannies of the Present

1. See Libet (1985). For a taste of the debate on free will Libet's work provoked, see Libet, Freeman, and Sutherland (1999). For cultural theoretical discussions, see Connolly (2002, 83) and Massumi (2002, 29–31, 195–97).

2. For a brief rundown of some of this research and a discussion of its implications in the theater of war, see "Perception Attack: The Force to Own Time," chapter 2 in Massumi (2015a). For a consideration of its implications for rational choice in the economic arena, see *The Power at the End of the Economy* (Massumi 2015c).

3. I suggest placing mirrors at inhabitual places in your home. But then that works only if *they* catch *you* unawares.

4. This is what makes Quentin Meillassoux's (2010, 10–20) problem of the "arche-fossil" a false philosophical problem. The true question, for Whitehead, is

not how we can know the reality of existences on timescales beyond the human. The more mysterious, and more metaphysically resonant question, is: When I am angry now, how do I know I was angry half a second ago? (Whitehead 1967a, 183–84). If we can answer that question—of how a continuity of experience bootstraps itself from the "influx of the other" in *immediate* experience—we have all the tools necessary to extrapolate a "historic route" to any others, on all scales. We do not have to ask how our knowledge moves beyond human presence. At each imperceptible interval, our experience has always just effectively done so, and we affectively know it so, in the life-extension we have directly felt. Meillassoux's question implicitly presupposes the cognitive continuity of an observing human presence under immediate conditions of givenness, in order to move the question away from what Whitehead calls the "becoming of continuity." The question of the knowledge of the other-than-human is thus displaced to what are in fact secondary issues drawn in overly general epistemological terms on macro-scales, while micrologically the "correlationist" human subject remains essentially in place.

5. The homunculus theory refers to the well-known problem that conventional vocabulary, for example, saying the brain "receives images" from an outside world, assumes that there is some sort of seeing-eye soul inside the cranium. Would there then be another seeing-eye behind the brain-dwelling soul's to receive its images? Any form of representational approach to perception in terms of image reception leads to an infinite regress of mythic corrections for blindness. One thing there is not "all the way down" is prosthetic eyes. You can go no further down than the synaptic gaps of the brain. One way or another, you always end up in intervals. On the relation of the brain to perception in a nonrepresentational frame, see Bains (2002, 111–14) (working from Raymond Ruyer) and Andrew Murphie (2010).

6. "What really exists is not things made but things in the making. . . . Put yourself *in the making*" (James 1996a, 262–63).

7. "Take it just as we feel it" (James 1996b, 48).

8. On the terminus, see also Massumi (2011, 4, 9, 29, 31–34).

9. For Whitehead, continuity is always a matter of mutual, differential immanence (1967a, 195–96).

Couplet 6. Dim, Massive, and Important

1. Peirce writes of the degree zero of Firstness as a quality of feeling, as a universe in itself, as if, for example, nothing existed in the world except the shrillness of an endless whistle, or this red. But Firstness of this purity is not an experienceable event. Every quality needs the contrast of other qualities, as well as the contrast between itself and its background, to actually occur and be held in existence. A monochrome visual field quickly blinks out. What is being brought up here are the two aspects of Possibility (a synonym for Firstness and Quality in Peirce): on the one hand, pure possibility, unactualized (what Deleuze would call the virtual,

with Firstness corresponding to his "singularities" and with what Whitehead would call the "pure potentiality" of "eternal objects"), and on the other hand, possibility effectively in-forming the unfolding of an actual taking place (Whitehead's "real potentiality").

2. Peirce describes Firstness as "Pure Self-Consciousness, which might be roughly described as a mere feeling that has a dark instinct of being a germ of thought" (1998, 161). The way in which Firstness is a "pure self-consciousness" is not as an a priori but as a germ, one without mine-ness yet, only an embryonically "dark instinct" for becoming my thought. It is best thought of in terms of Raymond Ruyer's (2016, chs. 9–11) immediate "self-survey" (survol) rather than phenomenology's prereflective field. In a formula Deleuze often repeats, this is not consciousness "of" something but a consciousness that *is* something.

Couplet 7. Going Kinetic

1. Describing the mood at a U.S. National Security Council meeting held September 13, 2001, two days after the attacks on the World Trade Center.

2. George W. Bush, *New York Times*, March 4, 2000 (quoted in Weisberg 2009).

3. George W. Bush, September 22, 1997 (quoted in Weisberg 2009).

4. Even one person alone having a thought is in virtual interaction with others whose place is held by the intrinsic activity of language. "There is no individual enunciation. Yet relatively few linguists have analyzed the necessarily social character of enunciation. The problem is that it is not enough to establish that enunciation has this social character, since it could be extrinsic. . . . The social character of enunciation is intrinsically founded only if one succeeds in demonstrating how enunciation itself implies *collective assemblages*. . . . It is the assemblage . . . that explains all the voices present within a single voice . . . the order-words in a word" (Deleuze and Guattari 1987, 79–80).

5. George W. Bush, Iowa Western Community College, January 21, 2000 (quoted in Weisberg 2009).

6. For a journalistic musing on the unspecified enemy, see "The Return of Mr. Unspecified Threat" (Preston 2003).

7. Bush in conversation with White House communications director Karen Hughes, September 12, 2001 (quoted in Woodward 2002, 41).

8. George W. Bush, meeting with congressional leaders, September 12, 2001 (quoted in Woodward 2002, 45).

9. This quote was widely attributed to Bush through email lists and on numerous websites but, as far as I can determine, without ever being referenced. It is also occasionally attributed to former vice president Dan Quayle, and is likely apocryphal. Apocryphal or not, it belongs effectively to the Bush oeuvre by dint of its public repetition.

10. Cover letter to National Security Strategy, quoted in Daalder, Lindsay, and Steinberg (2002).

11. When the short-circuiting of logical progression telescopes into a pure redundancy, the oxymoron's holding together of contraries abbreviates into a reduplicative of one term, held together with a variation on itself. The contrary remains implicit as a vague sense of something missing. This oxymoronic telescoping is numerically prevalent in compendiums of quotes circulated by purveyors of Bushisms on the scale of a minor industry: in addition to Weisberg (2009) and Miller (2002), Jacob Weisberg published multiple volumes of *Bushisms* in book form, including but not limited to Weisberg (2002, 2003, 2005, and 2007); see also Brown (2003). DVD collections of videos of the most infamous quotes were also marketed, for example Reeder (2004).

12. "Look at these different places around the world where there's been tremendous death and destruction because killers kill." George W. Bush, Washington, D.C., January 29, 2004 (quoted in Weisberg 2009). A no-nonsense Rumsfeld (2005) example: "When you're hunting for someone and you haven't found them, you haven't found them."

13. Vice Chairman of the Joint Chiefs of Staff General Peter Pace discussing weapons procurement and military strategy at a U.S. Department of Defense news briefing with Secretary of Defense Donald Rumsfeld. Rumsfeld (2002b) enthusiastically takes up Pace's bow wave image.

14. Donald Rumsfeld, interview with the *New York Times*, May 16, 2001 (quoted in Seely 2003).

15. George W. Bush, *Dallas Morning News*, May 10, 2000 (quoted in Miller 2002, 251).

16. "A being is the creature of its decisions, not their creator: An actual entity arises from decisions *for* it, and by its very existence provides decisions *for* other actual entities. . . . 'Actuality' is the decision amid 'potentiality'" (Whitehead 1978, 43). "Decisions are impossible for the nascent creature antecedently to the novelties [here, apprehended in the feeling of surprise] in the phase of its concrescence" (224). The cause of the decisions for the creature, from which it arises, is immanent: "The final decision is the reaction of the unity of the whole [experience] to its own internal determination" (28).

17. From the "axis of evil" speech where Bush (2002b) first made it known that his administration felt it was within its rights to preemptively invade Iraq.

18. George W. Bush, interview with Bob Woodward, August 20, 2002 (quoted in Woodward 2002, 341).

19. George W. Bush, Houston, September 6, 2000 (quoted in Weisberg 2009).

20. George W. Bush recounting a National Security Council meeting held September 25, 2001, in the aftermath of the 9/11 attacks (quoted in Woodward 2002, 118).

21. George W. Bush, aboard Air Force One, June 4, 2003 (quoted in Weisberg 2009).

22. George W. Bush recounting when he first learned of the September 11, 2001, attack on the World Trade Center (quoted in Woodward 2002, 14).

23. George W. Bush, pre-inaugural interview with *U.S. News and World Report*, January 22, 2001 (quoted in Weisberg 2009).

24. Quoting an AP reporter who was invited to jog with Bush at his Texas ranch.

25. George W. Bush, Reynoldsburg, Ohio, October 4, 2000, in response to a question asking him if he wished he could take back any of his answers in the first presidential debate (quoted in Weisberg 2009).

26. George W. Bush, *Austin American-Statesman*, November 2, 2000 (quoted in Miller 2002, 133).

27. Rumsfeld addressing a meeting of the inner circle of the Bush war cabinet, September 25, 2001 (quoted in Woodward 2002, 153).

28. On Reagan and George H. W. Bush, see Dean and Massumi (1992); also on Reagan, "The Bleed: Where Body Meets Image," in Massumi (2002, 46–67).

29. On operative logic, preemption, and the ecology of powers, see Massumi (2015a).

30. See Massumi (2015b, 2015c).

Couplet 7. Barely There

1. In particular as developed in the seminars: *Society Must Be Defended* (2003), *Security, Territory, Population* (2007), and *The Birth of Biopolitics* (2010).

2. [The concept of the "barely-there" is developed at length in my subsequent work under the term "bare activity." See Massumi (2011, 2015a, 2015b, 2015c).]

3. "Right of Death and Power over Life" in Foucault (1978, 135–59).

4. The mechanism of this becoming-immanent was the development of policing in tandem with the operation of normative institutions like the prison and psychiatry. On the becoming-immanent of carceral functions to the social field, see Foucault (1977, 296–306). On policing as the descent of sovereignty to the microlevel of detail, see Foucault (2007, 339–41).

5. The translation has been modified to restore "singular," which the translator renders as "individual"; the individual is a particular case of the general rule, whereas the singular is outside general relations of inclusion. On this point, see Agamben (1993a).

6. "There was a perceptible shift in attitude. Military action was now seen as inevitable. Bush wanted to remove Saddam, through military action, justified by the conjunction of terrorism and WMD. But the intelligence and facts were being fixed around the policy. The NSC had no patience with the UN route, and no enthusiasm for publishing material on the Iraqi regime's record. There was little discussion in Washington of the aftermath after military action" (*Sunday Times* 2005).

7. [On the politics of fear, see "Fear (The Spectrum Said)" in Massumi (2015a, 271–88).]

8. [See Massumi (2015a) for subsequent developments of these ideas.]

9. [For more on perceptual "filling in," amodal completion, and the saccadic nature of perception, with additional considerations on the "priming" that occurs in the off-beat, see Couplet 6, "The Crannies of the Present," in this volume.]

10. "Perception as a whole has its true and final explanation in the tendency of the body to movement" (Bergson 2004, 41).

11. [For ontopower in this and other spheres, particularly the theater of war, see Massumi (2015c).]

12. [The concept of affectively spurred collective individuation and the syncopation of the production of political effects are further developed in Massumi (2015a), ch. 6, "Fear (The Spectrum Said)," and ch. 3, "Perception Attack: The Force to Own Time," respectively).]

13. Woodward (2002, 1–64) gives a chronicle of these first days.

14. "Rendered into dust" were the words of the New York City chief medical examiner. "There are pieces," said a forensic pathologist, "but how do you identify and extract it from other similarly appearing pieces at the site—bricks, mortar, rubble?" (Pyle 2001). Bits of bone fragment "the size of small twigs" were found on the roof of a forty-story building near Ground Zero a year after the event, making the national news (Kugler 2002). Specks of human bone matter continued to be found years after. When it was learned that some fragments had been accidentally disposed of at a city landfill tauntingly named Fresh Kills an uproar ensued, spearheaded by the association of families of the victims. The families association wanted any rubble potentially containing unidentifiable human specks to be excavated from the landfill and ceremonially reburied at a more decorous site (Moore 2004).

15. This dynamic is expressed in the words of a mother who lost her son in the World Trade Center attacks, still struggling to comprehend three years later: "I want to know everything" about the moment of his death, she says. "This is the most important thing I will never know. . . . I try to imagine, but there is no imagining." She repeatedly revisits the site to attempt to get a glimpse of what she cannot see (Flynn and Dwyer 2004). This impulse was widely shared, even by those not directly affected. It led to the widely commented-upon phenomenon of "grief tourism" to Ground Zero and the field in Pennsylvania where Flight 93 crashed. The affective charge surrounding the agitated dialectics of seeing/not seeing, imagining/no imagining, critical commentary/pious observance fed a great deal of acrimony over the design of the memorial and museum at Ground Zero.

16. Sontag's commentary was searing, focusing on the affective politics underway. A sample: "The unanimity of the sanctimonious, reality-concealing rhetoric spouted by American officials and media commentators in recent days seems, well, unworthy of a mature democracy. Those in public office have let us know that they consider their task to be a manipulative one: confidence-building and grief management. Politics, the politics of a democracy—which entails disagreement, which promotes candor—has been replaced by psychotherapy. Let's by all means grieve together. But let's not be stupid together. A few shreds of historical awareness might help us understand what has just happened, and what may continue to happen" (Sontag in *New Yorker* 2001). Stockhausen, apparently responding to the media spectacle of the event, called 9/11 "the greatest work of art ever" at a Hamburg music festival. He was immediately removed from the festival and was reviled

around the world. [For a retrospective account written for the tenth anniversary, see Castle (2011).]

17. [On the unitary executive, see Calabresi and Yoo (2012).]

18. [For recent comments on the function of the face with respect to threat, in the context of the COVID-19 pandemic, see Massumi (2020).]

19. For an example that had high visibility at the time, a photo taken at the "Cincinnati Cares Freedom Rally" held ten days after the attacks, see Getty Images, https://www.gettyimages.ca/detail/news-photo/rachel-rasfeld-cheers-with-her-face-painted-red-white-and-news-photo/1165777.

20. For an analysis of this tension between unification and fragmentation as definitive of the dynamic of fascist and proto-fascist political process, see Dean and Massumi (1992).

21. "Bush Presidency Seems to Gain Legitimacy" was a September 16 headline of an editorial in the *New York Times*: "He sought to console the bereaved, comfort the wounded, encourage the heroic, calm the fearful and, by no means incidentally, rally the country for the struggle and sacrifice ahead" (Apple 2001).

22. "The next time they report I'm out riding, chopping or otherwise getting the old circulation going, why don't you get yourself out there and enjoy some exercise yourself? If all of us do, America will be in better shape too. I'll be thinking of you. Good health to you all" (quoted in Apple 2001).

23. [For a few preliminary notes on Trump and issues usually discussed in terms of political identification, see Couplet 8, "The Political Is Not Personal," in this volume.]

Couplet 8. Requiem for Our Prospective Dead

1. These are Pentagon estimates, as reported in the news media.

2. Iraqi violations of the southern "no-fly zone," declared by the UN and policed primarily by the US, received high-profile international attention. Relatively insignificant air flight and radar violations (for example, on June 30, 1993) made high-profile news as affronts to the world community, while Saddam Hussein's relentless ground operations against the southern Iraqi populations supposedly protected by the no-fly zone were hardly featured. These operations included wholesale ecological warfare: the systematic destruction by fire and drainage of the wetlands ecosystem that was the traditional home of the "Marsh Arabs" of the Tigris-Euphrates delta.

3. On "hybrid objects" combining the social and the natural, see Latour (1993).

4. On the fate of civil society under contemporary capitalism, see Hardt and Negri (1994, 217–61) and Hardt (1995).

5. The United Nations has encountered embarrassing difficulties patrolling its official "peacekeeping" vocabulary. All copies of a glossy Australian Department of Defence booklet entitled *Peacekeeping Policy: The Future Australian Defence Force Role* had to be recalled because the authors had used the word "peacemaking" in several

passages referring to operations in Somalia. The problem wasn't that the "peacemaking" recalled its etymological model, "warmaking." "Peacemaking" is in fact approved UN vocabulary, but it is carefully distinguished from "peacekeeping" and "peace enforcement" (the correct term for the Somali case). The authors of the booklet had failed to appreciate the subtleties of this array of neologisms, the effect of which is to annex mediation, military action, and police enforcement into a continuum subsumed by the concept of "peace" (*Australian* 1993b).

6. The evidence of the plot against Bush's life would not hold up in court. Iraq's ambassador to the UN accused the United States, quite accurately, of acting as "prosecution, judge, jury and executioner in its own case" (*Guardian Weekly* 1993). Saddam Hussein had a simpler defense, stating that Bush, already political dead wood, would not be worth the explosives.

7. Clinton said after his election that he would do "precisely what the Bush administration has done" in relation to Saddam Hussein. And that is precisely what he did—to the audible relief of many media military analysts. "Clinton has comprehensively embraced the US military's view of security" (a doctrine of military deterrence known as "forward deployment" [which foreshadowed George W. Bush's doctrine of preemption in his replay of the Gulf War a decade later]), cooed the *Australian*'s foreign editor, Greg Sheridan (July 15, 1993), in response to the Iraqi attack and Clinton's post–Tokyo summit statement in Seoul that North Korea would "cease to exist" if it attacked the South.

8. This has entailed a post–Cold War adaptation of intelligence agencies. Revelations in June 1993 that the French intelligence agency, after the collapse of the Soviet Union, its old nemesis and reason for being, had turned its attention to the high-tech secrets of political allies have led to a general recognition that industrial spying is the new priority in international intelligence across the board. See, for example, *Newsweek* (1993).

9. [This hijacking of ontological emergence is developed in later work under the concept of "ontopower" (Massumi 2015a).]

10. [In later work, I move to a model of the "more-than-human" as opposed to the posthuman. See Couplets 3, "Becoming Animal in the Literary Field," and 4, "The Supernormal Animal," in this volume; Massumi (2014); and "Capital Moves," chapter 1 in Massumi (2017a).]

11. See "Postscript on Control Societies" in Deleuze (1995, 177–82). On Deleuze's updating of Foucault in the context of the Marxist theory of real subsumption, see Hardt and Negri (1994).

12. On the current convergence between the figure of the statesman and that of the criminal, see Agamben (1993b).

13. [Working and reworking the distinctions and interplays between the modes of power (disciplinary power, biopower, sovereign power, control, and a new addition, ontopower), as part of an "ecology of powers," is a major preoccupation in subsequent work. See, for example, Couplet 7, "Barely There," in this volume; "National Enterprise Emergency: Steps toward an Ecology of Powers," chapter 2 in Massumi (2015a); Massumi (2015c, 37–40; 2018, 63–82).]

14. This is what Deleuze and Guattari call "machinic enslavement" (1987, 456–58).

15. Deleuze and Guattari develop the theory of capitalism as axiomatic in *A Thousand Plateaus* (1987, 460–73). They base their analysis on Robert Blanché's (1955) overview of axiomatic method.

16. Guattari (1995, 6–7, 38–42) elaborates from the work of Francisco Varela to develop an ontological model of "autopoiesis" which should not be confused with Luhmann's (1990, 1–20) communicational model of "self-referential systems" as "autopoietic."

17. On the singular as multiple, see Deleuze (1990, 58–65, 100–108). On the singular-multiple as generic, see Agamben (1993b).

Couplet 9. Tell Me Where Your Pain Is

1. "There is so much interaction between different brain centers . . . that there is no direct hotline from pain receptors to 'pain centers' in the brain" (Ramachandran and Blakeslee 1998, 54). Because of this "cross-wiring," there is no one-to-one correspondence between organic stimulus and quality of feeling. No feeling can be definitively located in any particular place in ordinary space or univocally "mapped" onto a single "center" in the brain, in spite of the existence of certain genetically determined cerebral specializations and connections. Feeling as such is fundamentally nonlocal (always implicated in complex feedback loops, as part of an open-ended process). Its nonlocalizable complexity accounts for its remarkable plasticity, as illustrated in such phenomena as the placebo effect, meditation-based pain-control techniques, and Ramachandran's uncanny ability to treat phantom limb pain with visual illusions.

2. This is an allusion to Peirce's "Firstness." For more on Firstness, see Massumi (2016, 2017b).

3. In this passage, James is referring specifically to a blind child. The principle, however, is the same for a sighted child, with the addition of a visual cross-referencing of the emphatic points that facilitates the separating out of the body part.

4. James's "emphatic points" return in Deleuze's concept of "remarkable points" in *Difference and Repetition* (1994).

5. "Sensations are not in space; on the contrary, space is enveloped in each sensation and develops connectively until it reaches its own confines. . . . The rumble of the thunder is no bigger than the prick of a pin" (Lapoujade 1995, 58).

6. James's "voluminousness" or "vague vastness" of experience before the differentiation of space and time is a Firstness of spaciousness. The concept is close to Deleuze's *spatium* (1994, 134–35). [On the role of this primitive voluminousness in the process of "bodying," see Erin Manning's analysis of DeafBlind experience in the context of the ProTactile movement, "Not at a Distance" (2020, 245–70).]

7. Processually, pain may be defined as a point of maximal contraction of the space-time of experience. The notion that the world emerges from feeling is not as off-the-wall as it might sound. It is, in fact, the founding insight of empiricist

philosophy, dating back to Hume. James's "radical empiricism" is a return to and development of that insight, influenced by C. S. Peirce's "pragmatism" (Peirce's "Firstness" is the vague qualitative volume of sensation discussed here) and further extended by Whitehead's "process philosophy" and Deleuze's post-Humean "superior empiricism." The translation of the quote from Deleuze ("place is not different from what passes through it") has been modified. The French phrase rendered over-literally here as "what passes through it" is "ce qui s'y passe," a colloquialism meaning "that which happens." Boundas's translation, "place is not different from what takes place in it" quite rightly foregrounds this connotation of eventfulness.

8. Everything, Bergson says, is attached to the rest of the universe by a "tenuous thread." "It is down this thread that is transmitted to the smallest particle of the world in which we live the duration immanent to the whole of the universe" (1998, 10–11). Whitehead: "Thus an event is a matter of fact which by reason of its limitation is a value for itself; but by reason of its very nature it also requires the whole universe in order to be itself" (1978, 194).

9. The brain regions involved in navigation "responded much more strongly to scenes depicting bare spatial layout (empty rooms and landscapes) than it did to faces, objects or multiple object arrays" (Epstein and Kanwisher 1998, 600). The authors conclude that the brain "uses the shape of the surroundings to determine current location," rather than using the location of objects to determine the shape of the space (600). In active orientation, landmarks function as indexes of the "shape of the space" rather than as specific locations. [This result is also discussed in "Strange Horizon: Buildings, Biograms, and the Body Topologic" (Massumi 2002, 177–207) as part of an analysis of the fundamentally topological nature of experience.]

10. Daniel Stern gives a beautiful account of the "sense of an emergent self" (1985, 37–68).

11. On habit as the first "passive synthesis" of experience, see Deleuze (1994, 70–81).

12. "Movement . . . cannot be perceived. However, we are obliged to make an immediate correction: movement also 'must' be perceived, it cannot but be perceived, the imperceptible is also the *percipiendum*" (Deleuze and Guattari 1987, 281).

13. [For more on modal perception (or completion) and movement, see Couplet 7, "Barely There," in this volume; for a critique of the limitations of the notion of the "filling in" of perception, see Couplet 6, "The Crannies of the Present," in this volume; for a reinterpretation of the filling in of perception as the production of a "semblance" (an abstract extra-effect taking off from the conditions of perception), see Massumi (2011, ch. 2).]

14. Neurological research shows that imagined sights activate the same brain regions involved in vision with corresponding sensory input (O'Craven and Kanwisher 2000).

15. [On cut and continuity, see Massumi (2019).]

16. Technically, indicators of place like "here" and "there" that have determinate meaning only in the context of the speaking event are "deictics." The "this" or

"that" of "this place/that place" are demonstratives. In this essay, I will use the term "demonstrative" nontechnically in order to access two connotations it has in its common dictionary definition: "pointing out" and "marked by a display of feeling." It should be noted that this account is consonant with Whitehead's assertion that "pure demonstration" is a "practical impossibility." "A proposition," he says, "about a particular factor in nature can neither be expressed to others nor retained for repeated consideration without the aid of auxiliary complexes which are irrelevant to it" (1920, 10). This is because the demonstrative implicitly presupposes and effectively "includes the general circumstances of its production" (9), i.e., the "simple total vastness" of movement potential that is the moving ground of experience.

17. [On the creative force of language, see Massumi (2011, ch. 4).]

18. Raymond Ruyer forcefully develops this point: "There is no subject, no observer, no super-retina, in a [supplementary] dimension, and yet all the points, all the details of the sensation are present, 'visible' at the same time.... Sensation is not 'at a distance.'... [It is] a void of distance.... My consciousness is never outside its sensations" (1950, 56–58). "There is no third eye. My visual field necessarily sees itself in 'nondimensional' or 'absolute survey.' It self-surveys without distancing itself" (Ruyer 2016, 97). "'I' am simultaneously at every place in my visual field" (94, translation modified). "The impression of distance is a by-product of the transformation of an absolute surface into a surface-object" (Ruyer 1950, 58). Ruyer's "absolute surface," from which objects and their positionings transformationally emerge, is James's "simple total vastness." The "absolute surface" is itself composed of "pure linkages" (pure transitions) in "superposition" (Ruyer 1950, 110–11). Ruyer's "void of distance" is closely akin to what was called earlier in this essay a quantum void of movement, minus the positions moved between (pure or "absolute" movement).

19. The nausea is caused by the "irritation" to the inner ear's sense of balance (Schilder 1950, 113). As we saw earlier, the vestibular sense is crucial to kinesthesis, which is crucial to making the synesthetic cross-connections between the other senses, which are in turn crucial to the success of visual in-fill.

20. That maps change is true down to the physiological level: "Large-scale changes in the organization of the brain occur in adult humans. The implications are staggering. First and foremost, they suggest that brain maps can change, sometimes with astonishing rapidity. This finding flatly contradicts one of the most widely accepted dogmas in neurology—the fixed nature of connections in the human brain" (Ramachandran and Blakeslee 1998, 31).

21. "When thinking about the categories I used to distinguish, in the accepted manner, the category of quantity from that of relation, since quantity and position (both of which are included in this category) seem to be produced by motion per se, and usually conceived by people in this way. But when I considered the matter more accurately I saw that they are mere results which do not constitute any intrinsic denomination per se, and so they are merely relations which demand a foundation derived from the category of quality, that is, from an intrinsic accidental

denomination" associated with a "power of transition" (Leibniz 1995, 133–34). This passage from Leibniz contains the argument of the present essay in a nutshell: position arises from motion (rather than motion connecting positions); the motion in question is purely relational minus the terms in relation (a pure potential or power of transition); the relation must be conceived as a quality of feeling (it is sensational or perceptual, even if atomically "indiscernible"); the quality is brought out and made in an accident, and the accident is "denominated" or demonstrated in a way intrinsic to it (it is expressed by language, whose distinctions it nevertheless encompasses); and through its expression it is made discernible (having undergone a transformation—so that its indiscernibility or "invisibility" subsists across its expression). The kinship between Leibniz's matter and Ruyer's "absolute surface" composed of "pure linkage" is apparent. Deleuze and Guattari, extending Leibniz, Ruyer, as well as Bergson, also argue that the thinking of change requires a notion of the intrinsic or "absolute" movement (1987, 255).

Couplet 9. The Art of the Relational Body

1. See, for example, Bannissy, Walsh, and Muggleton (2011).

2. I do not mean to suggest that the dangers of this model are unacknowledged, or that many authors do not consciously work against it. The point is that the difficulties of effectively surpassing it are considerable, and require a dedicated philosophical labor. An unintended return to the passive-reception model occurs frequently in the literature at critical points, piggy-backing on the vocabulary of representation, imitation, body image, and body map, all of which implicitly presuppose an inspecting, cognizing subject. These slippages are most palpable when the first-person pronoun is resorted to, for example in discussions of how "we" relate to the phenomenon under discussion.

3. I am borrowing the term "neurotypical" from the autistic self-affirmation movement, where it is used to refer to nonautistics. The term is beginning to gain wider currency among a number of communities whose "neurodiverse" perceptual or cognitive manners of being are considered, according to prevailing standards, to depart from the norm. See Manning (2013, 2016).

4. Although synesthesia is fundamentally involuntary, its rising to the conscious level of explicit experience can be acquired. As the next paragraph argues, this does not mean, however, that it becomes voluntary; rather, it has the status of an acquired automaticity (i.e., a habit). See Bor et al. (2014).

5. "Mirror-touch synesthetes have been found to show an increased tactile sensitivity, which is in line with evidence of heightened perceptual processing of the synthetic concurrent in other variants of synesthesia. . . . Mirror-touch synesthesia is a consequence of increased neural activity in the same mirror-touch network that is evoked in non-synesthetic controls when observing touch to another person and therefore may be mediated by the 'normal' architecture for multisensory interaction" (Bannissy 2013, 589).

6. Cut out the yellow band of the spectrum of natural light, as many LED lightbulbs do, and what you get is not more or less light but a different quality of light.

7. The central role of movement is seen in mirror-touch synesthesia in the fact that "observed touch to another person in a video evoked a significantly more intense synesthetic experience than observing similar touch in static photographs" (Banissy 2013, 587).

8. Whitehead on vibration: "We shall conceive each primordial element as a vibratory ebb and flow of an underlying energy, or activity. . . . Each primordial element will be an organised system of vibratory streaming" (1967b, 35; see also 131–36, 154–55). Bergson on vibration, the imperceptible interval of perception's arising, inhibition, the difference between intensive and extensive relations, and change:

> May we not conceive, for instance, that the irreducibility of two perceived colours is due mainly to the narrow duration into which are contracted the billions of vibrations which they execute in one of our moments? If we could stretch out this duration, that is to say, live it at a slower rhythm, should we not, as the rhythm slowed down, see these colours pale and lengthen into successive impressions, still coloured, no doubt, but nearer and nearer to coincidence with pure vibrations? In cases where the rhythm of the movement is slow enough to tally with the habits of our consciousness, as in the case of the deep notes of the musical scale, for instance, do we not feel that the quality perceived analyses itself into repeated and successive vibrations, bound together by an inner continuity? That which usually hinders this mutual approach of motion and quality is the acquired habit of attaching movement to elements—atoms or what not—which interpose their solidity between the movement itself and the quality into which it contracts. . . . Motion becomes then for our imagination, no more than an accident, a series of positions, a change of [external] relations; and, as it is a law of our representation that in it the stable drives away the unstable. (2004, 269)

Deleuze on vibration, event, and extension: "The event is a vibration with an infinity of subharmonics or submultiples, such as an audible wave, or an increasingly smaller part of space over the course of an increasingly short duration. For space and time are not limits but abstract coordinates . . . in extension" (1993, 77; see also 4, 95–96).

9. For more on the topology of experience, see "Strange Horizon: Buildings, Biograms, and the Body Topologic," in Massumi (2002, 177–207).

10. The five traditional senses are exteroceptive, or exoreferenced. Proprioception is the interoceptive sense par excellence. It is essentially endoreferential and must be understood topologically. As such, it is the actual sense functioning closest to the virtual body, whose geometry of internal relations it shares. See Massumi (2002, 58–61, 168–69, 179–84) and Couplets 5, "Sensing the Virtual, Building the Insensible," and 9, "Tell Me Where Your Pain Is," in this volume.

11. This applies equally to the "specular" and "anatomical" variants of mirror-touch synesthesia. Specular mirror-touch synesthesia is when the experienced location of a touch is reversed, as in a mirror, and anatomical mirror-touch synesthesia is when the reversal does not take place, so that a touch on the right side is experienced on the left. From the point of view developed here, even in the anatomical variant, where there seems to be a direct correspondence, there is still an underlying topological transformation folding sight and touch into each other.

12. The link between mirror-touch synesthesia and the virtual body is exemplified by the fact that the most common cases of acquired mirror-touch synesthesia occur in amputees who experience a phantom limb (Banissy 2013, 594). The mirror-touch effect occurs when touch is perceived on the corresponding limb of another body. It is as if the loss of the actual limb leaves the body with only a virtual body to operate with in that region of experience, and a striving to complete the circuit between the physiological and virtual body gives rise to a consciousness of the virtual body in the form of a virtual touch.

13. For an extended discussion of sympathy in this connection, working from David Hume's account, see Massumi (2015c, 60–65).

14. The scientific literature distinguishes between cognitive, motor, and emotional empathy. What I am referring to as sympathy integrally combines the motor and the emotional, and contrasts these taken together with the cognitive (here, the conscious peaking of experience). Giacomo Rizzolatti, one of the discoverers of mirror neurons, remarks upon the indissociability of the motor and emotional in mirror-neuron-related experience: "The fact remains that these [emotional and empathic] phenomena have a common functional matrix similar to that which intervenes in the understanding of actions" (Rizzolatti and Sinigaglia 2008, 192). Once again, I am not arguing that the concept of projection is universally accepted among researchers, or that the model of identification is never called into question. The issue, once again, is the tenaciousness of philosophical presuppositions and their tendency to return uninvited. The work of Vittorio Gallese (a codiscoverer of mirror neurons) on empathy understood in terms of a "shared manifold" that underlies and gives rise to the sense of self *and* other is close to the perspective advocated here, excepting its continued use of the concept of representation (2003). Freedberg and Gallese's concept of unmediated "simulation" of physical involvement with others' feelings, associated with mirror neurons, is allied to the philosophical concepts of reenaction or nascent action mentioned at the beginning of this essay (2007, 197–203).

Couplet 10. The Parable of the Cave (Blind Version)

1. The caves are more akin to Klein bottles than familiar Euclidean spaces, the difference being that they are not surfaces but have a voluminousness that a Klein bottle lacks. Klein bottles are pure topological surface. They have no interior or exterior but, embedded in a higher dimensioned Euclidean space, appear to have both.

Couplet 11. Urban Appointment

1. The HUMO Master Class was part of the "Interfacing Realities" project, a series of four master classes organized as part of the European Culture 2000 program. It was realized in cooperation with ENCART (European Network for Cyber Arts). Partners: V2_Organisation (Rotterdam), ZKM (Karlsruhe), C3 (Budapest), and Ars Electronica Center (Linz). The workshop was directed by Rafael Lozano-Hemmer and Brian Massumi; produced with the Ars Electronica Center/FutureLab: Eva Luise Kühn, Martin Honzik, Stefan Mittlböck-Jungwirt, Magnus Hofmüller, John Gerrard, Rüdiger Weibold; commissioned by V2_Organisation: Boudewijn Ridder, project manager; and was supported by PANI Projection and Lighting Vertriebs GmbH (Bernhard Höfert, lead technician) and Hartlauer Handelsgesellschaft mbH.

2. Participants: Julie Andreyev, Noel Douglas, Rainer Eisch, Johanne Gees, John Gerrard, Peter Grünheid, Martin Honzik, Maya Kalogera, Anya Lewin, Stefan Mittlböck-Jungwirt, Harald Schmutzhard, Flavia Sparacino, and Lorenzo Tripodi.

3. The HUMO workshop utilized the BP12 projector from PANI Austria. This projector has a 12,000 Watt HMI lamp that can produce images with over 100,000 ANSI lumen intensity.

4. [This notion of documentation as a dissemination of process seeds has been taken up and developed over many years by the SenseLab under the concept of the "anarchive"; see *The Go-To How-To Guide to Anarchiving* (SenseLab 2016), itself an anarchiving of a SenseLab event ("Distributing the Insensible," Montreal, December 2016) in the form of a book sprint.]

Couplet 12. On Critique

1. [This text was originally written as part of an online discussion thread that occurred in the transition between two SenseLab "research-creation" events held in Montreal: *Dancing the Virtual* (May 13–15, 2006, http://senselab.ca/wp2/events/dancing-the-virtual-2005/) and *Housing the Body, Dressing the Environment* (August 23–26, 2007, http://senselab.ca/wp2/events/housing-the-body-dressing-the-environment-2007/). For a discussion of the speculative pragmatist approach of this and other SenseLab events based on the first ten years of experimentations, see "Propositions for Thought in the Act," in Manning and Massumi (2014, 83–151).]

Couplet 12. How Do You Make Yourself a Proposition?

1. "The primary mode of realization of a proposition in an actual entity is not by judgment, but by entertainment. A proposition is entertained when it is admitted into feeling" (Whitehead 1978, 188).

2. "An element in this penumbral complex is what is termed a 'proposition'" (Whitehead 1978, 185).

3. "An actual entity has a perfectly definite bond with each item in the universe. This determinate bond is its prehension of that item. A negative prehension is the definite exclusion of that item from positive contribution to the subject's own real internal constitution. This doctrine involves the position that *a negative prehension expresses a bond*" (Whitehead 1978, 41, emphasis added).

4. "The feelings aim at the feeler, as their final cause. The feelings are what they are in order that their subject may be what it is. . . . It is better to say that the feelings *aim at* their subject, than to say that they *are aimed at* their subject. For the latter mode of expression removes the subject from the scope of the feeling and assigns it to an external agency. Thus the feeling would be wrongly abstracted from its own final cause. This final cause is an inherent element in the feeling, constituting the unity of that feeling. An actual entity feels as it does feel in order to be the actual entity which it is" (Whitehead 1978, 222).

5. For more on the practice of the SenseLab, see "Nestingpatching," in Manning (2020, 55–74), "Experimenting Immediation: Collaboration and the Politics of Fabulation" (115–44), "Practicing the Schizz" (145–97), and "Cephalopod Dreams: Finance at the Limit" (289–308).

6. We would like to thank for their participation Adam Szymanksi, Ana Ramos, Andrew Murphie, André Fogliano, Anique Vered, Bianca Scliar, Charlotte Farrell, Csenge Kolosvari, Diego Gil, Erik Bordeleau, Franciso Trento, Halbe Kuipers, Hubert Gendron-Blais, Jane Gabriels, Joel Mason, Leslie Plumb, Lone Bertelsen, Matthew Robin-Nye, Mattie Sempert, Mayra Morales, Olivier Bissonnette-Lavoie, Ramona Benveniste, Roberto Scienza, Ronald Rose-Antoinette, Siglinde Langholz, and Skye Bougsty-Marshall.

7. For an in-depth discussion of conceptual speed-dating and collective enunciation in relation to Peirce's theory of the sign, see "Collective Expression: A Radical Pragmatics," in Massumi (2017a, 111–43).

REFERENCES

ABC News (Australia). 2010. "Ngarrindjeri in Symbolic Walk across Hindmarsh Island Bridge." July 6. https://www.abc.net.au/news/2010-07-06/ngarrindjeri-in-symbolic-walk-across-hindmarsh/894792.

Abram, David. 2010. *Becoming Animal: An Earthly Cosmology*. New York: Pantheon.

Agamben, Giorgio. 1993a. *The Coming Community*. Trans. Michael Hardt. Minneapolis: University of Minnesota Press.

Agamben, Giorgio. 1993b. "The Sovereign Police." In *The Politics of Everyday Fear*, ed. Brian Massumi, 61–63. Minneapolis: University of Minnesota Press.

Agamben, Giorgio. 1998. *Homo Sacer: Sovereign Power and Bare Life*. Trans. Daniel Heller-Roazen. Stanford, CA: Stanford University Press.

Age. 1988. "Blacks Jeer Queen over Land Rights." May 10.

Alliez, Eric, and Michel Feher. 1986. "Notes on the Sophisticated City." *Zone*, nos. 1–2: 40–55.

Apple, R. W., Jr. 2001. "After the Attacks Assessment: Bush Presidency Seems to Gain Legitimacy." *New York Times*, September 16. https://www.nytimes.com/2001/09/16/us/after-the-attacks-assessment-president-seems-to-gain-legitimacy.html.

Arakawa and Madeline Gins. 2002. *Architectural Body*. Tuscaloosa: University of Alabama Press.

Attwood, Bain, and Andrew Markus. 1999. *The Struggle for Aboriginal Rights: A Documentary History*. Sydney: Allen and Unwin.

Austin, J. L. 1975. *How to Do Things with Words*. Cambridge, MA: Harvard University Press.

Australian. 1988a. "Mosaic Blesses All, Says Its Creator." May 11.

Australian. 1988b. "Queen Extends House-Warming Tradition." May 10.

Australian. 1993a. "Artist Digs Up His Parliamentary Mosaic in Mabo Protest." September 28.

Australian. 1993b. "Defence Gaffe Leads to Recall of Booklet." July 1.

Australian. 1995. "Pilot Shot Down over Bosnia Broke Rules on the Ground Too." July 8–9.

Bains, Paul. 2002. "Subjectless Subjectivities." In *A Shock to Thought*, ed. Brian Massumi, 101–16. London: Routledge.

Baker, J. A. (1967) 2005. *The Peregrine*. Intro. Robert Macfarlane. New York: New York Review of Books.

Bakhtin, M. M. 1990. *Art and Answerability: Early Philosophical Essays by M. M. Bakhtin.* Ed. Michael Holquist and Vadim Liapunov. Trans. Vadim Liapunov. Austin: University of Texas Press.

Bannissy, Michael J. 2013. "Synesthesia, Mirror Neurons, and Mirror-Touch." In *The Oxford Handbook of Synesthesia*, ed. Julia Simner and Edward M. Hubbard, 584–600. Oxford: Oxford University Press.

Bannissy, Michael J., Vincent Z. Walsh, and Neil G. Muggleton. 2011. "Mirror-Touch Synaesthesia: A Case of Faulty Self-Modelling and Insula Abnormality." *Cognitive Neuroscience* 2 (2): 98–133.

Barron, James. 2001. "Bush Says Attack Was 'First War of the 21st Century.'" *New York Times*, September 13. https://www.nytimes.com/2001/09/13/nyregion/bush-says-attack-was-first-war-of-the-21st-century.html.

Baudrillard, Jean. 1983a. *In the Shadow of the Silent Majorities.* Trans. Paul Foss, Paul Patton, and John Johnston. New York: Semiotext(e).

Baudrillard, Jean. 1983b. *Simulations.* Trans. Paul Foss, Paul Patton, and Philip Beitchman. New York: Semiotext(e).

Baudrillard, Jean. 1995. *The Gulf War Did Not Take Place.* Trans. Paul Patton. Sydney: Power.

Bazinet, Kenneth R. 2002. "Bush Message Edited to Few Words." *Montreal Gazette*, July 26.

Bell, Diane. 1998. *Ngarrindjeri Wurruwarrin: A World That Is, Was, and Will Be.* Melbourne: Spinifex.

Bennett, Jane. 2010. *Vibrant Matter: A Political Ecology of Things.* Durham, NC: Duke University Press.

Bergson, Henri. 1965. *Duration and Simultaneity.* Trans. Leon Jacobson. New York: Bobbs-Merrill.

Bergson, Henri. 1972. *Mélanges.* Paris: PUF.

Bergson, Henri. 1998. *Creative Evolution.* Trans. Arthur Mitchell. Mineola, NJ: Dover.

Bergson, Henri. 2004. *Matter and Memory.* Trans. Nancy Margaret Paul and W. Scott Palmer. Mineola, NY: Dover.

Bergson, Henri. 2007. *The Creative Mind.* Trans. Mabelle L. Andison. Mineola, NY: Dover.

Berkeley, George. (1709) 1957. "An Essay towards a New Theory of Vision." In *A New Theory of Vision and Other Essays*, 1–86. London: J. M. Dent and Sons.

Berndt, R. M., and C. H. Berndt. 1993. *The World That Was.* Melbourne: University of Melbourne Press.

Blanché, Robert. 1955. *L'axiomatique.* Paris: PUF.

Blanchot, Maurice. 1949. *La part du feu.* Paris: Gallimard.

Bohm, David, and F. David Peat. 1987. *Science, Order and Creativity.* London: Routledge.

Böhme, Gernot. 1993. "Atmosphere as the Fundamental Concept of a New Aesthetics." *Thesis Eleven* 36: 113–26.

Bor, Daniel, Nicolas Rothen, David J. Schwartzman, Stephanie Clayton, and Anil K. Seth. 2014. "Adults Can Be Trained to Acquire Synesthetic Experiences." *Scientific Reports* 4, article 7089. doi:10.1038/srep07089.

Bornstein, Marc H. 1978. "Chromatic Vision in Infancy." In *Advances in Child Development and Behavior*, vol. 12, ed. Hayne W. Reese and Lewis P. Lipsitt, 117–82. New York: Academic Press.

Braidotti, Rosi. 2013. *The Posthuman*. Cambridge: Polity.

Broadbent, D. E., and M. H. Broadbent. 1987. "From Detection to Identification: Response to Multiple Targets in Rapid Serial Visual Presentation." *Perception and Psychophysics* 42: 105–13.

Brookhiser, Richard. 2003. "Close-Up: The Mind of George W. Bush." *Atlantic Monthly*, April, 55–69.

Brown, Robert S. 2003. *Presidential (Mis)speak: The Very Curious Language of George W. Bush*. New York: Outland Communications.

Bruno, Giordano. 2000. *De la magie*. Trans. Danielle Sonnier and Boris Donne. Paris: Allia.

Buckley, Sandra. 1998. "Remaking the World Order: Reflections on Huntington's Clash of Civilizations." *Theory and Event* 2 (4). http://muse.jhu.edu/article/32531.

Bush, George W. 2001. "Remarks by the President in Photo Opportunity with the National Security Team." September 12. https://georgewbush-whitehouse.archives.gov/news/releases/2001/09/20010912-4.html.

Bush, George W. 2002a. *The National Security Strategy of the United States*. September. https://georgewbush-whitehouse.archives.gov/nsc/nss/2002/.

Bush, George W. 2002b. State of the Union Address. January 29. https://georgewbush-whitehouse.archives.gov/news/releases/2002/01/20020129-11.html.

Cache, Bernard. 1995. *Earth Moves: The Furnishing of Territories*. Trans. Anne Boyman. Cambridge, MA: MIT Press.

Calabresi, Steven G., and Christopher S. Yoo. 2012. *The Unitary Executive: Presidential Power from Washington to Bush*. New Haven, CT: Yale University Press.

Canberra Times. 1988. "Nation's Disgrace Burns Within." May 15.

Cappucci, Matthew, and Andrew Freedman. 2019. "President Trump Showed a Doctored Hurricane Chart: Was It to Cover Up for 'Alabama' Twitter Flub?" *Washington Post*, September 5. https://www.washingtonpost.com/weather/2019/09/04/president-trump-shows-doctored-hurricane-chart-was-it-cover-up-alabama-twitter-flub/.

Castle, Terry. 2011. "Stockhausen, Karlheinz." *New York Magazine*, August 27. https://nymag.com/news/9-11/10th-anniversary/karlheinz-stockhausen/.

CBS News. 2004. "Fierce Fighting in Fallujah." April 28. https://www.cbsnews.com/news/fierce-fighting-in-fallujah/.

Chait, Jonathan. 2005. "Bush's Obsession with Exercise Borders on Creepy." *Montreal Gazette*, July 26. Reprint of Chait, "The (Over) Exercise of Power," *Los Angeles Times*, July 22, 2005, https://www.latimes.com/archives/la-xpm-2005-jul-22-oe-chait22-story.html.

CNN. 2006. "Bush: 'I'm the Decider' on Rumsfeld Defense Secretary: Changes in Military Meet Resistance." April 18.

Connolly, William E. 2002. *Neuropolitics: Thinking, Culture, Speed*. Minneapolis: University of Minnesota Press.

Coole, Diana, and Samantha Frost. 2010. *New Materialisms: Ontology, Agency, Politics.* Durham, NC: Duke University Press.

Cronenberg, David, dir. 1986. *The Fly.* Century City, CA: 20th Century Fox. Film.

Daalder, Ivo H., James M. Lindsay, and James B. Steinberg. 2002. "The Bush National Security Strategy: An Evaluation." Brookings Institution, October 1. https://www.brookings.edu/research/the-bush-national-security-strategy-an-evaluation/.

Dean, Kenneth, and Brian Massumi. 1992. *First and Last Emperors.* New York: Autonomedia.

Debaise, Didier. 2008. "Une métaphysique des possessions: Puissances et sociétés chez G. Tarde." *Revue de Métaphysique et de morale* 4 (1): 447–60.

Debaise, Didier. 2017. *Nature as Event: The Lure of the Possible.* Trans. Michael Halewood. Durham, NC: Duke University Press.

Debord, Guy. 1996. "Theory of the Dérive." In *Theory of the Dérive and Other Situationist Writings on the City*, ed. Libero Andreotti and Xavier Costa, 22–27. Barcelona: Museu d'Art Contemporani.

Deleuze, Gilles. 1986a. *Cinema 1: The Movement-Image.* Trans. Hugh Tomlinson and Barbara Habberjam. Minneapolis: University of Minnesota Press.

Deleuze, Gilles. 1986b. *Foucault.* Trans. Paul Bové. Minneapolis: University of Minnesota Press.

Deleuze, Gilles. 1989. *Cinema 2: The Time-Image.* Trans. Hugh Tomlinson and Robert Galeta. Minneapolis: University of Minnesota Press.

Deleuze, Gilles. 1990. *The Logic of Sense.* Trans. Mark Lester with Charles Stivale. Ed. Constantin V. Boundas. New York: Columbia University Press.

Deleuze, Gilles. 1991a. *Bergsonism.* Trans. Hugh Tomlinson and Barbara Habberjam. New York: Zone Books.

Deleuze, Gilles. 1991b. *Empiricism and Subjectivity: An Essay on Hume's Theory of Human Nature.* Trans. Constantin V. Boundas. New York: Columbia University Press.

Deleuze, Gilles. 1993. *The Fold: Leibniz and the Baroque.* Trans. Tom Conley. Minneapolis: University of Minnesota Press.

Deleuze, Gilles. 1994. *Difference and Repetition.* Trans. Paul Patton. New York: Columbia University Press.

Deleuze, Gilles. 1995. *Negotiations.* Trans. Martin Joughin. New York: Columbia University Press.

Deleuze, Gilles. 1997a. *Essays Critical and Clinical.* Trans. Daniel W. Smith and Michael A. Greco. Minneapolis: University of Minnesota Press.

Deleuze, Gilles. 1997b. "One Manifesto Less." Trans. Alan Orenstein. In *The Deleuze Reader*, ed. Constantin V. Boundas, 204–22. New York: Columbia University Press.

Deleuze, Gilles. 2004. *Desert Islands and Other Texts, 1953–1974.* Trans. Michael Taormina. Ed. David Lapoujade. New York: Semiotext(e).

Deleuze, Gilles. 2005. *Francis Bacon: The Logic of Sensation.* Trans. Daniel W. Smith. Minneapolis: University of Minnesota Press.

Deleuze, Gilles. 2007. *Two Regimes of Madness: Texts and Interviews 1975–1995*. Trans. Ames Hodges and Mike Taormina. New York: Semiotext(e).

Deleuze, Gilles, and Félix Guattari. 1983. *Anti-Oedipus*. Trans. Robert Hurley, Mark Seem, and Helen R. Lane. Minneapolis: University of Minneapolis Press.

Deleuze, Gilles, and Félix Guattari. 1986. *Kafka: Toward a Minor Literature*. Trans. Dana Polan. Minneapolis: University of Minnesota Press.

Deleuze, Gilles, and Félix Guattari. 1987. *A Thousand Plateaus*. Trans. Brian Massumi. Minneapolis: University of Minneapolis Press.

Deleuze, Gilles, and Félix Guattari. 1994. *What Is Philosophy?* Trans. Graham Burchell and Hugh Tomlinson. New York: Columbia University Press.

Deleuze, Gilles, and Claire Parnet. 1987. *Dialogues*. Trans. Hugh Tomlinson and Barbara Habberjam. New York: Columbia University Press.

Despret, Vinciane, and Jocelyne Porcher. 2007. *Etre bête*. Paris: Actes Sud.

Dolphijn, Rick, and Iris van der Tuin. 2012. *New Materialisms: Interviews and Cartographies*. London: Open Humanities Press.

Dowd, Maureen. 2002. "Treadmills of His Mind." *New York Times*, August 25. https://www.nytimes.com/2002/08/25/opinion/treadmills-of-his-mind.html.

Edwards, Steven. 2002. "Inspired by 9/11 Tumbling Woman [Sculpture] Provokes a Public Uproar in New York." *National Post* (Canada), September 19.

Epstein, Russell, and Nancy Kanwisher. 1998. "A Cortical Representation of the Local Visual Environment." *Nature* 392 (April 9): 598–601.

Ewald, François. 1993. "Two Infinities of Risk." In *The Politics of Everyday Fear*, ed. Brian Massumi, 221–28. Minneapolis: University of Minnesota Press.

Faber, Roland, Michael Halewood, and Andrew M. Davis. 2019. *Propositions in the Making: Experiments in a Whiteheadian Laboratory*. Lanham, MD: Lexington Books.

Feuillade, Louis, dir. 1919. *Vendémiaire*. Paris: L. Gaumont. Film.

Flynn, Kevin, and Jim Dwyer. 2004. "Falling Bodies: A 9/11 Image Etched in Pain." *New York Times*, September 10. https://www.nytimes.com/2004/09/10/nyregion/nyregionspecial2/falling-bodies-a-911-image-etched-in-pain.html?searchResultPosition=3.

Foster, Charles. 2016. *Being a Beast: Adventures across the Species Divide*. New York: Metropolitan Books.

Foucault, Michel. 1977. *Discipline and Punish: The Birth of the Prison*. Trans. Alan Sheridan. New York: Pantheon.

Foucault, Michel. 1978. *The History of Sexuality*. Vol. 1. Trans. Robert Hurley. New York: Vintage.

Foucault, Michel. 1989. *The Archaeology of Knowledge*. Trans. A. M. Sheridan Smith. London: Routledge.

Foucault, Michel. 2003. *"Society Must Be Defended": Lectures at the Collège de France, 1975–1976*. Trans. David Macey. New York: Picador.

Foucault, Michel. 2007. *Security, Territory, Population: Lectures at the Collège de France, 1977–1978*. Trans. Graham Burchell. New York: Picador.

Foucault, Michel. 2010. *The Birth of Biopolitics: Lectures at the Collège de France, 1978–1979.* Trans. Graham Burchell. New York: Picador.
Freedberg, David, and Vittorio Gallese. 2007. "Motion, Emotion, and Empathy in Esthetic Experience." *Trends in Cognitive Sciences* 11 (5): 197–203.
Gallese, Vittorio. 2003. "The Roots of Empathy: The Shared Manifold Hypothesis and the Neural Basis of Intersubjectivity." *Psychotherapy* 36: 171–80. doi:10.1159/000072786.
Gibbs, Nancy. 2002–3. "Double-Edged Sword." *Time,* December 30–January 6.
Gibson, James J. 2015. *The Ecological Approach to Visual Perception.* Classic edition. New York: Psychology Press.
Gil, José. 1998. *Metamorphoses of the Body.* Trans. Stephen Muecke. Minneapolis: University of Minnesota Press.
Goethe, Johann Wolfgang von. 1970. *Theory of Colours.* Trans. Charles Lock Eastlake. Cambridge, MA: MIT Press.
Grattan, Michelle, ed. 2000. *Essays on Australian Reconciliation.* Melbourne: Black.
Guardian Weekly. 1993. "Missiles Cannot Plug Holes in Evidence." July 4.
Guattari, Félix. 1995. *Chaosmosis: An Ethico-Aesthetic Paradigm.* Trans. Paul Bains and Julian Pefanis. Bloomington: Indiana University Press.
Guattari, Félix. 2014. *The Three Ecologies.* Trans. Ian Pindar and Paul Sutton. London: Bloomsbury.
Hafed, Zian M., and James J. Clark. 2002. "Microsaccades as an Overt Measure of Covert Attention Shifts." *Vision Research* 42: 2533–45.
Hallward, Peter. 2006. *Out of This World: Deleuze and the Philosophy of Creation.* London: Verso.
Haraway, Donna. 2007. *When Species Meet.* Minneapolis: University of Minnesota.
Haraway, Donna. 2016. *Staying with the Trouble: Making Kin in the Cthulucene.* Durham, NC: Duke University Press.
Hardt, Michael. 1995. "The Withering of Civil Society." *Social Text,* no. 45: 27–44.
Hardt, Michael, and Antonio Negri. 1994. *Labor of Dionysus: A Critique of the State-Form.* Minneapolis: University of Minnesota Press.
Hardt, Michael, and Antonio Negri. 2000. *Empire.* Cambridge, MA: Harvard University Press, 2000.
Hayles, N. Katherine. 1999. *How We Became Posthuman: Virtual Bodies in Cybernetics, Literature, and Informatics.* Chicago: University of Chicago Press.
Improbable Research. 2016. "The 2016 Ig Nobel Prize Winners." Accessed January 8, 2017. http://www.improbable.com/ig/winners/#ig2016.
James, William. 1950. *Principles of Psychology.* Vol. 2. New York: Dover.
James, William. 1996a. *Essays in Radical Empiricism.* Lincoln: University of Nebraska Press.
James, William. 1996b. *A Pluralistic Universe.* Lincoln: University of Nebraska Press.
Jameson, Fredric. 1991. *Postmodernism, or The Cultural Logic of Late Capitalism.* Durham, NC: Duke University Press.
Johnson, Mary. 2005. "After Terri Schiavo: Why the Disability Rights Movement Spoke Out, Why Some of Us Worried, and Where Do We Go from Here?"

Ragged Edge Online, April 2. http://www.raggededgemagazine.com/focus/postschiavoo0405.html.

Johnson, Vivien. 1997. *Michael Jagamarra Nelson*. Sydney: Craftsman House.

Kaufman, Lloyd. 1979. *Perception: The World Transformed*. Oxford: Oxford University Press.

Kirksey, Eben, ed. 2014. *The Multispecies Salon*. Durham, NC: Duke University Press.

Kohn, Eduardo. 2013. *How Forests Think: Toward an Anthropology beyond the Human*. Berkeley: University of California Press.

Kugler, Sara. 2002. "Bone Fragments Discovered in Rooftops Near Trade Center Site." *USA Today*, August 30.

Lacan, Jacques. 1981. *The Four Fundamental Concepts of Psychoanalysis*. Trans. Alan Sheridan. New York: Norton.

Lapoujade, David. 1995. "Le flux intensif de la conscience chez William James." *Philosophie* 46: 55–76.

Lapoujade, David. 2018. *Powers of Time: Versions of Bergson*. Trans. Andrew Goffey. Minneapolis: University of Minnesota Press.

Latour, Bruno. 1993. *We Have Never Been Modern*. Trans. Catherine Porter. Cambridge, MA: Harvard University Press.

Le Corbusier and Amadée Ozenfant. 1920. "Purism." In *Modern Artists on Art*, ed. Robert L. Herbert, 58–73. Englewood Cliffs, NJ: Prentice-Hall.

Leibniz, Gottfried Wilhelm von. 1995. *Philosophical Writings*. Ed. G. H. R. Parkinson. London: Everyman Library.

Libet, Benjamin. 1985. "Unconscious Cerebral Initiative and the Role of Conscious Will in Voluntary Action." *Behavior and Brain Sciences* 8: 529–66.

Libet, Benjamin, Anthony Freeman, and Keith Sutherland, eds. 1999. *The Volitional Brain: Towards a Neuroscience of Free Will*. Exeter, UK: Imprint Academic.

Lovelock, James. 2016. *Gaia: A New Look at Life on Earth*. 2nd reprint edition. Oxford: Oxford University Press.

Luhmann, Niklas. 1990. *Essays in Self-Reference*. New York: Columbia University Press.

Lynn, Greg. 1999. *Animate Form*. Princeton, NJ: Princeton Architectural Press.

Manning, Erin. 2009. *Relationscapes: Movement, Art, Philosophy*. Cambridge, MA: MIT Press.

Manning, Erin. 2013. *Always More Than One: Individuation's Dance*. Durham, NC: Duke University Press.

Manning, Erin. 2016. *The Minor Gesture*. Durham, NC: Duke University Press.

Manning, Erin. 2020. *For a Pragmatics of the Useless*. Durham, NC: Duke University Press.

Manning, Erin, and Brian Massumi. 2014. *Thought in the Act: Passages in the Ecology of Experience*. Minneapolis: University of Minnesota Press.

Manning, Erin, Anna Munster, and Bodil Marie Stavning Thomsen, eds. 2019. *Immediation I and II*. London: Open Humanities Press.

Marcus, Ruth. 2020. "Trump Wants to Be King: Did John Yoo Just Hand Him the Crown?" *Washington Post*, July 21. https://www.washingtonpost.com/opinions/trump-wants-to-be-king-did-john-yoo-just-hand-him-the-crown/2020/07/21/a9a896fe-cb7e-11ea-bc6a-6841b28d9093_story.html.

Margulis, Lynn, and Dorion Sagan. 1997. *Slanted Truths: Essays on Gaia, Symbiosis and Evolution*. New York: Copernicus.

Martin, Jean-Clet. 1990. *Variations*. Paris: Payot.

Massumi, Brian, ed. 1993. *The Politics of Everyday Fear*. Minneapolis: University of Minnesota Press.

Massumi, Brian. 2002. *Parables for the Virtual: Movement, Affect, Sensation*. Durham, NC: Duke University Press.

Massumi, Brian. 2011. *Semblance and Event: Activist Philosophy and the Occurrent Arts*. Cambridge, MA: MIT Press.

Massumi, Brian. 2014. *What Animals Teach Us about Politics*. Durham, NC: Duke University Press.

Massumi, Brian. 2015a. *Ontopower: War, Powers, and the State of Perception*. Durham, NC: Duke University Press.

Massumi, Brian. 2015b. *Politics of Affect*. London: Polity.

Massumi, Brian. 2015c. *The Power at the End of the Economy*. Durham, NC: Duke University Press.

Massumi, Brian. 2016. "Such as It Is: A Short Essay in Extreme Realism." *Body and Society* 22 (1): 115–27.

Massumi, Brian. 2017a. *The Principle of Unrest: Activist Philosophy in the Expanded Field*. London: Open Humanities Press.

Massumi, Brian. 2017b. "Virtual Ecology and the Question of Value." In *General Ecology: The New Ecological Paradigm*, ed. Erich Hörl, 345–73. London: Bloomsbury.

Massumi, Brian. 2018. *99 Theses for the Revaluation of Value*. Minneapolis: University of Minneapolis Press.

Massumi, Brian. 2019. "Immediation Unlimited." In *Immediation II*, ed. Erin Manning, Anna Munster, and Bodil Marie Stavning Thomsen, 501–43. London: Open Humanities Press.

Massumi, Brian. 2020. "The American Virus." In "The Quarantine Files: Thinkers in Self-Isolation." *Los Angeles Review of Books*, April 14. https://lareviewofbooks.org/article/quarantine-files-thinkers-self-isolation/.

Maurer, Daphne, Laura C. Gibson, and Ferrine Spector. 2014. "Synaesthesia in Infants and Very Young Children." In *The Oxford Handbook of Synaesthesia*, ed. Julia Simner and Edward M. Hubbard, 46–53. Oxford: Oxford University Press.

McFadden, Robert D. 2001. "President, in New York, Offers Resolute Vows atop the Rubble." *New York Times*, September 15. https://timesmachine.nytimes.com/timesmachine/2001/09/15/198498.html?pageNumber=1.

Meillassoux, Quentin. 2010. *After Finitude: An Essay on the Necessity of Contingency*. Trans. Ray Brassier. London: Bloomsbury.

Merleau-Ponty, Maurice. 1964. *The Primacy of Perception*. Trans. James Edie. Evanston, IL: Northwestern University Press.

Merleau-Ponty, Maurice. 1968. *The Visible and the Invisible*. Trans. Alphonso Lingis. Evanston, IL: Northwestern University Press.

Michotte, Albert, Georges Thinès, and Geneviève Crabbé. 1991. "Amodal Completion of Perceptual Structures." In *Michotte's Experimental Phenomenology of*

Perception, ed. Georges Thinès, Alan Costall, and George Butterworth, 140–67. London: Routledge.

Miller, Mark Crispin. 2002. *The Bush Dyslexicon: Observations on a National Disorder.* New York: Norton, 2002.

Mitchell, Alison. 2000. "The 2000 Campaign: The Texas Governor; Bush Says That the Bottom Line on Gore's Proposals Would Consume the Surplus." *New York Times*, September 7. https://www.nytimes.com/2000/09/07/us/2000-campaign-texas-governor-bush-says-that-bottom-line-gore-s-proposals-would.html.

Moore, Martha T. 2004. "WTC Families Want Remains out of Landfill: They're Fighting to Get Debris Buried So Loved Ones Don't Spend Eternity Buried in Trash." *USA Today*, October 6.

Morrow, Lance. 2003. "The Right to Wear T-Shirts." *Time*, March 17.

Murphie, Andrew. 2010. "Deleuze, Guattari and Neuroscience." In *Deleuze, Science and the Force of the Virtual*, ed. Peter Gaffney, 277–99. Minneapolis: University of Minnesota Press.

Nagel, Thomas. 1974. "What Is It Like to Be a Bat?" *Philosophical Review* 4 (48): 435–50.

Nathan, Tobie. 1996. *Fiers de n'avoir ni pays, ni amis, quelle sottise c'était*. Paris: La Pensée Sauvage.

Nelson, Michael Tjakamarra. 2000. "I Am an Artist, Not a Politician." In *The Oxford Companion to Aboriginal Culture*, ed. Sylvia Klenert and Margo Neale, 482–83. Oxford: Oxford University Press.

Newsweek. 1993. "A New World for Spies." July 5.

New Yorker. 2001. "Tuesday and After: New York Writers Respond to 9/11." September 17. https://www.newyorker.com/magazine/2001/09/24/tuesday-and-after-talk-of-the-town.

New York Times. 1992. "The 1992 Campaign: Verbatim; Heckler Stirs Clinton Anger: Excerpts from the Exchange." March 28. https://www.nytimes.com/1992/03/28/us/1992-campaign-verbatim-heckler-stirs-clinton-anger-excerpts-exchange.html.

New York Times. 2002. "Full Transcript: Bush's National Security Strategy." September 20. https://www.nytimes.com/2002/09/20/politics/full-text-bushs-national-security-strategy.html.

Nietzsche, Friedrich. 1967. *The Will to Power*. Ed. and trans. Walter Kaufmann. New York: Vintage Books.

Nietzsche, Friedrich. 1997. *Untimely Meditations*. Trans. R. J. Hollingdale. Cambridge: Cambridge University Press.

Nietzsche, Friedrich. 2003. *Writings from the Late Notebooks*. Trans. Kate Sturge. Ed. Rudiger Bittner. Cambridge: Cambridge University Press.

Nietzsche, Friedrich. 2006. *Thus Spoke Zarathustra*. Trans. Adrian Del Caro. Cambridge: Cambridge University Press.

O'Craven, K. M., and N. Kanwisher. 2000. "Mental Imagery of Faces and Places Activates Corresponding Stimulus-Specific Brain Regions." *Journal of Cognitive Neuroscience* 12 (6): 1013–23.

Oettermann, Stephan. 1997. *The Panorama: History of a Mass Medium*. Trans. Deborah Lucas Schneider. New York: Zone Books.

O'Regan, J. Kevin, and Alva Noë. 2001. "A Sensorimotor Account of Vision and Visual Consciousness." *Behavioral and Brain Sciences* 24: 939–1031.

Parrhesia: A Journal of Critical Philosophy. 2009. Special issue, "On Gilbert Simondon," no. 7.

Peirce, C. S. 1931. *The Collected Papers of Charles Sanders Peirce*. Vols. 1–2. Ed. Charles Hartshorne and Paul Weiss. Cambridge, MA: Harvard University Press.

Peirce, C. S. 1935. *The Collected Papers of Charles Sanders Peirce*. Vol. 6. Ed. Charles Hartshorne and Paul Weiss. Cambridge, MA: Harvard University Press.

Peirce, C. S. 1992a. *The Essential Peirce: Selected Philosophical Writings*. Vol. 1. Ed. Nathan Houser and Christian Kloesel. Bloomington: University of Indiana Press.

Peirce, C. S. 1992b. *Reasoning and the Logic of Things*. Ed. Kenneth Laine Ketner. Cambridge, MA: Harvard University Press.

Peirce, C. S. 1998. *The Essential Peirce: Selected Philosophical Writings*. Vol. 2. Ed. The Peirce Edition Project. Bloomington: University of Indiana Press.

Preston, Peter. 2003. "The Return of Mr. Unspecified-Threat." *Guardian*, May 26. https://www.theguardian.com/politics/2003/may/26/terrorism.britainand911.

Prigogine, Ilya, and Isabelle Stengers. 1984. *Order out of Chaos*. New York: Bantam.

Prigogine, Ilya, and Isabelle Stengers. 1988. *Entre le temps et l'éternité*. Paris: Fayard.

Pyle, Richard. 2001. "WTC Victims Might Have Vaporized." *Montreal Gazette*, December 5.

Ramachandran, V. S., and Sandra Blakeslee. 1998. *Phantoms on the Brain: Probing the Mysteries of the Human Mind*. New York: Morrow.

Reagan, Ronald. 1983. "How to Stay Fit: The President's Personal Exercise Program." *Washington Post, Parade Magazine* supplement, December 4.

Reagan, Ronald. 1988. Farewell Address at the Republican National Convention. August 15. Accessed May 15, 2020. https://millercenter.org/the-presidency/presidential-speeches/august-15-1988-farewell-address-republican-national-convention.

Reeder, Elizabeth, dir. 2004. *George W. Bushisms*. St. Clair Entertainment. DVD.

Rizzolatti, Giacomo, and Corrado Sinigaglia. 2008. *Mirrors in the Brain: How Our Minds Share Actions and Emotions*. Oxford: Oxford University Press.

Rucker, Philip, and Felicia Sonmez. 2020. "Trump Defends Bungled Handling of Coronavirus with Falsehoods and Dubious Claims." *Washington Post*, July 19. https://www.washingtonpost.com/politics/trump-defends-bungled-handling-of-coronavirus-with-falsehoods-and-dubious-claims/2020/07/19/1b57cb3e-c9e6-11ea-91f1-28aca4d833a0_story.html.

Rumsfeld, Donald. 2001. US Department of Defense News Briefing with Secretary of Defense Donald Rumsfeld and Chairman of the Joint Chiefs of Staff General Richard B. Myers. October 12. Accessed June 14, 2020. http://www.defenselink.mil/transcripts/transcript.aspx?transcriptid=2068.

Rumsfeld, Donald. 2002a. U.S. Defense Department Briefing with Chairman of the Joint Chiefs of Staff General Richard Myers. February 12. Accessed November 15, 2005. http://www.defenselink.mil/ transcripts/2002/t02122002_t212sdv2.html.

Rumsfeld, Donald. 2002b. U.S. Department of Defense News Briefing on Defense Strategy for the "War on Terrorism," with Vice Chairman of the Joint Chiefs of Staff General Peter Pace. May 1. Accessed November 15, 2005. http://www.defenselink.mil/transcripts/2002/t05012002_t0501sd.html.

Rumsfeld, Donald. 2002c. U.S. Department of Defense News Briefing with Secretary Rumsfeld and General Pace. October 7. Accessed November 15, 2005. http://www.defenselink.mil/transcripts/2002/t10072002_t1007asd.html.

Rumsfeld, Donald. 2003a. Department of Defense News Briefing with Chairman of the Joint Chiefs of Staff General Richard Myers. February 28. Accessed November 15, 2005. http://www.defenselink.mil/transcripts/2003/t02282003_t0228sd.html.

Rumsfeld, Donald. 2003b. U.S. Secretary of Defense Senate Briefing on the Iraq War. July 30. Accessed November 15, 2005. http://www.defenselink.mil/transcripts/2003/tr20030730-secdef0482.html.

Rumsfeld, Donald. 2005. Department of Defense News Briefing with Chairman of the Joint Chiefs of Staff Gen. Richard Myers and Commander, U.S. Central Command, Gen. John Abizaid. May 18. Accessed November 15, 2005. http://www.defenselink.mil/transcripts/2005/tr20050518-secdef2861.html.

Ruyer, Raymond. 1948. *Le monde des valeurs*. Paris: Aubier.

Ruyer, Raymond. 1950. *La conscience et le corps*. Paris: PUF.

Ruyer, Raymond. 2016. *Neofinalism*. Trans. Alyosha Edlebi. Minneapolis: University of Minnesota Press.

Ruyer, Raymond. 2019. *The Genesis of Living Forms*. Trans. Jon Roffe and Nicholas B. de Wedenthal. London: Rowman and Littlefield.

Ryle, Gilbert. 1949. *The Concept of Mind*. New York: Barnes and Noble.

Sassen, Saskia. 2000. "Geographies and Countergeographies of Globalization." In *Anymore*, ed. Cynthia C. Davidson, 110–19. Cambridge, MA: MIT Press.

Schilder, Paul. 1950. *The Image and Appearance of the Human Body*. New York: International Universities Press.

Schmitt, Carl. 2007. *The Concept of the Political*. Expanded edition. Trans. George Schwab. Chicago: University of Chicago Press.

Schmitz, Hermann. 2016. "Atmospheric Spaces." *Ambiances* (April). https://journals.openedition.org/ambiances/711.

Schmitz, Hermann, Rudolf Owen Müllen, and Jan Slaby. 2011. "Emotions outside the Box: The New Phenomenology of Feeling and Corporeality." *Phenomenological Cognitive Science* 10: 241–59.

Scott, Ridley, dir. 1982. *Blade Runner*. Burbank, CA: Warner Bros. Film.

Seely, Hart. 2003. "The Poetry of D. H. Rumsfeld: Recent Works by the Secretary of Defense." *Slate*, April 2. https://slate.com/news-and-politics/2003/04/the-poetry-of-donald-rumsfeld.html.

Senior, Jennifer. 2002. "The Memorial Warriors." *New York Magazine* 35 (31): 26–29.

SenseLab. 2016. *The Go-To How-To Guide to Anarchiving*. Ed. Andrew Murphie. Lulu.com.

Shanker, Thom. 2002. "Traces of Terror: Rumsfeld's Search for a Way to Fight a New Type of Foe." *New York Times*, September 4. https://www.nytimes.com/2002/09/04/world/traces-of-terror-rumsfeld-s-search-for-a-way-to-fight-a-new-type-of-foe.html?searchResultPosition=1.

Simondon, Gilbert. 1964. *L'individu et sa genèse physico-biologique*. Paris: PUF.

Simondon, Gilbert. 1992. *Individuation psychique et collective: À la lumière de forme, information, potentiel et métastabilité*. Paris: Aubier.

Simondon, Gilbert. 2005. *L'individuation à la lumière des notions de forme et de l'information*. Grenoble: Million.

Simondon, Gilbert. 2009. "Technical Mentality." Trans. Arne de Boever. *Parrhesia* 7: 17–27.

Simondon, Gilbert. 2017. *On the Mode of Existence of Technical Objects*. Trans. Cecile Malaspina and John Rogove. Minneapolis: Univocal Press/University of Minnesota Press.

Simondon, Gilbert. 2020. *Individuation in Light of Notions of Form and Information*. Vol. 1. Trans. Tayler Adkins. Minneapolis: University of Minnesota Press.

Souriau, Étienne. 2015. *The Different Modes of Existence*. Trans. Eric Berenak and Tim Howles. Minneapolis, MN: Univocal.

Spuybroek, Lars. 2000a. Interview. In *Book for the Electronic Arts*, ed. Arjen Mulder and Maaike Post, 120–29. Rotterdam: V2_Organisation/de Balie.

Spuybroek, Lars. 2000b. Interview with Arielle Pelenc. In *Vision Machine* (catalogue), ed. Arielle Pelenc. Nantes: Musée des Beaux-Arts.

Spuybroek, Lars. 2001a. "Architecture of Interaction: An Informational Form." Interview with Im Sik Cho. ANC (*Architecture and Culture*) 244 (September): 111.

Spuybroek, Lars. 2001b. "Machining Architecture." In *The Weight of the Image: 4th International NAI Summer Master Class, 15–28 August 1999*, ed. Lars Spubroek and Bob Lang, n.p. Rotterdam: NAI.

Spuybroek, Lars. 2004. *NOX: Machining Architecture*. London: Thames and Hudson.

Spuybroek, Lars. 2016. *The Sympathy of Things: Ruskin and the Ecology of Design*. Revised and expanded edition. London: Bloomsbury.

Stengers, Isabelle. 2010–11. *Cosmopolitics I and II*. Trans. Robert Bononno. Minneapolis: University of Minnesota Press.

Stengers, Isabelle. 2015. *In Catastrophic Times: Resisting the Coming Barbarity*. Trans. Andrew Goffey. London: Open Humanities Press.

Stengers, Isabelle, and Tobie Nathan, eds. 2002. "Propositions de paix." Special issue, *Ethnopsy: Les mondes contemporains de la guérison*, no. 4 (April).

Stengers, Isabelle, and Ilya Prigogine. 1986. *La nouvelle alliance*. Paris: Gallimard.

Stern, Daniel. 1985. *The Interpersonal World of the Infant*. New York: Basic Books.

Sunday Times. 2005. "The Secret Downing Street Memo (July 23, 2002)." May 5. https://web.archive.org/web/20110723222004/http://www.timesonline.co.uk/tol/news/uk/article387374.ece.

Suskind, Ron. 2004. "Faith, Certainty and the Presidency of George W. Bush." *New York Times Magazine*, October 17. https://www.nytimes.com/2004/10/17/magazine/faith-certainty-and-the-presidency-of-george-w-bush.html.

Tarde, Gabriel. 1880. "La croyance et le désir." *Revue Philosophique de la France et de l'Étranger* 10 (July–December): 150–80.

Tarde, Gabriel. 1903. *The Laws of Imitation*. Trans. Elsie Clews Parsons. New York: Henry Holt.

Tarde, Gabriel. 2012. *Monadology and Sociology*. Trans. Theo Lorenc. Melbourne: Re.press.

Taussig, Michael. 1997. *The Magic of the State*. London: Routledge.

Thomas, Evan. 2004. "'I Haven't Suffered Doubt.'" *Time*, April 20.

Thwaites, Thomas. 2016. *GoatMan: How I Took a Holiday from Being Human*. Princeton, NJ: Princeton Architectural Press.

Time. 1993. "The Incredible Shrinking President." June 7.

Tinbergen, Niko. 1951. *The Study of Instinct*. Oxford: Oxford University Press.

Tinbergen, Niko. 1965. *Animal Behavior*. New York: Time-Life Books.

Tinbergen, Niko, and A. C. Perdeck. 1950. "On the Stimulus Situation Releasing the Begging Response in the Newly Hatched Herring Gull Chick." *Behavior* 3 (1): 1–39.

Tsing, Anna Lowenhaupt. 2015. *The Mushroom at the End of the World: On the Possibility of Life in the Capitalist Ruins*. Princeton, NJ: Princeton University Press.

Ulick, Josh. 2005. "Barely There." In Arian Campo-Flores, "The Legacy of Terri Schiavo," *Time*, Canadian edition, April 4.

Virilio, Paul. 1976. *L'insécurité du territoire*. Paris: Stock.

Virilio, Paul. 1987. "The Overexposed City." Trans. Astrid Hustvedt. *Zone*, nos. 1–2: 15–31.

Viveiros de Castro, Eduardo. 2004. "Exchanging Perspectives: The Transformation of Objects into Subjects in Amerindian Ontologies." *Common Knowledge* 10 (3): 463–84.

Vološinov, V. N. 1986. *Marxism and the Philosophy of Language*. Trans. Ladslav Matejka and I. R. Titunik. Cambridge, MA: Harvard University Press.

Webster's Ninth New Collegiate Dictionary. 1983. Springfield, MA: Merriam-Webster.

Weiner, James F. 1999. "Culture in a Sealed Envelope: The Concealment of Australian Aboriginal Heritage and Tradition in the Hindmarsh Bridge Affair." *Journal of the Royal Anthropological Institute* 5 (2): 193–210.

Weiner, James F. 2001. "Strangelove's Dilemma: Or, What Kind of Secrecy Do the Ngarrindjeri Practice?" In *Emplaced Myth: Space, Narrative, and Knowledge in Aboriginal Australia and Papua New Guinea*, ed. Alan Rumsey and James F. Weiner, 139–60. Honolulu: University of Hawai'i Press.

Weisberg, Jacob. 2002. *George W. Bushisms*. New York: Fireside.

Weisberg, Jacob. 2003. *Still More George W. Bushisms*. New York: Fireside.

Weisberg, Jacob. 2005. *George W. Bushisms V*. New York: Fireside.

Weisberg, Jacob. 2007. *The Ultimate George W. Bushisms*. New York: Fireside.

Weisberg, Jacob. 2009. "The Complete Bushisms." *Slate*, March 20. http://www.slate.com/articles/news_and_politics/bushisms/2000/03/the_complete_bushisms.html.

Westphal, Jonathan. 1987. *Colour: Some Philosophical Problems from Wittgenstein*. Aristotelian Society Series, vol. 7. Oxford: Basil Blackwell.

Whitehead, Alfred North. 1920. *Concept of Nature*. Cambridge: Cambridge University Press.

Whitehead, Alfred North. 1967a. *Adventures of Ideas*. New York: Free Press.

Whitehead, Alfred North. 1967b. *Science in the Modern World*. New York: Free Press.

Whitehead, Alfred North. 1968. *Modes of Thought*. New York: Free Press.

Whitehead, Alfred North. 1978. *Process and Reality*. New York: Free Press.

Whitehead, Alfred North. 1985. *Symbolism: Its Meaning and Effect*. New York: Fordham University Press.

Wittgenstein, Ludwig. 1978. *Remarks on Colour*. Trans. Lindal L. McAlister and Margarate Schättle. Oxford: Basil Blackwell.

Wolffe, Richard. 2020. "Don't Call It a Comeback: Trump's Tulsa Rally Was Just Another Sad Farce." *Guardian*, June 21. https://www.theguardian.com/commentisfree/2020/jun/20/donald-trump-tulsa-rally-crowd-empty-seats.

Woodward, Bob. 2002. *Bush at War*. New York: Simon and Schuster.

Woodward, Bob. 2004. *Plan of Attack*. New York: Simon and Schuster.

World Wildlife Fund and London Zoological Society. 2016. *Living Planet Report 2016: Risk and Resilience in a New Era*. Gland, Switzerland: WWF.

INDEX

Aboriginal Australians, 39–40, 46–47, 48–50, 52, 53, 54, 55–56; land rights movement, 35–36, 50; and secret, 42, 49

Abram, David, 90–91

absence, 274, 282, 291; near, 232, 324; and pure negation, 266. *See also* barely-there

absolute origin, 107, 109, 110, 111, 113, 114, 116, 117, 118. *See also* synergy; technical mentality; technical object

absolute surface, 441n18, 442n21. *See also* abstract surface

abstraction, 64, 86, 108, 153, 163, 165, 172, 312, 335, 336–37, 348, 371; and activity, 186–87; and actual, 159; and animality, 132; becoming as, 82; and body, 105, 340; and capitalism, 311; and concrete, 152, 157; and expression, 92; and flow, 19; and force, 172; and form, 109; and limit, 373; and literarity, 89; and map, 332; and material, 152; and model, 106; and nonsensuous, 199; of outcome, 64; and perception, 168; potential as, 22; and reality, 89; and schema, 335, 370; and space, 135–37, 331; and thinking-feeling, 199; and virtual, 135; and vision, 335; and worlding, 186; and writing, 82. *See also* abstract surface; concreteness

abstract surface, 140, 146; hyperabstract surface, 157; and light, 149; of movement, 148. *See also* absolute surface; abstraction

academia, 410–11, 413, 418–19, 423; and research-creation, 421

accident, 70, 325, 364, 441n21; and art, 399; of attention, 145, 146, 147; and instinct, 122, 124–26; and mapping, 330–31, 332; and virtual, 68–69

action, 155, 183, 197, 200, 225, 271, 381; action path, 265; and atmosphere, 203; and becoming, 316; and composition, 353; and expression, 316; and habit, 66; incipient, 87, 180; and knowledge, 199; and landing site, 388; and perception, 67, 165, 166, 168; pre-action, 217; social, 58; standardized, 20; and thought, 65, 66, 67; traditional, 225. *See also* activity

action-perception, 178, 181, 183, 185–86. *See also* action; perception

activation contour, 83. *See also* vitality affect

activity, 115, 183, 269, 350; antecedent, 7; emergent, 380; indeterminate, 225; intensive, 174; nonconscious, 379; and pattern, 196; and process, 197; pure, 247, 270; and stasis, 379. *See also* action

actual, 2, 4, 66, 69, 70, 95–96, 117, 152, 246, 407, 446n4; and abstract, 159, 371; anticipation of, 216–17, 380; and movement, 159, 162, 165, 170–71, 188, 205, 353, 379; and potential, 64, 156, 159, 206; and proposition, 415, 418; suspension of, 217; and thought, 213–15; and virtual, 94, 135, 145, 146, 147, 149, 151, 153, 157, 195, 213–15, 227, 256, 350

actual entity, 6, 13, 224, 434n16, 445n1, 446n3

actualization, 57, 69, 88, 101, 157, 168, 170, 213–15; co-actualization, 243; and movement, 165, 215, 366. *See also* absolute origin; catalysis; induction; synergy

adaptation, 125, 305; and capitalism, 302; counteradaptation, 319; cultural, 54; and evolution, 131; and life, 57

additivity, 14, 303, 306

advertising, 306, 393–96

aesthetic, 74, 138, 344; and atmosphere, 204; and becoming-literary, 88; and instinct, 119; and nature, 120; and the political, 317; and resistance, 320; and value, 74. *See also* aesthetic yield; ethico-aesthetic paradigm

aesthetic yield, 127–28

affect, 74, 88, 247, 251, 268, 291, 295, 312, 314, 316; affective circuit, 277; affective conversion, 279, 282, 322; affective distance, 90; affective involvement, 192;

462 INDEX

affect (continued)
affective legitimation, 278, 282, 297, 299, 302, 313, 314; affective modality, 117; affective propulsion, 127; affectscape, 91, 93; and autonomy, 313; and belonging, 59; collective, 274; and concept, 312; and decision, 221, 239; and emotion, 192, 274; and impersonality, 313; integral of, 87, 89; and limit, 240; and media, 294; and performative, 267; and the political, 317–20; and politics, 315–20; and power, 313, 315–22; and relation, 32; and social field, 42–43; and subjectification, 304; and violence, 293, 301. See also affectability; emotion; intensity; sympathy; vitality affect

affectability, 251, 272, 281; and facialization, 277; and image, 259, 263; and legitimation, 260; and literary, 87–88; and ontopower, 247, 258; and vanishing point, 244. See also ontopower; power: and affect; power: and the political; singular point; surplus-value: of emotion

affective attunement, 259, 315, 319, 320. See also affect: and the political

affective tone, 188, 271, 274, 284; and conformation, 197, 198–99; and proposition, 206, 414; as relatum, 195; and subjective form, 194, 200–201, 206. See also affect; affectability; atmosphere; emotional tone

affirmation, 7, 184, 316, 418; and negation, 9; and resistance, 320

affordance, 230; and affect, 316, 390; and landing site, 101, 388–89, 391; and urban art, 392, 396. See also landing site

afterimage, 264, 267, 279, 282, 286. See also image

Agamben, Giorgio: on state of exception, 237, 238

agitation, 224, 244, 284; and affectability, 251, 263; and life, 241; and surplus-value of emotion, 266. See also bare activity; barely-there

aim, 180; and proposition, 415–17, 419, 420, 422, 446n4. See also cue; lure; occasion; proposition

allagmatic, 97, 113. See also axiomatic; concept

Alliez, Eric, and Michel Feher, 18

ambiguity, 150, 219, 242, 413; and atmosphere, 194. See also indeterminacy; vagueness

amodal completion, 178, 253–59, 265–71, 275–79, 333–34. See also saccade

amodal perception, 333–34. See also amodal completion; saccade

analogical gap, 138–39, 141, 144, 151. See also architecture; constraint; topology: and architecture

analogue, 151, 170, 175, 246, 251–52, 269, 276, 364–65, 368–69; operative, 116–17, 170, 245–46; process as, 138, singularity as, 251–52; and virtual, 97. See also analogical gap

anarchive, 421, 423, 426; and minor gesture, 425. See also documentation; immediation; seeding

animal, 17, 72, 91, 131; and adaptation, 126; and art, 120, 128; elemental, 86; and evolution, 92; and human, 73, 76–78, 89, 128, 132; and improvisation, 125; and instinct, 119–21; and language, 92; and personhood, 81, 83; and play, 429n14; and the political, 320; and predation, 86, 90–91, 93; and sympathy, 129; and world, 77. See also becoming; becoming-animal; instinct; supernormal tendency

anticipation, 65, 110, 116, 162, 255, 290; and amodal completion, 268; and bow wave, 222–23; and habit, 334; and landing site, 388; and movement, 215; and novelty, 111; and perception, 214; and readiness, 212, 213, 220, 228, 230; and reflexive pullback, 220–22; and repetition, 112; and vision, 254. See also preemption; readiness potential

appearance, 85, 267, 268, 276, 279, 281; and background, 354; and reality, 184, 207; and vision, 254

appetition, 128–30, 210, 351–52, 419, 422, 423; and empathy, 221; and subjectivity, 351–52. See also belief; desire; kinesthesia; landing site; lure; proposition; sympathy; terminus

Arakawa, Shusaku, and Madeline Gins, 101, 161, 173, 175, 388

arbitrarity, 137–39, 140, 397. See also chance; constraint

architecture, 134, 158–59, 170, 172, 376; and abstraction, 170; and accident, 149; and complicity, 141; and deformation, 150; and design, 99; and disciplinarity, 102; and encounter, 100; and form, 136, 142; and gravity, 166; and landing site, 101; and philosophy, 152; and process, 99, 139–40, 143, 151; proto-, 173, 175; relational, 156; and time, 97; and urbanism, 101; and virtual, 100, 135, 149, 157. See also design; topology

INDEX

art, 127–28, 158; and abstraction, 170; and atmosphere, 204; Baroque, 140; and experience, 347, 390; minor, 22; and parasite, 391; and pure artist, 137–39; as simulation, 21; and synesthesia, 357; and world, 139. *See also* artfulness; urban art

artfulness, 345; and animality, 120; and difference, 88; of experience, 347–48, 357. *See also* art; becoming; neurodiversity; synesthesia

artifice, 79, 91, 93; and invention, 126, 429n13; literary, 82, 87–88, 92. *See also* power of the false; writing

assemblage, 23, 74, 429n9, 433n4

asymmetry: and becoming, 80, 82, 90–91; and belonging, 27, 29–31, 44, 92. *See also* becoming; sociality

atmosphere, 188, 192–94, 196–97, 204, 207; and background, 203; and object, 207; and personality, 206; and phenomenology, 189; and potential, 198; and reality, 207; and subjectivity, 189; and truth, 194; and untimeliness, 206; and vitality affect, 202

attention, 27, 168, 188, 223, 260, 396; and amodal completion, 178–79, 256–57; and confound, 146–47, 149; and media, 313; and ontopower, 247; and operative reason, 65; and proposition, 414, 417, 419; and sensation, 67, 68; and vanishing point, 244–46

attraction, 121, 160, 163, 283, 379; supernormal, 122; and terminus, 180, 185

Austin, J. L., 33

automatism, 28, 30, 241, 288, 295; and gut decision, 239; and habit, 66–67, 442n4; and instinct, 119–21, 126–27, 430n2; and self-conditioning, 106–7, 110. *See also* autonomy; habit

autonomy: of affect, 313; of apparatus of power, 296, 301, 302, 308–11; of design process, 137–39, 144, 151; operative, 106–8, 110, 113, 116; relational, 101; and supernormal tendency, bodily, 28–29, 126–27, 241–42; of technical object, 112. *See also* absolute origin; autopoiesis; intuition; operative solidarity; synergy

autopoiesis, 152, 311, 312, 439n16

axiomatic: and capitalist critique, 311–12, 439n15; and psychic individuation, 113

background: atmosphere as, 188, 189, 190, 202, 203, 204; and experience, 190–92, 196–97, 200, 348–49, 354, 432; and figure, 92, 121, 123, 256, 281, 329, 334, 336, 365; foregrounding and backgrounding, 347, 387, 394, 397, 415, 420. *See also* atmosphere

Baker, J. A., 78, 82–83, 90–93

bare activity, 129, 226; and governance, 224, 225, 230. *See also* affectability; agitation; ontopower

barely-there, 232, 240, 242, 251, 252, 258, 260, 263, 271, 275. *See also* agitation; bare activity; image; ontopower; vanishing point

basic fact: and affective tone, 194, 196; and relation, 193; and subjectivity, 189, 190, 191. *See also* atmosphere; inheritance; relation; subjectivity

Bateson, Gregory, 114, 115

Baudrillard, Jean, 15–16, 18, 23–24, 287, 293, 304

becoming, 21, 58, 61, 76, 80, 83, 94, 117, 127–28, 149, 159, 184, 316; and actual-virtual, 94; and being of relation, 57; collective, 22, 61, 320; becoming-different, 93; and differential, 90; and distance, 91; elemental, 86; ethics of, 118; latitude of, 112; literary, 88; negative, 21; nonintentional, 93; and novelty, 22; becoming-other, 73, 79; and people to come, 60; positive, 22; problematic, 52; quantum of, 109; relational, 73–74; and sympathy, 93, 129; and thought, 408; trans-, 82, 92. *See also* becoming-animal; double becoming

becoming-animal, 75, 429n9; and art, 120, 128; and empathy, 76–77; and literarity, 78, 82, 89, 92; and more-than-human, 128, 132, 429n14; and sympathy, 93, 129; and third term, 90–91. *See also* becoming; ethico-aesthetic paradigm; heterogenesis

being: and becoming, 150; formed, 57, 58; and nonbeing, 9, 10

being of relation, 58–59

belief, 39, 41, 128, 410, 428n5; disbelief, 38; and effect, 38; and ideological content, 38, 41, 61, 281, 301, 410, 428n5; and life, 275; and minor, 61; and politics, 281; and pure feeling, 128–29; and sympathy, 129; and violence, 301

belonging, 30–31, 33, 43, 59–60, 128. *See also* asymmetry; preindividual: preindividual field; sociality

Bénard instability, 65

Bergson, Henri, 125, 130, 344, 350, 440n8; on art, 120; on critical point, 65; on duration, 332; on experience, 353; on instinct, 126; on light, 149, 157, 431n5; on pure past, 332; on sympathy, 129; on the possible, 115; on vibration, 443n8; on the virtual, 134

biopolitics, 233, 235, 236, 237, 240. *See also* power: biopower
Blade Runner (dir. Ridley Scott), 17
Blanchot, Maurice, 196
block of sensation, 127, 129–30. *See also* becoming; object
body, 275, 314, 333, 339, 341; and activity, 379; and affect, 313, 315, 319; and affective tone, 206; and architecture, 100; and artfulness, 357; and attention, 68; body-object, 339, 340; and building, 100, 101; and change, 357; as code, 312; collective, 245; and city, 388; and death, 263; and design, 79; and duration, 332; exemplary, 251–52, 275, 277; and experience, 328, 345; and expression, 317; and feeling, 374; as field, 374; and form, 101; frame of, 223; as ground, 404; and habit, 68; and identity, 21; and immanence, 217; and immediate experience, 340; and impression, 193; and installation, 170; and intensity, 374; and kinesthesia, 379; and landing site, 101, 161, 388; of the leader, 279; and life force, 22; and light, 149, 157; and locatability, 328; and matter, 247; as milieu, 368; and mirror-touch synesthesia, 343; modification, 78; and mood, 203; and movement, 215, 350, 352; and othering, 276; and phase-shift, 101; physiological vs. virtual body, 354; and potential, 374; and potential movement, 170; and power, 245–46; and power of existence, 315, 318; and previousness, 369; and primitive chaos, 351–52; and readiness, 178; and relation, 356–57; and relationality, 368–69; and relational power, 315; shape of, 373; and singular point, 245; and sovereignty, 235–36, 240; and space, 328, 360; of the state, 259, 260, 267; and subject, 343; as system, 361; and vagueness, 374; and variation, 355; and vertigo, 164; and vision, 255; and world, 329; and writing, 87
body image, 164; and amodal completion, 259, 268; and body-object, 339–40, 374; and exemplary body, 251, 274, 277. *See also* body
body politic, 246, 247, 269, 275; and affective attunement, 259, 260, 275–77; and amodal completion, 276, 277; and exemplary body, 249, 258
body-without-an-image, 339–40
Bruno, Giordano, 34
Buckley, Sandra, 27

building, 387; as affordance, 175, 389–90; and double capture, 99–100; as environmental constraint, 398; and potential, 166; as processual end-form, 142, 144–45, 151, 153, 173. *See also* architecture
Burroughs, William S., 140–41
Bush, George W., 211, 216–19, 220, 224–31, 234, 238–39, 251, 261–62, 265–71, 275–82, 298, 302, 438n7

Cache, Bernard, 169
Cage, John, 140–41
capitalism, 16, 302–14; and abstraction, 311; and deterritorialization, 23; and Donald Trump, 321–22; and labor, 307; and life, 268, 274, 301, 306; and patriotism, 268, 274; and personhood, 321; precapitalism, 303; as quasi-cause, 21; and reason, 73; and urbanity, 393
capture, 69; adaptational, 306; of attention, 244, 271; and capitalism, 305; and double capture, 98; politics as, 316; refusal of, 45; and sense of self, 351. *See also* capitalism; double capture; resistance
catalysis: of relation, 59–60; and sensation, 69, 151, 278; and topological architecture, 136–37, 150, 151, 155. *See also* absolute origin; intercessor
causality: vs. conditioning, 207; and invention, 106, 107, 111; and quasi-cause, 19. *See also* quasi-cause
chance: and design, 137, 150, 175, 377, 397; and performative, 58; and virtual, 69. *See also* arbitrarity
change, 69, 99, 153, 246, 341, 367; and absolute surface, 442n21; as constant, 95; and iteration, 95; and life, 224; and power, 316; qualitative, 155, 157; quantum, 109; and truth, 55; and virtual, 94–95, 97
chaos, 178; and body, 350–52; and capitalism, 295, 309; quasi-, 186, 379
chaosmosis, 186
chaos theory, 63, 313
character, 83, 87, 92, 192, 199, 206, 258, 366, 418; transfer of, 81–82, 88–90. *See also* affective tone; becoming; double becoming
chiasmus, 81–82, 89–90
circulation, 15, 291; of affect, 313; and deterritorialization, 303, 306, 308; of figures, 309, 310, 311–12; and media, 293, 294, 304, 306. *See also* capitalism; deterritorialization; distribution

INDEX 465

Clinton, Bill, 221, 280, 282, 286, 298, 299–300, 302, 438n7
coding, 172, 303, 310, 313, 347; cross-coding, 100; decoding, 142–43, 159, 163, 165, 171, 173, 310; encoding, 155; and facialization, 276; recoding, 100
cognition, 187, 199; and artfulness, 344–45; and atmosphere, 194; noncognition, 111; prefit, 144. *See also* cognitive schema; technical mentality
cognitive schema, 104, 109–11, 113, 115, 117, 121; and abstract model, 105; and individuation, 116. *See also* body image; cognition; concretization, schema of; technical mentality; technical object
collective individuation, 258, 274, 419, 426; and proposition, 418; and thought, 424. *See also* individuation
colonialism, 35–36, 38, 47, 53, 54, 56, 298, 394; and cultural genocide, 40; postcolonialism, 292; and *terra nullius*, 47
color, 146; and animal becoming, 83–85; and brightness confound, 146–47; and phosphene, 402–4; as secondary sensation, 147, 152, 193; and synesthesia, 345–46; as trigger for instinct, 121–23. *See also* confound: brightness; contrast
command, 239, 295–96, 300–301, 304, 306–9, 337; and suspension, 238. *See also* control
common: politics of, 26, 27, 51, 53, 57, 61, 62
communication, 157, 296, 396; and capture, 51, 61; and circulation, 303–4; and disciplinary power, 50; and exchange, 33; as exchange, 28; and imperative, 52; imperative to, 52, 56, 60; and incommunicable, 31; intercultural, 27; and meaninglessness, 28; and mediation, 155; and preindividual field, 33; and repetition, 280; and translation, 61; and transmission, 78; and transparency, 154; and urban art, 397. *See also* noncommunication
complicity, 27, 269, 292; and capitalism, 309, 313–14; and design, 140–41
composition, 157, 201, 204, 206, 329, 331, 352, 354, 369, 372; becoming as, 127–28; of body, 375; co-composition, 87, 88, 92, 235; and movement, 353; and perception, 346, 347, 348, 350, 357; and world, 85, 415
compossibility, 243, 246
concept, 95, 115, 134, 186, 311–12, 322, 419, 421; infra-conceptual, 214; and invention, 113, 118; limit-, 186, 350; minor, 425–26;

models for, 96–97; qualitative, 192. *See also* axiomatic
concreteness, 3, 91, 199, 311–12, 314, 412; and abstract, 105, 152, 156–57; and emergence, 142; and potential, 135. *See also* abstraction; misplaced concreteness
concretization, schema of, 105, 110, 115, 116, 118. *See also* cognitive schema
conditioning, 7, 98, 99, 100, 109, 202, 318; vs. causality, 207; and effect, 109; and individuation, 112; past, 110, 112, 117, 118; and potential, 98; self-, 106, 108, 110, 113
conformation, 198–99
conformity, 105, 110–11, 126–27, 144, 151, 182, 253, 279. *See also* conformation
confound: brightness, 146–47, 149; experiential, 150, 155–57, 350–53
conjunction, 11–12, 64, 148, 351, 406, 408
consciousness, 130, 144–45, 178, 180, 183, 196, 213, 260, 426, 444n12, 444n14; and amodal completion, 256; and decision, 177; and Firstness, 194, 433n2 and perception, 68, 256–57, 345–48; primary, 120, 129–32, 441n18; and propostion, 415; reflective, 196; subject of, 190, 192; unconsciousness, 161, 241, 410, 412. *See also* nonconscious
consensus, 242, 248, 269, 296, 309, 423
consistency, 230, 246, 279, 335, 430n3; plane of, 131; self-, 124–26. *See also* threshold
constancy: and change, 95, 141, 143, 147, 311
constraint, 151, 397, 408, 409; and design, 137–41; and escape, 102; and eternal object, 195; and milieu, 125, 127; and novelty, 112, 151. *See also* analogical gap; arbitrariness
content: and architecture, 100, 103; and belief, 128, 428n5; and context, 58, 60, 166; and culture, 53–54; of the image, 158–59, 163, 169, 252, 260–62, 278, 380; and information, 114–15, 118; lived, 169, 175; logical, 411–12; and media, 245; objective, 7; secret, 42; semantic, 28, 30, 34, 39, 41, 43, 45, 214, 226, 281, 338; of sight, 255; speculative, 8; subjective, 313; verifiable, 43, 48–50, 55, 61. *See also* context
context: and content, 48, 58, 60, 166, 169; cultural, 41; urban, 398–99. *See also* content
contingency, 68–69, 295, 397, 398; future, 222; and virtual, 69

continuity, 135, 190, 267, 333, 363, 432n9; and break, 199; and difference, 107; and differentiation, 151; and discontinuity, 109; effective, 108; of experience, 186; and identity, 198; and novelty, 191; and transition, 336

continuous variation, 102, 143, 149, 346, 347, 362–63, 369

continuum, 201; of experience, 346–50, 354, 355, 361, 373; reality as, 11; and visual form, 256

contraction, 70, 180, 202, 328, 329, 331, 333, 334, 336, 339, 373, 439n7, 443n8

contrast, 30, 80, 121, 185, 201, 432n1; and eternal object, 195; and evolution, 131; and intensity, 122; and meaning, 240; and movement, 83; and preindividual field, 31; and supernormal tendency, 121–23. *See also* relief

control, 295–96, 300, 304, 306–7, 308–9, 400. *See also* command

Courchesne, Luc, 377–78, 380–81, 383

creation, 91, 120, 137, 181, 183, 191, 418; and animality, 92; co-, 85; and complicity, 139, 141; and constraint, 397; and evolution, 131; and instinct, 127

critical/bifurcation point, 65, 109, 112, 114

criticality, 63, 64, 67, 70

critique, 314, 406–7; capitalist, 302–3, 313

crossing point, 80, 82

cross-sensory, 345, 369, 372, 374

cue, 180, 181, 183, 186, 276; functional, 145; recue, 257, 258, 276. *See also* tendency; terminus

cultural theory, 135, 142, 145, 311

culture, 295, 428n6; Aboriginal vs. white, 42, 44; and difference, 42; as dynamic formation, 53, 54, 56; and heterogeneity, 43; vs. nature, 128

curve, 96, 167, 377

cut, 155, 181, 225; and continuity, 336; and decision, 224, 226; and life, 86; and movement, 350; and qualitative continuum, 349; and reality, 11

cybernetics, 104, 105, 114, 115, 308

Dancing the Virtual (SenseLab), 406, 409

datum, 410, 417

death, 289, 298, 307, 308; and absence, 264, 265, 266, 274; and capital, 301; and command, 295; and life, 86, 87, 93, 232, 244, 245, 263, 287, 292, 306, 311; and media, 290; and politics, 288; and potential, 295; and sovereign power, 235, 296; and surplus-value, 267, 268, 271, 275; and virtual, 69; and work, 70

decision, 209–11, 217, 222, 225, 434n16; and affect, 221; arbitrary, 138, 139; autocratic, 295; and contingency, 223; and cut, 230; and decision-making, 225; and factuality, 211; gut, 239; and intuition, 228; kinetic, 226, 228; and lag, 177; and life, 224; and nonvolition, 28; pre-, 218, 220, 238; and preacceleration, 216, 217; and present, 223, 224; and proactivity, 225; and readiness, 217; and reason, 223; and reflexive pull-back, 220; and shock, 223; and sovereign power, 240; subject of, 182; and subjectivity, 181; and time, 219

decoding, 142, 143, 159, 163, 165, 171, 173, 310. *See also* coding; interpretation

deformation, 143, 150, 155, 157; and desire, 127; and form, 135, 138, 139; and movement, 365, 368; mutual, 123, 126, 353; and supernormal tendency, 122, 123; and topological architecture, 136, 137, 144; and transduction, 171

Deleuze, Gilles, 9, 11, 16, 17, 23, 55, 69, 87, 120, 127, 149, 183, 314, 350, 407; on actual-virtual, 94–96; on architecture, 147; on Baroque, 140; on capitalism, 307; on creativity, 144; on critique, 406; on ethics, 141; on fabulation, 429n15; on intercessors, 60; on language, 430n6; on light, 431n5; on optical effect, 109; on parts and whole, 108; on powers of the false, 61; on society of control, 308; on stuttering, 27; on thought, 424; on vibration, 443n8; on virtual, 145, 243; on virtual occurence, 213

Deleuze, Gilles, and Félix Guattari, 6, 7, 12, 17, 18, 21, 22, 24, 82, 94, 113, 125, 126, 128, 129, 130, 132, 202, 303, 337, 430, 442; on the animal, 120; on becoming-animal, 78; on capture, 98; on consistency, 124; on desire, 127; on escape, 102; on faciality, 275; on order-word, 215; on plane of organization, 130; on simulation, 16, 19; on virtual, 134

depth, 146, 147, 148, 152, 166, 376. *See also* confound: brightness

derivation, 191, 199, 332. *See also* atmosphere; emotion; emotional tone; vector

Derrida, Jacques, 182

design, 79, 99, 100, 104, 108, 173, 175, 392; afterlife of, 145; and becoming-animal, 76,

82; and body, 78, 170; and conditioning, 110; and constraint, 151; and potential movement, 159; and process, 100, 151; and transduction, 171, 173
desire, 127, 128, 129, 130, 131. *See also* appetition; bare activity; supernormal tendency; sympathy
Despret, Vinciane, 59
determinability, 304–5, 310–11
determination, 8, 59, 98, 132, 168, 175, 244, 304; and affective tone, 188; and atmosphere, 192; and capitalism, 310; of content, 61; and determinabilities, 304; and duration, 99; in germ, 33; and judgment, 55; and language, 30; and movement, 353; and particularity, 312; and reality, 3–4; and relief, 347–48; and thought, 213; and vagueness, 174. *See also* determinability; indeterminacy
deterritorialization, 308, 311, 313; and art, 21, 23; and circulation, 303. *See also* reterritorialization; territory
detour, 390, 396. *See also* urban art
difference, 183, 369; agonistic, 234; and becoming, 90; and belonging, 409; and combination, 84; and continuity, 107; cultural, 42–44, 50–53, 56, 60–62; enactment of, 80; and eternal object, 195; and experience, 190; and fold, 350; intensive, 366; modal, 365, 367; negotiation of, 28; noncommunication of, 27, 61; qualitative, 364; and relation, 80; and simulacrum, 17; and solidarity, 219; and sympathy, 88; and unity, 60
differential, 44, 57, 74, 227, 259; and becoming-animal, 79, 80, 82, 90; and body, 327; and continuity, 432; evolution as, 131; as fundamental, 182; and inequality, 30; and operative solidarity, 106, 107; singularity as, 96; society as, 283; and time, 183; and writing, 91
differentiation, 60, 62, 295, 332, 345, 362, 363, 364, 367, 371; and capitalism, 302; continuity of, 151; cultural, 42; and experience, 372; and fusional continuum, 350; and indifference, 29; and integration, 51, 52; and locatability, 327–28; and movement, 367; and preindividual field, 31; and secret, 44; and simulacrum, 17; without separation, 57
digital, 16, 393; and architecture, 153–54, 156–57, 383

direct perception, 193–94, 198, 199, 203, 204, 423. *See also* atmosphere
discontinuity, 107, 109, 114, 256–57, 349. *See also* continuity
discourse, 30, 44, 45, 214, 270, 279, 281, 284
disjunction, 11, 351, 362–63, 406, 408, 416
disparity, 107, 108, 110, 111, 113, 114, 116, 117, 118. *See also* operative solidarity; concretization, schema of
distribution, 20–21, 58, 62, 252, 392. *See also* circulation
documentation, 392, 393, 395. *See also* anarchive; seeding
Dopplering, 145, 147, 155, 333, 402. *See also* architecture; confound: brightness; fog
double becoming, 21, 82, 88, 89, 91, 312, 429n9. *See also* becoming
double capture, 98–101. *See also* architecture; capture; operative solidarity; synergy; urbanism
down-beat, 257, 259, 268. *See also* amodal completion; off-beat; up-beat
duration, 66, 325, 327, 332, 336, 390, 440n8, 443n8; and advertising, 394; disjointed, 391; fusional, 389–90
dynamic form, 54, 55, 61, 96, 196, 197, 200, 202
dynamic unity, 30, 33–32, 60
dynamism: and architecture, 100; of body, 339, 368; and critique, 407; and culture, 53, 54, 57, 60; of experience, 332; and quality, 196; and relation, 107, 315, 317, 333; unity, 180; and virtual-actual, 94. *See also* movement

ecology: and crisis, 72, 73; of modes of power, 230; and perception theory, 101, 146; three ecologies, 421
ecology of practices, 60, 61
economy, 56, 295, 394, 395; and community, 53
effect, 108, 184, 420; and architecture, 99; atmospheric, 188; and autonomy, 127; vs. cause, 107; co-, 84; and cue, 180; and emergence, 183; and event, 181; follow-on, 222–23; and importance, 201; incipient, 64; ontological priority of, 109; optical, 109; and place, 95; and reality, 7, 12; and terminus, 325. *See also* holism-effect; special effect
emergence: assimilation, 305; and becoming, 120; condition of, 8; dimension of, 57;

emergence (continued)
of difference, 195; and habit, 147; and lure, 419; perceptual, 101; and the political, 316; and power, 316; of process, 186; quantum, 109; and resistance, 313; and self-conditioning, 108; social, 305, 306; tendency to, 29; and thought, 408

emergent collectivity, 420, 426

emotion: absorbing affect, 274; vs. affect, 192; and faciality, 272; and mirror neurons, 444n14; and personhood, 321; surplus-value of, 251, 266, 277, 283; as vector, 190, 191, 192. *See also* affect; derivation; emotional tone

emotional tone, 205, 414–17, 425. *See also* affective tone; atmosphere; penumbral complex

empathy: and human-animal relation, 76, 77, 78, 93; and mirror-touch synesthesia, 356, 444n14; and reflexive pull-back, 221, 223; vs. sympathy, 88. *See also* mirror-touch synesthesia; sympathy

emphatic point, 327, 330–31, 334–36. *See also* location; mapping

empiricism: classical, 194, 227, 440n7; radical, 11, 109, 149, 152, 184, 193, 329, 406, 440n7; superior, 149, 152

encounter: determining, 98, 329; and difference, 44–45, 60, 81; and expression, 100; intercultural, 53

enjoyment, 8, 14, 413; self-, 8–9, 13, 191, 413. *See also* occasion; proposition

entertaining subject, 416, 417, 418, 420, 423

entertainment: of potential by process, 8; of the present toward the future, 179; and proposition, 413–20; self-, 8

entrainment, 12, 271, 338

enunciation: as assemblage, 433n4; collective, 423, 426; effectiveness of, 38. *See also* performative; subject of the enunciation

environment, 73, 137; atmosphere as, 188; and biopower, 247; and conditioning, 98–99, 100, 101; and instinct, 124–25, 126; and power of existence, 315; and three ecologies, 421

eternal object: and Firstness, 432n11; as limit, 195; as virtual, 206

ethico-aesthetic paradigm, 74, 75, 76, 88, 91; and becoming, 93; and sympathy, 93. *See also* aesthetic; becoming; ethics

ethics, 74; and becoming, 118; and complicity, 141; and nonintentionality, 88; and relation, 59, 73, 74–75, 93. *See also* aesthetic

ethology, 119, 120, 124, 125; and instinct, 119

ethopoiesis, 59, 60, 61

event, 80, 149, 184, 247, 262, 339, 366, 390, 406, 408, 409, 421; affective, 318; and architecture, 152; and asymmetry, 30; and atmosphere, 204, 206; and chance, 58; and extension, 325; and exteriority, 367; and feeling, 326; and habit, 67; and language, 337; limit of, 325; and lure, 8; macro-, 245, 252; and minor gesture, 425; multiple-singular, 86; and novelty, 197; operationalization of, 275, 276; perception as, 181; and potential, 252; and presentiment, 162; and process, 198; and proposition, 412; and propositional force, 416; and SenseLab, 419; and seriality, 420; and singularity, 319; and substance, 82; suspended, 390, 391; and threshold, 367; and topology, 353; and violence, 318; virtual, 213; and virtual, 134; and virtual body, 355; and world, 420; and worlding, 85

evolution: and animality, 92; and becoming, 120; coevolution, 184; and creativity, 92, 126, 128; and differential, 131; and improvisation, 125

excess, 64, 129, 197, 297; affective, 274, 277; and auto-conduction, 124; and immanence, 123; and instinct, 120; and nature, 122; and optical effect, 109; and potential, 65; and real, 3, 6, 18; and self-referentiality, 64. *See also* surplus-value

exchange, 15; and communication, 296; and differential, 81, 428n2; nonexchangeability, 26, 30, 31; social, 28–30, 32–33. *See also* asymmetry; becoming; circulation

excluded middle, 219, 311

exemplary, 86, 90, 92, 251, 260, 267, 271, 275, 277, 279, 284. *See also* analogue

exfoliation, 168, 369, 374. *See also* body

experience, 14, 181, 192, 331, 332, 333, 335–36, 338–39, 341, 345, 347, 349, 355, 357, 374, 388; and abstraction, 88, 185, 186; and aesthetics, 317; and affordance, 389–90; and architecture, 101, 150; and artfulness, 347, 348; and atmosphere, 188, 190; and being, 149; and body, 340, 373; and building, 166; center of, 91; and chaos, 352; and confound, 155, 353; and continuity, 432n4; as continuum, 373; and creativity, 202; and cue, 180; and cut, 354; and decision, 177; and double registering, 354; and effect, 95; embodied, 101; and excess, 123; and extension, 364; extensive vs. intensive, 352; and feeling, 165, 194; field of, 181,

INDEX 469

328, 335, 370, 371, 372, 373; and fold, 350; and form, 148; and fusional duration, 391; and gravity, 164; and hyperorder, 353; image of, 380, 381; immediate, 179; and infra-instant, 185, 186; and intensity, 83, 316; intensity of, 82; liminal, 88; mode of, 75; and movement, 87, 340; nonhuman, 197; and novelty, 373; and potentiality, 373; prefigured, 144; and previousness, 330, 372; primary phase of, 194; primitive, 346, 371; prototype of, 392; pulse of, 191; qualitative, 372; and reading, 88; and reality, 12; and relation, 356; relational, 83; and self-identity, 191; space of, 331, 332, 348, 371; and subject, 340; and subjectivity, 340; and sympathy, 355, 356; and terminus, 186; and topology, 372; and urban art, 396; and vertigo, 164; and virtual movement, 215; and voluminousness, 328

expression, 186, 200, 203, 243, 315, 317; and affect, 316; and animal, 120; and becoming-animal, 89; collective, 234, 242; cultural, 53; and cut, 349, 353; differential, 98; and effect, 204; field of, 33; and life, 252; and movement, 350; and potential, 33; of potential, 99; and power, 234; pure, 89, 92; qualitative, 206; and real, 6, 7; resumption of, 29; serial, 205

extension, 64–65, 162, 179–80, 324–26, 351–53, 365, 371, 373; and iterativity, 363; non-spatial, 364; and perception, 66; and quality, 363; and reason, 64. See also intensity; space

exuberance, 315, 345

Faber, Roland, 410
fabulation, 429n15; abstract and real, 22; and culture, 54–55, 57; and form of life, 57; and power of the false, 61; and reality, 22; and simulation, 20. See also power of the false
facialization: and affective legitimation, 272, 282; and personalization, 274, 277; and whiteness, 275–76, 282
false problem, 182, 187, 431n4; truth as, 55
fascism, 231
fear: and life, 251; and nationalism, 248; politics of, 283
feedback, 104, 107, 288
feeling, 69, 87, 183, 200, 274, 324, 326, 329, 332, 333, 341, 346, 347, 374; and atmosphere, 189; direct, 336; and effect, 12; and empathy, 88; and experience, 165; and Firstness, 195; and image, 399; and intensity, 165; and location, 325, 326, 330, 439n1; and morality, 291; and movement, 352; non-actualized, 88; pre-, 161, 163; pure, 129, 131; and real, 12; self-, 152; and subject, 13; and sympathy, 88; and thought, 228; and truth, 194, 362; and variation, 149; feeling-with vs. feeling-for, 88

field, 366, 367, 368, 369; of color, 403; energetic, 107; experience as, 372; and extension, 364; and intensity, 371; and interiority, 367; and local-global resonance, 31; and place, 363; vs. space, 363

figure, 85, 123; and affect, 87; and background, 84; and contrast, 84; and determinabilities, 305; and the generic, 304; and language, 87; and movement, 83, 85, 87; nonfigurality, 365

Firstness, 194, 195, 432n1, 433n2, 439n6, 440n7; and Thirdness, 195

flow, 336; abstract, 19; of affect, 313; of body, 161; and cut, 11, 336; and elements, 443n8; of experience, 148, 335; of language, 28, 251; of movement, 332; of the past, 325; of the present, 223; regime of, 98

Fly, The (dir. David Cronenberg), 21–23
fog, 69, 145, 146, 155. See also architecture; confound: brightness; Dopplering
fold, 19, 155, 168, 350, 352, 355, 367, 380, 381; and criticality, 63; and habit, 67; infold, 65; and novelty, 349; outfold, 65; and virtual, 69
force, 170, 173; abstract, 171; and affect, 313; affective, 88, 90, 91; and architecture, 172; of attraction, 121–22, 185; attractive vs. mechanical, 127; and body, 171; and decision, 225; iterative, 230; ontogenetic, 114; and operative reason, 65; propositional, 414, 416, 424; real and abstract, 87; and sympathy, 89–90; and vector, 126

foreground, 101, 123, 200–203, 243, 256, 376, 420. See also atmosphere; background
form, 57, 58, 99, 100, 190, 334, 336, 339, 365; and abstraction, 335; and affective tonality, 194; and background, 256; and building, 99; as catalyst, 150; and conditioning, 98; and condition of emergence, 144; and depth, 147; and determination, 98, 175; dynamic, 61; empty, 60; and environment, 99; and experience, 148; of expression, 54, 60; and feeling, 329; and fold, 349; and formation, 97, 98; and function, 174; and generation, 125; germinal, 33, 59;

form (continued)
  and in-formation, 150; and intervention, 57; pregiven, 372; and process, 99, 135, 136, 173; reforming, 100; as sign, 137; static, 99; and supernormal, 122; and topology, 135; virtual, 149; visual, 281
form of life, 54, 120, 131; and adaptation, 57; and ethopoiesis, 59; and lived quality, 75
formation, 57, 243, 244, 245; and architecture, 99, 150; and being of relation, 57–58; and continuum, 359; and deformation, 155; of experience, 182, 354; force of, 202; form and, 98–100, 135; and information, 59; and iteration, 243; of perception, 344, 347; of reaction, 332; and repetition, 111; of social field, 246; and technique of noncommunication, 58; and tunneling, 156; and virtual, 144. *See also* dynamic form; emergence
Foster, Charles, 76, 77, 78, 83
Foucault, Michel, 232, 307, 321; on coup d'état, 237; on proposition vs. statement, 42; on sovereign power, 235
freedom: and accident, 69; and classified bodies, 305; and creation, 138–41; and decision lag, 177, 186–87; and determination, 22; and false problem, 182–84; free action, 203; and resistance, 319; and sensation, 68
function, 66; and aesthetics of instinct, 119; vs. aesthetic value, 74, 93; and behavior, 123, 174; as design constraint, 138, 139, 141; and designed space, 174; futurity of, 108; generic, 174; and landing site, 162, 163–64, 388–89; new regime of, 106–7, 110, 114, 116; as ontological ground of existence, 143–44, 145; and plane of organization, 130–31; vs. potential movement, 170–71; and reproduction, 21; threshold of, 117
fusion: felt present as, 180–81; of figures, 289, 304, 312; fusional duration, 389, 391; and heterogeneous unity, 363, 364; of life and death, 306; and movement, 363; of qualities of experience, 350; of senses, 353, 371; vision-touch, 348
future, 64, 179, 190, 293, 403; and anticipation, 220–22; back action of, 110; collective, 54, 320; and decision, 220; and event, 8, 413, 420; and fabulation, 57; and invention, 105–18; and knowledge, 211; and life, 273; and memory, 334; memory of, 59; and past, 94, 135, 148, 205, 288, 291, 293, 297, 304, 403–4; and potential, 322; and pragmatism, 55; and preemption,
218, 219, 261, 262; presence of, 64; and present, 180, 184; and surprise, 224; and transindividual, 320; and virtual, 94. *See also* future-past; past; present
FutureLab, 386
future-past, 95, 218, 220, 224, 227, 230, 255, 258, 334; and decision, 218; and virtual, 95. *See also* future; past

generality, 374; of city, 392, 393; and conventional proposition, 411, 412, 417, 419, 420; critical judgment as, 407; and particularity, 316; and singularity, 70, 189; and structural violence, 319; and Whiteheadian proposition, 415
genericness, 174, 198; and affect, 313; and figure, 303–4, 309, 310; humanity as, 306, 312; and infrastructure types, 387, 388, 389, 390, 391, 392, 393; and quality, 363, 371; and resistance, 312; and singularity, 305, 365; and whiteness, 275, 276. *See also* singular-generic
geology, 72, 96; of experience, 347, 348, 350, 357
geometry, 96, 123; and abstraction, 335, 348; and architecture, 152, 161, 168; and extension, 354; and mapping, 335, 339, 340; projective, 96; and space, 364; and topology, 353
gestalt, 123–24, 281, 365, 398
gesture, 43, 58; and intention, 81, 83, 89; micro-, 202; minor, 425; modest, 57, 132; and performative, 34, 337
Gibson, James J., 388
Gil, José, 29, 369
Gilbert, Kevin, 40–42, 44, 46
givenness, 7, 135, 191, 305, 432n4; atmosphere as, 194; pre-, 261, 328, 330, 331, 372; present as, 66–67; and proposition, 410, 414, 417; reality as, 5–6; space as, 356
globality: and atmosphere, 188, 189, 204, 206; and locality, 31, 32, 33, 39, 57, 327, 328; and singularity, 245, 295
Gore, Al, 221
governance: and bare activity, 224
gravity, 65, 66, 69, 70, 166, 172, 294, 329, 404
gridding: back-, 262; and disciplinary power, 246; representational, 21–23; spatial, 348, 349, 352–56, 370
Guattari, Félix, 74, 80, 120, 312; on autopoiesis, 439n16; on infra-instant, 186; on the three ecologies, 421
Guimbal turbine, 105, 106

habit, 66, 69, 148, 173, 180, 259, 336, 341, 348; and amodal completion, 257, 268; and architecture, 172; and contraction, 333; and cue, 145; and event, 67; and landing site, 161; and memory, 334; and perception, 146, 147, 256; perceptual, 347; and physical laws, 66; and possible, 66, 67; and potential, 67, 198; and repetition, 170; and sensation, 66; and situation, 68; and tendency, 255
haecceity, 202, 203
hallucination, 124, 125, 128, 169, 334
Hallward, Peter, 95
Hardt, Michael, and Antonio Negri, 26
hegemony, 259, 268–69, 271, 277, 279
heterogeneity, 43, 259, 335, 363–64, 366, 374, 397, 430n3; heterogeneous unity, 363, 364
heterogenesis: becoming-animal as, 80; and ontopower, 259
heteropoiesis, 312
hiatus, 66, 67, 69
Hindmarsh Affair, 48–51, 53, 56
history, 181, 271, 431n4; and atmosphere, 204–7; and infra-instant, 181; nonteleological, 293; and proposition, 412, 414
holism-effect, 108–11, 113. *See also* operative solidarity; resonance; synergy
homeostasis, 112, 113, 117
homogeneity: of nation, 276; of space, 365
homunculus, 182, 254, 432n5, 442n2
Housing the Body (SenseLab), 406, 408
Howard, John, 55, 56
human, 13, 76, 80, 181, 197, 276, 311; and animal, 77, 89, 92, 244; and animality, 128; and blackness, 292; and capitalism, 306; and climate change, 72; and death, 93; deterritorialized, 311, 312; and empathy, 76; human rights, 306; and language, 28, 89, 92; and literarity, 89; more-than-human, 21, 92; and nature, 72, 92; nonhuman, 131, 132; and nonhuman, 14, 73, 74; and personal, 274; and reason, 72, 73, 91; and reflection, 63; as relay, 310; and singularity, 132; and supernormal, 128; and technology, 73; and volition, 82; and whiteness, 275, 276. *See also* animal; more-than-human; nonhuman
humanism, 73, 77, 82, 89, 91, 306. *See also* posthumanism
Hume, David, 439n7
HUMO workshop, 386, 397, 400
hylomorphism, 105, 106, 113, 139

idealism: and bifurcation of nature, 196; Platonic, 94, 95; realist idealism, 105, 115, 117, 118; and substantialism, 196; and terminus, 185
identification: and charismatic leadership, 251, 278, 321; and interiority of experience, 356; and mirror-touch synesthesia, 444n14
identity, 22, 23, 180; abstract, 21; ideal, 19; machinic, 151; miraculated, 21; and movement, 327; and nonidentity, 427; and otherness, 190; processual, 198; and recognition, 131; and resistance, 320; self-, 11, 13, 179, 189, 190–92, 194–99, 201, 204, 205, 206; and territory, 295; and world, 191
ideology, 252, 259, 281, 293, 297, 301; anti-, 61; and atmosphere, 207; and identification, 251; and image, 278; and legitimation, 260; and urban art, 396
illusion: effective, 19, 20, 24; optical, 109, 150
image, 170, 252, 258–60, 262–65, 267, 269, 271, 276, 278, 336, 377, 379, 381, 386, 399–400; and affect, 277–78; affective, 266; and amodal completion, 253; and architecture, 159; and black hole, 379; and context, 260; of death, 266; and determination, 163; and event, 260; exemplary, 284; and experience, 380, 381; and indexicality, 270; itinerary of, 380; and kinesthesia, 379; and landing site, 170; and life, 274; and message, 278, 279; and more-than-visual, 380, 389; and movement, 158–59; as object, 381; political, 253; and postmodernism, 15; postponed, 173; and potential movement, 159; and power, 248; power of, 279, 283; and process, 260–61; as process, 256–57; as sign, 15; and site, 400; and spectacle, 262; still-, 169; vs. substance, 278; and urban site, 398; virtual, 254, 267, 269, 271; and virtual, 257; and words, 281. *See also* amodal completion; barely-there; body-without-an-image; synesthesia; vision
imagination, 334, 340, 343; and amodal completion, 253–54
imitation, 77, 79; and difference, 18; and movement, 85; and uniqueness, 17
immanence, 29, 34, 55, 70, 129, 215, 218, 236, 367, 418; and absolute origin, 113; and activity, 163, 165; of body, 370; and cause, 116; and desire, 127; and disciplinary power, 235; and end-form, 142; and excess, 123; and experience, 354; and experience formation, 100; and fabulation, 22; immanent center, 57;

immanence (continued)
immanent critique, 407; and improvisation, 125; and in-formation, 58; and infra-moment, 220; and limit, 69; and perception, 213, 214; and pragmatic truth, 43; reciprocal, 57; and schema of concretization, 110, 111; and sensation, 66; and sovereign power, 237; and technicity, 112; and world of experience, 186

immediacy: of belonging, 30; of body, 340; of culture, 54; of enjoyment, 8, 14; of experience, 179, 194, 198, 432n4; of feeling, 372; of habit, 148; of instinct, 125; of past, 11, 13, 180, 190, 195, 197, 199, 204, 205, 226, 325; of present, 11; of relationality, 356; of sympathy, 131, 132; of time, 220; of transition, 336. *See also* immediation

immediation, 114, 421. *See also* anarchive; mediation

immersion, 83, 92, 336, 339, 372, 380–81, 383, 385

impact: and importance, 201; and sensation, 66–69

impassibility, 69

imperceptibility, 268, 275, 281, 347, 349, 353–55, 432n4, 440n12, 443n8; and modesty, 132; and virtual, 144, 357

impersonal: and affect, 313; and facialization, 277; and mood, 206

importance, 188, 189, 192, 201, 406, 409. *See also* atmosphere

impress, and proposition, 414

improvisation, 125, 202, 319, 320, 408; vs. adaptation, 125; and novelty, 127

impulsion, 226, 227

inclusion, 64; communicational, 26; of feelings, 326, 327; of logical subjects, 416; physical, 63; pre-, 162

in-come, 367–68, 372, 374

indeterminacy, 33, 45, 59, 138, 150, 154, 163, 175, 202, 245, 305, 311, 391, 403; and art event, 390; assimilation of, 305; and capitalism, 310; and common, 26; and design, 137; and order, 24; and postmodernism, 15; and terrorism, 216; and vanishing point, 244; and virtual center, 246. *See also* determinability

indexicality, 17, 260, 270, 280, 281, 357, 368, 370, 403

individual, 83, 118, 321, 417, 435n5; and affect, 315; atomized, 53; and dividual, 85; as figure, 84; and preindividual, 33; and proposition, 418; and speciation, 418; and transformation, 84; and violence, 317; and whiteness, 275. *See also* personal; preindividual; transindividual

individuation, 32; affective, 275; and cognitive schema, 115–16; collective, 32, 258, 274, 426; and materiality, 115; and mode of thought, 113; psychic, 112–13, 117, 118; as speciation, 418; technical, 112, 117, 118; vital, 112, 113. *See also* preindividual; transindividual

induction, 31, 80, 90, 125–27, 203, 215, 226, 245, 257, 266, 269, 379, 430n4

in-fill, 178, 181, 333–36, 441n19

inflection, 26, 32–33, 58, 85, 198; and aim, 417; and juncture, 422; and minor gesture, 425

infolding, 64–65, 195–97

information: vs. appetite, 210; as content, 60, 411; as disparity, 114; and distributive power, 58; and experience, 156; vs. in-formation, 58, 59; and preindividual, 114; and tunneling, 155; and windowing, 154

infra-instant (infra-moment), 180–81, 185–86, 213–14, 217, 218, 219, 220. *See also* anticipation; future-past; propension; readiness potential

infralinguistic, 29, 33, 34. *See also* language; linguistics

ingress, 318, 319, 320

inheritance, 7, 111, 112, 190, 191, 192. *See also* novelty; occasion

instinct, 119–28. *See also* animal; supernormal tendency

integral openness, 195, 362

intensity, 63, 64, 66, 69, 163, 165, 170, 180–81, 185, 350; and aesthetic, 320; and affect, 316–17; and body potential, 317, 374; and contrast, 122; and experience, 347, 352, 357; vs. extension, 349, 443n8; of feeling, 327; and gradation, 201; and life, 86; and orientation, 371; and plane of emergence, 332; and potential movement, 162, 366; and qualitative domain, 349; and qualitative field of experience, 363, 373; reality as, 427n2; relational, 83; and singular point, 244, 247; situational, 319; and supernormal tendency, 123; and thought, 64; time-, 220; and vagueness, 174; and virtual, 97; and virtual body, 353, 354; and world, 85

intentionality, 81, 83; and artfulness, 348; and capitalism, 309; and object, 207; and phenomenology, 143. *See also* volition

interaction, 140, 148, 149, 150, 151, 157, 381, 380, 383

intercessor, 60, 428n8
interest, 417
interference, 64, 96, 180, 283, 304, 313, 391, 396, 398, 400, 423
interpretation, 41, 45, 142, 143, 154, 155
interruption, 28, 29, 33, 38, 39, 41, 45, 55, 57, 58, 63, 224, 257, 295, 296. See also saccade; stutter; suspension
intersection, 329, 336, 362
intertextuality, 140, 143
interval, 69, 177–78, 186, 246, 268, 425, 432n5; emergence of, 181; and infra-moment, 185; and stutter, 32; and virtual, 69. See also suspension
intervention, 33, 64, 106, 161, 202; affective, 313; as form and in-formation, 57–58; supernormal, 122; urban art, 390, 396, 397, 401
intuition, 131–32, 139; and decision, 228
invention, 106–8, 110–18, 155, 244; and becoming, 58, 59; cultural, 55, 57; and instinct, 126; and language, 78, 338; vs. novelty, 157; speciation as, 418
involution, 126, 128
iterativity, 209, 230, 242, 243, 271, 392; and feeling, 326; and virtual, 95

James, William, 179, 181, 182, 184, 191, 258, 344, 441n18; on arrival, 390; on body, 374; on pure experience, 195–96, 326–29, 332, 367, 439n3; and radical empiricism, 109, 129, 149, 440n7; on space, 373; on terminus, 130
Jameson, Fredric, 16
judgment, 8, 48, 61, 125, 188, 319, 428n5; and academia, 424; vs. affirmation, 418; vs. critique, 407; and disciplinarity, 50; and generality, 419; and proposition, 410, 414–15; and truth, 55
juncture, 422–23
juxtaposition, 95, 308, 349, 351, 369, 370

Kartinyeri, Doreen, 48
Kaufman, Lloyd, 163, 255
Kiesler, Frederick, 141
kinesthesia, 148, 161, 255, 335–36, 338, 346–48, 379, 388, 441n19; and synesthesia, 148, 333–34, 336, 338; and writing, 87. See also proprioception; synesthesia
knot, 242, 422
knowledge, 417, 432n4; and action, 199; and decision, 211; objective, 77; and present, 211; rational, 81; and retrospection, 210; secret, 48–51, 56; and world, 415

Lacan, Jacques, 17
landing site, 101, 161, 168, 170, 175, 388, 389, 390, 391, 397; and pre-feeling, 163; and vertigo, 165. See also affordance; Arakawa, Shusaku, and Madeline Gins
language, 244, 336–39, 433n4; and abstraction, 87, 337; and animality, 92; and architecture, 159; and becoming, 89; and becoming-animal, 78; and colonization, 40; common, 31, 51, 57, 62; and complexity, 45; and description, 87; and exchange, 28; infra-linguistic, 214; and invention, 338; and mediation, 43, 78; and order, 214; and performative, 33; and reality, 339; and repetition, 264; and sociality, 30; suspension of, 28; and synesthesia, 338–39; and thought, 214–15, 217; univocity, 24; and world, 34. See also infralinguistic; linguistics; writing
Lapoujade, David, 13, 131
Latour, Bruno, 61, 74
Le Corbusier, 136–38, 140
legitimation, 35, 252, 260, 278, 281, 286, 290–91, 294, 297, 300–301, 313–14, 408
Leibniz, Gottfried Wilhelm, 379, 441n21
Libet, Benjamin, 177, 179
life, 67, 85, 131, 182, 233, 287, 292; and abstraction, 86; and activity, 181; and adventure, 93; and affect, 240, 315; affirmation of, 316; and bare activity, 224; and capital, 301, 306; and co-creation, 181; and command, 307; condition of, 93; and consistency, 430n3; and continuation, 69; and crisis, 286; and death, 86, 93, 263, 266, 306–7; and divinity, 236; and double ordering, 131; and ethico-aesthetic paradigm, 93; and event, 181; and eventfulness, 69; and event horizon, 70; and experience, 181; and function, 130; and germinal consciousness, 120; and habit, 70; and homeostasis, 112–13; and imitation, 17; individual, 274; and insecurity, 251; and intensity, 86; and invention, 113; and matter, 241, 264; and metastability, 112; and more-than-human, 93; and movement, 373; and personality, 206; and the political, 320; potential, 271; and power, 246; and powers of the false, 54; and problem, 141; and recursivity, 130; and renewal, 92; and sensation, 69; and singularity, 70; and supernormal, 132; and system logic, 66; and vanishing point, 232; and variation, 92; and world, 329

light, 83, 254, 402, 403, 431n3, 443n6; and abstract surface, 149; and body, 157; and virtual, 146
liminality, 88–89, 91, 198, 203, 423
limit, 85, 185, 372, 407; absolute, 237; and experience, 186; immanent, 69–70, 186, 242, 258–59; optimal and pessimal, 84, 429n14; plastic, 124; processual, 185; and vision, 164
limit-event, 366, 367. *See also* event; limit
linguistics, 34, 214–15, 337–39. *See also* infralinguistic; language
literarity: and animality, 92; and becoming animal, 78. *See also* writing
location, 357; of feeling, 325, 327, 329; and language, 337; and mirror-touch synesthesia, 343, 355, 444n11; and orientation, 330, 440n9. *See also* mapping; position; simple location
locus: and proposition, 415
logic, 211, 311, 362; equivocation, 219; instrumental, 33; nonlinear, 219; oxymoron, 219, 434n11; tautology, 219–20
logical subject, 412, 416, 420. *See also* subject of the statement
logic of relations, 360–61, 370, 371–72
Lozano-Hemmer, Rafael, 386, 390, 396, 400
Luhmann, Niklas, 311–12
lure, 8, 14, 191, 201–2, 415, 417, 419–20; and proposition, 413–14. *See also* proposition
Lynn, Greg, 100

Macfarlane, Robert, 83
machinic, 137, 171, 288, 306, 311, 439n14; and analogue, 151; and relay, 310; and virtual, 144
magic, 34, 35, 57, 278, 291
manner, 92, 93, 204, 392; affective, 87; and novelty, 93
Manning, Erin, 132, 406, 429n9, 439n6; on preacceleration, 215
mapping, 330–33, 335–36, 339–41, 369, 441n20. *See also* location; orientation
market, 53, 288–89, 294, 305–6
Marx, Karl, 21, 303, 307
massiveness, 189, 192, 201. *See also* atmosphere
Massumi, Brian: *Parables for the Virtual: Movement, Affect, Sensation*, 97, 279; *The Politics of Everyday Fear*, 279; *Semblance and Event: Activist Philosophy and the Occurrent Arts*, 129
matter, 64, 65, 105, 110, 111, 113, 441n21; and becoming, 110; body as, 260; and habit, 66, 70; inert and irritable, 241, 245; and light, 149; and resonance, 113; sound, 264; and thought, 132
meaning, 23, 28, 81, 83, 89, 116, 150; and contrast, 240; and difference, 28, 29; and faciality, 272; and media, 245; and performative, 34; and postmodernism, 15; pragmatic, 43; propositional, 41; referential, 78; and stutter, 27; and style, 100
mechanism, 127; and instinct, 119
media, 244–46, 248, 269, 282, 290, 292–93, 296, 314; and absence, 291; and affect, 291, 294, 313; and coding, 303; and direct effect, 278; and Donald Trump, 322; and event, 245; and image, 253; and politics, 279, 280; and production, 259; and representation, 44, 302; and surplus-value, 252; and transduction, 245; and violence, 293; and virtual, 153. *See also* image
mediation, 31, 64, 105, 293, 297, 301, 309, 310; and communication, 154; and ontogenesis, 114. *See also* immediation
Meillassoux, Quentin, 431n4
memory, 180, 228, 291, 330, 332, 403–4; collective, 57; and experience, 255; and futurity, 334; and orientation, 331
Merleau-Ponty, Maurice, 144
metamodelization, 113. *See also* allagmatic; concept
metaphysics, 157, 181, 311, 432n4
Michotte, Albert, 360–61, 363, 365, 373, 374
middle, 84, 140, 151, 155, 157, 210, 216, 422. *See also* excluded middle
milieu, 125, 169. *See also* environment
minor, 202; artist, 22; concept, 425, gesture; 425; minoritarian movement, 61
mirror neurons, 343, 344, 352, 356, 444n14. *See also* empathy; mirror-touch synesthesia; sympathy
mirror-touch synesthesia, 343–44, 348, 352, 354–57, 443n7, 444n11. *See also* mirror neurons; sympathy; synesthesia; touch
misplaced concreteness, 185–86. *See also* simple location
mode, 282–83, 365; of affectability, 88; of existence, 57, 189, 193, 322; of reality, 9–10; and singularity, 80; of thought, 113
model, 123; abstract, 108; vs. description, 96; external, 15; and power of the false, 17; and problem, 96; and reality, 18; and simulacrum, 16, 18; and technical object, 105
modesty, 57, 93, 132
modulation, 58, 102, 179, 180, 181, 183, 184, 196, 201, 202, 245, 308, 309, 407, 422, 425

momentum, 180, 185, 409
monad, 367, 374, 379–81; transmonad, 372–73
mood, 203, 206, 219; anger, 198–201. *See also* atmosphere; impersonal
morality, 177, 230, 290–91; and capitalism, 321; and media, 294; and reason, 182
more-than-human, 21, 82, 92, 93, 132, 428n2, 429n14, 438n10
movement, 84, 152, 164, 166, 170, 363, 368, 370; absolute, 152; abstract, 159; and activity, 223; and actualization, 366; and affect, 313; and anticipation, 215; and appetition, 351; and architecture, 159; and body, 328; and brightness confound, 149; and color, 84; and cut, 226, 350, 353, 354, 366; and decision, 226; description of, 83; and differentiation, 366, 367; vs. displacement, 352, 366; as event, 364; and exfoliation, 369, 374; and experience, 372; and feeling, 327; and field effect, 227; and figure, 87; and geometry, 370, 371; and image, 257; and intensity, 353; intensive, 366; kinetic, 226–28; and landing site, 161; and life, 373; micromovement, 379; and mirror-touch synesthesia, 443n6; and movement-form, 365; and pattern, 174; and perception, 147, 256; and position, 371, 441n21; potential, 162, 163; and potential, 368; premovement, 215, 217; priority of, 371; and relation, 441n21; and rest, 374, 399; saccadic, 269; and self, 352; and senses, 165; and shared ground, 158; and singularity, 364, 365; and space, 148, 330; and stasis, 257, 379; and stillness, 162; and subjectivity, 351, 352; and thought, 228; and transition, 331, 336; and variation, 123; and vector, 270; virtual, 381; and virtual-actual, 94; and virtual center, 67; and vision, 254, 255, 333; of vision, 380; and world, 329. *See also* preacceleration
multiple-singular, 53, 90, 312, 321, 368–69, 371

nature, 17; and atmosphere, 192, 206; and becoming, 80; bifurcation of, 193, 196; and human, 72, 73, 128; and individuation, 113, 118; and instinct, 126; and Mind, 115; naturing, 87, 91; and sovereign power, 235, 236
neonate, 331, 341, 345
network, 117; postindustrial, 118
neurodiversity, 346, 442n3
neurotypicality, 345, 346–49, 442n3
nextness, 66, 334–35, 338, 362. *See also* previousness

Nietzsche, Friedrich, 12, 206, 426, 427n3, 429n14
9/11 attacks, 216, 221, 238–39, 247–48, 251–53, 259, 261–64, 267–72, 275–76, 279, 436n15. *See also* Bush, George W.; war on terror
node, 337; body-media, 322; central, 252, 258, 260; of collective expression, 234, 242; of decision, 295; nodal point, 130
noncommunication, 50, 52, 56, 58, 61, 314
nonconscious, 177–78; activity, 379
nonhuman, 311, 399. *See also* animal; human; more-than-human
nonlinearity: logical, 220; temporal, 95, 219, 293, 300, 304
nonlocality, 156, 333, 354, 393, 439n1; and advertising, 395; and infra-instant, 185; and sympathy, 356; and urban art, 392
nonsensuous, 199, 202
normativity, 308; and abnormality, 309; and exclusion, 62; and negative simulation, 20
novelty, 6, 7, 111, 114, 197, 419; and desire, 127; and inheritance, 112; and invention, 107; and potential, 198; and reality, 6

object: body as, 339–40; building as, 142; and critique, 314; and depth perception, 147; of desire, 127; effective, 43, 130; as event, 130–32; as making, 184; and multisense perception, 346–49; and orientation, 330–36, 361, 370; of power, 305, 306, 308; and recognition, 163, 166, 170, 173, 212; subject and, 143, 148, 152, 182; and subjectivity, 207; of sympathy, 120; of thought, 97
objectivity, 16, 76; of body, 339–40, 373–74; and feeling-location, 326, 328; objective content, 7; objective form, 158–59, 388; objective knowledge, 77; objective phenomenology, 77, 78, 91; pre-objective, 341; and primary qualities, 193
occasion, 195–97, 201, 206, 414, 418, 426; and antecedent world, 191; and event, 198; and intensity, 201; perishing of, 191; and potential, 191, 200; and proposition, 417; society of, 415
occurrence, 82, 118, 181, 207
Oettermann, Stephan, 376
off-beat, 177, 180, 185, 186, 192, 246, 257, 258, 259, 435n9. *See also* amodal completion; down-beat; up-beat
ontogenesis, 58, 101, 116, 118, 181, 184, 191, 246; and atmosphere, 192; and experience, 186; and location, 185; and novelty, 155;

476 INDEX

ontogenesis (continued)
and resistance, 313; and vagueness, 100. See also ontopower
ontology, 109; and emergence, 144; and ontogenesis, 191; and phenomenology, 143; and secondary quality, 193
ontopower, 247–48, 251, 258–59, 269, 279, 281
operationalization, 240, 248, 258–59, 275
operative solidarity, 108, 110–11, 113, 115, 116, 184–85
operativity, 84; operative logic, 230
order: and chaos, 63; and critical point, 65; and indetermination, 24; and perspective, 377; super order, 63–64; universal, 378
order-word, 214–15, 337–38. See also linguistics; performative
orientation, 66, 185, 329–41, 440n9; intensive, 371; and movement, 369; nonperspectival, 167; and reality, 4. See also mapping; space
otherness, 11, 20, 81, 91, 195, 200; and basic fact, 190; and event, 80; imitation of, 77; mutual, 88; and novelty, 13, 191; and sociality, 82; and synthesis, 91
Otto, Frei, 141, 175
outside, 372, 379; absolute, 314; immanent, 143

panorama, 376–79, 381
paradox, 95–96, 107, 195, 242–43, 377; and technique, 422; and time, 218–19
parasitism, 126, 252, 391, 392, 393, 396
particular, 85, 86, 377; and resistance, 312; vs. singular, 363. See also generality; genericness; singularity
passion, 129, 131, 247
past: collective, 293; and decision, 220; and future, 218; immediate, 11, 13, 179, 180, 190, 195, 197, 198, 199, 325; and inheritance, 192; past-present, 180, 181; and politics, 320; pure, 332, 334; and truth, 55; and virtual, 94. See also future; future-past; present
pattern, 196, 200, 254, 266, 351, 353; and orientation, 352
Peirce, Charles Sanders, 173, 344, 363; on Firstness, 194, 432n1, 433n2, 440n7; on physical laws, 66; on Thirdness, 195
penumbral complex, 204–7, 415–16, 419–20, 423, 425–26; and anarchive, 421; and historicity, 205; and proposition, 413, 414
perception, 154, 157–58, 163, 180, 183, 186, 214, 276, 343, 347, 392; and accident zone, 145; and anticipation, 255, 258; and architecture, 101; and artfulness, 347; bare, 425; composition of, 257, 346; and constraint, 397; edge of, 87, 88; event of, 404; extensive, 355; extra perception, 214; full-spectrum, 256; and fusional continuum, 346; and habit, 66; infra-, 212, 213; and lag, 178, 181; and light, 146; and mode of appearance, 347; and movement, 147; multi-sense, 168; neurodiverse, 442n3; neurotypical, 345, 348; nonconscious, 177; and nonlocality, 155; nonperspectival, 167; nonsensuous, 199; and optical illusion, 109; and politics, 278; primary, 184; and propensity, 213; and reason, 64; and recognition, 212; self-, 64; and sensation, 66; and space, 348, 349; subject of, 182; and synesthesia, 355; and thought, 67, 212, 214; underperception, 257, 258; and world, 344
performance, 45, 50, 51, 55, 119, 125, 377; collective, 57, 60; and interactive art, 381, 396; and performativity, 34, 38; pragmatic, 54; pre-, 162; and proposition, 412; of secret, 42; singular, 365–66; of sociality, 396
performance envelope, 390, 391–92, 395. See also urban art
performative, 46, 55, 262–63, 270, 337, 412, 427n2; and affect, 267; capture of, 50; and chance, 58; curse as, 39; and indetermination, 45; and magic, 34; and nontransparency, 42, 43; and quasi-cause, 33; and relation, 34, 39; and resistance, 318; and social act, 58; and trigger, 57; and virtual, 97; and war, 265; and white supremacy, 47. See also language; order-word
persona, 294, 322
personal, 275, 311, 412, 420; and faciality, 274, 277; and general, 412; and political, 320; and power, 321
personalization, 277, 282, 290, 320; and conventional proposition, 412, 420; and faciality, 274–75. See also facialization
person/personhood, 83; cross-, 81; and sympathy, 89
perspective, 148, 163, 166, 175, 370, 376, 377, 380; affective, 91; interior, 380; and navigation, 166
phase, 99, 139–40, 300, 308; dephasing, 108, 312; of event, 45, 325, 396; phase-shift, 101–2; of process, 100; transition, 98, 101
phenomenology, 144, 360; and atmosphere, 204; and empathy, 91; new, 189, 192;

INDEX   477

objective vs. subjective, 91; and substrate, 143; and topology, 144
philosophy, 14, 95, 193, 329; and affect, 317; and architecture, 152; empiricist, 439n7; of language, 32, 338–39; and multisensory experience, 344; of science, 125; and SenseLab, 421
phosphene, 402–4
physics, 21–22, 109, 149; laws of, 63, 66
plane: of emergence, 332; of operation, 106–7, 110, 117; of organization, 130
plasticity, 122–23, 126, 352, 439n1
play, 319, 429n15; and instinct, 126
point of indistinction, 234, 235, 241
politics, 216, 232, 295; and affect, 274, 294, 322; cosmopolitanism, 26; and death, 288; and decision, 212; and enemy, 26; identitarian, 306; and image, 279, 280; and magic, 35; and media, 294; micropolitics, 319; and negotiation, 59; and persona, 294; and personal, 320, 322; and the political, 309, 316–17, 320; political thought, 61; post-deliberative, 229, 230; and potential, 318; and power, 316; and uncertainty principle, 211, 220, 222; and war, 181. *See also* affect; power
position, 330–32, 336, 370–72, 408, 441n21. *See also* mapping
possible, 64, 68, 385, 387; and habit, 66; and potential, 65, 67, 115; and reality, 4; and virtual, 153. *See also* potential
posthumanism, 73, 76, 118, 306, 310, 438n10. *See also* more-than-human; nonhuman
postmodernism, 15, 140, 156–57, 302
potential, 58, 65, 98, 153, 183, 197, 200, 246, 331, 333, 336, 339, 353, 373, 392; abstract, 374; and actual, 64, 135; actualization of, 57; and affect, 315; and anarchive, 423; and atmosphere, 197, 207; and becoming, 21, 22; and command, 295; and conditioning, 112; and constraint, 397; energy, 115; and eternal object, 206; and excess, 64; expression of, 100; and field of belonging, 33; and future, 107; and haecceity, 203; human, 286; and identity, 21; and implex, 64; and infra-instant, 185–86; and materiality, 64; and movement, 365; multifunctional, 106; and nonlocality, 185; and novelty, 191; potentialization, 108, 112; potential movement, 159, 163–66, 168, 170–75, 255, 368; and proposition, 206; pure, 195, 205, 332, 336; and realist

idealism, 115; and reality, 2, 6, 8, 115; relational, 74; remainder of, 58; and situation, 68; and vertigo, 164; and violence, 317; and virtual object, 130; and vision, 254. *See also* possible; virtual
potentiation, 180–81, 183
power, 232, 234, 304, 318; of abstraction, 89; and affect, 313, 315; and affectability, 247; biopower, 235–36, 246–47, 291, 296, 307–8; and body, 246; and capitalism, 302; and change, 316; and classification, 305; and command, 296; and communication, 50, 52; constituent, 74; control-and-command, 305; cosmological, 247; counterpower, 320; destituent, 74; disciplinary, 50, 52, 56, 60, 62, 235–37, 240, 246–47, 269, 271, 307, 308; distributive, 20, 52, 58; of existence, 316; and life, 307, 316; ontogenetic, 58; and personal, 320, 321; and the political, 316; and politics, 316; power object, 306; power-to vs. power-over, 295, 315–16, 320, 322; productive, 304–5, 307; and singular point, 242; sovereign, 235–37, 240, 246–47, 296, 307; and violence, 317. *See also* affect; ontopower; politics
power of the false, 54, 427n3; and minor art, 23. *See also* fabulation
pragmatism, 31, 45, 51, 56, 139, 232, 313–14, 406, 440n7; and truth, 43, 55
preacceleration, 215–17, 226, 228. *See also* movement
preemption, 217, 218, 230, 248, 258, 261, 283, 290
prehension, 423; negative, 415, 423, 446n3; and reality, 13, 14. *See also* background
preindividual, 30, 59, 114, 117, 118; preindividual field, 29, 31, 32, 33, 59, 116. *See also* individuation; transindividual
present, 177, 183, 258, 297, 334–35; and anticipation, 293; and cut, 223; and futurity, 179, 218, 288; importance of, 55; and indeterminacy, 224; kinetic, 226; and knowledge, 210; and past, 179, 190, 197; and perception, 213; specious, 179, 180, 186; and world, 184. *See also* future; future-past; past
presentiment, 162, 163
previousness, 330, 334–35, 338, 362, 365, 369. *See also* nextness
primary phase, 194–97, 201–2, 344
priming, 154, 180–81, 268, 318, 322; and alter-priming, 318; and cue, 178, 180–81; and order-word, 337; and social field, 39

proactivity, 225; and reactivity, 322
problem, 39, 42, 56, 182, 184–86, 419, 422–23; affirmation of, 184; and criteria, 51; ethico-political, 55; and model, 97; pragmatic, 43; and singular point, 242; terms of, 183
process, 135, 260, 308, 367, 393; and activity, 197; and affect, 192; and architecture, 102, 139, 151; and atmosphere, 190, 207; and being of relation, 57; and co-determination, 98, 99; collective, 60; and conditioning, 98; and content, 48; content and context, 58; continuation of, 46, 56; and correspondence, 151; and extension, 98; and form, 138; and immediation, 192; and infra-instant, 186; and mentality, 115; and model, 97; next pulse of, 7, 8, 195, 198; and novelty, 7, 8; novelty and perishing, 58; open, 43; of perception, 276; and problem, 141; process philosophy, 192–93, 344, 439n7; processuality, 59, 143–44; and product, 144, 151; pure, 354; and reality, 6; and reenaction, 199; and reprocessualization, 58–59, 151; and self-feeling, 152; and singular point, 243; stalling of, 46; technical, 105; and time, 198; and trace, 145; and transition, 98; urban, 99; virtuality of, 139; and vision, 335
production: and circulation, 304, 308; cultural, 139–40, 145; and power, 259, 307; process of, 16; and reality, 7, 9–10, 19, 24, 183; and subject, 417, 426; of surplus-value, 252, 258, 261, 268, 271, 277
programming, 171–72; and design, 138; and indeterminacy, 137
propension, 204, 206–7, 213–14, 215, 218; suspension of, 217. See also anticipation; readiness potential
propensity: and atmosphere, 204, 206, 207; to perceive, 212, 213. See also anticipation; readiness potential
proposition, 191, 219, 410, 422, 425; and affirmation, 418; and event, 412; and individuation, 419; and intervention, 57; and locus, 415; logical, 411–12, 419; vs. logical statement, 206; and occasion, 417; and penumbral complex, 413–14; propositional field, 416, 426; and reality, 8–9; and research-creation, 421; and subject of the enunciation, 412; and undecidability, 45; and variation, 413; and world, 415–16

proprioception, 154, 161, 165, 168, 333, 348, 369, 371, 389, 443n10; and orientation, 368, 370; and vision, 148, 256
psychology: experimental, 146, 177; Gestalt, 281; neuropsychology, 179, 183
pure experience, 129, 196, 332, 367; and Firstness, 195; and space, 373
pure transition, 331, 334, 336, 339, 366, 369, 370. See also transition

qualitative, 74, 75, 84, 203, 345–46, 345–55, 352, 363, 364, 371, 373; experience as, 372; neighborhood, 122–25
quality, 98, 197, 326, 347, 349; and atmosphere, 189; and background, 432n1; and contrast, 83, 432n1; defining, 84; and determination, 331; and dynamism, 196; of experience, 89; and extension, 363; and field, 32; global, 204; lived, 75; primary and secondary, 193
quantitative, 114–15, 180, 345, 371
quantum: of effect, 114; of event, 96; of individuation, 332; leap, 106, 109, 111–13, 118; of subjectivity, 76; threshold, 111, 116; void, 332, 441n18; of worlding, 22, 109, 111, 332
quasi-cause, 20, 58, 60; capital as, 21; and field effect, 227; and magic, 34; and relation, 33; and stutter, 32; and trigger, 57

race, 22, 43, 288–89, 292, 318; and faciality, 276. See also whiteness
racism, 35, 38, 39, 276, 292, 299–300
radical empiricism, 109, 149, 184, 329, 406, 439n7; and nature, 193; and reality, 11; and topological architecture, 152
reactivity, 284; affirmation of, 322; and violence, 319
readiness potential, 178, 182–83, 210, 212, 213, 215, 220, 224, 226, 228, 230, 255, 258. See also anticipation; preemption; propension; propensity
Reagan, Ronald, 229, 279–80, 290, 298, 300, 302
reality, 181, 211, 227, 336, 355; and abstract, 132, 185; and actualization, 88; and appearance, 207; and atmosphere, 207; creation of, 228; and determination, 3; and effect, 7; and excess, 6; and experience, 95; extreme, 14, 184, 193; and feeling, 12; as given, 5; and hyperreal, 24; hyperreality, 15; and ideal, 115, 185; and imaginary, 20,

INDEX 479

24; and language, 339; mode of, 365; nonactual, 195; and potential, 2; production of, 18; and proposition, 8, 9; and pure transition, 340, 370; and relation, 11; and simulacrum, 18; and simulation, 20–21, 24; and speculation, 7; and virtual, 4, 246, 427n2

reason, 91, 182, 184, 291; instrumental, 63, 72; instrumental vs. operative, 63, 64, 69; operative, 64, 65

recognition, 131, 159, 163, 170, 212, 213, 258; and attention, 68; and difference, 322; and pre-feeling, 389; and repetition, 65, 170; self-, 192

recursion, vs. repetition, 156

reenactment, 111, 199–200, 202, 444n14

reflection, 67, 187; and choice, 63; and movement, 228; retrospective, 181

reflex, 91, 121, 241, 242; and decision, 239

regime of functioning, 106–7, 110. *See also* concretization, schema of; synergy

relation, 60, 73, 87, 100, 191, 317, 420, 423; and autonomy, 316; being-in-, 39, 45; and body, 356; and catalysis, 59; and co-creation, 85; and composition, 92; and culture, 54; dequalified, 28; and determination of potential, 107; and difference, 91; differential, 365; dimension of, 59; dynamic, 107; and excess, 5; extensive, 351, 356, 371; external vs. internal, 125, 126, 354; extrinsic, 64; and feeling, 441n21; and field, 31; healers of, 59; and immediacy, 54; and individuation, 32; and invention, 107; and movement, 441n21; and multifunctionality, 107; and potential, 74, 416, 419, 420; as primary, 32, 190; quantitative, 371; and reality, 11, 193; and reenaction, 199; relational complex, 420–21, 425; and relationships, 31; and schema of concretization, 110; superempirical, 91; and sympathy, 356; taking-effect of, 108; technique of, 31, 33, 45, 54, 58, 59, 408, 411, 421–26; terms of, 82; and Thirdness, 195. *See also* belonging; interaction; sociality

relatum, 123, 190, 191, 195, 201

relay, 22, 58, 162, 165, 168, 242, 271, 272, 288; intensive, 175; intersense, 166

relief, 83, 92, 347, 350, 351, 353. *See also* contrast

remainder, 34; of potential, 197; of processuality, 58–59; pure relation as, 31, 197; of reality, 3. *See also* excess

repetition, 65, 67, 130, 242, 254, 264, 267, 280, 301; and difference, 327; and language, 29; and movement, 367; and relief, 351; and vertigo, 164

representation, 23, 302, 343, 376, 378, 403, 407; and black hole, 377, 379; and copy/ model, 16, 18; and deterritorialization, 303; and generality, 407; and hyperreality, 15; and image, 24, 158; and knowledge, 377; and likeness, 88; and perspective painting, 380; and quasi-cause, 20

research-creation, 421, 445n1

resistance, 166, 306, 312, 313, 316, 318, 319, 320

resonance, 63, 66, 163, 180, 252, 283, 296, 322, 423; and matter, 113

rest, 22, 84; absolute, 374. *See also* movement; stasis; stillness

reterritorialization, 20, 23, 313. *See also* deterritorialization; territory

retrospection, 68, 177, 181, 210, 215, 270; and legitimation, 290; and projection, 65

rhetoric, 249, 251, 302, 407, 409

rhythm, 150, 230, 254, 443n8; and body, 247, 251, 340; emergent, 60; of image perception, 257; and movement, 123, 174; rhythmic inclusion, 326, 327, 333; saccadic, 261; and social field, 252, 258, 296; syncopated, 267, 276–77, 279; systolic/diastolic, 59; and vision, 254, 379; and writing, 88. *See also* down-beat; off-beat; saccade; up-beat

ritual, 35, 42, 81, 297; communication as, 314; and territory, 47; violence as, 291, 297, 300

Rumsfeld, Donald, 129, 209, 210, 211–12, 216–19, 222–23, 225–26, 229, 238, 282

Ruyer, Raymond, 5, 120, 124–27, 352, 429n10, 430n4, 433n2, 441n18

Ryle, Gilbert, 203, 212–16, 228, 241, 255; on frame of mind, 215

saccade, 178, 254, 256, 261–62, 267, 269, 277, 282. *See also* amodal completion; barely-there

Sassen, Saskia, 393

Schiavo, Terri, 232–33, 236, 240–41, 244–45, 251–52, 259

Schilder, Paul, 164

Schmitt, Carl, 237, 272

Schmitz, Hermann, 189

secret, 51; and differentiation, 42; form of, 42, 48–49, 52–54, 57; and performative, 44

480 INDEX

seeding, 393, 396, 401. *See also* anarchive; documentation
self: and capture, 351; and duration, 332; and empathy, 88; and other, 343, 355; as world, 91
self-enjoyment, 8, 13, 191, 413
self-iteration, 242, 392
self-referentiality, 65, 67, 156, 311, 335, 337–39, 439n16; and criticality, 63–64. *See also* autopoiesis
sensation, 439n5, 439n7, 441n18, 441n21; and anticipation, 212, 216; and atmosphere, 198, 388; and attention, 67; block of, 127, 129–30; and freedom, 68; and habit, 66, 67; and life, 69; multimodal, 345, 349; and perception, 66; primary and secondary, 147, 152; and reality, 14; of voluminousness, 330, 361
SenseLab, 410, 419, 425, 446n5; and anarchive, 445n1; and conceptual speed-dating, 425–26; and research-creation, 421, 445n1; and technique, 411, 421, 423–25
senses, 161, 256, 345, 443n10; and cross-modality, 346; and cross-reference, 337; in-sensing, 65; intersense, 164, 391; sense-impression, 199; sense perception, 194. *See also* perception; sensation
separation, 303–4; and depth perception, 147; and reality, 12
seriality, 111, 297, 301, 418
shape, 257, 403; and cut, 83
shock, 145, 178, 181, 245; and sensation, 67, 69
sign, 135; and ambiguity, 150; asignifying, 137, 142, 144, 150, 152; and conditioning, 318; dynamic, 407; as information, 15; and materiality, 152, 155; of the same, 52; as threshold, 151
signification, 143; and affect, 313; signifying structure, 46
Simondon, Gilbert, 29, 31, 33, 104–14, 117–18; on allagmatics, 97
simple location, 2, 185, 370. *See also* location; misplaced concreteness
simulacrum, 16–18, 23–24, 76, 427n1, 431n6. *See also* simulation
simulation, 15, 18, 20–23; and power of the false, 427n3; and virtual, 153. *See also* simulacrum
singular-generic, 306, 309, 311–12, 363–64, 366, 369. *See also* multiple-singular; singularity

singularity, 58, 200, 204, 246, 365–66, 370–71, 407, 408, 417–18, 432n1, 435n5; and black hole, 70; and chaos theory, 313; and common, 27; and event, 319; vs. generality, 70; and generic, 305; iterative, 230; and life, 70; micro-, 245; of mode, 80; and moment, 94; and multiplicity, 86; and occasion, 196–97; vs. particularity, 85, 363, 365; pure, 96, 364, 368; and state of exception, 237–38; vs. universality, 363. *See also* multiple-singular; singular-generic
singular point, 242–44, 247. *See also* singularity; vanishing point
situation, 66–70; and belonging, 30; and excess, 123
situationism, 385, 397; and *dérive*, 386; and *détournement*, 390
social: and affect, 310; and command, 296; and reason, 183; and self-definition, 28; social time, 300
social field, 46, 238, 300, 302, 307; agitation of, 243, 245, 266, 276, 284; and asymmetry, 51; and differentiation, 54; and exemplary body, 252, 258, 271; and polarity, 38, 283; priming of, 39, 322; and sovereign power, 236, 237–38, 240
sociality, 55, 293, 302, 392, 403; assimilation of, 310; and being of relation, 57; civil, 309; and differentiation, 29; and generic, 304; interrupted, 28; and nonexchangeability, 30; pure, 29, 59, 59; and urbanism, 396; without expression, 33
society, 82, 283; and art, 23; and asymmetry, 44; capitalist, 302; civil, 296; and cultural difference, 55; and exchange, 29; and negotiation, 38; and preindividual field, 33; and proposition, 418; propositional, 420; and publicity, 42, 49; and quasi-cause, 21; resegmentation of, 46; and settler colonialism, 39; and sociality, 31, 57; structure vs. process of, 45–46; whiteness and, 53
SoftOffice (Spuybroek), 174, 175
Sontag, Susan, 268, 436n16
Souriau, Étienne, 10, 120
sovereignty, 235, 321; and state of exception, 237
space, 324, 331–33, 335, 339, 369, 370; abstract, 334; and architecture, 159; and atmosphere, 189; and body, 340; Euclidean, 371; and experience, 185, 354; experience of, 349, 371; infra-, 364; interstitial, 425; and movement, 148, 351; nonlocal, 155;

and orientation, 332, 341; and possibility, 385, 386; and pure experience, 373; and spaceability, 331; spatialization, 336, 348; spatial order, 380; spatial schema, 329; and transition, 365; and virtual, 96. *See also* location; mapping; orientation; position

space-time, 95, 431n5

spatio-memorability, 331–32, 339. *See also* memory; space

special effect, 388, 390–91, 400. *See also* urban art

speciation, 418. *See also* becoming; individuation; species

species, 89; and affective attunement, 80; difference, 81; interspecies, 73, 74; species being, 83. *See also* speciation

speculation, 8

Spinoza, Baruch, 144, 315

spontaneity, 126; and instinct, 124; and movement, 175

Spuybroek, Lars, 88, 100, 158–59, 166, 169, 171–73, 175

stasis, 94, 98, 124, 379; and process, 99. *See also* movement; rest; stillness

state of exception, 237, 245, 272, 283

Stelarc, 156

Stengers, Isabelle, 26–27, 74, 406, 408; on ecology of practices, 60

Stengers, Isabelle, and Ilya Prigogine, 31, 65

Stern, Daniel, 201, 365. *See also* activation countour; vitality affect

stillness: and movement, 162. *See also* movement; rest; stasis

stimulus, 119, 123

Stockhausen, Karlheinz, 268

stratum, 303, 304

structure, 57; and adaptation, 58; and determinacy, 155; and world, 57

stutter, 27, 38, 41, 57, 62; and sociality, 29; and volition, 28. *See also* language; performative

style, 85, 100, 102, 204

subject, 179, 184, 332, 340; and belief, 128; and body, 339; deliberative, 182; and empathy, 356; and experience, 13, 148; of experience, 129, 340; and expression, 6–7; as false problem, 187; and legislation, 24; of life, 81; pre-formed, 185; private, 235, 343; and proposition, 417; and separation, 356; and sovereign power, 236; of state, 275; and superject, 129. *See also* self; subjectification; subjective form; subjectivity

subjectification, 304; cross-, 83

subjective form, 111, 196, 200, 201, 206; and affective tonality, 194; and background, 197; and Firstness, 194; and vitality affect, 202. *See also* subject

subjectivity, 77; and atmosphere, 189, 196; and movement, 352; nonhuman, 81; and otherness, 195; and perspective, 376; and property, 76; and quality, 193; and subjective form, 194. *See also* subject; subjectification; subjective form

subject of the enunciation, 40–41, 60, 411–12, 417, 427n1

subject of the statement, 411–12, 417, 427n1. *See also* logical subject

supernormal tendency, 121–22, 124–25, 129–30, 132; as attractor, 127; and vector, 126. *See also* animal; excess; instinct; surplus; tendency

superposition, 64, 364–65, 367, 371

surface, 15, 70, 398, 399. *See also* absolute surface; abstract surface

surplus: determination, 100–102; emotional, 415; of signification, 45. *See also* excess; surplus-value

surplus-value, 260, 308; of emotion, 251, 266, 277, 283; of legitimation, 252; of meaning, 241–42, 247, 251, 258, 266, 271, 277, 279, 283; of organization, 244–45, 247, 251, 258, 266, 271, 277, 283; of patriotism, 268; of perception, 258; of reality, 183; of vitality, 271. *See also* surplus

suspension, 29, 66, 168, 177–78, 184, 217–18, 237, 244–45, 260, 297, 390, 391, 396, 400; of communication, 39; and in-formation, 58; of meaning, 28; and potential, 32; and sovereign command, 238; system and, 63; and tautology, 219; and technique of relation, 31. *See also* interruption

sympathy, 120, 131–32, 444n14; and abstraction, 91; and animal, 129; vs. empathy, 88, 356; and event, 355; and intention, 89

syncopation, 259, 272, 276–77, 279, 284. *See also* saccade

synergy, 106–7, 175, 397. *See also* absolute origin; concretization, schema of

synesthesia, 67, 345–47, 349, 362, 441n19, 442n4; and kinesthesia, 148, 333–34, 336; and language, 338; mirror-touch, 343–44, 348, 352, 354–57, 443n7, 444n11; and movement, 152; and tunneling, 154. *See also* empathy; sympathy; touch; vision

synthesis, 90, 143, 283, 440n11
system, 63, 311; and self-adaptation, 104; and self-conditioning, 110; supersystem, 302, 305, 309, 311; and variation, 65

Tarde, Gabriel, 128–29, 252
Taussig, Michael, 35
technical mentality, 104–5, 110, 112, 115–18. *See also* technical object
technical object, 107, 111–12, 115–17; and mentality, 105, 108; and network, 104. *See also* technical mentality
technicity, 112, 116–18. *See also* technical mentality
technique: of relation, 31, 33, 45, 54, 58, 59, 408, 411, 421–26
tendency, 4, 30, 32, 58, 163, 180, 186, 201–2, 242, 259, 283, 407, 408; and anticipation, 255; in germ, 33; and landing site, 161; and movement, 162; presence in, 28; and priming, 318; terminal, 185; and virtual, 243. *See also* supernormal tendency; terminus
terminus, 4, 180, 184–86, 351; and virtual object, 130. *See also* tendency
territory, 18, 20, 22, 303, 311, 313, 322, 428n6; and art, 21; and figure, 305. *See also* deterritorialization; reterritorialization
terrorism, 38, 216, 276, 293, 303. *See also* war on terror
Thirdness, 195. *See also* Firstness
thought, 65, 99, 215, 228, 295, 408, 420, 423; and affect-body, 314; and amodal completion, 253–54; and analogue, 97; collective, 214; and collective individuation, 424; and extension, 66; and feeling, 228; infra-, 213; and language, 214; and matter, 64; and mimicry, 97; and movement, 215; movement of, 215, 217, 420–21, 423–24, 426; nonvolitional, 402; and novelty, 419; and operative reason, 64; and perception, 213–14, 228; and preindividual field, 116; and premovement, 217; and problem, 97, 184; and process, 96; and propensity, 213; and proposition, 416; and self-referentiality, 64; and subjectification, 304; of system, 64; thinking-feeling, 199; thought-effect, 97; thought-matter, 132; and virtual, 94, 213
Three Ecologies Institute, 421. *See also* SenseLab
threshold, 58, 99, 106, 107, 109, 111, 116, 232, 242, 245, 260, 281, 308, 316, 362, 366, 367, 369, 371, 417, 421; and consistency, 230; of consistency, 246; and critical point, 65; end-form as, 142; and lure, 420; passing of, 108
Thwaites, Thomas, 76, 78, 80–82, 89–90
time, 183–84, 192, 197, 331–33, 335, 339; and architecture, 159; and decision, 219–20; distortion, 390; and experience, 165, 185; experiential, 184; infra-temporal, 215; nonlinear, 95, 293, 300, 304; and politics, 220; and preemption, 218; and space, 98; and vector-form, 195; and violence, 297; and virtual, 96. *See also* future; future-past; past; present
Tinbergen, Niko, 120–26, 430n2
topology, 135–36, 138–41, 153, 354, 361, 367, 374; and architecture, 96, 135–57; and experience, 150, 372; and mirror-touch synesthesia, 444n1; and problem, 142; and sign, 137; and virtual, 96; and virtual body, 353, 355. *See also* architecture; tunneling; windowing
touch, 165, 336, 346–47, 354, 367, 389; and location, 355; and mirror-touch synesthesia, 343; and position, 369; and vision, 148, 255–56, 337. *See also* mirror-touch synesthesia
trace, 135, 145, 196, 267, 269, 329; anarchival, 426; of process, 58. *See also* anarchive; documentation; seeding
transcendence, 52, 191; of occasion, 191; plane of, 19; and sovereign power, 236–37, 240; truth and, 51–52. *See also* immanence
transcendental, 101, 144
transduction, 87, 117–18, 154, 156–57, 171–73, 175, 197–98, 245, 268, 414; of affective force, 88; and change, 157; and immediation, 421; and space, 155
transformation, 63, 69, 84, 171–73, 427n2; and being of relation, 57; and desire, 127; and integration, 61; matrix of, 84; and performative, 34, 39; qualitative, 85, 92; and sensing, 65; and survival, 60
transindividual, 320; affect as, 315; reality as, 12. *See also* individual; individuation; preindividual
transition, 3, 147, 155, 171, 327, 331–32, 335–36, 340, 362, 367, 371; and affect, 316; and continuity, 333; and expression, 98; quantum, 109; and virtual, 135
translation, 30, 49, 255, 381, 383; analogical, 138; of difference, 51; imperative to, 60; and literarity, 87; nontranslatability, 26; and sociality, 31

trigger, 43, 58, 65, 121–22, 325, 334, 338, 403; and becoming, 57; and system, 65
Trump, Donald, 229–31, 282–84, 321–22
truth, 41, 45, 52, 193; and affect, 43; and ambiguity, 194; and change, 55; declarative vs. pragmatic, 43, 55; general, 51; and minor, 61; and penumbral complex, 413; post-, 229, 321–22; propositional, 41; and transcendence, 51; and whiteness, 57. *See also* power of the false; proposition
tunneling, 154–57, 367. *See also* architecture; topology

unconscious, 241, 410, 412; and appetition, 346; and landing site, 161; and sympathy, 356. *See also* consciousness; nonconscious
up-beat, 246, 257, 266, 268. *See also* amodal completion; down-beat; off-beat
urban art, 386, 388–89, 391–93, 396–98, 401; and advertising, 395–96; and suspension, 390–91
urbanism, 99, 101; and advertising, 394. *See also* urban art

vacuum, 226, 227, 228. *See also* kinesthesia
vagueness, 70, 159, 172, 175, 224, 374; and atmosphere, 194, 197; and determination, 174; and dynamism, 173; and enunciation, 41; and fog, 146; and intensity, 174; ontogenetic, 100; and reality, 207; and recognition, 65; vague presence, 200–201, 203. *See also* atmosphere; fog; zone of indistinction
value, 81, 83, 89, 184, 195; aesthetic, 74; and capitalism, 303; and relation, 28
vanishing point, 163–64, 166, 232, 241, 244, 246–47, 291, 376–77. *See also* singular point
variation, 65, 85, 166, 181–83, 254, 283, 361, 362, 364, 366, 369, 371, 392, 420; axis of, 84; and chance, 175; collective, 123–26; and form, 135; and habit, 147; intensive, 219; and movement, 365; and mutual inclusion, 353; and proposition, 416, 417; punctual, 143; pure variability, 353; and reality, 7, 11; and rest, 374; and sameness, 130; and singular point, 242; and topology, 135. *See also* continuous variation
vector, 96, 124, 126, 180, 190, 198, 270, 422; and desire, 127; and experience, 191; truth as, 43
Vendémiaire (dir. Louis Feuillade), 18–20
vertigo, 161, 164–65, 168, 170, 172, 379

violence, 289, 297, 304, 322; and colonialism, 298; and ideology, 301; micro-aggression, 317, 319; and resistance, 319; and sign, 318; state, 286, 291, 296–97; structural, 317–19. *See also* politics; power
Virilio, Paul, 293, 385; on effraction, 393
virtual, 58, 367, 380, 432n1; and abstract, 153; and actual, 94, 96, 213, 227; actualization of, 69, 157; and analogue, 97; and architecture, 134; and death, 69, 264; and effect, 95; and eternal object, 195; and expression, 94; feed-forward of, 151; and form, 142, 144; and history, 206; and ideal, 94–95; and instantiation, 94; and life, 69; and light, 146; and machinic body, 144; as mode, 157; and model, 97; and movement, 147; and penumbra, 205; and potential, 153; and process, 96; and propensity, 213; pure virtuality, 314; reality, 350; and reality, 4, 66, 134, 149; and singularity, 96; and space, 95; supernal, 95; vs. technological, 153, 156; and terrorism, 216; and thought, 213; and time, 95; virtual enemy, 218, 222; virtual force, 139, 144; virtual movement, 215; virtual point, 66; and vision, 148. *See also* actual; potential
virtual appointment, 385–86, 389–90, 401. *See also* urban art
virtual body, 353–56; and mirror-touch synesthesia, 444n12; and reality, 356–57; and sympathy, 355
virtual center, 66–67, 246, 370
vision, 163, 341; abstract, 333–34; and accident zone, 145; and anticipation, 253–55; and death, 264–65, 274; and distance, 372, 376; and experience, 165; field of, 163; limit of, 165; and materiality, 140; and memory, 330; monadic, 379–80; more-than-visual, 279; and movement, 257, 346, 381; and optical effect, 109, 251; and other-sense, 152, 154, 164–65, 170, 255, 333–34, 379, 381; and periphery, 160–61, 163–64; as political principle, 279; and politics, 281; and proprioception, 148, 164; and self-referentiality, 335; and shock, 178; and space, 370; and touch, 347, 354, 381; and variation, 256; virtual, 255. *See also* amodal completion; image; saccade; synesthesia
vitality, 231, 267, 277; and barely-there, 271; and culture, 56; and war, 265. *See also* life
vitality affect, 201–2, 205, 365. *See also* activation contour

volition, 350–51; and experience, 348; nonvolition, 28, 93; and perceptive lag, 178. *See also* intentionality

Vološinov, Valentin, 6

voluminousness, 324–25, 330, 439n6, 444n1. *See also* atmosphere; space

wander-line, 422

war, 265, 268, 288–89, 291; and deterritorialization, 20; and life, 287, 292; pure war, 293

war on terror, 216, 221, 262, 268, 281, 283. *See also* Bush, George W.; 9/11 attacks

weather, 98, 204; and urban environment, 99. *See also* architecture; atmosphere

Weiner, James, 53–54

WetGRID (Spuybroek), 158, 166, 171–75

Whitehead, Alfred North, 109, 111, 179, 180, 181, 182, 186, 188–98, 329, 344, 419, 424, 426, 431n4, 432n1, 434n16, 440n7; on conformation, 190, 198; on consciousness, 256; on continuity, 432n9; on locus, 415; on misplaced concreteness, 185; on modes of reality, 9; on nature, 193; on object, 130; on penumbra, 204–5, 414; on prehension, 13; on proposition, 8, 410, 412–13, 422, 441n16; on proximate relevance, 2; on superject, 129; on vibration, 443n8

Whitehead Research Project (WRP), 410, 421, 424

whiteness, 38–39, 46–49, 275, 292, 299, 321; and faciality, 276; and market, 53. *See also* facialization; race; racism

windowing, 154, 157. *See also* architecture; topology; tunneling

Wodiczko, Krzysztof, 396

world, 317, 333, 403, 415; and absolute movement, 152; and atmosphere, 189; and basic fact, 190; and becoming-animal, 429n9; and body, 143; and co-creation, 86; common, 61; and event, 420; and experience, 144, 183; and expression, 7; and feeling, 13, 326, 328–29, 439n7; and form, 57; and identity, 196; and infra-instant, 186; and movement, 341; and novelty, 85; and otherness, 195; and penumbral complex, 414; and perception, 157; and performative, 34; and potential, 6, 58; and present, 179, 184; and proposition, 206, 416; and reenaction, 199; and relation, 90; and self, 91; and self-enjoyment, 191; and self-identity, 190, 194; and simulation, 20; and terminus, 186; and untimely, 206; virtuality of, 22

writing: and becoming-animal, 82; and movement, 87; and point of view, 91; and rhythm, 88. *See also* language; literarity

zone of indistinction, 41, 81, 83, 128, 168, 245, 247, 252, 260, 298

zone of proximity, 159, 175

SOURCES

Couplet 1

2019 "Extreme Realism: In Sixteen Series." Written for Zhang Ga, ed., *Topologies of the Real*, catalogue of the 2020 CAFAM Techne Triennial, Beijing, China, 2020; delayed due to COVID-19. Published here with permission.

1986 "Realer Than Real: The Simulacrum according to Deleuze and Guattari." Originally published in *Copyright*, no. 1 (1987): 90–97. Reprinted here with permission.

Couplet 2

2000 "On the Right to the Noncommunication of Cultural Difference." Originally published in French under the title "Le droit à non-communication de la différence," in "Propositions de paix," ed. Isabelle Stengers and Tobie Nathan, special issue, *Ethnopsy: Les mondes contemporains de la guérison* (Paris), no. 4 (April 2002): 93–131. The English version prepared for this volume integrates updates and revisions.

1998 "Event Horizon." Originally published in Joke Brouwer, ed., *The Art of the Accident* (Rotterdam: Dutch Architecture Institute/V2_Organisation, 1998), 154–68. Reprinted with permission.

Couplet 3

2017 "Becoming Animal in the Literary Field." Originally published in a condensed version in Bruce Boehrer, Molly Hand, and Brian Massumi, eds., *Animals and Animality in the Literary Field* (Cambridge: Cambridge University Press, 2018), 265–83. The full-length version appears here. Reprinted with permission.

2008 "The Virtual, Double Capture, and the Urban-Architecture Manifold." Originally printed under the title "Forms of Time," interview with Jason Nguyen and Mark Davis, *Manifold Magazine* (School of Architecture, Rice University), no. 2 (spring 2008): 17–30. Reprinted under the title "Brian Massumi on the Virtual" in "The Interview Issue," *Manifold Magazine*, no. 3 (Winter 2008): 13–26. An abridged version appears here. Reprinted with permission.

Couplet 4

2009 "Simondon's 'Technical Mentality' Revisited." Originally published in "On Gilbert Simondon," special issue, *Parrhesia: A Journal of Critical Philosophy*, no. 7 (2009): 36–45. Reprinted in Arne De Boever, Alex Murray, Jon Roffe, and Ashley Woodward, eds., *Gilbert Simondon: Being and Technology* (Edinburgh: Edinburgh University Press, 2013), 1–18. An abridged version appears here. Reprinted with permission.

2012 "The Supernormal Animal." Originally published in Richard Grusin, ed., *The Nonhuman Turn* (Minneapolis: University of Minnesota Press, 2015), 1–18. Reprinted here with permission.

Couplet 5

1997 "Sensing the Virtual, Building the Insensible." Originally published in "Hypersurface Architecture," ed. Stephen Perrella, special issue, *Architectural Design* 68, nos. 5–6 (May–June 1998), Profile no. 133, 16–24. Reprinted here with permission.

2004 "Not Determinately Nothing: Building Experience." Originally published under the title "Building Experience: The Architecture of Perception," in Lars Spuybroek, ed., *NOX: Machining Architecture* (London: Thames and Hudson, 2004), 322–31. Reprinted here with permission.

Couplet 6

2014 "The Crannies of the Present: On the Subject of Decision." Originally published under the title "The Crannies of the Present," in Stuart Grant, Jodie McNeilly, and Maeva Veerapen, eds., *Performance and Temporalisation: Time Happens* (London: Palgrave/Macmillan, 2015), 91–100. Reprinted here with permission.

2018 "Dim, Massive, and Important: Atmosphere in Process." Originally published in Friedlind Riedel and Juha Torvinen, eds., *Music as Atmosphere: Collective Feelings and Affective Sounds* (London: Routledge, 2020), 286–301. Reprinted here with permission.

Couplet 7

2005 "Going Kinetic: What Is Decision in a Post-deliberative Age?" Not previously published. Text finalized for this volume.

2005 "Barely There: The Power of the Image at the Limit of Life." Not previously published. Text finalized for this volume.

Couplet 8

1995 "Requiem for Our Prospective Dead: A Participatory Critique of Capitalist Power." Originally published in UTS *Review: Cultural Studies and New Writing* (Sydney), no. 2 (October 1995): 35–56. Reprinted in Eleanor Kaufman and Kevin John Heller, eds., *Deleuze and Guattari: New Mappings in Politics, Philosophy, and Culture* (Minneapolis: University of Minnesota Press, 1998), 40–63. Reprinted here with permission.

2017 "The Political Is Not Personal: Affect, Power, Violence." Originally published under the title "Affect, Power, and Violence: The Political Is Not Personal, Interview with Brad Evans," *Los Angeles Review of Books*, November 12, 2017. Reprinted in Brad Evans and Natasha Lennard, eds., *Violence: Humans in Dark Times* (San Francisco: City Lights, 2018), 249–61. Reprinted here with permission.

Couplet 9

2001 "Tell Me Where Your Pain Is: Pointing to the Body without an Image." Not previously published. Text finalized for this volume.

2015 "The Art of the Relational Body: From Mirror-Touch to the Virtual Body." Originally published in Daria Martin, ed., *Mirror-Touch: Thresholds of Empathy with Art* (Oxford: Oxford University Press, 2017), 191–209. Reprinted here with permission.

Couplet 10

2000 "The Parable of the Cave (Blind Version)." Not previously published. Text finalized for this volume.

2003 "Panoscopia." Originally published in French translation under the title "Panoscopie: La photographie panoscopique de Luc Courchesne," in "Vision," special issue, *CV Photo*, no. 60 (April 2003): 27–29. Reprinted here in the original English with permission.

Couplet 11

2003 "Urban Appointment: A Possible Rendezvous with the City." Originally published in Joke Brouwer and Arjen Mulder, eds., *Making Art of Databases* (Rotterdam: V2_Organisation/Dutch Architecture Institute, 2003), 28–55. An abridged version appears here. Reprinted with permission.

1999 "Purple Phosphene." Originally published in *Angelaki: Journal of the Theoretical Humanities* 4, no. 3 (December 1999): 219–21.

Couplet 12

2007 "On Critique." Originally published in Christoph Brunner and Troy Rhoades, eds., "Transversal Fields of Experience," special issue, *Inflexions: A Journal for Research-Creation*, no. 4 (November 2009): 333–40. Reprinted here with permission.

2019 "How Do You Make Yourself a Proposition? For a Whiteheadian Laboratory" (with Erin Manning). Originally published under the title "For a Whiteheadian Laboratory: How Do You Make Yourself a Proposition?," in Ronald Faber, Michael Halewood, and Andrew M. Davis, eds., *Propositions in the Making: Experiments in a Whiteheadian Laboratory* (London: Lexington Books, 2019), 3–18. Reprinted here with permission.

IMAGE CREDITS

FIGURE 5.1. *Field of View*, from James J. Gibson, *The Ecological Approach to Visual Perception* (London: Routledge, 2014), 112.

FIGURE 5.2. *Self-Portrait*, Ernst Mach, from *Beiträge zur Analyse der Empfindungen* (Jena: Verlag von Gustav Fischer, 1886), figure 1, p. 14. Internet Archive/Royal College of Surgeons of England.

FIGURE 5.3. Lars Spuybroek, *WetGRID*, overview, exhibition design for Vision Machine, Musée des Beaux-Arts Nantes, 2000. Courtesy of NOX/Lars Spuybroek.

FIGURE 5.4. Lars Spuybroek, *WetGRID*, interior, exhibition design for Vision Machine, Musée des Beaux-Arts Nantes, 2000. Courtesy of NOX/Lars Spuybroek.

FIGURE 7.1. Survivor, September 11, 2001, from Gilles Peress, Michael Shulan, Charles Trabu, and Alice Rose George, eds., *Here Is New York: A Democracy of Photographs* (Zurich: Scalo Verlag, 2002), p. 575.

FIGURE 7.2. Survivor, September 11, 2001, from Gilles Peress, Michael Shulan, Charles Trabu, and Alice Rose George, eds., *Here Is New York: A Democracy of Photographs* (Zurich: Scalo Verlag, 2002), p. 285.

FIGURE 7.3. Flag at Ground Zero, September 2001, from Gilles Peress, Michael Shulan, Charles Trabu, and Alice Rose George, eds., *Here Is New York: A Democracy of Photographs* (Zurich: Scalo Verlag, 2002), p. 531.

FIGURE 7.4. Onlookers, September 11, 2001, from *Life Magazine: The Year in Pictures. September 11 Before and After*, January 14, 2002, p. 84. Photo: Patrick Witty.

FIGURE 7.5. Bodies falling, September 11, 2001, from Gilles Peress, Michael Shulan, Charles Trabu, and Alice Rose George, eds., *Here Is New York: A Democracy of Photographs* (Zurich: Scalo Verlag, 2002), p. 232.

FIGURE 7.6. Kiosk with missing persons posters, September 11, 2001, from Gilles Peress, Michael Shulan, Charles Trabu, and Alice Rose George, eds., *Here Is New York: A Democracy of Photographs* (Zurich: Scalo Verlag, 2002), p. 232.

FIGURE 7.7. Ad on bus shelter, September 2001, from Gilles Peress, Michael Shulan, Charles Trabu, and Alice Rose George, eds., *Here Is New York: A Democracy of Photographs* (Zurich: Scalo Verlag, 2002), p. 103. Photo: Robert Spencer.

FIGURE 10.1. Panoramic photograph. Luc Courchesne, *Journal Panoscopique*, *Ogaki City*, November 2, 2000.

FIGURE 10.2. Panoramic photo viewing device. Luc Courchesne, *Panoscope V.1*. Photo: Richard-Max Tremblay.

FIGURE 11.1. Large-scale image projection. HUMO Master Class with Rafael Lozano-Hemmer, V2/Ars Electronica FutureLab, Linz, Austria, February 3–7, 2003. Image: Anya Lewis.

FIGURE 11.2. Large-scale image projection. HUMO Master Class with Rafael Lozano-Hemmer, V2/Ars Electronica FutureLab, Linz, Austria, February 3–7, 2003. Image: Harald Schmutzhard.

FIGURE 11.3. Nike advertisement, building wrap, Rotterdam, Netherlands, 2000, from Joke Brouwer, ed., *Making Art of Databases* (Rotterdam: Dutch Architecture Institute/V2_Organisation, 2003), p. 37.

FIGURE 11.4. Large-scale image projection. HUMO Master Class with Rafael Lozano-Hemmer, V2/Ars Electronica FutureLab, Linz, Austria, February 3–7, 2003. Image: Maja Kalogera.

FIGURE 11.5. Large-scale image projection. HUMO Master Class with Rafael Lozano-Hemmer, V2/Ars Electronica FutureLab, Linz, Austria, February 3–7, 2003. Image: Anya Lewis.

www.ingramcontent.com/pod-product-compliance
Lightning Source LLC
Chambersburg PA
CBHW060348250426
43667CB00051B/2465